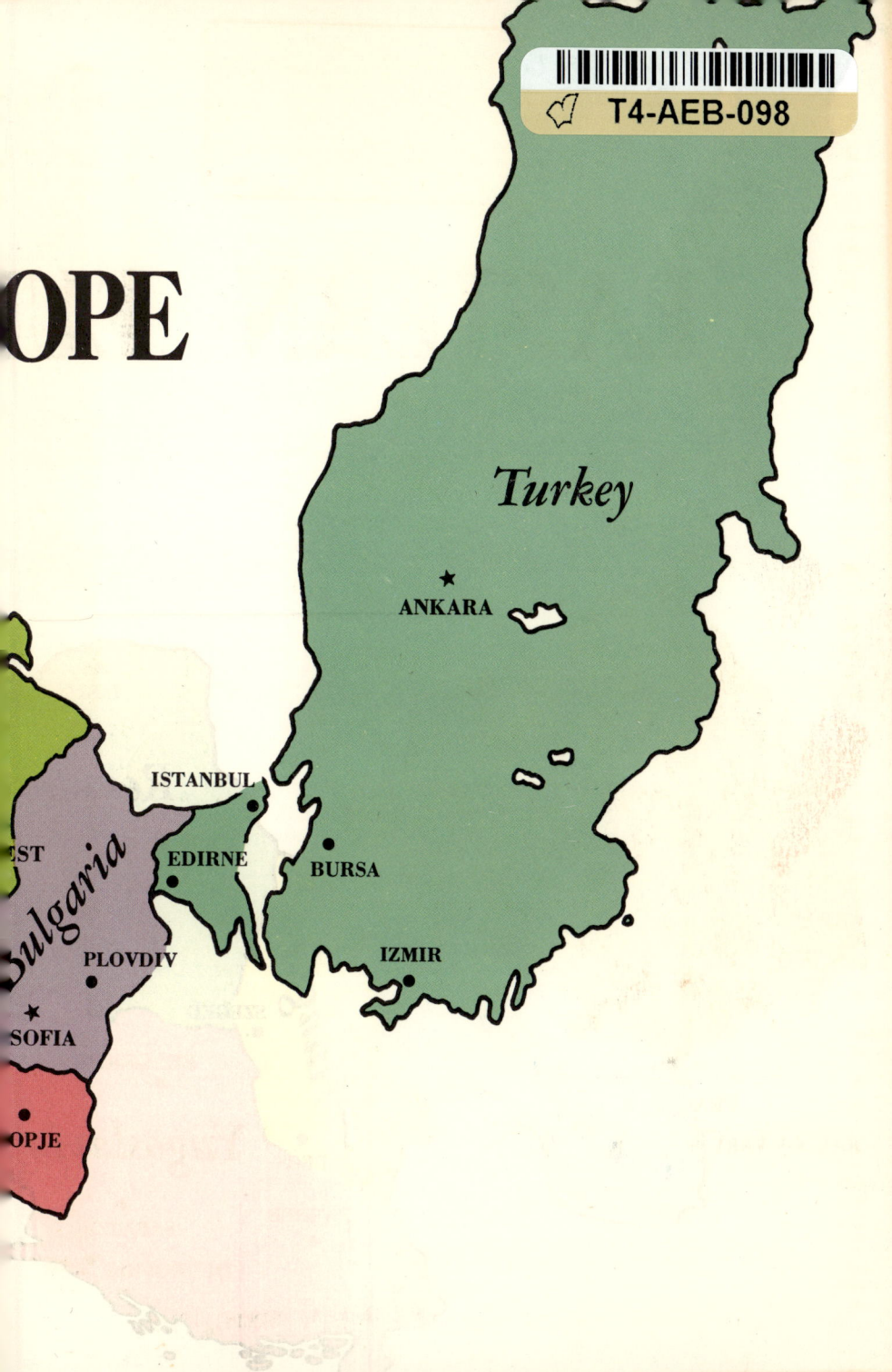

*Complete Guide
to
Eastern Europe*

COMPLETE GUIDE TO EASTERN EUROPE

DAVID H. EKVALL

Hart Publishing Company, Inc.
New York City

to Lisl

COPYRIGHT (C) 1970
HART PUBLISHING COMPANY, INC., NEW YORK, N. Y. 10011
SBN NO. 8055-1053-2
LIBRARY OF CONGRESS CATALOG CARD NO. 69-18898

NO PART OF THIS BOOK MAY BE REPRODUCED OR USED IN ANY FORM WITHOUT THE EXPRESS PERMISSION OF THE PUBLISHER IN WRITING.

MANUFACTURED IN THE UNITED STATES OF AMERICA

*Complete Guide
to
Eastern Europe*

Contents

BULGARIA	9
CZECHOSLOVAKIA	79
HUNGARY	133
POLAND	205
ROMANIA	277
TURKEY	347
YUGOSLAVIA	429
INDEX	520

Bulgaria

Bulgaria (about 43,000 square miles) is roughly the size of the state of Ohio and has a population of about eight million people. Yugoslavia borders Bulgaria to the west; the Black Sea forms the nation's 248-mile-long frontier to the east. Greece and Turkey lie south, and Romania lies north.

The Bulgarian countryside possesses such immense variety that a car trip through it is a must. Each turn of the road yields visual thrills, whether one is driving through the rolling countryside of northern Bulgaria, a grain-producing area nurtured by the Danube River, taking the scenic drive along the Black Sea coast from Varna south to Burgas, driving through the Schipka Pass to the Stolytov Monument, or perhaps touring the tobacco fields and thick pine forests on the way to the monastery at Rila. The landscape of Bulgaria is harsh-primitive in some aspects, but it is this very ruggedness that encourages one to go just a bit further. The air has an unusual sparkle, a zest, a healthful clarity that makes the moon seem closer, the sun feel warmer, the breezes more fragrant. Temperatures are mild, averaging between 68 and 80 degrees Fahrenheit in summer. Bulgarians seem to have acquired much of their temperament and naturalness from the landscape; clearly there is a close relationship here between the hardy, jovial people and their rugged, bright-colored, fascinating land.

HISTORY

The original Bulgar tribes were a people of Turkic extraction who crossed the Danube in the 6th century to settle in an area which was predominantly Slavic. In the late 7th century, after wars and much intermingling, the Bulgars and Slavs joined forces to build a nation based largely on the political code of the invaders. Between 893 and 923 A.D., under Simeon I, the Bulgarian nation achieved its maximum territorial limits while fighting against encroachments from Byzantium. In the year 1018 Byzantine forces gained control and for the next 200 years Bulgaria was a vassal state. This was just the first of many long periods of subjection by invaders.

In 1185 two Bulgarian princes of the town of Turnovo encouraged an uprising against the Byzantine troops which the next year resulted in the defeat of Byzantium and freedom once again for Bulgaria. For the next two centuries Bulgarians acknowledged their own king. During the 12th and 13th centuries, Bulgaria was a major Balkan power, reaching its zenith under King Ivan Aven II, who ruled from 1218 to 1241.

In the early 13th century, the Ottoman Turks began to invade Bulgaria, and by the late 1300's Bulgaria was completely overrun by the Turkish military. This bloody, hate-filled period of subjection lasted 500 years, until 1878.

After Russian military forces routed the Turks at the battle of the Schipka Pass in 1877, the Treaty of San Stefano divided the country into two sections; the northern part became an independent republic under Turkish suzerainty, while southern Bulgaria, known as Eastern Rumelia, remained directly under Turkish rule. In 1885, the north annexed Eastern Rumelia in a military coup, and consolidated the two economies. In 1908, Bulgaria declared its independence from Turkey and the ruling Bulgarian prince, Ferdinand of Saxe-Coburg-Gotha, assumed the title of tsar.

Four years later, Bulgarian ambitions, encouraged in part by Greece, Serbia and Montenegro, resulted in the First Balkan War, which gained for Bulgaria access to the Aegean Sea. A month later (June-July, 1913), seemingly not content to let well enough alone, Bulgaria turned on Greece and Serbia, and at the end of this flurry of military suicide lost her Macedonian provinces, and her northern territory, known as southern Dobrudja, went to Romania. Bulgaria's unwise decision to join with Germany in World War I resulted in the loss of her Aegean territories to Greece.

After this last debacle, King Ferdinand abdicated in favor of his son, Boris III. In 1935 King Boris assumed personal control. He sided with Germany in World War II in the hope of regaining southern Dobrudja, sections of Thrace, and the Aegean beaches. As a result, Bulgaria managed to reclaim southern Dobrudja (compliments of Russia) but was unable to annex western Thrace and the Aegean area. Three years after King Boris died, a People's Republic was proclaimed, on September 15, 1946.

When the Russians declared war on Bulgaria in 1944, the Communists rose to prominence. Georgi Dimitrov, a revered name in today's Bulgaria, became premier in 1946 and died in 1949; a visit to his tomb in downtown Sofia is a "must" for all foreign dignitaries. The only other political party in today's Bulgaria, the Agrarian People's Union, cooperates closely with the Communist Party.

LANGUAGE

Bulgarian is a Slavic tongue related to the Macedonian, Slovakian and Serbo-Croatian languages. "Old Bulgarian" was the first of the Slavic languages to be transcribed into the written word, by two Bulgarian monks in the 9th century. This transition was based on a new alphabet related to the Greek and known as Cyrillics, which translates as "you're on your own!"

Since tourist maps tend to use the Latin alphabet they are of little use when one is faced with street signs in Cyrillic characters. I suggest that instead of asking the waiter, "Which way to the opera?" that you have him draw a map or, better yet, that you buy an extra ticket and use him or a friend of his as a guide.

The Cyrillic alphabet is not such a problem in restaurants, as the larger ones have menus printed in four or five languages. Sufficient use is made of German, French, Spanish, Turkish, Russian and even English to make life easy for those who do not speak Bulgarian. Learn some basic words on a phonetic basis; it's not too difficult. Meanwhile, blaze your trail like a Boy Scout, memorize buildings, avenues and monuments.

CURRENCY

The Bulgarian monetary unit is the lev. There are 100 stotinki to the lev. Coins fall into denominations of 1, 2, 5, 10, and 50 stotinki, and the latter coin is rarely seen; 5 and 10 stotinki coins are the most common. Notes are in the following denominations: 1, 2, 4, 10, and 20 lev. The 1 and 2 lev notes are the most widely circulated.

At the tourist premium rate you will receive approximately two leva for one dollar. Money can be exchanged at all frontier entry points, at banks, large hotels and at some gas stations. Bulgarian currency cannot be imported or exported. When you change dollars into local currency, be sure to retain the slips given you at the transaction; border officials may ask to examine them when you leave the country.

VISAS AND CUSTOMS

Regulations governing entry of foreigners into Bulgaria change frequently, so check with the Bulgarian Legation, 2100 Sixteenth Street, N.W. Washington, D.C. or with your travel agent to find out whether or not a visa is required.

When you apply for an entry permit you will more than likely be asked to fill out a questionnaire in which you indicate the precise dates of your trip and the places you plan to enter and leave the country. This completed questionnaire will be inserted into your passport. When you enter Bulgaria the front section of the questionnaire, marked "Entry," will be retained at the border; the second section, marked "Exit," will be left in the passport. Hold on to it—it must be presented when you leave the country! Moreover, it must be left in the passport and shown upon registration at any hotel (the usual European police requirement).

Should you be in Greece, Yugoslavia or Turkey and decide to pay a visit to Bulgaria, a visa or entry permit can probably be obtained at the frontier for about $20; you may also need some passport-size photo portraits.

Bulgarian officials do not require you to submit a precise itinerary of your proposed trip; once inside the country you are pretty much free to move around as you please. Also, contrary to popular belief, it is not necessary to prepay your hotel and meal bills before entering Bulgaria; more about this where hotels are discussed.

Customs are no particular problem, formalities having been eased almost to the point of a cursory glance. All personal articles and souvenirs may enter duty free, as well as a typewriter, 250 cigarettes, two liters of wine or whisky, a radio, camera and film. There is a customs charge of about 20 leva ($10) for woolen and leather articles imported as gifts for relatives. During custom processing, be polite and cooperative and the chances are good that only the trunk of your car will be opened. I found the Bulgarian Customs officials to be firm but pleasant.

Before driving into Bulgaria or when leaving the country, be sure to establish ahead of time exactly which roads lead to the official frontier entry or exit points. A wrong turn can cost you time and trouble. Maps, particularly international road maps purchased in Western Europe, show roads crossing the border at a number of places. For quick reference, Bulgarian entry-exit points from Yugoslavia (Skopje); Gyueshovo; from Romania (Bucharest): Rousse; from the U.S.S.R. (Constanta): General Toshevo; from Greece (Salonica); Koulata. No other points of entry are now available to foreign tourists, except the international airports and the seaports of Varna and Burgas.

TRAVELING TO BULGARIA

By Air

Sofia, the capital of Bulgaria, is connected with Western European cities by KLM, Lufthansa, Austria Airlines and the Bulgarian State Airline, TABSO. There is daily service into Sofia's Virzhdebna airport by one or another of these airlines, usually on an alternating basis. In addition, Sabena in recent years has maintained air service from New York and Montreal, offering special 21-day excursion fares during the summer.

I suggest that when flying to Bulgaria you book on a round-trip basis. Be sure to reconfirm your departure once you have arrived in Bulgaria; this procedure may spare you considerable confusion during your stay and will permit you to plan your trip in greater detail with the assurance of a specific return date.

TABSO flies Iluyshin 18 turbo-prop planes on its international route which extend to the principal cities of Europe as well as to Athens and Algiers. Service is average, functional, safe—no frills, but convenient.

It is too bad that a greater effort is not made by Bulgarian authorities to provide incoming international guests with proper flight information, directions through customs and information regarding visa formalities, plane changes and the like. Passengers arriving at Sofia are often left to find out for themselves whether to check in at such-and-such a room, to wait on (or off) the plane in a continuing flight, etc. Moreover, help with luggage, particularly at night, is hard to find.

Foreign tourists traveling by charter flight directly to the Black Sea resorts frequently complete the customs procedures at Varna airport, whereas passengers on flights directed to Varna via Sofia complete customs procedures at the capital. In any case, remember to take your travel documents off the plane with you when disembarking, even if yours is a continuing flight.

By Train

Train service to Bulgaria is available several times a week from London, Paris and Lausanne via Yugoslavia on the Simpion-Orient Express. The Balt-Orient Express, which originates in Stockholm, travels via Prague and Budapest. Both these trains terminate in Istanbul. There is also the Tauern Express from London via Munich and Salzburg and the Danubian from Moscow.

TRANSPORTATION WITHIN BULGARIA

Air and Rail

TABSO has connecting flights, usually on a tourist fare basis, between Sofia and Varna, Plovdiv, Burgas and Rousse. Children under 2 pay 10 per cent of the adult fare; those between 2 and 12 fly at half price. Local train service is available between Sofia and all regions of the country. A one-way first class ticket from Sofia to Varna costs approximately $6; second class, the same trip costs a little more than half the price. Children under five travel free; those between the ages of five and ten at half price. Sleeping cars and restaurant cars are available on most trains. Bus travel in Bulgaria is not very comfortable.

By way of comparison, air service between Varna and Sofia costs a few cents less than rail tickets.

Motoring

All car-rental facilities in the country are under the supervision of Rodina, a division of the Bulgarian government's General Travel Board. It is possible to arrange in advance for a nicely equipped Volkswagen bus with driver—and if you wish, a guide—to be waiting at the airport upon your arrival in a town and to remain with you throughout the trip. These private buses are the *Dichtung und Wahrheit* of travel and are therefore expensive, the price depending on the length of your stay and the number of miles you travel. The guide's fee and maintenance is additional. Travel by privately rented Volkswagen bus is highly recommended for small groups of tourists, say three or four or more.

You can also rent a private car, with or without chauffeur. The basic charge (without driver) is 30c per hour plus 15c per kilometer, with an 85c per hour extra charge when the car is in your possession but not in use. This rate is for a five-passenger Russian model, which is really not comfortable when there are five occupants. But for a couple, it's fine.

For a self-drive car you can expect to pay, first, a deposit of $100. For one to seven days, the rate is about $12 daily plus 8c per kilometer in excess of 100. For over seven days, $10.80 daily plus 8c per kilometer over 100. These rates are of course subject to change.

If you are driving your own car or expect to rent a car, note that you do not need an international carnet, but that you must have an International Driver's License. At the frontier you will be required to buy automobile insurance to cover your stay in Bulgaria. White Cross Insurance is not valid in Bulgaria.

Traffic in Bulgaria (and in all of Middle Europe) drives on the right-hand side of the road, as in the U.S. The speed limit is 100 km. per hour in the country and 50 km. per hour near towns, unless different speed limits are posted. The roads really do not permit higher speeds as in many instances they are brick-topped, causing a good deal of vibration. Then, too, there is a lot of pedestrian traffic, farm carts, animals and the like. At times I have had the sensation of being the only car owner in the country, so empty were the roads.

On main roads, directional signs are printed in both Cyrillic and Latin characters, at least at the major junctions. Latin letters are also generally used at the entrance to town. Along secondary highways and within cities and towns the signs are frequently only in Cyrillic letters.

Motorists will find a fairly recent map called "Auto Map Bulgaria," distributed by the General Travel Board, very handy. It shows the principal highways, the secondary roads, customs control points, resort areas, service stations and the like. The map also lists the outstanding historical sights about the country and gives detailed plans of the principal cities. Other maps are available, but I have found them less satisfactory, particularly with regard to indicating topography and comparative road conditions. I once innocently embarked upon what I thought would be an uneventful trip from Assenovgrad to Madon. My map indicated a journey of 75 miles—but what miles they were! Mountains, very few gas stations, rugged terrain all the way.

Further miscellaneous tips for motorists: don't be afraid to ask for advice on road conditions, directions, etc; people are always kind and helpful. Exercise great care when motoring near the border; you can get into serious diplomatic trouble by inadvertently crossing (or attempting to cross) the frontier. Gasoline stations are found near every large town and scattered throughout the countryside. In the smaller towns, they are open from 6 A.M. to 10 P.M. and frequently close for 2 hours at midday; in the cities some stations are open around the clock. Gas, which may be purchased with leva or with foreign currency, costs about 25 stotinki per liter for high octane.

BULGARIAN TOURIST INDUSTRY

In Bulgaria, as in all the countries of Central and Eastern Europe, the travel business is directly under the supervision of the state. Private travel agencies as we know them do not exist. In some countries (such as Hungary) there are local "municipal bureaus" in towns and cities which are solely responsible to the capital for the care of tourists who visit that particular region, but in Bulgaria all lodging, feeding and transporting of the tourist is handled directly from Sofia.

Bulgaria's travel business is the responsibility of the General Travel Board, an agency represented on the Council of Ministers, Bulgaria's governing authority and the equivalent of our Cabinet. Directly under the General Travel Board are various agencies involved with the different aspects of the visitor's stay. Balkantourist, the agency responsible for the "Visit Bulgaria" campaigns throughout the world, is concerned mainly with the overall reception accorded you on your visit to Bulgaria and for your general well-being while in the country. Balkantourist constructs hotels throughout Bulgaria, furnishes guides, plans tours and is, in fact, your host during your stay. The Balkantourist desk in your hotel is the place to go for any and all information pertaining to your trip.

Tourist is that division of the General Travel Board that actually operates the hotels established by Balkantourist for Bulgaria's many visitors. Tourist furnishes the staffs, pays the wages and is generally responsible for the upkeep of the hotel and motel facilities.

Rodinatourist, another agency under the General Travel Board, is responsible for car hire, drivers and the like. You will deal with this agency if you decide to rent a Volkswagen bus or Chaika self-drive car. Rodinatourist operates through the auspices of Balkantourist.

Balkantourist must in my opinion become less "group oriented"! Without realizing it, the National Tourist Agency has arranged most of its facilities—bus trips, nighttime tours, airport facilities and restaurant accommodations—largely for groups of persons numbering 15 to 30 and up. As a result, individual visitors—responsible for their own passport formalities, table reservations and tour programs—are, to a large extent, left to fend for themselves—and, so to say, are at the mercy of a semi-disinterested bureaucracy. Informed hostesses at airports, bi-lingual receptionists in hotels, better restaurant accomodations for individuals—those things will all make Bulgaria more attractive to the tourist who travels independently.

Representatives of Balkantourist are located in the lobby of every first class and deluxe hotel throughout Bulgaria. Take your problems to these people, not to the hotel receptionists, who are empowered to do little but accept vouchers and hand out room keys. The Balkantourist representative takes care of making hotel reservations in other cities, handing out food coupons, planning nighttime tours of the cities—in fact, generally oversees the sojourn of the foreign visitor. On occasion, a separate desk under Balkantourist management handles local tours and trips to folk restaurants, particularly in hotels in Sofia. I have found the Balkantourist people to be, in the main, efficient, multi-lingual, patient and pleasant; they are not, however, infallible, so be certain that you have written confirmation of all hotel reservations.

Balkantourist maintains upwards of 31,000 beds for foreign visitors in Bulgaria and is hoping to more than double that number by 1970. Bulgaria entertained 800,000 foreign tourists in 1964. Income from the tourist industry is stated to be the equivalent of approximately $30 million, and roughly $20 million is being poured back into the development of tourist facilities. In its promotional activities, Balkantourist is stressing the Bulgarian Black Sea resorts (Golden Sands, Sunny Beach, Friendship, etc.) with secondary emphasis going to the sites of historically important ancient ruins. Some 65 towns and cities scattered about the country—Sofia is included in this final category—are less widely publicized.

Bulgaria is not yet sufficiently developed in its tourist functions, but matters improve. At the moment Balkantourist is working toward reducing visa formalities at the border to a 15-minute or less process and hopes soon to institute oral baggage and monetary declaration procedures.

HOTELS

Most of the hotels under Balkantourist sponsorship have the usual nightclubs, bars, cafes, lounges and restaurants. (I will mention some outstanding ones when I discuss specific hotels.) These hotels are divided into three principal categories—deluxe, first class and tourist class—plus two other classes which foreign tourists are generally not concerned with—super-deluxe, called "special," which is usually available only to persons prominent in the world of government or business, and third class, which caters to groups and consists of dormitory-type sleeping quarters.

Prices are standardized in Bulgaria. The following table will give you a fairly precise idea of what you can expect to spend in the various categories of hotels. Daily rates drop $1 after you have occupied a room for over seven days. Prices quoted apply presently in Sofia and are for full pension. Rates vary according to locale and are somewhat lower in certain resort areas.

	SINGLE	*DOUBLE*
		(per person)
Special	$12.00	$10.50
Deluxe	9.00	7.50
First class	8.00	7.50
Second class	7.00	5.50
Third class	6.00	4.50

You ask, what exactly is the difference between deluxe and first class? Bathtubs seem to play some part in the differentation; the number of apartments may also be involved. The designation deluxe also generally confirms the existence of a restaurant within the hotel instead of in a structure a short distance away. A restaurant within the hotel itself would provide room service—something of a rarity in the resort communities—thereby upping the rating given the hotel by Balkantourist.

If you wish to be assured of an apartment with bath and enjoy one or two meals in your room, then request deluxe accommodations. If any one of these three points is of little importance to you, request first class space as it is less expensive and quite acceptable. If you request deluxe, be certain to take full pension as your hotel will probably have one of the best kitchens in the area.

For those who may be a bit dubious about plunging into strange hostelries in far away places, let me assure you that the hotels in Bulgaria are generally hospital-clean, interiorally drab and politically safe. You will meet some Frenchmen, quite a few Scandinavians, small groups of Britishers and literally hordes of West Germans. There are so many in this latter category that at times one is hard put to judge whether one is in Varna or Hamburg.

Those who travel in a tourist category (second class) will have the opportunity to meet many more people from Eastern Europe than those who travel first class or deluxe. In the tourist class hotels, which I will describe below, there is a better opportunity for "nationality mixing," and to my way of thinking this is desirable. Tourists in first class hotels of course meet "easterners" in restaurants, bars and theaters, but there can hardly be the informal companionship so readily apparent in the tourist category, particularly in those places where the younger age groups gather.

Hotel reservations seem to me to be at least as advisable when traveling in Bulgaria as they are when traveling in Western Europe or even the United States. Advance reservations are particularly desirable if you plan to visit popular resort areas such as those along the Black Sea coast. To secure a hotel reservation simply ask your travel agent to book you into a deluxe, first or second class hotel for X number of nights and tell him whether you want full board or only breakfast. To simplify matters, request all your Bulgarian hotel reservations at the same time. Your travel agent will request confirmation of the space requirements from Balkantourist and upon receipt of same will ask you for full payment.

Unfortunately, the relatively simple procedure of securing hotel reservations in Bulgaria can be turned into a quagmire of misunderstanding and misinformation by uninformed travel personnel in this country and abroad. When I was planning my own recent trip I turned the matter of hotel reservations over to a well-known American travel firm; the reservations requested were finally confirmed but not before I received several bits of contradictory information. Keep this in mind: Bulgaria is a section of the globe about which travel agencies in this country have very little information and an almost total lack of working knowledge. Therefore, in order to insure against possible mixups, these agencies may tell you that a visa will not be issued *without* hotel reservations. This is not true in Bulgaria, Romania or Czechoslovakia; you need not have confirmed hotel reservations prior to entering these countries. Furthermore, there is no minimum per diem charge for entry into Bulgaria, nor is a specific itinerary required.

By encouraging you to make specific reservations well in advance and preferably in first class, if not deluxe category, the travel agent may be doing you a considerable disservice. First class or deluxe hotels may not exist in every town on your schedule; in Eastern Europe "deluxe" is something of a rarity anyway and first class is perfectly adequate. Once accepted by you, a coupon (or hotel voucher) for a hotel anywhere in Eastern Europe is not refundable *in dollars*. Local travel desks in Eastern Europe very kindly refunded to me (in Bulgarian currency) the amount I paid unnecessarily in New York for first class space when such accommodations were not available in towns on my itinerary. Learn what type of accommodations are available in the towns you plan to visit; don't pay deluxe rates for second class lodgings.

Tourists traveling on a prepaid hotel and meals basis must enter Bulgaria in possession of a coupon or some form of credential from a travel agent indicating that they have paid for their hotel reservations and meals in advance. Upon arrival, this coupon is presented to the Balkantourist representative at the hotel where the room is reserved for the first night. This representative in turn gives the tourist leva equivalent to the amount he paid in America for room and board *or* individual hotel vouchers for presentation to each hotel on his itinerary, plus food coupons. (Whether he gets cash or coupons depends on Balkantourist policy during the year of his visit.) Once in possession of these funds (or hotel vouchers and food coupons), the tourist is expected to pay his own hotel and food bills.

Balkantourist and the other Eastern European national travel services (and even the hotels themselves) have indicated to me that they are prepared to accept tourist reservations directly, by mail or cable, but my advice is that such matters are presently better handled through local travel agents in the U.S. There is still too much red tape and too many language problems for the average person to cope with efficiently. Tell your travel agent exactly what kind of accommodations you want and when you expect to arrive at each place and he will issue coupons stating that reservations have been secured for you for specific dates at specific hotels for each town you plan to visit.

Because there is such a lack of information about travel to Eastern Europe, I want to recapitulate the options the foreign visitor has in regard to hotel reservations.

(1) A trip with all hotel reservations, meal coupon and visas obtained through your travel agent at home and paid for prior to departing on your trip. Confirmed reservations for round-trip air transportation would be part of the package.

(2) A trip with some visas and hotel reservations prearranged through your travel agent, say for the first part of your stay, with the latter part being left free. Once in Bulgaria your visa will be extended and hotel arrangements can be concluded as you travel through Bulgaria.

(3) A trip totally devoid of reservations; in such an instance you will have that fine feeling of being free to drive to whatever hotel you

wish, to camp out, or perhaps to visit one of Balkantourist's motels.

Remember that when hotel reservations are confirmed you will naturally be required to make full payment for these accommodations. In the event that reservations must be cancelled, your travel agency must send a wire to Balkantourist requesting such cancellation. You will be required to pay a service fee for this cancellation and will, in all likelihood, lose from one quarter to one half of the monies paid, depending on the number of days or weeks before such reservations were to have been effective. Therefore, make every effort to avoid changes in your prepaid travel program that will involve cancellation of hotel space reservations.

Conversely, always get written confirmation from the hotel manager's office of an extension of your room reservation for one or more days beyond that time originally approved. There are frequent breakdowns in communication between members of the reception desk, and verbal approval of extensions are not binding.

Let us consider for a moment the pros and cons of reserving hotel space in advance. In favor of confirmed reservations is the happy feeling that your trip has been largely paid for and the certainty that you will be sleeping under a roof each night. The negative aspect is that if and when coupons are discontinued (as they already have been in other Eastern European countries) upon arrival you may be handed a large roll of bills which should be somewhat of a headache to stash away—especially if the trip is long. You will also have a tendency to dip into the "hotel and food money" to pay for souvenirs, guides, side trips and the like, with the result that eventually you'll be obliged to cash travelers checks to pay hotel bills. The "newly discovered wealth" aspect of this coupon-leva exchange easily results in the tendency to go on a spree during the first days of your stay. In addition when you have prepaid for hotel space, you cannot cancel without considerable monetary loss!

Should your stay be of two to three weeks' duration (and to really enjoy Bulgaria it should not be much shorter), give some thought to applying for a visa for the full length of your stay, while requesting confirmed hotel space for only *a portion* of your visit, perhaps paying the room and full pension charge for the first several days. This will limit the amount to be paid in advance, limit the amount of money you will be handed at the border, give you greater flexibility of movement about the country, allow you to choose some hotels on your own, and—most important—give you the advantage of any exchange benefits the Bulgarian Government might establish for visitors who elect to buy levas within the country. (Such benefits are now in effect in other Eastern European countries but not as yet in Bulgaria. Present exchange regulations give you the same amount of leva for the dollar whether you pay for your trip in advance or exchange dollars for local currency within the country.)

Bear in mind that the full pension plan does not require you to eat all of your meals in the hotel in which your rooms are reserved. You will be given leva (or coupons) in exchange for the money paid in the United States. You may spend the leva in any restaurant in which you may elect to eat, the coupons only in Balkantourist establishments.

Hotel rates throughout Bulgaria are based largely on a room plus meals, full pension basis. When you reserve hotel space you will probably find it convenient to pay for meals also.

FOOD AND DRINK

Bulgarian cooking is good. The vegetables, fruits, meats (particularly the grilled pork and lamb) are excellent. Salads, cheeses and desserts are for the most part tasty, healthful, inexpensive and, in many instances, downright delectable. Tarator soup, made of cucumbers, onions, olive oil and yogurt and served cold, is delicious; as is borsch, made of beets and sometimes potatoes. Bulgarian cuisine reveals a marvelous composite of the cooking skills of the Slavs, the Turks and, to a degree, the Austro-Hungarians. In the large hotels, almost every imaginable kind of food is served, from caviar to "miche-mache," a marvelous concoction of paprika, hard-boiled eggs, tomatoes and cheese mixed together. Try fried eggplant and paprika with cheese. For the main course veal, pork or beef. Grilled meats are particularly outstanding—for example, kebabs, grilled sausages, "schaschlik," as well as meat balls on a skewer with onions and/or yellow cheese. Desserts run the gamut from crepes suzette to tarts, creme caramel and all sorts of fruits and cheeses. Don't forget to try pitka, the delicious warm bread; don't slice it, tear off bite size portions with your fingers.

On the streets you may see folks eating banitsa, a long thin waferlike food with cheese or—in season—pumpkin or spinach filling. Your figure will suffer but your pocketbook will not. You can enjoy an average, wholesome meal even in restaurants where no English is spoken—just by indicating that you want food. Prices are minimal, almost startlingly so for the portions served. A good three-course dinner will cost in the region of two leva or less. You should tip about 10 per cent.

For a non-alcoholic delight try Ayran, a combination of yogurt and water, served cold. Soda water (ask for "syphon" and you'll get a large seltzer bottle) and bottled mineral waters are also available, clean, clear, tasteful and inexpensive. The plain drinking water is uniformly good throughout Bulgaria.

Beer is likely to be of East German manufacture and acceptable. Whisky is available, and Scotch sells for 12 leva the bottle or approximately 1 lev for a 50 gram "shot," a quantity somewhat less than our jigger. However, in one or two bars (notably the Hotel Trimontium in Plovdiv) I entertained the suspicion that the whisky I ordered tasted a little odd; the drink resembled brandy. Should you dote on Scotch and soda before dinner, I suggest you furnish your own Scotch and let Bulgaria provide the soda. Bourbon? Forget it, or again, bring your own. You'll have no problem bringing in a couple of fifths. In Bulgaria, the so-called English whisky ordered in a cafe will most likely be the real McCoy. However, should you simply order whisky, there is every chance that you will be served cognac. Pliska Brandy, a product of Bulgaria, is inexpensive and pleasant, straight or when mixed with soda. Mastika, a drink made from anise, is also to be recommended. There is also Slivova (Slivowitz) and a good grape brandy.

GUIDES

It is my suggestion that you employ guides in one of two ways; either set out on your tour of the country by auto with the best possible guide available, or employ guides on a local basis.

In the first instance, naturally more expensive, your guide would be able to point out the landmarks that dot the countryside. The second approach is less expensive but does not necessarily provide you with less information. Naturally you miss a few high spots along the road but there is a redeeming factor here and an important one at that: the presence of a guide will tend to isolate you from the local people. You will find yourself relying on the guide to make your table reservations, book seats at the theater, order your meals, etc. When traveling across the country the local people will naturally approach your guide, not you.

It must be emphasized that even though you may make a day's trip through Bulgaria without a guide, once you have arrived at your destination a guide is a "must." Local guides can be supplied by Balkantourist.

Guides are seldom adequately informed on *all* the regions of their country, and for this and other reasons I prefer to hire a new guide in each region, rather than keep one guide throughout my trip. In any case, you will be paying a considerable sum of money for your guide. If he proves to be a "bust," contact the nearest National Travel Office and demand a new guide. I emphasize this point for it is useless to bumble about the country or a city in the company of a so-called guide who obviously knows little more than you do about the places you see. You pay dearly for this service so expect good value.

GROUP TOURS

Should you be a member of a group of tourists visiting Bulgaria, the entire program complete with reservations, meals, guides, side trips, transportation and the like, must be paid for in advance and cannot thereafter be altered although prices, itineraries and daily programs are naturally subject to variation. Most tourist organizations provide a small cash outlay to their clients during the trip to enable them to purchase souvenirs, have a beer and so forth. Members of the touring group can spend what they wish from their own funds carried along in the form of travelers checks, cash, etc. Touring groups usually eat together at hotels at tables set aside for their use. Meals are planned in advance and little leeway is permitted in the selection of courses. Inexpensive wines are usually included with the evening meal. But once again, it all depends on what price you have paid for your tour— whether it is to be a deluxe or first class trip. As a rule, passports and hotel coupons are handled by the guide who works in collaboration with his Bulgarian counterpart. This relieves those on tour of some responsibilities and red tape.

PHOTOGRAPHY

You may be asked at the border if you have a camera, typewriter and the like in your possession. Much as we might like to think so, this question carries with it no overtones of spine-tingling espionage. Rather, the Bulgarian government is simply making an effort to discourage the sale of these items in the country, and accordingly the border officials will make a note in your passport of the fact that you have certain items in your possession. As long as these things are still in your possession when you leave the country, there will be no trouble.

As far as what you may photograph, fire away at will—stills, movies, close-up shots, the works. I do suggest, however, that you suppress the urge to capture on film a warship as it cuts its way through the sunlit waves outside the harbor of Varna. Bulgaria offers splendid scenic shots, so take as many pictures as you wish—but use some discretion when you aim your camera.

MAIL

Very frequently the reception and mail desks in hotels are combined. This arrangement does not present any difficulty in obtaining one's mail. However, when the mail desk is combined with that of the concierge, I suggest that before surrendering your passport to the clerk at the reception desk you hand it to the person in charge of the mail desk so that he can properly identify your correspondence. Neither the diction of Maurice Evans nor the tones of a baseball umpire will achieve the same result as a clearly typed name on a page of your passport.

I suggest that you allow a full 10 days for mail from the U.S. or Western Europe to reach you in care of a Bulgarian hotel. Outgoing mail takes, minimally, one week to North America; two to three weeks is the average.

SOUVENIRS

You might like to take home a bottle of the rose oil for which Bulgaria is famous. Rose liqueur is also available. Items carved out of wood (cigarette holders, cigarette boxes) make nice, inexpensive gifts. Embroidery too can be quite well done. Earthenware jugs, ashtrays and the like (often hand painted) can be interesting and inexpensive.

TIPS ON TABLE-SHARING

Trained waiters and waitresses are in short supply throughout most of Eastern Europe. A number of countries have inaugurated programs enabling them to send hotel employees to London, Paris and other large cities for training. Bulgarian restaurant facilities are overburdened by the increased patronage of local citizens, whose standard of living has risen, also by the influx of tourists attracted by the lure of an inexpensive vacation.

Because of this overcrowding you may expect the headwaiters of some restaurants to ask if they may seat other guests at your table. American tourists are expected to react kindly, or, at the least, with civility. A non-English speaking would-be diner may simply indicate, without benefit of headwaiter, that he and his party would like to occupy the empty places at your table. May I offer several rules:

(1) Say yes if at all possible!
(2) Mind your own meal in pleasant fashion and resist the temptation to comment on the manners, appearances, etc. of your tablemates who may understand some English.
(3) Those who sit down will inevitably be curious about your nationality and about your personality. Only in these public places do they have much opportunity to come into contact with foreigners such as yourself. If they make comments about your clothes, cigarettes and the like, pretend not to notice their interest unless they direct a question to you.
(4) Do not feel that you must make conversation. Eastern Europeans are accustomed to such situations; if they are anxious to speak with you, believe me they will originate the conversation at the earliest possible moment.

SOFIA

At the base of the Vitusha Mountains in West Central Bulgaria, prior to the year 29 B.C., the Thracian tribes defended their empire against the expansion of Rome. Nonetheless in 29 B.C. the Roman armies overcame a Thracian tribe called the Serdi; at the site of the battle a strategic Roman fortress was constructed and given the name Serdica. The Roman Legions were eventually eliminated from Bulgaria by armies of the Visigoths and Huns. During a later period of the Byzantine Empire, Serdica was renamed Triaditsa, and in 1808 a Bulgarian Khan annexed the city, changing the name to the Slav Sredeta. Today we know this site as Sofia.

The city of Sofia has always been guarded by battlements and fortresses located on the hills and mountains surrounding the city. With the Ottoman conquest of the Balkans, the town of Sofia experienced a tremendous building program which included fountains, mosques, stone bridges and minarets. Christian churches had to be built in inconspicuous fashion if not actually constructed underground. After 1879, the date of Bulgaria's liberation from the hated Turks, a new intensive building program began that was also to eliminate many of the Oriental characteristics of the city.

At first glance, visitors to Sofia see little but the new architecture — those buildings built in the period from 1890 to the present. Yet any walking tour of Sofia is bound to introduce the foreign visitor to the historical charms of this city.

Listed below are some of the more outstanding points of interest of today's Sofia.

Sightseeing in Sofia

ALEXANDER NEVZKY MEMORIAL CHURCH This splendidly constructed edifice, its golden domes reflecting sun and moon alike, is located in the center of Sofia. The Bulgarian Orthodox Church is named for the patron saint of Czar Alexander II of Russia, and is notable for its fine paintings, frescoes and an excellent collection of icons and church relics dating from the 10th century. In the crypt are the solid gold treasures, relics of the ancient Thracian Kingdom.

CHURCH OF ST. SOPHIA A very interesting 10th century church. Orthodox services are held both at Alexander Nevzky and St. Sophia at the times posted on the doors.

THE RUSSIAN CHURCH · Opposite the Hotel Bulgaria.

THE NATIONAL ART GALLERY A former royal palace as interesting for its architecture as for its contents. The collection consists of the work of Bulgarian artists principally. Folklore exhibits.

THE GEORGI DIMITROV TOMB All foreign dignitaries visit the resting place of contemporary Bulgaria's foremost statesman.

ETHNOGRAPHICAL MUSEUM One block behind the Hotel Balkan. Interesting collection housed in a former mosque.

BUYOUK MOSQUE Representative architecture from the days of the Ottoman Turk.

CHURCH OF BOJANA This delightful museum is located in a cool pinewoods in the village of Bojana, 10 minutes or less by car south of Sofia on the Athens highway. A must for everyone interested in antiquity, in fresco painting, and in 13th-century architecture. The second (center) section was built in 1259 and the third was completed in 1882. Excellent frescoes all from the 13th century—not restorations! The outside of the building has been restored, however.
NOTE: Only 10 or 12 people are allowed in this church at one time because the government fears damage to the frescoes from humidity.

PARKS; BATHS; STATUARY Any guide will point out the five-story memorial to the Russian troops of World War II; nearby there is a particularly fine statuary piece commemorating the victory over Ottoman Turkey in 1879. Be sure to visit the public mineral baths housed in a fantastic building located near the Tsuom Department Store, which is also worth a visit. See the parks and the zoo.

Hotels

Hotels in Bulgaria fall into two categories: those built between 1952 and 1956, before the great interest in tourism, and the more recent high-rise structures, somewhat suggestive of the glass boxes along New York's Park Avenue. The pre-1957 hotels, of which the Hotel Balkan is most certainly a prototype, have an institutional appearance that can only be called formidable! Of medium height, square, bleak, they exude all the warmth and intimacy of Grand Central Station.

BALKAN The Balkan is part of a large complex of buildings located on Lenin Square in the heart of one of the best sections of downtown Sofia. The hotel does not occupy the entire structure; the rear section is headquarters for a government department. The Tsuom Department Store is across the street.

The Hotel Balkan is one of the best hotels in Sofia; it is very popular, so reservations are necessary.

Besides the large stone and marble lobby, there is a lounge, souvenir shop, cocktail lounge and French restaurant. Opposite the main entrance is a restaurant largely reserved for group dining. Since there are always large packs of tourists in town, this room is usually jammed. Off of this restaurant the management has set off an area resembling a typical country wine cellar (a "mechana" in Bulgarian) with small rooms and music for dancing.

A cocktail lounge off the central lobby serves coffee until 11 P.M. or so as well as cocktails, brandy, etc. The French restaurant is open all day. Very good food, and average to good service. Designed for individual dining, couples and small groups, it is one of the best in the city.

The girls at the Balkantourist desk in the lobby speak several languages and can answer all questions concerning your stay. The Balkan Hotel has 187 rooms including 5 large apartments and 25 smaller units; 65 singles in all, the other rooms being doubles. As the building has a courtyard to the rear, you might avoid the not inconsiderable street noise of Lenin Square by asking for a room here facing the courtyard. Perhaps you would like a *garçonniere*, a bedroom forming an alcove off a small living room. Large apartments have TV; radios are in most of the rooms.

Rooms are pleasantly furnished and clean. Room service is available for all meals. Bathrooms (with tubs) are available throughout the hotel; they are clean with hot water, wall showers, and hand showers, but the various bathroom apartments have on occasion been out of order.

A barber shop is located in the hotel. A haircut costs 30 stotinki; with a shave, etc., about 50 stotinki. The Balkantourist desk in the lobby can direct the women to hairdressers.

Letters should be delivered to the concierge desk. Attendants here will weigh the mail and you can pay them immediately instead of putting it on the bill. Telephone and telegraph facilities are also available. Personal laundry is done in the hotel; pressing taken out. Prices for laundry and pressing are very low, and clothes are returned in good shape.

Save time by breakfasting in your room. The meal consists of tea, sour bread (toasted) and jam.

My second choice of hotels in Sofia fluctuates between the centrally located Hotel Rila and the very new, ultra-modern Hotel Pliska, located some six minutes by car from the center of town. Let's discuss the Hotel Rila first because of its central location.

RILA The Rila does not have the swagger of the Balkan but is certainly much quieter than its older, flossier sister hotel. Constructed in 1963, the Rila is a 12 to 14-story structure located dead center in the better shopping center of Sofia, close to the opera, to museums, and to the better restaurants. A small bar and barbershop are off the lobby.

There are 160 rooms, only 10 with full showers. The other 150 rooms have bath with hand shower. Rooms on the south (park) side—the best location—have small balconies. There are 60 doubles and 30 singles; all rooms are about the same size and seem somewhat smaller than those at the Balkan. Suites are generally located at the corner of the building; they are not large either, but are pleasant and furnished with a large double bed.

The call buttons often don't work, but you can phone for room service, which is available for all meals. The main restaurant serves good food and an orchestra swings from about 8 P.M. There's a small, nice restaurant on the second floor, too. A more intimate place (no music) with an attractive view of the park. The "keller" is nothing outstanding, but pleasant for 9-to-12 dancing.

If you don't go for swank atmosphere and like a measure of tranquillity, you will prefer the Rila to the Balkan.

PLISKA An ultra-modern 14-story structure completed in late 1965, the Pliska is located in a new housing development two miles from the center of Sofia and directly on the international highway between Belgrade and Istanbul. The cocktail lounges at the top (for guests only!) offer a fine view of the city and surrounding countryside. The main lobby is colorful and attractive.

Rooms are on the small side with most beds in the foot-to-foot arrangement so popular in Europe today. All rooms are doubles with the exception of three apartments. Doubles have showers directed at the floor; apartments have bath showers. Furnishings are more practical than comfortable. Full room service, laundry and pressing services are available. You will pay the maid who does the work.

The lobby of the Pliska contains a souvenir shop, money exchange booth and a cafe, in which the Bulgarian architectural touch of including garden areas within the interior space is nicely carried out. The second floor contains a smart, modern cocktail lounge and a cafe seating 500 persons. Meals here are very good, and menus are in French and German.

The Hotel Pliska's location, some distance from the center of town is a disadvantage if you have to rely on taxis, since these are rather scarce. However, bus lines and trams run from the hotel directly to central Sofia. There is also bus service to and from Sofia airport. There is ample parking space in front of the hotel for guests' cars.

Near the hotel are a movie theater, shops and a post office, all part of the housing development in which the hotel is situated. The Pliska is not as dressy as the Balkan, nor as folksy as the Rila; it is quiet, smart in appearance and quite comfortable.

BULGARIA In this old edifice the dining rooms have been completely redecorated and now feature dining and dancing in a rather too brightly lighted atmosphere—modern, complete with mezzanine.

Built in 1935, this hotel is located directly in the center of historical Sofia quite near the National Art Gallery (former royal palace), the Georgi Dimitrov Mausoleum and the Alexander Nevzky Memorial Church.

There is a small but neat lobby where a souvenir shop and a money exchange desk are located. A bar can be found in a large lounge. Parking is available in front of the hotel.

There are 100 rooms, all with bath and shower. Both front and back rooms are acceptable, but the latter are somewhat quieter. Room service, laundry and pressing are available. Double rooms can be large or small, so be specific when reserving.

I found the personnel here to be very pleasant and interested in their work. The entire atmosphere of the Bulgaria is on the intimate side. I would rate this hotel after the Balkan, Rila and Pliska, although with renovations (and an improvement of the parking problem) the Bulgaria could be very pleasant.

SLAVIA Five minutes by car from downtown Sofia, the Slavia is right on the Sofia-Athens-Belgrade highway. It is a suburban hotel of four stories with a pleasant lobby, ample parking and a neat, sunny restaurant. Music at night. Exchange desk, elevator, bar and TV in the lobby. Approximately 75 rooms; all accommodations have a shower and telephone. There is room service for breakfast, and laundry and pressing service.

KOPITO (VITUSHA) Driving south from Sofia on the Athens highway, you will pass on your left the suburban village of Bojana. Drive through Bojana village, straight up into the Vitusha Mountains to the Hotel Kopito.

The Vitusha Range can be seen easily from Sofia; low-lying mountains which reflect the haze, the sun, the moon, as well as the snow's blueness in wintertime. The drive up to the Kopito takes roughly 15 minutes. There is also a cable car. The Kopito is a modernistic structure combining a restaurant and the hotel. There are only 22 rooms, with only the second and third level rooms boasting showers. No radios or telephones in rooms. Laundry and pressing services are available. Rooms are very clean and functional — similar to a modern chalet in the Alps.

Rooms have balconies with spectacular views of the city below. Be sure to book on the top two floors. Room service for all meals.

A lounge on the second floor connects with the restaurant which seats roughly 250 persons. It is intimate in decor and design. There are terraces for out-of-doors dining with that view overlooking Sofia. Those who have frequented Vienna's Kahlenberg will find the view somewhat similar, though the restaurant at the Kopito is decidedly more pleasant, less formal.

As appealing as it is, the Hotel Kopito is *out* if you are in Bulgaria mainly to tour-view Sofia and the like. If this is the case, settle for lunch there. However, if you really want to get away from it all, rest, hike, and yet remain within a half hour's car ride of Sofia, try the Kopito.

Restaurants

Hotel restaurants at the Balkan, Rila and Pliska are difficult to beat. I did not have the opportunity to try the food at the Bulgaria or Slavia, but judging from the surroundings, I would guess that these restaurants provide average to good food. The restaurant at Kopito is very good. Other restaurants in the Sofia area include the following:

HUNGARIA This establishment is roughly a 10-minute walk from the Balkan and Rila hotels but it might be a bit difficult to locate unless you are acquainted with the city. It is situated on one of the main boulevards of the capital, Rakovska Street, and is in two large sections. To the left is a cafe and to the right a dining area offering gypsy music in the evening. Large windows front directly on the walk; the rooms are low-ceilinged and include deep booths on the far wall and medium-sized tables throughout the rest of the restaurant.

Although others have enjoyed their food here, I did not! I found the service slow, the food mediocre, the atmosphere not unlike that of a third-rate saloon. It was noisy, cluttered and full of smoke.

The gypsy orchestra is very much with you as the tables run right up to the podium. Since there is not a great variety of restaurants in Sofia, you might try if you're in town for some days. Otherwise, I would eat elsewhere. I can't recommend the Hungaria on the basis of my evening there.

THE RUSSIAN CLUB Not Russian, not a club. Try this place, for it is attractive and provides good food, served in pleasant fashion by most efficient waiters. It is located in an old home a short distance behind the National Opera on Dobrudja Street, directly on the corner. There is a pleasant garden to the rear for summer dining. No music. Conventional dress for evening dining. Be certain to reserve ahead, and go early, about seven-thirty as it gets crowded.

TSUOM STATE DEPARTMENT STORE This large store—with restaurant—is located across the street to the right of the Hotel Balkan. It isn't Marshall Field's but it is worth trying simply for the experience. Open at noon; in the evening music is provided for dancing. In any event, the store is something to see.

BERLIN Opposite the Parliament Building on Boulevard Rouski. I did not have an opportunity to visit this restaurant but understand that it is popular with local people, which we all know is a good sign. It is reportedly on the dressy side.

PARK OF FREEDOM RESTAURANT This indoor-outdoor beanery is located near the television tower. Try it for a beer.

ROPOTAMO The Ropotamo Restaurant is named after the delightful river that enters the Black Sea in southeastern Bulgaria.

BOJANA RESTAURANT FOLK EVENING Several times during my stay at Sofia's Hotel Balkan I noticed a sign on the Balkantourist desk to the rear of the lobby, something about "Folk dancing—a night in a 'mechana'—buy your tickets here!" I dislike that sport known the world over as folklore night or "see Bessarabia by night," but I signed up in the interests of complete and factual reporting. Twelve leva per person and you will receive a receipt entitling you to a round-trip bus ride and a tasty dinner of sizeable proportions, including brandy before, wine with dinner and rose liqueur following dessert *if* you can find, handle, much less raise the glass by that time. "Mechana" is the name given to a rustic country inn Bulgarian style; wood paneling, chintz or gingham table covers, wooden furniture, waiters in national costume, folk music—the works! Here at Bojana, located at the foot of the picturesque Vitusha Mountains Range some 10 minutes from downtown Sofia, I spent a truly interesting, amusing evening handled with a maximum of enthusiasm, tact and charm by three attractive hostesses. I especially recommend this charming restaurant to tourists who are in transit through Bulgaria, stopping only a night in Sofia, for here is a chance to gain a peek into the country's folk patterns, national dances and the like. Don't miss it!

BOREVETS MOUNTAINS

HOTEL BOR Borovets, or "Pine Trees," depending on which language you speak, is a delightful hotel located in the center of one of Europe's most lovely pine forests, which is the Bulgarian headquarters for winter ski trips or summer hiking vacations. Not that the Hotel Bor is located a rugged mile off the main track—quite the contrary! The hotel is but a two-hour drive from Sofia along one of Bulgaria's most beautiful highways.

Built in 1961, the Bor is located on a small rise surrounded by gardens, terraces and pine trees. Drive your car to the rear of the hotel for it's quite a climb up the steps in front—at least too much climbing for baggage transfer. The fourth (top) floor consists of a dorm for groups of hikers; the first two floors comprise 60 nicely furnished double rooms (no singles) and three apartments which can be set up as a bedroom-sitting room or adjoining bedrooms. No elevator. Full-length mirrors and dressing tables. Showers are directly onto floor but fortunately recessed. Apartments are located on corners of the building for better ventilation; they have showers (not baths) and bedrooms which are a bit larger. On the third floor, there are rooms with balconies along the front side. Be sure to ask for front side exposure. Back rooms are pleasant, though somewhat darker. Beds in doubles are foot-to-foot.

Laundry and pressing are done on the premises—see your maid. Complete room service. Assistance with baggage during the season (summer months and mid-winter). A large restaurant and terrace off the lobby. The food is good, service is acceptable. Under the restaurant and off the ping-pong area there is a small souvenir shop with some interesting Bulgarian woodcarvings, hand-painted cocktail napkins, cigarettes and the like. Below this ping-pong area there is a small bar, a mighty "sympatisch" room with a complete line of drinks and a Wurlitzer. A fine little hotel and well worth the visit. Great for a rest and walking. Be sure to make reservations here, particularly in midsummer or during the ski holiday period.

If you are "doing Bulgaria," I would stop here for lunch. Run over from Sofia or on your way to Plovdiv. But if you want a break from a tough schedule or simply a few days' relaxation, take a front room with balcony, a book and you'll have it made! I understand that a somewhat larger hotel is planned for Borovets—200 rooms. Same style (rustic) but larger. Possibly to be named the Rila. Look for it!

HASKOVO

Hotel

BALKANTOURIST Haskovo is a pleasant little town situated approximately an hour's drive from the Turkish border. I recommend the hotel here for it is modern, clean, offering very comfortable rooms plus a restaurant with good food, well served.

A comparatively modern structure directly in the center of town, the hotel has ample parking, a very pleasant lobby and elevator. Attendants at the reception desk, where money can be exchanged, were most helpful during my stay. All rooms are doubles with shower or bath and are clean. There is nothing of historical note here. A walk around the town in the evening might be interesting to you. I always enjoy looking at the architecture, into the shops and generally seeing what the folks in each town do during their evening hours. In the mood for a movie? There is a theater just to the right of the hotel entrance.

PLEVEN

Hotel

KAILUKA Located some 10 minutes by car from the center of town, the Kailuka Hotel is situated in a natural park area surrounded by rock bluffs. Modern tourist cabins are located to the rear of the hotel; small and without baths (but with washing facilities nearby), they are neat and clean. The hotel has a large reception area and pleasant restaurant located beside a large garden in which guests may dine. The restaurant is inclined to be crowded in cool weather. Music in the evenings. The food is generally good.

Bedrooms at the Kailuka are relatively spacious and nicely furnished. The restaurant service is adequate. No room service. Bus service to the town.

Restaurant

GROTTO To visit the Grotto Restaurant operated by Balkantourist, take the bus which stops in front of the Kailuka Hotel. Get off at the first stop after leaving the hotel.

Sightseeing

To be seen at Pleven: the Russian Memorial Church dedicated to men who died during the Russian-Turkish War in the late 1800's.

PLOVDIV

Known to the Greeks as Phillippopolis (after their hero Phillip of Macedon), to the Romans as Trimontium (after three of the six hills on which they lived) and to the Turks as Felibe, Plovdiv is one of the most attractive cities of Europe. Besides its tourist attractions Plovdiv has in its immediate surroundings a spare parts works, a shoe factory, a textile mill, tobacco factories and so on. Plovdiv is called Bulgaria's second capital.

Put on your walking shoes, make it an early breakfast and begin your tour of this interesting, attractive old city, which sprawls along the banks of the Maritza River on the central Thracian plain in southern Bulgaria. The old town is best appreciated, explored, enjoyed by those folks who put legwork over horsepower. There are certain sections of the town more easily reached by car (the fair grounds; Liberator's Hill) but these are individual sites, and in all fairness to history I would not call them an intrinsic component of Old Plovdiv.

Visit the mid-1800 merchants' homes; their interesting architectural style is a good example of the Revivalist Period in Bulgaria. One of the most intriguing of these houses was built in 1847 and is presently occupied by the Ethnographical Museum. The building itself impressed me as much as the articles on display. Then too there is the Archeological Museum containing many wondrous gold vessels, including amphora (used for storing wine) and the gold sheets from which these magnificent Thracian pieces were made. Not far from the Ethnographical Museum is the house occupied for some days by Lamartine, the French poet, on his return from the Orient in 1833. Near this house is the small park which overlooks the Maritza River, the fair grounds and a large section of Plovdiv.

An outstanding example of the Bulgarian architecture of the early 1800's is the Georigiadihouse. And let's not forget that during this period Bulgaria was occupied by the Ottoman Turk; therefore, many houses as well as churches reflect the oppression and Orientalist flavor springing from the 500-year occupation. See the clock tower on Vassil Kolarov Hill, a heritage from the Ottoman era. And then there is the ever-present mosque located on Alexander Stamboliski Square. The name? Well, it's Djumaya Dyamiya.

The architecture of the small church of Constantin and Elena (circa 1830) reflects the determination of the Turks to suppress the Christians. No towers; low-to-the-ground construction. The residents of 19th-century Plovdiv saw no reason to infuriate the Ottoman unnecessarily. Visit the Church of the Holy Mother built in 1844, with a bell tower from 1888; note the beautiful icons, particularly the miniatures standing beneath and in front of the larger altar painting by Alex. Dospevski. The churches, Lamartine's house, the Ethnographical Museum and many of the other interesting sights of Plovdiv are centered in one small area. The views of the city from these hills, the narrow streets and old Revivalist houses, the age-old steps and lovely vines and fruit trees make a walk through Plovdiv a treat for young and old.

Sightseeing

THE RUSSIAN SOLDIERS' MONUMENT — Standing on Liberator's Hill, it dominates the entire city. You can drive up to the top or, if you are feeling particularly energetic take one of the many trails leading up to the monument. Benches line the trails with trees, flowers and one or two little cafes into which you may stagger for a mid-hill pick-me-up.

THE MONASTERY OF BATCHKOVO   Built in 1083, and restored during the early 19th century, it is under the custodianship of local monks who live within the walls. Located about 18 miles from Plovdiv, Batchkovo is near the town of Assenograd, which is in turn on the highway to Chepellare. The roads are good. A sign in French at the base of the road leading to the monastery will direct you to the main gate. Cars must be left outside! Inside the monastery grounds you will see the Church of St. Nicholas (1840) and the Church of the Holy Virgin (17th century). The latter contains an icon from Georgia, the face of which was painted in the 12th century and is surrounded by a halo of 13th-century silver. The chandelier in the Church of the Holy Virgin was made in the 17th century. Icons in this church are from the 18th and 19th centuries; frescoes on the walls were painted by Greeks whose names are unknown. The inside paintings are from the year 1643; those outside date from 1850.

There is the two-floor Church of the Archangel (12th century) which is closed, with frescoes by the famous Bulgarian painter Zograf. The frescoes in the former dining hall of the monastery are being restored. In 1929 some dull-witted "artists" painted directly on and over the frescoes dating from the 16th or 17th centuries.

NOTE: After visiting churches and monasteries in Bulgaria it is customary to leave a small memento of your visit, or your appreciation. It's a nice gesture to leave a handkerchief, gloves, even money (Bulgarian leva) somewhere near the icon; it doesn't have to be much; the thought counts most here.

Hotels

TRIMONTIUM Plovdiv is a six-hilled town, three of which were occupied by the Romans, therefore "Trimontium." This large, very pleasantly decorated and comfortably furnished hotel is directly on the Sofia-Istanbul highway. As the street in front of the Trimontium is one way, running toward the highway, should you be coming from Sofia, pass by and come up on the hotel from the rear side. Parking is permitted on the sidewalk in front of the main entrance.

Built in 1953, the Trimontium closely resembles its sister hotel, the Balkan in Sofia. Although cavernous, ponderous and rather lacking in style, it is clean, roomy, comfortable and convenient to the town. The hotel is also very crowded; reserve well in advance, particularly if you should be in Plovdiv during a year when the International Fair is being held, which is every other year.

Money exchange and souvenir stands in the lobby. Four floors with 162 rooms, 350 beds—96 of these rooms have bath or shower while 60 others have showers built into recesses in the floor. Only two rooms on each floor have double beds; the remainder have twin beds. The double rooms on the court have only showers. These court-side rooms suffer because of considerable noise from the Garden Restaurant. No radios in the rooms though there is a television set in the large conference room.

The first floor has 18 singles plus the apartments, 6 apartments in all. The furnishing of these large units is quite complete. In the two rooms are couches, chairs, a desk, radio and refrigerator; a double bed, bath and two showers. There are telephones in all rooms and complete room service. Figure 15 minutes for breakfast—cost 55 stotinki. Laundry and pressing are well done. Noise is no problem here, though I would shy away from the highway end of the building.

Off the main entrance is a cafe where breakfast is served. Although badly decorated, the room is popular with local people. It is most pleasant to sit in this room on a Sunday morning or Saturday afternoon and observe the young and old citizens of Bulgaria enjoying their cigarettes, coffee or beer.

Also off the lobby is the main restaurant, closed during summer months except for private parties. Use the summer garden room. There is no direct entrance to the garden from the lobby area; it can be reached by following the terrace to the back of the hotel. Here you will find the many terraced garden where the orchestra is good, dancing is encouraged and the food is well served.

The garden room would be more enjoyable if two amenities were observed: (1) The management should save some small tables for the individual tourist. Large tables are always reserved for prominent guests and large parties, while all of the small tables are taken over by tours. (2) A room should be set aside for those travelers who do not wish to eat in the rather night-clubby atmosphere of the garden room every evening.

Be sure you reserve well ahead for a table in the Garden Restaurant.

The Trimontium is a good hotel. Reserve well in advance as it is very popular with Bulgarians and, as it is only a two-hour drive from

BULGARIA Just off the main street, its location is actually rather poor. There are two sections—the first built in 1931, the newer wing in 1963. The older section is not acceptable. There are baths in the older section but they have short tubs and the bathrooms are third rate. So are the rooms.

The 1963 section is acceptable but not outstanding. One elevator; phones in all rooms. I understood that there were four apartments, but I saw only one room set up as an apartment. The remaining apartments were actually two rooms with a curtain divider and four beds. Call buttons work. Single rooms are sparsely furnished and rather grim, but clean; 189 beds in all. Assistance with luggage in the small, rather garish modern lobby. Noise is no factor here. Pressing done in the hotel; laundry out.

There is a good restaurant here though the atmosphere is a bit bleak, and it is mobbed at noon. Service is poor to average, the food good though certainly not spectacular. Music in the evening. The Keller Bar in the hotel basement is open from 7 P.M. until 2 A.M.

A new wing is to be built soon. Hopefully it will take the place of the older section. The Bulgaria is an acceptable hotel; clean but furnished in mediocre fashion. If you cannot find a room at the Trimontium, book into the new section here.

MARITZA The new Hotel Maritza was opened in 1966. Located across the Maritza River from the main part of the town, the Maritza is a 14-story structure which rates, in my opinion, above the Bulgaria. The Maritza is directly across the road from the fair grounds and would, therefore, be a good choice for those persons concerned with fair activities.

Restaurants

I can vouch for the food at the Trimontium and also the Bulgaria; ask your guide for other suggestions.

POMPOROVO

Hotels

ORPHEUS My idea of a mighty fine resort hotel! Congratulations to Balkantourist, the architect and the very capable management of the Hotel Orpheus. When driving southeast from Plovdiv through Assenograd and up to the Batchkovo Monastery, keep going up and up—the road will lead you through steep gorges, valleys filled with flowers, past streams. There will be an occasional village and not more than two gas stations. The drive is roughly two and one half hours from Plovdiv.

High in the Rhodopes Mountains, this modern hotel is set on a small rise in the mountain resort region of Pomporovo. The Orpheus blends the sporty with the comfortable, its decor is in harmony with the surrounding lakes and pine-covered slopes. Open summer and winter, the hotel has a pleasant lobby leading into a neat little bar (open 4 to 6 P.M.; 10 P.M. to 1 A.M.) Take note of the wood carvings that separate the bar from the lobby. They were done by a Bulgarian student as part of his graduate work. The ceramic designs in the restaurant are also his work. There is the Blue Room for touring groups, and a separate restaurant for individual tourists. The food is good. Music and dancing in the evening. Service is very good. I would say the entire atmosphere of this restaurant and hotel is definitely erste—premiere—first class! There are three private party rooms, at least two with fireplace. Beneath the restaurant, a fine little bar (or keller), Bulgarian style, complete with hewn log for the bar and rustic tables and chairs. Music by record. Open 10:30 P.M. to 3 A.M.

The hotel is steam-heated throughout and the restaurants are air-conditioned. No elevator, but it is really not necessary here. The front part of the hotel has two floors, the rear section three. All rooms have fine views. Two apartments with baths, 10 singles with shower and 75 doubles with shower. Ten other rooms have three beds and shower. No telephones. TV and radio in the lobby. Singles cost a bit more but have rather wide beds; moreover, singles seemed to me to be better furnished. All bathrooms are the same size. Double rooms have beds in a foot-to-foot position. Apartments are nicely furnished with twin beds against an angled wall facing a small sitting room which is furnished with desk, couch, chairs and tables; also a balcony. Room service.

Ask for eastern exposure on the second floor. These rooms have balconies with a fine view. Specify: "East Balcony." On the top floor is a solarium for cool-day relaxing in the sun and a game room (pingpong). The woven walls are a neat touch! Assistance with luggage. Laundry and pressing service. Souvenir desk and money exchange booth. For skiing, two chair lifts and one hand lift. Not Arosa nor d'Ampezzo as far as ski-runs are concerned, but the runs are here and they seem okay.

Costs—apartment: about $14; single bed in double room: $4.50; double: $8.50; single: $5.50. These prices include full pension.

If you are looking for a good rest in a pleasant atmosphere, with good food and service equaling the food, Pomporovo has my hearty recommendation. I suggest a stay here of at least three days. You'll be sorry if you leave too soon! There is not much here outside of walking, skiing and hotel life, but that's what you came for, wasn't it?

SNOW WHITE A clean, functional, uninterestingly decorated 45-room hotel with ample parking, laundry-pressing service, room service, but no baggage assistance. Built in 1961, the Snow White has a large restaurant with music (nightly) and a keller open 4 P.M. to 7 P.M. and 10 P.M. to 2 A.M.; music by record. There is a TV in the lobby. Apartments have twin beds, two rooms, a small bathroom with shower onto the floor. Nicely if somewhat sparsely furnished. The best rooms are on the third floor and have balconies. Four apartments, 32 doubles and no singles.

The Snow White is a bit too institutional for me. However, if you are up at Pomporovo for one or two nights and the Orpheus is not available, accept the Snow White without hesitancy. A good hotel; it simply has no *oomph!*

RILA MOUNTAIN AREA

Sightseeing

RILA MONASTERY Rila Monastery is located about two and one half hours drive south of Sofia on the new improved road to Athens.

After the well marked turn-off, it is a pleasant twenty-minute drive, over an asphalted road through tobacco-raising areas, up to the monastery.

The monastery was named after a 10th-century monk, Ivan Rilsky, who settled in the Rila Mountain area as a hermit, living in caves and trees. Apparently revolted by corruption among the Bulgarian nobility and clergy, Ivan of Rila built a small sanctuary which was destroyed in the 14th century. A feudal ruler named Hrelyu moved the monastery to its present site, turning it into a stronghold. The present bell tower, the principal structure within the walls, carries this early strong man's name and is the only section which survived three separate pillages during the days of the Ottoman Turk. The present restoration was completed in the mid-19th century. In the 400-room structure you can visit the Church of St. John Rilsky, decorated with the frescoes of two of Bulgaria's most famous painters, Zograf and Dospevsky. Magnificent! There is the library of 16,000 theological books (available to scholars only), plus a museum of religious objects of great value and interest. Note particularly the wooden cross made by the monk Rafil who working with *pins* cut out the small wooden figures (he went blind soon after the work was completed). This was an extremely wealthy monastery. Be sure to visit the kitchens and reception rooms, for they provide an intimate glimpse into 18th-century Bulgarian life. The monastery is now a state museum, though the Primate of the Bulgarian Orthodox Church still maintains apartments here.

Hotels

RILA (near the Rila Monastery) In the Rila Mountains, famous for not only the monastery but for excellent hunting opportunities as well, you will have a choice of two hotels, The Rila and the Balkantourist Hotel at Rila Monastery itself.

The Rila Hotel is terrible and under no circumstances should you consider booking here. It was built in the early thirties and time has not been kind—it is old, dark, grim! No baths, no showers, either! Most rooms are for five or six persons. The third floor consists of a dorm for hikers.

The restaurant at the Rila Hotel is quite another matter. Not too fancy, but good food, fair service, nice view, interesting companionship and a Wurlitzer. Breakfast, lunch and dinner are served; the only eating facility in the area.

Renovations are planned and there is talk of a new Balkantourist hotel nearby.

BALKANTOURIST HOTEL (in Rila Monastery) Rila Monastery is now a museum, but Balkantourist has constructed a small hotel within the monastery proper. I have visited these rooms, completed the summer of 1965, and found them delightful. Nothing elaborate, though the apartments are furnished with sofas, large tables and other rather deluxe items. All bedrooms overlook a small creek and wooded hills. Thirty rooms in all covering two floors. Bulgarian themes have been incorporated into the decor. Comfortable beds; heavy blankets against the mountain chill. Showers, toilets, etc. Apartments have an extra luggage room and generally larger accommodations. Most rooms have stools, tables and double beds. From the covered walkway in front of your room you look down into the Monastery courtyard.

Every three hours, 6 A.M. to 6 P.M. only, the chimes of the monastery play lovely and intriguing melodies, which make the old monks seem not so very far away.

This hotel is a wonderful bet for a one- or two-night stay. There is good shooting in the area — boar, stag, rabbits and perhaps bear — and climbing paths for hiking. Meals are taken at the nearby Hotel Rila.

SCHIPKA PASS

In 1877 the Turkish armies attempted to move north through the Schipka Pass in an effort to relieve garrisons under attack in northern Bulgaria. The Turks were met at the Pass by a combined force of Russian troops and Bulgarian partisans. Defeated, the Turks began their withdrawal and the 500-year occupation of Bulgaria by the Turks came to a close soon afterward. To commemorate this event, a cenotaph was erected on Mount Stoletov. Nearby is located the Balkantourist Hotel, not far from the ascent to the height bearing the memorial.

The cenotaph is a five-minute car ride above the hotel. The road through the Schipka Pass has quite a bit of traffic—watch the hairpin turns and go slow! Be sure and stop at the Schipka Church, built in memory of Russian troops who fell fighting the Ottoman Turks, a beautiful site located at the base of the Pass. The drive through the entire Pass takes about two hours, including a stop at the cenotaph.

Hotel

BALKANTOURIST Neat, clean and entirely functional, including apartments and double rooms. Some rooms have two or three beds. There are no bathing facilities of any kind beyond wash bowls. Twenty rooms with wash bowls; the apartments have toilets.

The apartments are not bad—two rooms with wash bowl, the toilet centered between the closets; double bed. An apartment rents for about 13 leva; doubles are about 3 leva.

The restaurant is designed in chalet-style with wooden chandeliers; in the summertime (especially at noon) it is very busy. A private dining room adjoins. Recorded music. Food fair to good; service acceptable.

TURNOVO

Sightseeing

Turnovo was the capital of the Second Bulgarian Empire. You must visit the site of the former royal palace on Tsarevets Hill; this island of rock, bordered on three sides by the Yantra River, is dominated by the large, square Baldwin Tower. Visit the excavated ruins of the royal palace as well as the patriarchal Church of the Ascension.

Directly across the gorge from the Balkantourist Hotel was the Trapezitsa, the walled fortress settlement of the nobles. Ruins of 17 churches have been discovered there.

Take a car to the unique Arbanasy district high on the hills overlooking the town. Here lived the wealthy merchants in a splendor unequaled by 18th-century Constantinople. A number of the homes have been restored, so you may see exactly how the well-to-do Bulgarian family lived in the late 18th and early 19th centuries. Here is the remarkable Birth of Christ Church built in the 17th century; it was evidently constructed around an earlier structure, for within the church are found, very well preserved frescoes dating from the 14th century. The architecture of this building is fascinating. Keep in mind that the Turks, being Moslems, wanted no part of churches; they permitted the construction of the Lord's House but they didn't want to have reminders of Christianity thrown into their faces every day by additions of steeples, crosses and the like. The Birth of Christ Church is one fascinating result of such conditions.

Just outside of Turnovo in the Assen Quarter you may visit the Church of the Forty Martyrs, containing the famous column of Omourtag with inscriptions in Greek plus mural paintings, one of which reputedly constitutes the oldest specimen of the illustrated calendar on the Balkan Peninsula. See the Church of Peter and Paul with its fine frescoes and the Saints Constantine and Helene Church designed by the self-taught architect Nikola Fichev. (You will hear a lot about Fichev in northern Bulgaria as people are justly proud of him.)

At Dervent, some four miles outside of Turnovo, visit the Preobrazhensky Monastery, the entire grounds a monument to Bulgarian art, courage and architecture. Somehow the monks at this monastery and its sister unit, the 11th Century Trinity Monastery, managed to stave off Turkish efforts to destroy totally all the art, literature and precious mementoes of the early Bulgarian Empires. Here you will see books, letters, frescoes and reliquaries dating from the 15th, 16th and 17th centuries, as well as photos of the beloved partisans who fought the Turks and were in turn hidden by the monks in the caves and cellars of Preobrazhensky. Look up at the cliffs hanging over the forested grounds of the monastery and you will see those caves where monk and partisan alike took refuge from the Turks. You may also see crosses built in memory of the monks killed by the Turks.

Go down into an underground vault under the main building to see the altar valued at two million British pounds. Many gifts to this monastery came from Tsar Alexander II of Russia as a token repayment for the medical assistance the monks gave to Russian soldiers fighting the Turks. The tsar is reported to have once visited this monastery. The Church of Saint Andrew is remarkable for its frescoes by Zahari Zograf. The frescoes on the outside of the little church date from

1849 and depict scenes from the Old Testament. The church itself was built in 1825.

From these few references to history, you can easily understand that Turnovo is not simply a night's stop on the way to Sofia. There is a savage, brilliant, exciting quality to this town and its people. When I arrived at the height of September Exposition, "A look into the Middle Ages," church bells were ringing, torches were flaring yellow, fireworks and costumed actors from Sofia's National Theater were performing and I felt myself transported back to the 12th century when Tsar Ivan Asan II ruled a noble land from his fortress palace overlooking the Yantra River. If you haven't seen Turnovo there is really a splendid treat ahead for you and the family. Plan to spend at the least three nights here.

Turnovo, a natural night's stop en route to Sofia by car from Bucharest, is one of the most unusual, attractive, charming towns I have ever visited, bar none. Built on the sides of a gorge carved by the Yantra River, no two views of the city are alike. It is a fascinating town.

Hotel

BALKANTOURIST Located just to the left as you drive into the first square coming from the north. Should you have trouble finding the hotel, try saying "Balkantourist," for it comes out the same in Bulgarian. You will find the people very willing to help.

Built in the early sixties, the Balkantourist Hotel is located on the edge of a gorge overlooking the Yantra River. What a spectacular view! A medium-sized lobby, neat lounge, souvenir stand and a Balkantourist desk where tours of the town may be arranged, money exchanged, etc.

A small cafe located directly off the lobby is very popular with the younger Turnovo set and is a good place for an introduction to Bulgaria. The three upper floors are served by an elevator. Baggage assistance; limited space in front of the hotel to park your car. Lounges on each floor, at least one boasting TV. The hotel is heated. Baths only in apartments. Rooms are clean. Be sure to reserve on the river side, for the opposite side of the hall overlooks a very narrow and noisy street. Showers in all rooms, directed onto the floor, as usual.

Beds are comfortable and rooms sparsely but neatly furnished. While reserving on the river side, ask for a room on the second or third floor; this gets you a bit away from the restaurant also located on the off-street side.

Incidentally, the second floor apartment is quite large. I suspect it may be reserved for visiting delegations. However, if you need such a suite, I am certain the management will give your request consideration.

A long, nicely furnished restaurant complete with outside dining terrace is one floor below the lobby and may be entered either through the hotel or directly from the street. Here you will have a mighty romantic view of the town by night. The food is good, the service very good. I would suggest you take all your meals in the restaurant; I doubt that room service is possible except in emergencies. There is a real swinging band at night for dancing. Do they twist in Bulgaria? They *sure do*! Fact is, here at Turnovo and at Golden Sands, I frequently felt the room literally swaying along with the superheated dancers. Breakfast on the terrace as the mists clear over the Yantra River Valley can be like entering a new day with your future secure.

VARNA

Founded some 3,000 years ago as Odessos, this lively port city (possibly renamed after the nearby river Vrana) is a large town of varying styles of architecture. There is a large and beautiful seafront park directly across from the leading hotel (see Hotel Varna). In this park and directly adjacent to it are an aquarium and the Naval Museum respectively.

In the center of town are the Archeological Museum and the Church of the Holy Virgin. Beaches are nearby, but the sun is usually not, and Varna provides little encouragement to those seeking an entertaining vacation. A day, perhaps two, would be sufficient here. Try the side trip to Dikilitash—a petrified forest located on the road to Turnovo.

Hotel

VARNA The best available. It is clean and comparatively comfortable, and provides the weary traveler with a pleasant, modern restaurant serving very good food.

The lobby of this 96-room, 189-bed hotel is grim. An elevator; telephones. All rooms have showers except three small apartments with baths on a corner somewhat removed from the rather noisy terrace below. Ask for a front location on the third floor. Rooms on the back are far quieter, though warmer in summer as they face west. The approximately 29 doubles have beds located "foot-to-foot." There are radios in all rooms but reception is poor. The restaurant is very popular with the local people, particularly on weekends. Plan to be in the restaurant for dinner by seven-thirty. There is a cafe off the lobby—a good place to meet the younger Varna crowd.

ADDITIONAL HOTEL LISTINGS

It was obviously impossible for me to inspect every hotel available to the foreign tourist in Bulgaria. What follows is a list of recommended hotels other than those discussed above. The asterisk denotes first class facilities.

TOWN	HOTEL
Blagoevgrad	Predela
Blagoevgrad	Volga
Bourgas	Primorets*
Dimitrovgrad	Moskva
Gabrovo	Balkan*
Mramor	Verkovitsa
Rousse	Dounva*
Stara Zagora	Balkantourist*
Vidin	Balkantourist*

*(Restaurant recommended)

MOTELS

It has been a long, slow climb to success for the motel business in

Europe, in the West as well as in the East. The vast majority of Europeans obviously prefer a hotel, "le camping," or the warmth of their own hearths to a motel. Judging from a few of the West European motels I can't say I blame them. Therefore, it was with considerable surprise that I walked through my first Balkantourist Motel near Plovdiv. It was a hot day, and I squirmed at the idea of touring what I was sure would be a row of cabins along the road, circa 1935, U.S.A. I was wrong! Located on the western edge of Plovdiv, just off the principal highway between Sofia and the Turkish border, the motel sits back in a small park some 20 yards from the road. A neat, clean, rather small unit of approximately 30 rooms on two levels (two more stories are to be built soon). Accommodations are comfortably, though not elaborately, furnished, with shower and twin beds. The price is about three and one-half leva per person a night. You can park directly in front of your room. Rear windows look out on a woods. A very comfortable lounge and reception room offers TV and radio.

A restaurant one minute from the reception room provides indoor and outdoor dining, music in the evening (a jukebox). I did not take a meal here, but the room looked promising and the setting in the small wood was pleasant.

There are "bungalows" to the rear of the motel, available at a cost of about two leva per person. I do not recommend these accommodations as they are extremely small, have no washing facilities nearby and are hot during the late afternoon.

Similar Balkantourist motel facilities are located at Kapitan Andreevo (Turkish border), near Dragoman (Yugoslavian border), and on the Black Sea at Arkutino.

CAMPING

For those of you who prefer the great outdoors to hotel or motel life, camping areas have been established at or near the following towns or beaches: 9 kilometers from Sofia on the Plovdiv road along the Isker River; 45 kilometers outside of Sofia on the road to Samokov, at the Isker River Dam; near the Balkantourist motel at Plovdiv; near the Stoletov Monument on the Kazanluk-Gabrovo highway; near Teteven at the Boaza Gorge; en route from Sovia to Varna on the Varna Vit (reputedly quite attractive scenery-wise); at Zlatni Pyassatsi; at Drouzhba; 30 kilometers south of Varna at the mouth of the Manchia River; at Slunchev Bryag; at Kavatsite near Sozopol; at Arkutino (near the Ropotamo River); and at Primorsko Village near Bourgas. Camping is permitted only in areas officially established for that purpose by Balkantourist. Keep to the spots listed above or such new ones as may be opened. Small road signs indicate the way to official camping sites. Tents of various sizes and bedding equipment can be rented for nominal fees; Balkantourist offices will give you the details.

The Black Sea Resorts

Built within the past 10 years, the resorts on the Bulgarian seacoast are modern in design, the hotels tall in structure, the location delightful in every sense. Let's give these vacation lands their English names: Zlatni Pyassatsi ("Golden Sands"); Drouzbha ("Friendship"); Slunchev Bryag ("Sunny Beach").

The drive up the Black Sea coast from Varna is through orchards, past large official residences, along a road lined with trees and flowers. A bend in the road brings you to a sign "Zlatni Pyassatsi" and before you is the Hotel Moscow, a 12- to 14-floor modern structure which dominates the south end of the resort. Here the road winds between the hotels (41 of them) and the sea—past shops, restaurants, camels (yes, camels!), casinos—and all this built since 1956!

The summer water temperature along the Black Sea beaches varies between 68° and 88° while the air temperature remains in the 70's and 80's. There is minimal rainfall during the summer months. The slope into the water is gradual—no rocks. The beach is cleaned and rolled daily.

The beach at Golden Sands is wide, clean, and lives up to its name; no rocks and a gradual slope into exceptionally clean water. Hotels and restaurants do not lie directly on the beach, but are very attractively located among the trees and gardens that cover the rolling hills which follow the shoreline as it winds north toward Balchik and the Romanian border.

The three resorts, Golden Sands, Friendship and Sunny Beach, are quite different geographically, structurally and socially. Golden Sands is perhaps the most lively: there is more activity, it is larger, more colorful. Friendship is quieter, not directly on the beach but on a bluff overlooking the sea. Sunny Beach is in a flatter region, though the beach itself is covered with dunes and seems less cosmopolitan than the other two resorts.

Tourist facilities at each one of the resorts are substantially the same. Hotels fall into three categories: deluxe, first class and tourist class. Of the 41 hotels at Golden Sands, only three or four have restaurants within the building. All others have either a restaurant adjoining the premises or share a restaurant with a neighboring hotel. These restaurants have both attractive indoor facilities and outdoor terraces and can handle 200 to 300 guests. They are open for three meals a day, and in the evening serve as nightclubs, with music and dancing.

Along with the hotels and hotel-restaurants, there is another very original approach to tourist entertainment at these resorts, the "folk restaurant." There are four or five of these attractive inns at Golden Sands, one at Friendship and two or three at Sunny Beach. Built strictly for tourists, they are the best example of this type of entertainment I ever hope to see — vivid illustrations of the tremendous efforts the Bulgarian people have made to attract foreign guests to their country.

Also at these resorts are shops selling furs, cigarettes, foodstuffs, souvenirs and beachwear; hairdressers and barber shops; gambling casinos and flowered terraces for lunch; bars; at least two small coffee shops for afternoon tea or brandy. On the beach: paddle boats, row boats, speed boats, deck chairs, umbrellas, etc. There is a donkey cart and there are two camels onto which you can climb, complete with Arab robes and fez, to be photographed beside a papier-maché palm tree. Water skis, volleyball courts, tennis courts and children's swimming pools; all these things and more are readily available. You can rent the necessary equipment very inexpensively.

I found the hotels at Golden Sands, Friendship and Sunny Beach to be as clean as the surging, exuberant guests allowed. In atmosphere, the hotels run from average to very pleasant.

The line between deluxe and first class is particularly hard to nail down. All having bathing facilities, restaurants nearby, use the same sea and in many cases have identical room sizes and styles of interior decoration. The first differentiating factor seems to be proximity to the beach; the second can be in milady's chamber appointments, e.g.

thickness of towels, the presence of a full-length mirror, the availability of room service. Another factor seems to be the presence of a restaurant inside the hotel rather than in an adjoining building.

As a rule, tourist units have smaller lobbies, some rooms on the rear side have no baths or balconies and are, on occasion, somewhat distant from the beach. Yet a number of these beachless tourist hotels have attractive locations in gardens, on small rises, etc.

The entire resort development has taken place since 1947 or 1948. The majority of the buildings have been completed during the 1960's and building continues at a great rate. The Bulgarian Black Sea resorts are very popular with the Germans. Russian tourists are five per cent to Germany's 80 per cent, with the remainder divided between the English, Scandinavians, a smattering of French and the virtually extinct Americans.

Deluxe hotels have the following services or conveniences in common: help with baggage; laundry and pressing; immediate access to restaurants; large, pleasant lobbies, radios in public rooms; cafes and bars located nearby; adequate parking areas; apartments; baths.

The season at Bulgaria's Black Sea resorts stretches from May until the end of October. Many of the restaurants are out of doors, so should you plan to arrive later in the summer, bring along some light woolen clothing. The days remain as wonderfully warm as in July or August, but evenings are cool.

TIP: Bathrooms are usually quite small, containing little more than a toilet and washbowl, a hook on the door and two towel racks. There is a drain in the floor over which, from high on the side of the wall, extends a pipe covered by a nozzle: this is the shower. A rubber or plastic shower mat is provided. Quite naturally, when you wash you can expect to soak everything in the room. Showers are available on the beach and, at Golden Sands, *mineral* showers to boot!

ZLANTNI PYASSATSI (Golden Sands)

You can reach Golden Sands in short order by driving along these routes: south along the Black Sea from Constanza, Romania; east on the Bucharest-Rousse-Kolarovgrad route to Varna; from Sofia via

Turnovo; and from Turkey via Kapitan Andreevo-Stara Zagora-Silver-Bourgas. There is frequent train and plane service between Sofia and Varna: the principal terminus is just 15 miles from Golden Sands. A good asphalt road connects the city with the resort. From Varna Airport to Golden Sands by taxi costs approximately 12 leva round trip, less if the cab is shared with another person.

There are 41 hotels in all. The Moscow, Metropole, Astoria, Morskie Oko and Zlatni Kotva are the "skyscrapers" with up to 14 floors. I understand the new International will have 17 floors. Other hotels average from 2 to 4 floors.

Hotels

ASTORIA The Astoria is a deluxe hotel with a restaurant within the building itself; also a cafe and a nightclub. Two elevators are located off a large but rather dark lobby; there is room service for all meals. Eighteen apartments, 69 singles, 35 doubles. All rooms include bath, radio, phone service, plus hand and wall showers. Apartments are very nice with separate living room, including an extra bed. Parking directly in front of the building and prompt assistance with baggage.

The restaurant here is good-sized, built in a rectangular shape around an enclosed court. Very good food, and a large varied menu. Service in this restaurant is above average.

The small, German-style cafe is extremely popular with young and old. Directly above it is a nightclub open from 11 P.M. to 4 A.M. This club is a popular spot, also, and I suggest reservations.

The Astoria has the best all around facilities at Golden Sands and moreover, is centrally located. There is considerable walking to be done at this resort, so the most central location is the best. The Astoria is not directly on the beach but only about a two-minute walk away. However, it is possible to drive to any location around the resort. Stay away from the main drive along the Sea. It is off limits for the cars of visitors. The hotel is very popular with West Europeans who return year after year, and the restaurant is jammed nightly.

ZLATNI KOTVA (GOLDEN ANCHOR) A deluxe hotel located 100 yards from the beach, adjacent to many of the resort attractions. There is ample parking space. The Zlatni Kotva features a large, modern lobby decorated in appealing style, a cafe and restaurant directly adjoining the hotel, and room service for all meals. Bedrooms include telephones and radios and electric outlets. Apartments consist of two separate rooms. Single rooms include an extra bed. This hotel was built in 1957 and is somewhat newer than the Astoria.

SOFIA A comfortable five-year-old structure situated on a small hill about five minutes from the beach and directly across from the casino. Front rooms overlook the sea; those on the opposite side face a small park. The restaurant in the hotel has a terrace affording a good view of the sea. There are 72 rooms with 162 beds; apartments on each floor with double beds. Showers are not the latest tiled compartments but somewhat better than what one finds in other hotels. Comfortable furniture, comfortable atmosphere! No frills, but clean, pleasant and nicely old-fashioned! Apartments have large bathtubs; all rooms with balconies. A small elevator is available. Broad staircases lead to a pleasant, homey lounge on each floor. Room service but no phones — contact desk regarding service. This building houses a training school for Balkantourist guides during the winter, so it is a good, all-year-round structure, well maintained.

RHODIN Located just a few steps from the sea, the Rhodin is the hotel for those who enjoy being comfortable in a traditional unpretentious atmosphere. It is a four-story structure, and a wide "easy-to-take" staircase serves in place of an elevator. A pleasant lobby and fine little cafe and terrace face the main square of the resort. Noise is no problem here. The cafe boasts a jukebox and is a fine place for afternoon tea or a cocktail. There is no restaurant within the building; however, there are numerous restaurants within walking distance. The entire hotel has a rather West European — even Swiss — atmosphere.

The Rhodin is right in the center in the resort area and is certainly one of the pleasantest of all the 40-odd hotels. You may prefer it to the Hotel Sofia if the lack of restaurant facilities does not bother you. The Rhodin is just off the beach.

MORSKIE OKO This popular first-class hotel is a high-rise, modern building. Rooms on the south are great for sunbathing. Small balconies; telephones in rooms; showers.

Apartments are to the front of the building overlooking the sea. All rooms are on the small size, but neat. Your single may have another bed for which you will not be charged. Just be certain that you *do* have a single! A partially open-air cocktail lounge on the roof is available to guests after 11:30 P.M. and offers a fine view of the resort. There is a restaurant and a bar adjacent to the hotel.

Located quite near the hotel is a mini-golf course, tennis courts, an open-air theater and a children's swimming pool. The Morskie Oko is a pleasant, comfortable, unexceptional, nicely run hotel with no frills, and a relaxed atmosphere. It has a considerable following among West Europeans. Its central location is quite an asset. Be certain to reserve.

GLAROUS Located at the far north end of the beach, this hotel provides tourist accommodations for those wishing to get away from it all.

MOSCOW Opened in 1956, the first class Moscow Hotel has modern elevators, fair-sized rooms, pleasant halls and lobby, and is well illuminated. There are 160 rooms with a total of 320 beds; approximately 13 rooms per floor. Singles are available only above the sixth floor; apartments and doubles are located throughout the hotel.

There is no room service here, as the restaurant is across the street. For laundry and pressing, see the maid. No phones. Baths perhaps, though I saw only showers.

The rooms at the Moscow are clean and neatly maintained, but I consider it a typical example of what I fear may become a Bulgarian trend. High-rise buildings, built in too much of a hurry with the aim, seemingly, of making an impression rather than of providing a maximum of comfort in an atmosphere of true Bulgarian hospitality. There's little hospitality at the Moscow; shower pipes shudder as they strain to spray water over the entire bathroom; toilets pop, gurgle and emit odors strange for such a new hotel; windows jam. No, I'm sorry but this hotel is not for me, at least not again!

LILLIA A neat little tourist hotel not far from the sea. Showers only in front rooms; back rooms have only toilet and washbowl. The public showers and toilets are well maintained. No elevator; nice lounges; comfortable beds. Young people and travelers with economy uppermost in mind, take note.

MELANA Here is another pleasant little tourist hotel for those who want to swim, sun, lead the sporting life and ignore the surroundings. Clean, spartan, homey! There are 60 rooms with a total of 194 beds. Curtained wardrobes; beds foot-to-foot. Rooms to the back are not acceptable. For "apartments" here, read "dorms"! Showers in rooms; also public showers. All facilities are clean. Rooms with showers and balconies are on the front side only.

HOTELS BRIS; HORIZANTE; EDELWEIS; PEARL These hotels are similar in size and design to the Melana. All are small and nondescript, but clean and comfortable—tourist class. The Horizante and Edelweiss are rather far from the beach, situated on a small hill overlooking the resort. All these hotels are quiet and their lobbies uncrowded. You won't find baths, elevators, telephones, radios or baggage help here. When reserving space, request a room with a shower and a balcony and tell Balkantourist whether or not you wish to be near the beach.

Tourist hotel rooms are on the small side and certainly far from opulently furnished, but they are clean with comfortable beds. These small hotels impressed me favorably. Keep to those mentioned in this book until you have a chance to look about for yourself.

Restaurants

There are four types of restaurants at Golden Sands: (1) those within hotels (2) those in the immediate vicinity or adjacent to hotels, e.g. Moscow and Rhodina; (3) the Casino (no gambling here) which serves lunch and dinner; (4) the folk restaurants or mechanas.

Hotel restaurants are generally the best and for this reason I encourage you to try for a reservation in one of the hotels which include a good restaurant, e.g., the Astoria or the Sofia. Tables can be reserved for your stay, and meals vary from average to excellent. Service is adequate to very good. Menus are varied; prices are a little high, but not expensive.

Large groups usually eat in the over-sized beaneries of Category 2 which seat several hundred people. Most have inside dining rooms and also open-air terraces. These restaurants seemed to be open on an 18-hour basis. The food is acceptable but not outstanding. I don't recommend these restaurants unless you want a bit of variety. Service is poor to fair.

Folk restaurants are open mainly in the evening. Each restaurant is unique, and you will be amazed at the originality of design and construction. Each one offers very tasty Bulgarian dishes served by efficient waiters in national dress. Music and entertainment is also Bulgarian, though in two or three of the restaurants one can also enjoy dance music. These folk restaurants are scattered all over the resort, from the beach to the hills, so inquire about locations at your hotel before setting out.

THE CASINO   Located near the Balkantourist offices in the central section of the resort, consists of a small bar and a medium-sized dining room with terrace and balcony. The food is okay; service fair. The Casino is quite close to the Astoria.

VODENITSATA ("The Mill")   This is my favorite folk restaurant. About a 10-minute walk from the central section of the resort, the Mill is situated in a small wood a bit off the main resort drive. Parking is available. The architecture vaguely resembles a California Spanish-type home. The small, arched entrance leads into a medium-sized patio. A lower level of this patio-terrace provides another open-air dining area around a small pool and close by a waterwheel. There is music for dancing on the upper terrace.

The Mill proper features at least one fireplace and small rustic tables and stools scattered about the several rooms in this building. The entire structure is built of stone and tile. The food at the Mill is excellent.

Go up to the Mill after eight (be certain to make a reservation). Let me call your attention to one minor point here: desk clerks in Eastern Europe, especially in resorts and smaller towns, seldom feel that dinner reservations are necessary. "There is always a place!" Don't believe them; insist on a reservation being made in your name. During the summer, resort restaurants are mobbed, especially at Golden Sands.

KUSHLATA ("The Sheepfold")   is hard to locate, for this place is not on any resort map. Take a car and follow the main resort road past the Mill; make a left at the tourist bus garages. You'll pass a small gas station on your right and soon after you'll see a small parking area on the right. Leave your car and follow the trail — and the sound of a shepherd's horn!

After fumbling along the stone path, your way lighted by small lanterns, you will come to the sheep corral. To your right will be a cluster of rounded, plaster and thatched huts, their front sides sliced off to expose their colorfully decorated interiors to the full view of the dance floor around which the four or five "half-huts" are located. These smaller huts are available for private groups or small parties of tourists traveling together. A bit to the left of the huts (which seat six to eight people) is a large semi-circular, conical shaped building; in the center of this room there blazes a brazier on which turns a spitted roast lamb. Tables, stools and benches are arranged in concentric circles about the room which seats roughly 200 people.

The orchestra plays Bulgarian music and the waiters urge guests to get up and dance by leading them to the floor. After a circle is formed, the lead waiter uses a large scarf to signal the movements of centuries'-old dances. The dance floor becomes so crowded that only those people in the huts outside have an unrestricted view of the entertainment. Around and around the dancers go, bobbing up and down, turning right and left as the primitive music, played largely by flutes and drums, beats through the still darkness.

The food here is likely to be rather limited in choice. Grilled meats are featured, and they are accompanied by various types of salads. The meat tends to be "Variations on a Theme Called Lamb." For dessert, try fruit, caramel custard or perhaps yogurt. At the Sheepfold food takes second place to atmosphere.

Prices at both the Mill and the Sheepfold are a little higher than at the regular restaurants near the hotels.

GORSKI KUT ("Forest's Corner") The dining area walls in this unusual structure are made of wooden blinds that may be angled or closed, depending on the weather. The entire restaurant has been built not only in the woods but encircling the trees themselves. Candlelight, rather intimate dining, with good food and service. A long bar is constructed from a rough-hewn tree trunk. Very smart in appearance; quite intriguing.

This restaurant *may* be reached by foot, but I advise that you drive or take one of the carriages available at the resort in the evenings. Reserve! Dress well; carry some sort of warm wrap as the location is rather high above the beach in an area that can be damp in the late evenings and downright cool in late fall.

KOLIBITE ("Indian Village") Located directly behind the Gorski Kut, this small settlement of huts is actually an adjunct of the restaurant. The village includes huts with seating arrangements for several couples, a dance floor built over a large pool, other tables grouped near the pool and a very small bar with swings for seats. Only drinks are served at Kolibite. A dance orchestra and floor show provide the evening's entertainment. A small entrance fee is charged.

The Gorski Kut and Kolibite are only a few yards from one another. There is ample parking and I recommend these places for a full and entertaining evening. Don't forget to make reservations!

GEMIYATA ("The Ship") This restaurant is located on the north end of the resort, directly on the beach. I did not have an opportunity to visit here but understand the atmosphere is informal. The place is designed to resemble an old sailing ship and specializes in fish. There is a bar.

KUKIRI Primarily a night spot, this strikingly modern structure constructed rather like an amphitheater, is located at the north end of Golden Sands on a high bluff overlooking the resort area. All tables share a magnificent view of the resort, the Black Sea and the city of Varna in the far distance. This panorama provides a backdrop for nightly performances by local folklore groups and singers from the Varna opera. This place is best for drinks, dancing and the show, rather than for dinner. There is a cover charge and reservations are a must! Don't pass up this beautiful night spot where the Kukiri ("Devil's Masks") and Fire Dancers provide thrilling entertainment. You can't miss Kukiri because its pointed white towers dominate the north end of the resort.

ROULETTE CASINO This is a small, rather elongated structure directly on one of the back streets of the resort. It should not be confused with the large structure called the Golden Sands Casino. Accommodations at the Roulette Casino include a small lounge, a decrepit bar and two curtained gaming rooms, each furnished with two roulette tables and some chairs. Even the croupiers seemed timid. You will have to show your passport to enter the gambling room.

DROUZHBA *("Friendship")*

This Black Sea beach resort lies some seven to eight miles north of Varna and roughly eight miles south from Golden Sands. Though Friendship was the original beach development of Balkantourist, it has only 13 or 14 hotels scattered along a beach area of about a mile and a half. The terrain at Friendship is less romantic though just as attractively landscaped as Golden Sands. This is evidently a quieter resort. All restaurants are separate from the hotels.

Hotels

TCHAIKA ("Seagull") The Tchaika was built in 1950 which makes it the granddaddy of all hotels in the three resort areas. A sprawling, three-storied structure, it is located at the north end of the beach, with a prim lobby and a very pleasant bar which also serves as a breakfast room. No elevators or phones. The lower floors offer deluxe or first class accommodations, but there are no baths. Only the apartments and singles have radios.

Upper floor rooms and all rooms at the rear have only washbowls. Laundry and pressing is done in the hotel. A restaurant is a four-minute walk from the Tchaika. This hotel has nicely landscaped grounds and ample parking. Its chief drawbacks are a lack of food facilities within the building, a rather staid atmosphere and an almost total absence of up-to-date, practical guest facilities—such as baths, baggage assistance, elevators and the like.

RUBIN The Rubin, at the south end of the beach, is a new highrise hotel complete with elevators, attractive lobby (containing a billiard table), and a small bar that appeared well staffed and very popular. All rooms here are doubles, rather on the small size but neat in appearance and clean. No baths—each bathroom contains a toilet, washbowl and hand shower. Laundry and pressing; no phones or radios. There are two nice restaurants nearby.

Restaurants

The eating facilities here seemed extremely pleasant. Nice locations, attractive buildings and good food.

VARNA Set in a small wood, the Varna has inside and terrace facilities and is most attractive. It is rather casual—a nice place for a leisurely meal.

MONASTIRSKA MECHANA *("The Monastery Tavern")*
An extremely pleasant little folk restaurant somewhat less grand than the Mill and the Sheepfold at Golden Sands. There is a split-level terrace for dining as well as inside facilities and a keller (wine barrels in the wall) for group parties. Music. The food is good. Open for lunch. A very nice place on a warm sunny day.

ALADGA MONASTERY

This 14th-century monastery is carved directly into the rocks in the hills behind Golden Sands. It is an interesting sight and certainly a monument to the determination of the monks who lived there for centuries prior to the Turkish occupation. You can drive part of the way, then walk through the beautiful woods surrounding the monastery.

En route to Balchik from Golden Sands, be sure to ask your driver to stop at the Ottoman Turkish tomb of the priest *Yakasal Baba,* buried in the then Turkish province of Bulgaria during the 16th century. Yakasal was of the Mevlana sect whose origins stemmed from the central Anatolian town of Konya. The Mevlana is better known in the West through its association with the "Whirling Dervishes," a religious sect employing a form of twisting motion as part of its devotionals.

The Turbe, or tomb, has seven sides. Archaeologists determined that the body was probably removed from the tomb by the Turks before their departure in the 19th century. Nearby are the ruins of an old inn also designed with seven walls but destroyed during the First Balkan War. With only a little imagination you can actually picture this center of Ottoman social and religious life during the 18th century.

TENHA YAVA *("Quiet Nest")*

Calling all members of America's Garden Clubs, irrigation experts and lovers of the remote, the unique, the tranquil: Tenha Yava is truly one of the most restful, charming spots I have seen in many a year. Between the years 1926 and 1931, Queen Marie personally supervised the construction of this miniature summer residence and its wonderful gardens, artificial waterfalls and small Orthodox Church. The home reflects in its gardens and its small minaret a distinct Eastern influence. The gardens and home are open on Mondays, Wednesdays and Fridays. A former servants' wing and a guest house are now used as retreats for Bulgarian writers and artists.

The small chapel contains frescoes of Queen Marie as well as of her favorite daughter. The chapel also contains an Iconoclast originating on Cyprus in the 16th century. The Queen was buried here after her death in 1937, but was reinterred in Bucharest when the region known as Southern Dobrudja was reoccupied by Bulgaria.

Here at Tenha Yava, the waterfalls and artificial streams are delightful. Be sure to visit the Garden of Alak, a beautiful display of summer flowers. Make this trip only on a sunny day.

SLUNCHEV BRYAG *("Sunny Beach")*

This resort runs a very poor second to Golden Sands and really cannot be recommended unless you particularly want to visit the ancient town of Nessebur nearby or the sea coast areas to the south. The best hotel, the Globus, is comfortable and clean though the restaurant in the hotel is terrible. The drive from Varna to Sunny Beach takes roughly one and a half hours on a good road through some very attractive countryside dotted with a few colorful villages, rolling hills, winding curves and affording an occasional peek at the Black Sea. Spread out to the south along the beautiful coastline are the hotels, restaurants and beaches of Bulgaria's second largest summer resort. In the distance you will see the outline of Nessebur, the fabled "island city" founded six centuries before Christ.

Should you be approaching Sunny Beach from the south, coming from Turkey (via Haskovo) or from Sofia (via Kazanluk), you will reach the Black Sea at Burgas. Turn north and the road will wind through the mud flats (containing minerals for which Burgas is famous), past farms and orchards until in the distance you will see the outline of the first of the 30-odd hotels which comprise this resort.

The Balkantourist office is directly next to the entrance to Sunny Beach. All hotel buildings are accessible by car. Sunny Beach offers an even wider range of sleeping accommodations than does Golden Sands. There are the high-rise units; rambling ranch-style buildings of four to five floors; six-story hotels with bachelor apartments which include wide terraces for sunning; buildings of ultra-modern design constructed in such fashion as to permit each room a view of the sea. You will also find individual bungalows and "community units" of one room each with common showers available to the guests.

At Sunny Beach, hotels are much closer to the beach and in most cases, have direct access to the dune-covered shoreline. One or two hotels are actually constructed on a split-level basis providing guests on the first and second floors with access to the beach. The shore line at Sunny Beach is covered with small dunes permitting sun bathers a unique form of privacy. Bulgaria gives us the opportunity to choose between the straight, very wide and flat beach at Golden Sands and this rolling shore of Sunny Beach. Life at Sunny Beach is a bit more casual than at Golden Sands. There is a more tranquil atmosphere here, though surprisingly enough the night life is somewhat more sophisticated.

Because of the close proximity of the hotels, bungalows and the like to the beach, there is less vehicular movement, hence a more quiet environment. Hotels may be separated from the beach by a road, but this roadway is seldom used by vehicles. Unlike the main thoroughfare at Golden Sands (actually a terminating point of a secondary road from Varna), this roadway is only a resort road running from the north to the south end of Sunny Beach. The closeness to the bathing facilities allows for more casual dress, which in turn encourages a more relaxed atmosphere. Restaurant facilities are not equal to those at Golden Sands and are visited by guests dressed in more casual fashion.

The "sophistication" stems from the availability of one or two smartly designed supper clubs, which require more fashionable dress. Folk restaurants, the *mechanas,* are less in evidence here.

You will find many small shops located throughout the Sunny Beach resort areas offering everything from liquor to antiques. Shop around—you may pick up some interesting souvenirs!

Hotels

GLOBUS This is a medium-height deluxe establishment located directly on the beach (actually separated from the sand by a little-used resort road). It has a pleasant lobby and a nice restaurant on the second floor. It was built in 1960. All rooms are doubles with balconies. The rooms to the front afford fine view of the sea, whereas those to the rear overlook a park. A number of rooms with baths. Apartments are also available but are not particularly outstanding. Some doubles are larger than usual and have small dressing rooms and baths — something like a small apartment.

No TV, telephones or radios here; pressing and laundry are done in the hotel. Limited parking space is available in front of the building.

For quiet, reasonably normal dining in the restaurant, be sure you are seated by seven-thirty at the latest. The orchestra is overly loud, the service bad. At any time, the food is none too good; breakfast and lunch are considerably better served than dinner. A small bar off the private dining room can be pleasant and offers taped music — comfortable atmosphere for a late evening cognac.

PHOENIX This modern building about a five-minute walk from the beach has a large parking area, a restaurant and a shopping area just outside the main entrance. Built in 1962, the 320-room Phoenix features a large, comfortable lobby with TV and a souvenir stand.

Take a double or single; the latter are small but comfortable. If you require an apartment, ask about the "special" or "deluxe" apartments; as a rule they are held for Bulgarian officials, but one might be made available to you. Double rooms are L-shaped. Laundry and pressing are done in the hotel. The Phoenix is centrally located with immediate access to shops and restaurants. It is a comfortable hotel, not so much in design as in atmosphere.

NESSEBUR Completed for the 1966 summer season, this hotel is very intriguing in design but its interior is like a barracks. The rambling yellow-brick and split-level wood structure is located *directly* on the beach, some 30 yards from the sea. Only four stories high, the hotel is built around patios, parking areas, shops and a restaurant. Because of the dunes and the various levels of the hotel it is difficult to say which floor would be best; the upper floors would seem preferable for an unobstructed view of the sea. In any event, ask for the east side facing the sea. A bar and pleasant restaurant are in this hotel. Rooms include showers and toilets. Bedrooms are of a modern, stark and totally functional design with balconies. I prefer the Hotel Globus for location and general overall appearance. The Nessebur seems better suited for groups.

PIRIN Located toward the northern end of the resort, the Pirin is set back in a small wooded area with its sister hotels (tourist class), the Vitusha and the Rila. The hotels are named after Bulgarian mountain ranges. The Pirin, located quite near the beach, though some ten minutes' walk from the central section of the resort, is rated first class. With 58 doubles, 10 singles and 6 apartments, it is not a large hotel. There is luggage assistance; elevators, but no phones. A small bar is just off the lobby. Guests may have breakfast in their rooms (tea or coffee, a variety of breads, jam, cheese), but no other meals are served within the building. The Akheloy Restaurant is a four-minute walk from the Perin.

All rooms have showers. Laundry and pressing services are available. The six apartments have small shower rooms and double beds. All double rooms have beds in the foot-to-foot arrangement. Most rooms have balconies. The hotel faces the sea so ask for a southeastern or seaside exposure. The beach is only a short distance away. The Perin is a nice little hotel if you don't mind the short walk to meals. The informal, intimate atmosphere is appealing.

YANTRA, MARITSA, ARDA These three sister hotels, named after Bulgarian rivers, are some distance from the beach (this means an eight-minute stroll) but are particularly nicely furnished and pleasant. They are exactly the same. Each hotel has 9 apartments, 97 doubles and 14 singles, all with showers. Beds are placed foot-to-foot. Elevator. There are no radios. A money exchange desk is in the lobby and there is a breakfast room on the second floor. A small bar off the lobby is open only in the day. These three hotels have a certain rather inexplicable appeal. Perhaps it is because the management is particularly efficient.

CHAIKA The deluxe four-story Hotel Chaika has no elevator.

There are 2 apartments and 50 doubles. Central location; assistance with baggage; laundry and pressing. The apartments with a direct view to the sea are particularly pleasant; they consist of two bedrooms with twin beds and a sitting room. There are no telephones in the hotel.

The view from the top floors is quite spectacular. The top floor contains some small rooms with two beds; no private showers or toilets here (the latter are located just down the hall). These rooms are perfect for those who do their bathing in the sun. They have very large balconies which are easily converted at night into great places for cocktail parties.

A small bar is off the lobby. The Chaika is roughly a five-minute walk from the Globus where guests may eat their meals. Breakfast is served in the hotel, possibly in your room.

OLIMP The Olimp is a smart, new high-rise hotel with five apartments. The singles are especially nice here. There is no room service but laundry and pressing services are available. The building features a pleasant lobby and is about a five-minute walk from the beach. Rooms have balconies and are clean and comfortable but lack such facilities as telephones and radios. Elevators, certainly! Bathrooms are usually inside (without windows) and tend to be musty.

EUROPA The Europa opened in 1965. It is located on the beach; in fact, it is surrounded on three sides by sandy dunes. Because the Europa is built at right angles to the sea, most of the rooms do not face the water. No singles; all doubles built in an L-shape. There is a large parking area nearby and a good-sized lobby. An attractively decorated bar is to the rear of the lobby. Laundry and pressing services; baggage assistance; modern elevators.

BALATON and BIKEL These hotels have special rooms for language classes, historical discussions and the like. They specialize in handling group tours. No restaurants. I recommend these hotels only for younger people. They are too cold and institutional for me.

Bungalows

If you prefer to go in for "family living" in a semi-independent unit, try one of the bungalows. Ask for a unit with a lawn toward the street; this will allow you to park your car close to the building. The rooms are very small, with twin beds and washbowl. There are toilets and showers available for Bungalow renters. There are about four or five sections, with 180 bungalows to each section, scattered through the central area of the resort. It is a park-like environment surrounded by large trees and winding streets. A separate office administers each section and is open until midnight.

This arrangement can be nice for a family trying to economize or for teenagers on a summer's trip to the Black Sea. A number of restaurants are scattered about nearby.

Other Hotels

Should you not have a hotel reservation, I would suggest that you drive very slowly through the resort, examining each of the many types of hotels available (I am speaking of architecture, height, access to beach, etc.) and thus determine for yourself which hotel seems to fit your needs and preferences. Then drive to the Balkantourist office near the main entrance to the resort. I am certain the hotel reservation clerk will do everything possible to reserve a room for you in the hotel of your choice. Keep in mind, though, that in the season this resort is packed!

Restaurants

Attention should be paid to the hotel-restaurant arrangement here at Sunny Beach. Unlike Golden Sands, which provides restaurants at the side of practically each hotel, the restaurants at Sunny Beach are located mainly along the beach road whereas most hotel facilities are somewhat away from the beach areas. Therefore, guests must use the beach restaurants as regular eating facilities. Some are good; some rather poor.

There are three folk restaurants at Sunny Beach. The Ribarska Hizha ("Fisherman's Hut"), the Buchvata ("The Barrel") and Tschuchura ("The Fountain"). I had no opportunity to visit the first two of these restaurants. I have also heard of some sort of "Venetian

Nights" creation at the mouth of the nearby Hadjiiska River, the restaurant complete with lanterns and gondolas.

TSCHUCHURA This restaurant is located south of the resort, roughly 200 yards from the main entrance. It is not easily seen at night from the highway, so drive slowly. On cool nights ask for the first room; on hot evenings, the garden patio. There is a limited menu but the food served is good; service is average to good. Local costumes; folk music and singing. Good for a single visit. A definite "break" from the weary restaurants at this resort. Reserve, and also go a bit early, say seven at the latest. There is a small wine-tasting inn, the Buchvata, directly across the road from the Tschuchura.

CASINO Directly to the south of the Hotel Globus, just to the right of the hotel, is a long white structure providing dinner-dance facilities on an open terrace facing the Sea. Recommended only on warm nights, for the entire dining area is exposed to the elements. There is an entrance from the front and a more formal entrance on the west side of the building.

Service is fair; the food is average. There are such distances for the waitresses to travel here that the food is inclined to be C.O.D. (cool on delivery). The terrace is covered. Informal clothes, but no slacks for women. Inexpensive; go after seven-thirty. This is a restaurant — no gambling here.

LOTUS CASINO A large restaurant located in the upper portion of a two-story building, the first floor of which features the roulette casino. The restaurant and casino are located in the south-central portion of the resort near the Hotels Europa, Nessebur and the Yantra-Arda Hotel complex for which, in part, the Lotus provides meal facilities.

The Lotus is not at all intimate, but pleasant. It is inclined to be a bit breezy on cool evenings. The green walls, tiered table areas and clean tablecloths all do much to make the Lotus an attractive eating place. Dress informally. The food and service are average. There is music in the evening.

The gambling rooms appear modern and well-designed. I am under the impression that the casino here has a bar, and provides music for dancing.

NIPTOUN A few minutes' walk south of the Globus and directly across the road from the beach is the Niptoun. It is a pleasant restaurant built on several levels, and is best visited on a warm evening. The Niptoun sports striped awnings and small gardens, giving rather the effect of a large country house. The cellar of the Niptoun boasts a "wine feast" for those who like to march in early and stagger out late. Wine is "tasted" from large barrels. But don't plan anything for the next morning!

DUNI Located smack on the beach just north of the Globus and a bit south of the Chaika, the Duni has enormous rooms totally devoid of atmosphere. Even locals are loud in their criticisms of this place. Used largely for tours.

AKHELOY This informal, pleasant restaurant is directly north of the Hotel Chaika. Music is available for dancing. This place is acceptable — nothing fancy but substantial and not institutional. Inside dining and also an open-air terrace.

ORFEY A fairly large place located right on the beach. I found it to be only one degree better than the Duni. The Orfey is convenient for lunch on a hot, sunny day, for you can come straight in off the sand. There are several rooms here, of which the comparatively small area upstairs is the most pleasant. This restaurant and others like it have lengthy meal service hours.

LAZOUR Located directly on the beach, south of the Orfey and just north of the Hotel Europa. It is similar in style to the Duni and Orfey.

ROUSSALKA PASTRY SHOP AND BAR A small rambling structure surrounded by wide lawns, terraces and gardens, located just south of and somewhat behind the Casino restaurant. During the day, a typical teahouse with pastry, soft drinks as well as liqueurs, brandies and the like. A small cover charge admits you to a medium-sized oval room with roughly 80 small tables surrounding a dance floor. At night a very lively place with music and a floor show at about 12:30 A.M. Reservations are advisable.

VARIETY BAR Here is a surprise in the casual, tranquil, almost rural Sunny Beach to find the rather sophisticated, formal, cosmopolitan atmosphere of the Variety Bar. I feel, and perhaps you'll agree after a visit here, that this colorful spot might better be named "Lido Sofia." I don't think its present name does it justice!

Reserve a table and go late, certainly not before ten in the evening, and that's on the early side. As I noted before, entertainment in the Eastern European resorts starts about 10 P.M. and picks up momentum, usually carrying the fun through until dawn. Here's the place to visit with a group of friends, the wife, boy friend or whomever you're traveling with at the moment. A well-decorated, interesting, comfortable and colorfully illuminated nightclub par excellence.

A five leva entrance fee is charged, but you will drink this up as the entrance fee is deducted from your bill. A short ramp will take you into a well furnished lounge from which you enter the "theater club" proper. The building is circular in shape and modern in design; though rather uninteresting in appearance on the outside during the day, the architecture takes on its real meaning by night. Rows of tables range around three sides of the rather large rooms on various levels so that they all look in the direction of the large stage, which is built on an angle and covers the fourth side of the room. The orchestra plays from a raised stand to the right of the stage.

I believe the Variety Bar serves only light meals, sandwiches, canapes, and the like. Beverages of all tastes, strengths and national origins are available. Service is good. The floor show (there are two performances both after eleven-thirty) was one of the best I have ever seen.

Picnics

A "picnic" at Sunny Beach is like no picnic I've ever seen before. Sign up for one, they are a lot of fun.

A bus leaves the Balkantourist office at Sunny Beach around noon. On arrival at the picnic site you will find small thatched huts, wooden tables, a delicious-looking barbecue and waiters in national dress serving brandy and Mastika to the tune of Bulgarian folk music. There are even benches built into the trees. The typical meal consists of barbecued meat, shopska salad, bread, potatoes, wine and a delicious dessert. This is not a buffet; no standing in line! Later there are Bulgarian folk dances led by some of the musicians. The picnic site is in the hills behind Sunny Beach in a region called Partizanska Polyana, so named from partisan activities there during the last war. There are also barbecues here in the evening.

Outdoor Theaters

There are outdoor theaters at both Sunny Beach and Golden Sands. Plays and operas are performed, and sometimes movies are shown.

Side Trips from Sunny Beach

NESSEBUR This small island, clearly seen at the south end of the Sunny Beach resort, was founded in the 6th century B.C. and is now connected to the mainland by a two-lane causeway. Occupied by Thracians, Greeks and Slavs, Nessebur gained much of its fame through the manufacture of amphora jugs in which wine was shipped to Western Europe. Here is a marvelous spot to just stroll about, examining the ruins of buildings built as early as the 4th century A.D. Numerous churches, about 40 in all, were built by wealthy merchants and nobles; 10 of these ancient buildings are well preserved. Look for the Church of the Pantakrator (14th century), Saint Parasheva (built in 1314), and the Church of Metropoli (6th century). Many of these structures are decorated with the original ceramic friezes for which the island is famous. I recommend you spend at least half a day here, or perhaps an entire day.

Near the entrance to the island you can see the restored fortifications. Look back along the shore line for a splendid view of the Balkan Mountains framing the resort of Sunny Beach. To the south you will see the large port of Burgas.

The Nessebur restaurant is clean and fairly large and is located some 20 steps from the east end of the causeway, on your right just behind a small plaza. On a hot day try the Ayran (yogurt and water) — cold and so tasty!

KAVATSITE At this beautiful, undeveloped beach area some 15 miles south of the southern Bulgarian city of Burgas, Balkantourist has built a small hotel and restaurant for what would seem to be the express purpose of satisfying the soul of those visitors who desire nothing more than rest, good food, a sunny beach and absolute tranquillity. The hotel has 50 rooms and 2 apartments. There is no elevator but help with baggage is provided. No radios or telephones. Laundry and pressing service is available. All doubles have comfortable beds (arranged in a foot-to-foot fashion); the apartments have beds in both rooms. There are no single rooms. Bathrooms have toilets, washbowls and hand showers; no baths.

The two-story hotel is some 150 yards from the restaurant. A small lobby adjoins a bar area.

There is an inexpensive camping ground nearby. Bungalows are also available and cost about two leva per person.

The restaurant which like the hotel is located directly on the wide, clean and sunny beach serves very good food on open terraces overlooking the water.

Kavatsite is located right on the main road running from Varna toward the Turkish border and is really delightful. Very informal, very clean—a perfect place for a break in a hectic summer's trip.

ARKUTYNO (ARKOUTINO) The drive south from Burgas is truly a back-to-nature trip, affording the opportunity to see nature from the surface of a well-asphalted road. As you travel south, to your right will be rugged bluffs and forests, punctuated here and there by camping areas and youth hostels. To your left, broad expanses of carving beach; a large bay provides a haven for fishermen and swimmers alike. Sea gulls, sand, few cars, small groups of cabins—this stretch of shore line is surely one of the most naturally lovely and non-commercialized areas in Europe.

As you leave Burgas, a large town of no outstanding significance tourist-wise, you will pass west of Sozopol, which is a very interesting old fishing town through which you should take time to walk a bit. Old houses, churches and a magnificent view of the sea from the bluffs.

The next town is Kavatsite (the hotel and restaurant mentioned above) and then on to Arkutyno, which is situated east of the main road near the Black Sea but not directly on the beach. Here you will find a Motel-Restaurant located just north of the beautiful Ropotamo River. Built in 1963, the 57-room 99 bed motel facing the sea has two floors. No baths or telephones; limited covered parking. The rooms are clean but dark. I would describe the units as functional. Keep in mind that this is a beach motel. A good place for a one or two nights' stop when you are visiting the Ropotamo region.

Nearby are 200 bungalows and a camping area. The restaurant, 100 yards or so to the left of the motel, serves average food. Music in the evening. The atmosphere is restful and quite attractive.

There is boating on the Ropotamo River, a stream that runs through beautiful countryside of primitive serenity. Boats can be found at a dock just off the main road.

BLACK SEA TRIPS

During the months of May through September Balkantourist offers Black Sea excursions aboard Bulgarian ships which depart from Varna and sail to Istanbul, Yalta and Odessa. Excursion prices are about $90 (single deluxe) or $55 double (per person); about $42 per person (tourist) for a room for four persons. Round-trip excursion voyages from Varna through Istanbul to Odessa and return cost: about $150 for a single first class; about $125 in tourist class. Should you be interested in an excursion air trip to Athens, Balkantourist will provide you with a ticket (all are tourist class) on an Iluyshin 18 for about $85, which includes meals for two days and tours of the Greek capital. There are seven flights a month in June and September; ten flights per month in July and August.

Most of the excursions to Istanbul are by ship. Note that excursion fares to Istanbul by ship also include meals (aboard the vessel) and two half-day tours of the Ottoman capital. The $68 per person trip to Odessa includes a two-day visit to this Russian port city, plus one or two tours in the Soviet Union. The seven-day trip to Turkish and Russian ports includes half-day tours of historical sites at each port of call.

Balkantourist plans some of their excursions in conjunction with ships of other registries. The Bulgarian ships are preferable. The "Nessebur" and "Vassil Kolarov" are Bulgarian registry and it is to these ships that the above prices refer.

These excursions are inexpensive and a fine way to enjoy a close-up view of the Soviet Union and Turkey.

NOTE: You can keep your room at any of the Bulgarian seaside resorts while on such excursions. This eliminates a baggage problem.

Additional Interesting Attractions

The Ledenika Cave (Vratsa).
The Belodgradchik Rocks (near Vidin).
Kazanluk, "The Valley of the Roses," particularly in May.
Berkovitsa, a resort hotel near Belogradchik.
The Magoura Cave (near Belogradchik).
Predel, a new Balkantourist hotel in the Pirin Mountains.
Koprivshtitsa, an extremely interesting old town, one of the only inhabited settlements not destroyed by wars. Tourists get a fascinating glimpse into 18th-century Bulgaria. The scene of the mid-19th century uprising against the Turk.

I want to note my admiration for the no-nonsense, "let's get on with the job" approach at Balkantourist offices, hotels and restaurants and among their employees. These people are refreshingly frank and hard-working, and dedicated to their jobs. Their aggressive approach to their work, their determination to provide modern, comfortable tourist facilities for Bulgaria's visitors is truly impressive.

Czechoslovakia

Czechoslovakia is composed of Bohemia, Moravia, Silesia and Slovakia. In these regions you'll find fishing, hiking, hunting, and mineral baths; cable cars to the peaks of the windswept Tatras; dark tunnels dipping deep into the Demanovska Grottos. You'll see Brno's Spillberk Fortress, the castle at Bratislava which commands a magnificent view of the Danube — and provides a glimpse of three countries. Here are the wondrous palaces at Olomouc and Kromeriz; the delightful 18th century country estates at Slavkov and Buchlovice. In fact, the number of castles, summer houses, palaces and hunting lodges defies accurate count. The landscape is covered with them. And scenery? You name it — it's there.

Mountains, rivers, wooded hills and sun-drenched plains, abound, and the last-named offers some of the finest vineyards in the world. You can ride the narrow-gauge railway running through the deep forests surrounding Tatranska Lomnice and Stary Smokovec or drive the broad highways running north of Bratislava to the famous bath town of Piestany and on to Trenchin, later to turn west into the beautiful Moravian hills. Tour the fantastic old town of Cesky Krumlov where time seems to have stopped in the 16th century. You won't want to miss one of the churches or cathedrals, the museums or art galleries! And when you have toured the entire country, when you are certain that neither nature nor man can provide further surprises or greater beauties to amaze your satiated senses, then, my friends introduce yourself to Prague. The architectural and natural beauty of Czechoslovakia's capital city will take your imagination on a flight of fancy you believed no longer possible in this world of moon rockets and undersea explorations.

Czechoslovakia is indeed sightseer's paradise. For those interested in architecture, the entire country provides a symposium on design dating from the 14th-century early Renaissance to the steel and glass structures so prevalent today. There are beautiful examples of Renaissance, Gothic, Baroque and Neo-Gothic edifices. Just imagine having the opportunity to study history through the medium of architectural design!

For those who love the great outdoors, the heavily forested hills of southern Bohemia offer many fine excursion sites; eastern Moravia provides equally delightful recreational facilities. My favorite vacation spot is all of Slovakia from Bratislava to Presov from the Danube to the Tatra Mountains. Slovakia is just great for fishing, hunting, winter and summer sports. A trip to Czechoslovakia cannot be complete without visiting a region that has, in my opinion, too long played second fiddle to Bohemia. Should you miss seeing the eastern sections of Czechoslovakia, you will have missed one of the most outstanding parts of the journey. And for hospitality, you will seldom find an equal to the greeting awaiting you east of the River Moravia, north of the Danube.

If you think of Czechoslovakia in terms of Prague, Bratislava or maybe Karlsbad, you had better be prepared for considerable re-orientation. You should also be prepared to spend more time here than you perhaps originally intended, for Czechoslovakia is one grand tourist exhibition. When I mentioned to CEDOK, the National Travel Office, that I intended to begin my trip in the Tatras, drive to Banska Bystrica, to Bratislava, etc., they sent me a long letter giving the location of various sights to see along the entire route. At no time did I make much headway in one specific direction. Instead of west from the Tatras toward Prague, I drove east to visit Dobsina and Levoca. West from Bratislava toward Brno. Not at all! I drove east to take in Piestany and then north to the new city of Gottwaldov. Instead of going directly from Brno west to Prague, I first drove east and north to see Slavkov (Austerlitz), Kromeriz and Olomouc. I'm certain you will have the same temptation to travel off in all directions at the same time.

There is so much to see! Even when there is no small town on your itinerary and you think, "Now at last we can stay in the car for at least an hour!" there on the right will be a fabulous turreted castle high on some hill; across the river to your left, a magnificent country house which must not be missed. There is always something to see, to do in Czechoslovakia. You will arrive at that point where you won't look, just to give yourself a chance to rest up.

Such is the tremendous variety of scenery to be witnessed within the borders of Czechoslovakia, one of Europe's smallest countries, that it might well be called the Switzerland of Eastern Europe. The country side, the many small villages, beautiful green trees, sparkling air, the fast mountain streams and brooks running through fertile pastureland are scenery par excellence! The Tatras don't rival the Swiss Alps, certainly, but they are striking, rearing-up out of the steppe land as they do. Rivers? The Danube literally surges through the heart of Bratislava; while the Vitava, a liquid mirror reflecting old Prague castle on misty, moonlight nights, certainly accentuates the beauty of the Czech capital city. The sight of the Hradcany silhouetted against the stars or against a stormy sky is unforgettable. The forests of Bohemia, the vineyards of Modra—history! In no other country have I felt myself so close to a past which books tell us was there, but which in this modern world sometimes seems to be impossibly distant. There are Karlstejn, that magnificent feudal castle dominating the entire countryside, and Buchlovice, the delightful Italian Baroque villa with its 17th-century interiors where the Austrian and Russian foreign ministers met in 1908. The Royal Castle of Buchlov, originally constructed as a fort in the 13th-century, is also not to be missed.

Dolna Krupa, the castle that once housed Beethoven, is another lovely place. In 1899 Count Paliffy restored this former historical ruin of the 13th century. The styles of architecture in popular usage throughout central France during the 14th-century were employed to transform this ancient castle into a palace that might have been transported from the French "Moyen Age." See also Vranov and the baroque church housing the family vaults of the famous Liechtenstein family. The list of noteworthy and beautiful places is endless.

The Czechs are efficient, helpful, very candid, hard-working, and honest, and they operate some of the best hotels in Europe—West or East. When you visit Czechoslovakia, you can be certain that approximately 14 million people are prepared to make your stay a pleasant one, one worth the effort and expense you have put into your trip.

GEOGRAPHY

Czechoslovakia is about as large as New York State, with a population of about 14 million. Czechoslovakia borders Poland, the Soviet Union, Hungary and Austria. Although landlocked, Czechoslovakia has great rivers which give her access to the Black Sea, North Sea and Baltic Sea.

The western area of the country, which borders on the two Germanies, is rugged and stark—gradually becoming more settled, fertile and rolling to the east. This western region is known as Bohemia and within its confines lies Prague, the capital of Czechoslovakia.

The second of the three geographical divisions is known as Moravia-Silesia, with highlands to the north and west and the Western Carpathian Mountains on the east. Rolling plains are found throughout the center of this region and in the east dense forests.

CURRENCY

The unofficial rate presently stands at 30 Crowns (Kcs) to one Dollar. That gives you some idea about this bonus bit. (I would not call Czechoslovakia a particularly good deal tourist-dollar-wise.)

Coins are called "hellers," 100 hellers equalling 1 crown. Coins are in the denominations of 3, 5, 10, 25, and 50 hellers, plus 1 and 3 crowns. Bank notes of 3, 5, 10, 25, 50, and 100 crowns are in circulation. Tourists in Czechoslovakia must spend not less than $3 per day per person. And I can assure you that even though this minimum per diem does not run as high as in some of the other Middle European countries, hotel and restaurant rates in Czechoslovakia can be rather steep. Example: deluxe at $14 (single) with breakfast. This $14 spent per night won't result in your exactly roughing it, but then again I don't feel you will get your money's worth either.

The import and export of Czech currency is forbidden. You will be expected to declare all foreign currencies (including Czechoslovakian crowns) that you plan to bring into the country. Before crossing the border or landing at Prague's Ruzyne Airport, etc, you'd better make an exact count of those dollars, travelers checks and the like in your possession. Should your declaration not be exact when entering the country, you may be hard-pressed to give officials a correct total on your declaration form when leaving.

IMPORTANT: When you enter the country, your visa will be stamped onto a page of your passport. There will also be a small, two-paged slip of paper clipped onto the page bearing this visa. Part of the slip will be removed when you enter the country; the other section is retained in your passport. A portion of this second section includes your monetary declaration, also your photograph. Lose it and you'll have a lulu of a mess trying to exchange money, so be sure the slip is well attached to your passport. Too bad CEDOK, the National Travel Agency, cannot arrange to have these monetary declarations written directly on to the page containing the visa; it would be so much easier for all concerned.

VISAS AND CUSTOMS

Visa application forms may be obtained from authorized travel agents or from the Czechoslovakian Embassy, 2349 Massachusetts Avenue, N.W., Washington, D.C. 20008. The cost of an ordinary tourist visa is $4. Two passport-size photographs must accompany the application as well as your passport and visa fee. Persons requesting two-way transit visas must submit two separate applications. All visas are issued in a very short time. When I visited the Embassy, I received my visa in roughly five minutes. Mail applications are generally processed in four or five days.

Adults applying for two visas but using a joint passport will be treated as two separate individuals and must submit separate applications as well as separate fees. Children under 15 years of age included on their parents' passports are charged no fee, and no separate applications are required. However, any child who has a separate passport is treated as an adult.

All visitors—except children under the age of 15—are obliged to exchange a minimum of $3 per day for each day of their stay in the country, unless they have prepaid their hotel accomodations. Such funds will not be re-exchanged unless the visitor's stay is unexpectedly *shortened*. To meet the minimum per diem, you may exchange dollars for crowns at the border, the airport in Prague or at any point of entry. New citizens of Czechoslovakia who now have U.S. passports are charged only $1.50 per day.

Visas are valid for five months from the date of issue. There is no limit to the number of times you can visit Czechoslovakia within a year, though you may be asked by frontier officials whether you have made previous trips to the country prior to a particular day of entry. One stay is limited to 90 days, but extensions can be obtained in Prague.

Forty-eight-hour visas may be issued by authorized travel agents with offices in large West European cities. The travel agent would no doubt need to refer to your passport when filling out the visa application form, but the passport need not be submitted to Czech authorities. No photos are necessary for 48-hour visas. Two days after requesting a 48-hour visa the document may be picked up from your travel agent. There will be no notation made in your passport until you reach the Czech border, at which time frontier officials will take half of the two-section form and stamp entry permission. You may enter at any authorized point with this 48-hour visa and may travel to any location within the country. Note that the 48-hour time period of this visa refers to the exact hour you cross the frontier into Czechoslovakia.

Regular tourist visas may be secured not only from authorized travel agents but also from CEDOK or at Prague's Ruzyne airport. Visitors passing through Czechoslovakia on a basis of two or three hours need no visa.

You may bring into Czechoslovakia your personal belongings, 300 cigarettes and a fifth of liquor, duty free. For the importation of weapons or ammunition, you must request a permit from Czech officials abroad. Gifts and souvenirs up to the limit of 200 Kcs.

If you enter Czechoslovakia by auto, at the border you will be asked to park near a customs building and to present your passport and green insurance paper. Your money exchange slip will be completed and returned to you following customs inspection. At some of the Czech frontier stations, you may not find facilities for cashing travelers checks, vouchers and the like. Therefore, better have the car gassed-up in Austria or Germany to enable you to "make" the bank or money exchange desk at some hotel in the first large city.

When I entered the country by car, only a cursory check was given my vehicle. However, when departing from Czechoslovakia into Austria, my car and baggage were given one of the most systematic goings-over that I have seen in many a day, in spite of weather so wet that even a duck would have taken cover. The young female in charge was decidedly eager! Her associates were soaked and, I suspect, unhappy about the whole thing; the industrious little lady was wet to the skin. Let's hope this incident was exceptional, for it certainly was ridiculous. When I flew into Prague's Ruzyne airport, the official in charge of customs control glanced briefly at my passport and then I was waved through without any baggage inspection whatsoever. It was equally simple when leaving the capital.

When leaving Czechoslovakia you must be prepared to show your passport several times: at least once at baggage control, twice when entering the waiting room and once more when leaving the building for the aircraft. A tiresome routine, requiring some patience on the part of the tourist.

Should you be in transit through Czechoslovakia enroute to the Soviet Union or Poland, unexpended Czech crowns may be deposited at offices of the National Bank of Czechoslovakia located at border control stations. In return for the money you will receive a paper noting that such crowns as you have deposited are to be refunded to you on your return to Czechoslovakia. Should you be leaving Czechoslovakia with no plans for an early return, the rules call for a return of dollars equivalent of those crowns unexpended in Czechoslovakia (providing, of course, that the tourist has in his possession an exchange slip showing that the crowns were legally obtained in Czechoslovakia). Whatever the rules, the actual practices seem to be quite another matter. I deposited my extra Czech crowns in a bank at the Kudowa (Bohemia) frontier station in return for a slip issued by the National Bank of Czechoslovakia, but frontier officials at Javorina, Slovakia, refused to re-exchange the slip crowns when I re-entered Czechoslovakia. It was only when I departed from Czechoslovakia, at Bratislava, that my money was refunded—and then in Austrian schillings, not dollars. It is quite probable that the offices of the National Bank would have refunded my crowns, but when I was making time across the country I did not find it convenient to stop in some small town and search for the local bank. Suffice to say that I would either make a firm effort to use up my extra crowns before leaving Czechoslovakia or insist on an immediate refund in dollars, even though I was planning a return visit.

Keep well in mind that the importation or exportation of Czechoslovakian crowns is strictly forbidden. Lay off the temptation to import undeclared amounts of local currency, dollars, marks, etc. I would further dissuade the reader from engaging in any "sentimental enthusiasms" prompted by Czech citizens who request illegal actions such as bringing in money or gifts from relatives in the States. Certain types of gifts are allowed but I would be very sure of regulations before attempting any actions which smack of the "extracurricular."

Border crossings into Czechoslovakia may be made at the following points:

By car
West Germany	Waidhaus; Schirnding
Austria	Wolfethal; Drassenhofen; Klein Haugadorf; Gmund; Wullowitz
Hungary	Satoraljauhely; Hidasnemeti; Balassagyarmat; Komarom; Rajka
Poland	Kudowa-Stone; Chalupki; Cieszyn; Lysa Polana; Jakuszice
the Soviet Union	Uzhgorod

By rail
West Germany	Schirnding
Austria	Marchegg; Hohenau; Gmund; Summerau
Hungary	Satoraljauhely; Hidasnemeti; Somoskoujfalu; Szob; Komarom
Poland	Miedzylesie; Zebryzydovice
the Soviet Union	Chop

Ruzyne Airport at Prague is also considered a point of entry.

Keep in mind that issuance of a visa for Czechoslovakia does not depend on your possession of a voucher indicating confirmed hotel space in that country.

TRAVELING TO AND IN CZECHOSLOVAKIA

The obvious approach to Czechoslovakia for Americans and West Europeans, whether by car, plane or train, is through West Germany or Austria (points of entry are listed above). I continue *not* to recommend travel through the eastern zones of Germany. A "swing" from Vienna through Hungary and up into Slovakia has proved quite delightful. Scenery along the Hungarian-Slovakian border is extremely attractive.

By Car

An international garnet is not necessary in Czechoslovakia. It is sufficient if you are in possession of the proper insurance—the so-called green card—and an International Driver's License. A notation will be made on your passport giving evidence of possession of a car, the engine number, make, etc., so don't be tempted to make a fast sale while in the country; you'd look kind of funny waltzing out of Prague by air with that notation about the car staring Ruzyne Airport officials in the face.

Highways in Czechoslovakia are relatively good and well maintained. Traffic moves at a comparatively fast pace and never has the motto "Keep your eye on the road" been so applicable. Quite literally, glue your eyes to the road as well as on the other cars, pedestrians, motorcyclists, etc. The roads here are usually well constructed and well planned. Should you see in the distance a couple on a motorcycle, Moped, bicycle or any other small two- or three-wheeled vehicle, better honk from some distance away and, on approaching them, slow down. Be fully alert! Deafened by the noise of their own motors, several youngsters swung left directly across the road in front of my car. In one Slovakian village an elderly gentleman ran his bicycle into my right rear fender. I don't know which is the greater hazard, the other car or the cyclist! Be cautious at all times when driving.

By Plane

The in-season roundtrip airline fare from New York to Prague is roughly $615. The one-way fare, off season is approximately $275. Czechoslovakia is served by major European airlines such as Austrian Air Lines, Swissair, KLM, Air France, Aeroflot (the Soviet Union), Sabena as well as Air India and Lufthansa.

Though Prague's downtown International Air Travel Officers are very well organized, I consider it a good policy to have in hand confirmed return space (or continuing space) prior to arrival in Prague. Once in Czechoslovakia you need only confirm.

For confirmations, ticket purchases and the like, go to the Czechoslovakian airline's downtown office at #8 Namesty Republike. Czechoslovakian Air Lines handles space on all flights out of the country. Airline offices of say, Sabena, AUA, etc., are mainly information outlets and are not authorized to make actual ticket sales. Should you not have return space, determine on which day you wish to leave and then contact CSA (Czechoslovakian Air Lines) to determine which line has a flight on that particular day. The CSA clerk will make reservations, arrange for payment (if necessary) and issue a ticket.

CSA has very good regularly scheduled flights to points throughout Czechoslovakia and Europe. Soviet-built Tupelov or Ilyushin airlines are used. Domestic flights cover all the large towns and cities of Bohemia, Moravia and Slovakia. Transportation from the terminal to the airport is reported to be without charge.

I had the opportunity to fly from Prague to Zurich aboard one of CSA's Tupelov 104 prop-jets and enjoyed the very pleasant, uneventful hour's flight. The new airport terminal building at Prague should be quite an improvement; Prague's Ruzyne airport already boasts some of the longest runways in Europe.

Seats (in the international flights) are "three and two" as you fly at 9,000 feet in a seemingly semi-pressurized cabin. There are few announcements (to me, a blessing), though a flight report is passed among the passengers midway through the trip. Clue to happiness: the front of the plane is quieter! The stewardesses are attractive, efficient. A cold and tasty lunch is served, which includes the wonderful Pilsner beer. Souvenirs are given away on the flight (chocolate and CSA pin) cigarettes of all types are sold. There is, incidentally, a "free shop" at Ruzyne airport in case you want to pick up a few extra items on your way home. I do recommend CSA and want to emphasize here that you need have no qualms about flying with this particular airline.

By Train

Situated as it is in the heartland of Europe, Czechoslovakia is accessible from literally all points of the compass. The *Orient Express* runs from Warsaw via Prague to Nuremburg and on to London, Stuttgart or Paris. From East Berlin one can make connections via Prague with Vienna aboard the *Vindobona* motor express. The *Balt-Orient* runs from Warsaw to Belgrade to connect with the *Simplon-Orient Express* with further connections to Bucharest and on to Istanbul. Trains to almost any country in Middle Europe cross Czechoslovakia at some point. Motor trains also run between Vienna and Bratislava, but I have found the latter route to be largely a milk run serving the farming areas east at Vienna. Moreover, the departure hours from Vienna's South Station are notable for their lack of convenience. Trains leave Vienna for Bratislava at something after 6:00 A.M., and in the evening at approximately 7:00 P.M. The trip takes an unnecessarily weary five hours.

Prague's principal station lies quite near the Hotel Esplanade and the Smetana Theater, not far from the upper end of Wenceslaus Square. Sleeping car tickets may be secured either at the station or at CEDOK; I would urge that you make your purchases at CEDOK. Accommodations are clean and well maintained. A trip from Prague to Poprad (Slovakia) can be an interesting experience. Arrange to travel by day, for the whole of Czechoslovakia will be spread before you during the trip. Dining car service is available on most international trains.

By Bus

Daily bus service is in effect between Vienna and Prague, Vienna and Bratislava. This is an inexpensive, scenic mode of travel! CSAD is the abbreviation for the Czechoslovakian bus lines. Should your car break down or that hiking trip become less interesting with each succeeding painful step, head for the CSAD sign posted at intervals along all major roads.

All in all, it can be stated that between the dense network of international highways, the international system of railways and the airlines operating through Czechoslovakia, you will have no trouble finding transportation to almost any point within the country, to any border, at any time. Your passage arrangements will be handled in efficient fashion by CEDOK, CSA and their affiliates. In Czechoslovakia, you'll travel well.

Car Rentals

To give you some idea of costs, a four-seater Skoda Octavia or Skoda Felicia (convertible) rents for about $2 per day up to seven days and $1 per day for eight or more days, plus 5c a kilometer. (This is a rough estimate; rates have probably gone up some in the past year or so.) Costs include insurance, oil and repairs. You're on your own when it comes to gas. A deposit of $100 must be left by the person renting the car; the amount is refundable when the car is returned. There is a daily minimum of 100 kilometers which must be driven (80-odd miles; it goes fast!). Should you be wanting a car with chauffeur, you will pay about 20c a kilometer in Prague with one half hour's waiting time costing 70c. Outside of Prague, with a minimum of 150 kilometers and an hour's waiting time at 70c, the kilometer charge is 15c. You can even hire a Micro-Bus (seating up to seven persons) for a minimum of 150 kilometers for 15c a kilometer; an hour's waiting time costs 60c.

My recommendation? Whether driving yourself or with chauffeur (be sure his papers are in order!), I would rent the car in Western Europe and hire my driver there too. The car will be more comfortable and should you want to tour the country (and you must!), you can always hire a guide locally.

Car repairs are handled very efficiently in Czechoslovakia, although there are, of course, shortages of certain types of parts for American and West European cars. If you can, carry with you extra oil, transmission and brake fluid, additives for your gas (if you use special fuels), and a spare can of gas for emergencies. Sometimes the distance between gas stations becomes a bit stretched out.

You will be able to buy the standard gas 72 octane at about 4 Kcs. per liter. Special gasoline is available in all the large towns and in resort areas.

Tuzex (see below) sells vouchers abroad for fuel and oil. They are available at all borders, the offices of the state bank and Tuzex stores throughout Czechoslovakia (as well as in the U.S.A. at Utsch and Assoc., 39 Broadway, New York). These vouchers will provide you with 7 liters of 84 octane gas for $1. This can be a good deal but you should first inquire whether a greater saving can be realized by first exchanging the dollars for crowns and then paying for the gas.

CEDOK

CEDOK is the abbreviation for the Czechoslovakia Transport Bureau, your host in Czechoslovakia. From offices at 10 East 40th Street in New York, and through its affiliations with travel bureaus throughout the United States and Europe, CEDOK takes care of hotel reservations, bus tours, guides, theater tickets, visa information and all facets of one's stay in Czechoslovakia. It's even possible to make charges on one's Diners' Club card in Czechoslovakia! The credit for this progressive step goes to CEDOK and its hardworking, efficient staff in Prague.

Should you have any accommodations problems while in Czechoslovakia, contact the CEDOK office at your hotel for the Interhotel organization that controls all hotels in Czechoslovakia and a subsidiary of CEDOK. Interhotel manages all the first class tourist accommodations in the country; CEDOK itself is responsible for reservations, for general over-all management. The CEDOK gal in your hotel will see to your every wish. Should you be in Prague, call at the main CEDOK office at Na Prikope 18. Here you will find special representatives for each country. If there is really something serious that must be settled, the very capable Regional Manager for the U.S.A. will be glad to step in personally and help you out.

Located around the corner from the main CEDOK office is a reservation center for the Interhotel chain. There, in modern surroundings, you will be able to make immediate reservations for hotels throughout Czechoslovakia. Incidentally, plane transportation can be arranged on the second floor of the CEDOK offices.

HOTELS

Interhotel and CEDOK have done an excellent job of updating the older hotels in Czechoslovakia as well as maintaining, staffing and equipping all other hotels throughout the country from the smallest town to the largest city. I would say their efforts have evidenced greater success in Slovakia than in Bohemia. On an overall basis, personnel are very pleasant, the rooms clean and food average to excellent. Service, particularly in hotel restaurants, is unusually prompt. Room service, where it exists, is reasonably quick. Additional service in hotels such as stamp purchases, theater ticket reservations, railroad ticket purchases, city tours and money exchanges are well managed. Hotel rooms in other cities are confirmed to you with remarkable dispatch when one considers that reservation personnel have the added headache of marginal telephone connections across the country. Long distance calls are handled with maximum dispatch. Porters are helpful. Tips are graciously accepted.

I found hotel and restaurant personnel to be helpful, kind, informative and disarmingly frank. The Interhotel desks are in most instances staffed by charming young ladies who take their jobs quite seriously.

In this chapter I have not concerned myself with listing certain functions of the hotels—baggage assistance, elevators, telephones, laundry and pressing, room service, etc.—because the Czech hotel industry has developed to such a level that these facilities are generally to be found, at least in the deluxe and first class domains of the Interhotel chain. Without a doubt, there are exceptions—no phones here, no laundry there, etc.—but on the whole you will find almost every convenience available to you if you stay in Interhotel accommodations.

It has been widely reported by CEDOK, as well as other national travel officers, that hotels will accept reservations made directly by the client, by letter or wire. I have tried out this system and find it impractical, as one seldom receives an answer to his request for reservations. I never did!

Therefore I suggest that reservations be made and paid for in advance at a local travel agency either in the United States or in one of the principal cities of Western Europe. Telex systems are frequently used in Europe, thus speeding the reply. By arranging your reservations in advance you can enter the country "prepaid," always more convenient when traveling in so foreign a surrounding. Travelers checks should be set aside for the purchase of souvenirs or for emergencies. Keep in mind that the national travel offices of Eastern European states located in such cities as New York, Vienna, Paris, etc., are not authorized to sell tickets, make hotel reservations and the like. They are merely information centers. To make your hotel reservations, to purchase plane tickets and the like you must visit authorized travel agencies such as American Express, Thos. Cook and, in Vienna, Cosmos, as an example.

CEDOK and Interhotel seem to have made a noble effort to reach out across the country, building hotels and restaurants, furnishing transportation to remote areas so that the tourist trade may be circulated to all regions of the country. It is possible that tours of Prague and that capital's environs have been over-played; that a full enough accounting has not been made of the Slovakian resort areas. But then, Prague is a fabulous city which I really feel cannot be over-rated. And in this book I have tried to throw a brighter light on the delightful vacationlands to be found east of the Moravian Gate.

Hotels in Czechoslovakia are divided into categories; however, this book is concerned only with deluxe and first class. Typical prices with full board run approximately as follows: Single deluxe with bath, $15; double occupancy, $13 per person. First class single, again with private bath, $10; $8.50 per person, double occupancy. These are in season prices (June 15 to September 15.) There is a 50% discount for children under 10 (30% discount for children under 10 if they occupy a separate room). During international fairs or other special events some hotels charge higher additional fees.

Arrangements can be made for rooms with breakfast and one main meal. Per person rates for groups of 12 or more are considerably lower than those charged individual tourists. CEDOK asks that you contact them for such rates.

Regarding the correlation between visas and hotel reservations, it was a wise move when the governments of Czechoslovakia, Romania and Bulgaria dropped the requirement that foreign visitors have prepaid confirmed hotel space before they would permit their officials in Washington to issue a visa. It is always a nuisance to wait for some national travel office thousands of miles away to confirm hotel space before permitting their embassies to issue visas. It ties everything up until the last minute. Poland and Hungary are the chief offenders in this category! The elimination of the hotel space requirement speeds up the issuance of the visa; thus one's passport is available for travel or presentation to other embassies or legations, instead of being held somewhere while hotel space is arranged.

Nonetheless, I would not leave for Czechoslovakia, except in instances of emergency, without confirmed hotel space. Reservations are necessary! Prague, in particular, is jammed during the summer months. Hotels are few; first class hotel space is mighty scarce. West Europeans know what Czechoslovakia has to offer the visitor and tourists from the West are traveling to the spas of Bohemia and the cool slopes of the Tatra Mountains in increasing numbers. Europe is on the move during summer months, so better be prepared to compete with others for hotel space.

And so what about hotel reservations; how do you arrange them? Your travel agent will work with you, help you plan an itinerary and select appropriate hotels. Decide which areas of the country you wish to visit, in what category (deluxe or first) you wish to travel. And don't automatically say deluxe! Most large towns do not even have deluxe facilities; result—you will limit yourself to the capital city, the large commercial centers, and perhaps a few resort areas. Or worse yet, you will be obliged to pay the deluxe rate for each day of your stay, and when deluxe facilities are not in existence, you will receive back in local currency the difference between the cost of deluxe accommodations and the price of the space you actually occupy.

I want to note here that as of this writing there is a weary lack of rapport between travel agencies in this country and the national travel office of Middle Europe. Local agencies have a yen for deluxe, and Middle Europe seems loath to state that in many of their cities deluxe facilities simply do not exist. Voila—your agent hands you a voucher stating that you are booked deluxe. You arrive to find that no deluxe accommodations exist in five out of eight towns on your agenda, and that you are actually in second class rooms in several towns along your route. Back comes all your hard earned currency in Czech crowns! So reserve in first class or even tourist if you wish! Select a specific hotel whenever possible. But above all know what type facilities the hotel of your choice has to offer. Do not accept any flat daily fee to cover your stay in Middle Europe. Many travel agents charge such a fee and it just is not fair. Learn the current charges for board and room (deluxe, first or tourist) in Czechoslovakia and then pay only those specific rates plus the agent's service fee. One travel company in this country charges a fee of $15 per day for every day the client is in Middle Europe despite the fact that only Hungarian deluxe and first class charges actually warrant this amount. And that particular agency also slaps a service fee on top of the exorbitant per diem charge.

Once the reservations are confirmed, your agent will issue a hotel voucher stating that you have paid so much for accommodations on specific dates in such and such towns. On your arrival in Czechoslovakia present this voucher to the first hotel reception desk or CEDOK facility you encounter. The clerk will return to you in local currency the total amount you paid your agent in the United States (less his commission), and you will then be expected to pay for those hotel rooms reserved in your name. Keep in mind that you have paid for specific accommodations in specific hotels. Don't reroute yourself in mid-trip without giving CEDOK plenty of time to cancel one reservation and set up another hotel.

Should you be traveling about without reservations, simply exchange travelers checks as your needs require.

FOOD

In general I found the food in Slovakia to be much more to my liking than in Bohemia. I have argued with myself that perhaps my liking for spicier foods could have resulted in a criticism of Czech cooking. But it isn't that; I simply did not eat as well in the Czech areas. In Slovakia I moved from town to town, restaurant to restaurant, and found myself eating well everywhere I went. After traveling west from Brno, it became a question of a good meal here, a poor meal there.

All of this is to say that you darn well better travel the length and breadth of this wonderful little country before making any final judgments about the food. And keep in mind that the "German kitchen" has left a mark on Czech culinary arts, while one thousand years of Hungarian rule have certainly made a lasting imprint on the cooking habits of the Slovakians.

I ought to say that the restaurants in the Hotel Alcron in Prague and the Hotel Continental in Pilsen—and perhaps also the Hotel Esplanade in Marionske Lazne (Marienbad) serve delicious meals. However, these hotels boast "international" cuisine. The menus appear in several languages and offer an excellent fare much like what you would find in Los Angeles or Rome. Therefore, I feel these restaurants do not typify the Czech kitchen to the extent that, say, the Hungarian Restaurant in Kosice typifies the Slovak method of cooking.

If you want to eat well in Prague, be sure to try the *U Loretty* up in the old city off the Mala Strana. To me, this is Czech cooking at its best. This area of Prague has several delightful restaurants.

So what will you eat? In Bohemia, the dumpling; in Slovakia, the boiled potato. While the Czechs are enjoying their delicious pork chops, the Slovaks are delighting in a plate of beef goulash. Czechs: sauerkraut; Slovaks: paprika. The food makes one doubly aware of the cultural differences between the western and eastern sections of the country.

The Slovakian *strapacka* is made of flour and mashed potatoes and is a sister food to the Czech dumpling; it is served as a side dish with meat or as a dessert with a filling of cherries, plums or apricots. You'll get fish from the nearby rivers. Goose is a great delicacy. Praguer ham is delicious and the Liptovsky cheese of Slovakia is a delight. Many people like Oscepek, a delicate cheese with a slightly smoky flavor.

Prices are reasonable in all restaurants throughout the country. You can figure on an average of $2 for lunch and about $3 for dinner.

You can have a choice of breakfasts; the light, continental style with jam, rolls, coffee (with chicory) the English "Pickwick" tea, or one which includes eggs and delicious Praguer ham.

From the above it is clear that one eats well in Czechoslovakia, and at reasonable prices. In fact, the Czechoslovakian food should be one big drawing card for the tourist—there really is no better eating in Middle Europe. I don't want to forget to mention the "horke parky," those fat frankfurters sold from street stands, at railroad stations and during public events such as sports rallies. If you want to cut down on food prices, this is one way to do it, for these frankfurters, complete with rolls and mustard, are darned good and plenty filling.

Dubonnet, Campari and vermouth are served as aperitifs, and *Pilsner* beer is available in most restaurants. Don't miss the famous Slovakian *Silivovic* (Schnapps), which has 60% to 70% alcohol content. It's good but watch out—it makes for fiery tonsils! Incidentally, don't be jolted by the labels on the beer bottles. One day they read in French, the next German and later the labels become completely undecipherable unless you're up on your Cyrillic alphabet. The beer is evidently shunted onto the local market bearing labels intended for the export trade. In other words, if you turn "beer conscious" at a time when shipments are being made to Russia, you get beer with Russian labels.

In Bohemia, try the wines of *Melnik* and *Roudnice*. In Slovakia (particularly around Bratislava) I recommend *Malokarpacke Zlato*—

white, light, dry! *Postbraten Rakocsi* is very good and so is *Ludmila*, another dry white wine.

Wines at Czechoslovakia's Interhotels cost between 6 and 30 crowns per bottle. Meals at these hotels cost about 50 crowns for a light lunch and about 80 crowns for a hearty dinner with beer.

Tips are not included on restaurant bills but plenty of taxes and surcharges are! Figure that the cost of your meal will be several crowns more than the price stated on the menu.

SHOPPING

Tuzex shops sell many items—foods, hardware, souvenirs—articles to be purchased by foreign tourists either with their own currencies (since 1964) or with coupons. But don't buy the coupons or you'll lose your shirt in the process of the exchange; they are purchased at the unrealistically low official rate of about 7 crowns to the dollar. Czech citizens use the coupons to make purchases in the *Tuzex* shops after exchanging dollars received from relatives in the United States. It is amazing how many "unique" items end up in these *Tuzex* stores: Scotch whisky, Nescafe, Swiss chocolate, Havana cigars and French cosmetics. *Tuzex* is a good place to replenish your supplies of cigarettes, coffee, etc., should you be on an extensive trip and run short of such items. *Tuzex* stores also stock souvenirs and locally produced arts and crafts as well as garnets, Pilsner beer, Prague ham, Slivowitz, records and art books. But souvenirs are also available at other shops; so are the hams, the beer, the garnets and crystal. Some of the best buys I was able to make in the souvenir line were from country women who were selling handmade articles from small shops located in provincial towns. The prices were reasonable, too.

GUIDES

Fees charged for guides are high. A guide to accompany a tourist during a three weeks' visit costs in the area of $350.

When you travel with a guide, local people tend to shy away, as they feel you are in capable hands and in need of no further assistance. Of course, there are always those tourists who want to be assisted every inch of the way, who want nothing left to chance—for them a guide is a must. But for those of you who want to meet the people, I suggest that you travel by private car, bus, train or plane from one area to another and then employ guides locally in those specific towns you wish to tour in a more thorough fashion. In this way costs are kept down and one also obtains guides who are thoroughly familiar with the area. In between times fend for yourself. You'll learn more and be closer to the people you traveled so far to visit.

Guided bus tours of Prague are available through the CEDOK office. The cost runs around $2 per person and the tour takes roughly three hours. After you've covered the town by bus, consider hiring a private guide to cover places of particular interest. A half-day tour of Prague by bus with an English-speaking guide costs $2; a full day tour complete with lunch and a visit to castles outside of Prague costs little more than $5. A three-day visit to Northern Bohemia (14 days advance notice required)—costs about $30 per person. A tour of Czechoslovakian spas and folklore lasts four days and costs $40; a seven-day tour of Bohemia and Moravia costs about $70; a twelve-day tour of Czechoslovakia for $125 takes you all the way to the top of Slovakia's Tatra Mountains.

Should you be wanting to tour Prague by private car the cost is about $13 for half a day.

AUTO MAPS

CEDOK has issued a very good tourist's map of Czechoslovakia showing the roads and points of interest throughout the country. It is titled "Road Map of Czechoslovakia." Maps made in Western Europe quite frequently do not give enough attention to Czechoslovakia and are thereby impractical for local use. The CEDOK map shows where the castles are located, the best hunting areas, camping sites, hiking trails and thermal baths.

CEDOK has also put out a neat little series ("Auto Atlas") of regional maps highlighting specific areas in Bohemia, Moravia and Slovakia. Routes and points of interest are clearly outlined through the use of photos and diagrams. A distance (kilometer) chart is also included.

PHOTOGRAPHS

There are no specific restrictions on taking photographs in Czechoslovakia. However, the international understanding that military bases, dock and harbor facilities and airports are off limits to camera addicts applies, of course. One or two cameras (movie and still) can be taken into the country without upsetting any laws. I would not clank into Czechoslovakia with several large commercial-type cameras complete with telescopic lens and the like without first requesting permission of the Czech Embassy or clearing such equipment with CEDOK. Take along as much film as you like; it can be removed from the country undeveloped.

GROUP TOURS

This book is directed primarily at the individual visitor to Czechoslovakia who will plan his trip independently, without involvement in a group tour. Group tours certainly do exist, though they are organized largely through the local offices of European travel firms. Example: go to Vienna and you will immediately read of "Three Days in Budapest," "See Bratislava" or "Old Prague and Western Bohemia." You must first, however, make the jump to Europe; such tours are not given too much play in travel news within the United States. These group tours organized in Western Europe can be excellent introductions and can serve to demonstrate that travel east of Vienna is entertaining. But you must keep well in mind that such tours are pretty much cut and dried.

MOTELS AND CAMPING

The most outstanding motels are located in the following areas: Karlovy Vary (Karlsbad); Konopiste (outside Prague); Brno (Brunn); the Tatra Mountain area (near Tatranska Lomnica). Motel prices per person, including a service charge for bed and breakfast, are about $4.50 during the season. Facilities include two beds with extra space for a third accommodation, "warm" and cold water, plus a covered area for cars. There is usually a restaurant nearby.

Campers will find many campsites located throughout the country. The international symbol for camping placed along highways (white background; tent and trailer in black outline) can be seen time after time, by rivers and in forests. Rates begin around 75c per person (minimum) and may include the use of tents. Open from June 1 to September 15, the 32 (or so) campsites may include sports facilities, permanent chalets, grocery stores, swimming pools, restaurants and, frequently, car washing facilities. Ask the local CEDOK office to give you a complete list of camp sites and the specific facilities available. The "Road Map of Czechoslovakia" provides symbols indicating where camp sites may be found. You might also inquire for the Special Camping Map available from CEDOK, giving details on camping and the specific sites of the camps and camping areas throughout Czechoslovakia. These cabins may be rented fully or only partially occupied; prices remain the same. The 3-bedded log cabin has a living room and veranda, though toilet and showers are in a separate building. In the 4-bedded unit, a hall, living room and a toilet are incorporated into the building.

Tent camps have food shops and restaurants nearby, and are operated from June 15 to September 15.

SPAS

Want to revel in mineral baths? Watch geysers shoot alkaline-saline water of 160° F. 36 feet into the air? Want to enjoy radon baths and electrotherapy? Or what about a game of golf, some horseback riding, hiking or a little fishing? You can have a delightful time at any one of Czechoslovakia's numerous bath resorts. Prices range as follows:

For first class space, you would pay for a single (bath) about $160, for a double (also with bath), $140. The above are in season rates. Off season rates run approximately $30 less in first, $20 less in second class. These rates cover a 20-day stay and include accommodations and meals. Medical treatments are extra and run approximately $10. Beverages and surtax are also not included. Should you prefer to live in a hotel, there is a daily surcharge of $2 for treatments and medical attention. Those persons accompanying the patient are allowed a $35 reduction.

The principal spas are: Karlovy Vary (Karlsbad); Marianske Lazne (Marienbad); Frantiskovy Lazne (Frantisek Spring); Teplice Lazne (Teplitz-Schonau) where, incidentally, the emperors of Russia, Austria and Prussia met in 1813 to conclude an alliance against Napoleon; Jesenik (Grafenburg); Janske Lazne; Piestany located in Slovakia. Dining facilities are available in many hotels for those persons enjoying a "cure," who do not wish to live in the sanatorium.

HUNTING AND FISHING

Czechoslovakia is a sportsman's paradise. The mountains, pastures, valleys and rivers abound in game of such variety to tempt huntsmen. In Czechoslovakia you can find the red deer, fallow deer, wild boar, hare and chamois. Birds such as the bustard, partridge and pheasant; bear can be tracked in certain sections of Slovakia, while wildcats live in the Tatra Mountains.

Shoots can be arranged through the cooperation of CEDOK. A number of former private hunting lodges are now available to foreign visitors and regular group hunts can be arranged for eight or more persons (for partridges) and for groups of ten (for pheasants and hare). Season: August 16 – September 30 (partridge); August 16 – December 31 (pheasant and hare); August 1 – November 30 (wild duck). A hunting permit is naturally required and can be obtained through CEDOK.

CEDOK can supply you with literature listing the various hunting seasons, the per person limits to the shoot and costs.

THE SPARTAKIADE

A sports event en masse, the four-day exhibition involves mass demonstrations by thousands of Czech men, women, girls and boys selected through competing events from all over the country. Assembled in Prague in mid-June, the participants perform mass gymnastic feats before roughly 200,000 people in Prague's Strahov Stadium. The event lasts four days and is topped off with a gigantic parade through central Prague on the final day.

CABLES, WIRES AND TELEPHONE CALLS

See your hotel reception. At Prague's Hotel Alcron the message center, equipped for telephone calls, wires and mail, is located around the corner from the porter's desk. Telephone calls from Czechoslovakia to Western Europe take a short time to be completed; costs are minimal. For all daytime telephone service you might visit the General Post Office at Jindriska ulice 14.

SOUVENIRS

There are small shops throughout the country selling linens, wood carvings, inexpensive strings of crystal beads and the like. Prices for quality merchandise are definitely not low; prices are quite naturally based on the quality of the merchandise. Try the small shops located in the Gallery in Marianske Lazne. Prague also offers some merchandise of average quality in shops where you might pick up some interesting items. This is especially true in the area of *Staromestke Namesti*, near Old Town Hall.

ANTIQUES

Should you gaze into some antique store window and chance to spot a magnificent Meissen fruit compote about three feet high selling at $90, or a stunning piece of Bohemian cut glass crystal priced at $40, look further. You will most likely see a sign stating in three or four languages: "Goods in this store not for export!" Look well! Genuine antiques may not be removed from Czechoslovakia.

PRAGUE

In Prague, one of the world's great museum cities, at every turn of the street, across every bridge, around each corner stands some magnificent buildings, some wondrous panorama which demands exploration. You will need days to see Prague. You will look and look—and you will want to return!

Sightseeing

BETHELEHEM CHAPEL Here's where Jan Hus spoke in the 15th century.

WENCESLAUS SQUARE Fronting on this square are the National Theater and the National Museum.

OLD JEWISH CEMETARY According to tradition, a pebble laid on a grave will encourage the fulfillment of your dream. Here, too, is a beautiful, sad memorial to Jews killed by the Nazis.

PRAGUE SYNAGOGUE One of the oldest in Europe.

ROYAL PLEASURE PALACE Not to be missed. A lovely garden. The views are fabulous from the Vitava up toward the hills dominated by the Hradcany and from the hills down across the river in the direction of Central Prague.

PRAGUE CASTLE This seems to float in the mists above the river. Visit the Spanish Hall with its magnificent chandeliers. The residence of the President of Czechoslovakia is located in one wing. Go see the "Golden Lane," situated behind the castle.

ST. VITUS CATHEDRAL Here is the tomb of St. Vaclay.

SGRAFFITO PALACE This is now occupied in part by the War Museum.

CHARLES BRIDGE Noted for its magnificent statuary, placed there as early as the 15th century. The most prized are a grouping of Saint Luitgarda. The most famous is Brokoff "Turk" commissioned in honor of the Trinitarian Order who ransomed roughly 400,000 Christians from the Ottoman Turk during the early 18th century. Looking at the figures, you understand the feelings of the people regarding the Turks back in 1714.

BASILICA OF SAINT GEORGE A Romanesque building not to be missed.

OLD TOWN HALL Famous for is fabulous clock.

PALACES The most famous are those of Furstenburg, Ledeburg and Wallenstein families. Also recommended is the Cernin Palace.

MALANA STRANA A 700-year-old street in the Mala Strana district. One could wander here day after day without losing interest.

SMETANA THEATER Located on the banks of the Vltava. Home of the Czechoslovakia Philharmonic.

LIBERATION MEMORIAL Impressive in its panoramic location.

DALIBOR TOWER This is the subject of Smetana's opera. It is located near Prague Castle.

Excursions

Beyond the city limits of Prague, one should go to see Lidice, a town cruelly razed, its inhabitants slaughtered by Hitler; the magnificent Castle of Karlstein, built by Charles the Fourth in 1348; Kutna Hora, the cathedral and ancient mint; the Giant Mountains; Melnik, the castle and picture gallery; Konopiste Castle containing collections of the Austro-Hungarian aristocrat Ferdinand d'Este. These are only the more outstanding of the many sights to be seen in the immediate environs of Prague. Most are included on regular CEDOK tours.

Hotels

ALCRON Located on a busy side street approximately one block off Wenceslaus Square, the Alcron has my vote as the best in the city. The Alcron is comfortable, it is elegant, it is convenient. The Alcron offers all the conveniences one could ask for, starting with a very efficiently run reception desk, concierge, post office and cable desk. There's a Snack Bar and a Tuzex Shop on the main floor, and here too, is the main restaurant where gypsy music is played during the evening in summer, and dance music during the off season. The food and service at the Alcron Restaurant are excellent. English is spoken by most of the staff.

Rooms in the Alcron are commodious, traditional, comfortable, offering all facilities. A large apartment rents for approximately 330 Kcs. and consists of two living rooms, double bedrooms, a large bathroom and separate toilet; TV, radio, desk and davenport. A conference room is included in the larger apartments. A smaller apartment rents for about 260 Kcs., with an extra charge for a third person. There are 18 apartments in the Alcron.

Doubles rent approximately 160 Kcs. to 195 Kcs. Singles for about 100 Kcs. to 125 Kcs. All rooms have bath or shower. Corridors are wide, appointments nicely selected.

Groups are not accepted at the Alcron on weekends or during the Spartakiade.

JALTA A deluxe hotel and highly recommended. Not the traditional atmosphere of the Alcron but all that one could ask in accommodations. The Jalta faces directly on Wenceslaus Square, that is, fronting west. Noise is definitely a factor—cars, streetcars, the usual street noises. Also, front rooms are very warm in summer. Reserve a room to the back which is not only cooler but much quieter. The front or back rooms have the same furnishings.

Off the lobby is the reception desk, a Tuzex shop, and the lounge where cocktails and coffee are served day and evening. To the rear of this lounge is the restaurant. To the other side are a small bar and coffee shop. There are two nightclubs, one on the mezzanine, which is intimate, with a good orchestra, nice decor and small bar. The second club, located in the basement, is more of a dance palace. It is large, a bit more brassy and livelier. Two private dining rooms each seating about 35 persons are located on the mezzanine.

Apartments are on the seventh floor of the hotel. They rent for approximately 260 Kcs. plus tax. Frequently there is confusion about the type of accommodation the management feels it has given you and what you think you are in. Does that long day bed mean you are in a double? A single? Does the couch and desk indicate an apartment? Find out before settling in the room. The five apartments have a small balcony, French double beds, TV, radio and large baths. Doubles, average-sized bedrooms, rent for about 160 Kcs., and include a radio and two wardrobes. All rooms at the Jalta have bath or shower. I found the rooms at the Jalta attractively furnished in very good taste. The atmosphere of the entire hotel is modern with clean rooms and efficient service. It lacks, however, the relaxed atmosphere of the Alcron.

The restaurant at the Jalta is quite large, attractively furnished with beautiful and unusual cut-glass windows. The food is mediocre to good. The menu reads like a bill-of-fare at the U.N. Service is acceptable but not outstanding. In the lounge one can relax in comfortable chairs, enjoy a Campari, a Dubonnet or coffee.

ESPLANADE This hotel is on the conservative side with a genteel shabbiness similar to the surroundings in many of the old hotels just off the Champs Elysees or Picadilly Circus. The Esplanade takes its name from its pleasant location on Washington Avenue, directly across the street from the broad band of green grass, flowers and trees that separate "Washingtonova" from the main road passing the Smetana Theater and the central railroad station. Washingtonova and the other main roads separate well before reaching the hotel; therefore, noise is really no factor here. The hotel is two blocks from the railroad station and three blocks from the end of Wenceslaus Square and the main shopping center of Prague.

There is more of a view from the front rooms and a bit more air. Five apartments rent approximately at 255 Kcs. per night. The usual equipment of the room includes French double beds, TV, radio, good-sized bath. There are desks in the living rooms, and considerable closet space in inset wardrobes. Doubles rent for about 160 Kcs. a night plus a fee for an extra person. A single with bath rents for about 100 Kcs. a night; a single without bath about 72 Kcs. Singles with bath have couches in the room and are well-furnished and clean. There are radios in all rooms.

The food in the main dining room is very good, and the service acceptable. The dining room is small but comfortable, perhaps a bit too brightly lighted. In the evening, a nightclub called the EST Bar is open from 9 to 3 A.M. for dancing. There is also a lounge-cafe with an outside terrace overlooking the parkway.

There is the usual help with baggage and all types of room service. I found the employees at the hotel pleasant and helpful. English is spoken by many of the staff.

AMBASSADOR The hotel is located on Wenceslaus Square in a first-class quarter of the city. There is a western exposure, with front rooms suffering the disadvantage of noise coming from the very busy street. The lobby is small and cluttered, and one must climb stairs to mountainous heights.

The Ambassador is not unlike many of the little old hotels circa 1890. Rooms are located off courts, there are endless corridors, and there is a French atmosphere. Accommodations are of average size; rooms are clean and comfortable, service good. Room service is available and there are telephones. There is a fire potential — the only exit I could see was around the central elevator well.

The restaurant is about ten to twelve steps up from the main first floor lobby; the food is very good, the service equally fine. In summer the room is uncomfortably hot. A large portion of the restaurant is reserved for touring groups, while guests of the hotel are penned into one small area with far too few tables. Off the restaurant area is a "second category" restaurant, called the "Pasaj Kavarna," overlooking Wenceslaus Square. You can have an equally good meal here at lower prices, but a knowledge of Czech or at least German is a "must." There is dancing to an "oompha-oompha" style orchestra in the evenings.

Off the floor lobby is the Bar Budapest which is not recommended. A flight of stairs leads to a dark, rather dusty, clumsily decorated room where music for dancing is provided by an orchestra that makes up in brass what it lacks in rhythm.

INTERNATIONAL This place is located some ten minutes by car from the main section of the city, and sits among new apartment houses on the northwest edge of the capitol. A wide Baroque-styled flight of stairs leads to the restaurant areas. A bar is located through a door marked "International Club." A nightclub is on the 12th floor, while five or six private dining rooms adjoin the small but pleasant restaurant located on the second floor. The breakfast room is on the mezzanine.

Rooms are clean and pleasant, if a bit on the functional side. Rates run about the same as those at the Esplanade.

This hotel is too far out of town and in a district that can, for the tourist, only be called uninteresting. The entire hotel looks more like a museum than a public sleeping accommodation. Its one advantage is its proximity to the airport.

Restaurants

Prague has several different categories of restaurants: the international eating places represented by the hotel dining rooms; the typical Czech restaurants, and the small "Inns" of the Mala Strana District. CEDOK has issued a small pamphlet outlining the various sights of Prague and listing those restaurants to be visited throughout the capital. There you will find the best restaurants with addresses and brief descriptions of eating facilities. I would also recommend that for all restaurants you obtain reservations in advance through your concierge. This is particularly necessary in the Mala Strana District where the restaurants are small and (note!) open only in the evenings.

For descriptions of the various hotel restaurants, see the listing of hotels above.

U MARKYSE Located at Neka Zanka 8, near the main CEDOK office building, it consists of one very small room with black wooden furniture. The food is average. There is a small bar. I would make reservations to assure a seat. Roughly a fifteen-minutes' walk from the Alcron.

U LORETTY This restaurant is located in the Loretto Monastery and is well worth visiting. The address: Loretanske nam 11, near the Mala Strana. Open Sunday noons; serves lunch late; excellent food and good service in two or three small rooms; pleasant surroundings.

U KALICHA Located at Na Bojis i 14 in the Nove Mesto and

known as the habitat of one of literature's most famous characters "The Good Soldier Schweik." Good food.

VALD STEJNSKA HOPSODA The address is Tomasska 20 near the Mala Strana. Small rooms; bar; very good food.

U MEDEMASE In such an intimate atmosphere as this Prague really shines. It is located across the Vltava in the Mala Strana district. Actually it is a wine cellar, Czech version. Paneled, nicely decorated, with good service and average food. Taped music. Reserve in the second room, to the back — it is far more elegant and cozy. Plan on dinner about seven-thirty to eight. Many of these places close at eleven. Not dressy, but elegant in an informal manner.

GOLDENER BEARN One of the best restaurants in Prague. Located near the Hradcany on New World Street, this is intimate, charming and very small. Open only in the evenings. Be sure to reserve. Dress well but casually. There are several small rooms, almost a family dining room atmosphere to the place. Good service; fine food. Dinner at eight here also, though you can go much earlier if you like. It is ten minutes by car from Wenceslaus Square.

PRAHA This is a modern, very elaborate strcuture up on the hills across the Vitava from central Prague. There is a beautiful view of the city from all dining tables. Summer gardens; outside bar; fountains; flower beds — plus the French Restaurant. It is easily the most dramatic eating place in Prague. Dress well and be certain to reserve in the French Restaurant on the second floor. Tables there are on a reserved basis. The management calls their pleasant lower level dining room a second class restaurant, but this is a technicality of classification, little more. In the French Restaurant you will read from menus written in several languages and pay more for food similar to that served downstairs. There is music in the French Restaurant. Dress well. Plan on a seven-thirty to eight o'clock meal, for the restaurant closes at eleven. Again, be sure to call that cab before setting off for the hotel.

Bars and Nightclubs

Visitors to Prague may expect to eat and drink well at reasonable prices. A tour of popular nightclubs in the city indicates that prices of imported whiskeys and cognacs remain much the same throughout the town, though you will pay more for them in the posh hotel nightclubs. The latter are generally lacking in intimacy and are definitely geared for the innocent visitor.

KLOSTER WINE STUBE A not unpleasant dining spot about twelve minutes' walk from Wenceslaus Square and most of the large hotels. There are two medium-sized rooms, decor nondescript. An outside garden is located directly along the sidewalk for before-dinner aperitifs. Service is fair; food average. Very popular with locals and tourists alike. I would reserve in the front room. Informal dress.

CASCADE This very pleasant dance spot is located in the Hotel Central one block or so behind the Czechoslovakian Airlines Main Offices. There is a small cover charge. This place has no pretenses. The small bar is presided over by an affable bartender and his cocktails are tops. The medium-sized, high-ceilinged room is nicely decorated. The music is good and there is a fair-sized dance floor. This place is quite popular with both Czechs and tourists, but I don't think reservations are necessary. Dress moderately. It is a very pleasant spot in which to talk, have a good drink, dance and generally relax.

BAR MEMPHIS This is located in the Hotel Belvedere. You might like it for a sporty drink in an atmosphere of international comradeship.

OLYMPIA This night-time-only dining and dancing spot is located across the Vitava, a five-minute ride by taxi from the centrally located hotels. I would make reservations. It is not at all dressy. You will pay a small cover charge to enter. There are two large rooms at the basement level. Small bar. The atmosphere is rather dark; booths and tables. There is a good-sized dance floor and agreeable music of the dinner-dance variety. I would suggest the Olympia for an after-dinner drink, particularly if you enjoy dancing.

BRNO

This is a town of 300,000, the cultural and economic center of Moravia. Here you'll find a fortress on the Spillberk, with dungeons, torture chambers— and a fine restaurant; a 17th-century church (this as well as the castle can be seen for miles around); and within the town, the Dragon of Brno swinging above the entrance to the Old Town Hall. The former Dietrichestein Palace, now the Moravian Museum, contains some outstanding works of art by the great masters and contemporary artists. Near the museum is a fountain by Vienna's Fischer von Erlach. The Jesuit Church is remarkable for its architecture—a Baroque edifice containing statuary and pictures of note. Saint James Church, with a 300-foot tower, is a fine Gothic structure. You'll see the Augustine Monastery, with its Gothic Church, where Gregor Mendel is said to have completed experiments. Also visit the Dominican Church. The Fair Exposition Grounds (Brno Industrial Fair) contains exhibitions open all year round.

Outside of Brno are many important towns, castles and museums which should not be missed. You'll be busy! There is Olomouc the palace and church, university and Town Hall; and the beautiful Lounic Castle; the Peace Memorial on Pracky Hill which commemorates a Napoleonic victory over the emperors of Russia and Austria. At Bucovice, a Renaissance Castle which is architecturally outstanding.

Hotels

INTERNATIONAL This hotel certainly is in a star category within the framework of the Interhotel chain. Opened in 1966, the ultra-deluxe, modernistically designed hotel provides every possible convenience. Spacious modern lobbies give access to large cafes, bars, and attractive restaurants. There is a large municipally operated underground garage with a capacity for 160 cars; you can have your car washed and repaired here. The hotel has a smart gift shop and a hairdresser. A barber shop is nearby.

There are 655 beds in 256 rooms, each room with bath or shower, all quite attractive. Special closets in the doors to the rooms hold suits or dresses you might wish to have pressed. Large windows provide a good view of Brno to the east, Spillberk Castle to the west. Single room has a radio and modern bathroom; all furnishings are functional but comfortable. Several doubles are air-conditioned.

The main air-conditioned restaurant is located on the ground floor and seats 135 persons. It is nicely decorated and offers good food, average service. An adjoining dining room is called a "Second Class Dining Room"; the menus are in Czech. If you speak the language you will save money by eating there. Off the main restaurant, a terrace is open for cocktails from three until ten. Tea, coffee, beer, etc., are also served here. No food. Music for dancing three times weekly. This is a very pleasant spot where one could spend several hours on a summer evening before or after dinner. There is also a breakfast room located on the west side of the hotel. Beverages are served here later in the day. Be sure not to miss the nightclub which is a very large, attractive room, with smart decorations and a dance floor.

The season here is May 1 to October 1; as an example of prices, an apartment rents at about 320 Kcs. in season; a double at 130 Kcs.; a single with bath at 110 Kcs. and a single with shower at 65 Kcs. Doubles do not have showers.

The hotel is located in the immediate center of the city about five blocks from the railroad station and on the edge of the very beautiful park surrounding Spillberk Castle. Most of the principal churches and museums of Brno are quite near.

GRAND This fine hotel has the classic problem of street noises, though the rooms overlooking the side and rear are remarkably quiet.

Off the newly decorated lobby are a cafe, a second class dining room, a French dining room and a very pleasant garden restaurant. The last is quite small, with only seven or eight tables for six persons situated around a small pool; a room to the side seats parties of two and three. Unless you want to share a table with others, better be in the Garden Room by twelve-thirty. The side room closes at 2:30 P.M. I had lunch here and found the service pleasant and efficient, and the food quite good.

There are 120 rooms in the hotel including four apartments, the latter with radio and TV. The apartments have large bathrooms, bidets and French double beds. They also have a front location. Keep this in mind when making reservations. On the four corners of each floor of the hotel are large double rooms with bath described as "Lux"; they have very good cross ventilation. They rent for approximately 160 Kcs. Average-size doubles rent for about 100 Kcs., plus an extra amount for a third person and can be found in the quieter location. A single with no bathroom for about 55 Kcs. A single with bath is 65 Kcs. Corridors are large and well-lighted. Rooms are clean and quite airy. Laundry and pressing services are available.

CONTINENTAL Built in the shape of a 12-story cross, this hotel towers above Brno, providing guests with a breathtaking view of the city. It was completed in 1965 and has 121 single and 108 double rooms. On each floor there is only one single room with bath; all other rooms have showers. This lack of baths seems to be the principal reason why CEDOK has given this hotel a lower rating than it would, on inspection, seem to deserve.

A single room with shower costs approximately 50 Kcs., complete with radio and telephone. Singles to the east and southeast have small balconies, and truly a beautiful view. A double costs about 72 Kcs. Rooms are on the small side, rather stark but comfortable in the style of a school dormitory. There is a large central lounge on each floor.

A private dining room seating 30 people is located off the main lobby. There is a snack bar near the main lobby. No nightclub or bar.

In summation, I would say the Continental seems to have been geared for Czechs or their neighbors. Still, some of you may prefer the Continental to the Grand because of its view and modern decor. The Continental also has more car parking space and is in a pleasanter section of town.

SLOVAN Located around the corner from the International, this is the typical overstuffed, understaffed, boarding house style European lodging of the 1800's. The lobby is small, the halls long, the elevators non-existent. Only apartments have toilets, though many rooms have baths. Rooms are clean, however, and the staff is quite pleasant. The hotel seems reasonably popular with Western Europeans. There is little parking space for cars in front. A small restaurant moves out of doors in the summertime to serve food in a sidewalk cafe.

SLOVAK Readers please note the name of this hotel is the Hotel Slovak, not to be confused with the Hotel Slovan. Not recommended.

Restaurants

CERNY MEDVED Three blocks to the east of the Hotel International is the Black Bear. Extremely intimate in atmosphere, its two small rooms are most appealing. Rather rustic furnishings, low lights, low ceilings; comfortable; music from recordings. The restaurant is recommended by CEDOK. Give it a try. The atmosphere is a pleasant change from the usual hotel surroundings.

SPILLBERK CASTLE Don't miss a meal or at least a drink in the very attractive restaurant located within the walls of Spillberk Castle. One can drive or walk up to the Castle which is located directly behind the Hotel International. The restaurant opens at five, occupies several well-furnished rooms and has an extremely pleasant atmosphere. Very good management. Good service. A beautiful view of all Brno is offered here plus an atmosphere of complete relaxation amid trees, flowers, and fountains. You might want to take a taxi up to the castle, for the road can be a bit tricky at nights.

NOTE: People will suggest that you visit Spillberk Castle for a glass of wine during the afternoon. On the paths up to the Castle you will find one or two small wine houses where you may enjoy a beer or a glass of wine. But don't make the mistake of going directly to the restaurant in the Castle before five; the restaurant is strictly an "after six" even accommodation.

MYSLIVNA Situated some 15 minutes west of Brno, this is a well-known spot for luncheon or dinner with a fine view of the city. One can drive to Myslivna or take the train to Pisaky and walk up through the elaborate gardens surrounding the delightful restaurant.

CESKY KRUMLOV

This is a very small, 15th century town located seemingly in the heart of nowhere, though actually it is but two and a half hours by car from Prague and approximately two hours from the Austrian industrial capital of Linz. A by-pass highway swings around the town, planes fly over and politics take little interest. So Cesky Krumlov remains pretty much as it did five hundred years ago. Take time to wander through this medieval setting, a town that during the 1600's was owned by the Austrian Emperor Rudolf II. The town was later the seat of the

Schwarzenberg family. Be sure to visit the revolving theater where you, the audience, do the circling.

Hotel

KRUMLOV This is in the center of town and occupies three buildings. There is no elevator, but one is largely unnecessary. There are 22 rooms and 63 beds. Most of the rooms are quite large. The apartments are especially attractive, containing a small anteroom and very elaborate furnishings. No baths in the apartments, however. The entire building is quite intimate, simply designed, neat and very clean. The hotel was recently renovated. The third floor is a dormitory, accommodating group tours. Radios are available in several of the bedrooms. Apartments rent for about 55 Kcs. Doubles without bath are the same price. Doubles with bath rent for approximately 72 Kcs. while singles with bath or shower are about 50 Kcs. Singles with no bath are 38 Kcs.

The restaurant is a large room seating 100 or more people in a cheerful but businesslike atmosphere. Good food at reasonable prices. Service is prompt. The cafe is interesting in style and intimate in atmosphere. Mainly drinks and coffee are served but meals are available on request.

All in all, this is a pleasant, well furnished, interesting little hotel in an extremely charming old town. There is outside noise to a limited degree because of the very old and narrow streets, but activity is limited to the daytime and is mostly pedestrian.

GOTTWALDOV

Hotel

MOSKOVA Part of the Interhotel group. There are five apartments; single and double rooms with bath, restaurant; cafe; cocktail lounge; summer terrace. The location is near streetcar and bus stops; not far from the railway station.

KARLOV VARY (Karlsbad)

Moving further into Bohemia and west from Prague we come to many delightful towns, spas and historical sites. Karlovy Vary (Karlsbad), Plzn (Pilsen), the famous Marianske Lazne (Marienbad) and nearby, Kynzvart, the very beautifully maintained summer palace of the Metternich family. Goethe, Dumas the Elder and Beethoven were guests at this palace. Here are the old historical Gothic town of Cheb and Loket, with its 12th-century royal palace situated in a beautiful forest. Bohemia is a delightful place for any summer's drive. A view of the hills, forests, the natural setting of the entire countryside is an occasion not to be missed. And, there is Karlovy Vary (Karlsbad) with its baths, restaurants, fine hotels and famous Moser Glass Factory. Surely you know someone who has at one time owned some of the beautiful, rich, ruby glass seen so infrequently nowadays. Well, here is your chance to see a fine exhibition of it at the Moser Factory located just west of Karlovy Vary.

Hotels

GRAND HOTEL MOSKVA The ultimate! Built in the late 19th-century, the Moskva (formerly owned by the Pupp family) was nationalized some years back along with the rest of the tourists' Karlsbad. Now the management is making a strenuous effort to regain some of the hotel's former international reputation.

There are eight apartments and 498 rooms. A number of the apartments are quite elaborate and include marble baths in which you can revel at about 250 Kcs. a night. A double with bath costs approximately 145 Kcs.; doubles without bath are 55 Kcs. and singles without baths are 38 Kcs. Prices are a bit higher than the usual, but the hotel is certainly worth a visit. All rooms are large. TV is available on request. You will find the appointments of your room quite pleasant.

When reserving, I would let price and the size of room be your ultimate guide vis-a-vis location. Good rooms are scattered throughout the hotel.

The hotel has a large lobby, pleasant reception rooms and restaurants. The Mirror Room is reserved for those guests taking the cure, meaning that it is a controlled diet restaurant. Adjoining the Mirror

Room is the French Restaurant, where the service is excellent, the menu reads well and the food is decidedly mediocre. A medium-sized salon near the reception desk is used as a cocktail lounge and for after-dinner dancing. Beer drinkers in the crowd? Don't hesitate to explore, for there is a wealth of public rooms, restaurants and for any suds sippers, a special room to the rear of the hotel. There is a terrace for breakfast and afternoon tea. Don't miss seeing the Florentine Room. A first-class night spot tucked away in such a location that you will need a guide to show you the way in. The room is well-decorated; waiters provide good service. It is very popular with the local younger set, and a nice spot for after-dinner cocktails and dancing.

HOTEL PARK AND SEVASTOPOL This and the Moskva are under the same management and guests of the Moskva may also be housed here. The Park, with its own restaurant and bar, is directly at the side of the Moskva. An annex to the Hotel Moskva is the Hotel Sevastopol which houses the overflow from both the Park and Moskva.

The bedrooms and public rooms, restaurants, etc., are most pleasant at the Moskva. Its quiet location at the end of a main street plus the immediate accessibility to shops and baths make it a good bet.

CENTRAL A very pleasant B Class hotel; no pretensions, but ideal in location and efficient in management. Reported to have been the cure locale for Alexander Tolstoi. Located near the center of town and very close to the principal baths, it has two restaurants: one for guests, the second opening only at noon for touring groups. In the evening this second restaurant becomes a nightclub with dancing, open until 2 A.M.

There are 76 rooms, 13 with bath. An apartment rents for about 72 Kcs. A double without bath runs abut 55 Kcs. There will be a washbowl in the room, also radio and a double wardrobe. A single rents for approximately 38 Kcs. and is quite pleasant with radio but no bath — no singles in this hotel have baths. Baths and toilets off the halls are in good condition.

This is a very pleasant hotel, nondescript but adequate, with good food.

ATLANTIC Located immediately over the CEDOK offices in central

Karlovy Vary, this hotel has no restaurant, only a cafe. Bookings must be made through the Hotel Central and meals taken at that hotel. Not recommended.

MARIANSKE LAZNE (Marienbad)

In a toss-up between Karlovy Vary and Marianske Lazne, the latter town, with its green lawns, white colonaded buildings, attractive promenades and surrounding rolling wooded hills certainly would be my choice of two famous Bohemian watering places. While the spa section of Karlovy Vary is located in a small canyon, the entire town of Marianske Lazne is situated among the forested hills and gentle slopes of some of Western Bohemia's most beautiful countryside. The air, like its mineral waters, seems to have a certain sparkle, a tingle that compliments the charming melodies of Strauss and Lehar played each morning at eleven in the central promenade by the local band. The broad avenues, the gardens colored by cannas and zinnias, the small shops, white bath buildings and fine hotels make this little spa a truly delightful tourist attraction.

Hotels

ESPLANADE Located in a beautiful forest well above the main section of Marianske Lazne, but a short walk down to the baths and central promenade, is the Esplanade. Off a small lobby there is an attractive little cocktail lounge. Adjoining dining rooms are to the rear, overlooking a tree-shaded valley. The room to the far left doubles as a nightclub with music. There is also a French restaurant. Intermediate rooms are used for group tours and breakfast. This hotel appears big, but is actually rather small, with only 68 rooms. There are adequate parking facilities. Assistance with baggage is available.

All rooms have couches, cosmetic tables, telephones and radios; apartments have TV. Most rooms have balconies and are commodious. Bathrooms are large. The apartments have two large rooms, a dining table and a lovely view of the valley. Apartments rent for about 170 Kcs. The 17 singles without bath rent at 55 Kcs. The three singles with baths cost approximately 65 Kcs. Doubles wthout bath rent for about 75 Kcs; with bath, 100 Kcs.

Adjoining the Explanade is an annex called the Campanella which has 29 rooms, all without bath. No meals are served. This annex is Grade B category and is not recommended.

The French Restaurant at the Explanade is attractively decorated, the waiters serving good food in a pleasant and efficient manner.

This hotel's attractive decoration, pleasant location, efficient staff, the good food and service will make your stay a pleasant one.

PALACE The hotel has a Main Street location and is a 10-minute walk away from the baths and colonades. It is a turn of the century building with a cafe, a restaurant and dancing in the evening. The lobby is small; upstairs halls are rather grim. Telephones in all rooms. Radios on request.

Doubles with bath cost about 100 Kcs; without bath, around 80 Kcs. All singles are without bath, costing 55 Kcs. The one apartment costs approximately 100 Kcs. Doubles are large and quite attractive. High rooms are recommended because of the street noise outside the front of the building. Rooms are pleasant, clean and adequate in size.

The restaurant occupies an oddly shaped building next to the hotel. Here is also the Cafe Ludwig and the nightclub. Go to the rear section of the restaurant—the front rooms are usually reserved for tours. Food is plain but good; service is pleasant—efficient. Menus are in German as well as English.

CRISTAL Rated comparable to the Esplanade and Palace Hotels by some Czech authorities, this hotel is situated on the main street of Marianske Lazne. It is a few minutes walk from the baths, the main shopping area and the theaters.

CORSO AND EXCELSIOR HOTELS These hotels are situated just down the street from the Hotel Palace. Both are Interhotels, both appear to be pleasant and clean.

Restaurant

CAFE LIL For a little late drinking, some cold snacks, a bit of dancing and local atmosphere, try this cafe located in an old home surrounded by a park. It is opposite the Cristal Palace Hotel. The cafe is open from 5 P.M. to 2 A.M.

OLOMOUC

Hotel

DRUZBA I have heard this name frequently mentioned by Czech associates; reports indicate that it is quite pleasant. The hotel is located in a charming and historical town of eastern Bohemia.

OSTRAVA

Hotel

OSTRAVA If you journey to this town located not far from the Czechoslovakia-Poland border, you will find a hotel with two apartments, double rooms with bath, single rooms with and without bath. The Ostrava boasts two restaurants plus a keller featuring dance music nightly. It is located one mile from the railway station.

PLZN (Pilsen)

Recollections of Plzn: An old city, narrow streets jammed by streetcars and pedestrians; parks and circuses; a few broad boulevards; sun on dust and grime. This second city of Czechoslovakia's Bohemia produces one of the world's best beers.

Hotels

CONTINENTAL The hotels in Plzn are marvelous examples of the expression, appearances are deceiving. The Continental is located directly on the east-west highway connecting Prague and Plzn—the dead-center of the town. Streetcar tracks pass in front of the hotel. The hotel building is grim-appearing on the outside, the lobby most unimposing.

Roughly 53 rooms, only 16 with bath. Few overlook the streetcars. A TV is located in a public lounge. An apartment consists of two double rooms, a bath adjoining. An extra couch-type bed is available on request. Singles are equipped with two types of radios, one of them centrally operated. Large wardrobes, cosmetic tables and lounge chairs are included in the furnishings.

An apartment rents for approximately 150 Kcs., a double, 99 Kcs.; a single with bath for 65 Kcs. A double without bath runs about 75 Kcs., and can be large, airy and nicely furnished. After October 1 prices drop 20 to 30 percent. Rooms are comfortably furnished in a traditional fashion.

Meals in the restaurant are good; service is pleasant and efficient. English is spoken. Music in the evening. Sit in the rear section of the restaurant, as the front area is more or less a cafe. This restaurant is one of the best I encountered in Bohemia. Breakfast is served in the cafe. A tavern night spot in the basement is open from eight until three.

SLOVAN The Slovan, an 80-year old hotel, is situated on a quiet parkway in central Plzn. The hotel has an inviting exterior and a pleasant atmosphere within. Limited English is spoken. The main drawback is that out of 115 rooms, there are only three rooms (doubles) with·bath.

Doubles with bath run about 75 Kcs., and are large with radio, telephone, two wardrobes, a couch and TV. Doubles without bath run 55 Kcs., and appear about the same size. A single costs around 40 Kcs. Furnishings include washbowl, radio and couch.

The attractive restaurant is open at six for dinner; lunch and breakfast at regular hours. The Slovan also has a cafe; music nightly from eight until two. There is no nightclub.

Slovakia

Just one grand vacation spot packed full of resorts to visit, mountains to climb, sights to see, food in which to delight, wines to sip, and fine hotels.

I would recommend that you see Prague and her environs first. Then, if time permits, meander through eastern Bohemia, through Moravia, dip down to Bratislava and then drive along the highway through Nitra, up to Banska Bystrica and on (via Tale for a night's stop) to Stary Smokovce or Tatranska Lomnica. It is truly a beautiful drive, particularly between Podbrezova and Tatranska Lomnica.

On your tour of Slovakia, don't ignore the old town of Kosice with its churches, museums and good restaurants. It's a fine drive from the Tatras down through Levoca and Presov, the latter city a good example of modern Slovakia. Near Poprad, visit Klastorisko, a gypsy village situated near unique natural formations which include canyons and waterfalls. On a warm day, the Hornad River region is delightful with its old trees and small hills. At Levoca, see the old church with its elaborately carved altar. The lake at Strsbke Pleaso encourages a summer's stroll; nearby at Tatranska Lomnica try the cabin lift to the High Tatras. The entire Tatra area is truly beautiful. The pines, the cold lakes, the little open trains that run through the forests are tourist attractions of the first order.

Throughout Slovakia there are many beautiful natural scenic spots; for example, the Demanovska Grottos and Liptovsky Mikulas, an outstanding natural grouping of caves first opened to the public in 1924. Mentioned in writings of 1299 and first explored as early as 1719, the entire series of grottos is nearly eight miles long.

BANSKA BYSTRICA

The entire town of Banska Bystrica is worth seeing. Here the architecture of the 15th and 16th-centuries is remarkably well-preserved. See the District Museum located in the Gothic home of King Mattias. Local churches contain valuable interior furnishings from the Baroque Period.

Hotel

NARODNY DOM This is an Interhotel unit and you can be assured that all should go well during your visit to Banska Bystrica, although the hotel is in a Grade B category. Located near the center of town on the west side, this is best reached by foot from the main thoroughfare. The main floor is occupied solely by a restaurant and cafe, the reception area is on the second floor. The lobby is generally dark and emphatically gloomy. Singles should run around 40 Kcs., and two-bedded rooms about double that price. Rooms are clean, functional and provide adequate convenience for one or two nights' stay.

The restaurant consists of a large front room—not used in the summer—and a medium-sized side room very crowded during the summer months. On the small terrace at the front of the hotel one may have coffee and liqueurs. The food is generally good, substantial and well-served. The restaurant is very popular with local people.

BRATISLAVA (Presburg)

From Bratislava Castle high on a hill overlooking Slovakia's largest city, you will be delighted by the exciting view of the Danube, the city and, at not too great a distance, Austria and Hungary. It is both educational and entertaining to wander through the old town. There is the Primate's Palace with its Hall of Mirrors in which the Peace of Pressburg was signed between Napoleon I and Emperor Franz of Austria. In this building see the famous Gobelin Tapestries depicting the stories of Leander and Aphrodite. Here also are paintings by Breughel, Pietet, Murillo and Kupicky. The sculptor Donner is represented by some outstanding pieces.

Nearby, the Old Town Hall contains some interesting art objects from the past 500 years of Bratislava's history. Note the ceilings and walls of this building, for they are as interesting as the exhibits. Don't miss the magnificent Grassalkovich Palace built in 1760. The gardens date from Maria Theresa's time. Statues by Rafael Donner shown here depict the four seasons. This Palace is not far from the sightseeing boat docks located along the Danube River in the central section of the City.

In a state of semi-disrepair, the interior of St. Martin's Cathedral is nonetheless worth the visit. Note the animal head carvings on the seats near the altar and the magnificent statuary grouping by Donner hidden in the dusk to the right of the altar. This Cathedral was begun in the 14th century and completed one hundred years later. In 1563 the Cathedral was the Coronation Church for the Hungarian King.

Near Bratislava are the vineyards of Moors and the castle and vineyards of Pezinok where a sip of wine is waiting for you. Visit Dolna Krupa, the castle in which Beethoven vacationed. Nearby is Piestany Spa, a famous Slovakian health resort.

Hotels

DEVIN Your stay in Bratislava will be doubly enjoyable if you can arrange to stay at this hotel, an extremely attractive establishment located near the banks of the Danube. Built during the past few years, it offers outstanding accommodations for the visitor to Czechoslovakia. It is situated immediately off a quay, paralleling the Danube, and is separated from the quay by a small grassy area. The view from the front rooms on the higher floors is most pleasant, as one can see people boating, swimming and fishing on and in the Danube.

A small but pleasantly appointed French dining room opens from the north side of the spacious lobby. A cafe is situated along the front of the building facing the Danube and has an open terrace with garden chairs, tables and colorful umbrellas. Here one may enjoy snacks, coffee or an aperitif during the afternoon and early evening hours. Three banquet rooms are located on the second floor. Two are small rooms, one for cocktail parties, the other for a sit-down meal; a third room is much larger, seating 200 people. On the lower floors is an attractive nightclub with dance music nightly except Friday; floor shows from all over Europe are featured here. A bar is located at one end of the club.

Clean, pleasant sleeping accommodations occupy five floors. On the first floor front are two extremely elaborate apartments consisting of two rooms and two baths each. They are arranged so that the two apartments may be connected. The second apartment has a paneled bedroom representative of Slovakian woodcraft, featuring bookshelves, TV, a couch, plus a rather small bed. There is a very large living room and two baths. At the end of the first floor corridor are smaller apartments, the one to the south being particularly pleasant with central living room and single bedrooms to each side. Regular double bedrooms are very pleasant with good-sized baths. (All rooms in the hotel have bath or shower.) If you are traveling alone, try for the single rooms on the fifth floor with bath or shower. These fifth-floor rooms, whether facing the Danube or not, are rather large and have good-sized balconies.

CARLTON This enormous structure is located about two blocks from the Danube. Off the main lobby is a restaurant where the food is average. Below the lobby, the Cercle Bar is quite pleasant for entertaining. It is a large room with orchestra; somewhat formal in decor. Also available is the Lotus Club, a bar with Chinese motif which is rather small. A pleasant cafe is located off the lobby. The Palm Court opens in the summer and offers music from four in the afternoon.

The rooms are clean and well maintained, though in some instances they are overly furnished. The hotel as a whole has a European atmosphere circa 1909. Apartments consist of two large rooms; living room and bedroom. Singles can be quite pleasant and include radio and phone. A garconniere has the bedroom separated from the living room by a curtain; large bath.

With no view, and age not in its favor, the Carlton has to push to keep going. Few people speak English here but I don't think this is too great a problem. Do not hesitate to try the Carlton. Its staff will make a considerable effort to make your stay a pleasant one.

Restaurants

ZOCHOVA CHATA Some fifteen to twenty kilometers outside of Bratislava, this typical Slovak-style restaurant was highly recommended to me. It sounds like it would be great fun, with gypsy music, good wine, spicy food.

CAFE KRYM This restaurant is located not far from the Hotel Devin at the southeast end of the Danube Bridge. The small cafe, surrounded by a lovely garden, opens in mid-afternoon and boasts a good Hungarian orchestra. Patrons sit beneath trees, amidst flowers, sipping good local wines or Pilsner Beer. There are comfortable seats and good service, after a day of touring. Open in the evening for dancing.

KOSICE

Hotels

SLOVAN I was told the building housing the present "Hotel Slovan" is actually the former Imperial Hotel, though there is nothing whatever imperial about the place.

There is a large, pleasantly furnished cocktail lounge. The restaurant is not outstanding in decor, but is extremely popular with local folks; good food is served in prompt fashion. To fully enjoy it, one should speak German or Czech.

This Interhotel is in the B category. Corridors are narrow but fairly well lighted. Rooms are plain, clean, though somewhat on the grim side. Rooms overlooking the courtyard are noisy. In this hotel there are but two singles and two doubles with bath, plus those bathrooms connected with the three apartments. The apartments have TV and telephone, a couch, living room and a front location (the street below is not too noisy and has little traffic). A double with bath rents for about 65 Kcs., a single with bath, 55 Kcs. Doubles without bath, 50 Kcs., singles without bath, 35 Kcs. With the exception of the apartment, rates in season may be slightly higher.

HUTNIK This hotel is modern, sizeable and impressive. Appearances are, however, totally deceiving. This comparatively new structure is not recommended. There is a large lobby, bleak in decor. I understand beds are built in bunk style, one above the other. On the second floor there is a night spot, usually quite crowded; a fairly good dance orchestra plays each evening. This place is quite popular with local university students. Go early and be prepared to share your table. The hotel is roughly a five-minute drive from the business section of Kosice. It enjoys a quiet location situated in attractive surroundings.

Restaurant

HUNGARIAN RESTAURANT Here is interesting architecture within and without. Built in Gothic style with low-ceilinged rooms, the

Hungarian is located across from the Opera House. Hungarian-style food. It is a small-town restaurant with average prices. The tables are limited, so for lunch or dinner plan to arrive early. You probably will have to share a table with others in any case.

PODBREZOVA (Tale)

Driving through central Slovakia you will have occasion to take Route #66 from Poprad to Banska Bystrica. Some 50 kilometers east of Banska Bystrica you will come to the village of Podbrezova, located in a beautiful if somewhat sooty valley paralleling the Hron River. There is a great deal of mining activity in this region. (Podbrezova is also an important transportation center.)

Hotel

SPORT HOTEL PARTIZAN The hotel is located some five miles into the hills above the town of Podbrezova. Actually the hotel has no connection with the town. The resort lies some fifteen minutes' drive up a lovely mountain road in the resort area of Tale. The name Partizan relates to the area surrounding the hotel which was a center for the August 1944 Slovakian uprising against Hitler.

Built in 1961, the hotel stands on a small bluff or plateau overlooking acres of pasture, pine trees, numerous small cabins and a man-made lake for swimming. Facing the many small hills of the Lower Tatras, the hotel has access to numerous trails, roads, streams and hunting areas. Motel and camping grounds are located nearby.

There is a wine-cellar bar where one may hear a good orchestra and enjoy an evening of "slivovitzing and dancing." A very pleasant and efficiently staffed restaurant occupies the western end of the building. Surrounded by a wide terrace, the front part of the restaurant is maintained as a reading room where coffee and spirits may be served; the other section of the room is the restaurant proper with excellent food and good service. The view is really beautiful. The restaurant is open all day, serving local dishes as well as international cuisine.

The first-floor rooms of the hotel which face the valley or front of the hotel have balconies. Only double rooms have baths. Doubles without baths, as well as singles, have toilets and washbowls. All rooms are furnished in chalet modern—colorful and in good taste. Bathrooms, though small, are very clean.

The hotel is a very pleasant, leisurely drive of about two hours from Tatranska Lomnica through a beautiful section of eastern and central Slovakia. The hotel is delightful and deserves special consideration. Winter sports activities are also held in the area of the hotel.

STARY SMOKOVEC

Hotels

GRAND The road may be bumpy, but the scenery more than makes up for the ten-minute car drive from Tatranska Lomnica to the resort village of Stary Smokovec, both villages located in a resort area of the High Tatras in north central Slovakia.

The Grand gives the impression of being a little less formal and perhaps just a bit more polished than its sister hotel the Grand Hotel Praha in Tatranska Lomnica. It is also a member of the Interhotel Tatry group and has the advantage of being located near the various resort activities centered about the town. It has shaded lawns, large parking area, rustic exterior and a general overall simplicity of style. Off a spacious lobby there are several large public rooms including a very attractive cocktail lounge and two dining rooms. Nonetheless I enjoyed a very good meal at the restaurant—well served and complemented by a wide range of aperitifs and wine.

I would suggest that in booking you request rooms facing village, for the view from the south side is really attractive.

Located not far from the Grand and operated in conjunction with it is a small cabin-like structure called "The Koliba" where in typical Slovakian surroundings one can enjoy tasty grilled foods, wine and gypsy music. Open about five o'clock, it serves guests until late in the evening. Very fine for small groups and private parties.

To help you in making a choice between the Grand Hotel Praha and the Grand Hotel at Stary Smokovec, let me point up this fact:

The Grand Hotel Praha is situated on the edge of a very small village, so if semi-isolation, a view and a complete dependence on hotel life is your aim, then I would suggest you go to the Grand Hotel Praha. For the younger, livelier resort life, a mid-village location with more activity, more sights to see, but far less of a view, your choice should be the Grand Hotel at Stary Smokovec.

BELLEVUE This modern structure located on the edge of Stary Smokovec is set well back from the main road. The Bellevue opened in May 1965 and is in the best possible taste. There is a large, attractively designed lobby behind which is the main restaurant, also most attractive with a view toward the valley. A grill room is located on the lower level. Smart decor. The latest methods are employed in preparing meals in the hotel kitchen.

There are 220 beds; front rooms decorated in good taste open onto balconies. Apartments have two baths. Most single rooms have showers; double rooms have bath and hand showers.

TATRANSKA LOMNICA

Hotel

GRAND HOTEL PRAHA Built in the mid-Twenties, this hotel retains the finest tradition of Slovakian hospitality. The hotel site atop a small rise providing all front rooms with a delightful view of the surrounding pine-covered hills, the distant village and the Tatra Mountains. Terraces and restaurant have a similar exposure.

The hotel is located roughly a half hour from the Polish-Czech border at Javorina. The rustic, very small village of Tatranska Lomnica above which the Grand Praha is located, is roughly forty minutes from Poprad, a rail junction connecting the Tatra area with Prague. There is not too much to see in the village except the usual souvenir shops, the narrow-gauge railroad which hauls passengers to the nearby vacation village of Stary Smokovec and beyond. It's lots of fun to ride this train, its open-sided carriages providing passengers with a splendid glimpse of the surrounding forests.

The Grand Praha, a member of the Interhotel Tatry (CEDOK) group, is built on the side of a hill, just about the terminus of the cable cars lifting passengers to the hiking (or skiing) stations high on the peaks of the mountains. The Tatras tower over the entire area, their northern side in Poland, the southern slopes in Czechoslovakia. The season here is May 15 to September 15, with high season in July and August.

Owing to the particular location of the hotel, the main entrance and first floor (rear) bedrooms are on ground level just off the large parking area. The lobby is small but adequate. Rooms are good-sized, though accommodations on the parking lot side are more cramped and without bathing facilities. On each upper floor you will find a small pantry from which guests may buy tea, cookies, chocolate, cigarettes, and even sandwiches. The furnishings of the bedrooms are adequate though scarcely elaborate. Singles as a rule have a davenport which converts into beds. Rooms with bath all face away from the parking area and toward the valley and mountains. I do not recommend the top floor rooms. Stick to the first and second floor accommodations away from the parking area.

There is an excellent restaurant—three large rooms just to the right of the ground floor lobby, the last room available for parties. Waiters are efficient and very pleasant; the menu, large and varied. Food is delicious. Aperitifs are served in both the lounge and restaurant. The entire atmosphere of the restaurant is on a par with the best resort hotels anywhere in the world. Breakfast is served in the restaurant. "Tea complete" is served in the lounge after breakfast hours. Coffee and liqueurs are served in the lounge following dinner. There is music for dancing later on in the evening.

In summation, the Grand Praha is a fine hotel, well managed, adequately staffed, with average to good accommodations and excellent food. Recommended.

Side Trips from Tatranska Lomnica

You might enjoy the fifteen minute drive from Tatranska Lomnica through Stary Smokovec to Strbske Pleaso to see the lake, to hike, to sun; drive to Poprad to see the horses race or view the canyons and waterfalls surrounding the Hornad River region. There is Levoca with its old church and, at a greater distance, Kosice with its churches and museums.

We have already mentioned in the introduction to Slovakia that throughout that region there are many outstanding natural scenic spots. As an exciting example, there is the Demanovska Grottos near Liptovsky Mikulas. This is a spectacular natural grouping of caves first opened to the public in 1924. Mentioned in writings of 1299 and first explored as early as 1719, the entire twelve-kilometer long series of grottos are magnificent. A lot of walking and climbing is required for a ten minutes walk up (if the chair lift is not working), then a steep descent; again a rough ascent inside the Grottos. You will eventually exit above the spot where you originally entered. Take along overshoes (for some protection) and a warm, winter jacket.

Hungary

The country; lakes (some big ones, too!); rivers; rolling, tree-covered hills; flat plains where graze fine cattle; magnificent horses. White plastered walls, red roofs, and storks' nests. Mud! Dust! Gypsy carts rumbling along a stretch of hot macadam road. The smell of mint in a cool, dark forest. Color everywhere—red poppies, tulips, purple grapes clustered on a leafy green vine. A brown and white church steeple outlined against the bluest sky. A wisp of cloud forming a shadow against the trim, rakish prow of a lake steamer. Sun-browned bodies on a sandy beach. The sour smell of a dank wine cellar. Violins!

Describe the Hungarian, the Magyar? Many of the women are strikingly beautiful, chic, fashionably dressed. Not all of them. Many are fat, old, ill-clothed, terribly tired. Wars! Revolutions! Harsh suppression! Don't look at the body or the clothes—look at the eyes. Yes, it is certainly a fact in Hungary that the eyes are truly "a window to the soul"—blue, brown and green reflections of Hungary's past—her future! The bodies are tired, the hair perhaps grey, but the eyes? Proud! *Always* proud! Pride *is* Hungary!

The men? Faces and physique are unimportant. Clothes tell us nothing, nothing at all! Once again, look at the eyes! Tired? Perhaps. Determined? Very possibly. Proud? The entire manner of the man, of the Magyar, tells us that this Hungarian, whether he works in a factory, at a hotel reception desk, or as a cowboy out on the Puszta, is *proud*. Proud of his country, his home, his family, his ideals! He is a *Magyar*!

Much, much, much too much has been written, particularly in the travel pages of our Sunday newspapers, concerning the "gyeepsy moozik," the "vunderfool nights in Old Budapest, the wine, the ladies to whom a man cannot help but lose his heart, his soul." True! True! True! The gals, not only in Budapest but all over the bloomin' land, are visual delights! And the wine? *Wow!*

But what about the vodka frequently served with coffee at 10:30 in the morning! And Slivowitz! That liquid fire will really perk up your senses during some mid-morning slump. Why not speak of the "Street of Beautiful Women" in Eger, where tantalizing wines are sold from row upon row of underground caves whose damp interiors are dimly lit by candles or 10-watt bulbs. As for the "gyeepsy violins," why stick to commercialized Budapest? These gypsies get around, you know! In fact, it seems to me these folks are really the original travelin' kind! Go on out to the Puszta (the steppe, the cattle country) to the gypsy camps, to the restaurants of Debrecen and Kecskemet. There in the gypsy's true environment, over a glass of *Rizlinz Badacsonyi* (a light, white and dry wine), those violins will more than sing. They'll pull at your heart, twist it around a few times, bring tears to your eyes and fire to your soul.

But let's get away from wine, women and song for a moment. Like horses? How's about a Hungarian Riding Tour? Ten-day trips originate at various points throughout the country during the summer months. Roughing it? Not exactly, for the buses which accompany the tours provide every comfort to the weary rider. Actually, I don't know how the tourists find time to ride for they are treated to rodeos, barbeques, exhibitions of riding skill by Hungarian National teams and (here we go again!) visits to regional wine cellars where they are invited to sample local vintages.

Hydrofoils, anyone? $6.80 will take you in four hours from Budapest to Vienna on the hydrofoil *Siraly*; 90 feet long, 64 passengers, traveling at 34 knots. And what scenery you will pass as you travel around the Danube Bend cities of Visegrad and Estergom!

You see, there's one heck 'uva lot more to my Hungary than can be found in the over-played environs of Budapest. "Hungary" is not Budapest! The Hungarian capital is mighty fine, but no better than the proud land lying just outside the city's boundary lines.

GEOGRAPHY AND CLIMATE

Hungary is about equal in size to the state of Indiana, with a population figure approximating that of Illinois; 35,919 square miles and 10 million persons. Completely landlocked, Hungary is bordered by Czechoslovakia on the north, Austria on the west, Yugoslavia to the south, and Romania on the southeast. There is also a smaller border with the Soviet Union to the northeast. The highest mountains range up to 3,329 feet, and at its lowest point Hungary is 256 feet above sea level. Hungary is bisected by the Danube and Tisza Rivers, both flowing in a north-south direction. Lake Balaton—about 48 miles long, and approximately three miles wide (though at one point the lake is almost bisected by the Tihany Peninsula) is the largest lake in Central Europe. The Balaton is very shallow, only 11' to 14' deep. The northern portion of the lake is only 70 miles from Budapest, the capital of Hungary.

Hungary experiences quite cold winters as well as hot, dry summers. The western portions of the country are very fertile and boast vineyards, meadows, orchards and sugar beet farms. Plants for the production of food oils are grown here. You will experience many delightful views as you drive through the rolling green countryside past Lake Balaton, the vineyards and summer resort towns. Western Hungary is drier, a flat tableland dedicated largely to the growing of wheat, corn, rye and barley. Hogs, cattle and poultry, prominent export items, are raised here. Magnificent horses as well as fine breeds of cattle are raised in Eastern Hungary, near Debrecen in an area called the Puszta. You can say that Hungary's east rather resembles our western plains states. The Puszta is flat as far as the eye can see. At the Szilvasvarad stud farm you may see the famous Lippizan horses.

The largest cities of Hungary are its capital, Budapest, and Miskolc, Debrecen, Pece and Szeged; each of these places has a very definite character of its own. Hungary is not a large country, yet the extremely varied scenery which changes at the turning of a road, topping a rise or rounding a lake is an endless source of pleasure for the traveler. This is a country best seen and understood by means of car travel; or "horse travel," for Hungary is a horseman's paradise. Good fishing here, too!

HISTORY

In 895-896, the Hungarians also (known as the Magyars), the original settlers of an area usually described in history books as "beyond the Urals" (referring to a central mountain chain in Russia), invaded the Moravian Empire from the east and by so doing separated the Slav races, isolating the Czechs from the Slovaks. The Magyars were Christianized in about the year 1000 while under the rule of Stephen I. This great king was later canonized (1083), and his crown became a national symbol, the Holy Crown of Saint Stephen! Hungary reached the zenith of national power under Louis the Great (1342-82) who established effective control over Transylvanians, the Southern Slavs and the Slovaks as well as other tribes in neighboring areas. Another great ruler following in the footsteps of King Louis was Mattias Corvinus (1458-90). All these kings are venerated in today's Hungary. Statues, cathedrals, poems and songs attest to the esteem in which these men of olden times are held in the hearts of all Hungarians.

As is the case with almost all East European countries, no historical review can be complete without stirring-up the Turkish bogeyman. In 1453 the Ottoman Turk, under the leadership of Melmet the Conqueror invaded Constantinople from the north, east and west; the western approach proved particularly disastrous for the Byzantine metropolis because the Turks moved in large cannons which had been constructed in Adrianople, a town west of Constantinople. Down went the walls and in through the gate still used today and known as the "Edirne Kapi" (Door to Edirne) marched the "terrible Turks." History's gate was knocked off its hinges as the awesome, powerful "Yeni Cheri" or Janissary armies turned north; Greece fell in 1453, Bulgaria fell even before Constantinople, around 1370; Romania was under Turkish suzerainty by 1473; and next came Hungary.

Numerous battles raged between the Turks and Magyars during the late 14th and early 15th centuries. The year 1526 found Hungary ruled by a dissipated nobility; peasant uprisings resulted in a further weakening of the country. Finally, at Mohacs (a town located in what is now southern Hungary) the Hungarians suffered a defeat for which word "disastrous" is mild indeed. The Hungarian army, surprised and outnumbered, engaged the Turks in fierce combat on this plain not far from the Danube River. Result: the Hungarian army was almost totally annihilated; the nobles were lost almost to a man and King Louis was slain. For the next 150 years the Turks occupied the country. To us tourists the minarets, mosques, tombs and arms are colorful, interesting trophies of bygone wars. To the Hungarians, however, these mementoes will seemingly never cease to be other than hated reminders of a period in their history when the cultural link with their pre-14th-century heritage was partially severed, almost totally destroyed.

The year 1683 saw the Turks brewing coffee outside the gates of Vienna. Following their defeat by the great Polish General Jam Sobieski, the Turks withdrew from Hungary, eventually establishing themselves south of the Carpathian Alps in what is now Romania. In time the various warring factions in Hungary were tamed, at least temporarily, and the Hapsburg rulers (drawn to Hungary during the Turkish Wars) drew up the so-called Pragmatic Sanction binding Hungary to the Hapsburg domains. So stood Hungary in 1723.

The year 1848 is a much-revered year in Magyar history. Lajos Kossuth and Ferenc Deak led a revolt against the Hapsburgs which resulted in a short-lived (one year) republic. This autonomy was suppressed by Austria with the aid of Russian troops. Austria, engaged in one of her frequent hassles with Prussia and thereby somewhat off guard, gave in to Hungarian nationalistic aims and the Ausgleich (or "Compromise") of 1867 provided Hungary with a degree of self-government and established the Dual Monarchy.

World War I saw the collapse of the Austro-Hungarian monarchy and the beginning of three decades which would see Hungary become something of a "territorial football," increasing and diminishing in size throughout the years. The year following World War I saw the establishment of a democratic regime under the leadership of Prince Michael Karolyi, while 1919 introduced the short-lived Communist government of Bela Kun, suppressed by troops dispatched from neighboring Romania. In 1920 Hungary was once again a kingdom, albeit "kingless" (Admiral Nicholas Horthy was regent). It was during this year that the post-war Treaty of Trianon loosened non-Magyar nationalities from Hungarian domination; such areas as Transylvania and Slovakia were (seemingly) irretrievably lost. Between the wars, the return of the "lost" territories became a cornerstone of Hungarian foreign policy. Hitler fanned old antagonisms and new sentiments in Eastern Europe, and as a result most of Eastern Europe joined Germany and Italy during the early years of World War II. (It is well to remember here that Hungary, Romania and Bulgaria were monarchies with German ancestries prior to World War II; the largely pro-German acts by these governments seldom reflected the popular sentiment.)

For a time Czechoslovakia, Romania and Yugoslavia were forced to return to Hungary the lands originally controlled by Hungary. German troops eventually occupied Hungary in 1944 but were forced to leave a year later. The departure of German troops from Hungary was a bitter interlude; it resulted in tremendous damage throughout the country but particularly in Budapest where all bridges across the Danube were dynamited, palaces were burned and gutted and priceless antiques were destroyed. In 1946 Hungary was declared a republic. One year later a peace treaty was negotiated which required that Hungary return all territories acquired after 1937, thereby establishing the geographical limits of today's Hungary. Considerably smaller than before World War I but at least totally Hungarian, the country is now populated by a people of whom only four per cent are of other national backgrounds.

The Hungarian Workers Party took power in 1948; industry was nationalized, land collectivized and the general economy and constitution patterned after that of the Soviet Union. Policies originated prior to the 1956 uprising still constitute the basis for local government control. A status of forces agreement between Hungary and the Soviet Union in effect since May 27, 1957 permits the latter country to maintain forces on Hungarian soil as long as the two governments deem it necessary. The Soviet troops live in special camps, separated and secluded from the Hungarians.

LANGUAGE

Gee, whatta' deal! Hungarian is a branch of the so-called Finno-Ugaric language group, which also includes Estonian and Finnish. The alphabet consists of Latin characters. The Hungarian language was reformed during the late 18th and 19th centuries, better adapting it to a modern usage. Grammatical gender is unknown in Hungarian. All this is to say, use your English! Many Hungarians speak our language as well as French, German and largely since World War II Russian. Hungarian is laced with traces of French, Slavic, Turkish and Latin words. Now some samples of the challenge ahead!

Vowels and Consonants Division: there is a big difference here! The letter *c* is pronounces *ts*. The combination of letters *cs* results in a sound similar to the *tch* in our word *match*; *gy* results in a *due*; *sz* is soft as in *son* while *zs* ends up as a *su* sound as in *measure*. The several variations of the letter *o* are designated by symbols shown over the letter; *a* and *e* are each employed as two different sounds.

In Hungarian, the stress is always on the first syllable. Care for a run through? Okay! Try this for size: *Mi ez magayrul? Ketto levelzolap. Koszonom szepen!* The last two words you had best commit to memory: pronounced rather like *kussanem sayper*, the phrase means "Thank you very much." You will hear it again and again and again! The first two Hungarian phrases: "What is this in Hungarian? Two postcards."

Nem is no; *egen* means yes. *Ferfiak* is where the gents go when, in the cocktail lounge, they must wash their hands; gals head for the *nok*!

Budapest is but a five-hour car ride from Vienna, so rather naturally there is no great problem in finding a local person who can speak German (in particular). In the main hotels and travel bureaus French and some English are spoken. You will be surprised at the number of Americans, West Germans, French and other Europeans you will meet there. In the meantime, the best way to attack Hungarian is through phonetics. Listen to the words used about you, to you, to friends. You'll be surprised at the number of phrases you will be able to pick up this way.

Final important point: Hungarian names are usually written with the family name first: e.g., Smith, John. Don't be misled, as I was, into addressing the man as Mr. John. It is surprisingly easy to make this mistake in a country where the names are quite unfamiliar in sound and spelling.

CURRENCY

The equivalent of our word dollar is the Hungarian *forint*; our cents are their *fillers* pronounced "fillays"). Coins are in the denominations of 2, 5, 10, 20 and 50 fillers, plus 1, 2 and 5 forints. Notes are in the denominations of 10, 20, 50 and 100 forints. The exchange rate, presently 23.30 forints to the dollar, is not overly beneficial to the American visitor, particularly considering the exchange rate of some of Hungary's neighbors.

There is no restriction on the amounts of foreign currency which may be imported into Hungary. Be sure that you declare your foreign monies, travelers checks, letters of credit, etc., when entering the country. The import declaration (provided at the border) is usually requested when you plan to exchange funds within Hungary. Only 200 forints may be imported into Hungary and this in the form of 10 and 20 forint notes. There is no restriction on foreign currencies removed from Hungary within three months of your date of entry.

Should you be leaving Hungary for Romania keep well in mind that Hungarian currency is not acceptable in the latter country. So count your fillers carefully and don't exchange more than you will need those last few days before your departure. The same goes for Romanian currency in Bulgaria and Bulgarian lei in Romania; let's say they all love each other but . . .

Upon departure, should you arrive at one of the frontier stations with Hungarian currency, it may be exchanged at half its face value providing the total amount to be exchanged does not exceed $100. In short, at $100 you'll get fifty bucks back, so take care. Moreover, should you be on an international train, the confusion of border formalities may be such that you arrive in Austria complete with forints. I would complete this re-exchange at the IBUSZ desk at your hotel before leaving for the station. Bear in mind one important point: in many of the Eastern European countries your dollars exchanged at the tourist rate are not redeemable. This may also become the case in Hungary despite previous statements.

VISAS AND CUSTOMS

Visas may be obtained through your local travel agent or at the Hungarian Legation, 2437 15th Street, N.W., Washington 9, D.C. The visa fee is $4.50. You will be asked to fill out in duplicate two visa applications; two passport-size photographs are also requested. The visa is valid six months from the date of issuance. As stamped into your passport, the visa will be limited to a 21-day visit; however, this period may easily be extended through your hotel reception desk once you are in Hungary.

For the convenience of persons visiting Hungary, officials of the

Hungarian Legation in Washington have made it clear by word and deed that they will make every effort to expedite the completion of visa formalities at the earliest possible date after receiving the applications (carefully completed), photographs, visa fee and passport. I was surprised and pleased at the effort made by this legation's staff in providing all possible assistance toward the completion of my visa formalities.

Visas are also available at the border to visitors entering Hungary by car, plane or Danube boat. You will be asked to submit two visa applications and two photos; the former should be filled out prior to arrival at the border or airport. No visa is available at the border for travelers arriving in Hungary by train. (Note well those tourists arriving from Vienna!)

All visa applications must be accompanied by a "forint order" or voucher from your travel agent on which is noted the fact that you have confirmed hotel reservations for the entire length of your stay. The issuing agent at the Hungarian border or at the Ferihegy Airport will retain a copy of this voucher.

Should you not need hotel reservations for your stay, you will be asked to buy a forint order costing about $6.50 for each day of your stay between May 1 and October 31. This amount will be refunded to you in Hungary at the rate of 150 forints for each day. Between November 1 and April 30, a forint order will cost you $5.20 for each day of your stay and will be refunded in the amount of approximately 120 forints per day. The minimum pre-payment is for three days and there is a service charge of $6. Remember: forint orders relate only to persons entering Hungary without hotel reservations.

Persons who visit relatives in Hungary for 21 days must purchase a forint order costing about $52 plus a $6 service charge. This money will be refunded in Hungary (approximately 1,200 forints). If you visit relatives for a shorter period of time you will be required to purchase a forint order costing $6.50 for each day (refunded at the rate of 150 forints per day). Forint orders for visiting one's family may be extended without additional charge. Direct members of a family (spouse or children over 16 years of age) pay $4.30 per day per person (refund — 100 forints per day). Children under 16 years of age are exempt from the purchase of forint orders but are required to fill out two visa application forms.

And what are my personal observations regarding the visa requirements mentioned above? Perhaps the best response would be a referral to the entry requirements presently practiced at the Romanian and Bulgarian frontiers; neither country charges a minimum per diem; you have only to apply for a visa. When the visa has been issued you may enter the country without paying a per diem (or purchasing a forint order), and, if you are so inclined, without hotel reservations.

But this is Hungary, so the above regulations remain in force. Keep in mind that before visiting Hungary, you *must* obtain confirmed hotel reservations. Hungary is one of the few countries that make the issuance of a visa contingent on the confirmation from Budapest of confirmed hotel space. Frankly, I would skip this business of forint orders unless, of course, you are visiting relatives. Secure your hotel space through a travel agent. The Hungarian Legation will be advised by your travel agent that the hotel space has been set aside for you and — upon presentation of the visa fee, your passport, the applications and the photos by the travel firm — will issue a visa.

Do not concern yourself about the 21-day limitation. As I mentioned above, the visa will be extended with ease after you arrive in Hungary. You need only pay the minimum per diem for each additional day of your extended stay.

Entry points for Hungary are as follows:

> *By car* (from Austria): Hegyeshalom; Sopron; Rabafuzes; Koszeg.
> (from Czechoslovakia): Rajka; Komanom; Tornyosnemti; Balassagyarmat; Satoraljaujhely; Somoskoujfalu; Banreva; Parassapuszta.
> (from the Soviet Union): Zahony.
> (from Romania): Artand.
> (from Yugoslavia): Roske; Letenye.

> *By rail* (from Austria): Hegyeshalom.
> (from Czechoslovakia): Komarom; Szob; Midasnemeti; Banreve.
> (from the Soviet Union): Zahony.
> (from Romania): Biharkeresztes; Lokoshaza.
> (from Yugoslavia): Kelebia; Gyekenyes.

Additional points of entry are Budapest's Ferihegy Airport and, for those traveling to Budapest by ship, the Belgrad Rakpart.

Should you wish to visit Hungary while visiting, say in Vienna, Paris or some other principal European city, inquire at any reputable travel agency. For a minimal fee these firms will make all arrangements necessary for your trip. Important: the travel services of Eastern European countries located in Western Europe do not have the authority to issue visas. You must secure your hotel accommodations and visas through authorized local travel agencies.

If you do not have a visa and intend to pick one up at the border, don't be rushed through. Check with the guard, then pull into the parking lot. There is a building nearby where, against payment of the minimum per diem, the presentation of applications and passports, a visa will be issued in about twenty minutes. But take my advice. If you are traveling independently by car, train or air, secure your visa at home or in some principal city before setting out for Hungary. There is just too much confusion at border points.

Every hotel will ask that your passport be left at the reception desk for at least the first night of your stay in any one town, sometimes for "the duration." Don't forget to ask for your passport when checking out. In the event that you must make use of your passport at some time before leaving the hotel, be certain you return it to the concierge for his stamp and signature before your departure. This is a formality more than anything else but I encourage you to "subscribe to the rules."

I have been trying to think of a description that suitably and honestly fits the entire Hungarian posture with regard to the import and export of currency, customs formalities, hotel reservations and food payments. In other words, what actually is the attitude of the Hungarian government with reference to tourist travel in Hungary? Several words come to mind: business-like, concise, helpful, strict. The Hungarians will tell you "the rules" and assist you in every way possible to abide by such rules. They will provide you with mountains of well-prepared literature to explain the country, to make you feel at home in Hungary. In turn they will expect you not to stray from the prescribed "path" as outlined in their rules, literature and tempered explanations. I would urge that their words and mine be given maximum consideration.

In addition to the previously mentioned 200 forints, visitors to Hungary are allowed to take in 500 cigarettes, two quarts of wine, one quart of liquor, three quarts of liqueurs, one movie, one regular camera and an unlimited amount of film (which may be removed from the country developed or undeveloped). Radios, tape recorders and any other forms of "household machine" are subject to customs duty if their value exceeds 1,000 forints (approximately $43). As a general rule, a notation will be made in your passport in reference to your cameras and typewriter.

Should you be traveling by private car, the vehicle's motor or identification number will most likely be noted in your passport or on your visa card. Gifts may be imported up to the amount of 4,000 forints free of duty; gifts valued at between 4,000 and 8,000 forints are subject to duty and are restricted to products of a non-commercial character. Commercial articles over the value of 8,000 forints cannot be imported into Hungary even though the person entering the country offers to pay duty. Special licenses must be obtained from the National Bank of Hungary or the Chief Administration of Customs before this type of material can be imported.

Except for precious metals, stamps, large quantities of food, liquor or tobacco, all personal articles—including one liter of spirits, 200 cigarettes and two liters of wine—may be taken out of the country. Duty-free luggage should not weigh more than 50 kg. (140 lb) per person.

When I crossed by car from Austria I found that a long line of cars carrying tourists bent on a summer's holiday moved through customs quite rapidly. Oral declarations were accepted. Suitcases generally were not opened. In most cases passengers were not required to leave their cars (except those who obtained their visas at the border). Customs officials are most serious about their work but polite. The day may be bright, the flowers in bloom and the wheat "brown ripe" against an azure sky when you cross the Austro-Hungarian border. Nevertheless, even with all the modified customs procedures and the semi-nonchalant manner of the border guards, I must emphasize this is one country where you would be very wise to treat seriously the matter of tourist entry—by car, train or plane. The language problem makes for something of a headache, therefore don't be too frisky or try to pull some illegal maneuver. To speed matters up, before approaching the border determine the amount of dollars or other currencies in your possession and ascertain which of your possessions (e.g. typewriter; camera; etc.,) you will be obliged to declare.

TRAVELING TO AND IN HUNGARY

Hungary can be reached by train, plane, car, touring bus, river boat—even by hitch-hiking. Traveling by car? Okay—lunch in Vienna; cocktails in Budapest! Roughly a six-hour ride, customs formalities included.

By Air

Traveling by air? Austrian Air Lines, Sabena and KLM maintain weekly service to Budapest's Ferihegy Airport. These West European airlines also maintain offices in Budapest, but remember: MALEV, Hungary's national airline, controls all actual ticket sales (along with IBUSZ). Other lines serving Hungary are CSA (Czechoslovakia), TAROM (Romania) and AEROFLOT (the Soviet Union). All maintain offices in Budapest. MALEV maintains services to several West European capitals.

You will indeed be a wise traveler if you arrive in Hungary with confirmed return or continuing air reservations subject only to re-confirmation. However, should you need to purchase a ticket in Budapest, contact either IBUSZ or MALEV to determine which domestic or foreign airline is flying to your destination (or to a city from which you can continue your journey). Contact the airline people well ahead! Bookings are usually quite solid at all times of the year. IBUSZ or MALEV will advise you of the carrier leaving on your particular date (the airlines service Eastern European capitals on something of a rotation basis, AUA one day, MALEV the next, Sabena the next, etc.) Book and purchase tickets accordingly. MALEV maintains domestic service from Budapest to Pecs, Debrecen, Szombathely and Zalaegerszeg. Flying time between Budapest and Vienna: 50 minutes; Paris: 3 hours 30 minutes; Zurich: 1 hour 55 minutes and Rome: 2 hours 30 minutes. MALEV maintains a fleet of Ilyushin 14's and 18's. Stick to the Il. 18's if possible. The smaller Il. 14's are subject to weather conditions enroute.

A customs free shop and a transit hotel are located at Ferihagy Airport. Bus service between downtown Budapest and the airport is maintained. Passengers will pay 4 forints each way. There is no charge for such airport services as baggage handling, airport tax and the like.

One way fare to London: $131.40 (first class), $96.20 (tourist); to Vienna: $24.70 (tourist only); to Paris: $103.90 (first class), $74.20 (tourist).

Ferihegy Airport

Arriving passengers at Budapest's rather small but up-to-date Ferihegy Airport are met by bus at the foot of the exit from the aircraft. They are chauffered to the modern terminal building and introduced to visas and customs procedures by some extremely charming ladies in the Arriving Passengers Lounge located just inside the main door of the airport. Passengers arriving without visas obtain their entry permits at a booth on the opposite side of the room from the Passport Control. No one is allowed through Passport Control until he has his visa.

I emphasize that I found the personnel in this visa-issuing section to be very pleasant and most anxious to provide assistance. Upon completion of your visa application form, be sure to have immediately available your hotel voucher or prepaid per diem coupon, plus the $5 fee. (The visa fee will be requested in dollars.) Authors and writers please note that it is a good idea to list your profession as something other than the "true facts" for there seems to be a delay in granting visas to passengers who are professionals in the literary field. The actual approval of the visa takes but a few minutes. Following the receipt of your passport with the Hungarian visa, present your passport to the Passport Control, a process which takes but a minute or so, and proceed on through Customs. I did not find the Customs people overly eager to open my luggage, in fact, not one of my bags was checked.

I suggest that you take a taxi directly into Budapest, although bus service is available. By car, the trip from Ferihegy Airport to Budapest takes approximately 30 minutes and costs 50 forints. A freeway has been constructed part of the way between the airport and the capital so as to permit incoming and departing passengers along this road to proceed unhampered by local traffic. Tourists departing from Budapest should be very conscious of the fact it is a full half hour's ride to the airport, provided there are no traffic delays.

Actually, I always leave my Budapest hotel not less than an hour and a half prior to the departure of a flight. Departure procedures at Budapest's Ferihegy Airport are considerably more involved than those for arriving passengers as a result of the rather poorly managed processes through which departing passengers are expected to proceed. Passengers should keep in mind that at all airports in Central and Eastern Europe you are not expected to go to the check-in desk of the airline on which you are traveling. Check in at any ticket desk that happens to be open. The departure procedures for all flights out of Budapest are under the control of the MALEV authorities, that is the Hungarian National Airlines. Baggage will be weighed, excess baggage charges paid and tickets checked; only then can you proceed into a short corridor where you will line up for Passport Control. Passport Control is normally a short process but sometimes becomes needlessly long.

Bus service is available from the customs area directly to the plane. International flights depart promptly from Budapest and since it takes roughly twenty minutes to half an hour to complete ticket, passport and customs procedures and half an hour to get to the airport, passengers should leave their hotel definitely not less than an hour and a half before the departure of their flight.

By Train

Comfortable service to Hungary is provided from all European cities. From Paris and Vienna there is the Orient Express; from Vienna and Zurich, the Wiener Waltzer. The Balt-Orient Express runs to Dresden and Prague; the Pannonia to Berlin and Prague. The Borsod Express carries passengers to Miskolc in northern Hungary for connections to Czechoslovakia's Tatra Mountain region. Trains running between Budapest and Austria, Romania, Czechoslovakia and Yugoslavia leave from the Eastern Station in Budapest. Destination the Soviet Union?—use the Western Station. Some trains from Yugoslavia also arrive at the Southern Station. Kelenfold Station is a stopping place for trains arriving and departing from Budapest's Eastern and Southern Stations. Vienna is 4 hours traveling time away; Prague 10 hours and Warsaw 16 hours. Belgrade is 8 hours away.

Rail tickets may be purchased at the main IBUSZ office in downtown Budapest. Passengers traveling to Vienna or Paris or any other western European city should not accept the suggestion advanced rather frequently by the IBUSZ employees that first class is not available so "why not buy second class accommodations?" They often advise tourists to "attempt an improvement" of their accommodations once on the train. Well, the chances of "improving" are almost nil. Second class is jammed and first class carriages are as much sought after as seats in the last lifeboat off the Titanic. Wait for that train on which you can obtain signed, sealed and confirmed in writing first class space. Second class is adequate if you don't mind the garlic sausage, the "Please-pass-the-Slivowitz" crowd. There is little room for luggage, and the air, particularly on a rainy day, will discourage dinner on arrival.

Obtaining a rail ticket at IBUSZ is something of a lengthy procedure for which a morning should be set aside. First see if you cannot arrange matters through your hotel; this will save standing in several lines for tickets, for seat reservations and for payment. Very confusing! Better yet, make your reservations in advance, stopping in at IBUSZ only to *re*-confirm. (Same goes for air travel.) The more complete your return and continuing reservations when entering Hungary, the more pleasant will be your trip. Employees are helpful and as pleasant as the demands on their time permit, but now—those crowds!

Wagons-Lit Cook maintains an office at the side of the Eastern Station. Keep this in mind for checking up on those sleeping accommodations. Local trains operating largely over electrified routes maintain clean and comfortable first class accommodations. Restaurant cars provide substantial and tasty meals.

If you decide, as I did, to meet Aunt Lottie on her arrival from Vienna at Budapest's East Station, make note of the following: before departing from your hotel be certain you have well fixed in mind the arrival time and the number of her train, as well as that town at which she crossed into Hungary. Be at the station at least ten minutes before the train's arrival and take up a position from which you can view all incoming trains, then, by some process of inner chemistry, attempt to determine on which of the arriving trains Aunt Lottie may be found.

The East Station boasts one primitive information booth, several down-at-the heel waiting rooms, a sad little buffet and multitudinous doors and windows through whose cracked panes and lintels the wind blows cold on even the warmest nights. Announcements of arrivals and departures are rather naturally provided in Hungarian; no signs, to my knowledge, give indications of the track on which trains are to arrive. In short, bedecked in your best and with the welcoming bouquet of roses tucked under your arm, prepare to canter up and down the spacious station in a frantic effort not to miss Lottie among the throng.

Outbound passengers should be prepared to carry their own luggage from taxis or cars to the train. Porters are scarce.

River Boat

If you're in Vienna and decide to "probe" the vacation life in nearby Hungary, board the hydrofoil *Siraly*. Departures: Tuesday and Saturday from Vienna; Monday and Friday from Budapest. Season: May 15 to September 15. All aboard at 8 A.M. The trip takes roughly four hours. In Budapest you will be deposited at the Belgrade Rakpart. Tickets are obtainable at IBUSZ as well as at various ticket offices abroad. Refreshments served. One-way fare: 158 forints or 163 Austrian shillings.

By Bus

There is no scheduled bus transportation between Hungary and neighboring countries. Domestic bus service is quite good and covers most of the country. Ten-day passes are available at a cost of approximately $9.50. Hungarian buses (locally produced) are short on frills, but substantially built. Distances are short. I do not hesitate to suggest that you travel by bus if your plans call for extensive touring about the country.

Hitch Hiking

Hitch-hiking? So okay! For those in the young-at-heart category, it is perfectly acceptable to hitch-hike your way across Eastern Europe.

It's done all the time, but first a word of advice! If you manage a ride as far as the border, be smart—leave the car of your host a bit before the red and white arms of the border control gate loom in the distance. In short, arrive at the border under your own power. Why? Because your host driver will not want to be bothered with any unknowns while tromping through the official red tape. He doesn't know you and will most certainly be unreceptive to the idea of having border officials asking him who you are.

Then again, self-preservation would seem to affect your decision against staying in the car with a driver that you don't know. What if he is smuggling something into or out of some country? You'd sure look mighty sick sitting there when the customs men uncover the smuggled items; and this happens, unfortunately rather frequently.

So hitch-hike, "auto stop," whenever the spirit moves you and the state of your finances demands. But be a bit selective in your choice of companions and leave them before you reach the border!

Motoring

High (82-85) octane gasoline runs something over 3.70 forints per liter; regular gasoline is about 2.70 forints per liter. Use the super by all means unless you drive better to the tune of crashing profundos from your carburetor. Filling stations are located at important junctions outside of cities and at main intersections throughout Budapest. Rule of thumb: do not leave the immediate environs of any town with a partially full tank. The lines at gas stations near your hotel may be long, but don't become discouraged. Better to wait it out there than down the road a piece with an empty tank and sorely frayed nerves. Lines at gas stations are commonplace, but attendants work quite rapidly.

I suggest packing your own oil. I carried six quarts of oil in the trunk of my car, plus a gas additive, brake fluid, transmission oil and a good supply of tools. I avoid oil change and prefer to add good oil to that already in the tank; this conserves my supply and eliminates the need for using much of the local product.

Service station and garage attendants cannot be called less than enthusiastic regarding their task. Unfortunately, however, enthusiasm cannot make up for an absence of proper equipment or lubricants. Their body work is fair. Again the problem of absent equipment. Pack the extras, keep the spare tire well inflated and drive carefully.

Rented cars are available and may be contracted for at the main IBUSZ office, Ferihegy Airport and at all leading hotels in Budapest. There's quite a selection, too! In Hungary the choice of cars which you may hire extends bit beyond the gut-shaking Soviet models.

Listed below are the cars available and the prices asked for each model. All prices, are of course, subject to change. You will be required to sign a contract with IBUSZ, the sole agent for all car rentals in Hungary. A deposit of $100 (in dollars) is required. Minimum period of hire is 24 hours. Fuel is to be paid by the renter who must be in possession of a valid driver's license. Cars may be picked up and returned only in Budapest. Usage cannot extend beyond Hungarian borders. Note: your local driver's license is acceptable in Hungary.

		Daily	*Weekly*
Volga	(5 person)	$6.50	$40 plus per kilometer 7c
Simca 1300	(4 person)	$5.00	$32 plus per kilometer 6c
Fiat 1500	(4 person)	$5.00	$32 plus per kilometer 6c
Peugeot 403	(3 person)	$5.00	$35 plus per kilometer 6c
Plymouth Valiant	(5 person)	$10.00	$65 plus per kilometer 10c

If you drive your own car you will need the green card issued in conjunction with the White Cross Insurance available to international travelers through the American Automobile Club. Should you not already have such third party coverage, there is a fee of 30 forints for a stay of eight days. Buses must pay 55 forints for a stay of similar length. Tourist cars are exempt from local taxes providing they make but one visit to Hungary in a year. Point out your car radio to the customs officials. It is not taxable and will cause you no difficulty at the border. I certainly would not suggest entering Hungary with any type of fancy radio or telephone apparatus installed in your car. Repeat: an International Driver's License is not required. Your local license is acceptable.

CHAUFFEUR

A *Volga* (three seats) for a minimum of ten hours or 150 kilometers is available in Budapest with driver for about $20 plus 13c per kilometer. The renter is also responsible for the driver's expenses out of Budapest.

Thinking of lending your car to a Hungarian friend? Don't! And don't try giving it away or selling it either. This means trouble with local authorities.

The *Magyarorszag Autoutterkepe* road maps are quite good; you'll have no problem reading them. You can be sure the roads are as marked. Stick to the roads marked by red and heavy green lines; these are the best roads, those that you can travel without fear of bumps and detours. Watch out for roads shown by narrow green lines; they may seem more direct but may consist of mile after mile of holes, puddles and cart tracks.

Eight main highways fan out from Budapest in the direction of neighboring countries. These roads, marked with white shields and with the numbers 1 through 8, take precedence traffic-wise except in towns, where traffic markers should be carefully noted. Highway #1 leads to Vienna; #2 to Warsaw via Czechoslovakia; #3 to Czechoslovakia; #4 to the Soviet Union; #4-A to Bucharest; #5 to Belgrade, and so on.

In inhabited areas the speed limit is 50 kilometers per hour; in the country there is no speed limit for cars, but buses are limited to 80 kilometers. Horns may not be used in Budapest between the hours of 10 P.M. and 6 A.M. Traffic keeps to the right; at intersections the car to the right takes precedence. Ambulances and fire trucks have the right of way. Laws regarding the combination of alcohol and driving are very strict; when you drink, take a taxi or bus.

IBUSZ

In Bulgaria it is Balkantourist; in Czechoslovakia we have CEDOK. Coming to Hungary, the alphabetical potpourri provides us with the word IBUSZ. In most instances these words are abbreviations of some long title in the local language.

IBUSZ is Hungary's national travel office, the "folks to see" if you want to travel about, reserve in or come to Hungary; should you wish to hire a car, employ a guide or just gain some information, for all visit IBUSZ!

IBUSZ was founded in 1902 as the home away from home for guests of the Dual Monarchy. The main office in Budapest is located at Budapest V. Felzabadulas ter, 5, not far from the Pest side of the new newly completed Elizabeth Bridge. Constructed in a Revivalist Style (and vaguely reminiscent of Arabian Nights) this building is headquarters for the IBUSZ administration, for the purchase of air and rail tickets, for general information about travel throughout Hungary as well as for reservations for trips outside the country.

In 1964 the OIH, or National Travel Office, was formed and is today Hungary's chief spokesman for tourism. IBUSZ is under the immediate direction of OIH; in turn, under IBUSZ are two other offices, *Hungaria* and *Pannonia*; the latter is concerned with the direction of local restaurants. There is yet another agency in Hungary whose function is directly related to you foreign tourists. It took some figuring on my part to get this name and I'm still not sure I have it straight but here goes: IDEGENFORGAIMI HIVATALA!

Above I have noted that for air tickets, hotel space, car hire, train tickets, etc., you must contact either the main office of IBUSZ or the IBUSZ representative at your hotel. However, once you have settled in Budapest, Eger, Debrecen, Pecs and the like, you will find that your tourism activities are under the direct authority of the local Municipal Tourist Office, for the life of me I cannot pronounce the name of this agency (spelled above). But it would be well if you memorized the spelling and consigned this name to memory.

The IDEGENFORGAIMI HIVATALA is the place to go in every city and town with reference to local hotel reservations, to learn of the best local restaurants, for local guides, tours, the works. Want to do a little wine tasting? See IDEGENFORGAIMI HIVATALA! Horseback riding? Right! IDEGENFORGAIMI HIVATALA! Do *not* go to IBUSZ though the two offices may be vis-a-vis or door to door. A bus tour of Budapest? Visit the MUNICIPAL TOURIST OFFICE on Roosevelt ter. near the Chain Bridge.

Don't confuse the two offices; instead keep this rule in mind: If you are planning a trip within Hungary or, if in Hungary, a trip beyond its borders, see IBUSZ. If you want to reserve space in a hotel within Hungary or abroad, it's IBUSZ. Rail or air space? IBUSZ. But for any local activity within a specific town, see the almost always pleasant, helpful staffs of the local municipal tourist office (usually located in the immediate area of the best hotels). Money exchange matters relate largely (but not always) to IBUSZ. For cross-country horseback riding trips again see IBUSZ.

PLANNING YOUR TRIP

Travel to Hungary is about as easy as travel to many other European countries. There are no unusual shots to be taken; your smallpox vaccination is adequate (though be sure to return to the States within three years of the date of your most recent vaccination). That's it medical-wise. Any special medicines that must be taken along? Nope, unless they are required at home as well! Why not take along some Band Aids, aspirin, extra cosmetics, including soap, toothpaste, etc. You'll probably want an occasional swallow of your favorite anti-acid as the food in Hungary runs on the heavy side. Anything else is strictly up to you!

A visa you'll need; this is available through your local travel agent or the Hungarian Legation. The visa will cost you $4.50.

In Hungary there is a definite correlation between the issuance of a visa and the confirmed acknowledgement of hotel space. Should you have no confirmed hotel space you will be charged, during the summer season, $6.50 per day for the length of your stay.

With regard to hotel reservations, ask your travel agent carefully to determine in which towns deluxe or first class accommodations are actually available. Do not simply indicate that you are prepared to book deluxe or first throughout the trip without first determining if deluxe or first class accommodations actually exist in the towns you plan to visit. And before your departure, be sure that the advance payments you make for your accommodations and meals enroute are in fact based on existing deluxe, first, possibly tourist type space as specified for each town on your itinerary.

Some travel agencies in this country charge a flat rate for every day of your stay in the countries of Eastern Europe. In some cases these charges (which do not include the agency's service fees) run as high as $15 per day. Frankly, I feel such requests are exorbitant and self-defeating for they tend to discourage travel to Eastern Europe. When Hungary charges a daily minimum of $6.50, this $15 out-of-the-air per diem is bad enough; but in Romania and Bulgaria, where no per diem is necessary this $15 charge is totally absurd. Naturally, your hotel space is included in these agency charges, but in Hungary even deluxe space seldom runs much over $11 per day. In any case, you should know well in advance where you are going, where you are staying and the type of accommodation available in the towns along your route. Work with your travel agent! Rely on this book! I feel your personal efforts will vastly improve the chances for a pleasant trip and a less expensive one.

Now, what to do with the slip showing confirmation of your hotel space? One copy must be presented to the Hungarian Legation along with the visa application forms (or at the border when applying for your visa). Retain the second half (usually enclosed in a small booklet along with other similar vouchers), and present it to the IBUSZ desk in the first hotel in Hungary at which you stay. And what will the IBUSZ representative in Hungary give you in return for the total amount paid in New York, Chicago, Los Angeles or London, etc.? Keep the following information in mind; the procedure can be confusing if you enter Hungary unprepared.

(1) The payment for the full length of your stay at the hotel in Budapest will automatically be deducted from your voucher.

(2) In cash you will receive 100 forints a day for your meals for each day of your stay in Budapest.

(3) You will be given a coupon for each of the other hotels in which you will stay outside of Budapest. These coupons include breakfast and lodging for each night in the individual hotels. That is to say, one coupon for your three nights in, say Eger; the second coupon for your two nights in Debrecen, and so on. The coupon bearing the name of the hotel should be presented to the receptionist at that hotel in each of the towns.

(4) You will receive a book of food coupons totalling once again 100 forints per day per person for each of the towns you plan to visit; specifically, one coupon book for your three nights in Eger will be

worth a total of 300 forints. The individual coupons will be in amounts of 10, 20, 50 or 100 forints. You will be obliged to rip out the appropriate amount when presented with your bill at restaurants in the Eger area. The next coupon book, for your two-night stay in Debrecen, will include a total of 200 forint coupons of various denominations to be applied against meals in that area. And so it goes for each town on your itinerary. A five-town visit (plus Budapest) means five books per person.

IMPORTANT: By checking the small print on the back of each coupon book you will find that, for example, Eger coupons may also be applied against meals in Debrecen. The back cover of the coupon book lists all the hotels, restaurants and pastry houses at which the coupons in that particular book may be used. Therefore, should you fast in one town, chances are good that you can spend the unused coupons somewhere else. Be careful, however, for there is one rub to this business: Hungary is divided into various restaurant districts, and coupons for eastern Hungarian towns are not applicable for restaurants in the Lake Balaton region, etc. Be certain to use up the coupons for one "district" before moving into another.

Tourists will find that in some towns it is rather easy to stay within the combined forint coupon allowance for the meals they will eat. At another stop it is quite possible they will run over the allotted sum, or even fall below the allowance. By watching your step, by reading the back of the coupon book and by using travelers checks when you decide to celebrate Grandma's 105th birthday, it should not be too difficult to make the most of the coupon books. Remember: these books simply represent a part of the amount you prepaid for your trip.

I recommend that each tourist have his own voucher for food and lodging. Ask your travel agent to issue one voucher for each person and plan your trip so that your first night in Hungary can be spent in Budapest. This course of action will enable you to cash the stateside vouchers for Hungarian hotel and food coupons.

Single vouchers issued in the United States show the amount to be paid at each hotel enroute. The price typed onto the coupon in the U.S.A. is the result of instructions from IBUSZ in Budapest. These individual prices are a breakdown of the total amount you have paid for room and board for your trip in Hungary. There is, however, the inherent risk that too much will be allocated for one hotel, too little for another, with the result that you will be short in one town and overpaid in another. The local IBUSZ offices are not authorized to return unspent funds, even in forints.

Again, and in summation, I urge that each tourist enter Hungary with a single travel voucher giving his itinerary, the specific hotels reserved and the price of the accommodations in each, and the total amount he has paid to his travel agent, an amount which is subsequently transferred to Hungary (minus the agent's fee, of course). Plan your itinerary so that your first night will be spent in Budapest and work out your hotel and restaurant payments with the local IBUSZ representative situated in your hotel.

Let's Recap: For the money you pay prior to your departure (assuming you arrange to travel with a single voucher for each member of your party), the IBUSZ desk in the first hotel you visit in Hungary will automatically deduct your Budapest hotel funds and give you cash for your meals totalling 100 forints per day for each day of your stay in Budapest; issue vouchers for room and breakfast in each succeeding hotel outside of the capital; issue food coupons in the amount of 100 forints per day for each day in each town outside of Budapest.

Your voucher from the travel agency will state exactly how much you have paid for your stay in Hungary. IBUSZ has only to translate this payment into forints and break it down into individual payments (coupons) for the various hotels, plus the number of "meal days," for the purpose of issuing your food coupons.

You can see by the above why it is essential that your travel agent not simply book you deluxe throughout Hungary and charge you accordingly. This would reduce the IBUSZ representative to a jibbering, jellied mass of nerves while trying to determine for which cities you have been overcharged. You will be given a refund in forints for those nights when you are obliged to sleep in first or tourist class accommodations. This refund can be avoided if your agent (or you) know which towns have deluxe accommodations, and which have only first class rooms.

In Western Europe you can travel all over the map and sleep in whatever class hotel facility you wish. Not so in Eastern Europe. If you choose to keep to deluxe, you may do so, but frankly I see no purpose to your trip as three-quarters of the geographical area of Eastern Europe has no deluxe space; only a little more than half of the area maintains first class facilities. A determination to travel deluxe simply means that you will live largely in the cities. Moreover, I feel certain that your idea of the word deluxe and the space offered in that category are very dissimilar.

So, what should you say to your agent? Let me recommend the following: throughout Eastern and Central Europe specify first class accommodations wherever these are available. When first is unavailable, let your agent determine what type accommodation does exist in those towns you elect to visit. On the basis of his findings you can determine whether tourist class accommodations are acceptable.

The hotels and restaurants that follow are known to the writer; I have walked through them, usually floor by floor, kitchen by scullery. I know them, and on the basis of my "tour," I do or do not recommend hotels and restaurants. These establishments are located throughout the city of Budapest, throughout Hungary. I believe that after reading these pages you will have a fairly definite idea of where to visit, what to avoid, what to see and in general how to enjoy your stay in this delightful country called Hungary.

HOTELS

The hotels are generally clean, are staffed in a fashion that meets the minimum requirements of foreign guests, and out of Budapest are located in quite attractive surroundings. Except for the Lake Balaton region, most of the hotels maintain restaurants on the premises, have adequate parking facilities and were constructed during the thirties or slightly before. A number of modern structures have been built along Lake Balaton during the sixties. The steel and glass Balaton hotels offer more up-to-date facilities but not necessarily the comfort or conveniences of the older buildings.

One cannot possibly judge the hotels in Hungary without benefit of a first-hand survey. Ratings which classify hotels as deluxe, first and second class mean little, for the world over the best at The Best can frequently be termed a disaster. Hotels in Hungary are certainly no different. Your activities, your sleeping schedule, your knowledge of an area, the length of your stay, these points and others will necessarily play a part in your selection of a hotel. There is even that not unimportant dictate called snobbism which frequently enters in, sending a guest to the more social hotel rather than to the most comfortable place. Another frequent consideration is where Aunt Josie spent her holiday.

As an out-and-out criticism of IBUSZ policy, I feel the Lake Balaton area has been vastly overrated. Throughout Europe tourist literature urges the summer traveler to vacation at Balaton. As a result, during the summertime the towns and shores of this delightful 48-mile-long lake take on the appearance of an international Coney Island or Jones Beach. The lovely vineyards, forests and rolling hills fight for survival, their natural beauty almost obliterated by the thousands of sun-oil soaked vacationers of every nationality who jam the over-taxed hotel and restaurant facilities from June through September. It seems to me a question of the "over-sell." Hungarian tourist representatives throughout Europe have outdone themselves in promoting Lake Balaton; the Hungarian government seems to have failed to appreciate the drawing power of its own tourist propaganda. By over-emphasizing the Balaton region and underselling such beautiful spots as Eger, Szeged and the Puszta, the government has created one massive tourist jam at the lake and left the rest of its mighty charming countryside almost totally devoid of visitors.

I would be wrong indeed to suggest that readers of this book plan to spend more than three or four days at the Balaton between mid-June and mid-September. To the contrary, I urge that you travel away from the Balaton, out to the beautiful hills near Miskolc, to the wine sellers' caves at Eger or for a gallop across the Puszta. This over-crowding at the Balaton is really rather sad, for I fear many tourists, tired of the crowded restaurants and beaches and the poor service will carry away with them a wrong impression of Hungary; they will never guess that just beyond the hills to the east lies the true Hungary. The polyglot periphery of the Balaton certainly represents little but an updated version of Babel! Be smart! Look beyond Lake Balaton to see Hungary!

Above I have noted that many of the hotel buildings were constructed in the late twenties or early thirties, but don't for a minute picture over-aged structures or out-dated facilities beyond repair. With only one or two exceptions, these older buildings really offer delightfully pleasant interiors that blend well with their "Old World" surroundings.

Restaurants in the hotels are generally good. (At Lake Balaton, with one exception, the hotels do not have restaurants on the premises.) As in many recently constructed hotels throughout Eastern Europe, restaurant facilities remain across the street, up the road, or over by the beach. I found the food in hotel restaurants to be acceptable — also the service. Prices vary, depending on the category of the hotel. Groups naturally get the benefit of lower prices. All figures here are for the high season which lasts from May 1 to October 31 and are subject to change; be sure to check with IBUSZ or your travel agent. Budapest prices listed below will give you a good idea of what to expect. Prices tend to be quite a bit lower outside of Budapest except at Lake Balaton during the high season. During the high season only reservations including full board are accepted by IBUSZ. Hotel rates in Hungary, in general, are higher than in other Eastern European countries.

The figure before the slash represents the approximate usual charge for a single room with private bath; the figure following the slash is for a double room with bath. Single rooms without bath run about $3 cheaper; doubles without bath perhaps $4 and $5 cheaper. All quoted rates include full board.

Deluxe		$14/$26
Category A	(first class)	$13/$23
Category B	(tourist class)	$12/$22

While visiting in Western Europe you may, on the spur of the moment, decide to fly to Eastern Europe for a short holiday. In anticipation of such a trip, you will arrange for hotel reservations to be made in Eastern Europe through a travel agency located in some Western European capital. When such reservations are confirmed, full payment must be made for the entire duration of your stay. In the event that your reservations must be cancelled, the travel agency sends a Telex to the Eastern European country concerned requesting cancellation of space. For this service you will be required to pay a fee and will, in all likelihood, lose a quarter to one half of the monies paid, depending on the speed with which your cancellation is put through. You should, therefore, make every effort to avoid any change in your Eastern European travel program.

The listing of a particular hotel in a city does not mean to imply that it and no other is suitable for guests from abroad. Quite the contrary; criticism of some of the hotels listed provides ample evidence of their unsuitability. I made no attempt to visit the various thermal bath facilities located in almost every portion of Hungary. Sites such as Harkany, Hajdo and Paradsasvar are truly beautiful, but I feel are of limited interest to tourists in general.

I limited my trip to the larger, more prominent towns in and around which can be found attractions of interest to the foreign tourist. Moreover, I covered a large part of the country, thereby permitting the reader to move about with me and thus review more of Hungary than would be the case if this book dwelt at length on only one or two sections of this historic land.

DINING

The food in Hungary can be tasty and is usually more than adequate. Service, not unlike any other country, depends generally on the restaurant visited. Ditto, kitchens. Generally speaking, the kitchens are maintained in acceptable fashion. As a rule you will be eating in restaurants frequented by many foreigners. You can figure the Hungarian government demands the maximum from its employees in such places.

And prices? Again, it depends on where you go. Pick and choose with great care and chances are you will easily stay within your coupon budget. But whoop it up once or twice at the *Fortuna* or *Alabardas* restaurants and your coupons will melt away like the spring snow.

Before mentioning a few typical Hungarian dishes readily available in the majority of restaurants throughout the country, a word of advice: prepare for dishes that emphasize spices and sauces and that are generally on the heavy side. Oh, naturally, there are fruits, soups, cheese and ice creams that steer clear of the hot and heavy but speaking in general fashion, Hungarian dishes are not designed for the diet conscious, believe me!

Take *Szegediner Goulash*: here we have bits of well-cooked meat laced with the small bite-sized granulated pastry called Tarhonya, made of flour and egg. Tarhonya is used in soups, with potatoes, and is combined with other vegetables and meats.

And there is the delicious stuffed cabbage with a rich, creamy paprika sauce. Minced beef, minced pork and bacon is seasoned and rolled into cabbage leaves so that each of the stuffed cabbages is almost bite size. Sour cream seasoned with cabbage juice, onions and paprika is poured over the dish. And as if this were not enough, slices of pork or smoked sausage may be served to compliment the cabbage.

Good old goulash prepared with red onions and sweet paprika plus salt, pepper and caraway seeds and perhaps a few noodles makes a mighty fine dish. Porkolt is a fine stew and made of vegetables and chicken, pork, hare or beef. Porkolt with clotted cream becomes *Paprikas*. Should the pangs of hunger be raging through your stomach, try *Kolozvari Rakottpakszta* (and better make it a cool day for this dish is H-E-A-V-Y!)

Fish Soup! Now I'm not much for fish or soup, but this dish is truly delectable. It's a spiced, very hot Hungarian traditional dish which must not under any circumstances be missed. Should you be in Szeged, along the banks of the Tisza River, both the fish soup and the Szeged salami should be tops on your list. For my money the latter has never been surpassed.

Kessel goulash is frequently served in Hungary, most often from an iron kettle suspended over a roaring fire or from small kettles over a can of Sterno-like substance right at your table. Then there is *Paprika Chicken* and *Fatanyeros* (or mixed grill); *Fogas* (the fish from Lake Balaton) or *Racponty* (deviled carp). Don't forget, carp in Europe is generally a hot-house fish direct from the hatchery, not from some brackish canal.

In the dessert category, *Baratfule, Dobostorte, Indianfank* or my favorite *Retesh*, which in some areas can be bought from street stands. Retesh is a form of very flaky strudel.

Hungarian fruits can be delicious. *Turos Csusza*, small strips of boiled pastry covered with sour cream will really fill you up in delightful fashion.

Want something with which to wash down this flood of food? Well, let's see: there is the *Medoc Moir* from Eger; the Sopron vineyards yield the delightful *Kekfrankos*; Pecs boasts of her *Cirfandli*; *Tokay* (Tokaj) can be *furmint* (sweet) or *szamorodni* (dry). Other favorites of mine are *Rizling, Bedacsony* (white, dry), *Szeksardi Olasrizling, Puzstamergesi Rizling* (in Szeged) and *Veltingreer*. Try also the red, hearty *Bikaver* wine.

Of course, there are also the usual restaurants favoring French and German cuisine. There is even a play for American and English tastebuds.

And what about aperitifs, beer, brandies and the like? Well, Martini and Cinzano vermouths are available at about $1 a drink. For beer, run, do not walk for the Pilsen Export variety. *Remy Martin* and *Hennessy* cognac can be purchased by the drink for $1.25, *Grand Marnier* and *Benedictine* are available at the same price. *Vat 69* and *Johnny Walker Scotch* sell at 80c or so a drink. A number of cocktail lounges and bars in the better hotels offer cocktails in the white lady, gin fizz, and martini category at $1 or less. Should you enjoy tonic water with your vodka or soda with your scotch, be sure you bring these items into Hungary with you. Rarely was I able to locate a bottle of soda water, not even those good old syphon bottles now seldom used in the United States though still common in Western Europe. Mineral water was the usual mixer, and in some instances a mighty poor catalyst it proved to be. The mineral water varies from bottle to bottle, some is acceptable and some smells like dead fish.

Generally I found the food to be good; on the heavy side, but tasty and adequate. Lunches tend to be rather overpowering, but if you stick to omelets, salads, cheese and perhaps a fruit dessert you'll still manage to make the two o'clock tour.

As a tip, add 10% to the restaurant bill. Service is usually willing, but as a rule the waiters are inadequate in number and puffing to keep up with demand. Budapest's variety of restaurants runs from small snack shops in downtown Pest to pleasant hotel restaurants. Up in the hills of Buda one will find a number of good restaurants where a couple can dine, wine and dance themselves into a couponless state within a few hours.

SHOPPING

There are food shops and there are antique stores. Usually the two are located rather near each other, at least in Budapest. Purchases may be made only in foreign currencies, meaning the monies of Western Europe as well as those of individual countries of Asia, Africa and South and Central America. And so what's available!

In the food shops: wines and brandies; sausages and paprika chicken; cordials and chocolate. In the antique (china and silver) shops: Herend china and beaten silver; wood carvings and needlework; popular folk art, dolls and ceramics. These foreign currency shops in Hungary are known as *Konsumtourist*. Make note that no discounts are authorized. Keep the small slips given to you at the time of each purchase; customs officials may want evidence of proper purchase and the money exchange involved.

This business of antique sales—don't get all excited. In the shops displaying antiques as well as contemporary merchandise, you will see tags on certain articles. As I recall, these tags indicate that the article is not for export. We were told that goods over eighty years old may not be exported from Hungary—and a darn good law it is! Many beautiful items are available for sale; but keep in mind that local people, the Hungarians, are also authorized to make purchases in these shops providing they buy in foreign currencies. I think you will heartily agree that it is far better that local people have "first swing" at those goods which are, after all, part of their heritage. Better this than an antique dealer from Hogmoose Junction taking advantage of the rate of exchange to stock up his shop for Christmas buying. Moreover, my friends, I would ask you to consider the source of these antiques, the possible manner by which the goods arrived in these shops and then, perhaps, you will even more readily agree that the Hungarian shopping public should take its place at the head of the line for antiques.

How do I feel, generally speaking, about the quality of the goods displayed? Not over enthusiastic. If you think in terms of goodies for Aunt Minnie you'll stand a fair chance of picking up some nice little items. But then, you might as well make such purchases along the smart shopping streets of Pest. A number of attractive shops sell good-looking handwork, ceramics (modern and traditional) and wood carvings. Why use your foreign currency! In the regular shops you make your purchases in forints. For purchases of food articles, you might pick up some good buys—something rare in the States that you particularly like.

Konsumtourist sells certain brands of American liquor plus some French brandies and cognacs; foreign cigarettes and cigars are also available. As I stated in another section of this book, I am not overly enthusiastic about purchasing foreign liquors, brandies and the like in these shops. However, if you consider yourself affluent enough to pay the price and have foreign currencies to spare and are the kind of man or woman who is never, never taken for a ride, particularly regarding matters of labeling, then buy away! As for me, I'll stick to the local firewater and save the money for that first shot on the ship or plane.

TAKING PHOTOGRAPHS

Hungarian regulations state that you may take into Hungary one still camera and one movie camera. It is my personal impression that these regulations are not strictly enforced, at least with reference to the ordinary tourist. Naturally, a back seat full of cameras, film and lights will certainly cause a stir at the border, for authorities will believe you to be either in the motion picture business or prepared to sell the equipment in the country. Do as you would the world over, in Paris or Yosemite National Park! Take along the camera equipment usually needed by your family and I am sure there will be no problem at the Hungarian border.

Pictures of airports? You would probably have no difficulty photographing Aunt Clarice as she enters the terminal building, but I would rather have you complete your photographic chores on the old gal before taking her out to the Ferihegy Airport. Do not attempt a photo of your relatives or friends as they board the plane, for there is a 50-50 chance your film might be confiscated; it all depends on what type aircraft equipment is sitting about the airport the day you choose to snap your photo.

Lay off of ports, railyards and (need I say?) military installations.

GROUP TOURS

Many people choose group tours because they do not have time to set up the trip for themselves and prefer to place all such details as visas, tickets, etc., in the hands of travel agencies. Bus tours from Vienna to Budapest is a case in point. Tourists travel to Hungary in a group, eat in a group, tour in a group, sleep in adjoining rooms and then return in the same bus to Vienna. Remember: such tours have been carefully planned by touring agencies on both sides of the border. For those of you who want a peek at Hungarian life as an adjunct to your trip through Western Europe, group tours provide a fine opportunity. However, I urge all of you having the time to travel to Eastern Europe independently!

I refer readers to their travel agencies for information concerning group tours. In all large European cities a number of reputable travel agencies are able to provide you with more specific information regarding trips to Eastern Europe. European travel agencies are better informed regarding travel in Eastern Europe than are their American counterparts. Don't forget, only travel agents are authorized to handle visas, reserve space in hotels and plan tours for you in Eastern Europe. Travel offices of the Eastern European countries serve as information centers, nothing more. Incidentally, IBUSZ admits every 21st person traveling in groups (minimum for a group is twenty) free of charge (transportation excepted).

GUIDES AND INTERPRETERS

I most earnestly do not believe the independent tourist need hire a guide for cross-country travel in Hungary. Distances are short and local municipal tourist offices are most helpful and full of interesting information which the staff are most enthusiastic to share with you. Contact the tourist office in each town you visit. Inquire about the rates for guides and I know you'll have a darned interesting, really exciting, informal tour of the town. But you'll end up in a wine cellar somewhere along the way, too!

Guides and interpreters are available in various foreign languages. Costs are reasonable, though not cheap. Don't forget you may wish to invite the guide for lunch, dinner, etc. In Budapest the cost for a half day is $5; full day, $10. For a half day, for each additional person in your group add 25c to the bill, 50c per person on a full day's tour. A bus tour of Budapest takes half a day and costs for two persons about $11. The remainder of the day you can tour the city at your own leisure or with a guide revisit the sights which most interested you during the bus tour. Outside of Budapest a guide costs about $15.

In line with the above, I suggest that when touring outside of Budapest you simply contact the local municipal tourist office and through this bureau arrange for guide service. You will be assisted by a local person; this will not involve the high overhead involved in bringing someone along from Budapest and besides the local folks are much more knowledgeable and enthusiastic regarding their own regions or towns.

YEARLY EVENTS IN HUNGARY

The following events take place every year. To determine whether attractions of particular interest to you are being staged during your visit, contact your tourist agent. (*Note*) the dates listed below are subject to change.

International Gypsy Ball (February)
Anniversary of the Liberation of Hungary (April 4)
Budapest International Fair (May 21-31)
Sopron Festival Weeks and Costume-Pageant in the Castle of Kőszeg (June-July)
Costume Pageant in the Castle of Gyula (July)
Szeged Open-Air Festival (from mid-July to mid-August)
Beethoven Concerts at Martonvasar (last Saturday of June, July, August)
Tournament at Nagyvazsony (mid-August)
Concerts at Fertőd (the Esterhazy Estate near Sopron) (August)
Savaria Days at Szombathely (August)
International Regatta on Lake Balaton (August)
International Danube Cup Motor Race (July-August)
International Boat Tour on the Danube (from mid-July to mid-August)
Alba Regis Days at Szekesfeherver (September)
Vintage Festivities and National Horse-Show at Kecskemet (end of September)
Hairdressers European Championship and Ball (October)
IBUSZ International Ball (New Year's Eve)

CAMPING

Camp sites can be found throughout the country. Around Lake Balaton alone there are some 22 first class camps and roughly 10 second class camp sites. (The differentiation has to do with the size and overall development of the area; that is, first class equals permanent cabins for four persons, permanent cooking facilities, permanent shower facilities, and the like. Camping in Hungary is permitted only in specified areas. Camps are open from May 15 until the end of September. As a rule they accommodate 400 persons and cover two and one half to three acres.

A recently constructed campsite is north of Budapest, near Szentendre, along the Danube River. This first class site is called *Roman Camp* and has permanent facilities. We have already discussed the camping area near Pecs in the Mecsek Hills.

Prices run as follows: for a single person (in a cabin), 20 forints plus 10 forints for car space rental. Campsites rent for 18 forints a day, plus 7 forints per person.

At most of the smaller camps, after registering with the official at the gate you are free to choose your own campsite, but come after July 15 and you may well expect to find the best spots gone. Second class camps naturally do not occupy the best locations; better visit a number of them before making your selection. Here you will be expected to provide your own camping equipment. Second class camps have only the basic facilities. All camping areas are subject to international regulations. In the second class camps, officials are available only for a few hours each day. At all camps, open fires can be made only at points designated for such purposes. No noise is allowed between 10 P.M. and 7 A.M.

The first class compsites are usually maintained by officials speaking several languages. The following items are available: kitchen utensils, electric outlets and telephone (centrally located). There are also tents, rubber mattresses and gas stoves for rent. Postal services, sports equipment, money exchange offices and excursion programming offices are located at the sites. Cold foods may be purchased at stores and snack bars.

For youngsters traveling with their own equipment, either type camp is acceptable. Those of us straddling middle age will probably want to stick to the first class camps.

Campsites are identified on all main roads by the international symbol, the black outline of a tent and trailer superimposed on a white background. Usually the word camping is on the signs.

HORSEBACK TOURS

Tours of Hungary by horseback have been arranged by IBUSZ for (1) those who like to ride; (2) those accompanying someone who likes to ride; (3) those who enjoy a "horsey" environment but prefer to remain ashore. Under the title "Hungaria Riding Tours," IBUSZ has arranged four different trips which take place throughout the summer and cover different areas of Hungary. Specifically, the tours cover the area of the Matra and Bukk Mountains; Lake Balaton; through the Bakony Forests; Gemenc Forest and the Mecsek Hills. With commendable forethought IBUSZ sees that you take the tour which brings you to a particular region when the entire countryside is at its best.

Now, what do I mean when I refer to "those accompanying someone who likes to ride?" Well, you don't exactly rough it on these tours nor do you spend your entire time in the saddle. Special rates are offered to persons who wish to enjoy the "splendor of the chase" without suffering sore backsides and bowed legs. Such persons may accompany the riders by means of a special bus (which, I assume, is also available to those who have over-estimated their capacities and "give up" after two days on the trail).

The tours cover some 10 to 11 days out of which 6 days are spent riding, 2 days in Budapest. On Sundays, should you be in the provinces, you are left to attend church or quite possibly to apply various unguents to those sections of your anatomy most affected (or afflicted). The minimum number of riders is ten. The price for a 10 days' stay (for riders); $165; for 11 days, $173. For those of you tagging along, 10 days will cost $120 and 11 days approximately $130.

Included in these prices are the following: transfer to and from the airport; full board (breakfast and dinner usually taken in restaurants, luncheon out-of-doors); accommodations in double rooms with bath in Budapest and in category A hotels in the provinces (unless the itinerary calls for some other arrangement); charges for the use of horses, saddles and grooming (though you may use your own saddle); transfer of luggage and riders (plus the tagalongs) during the tour; an extra motor coach to escort the group for the purpose of transporting riders et. al. to rest places during the tour; entertainment and wine-tasting events; as well as sight-seeing in Budapest and throughout the provinces.

During your free time individual programs are arranged; e.g., visits to museums, churches, tourist attractions. Those of you not actually taking part in the riding will have special programs designed just for you. Riding parties are guided by bi-lingual riding masters (who are, I trust, adept in practices usually associated with functionnairies of roadside clinics).

THE MATRA-BUKK TOUR Originating at Gyongyos on to Eger; after leaving the Bukk Mountains a ride across the Puszta and along the Tisza River. You will be entertained at vineyards and stud farms and will visit the famous Seilvasarad stud farm, home of the Lippizan horses. Three nights (deluxe) in Budapest; 6 nights at the Eger Hotel (rooms with bath). Riding roughly 100 miles in all, you will be mounted 3 to 5 hours a day; the daily ride covers 15 to 20 miles. This tour begins in mid-May and mid-October. For more details contact your travel agent.

LAKE BALATON Starting from Siofok, by ferry to Tihany and on to Nagycazony (a visit to a 16th-century castle built by Pal Kinizsi, a Hungarian warrior who fought against the Turks); through the low mountains to the Balaton Shore. Tour the Radihaza stud farm, on to Heviz for (much needed, perhaps?) medicinal baths. Accommodations at Tihany the Kezthely "summer hotel" (meaning motel). 100 miles in 6 days. Mid-June and early August.

THE GEMENC-MECSEK TOUR The starting point is Baja. Riders are taken to this point from Budapest by hydrofoil. Across the Danube by ferry from the Baja stud farm and into the Gemenc Woods, a famous game preserve, to arrive for the hart belling season. (I didn't take this tour and would like to know: (1) what is a "hart" and (2) how and why does one "bell" it?) Through the vineyards of Villany to Siklos Castle and the Harkany Bath. Destination is Pecs. Accommodations at Harkany and Baja. 100 miles. Starting date is late September.

THE BAKONY MOUNTAIN TOUR You depart from the Komarom stud farm on the Danube. Visits are made to these stables where some 100 years ago the famous English Derby winner Kisber was reared. Through the Czuha Brook to the forest of Bakony. To Kinizsi Castle at Nagyvazsony where participants have an opportunity to witness a tournament held in costume. Following this event, down to Lake Balaton and Tihany Peninsula. Accommodations are at Komarom (a hotel) and at Nagyvazsony (the "castle" hotel); at Tihany mention is made of private bathrooms, so I sense such facilities are not available at the other "halts." 95 miles in 5 days. Several days are spent at Balaton swimming and fishing. Busman's Holiday? During the break you can attend the Tihany Riding School. Are they *kidding*!!! This tour takes place in mid-July.

Luncheons by the side of the Road

As in Poland and Czechoslovakia, distances in Hungary are frequently such that it is more convenient for one to plan lunch by the side of the road. Not only will you thereby enjoy the pleasures of literally dining out, but you will be saved the necessity of exploring every small hamlet for a suitable place to eat. Before checking out of your hotel, perhaps while ordering breakfast, ask your waitress to fix up a small package including hard-boiled eggs, tomatoes, cheese, bread, and if you have a thermos, some hot tea or cold lemonade. I'm sure the girl will be glad to do this and at minimal cost.

A picnic by the road, perhaps on the banks of a small brook, under some shady trees with some ducks, geese, chickens or horses as guests, makes for a delightful, certainly convenient, lunch-time break during a long car trip. Added recommendation: why not take along on your trip a small picnic basket complete with cups, thermos, a container for sandwiches, etc. I can assure you it will be a great asset throughout your entire journey.

Boat Charters

At Lake Balaton, naturally, sailboats, rowboats, canoes and peddlecraft can be hired for daily use. See any Municipal Tourist Office representative or the reception desk of your hotel; or inquire of the official in charge of your motel or camping area.

On the Danube (out of Budapest) boats carrying approximately 50 passengers are available for local charter, total charges run as follows: to Visegrad (Danube Bend region) with one hour sightseeing, $140 to Estergom (Danube Bend) with three hours of sightseeing, $215; to Dunaujvaros (south on the Danube) with three hours sightseeing, $215.

A small version of the *Siraly* hydrofoil, called the *Fecske* (swallow), is also available for local hire. Five persons (out of Budapest) at a rate of $9.50 per person.

Regular pleasure boat cruises are scheduled out of Budapest during the season: on weekdays at 5:30 P.M. and at 8 P.M.; Saturdays at 3 P.M. Sundays and holidays boats leave at 11 A.M., 1 P.M., 5:30 P.M. and at 8 P.M. Twenty cents per person, and it's a delightful trip. Food served aboard. Inquire at your hotel for the correct point of embarkation.

HUNTING AND FISHING

Deer hunting is one of the most prominent sports in Hungary. Herds of these animals can be found in the forests of Bakony, Bukk, Matra and in the flooded areas of the Danube, such as the Gemenc Forest near Mohacs. Roe-deer may be found on the edges of the above-mentioned forests as well as in the agricultural areas of the Great Plain and Transdanubia. Roe-buck may be hunted from May 1 to October 15; the Roe-deer, on a restricted basis, from October 1 to January 31.

Boar can be hunted throughout the year in the slightly forested areas, as well as in the deep forests (especially for those big tuskers!). The Matra, Vertes and Borszony forest areas are specifically suggested.

The spiral horned moufflon and fallow deer may be hunted only by special permit, as the Hungarian government is interested in safeguarding their breeding. These animals have been domiciled in Hungary only for the past 60 years. The largest moufflons can be found in the Matras and Pilis Hills.

Closed season for the hare runs from October to the end of January. The best stocks are to be found on the Great Plain area. The most common birds are the pheasant and partridge; shooting season from October 15 to December 31. Special permits needed for partridge. Restrict your "bag" in the Great Plain area. The wild goose shoots can be undertaken at Lake Velence, the southern part of Lake Balaton and in the shallows of the Danube Islands. Wild duck is also available. Also the bustard.

Trout can be found in the Bukk Mountains and in the streams of Transdanubia. Pike, pike-perch and catfish (the latter are particularly large) are to be found in streams near Gyor, Ganyu, Kalosca and near Gemenc.

Double-check with IBUSZ authorities for the seasons for all these animals as well as for the best fishing seasons. Inquire specifically regarding the importation of guns and ammunition.

CABLES, WIRES AND TELEPHONE CALLS

Regarding international cables, wires to Europe, postcards, etc., contact the reception desk in your hotel. If you wish some special information, inquire at Budapest's East Railway Station or at the main post office at Varoshaz Utca (Budapest 4).

Local public telephones are operated by special coins which can be purchased in post offices, tobacconists and restaurants. To give you an approximation of long distance charges, a telephone call from Budapest to Vienna costs a bit over 60 forints for five or six minutes. All too frequently telegrams sent from one point to another within Hungary, fail to be delivered.

BUDAPEST

To see Budapest, to understand Budapest from an historical vantage point, to appreciate Budapest as a new city, contact the Municipal Tourist Office IDEGENFORGAIMI HIVATALA located at the end of the

Chain Bridge in Pest. Comfortable open topped buses leave this office at frequent intervals during the morning and afternoon for a tour of the entire city. You will first drive across the Danube to Buda and Gellert Hill through the Fortress District (or Castle Hill) to see the Royal Palace, Matthias Church, the Fisherman's Bastion, the Vienna Gate, the Gothic Houses, the Magdalene Tower, Lutheran Church, the statues, pastry houses and restaurants. On to the more modern sections of Buda through the tunnel construction by Adam Clark as a shortcut from the Danube under Castle Hill. Mr. Clark, an Englishman, also constructed the Chain Bridge; the work was begun in 1839. Fo Utca (Main Street) is the principal traffic artery running from the Chain Bridge through Buda behind the hills, a district of 18th century homes. Located not far from the tunnel is the Capuchin Church built from the ruins of a Turkish Mosque.

Then on to the northern end of Buda, to Saint Anna's Church, to the house where Bartok once lived and the small concert house in which Franz Liszt played his magnificent, fiery melodies during the 19th century. There you will see the Tomb of Gul Baba, an Ottoman Turkish Priest and Dervish who resided here in the 16th century. Perhaps you will take the Arpad Bridge (the most northern of the bridges connecting Buda and Pest) and then drive the length of Margaret Island. Originally called Hare Island, this bit of land was renamed for the daughter of King Bela who once lived in the Royal Palace so that he might be near his daughter. The princess had chosen to live out her life in a convent on the pleasant island centered in the Danube River. Then you go back across the Chain Bridge past the Statue of Istvan Szechenyi, a leader of the 19th century Hungarian National Revivalist Movement. You will also see a statue of Ferenc Deak, a Hungarian statesman who was the force behind the Ausgleich which provided a nominal autonomy for Hungary, a "partnership" rather than a subjugation to the Hapsburgs in Vienna. There are the concert hall and the Corso with its statue of Sandor Petofi, Hungarian poet and revolutionary, the 12th century Belvarso Templom, or Church of the Inner City; the Greek Orthodox Church, the main shopping streets (Rakoczi ut; Kossuth Iajos ut.), Saint Stephens Cathedral, and the Parliament building, the latter in neo-Gothic style facing directly onto the Danube. At night the facade of the Parliament is beautifully illuminated. The modern building just north of the Parliament provides offices for the Council of Ministers, the principal leaders of present-day Hungary. There are the concert halls, theaters, City Park (with its Disney-like Castle of Vajadhunyad), Vidam Amusement Park and the Zoo, the latter including the famous Gundel Restaurant. The tour will end at the Stadium.

Once you have completed this tour of the capital, I am certain you will feel more at ease. While touring on your own I recommend that you visit:

NATIONAL MUSEUM A beautifully designed building containing many rich and interesting mementoes of Hungary's past. Included are a crown of the Byzantine Emperor Constantine, plus furniture shipped to Hungary as a gift from Louis XIV of France and a piano belonging to Beethoven.

MUSEUM OF FINE ARTS Here you will see quite a few masters of the Spanish and Dutch schools: Goya, El Greco, Giorgione, Titian, and so on.

THE BUDA HILLS Truly beautiful and should not be missed. You will find the woods delightful; many streams and small inns and restaurants are located in the area just beyond Buda.

Excursions Outside Budapest

ESTERGOM No visit to Budapest would be completed without a trip to the so-called region just north of the capital. The name stems from the southward curve taken by the Danube River as the waters come in from Vienna and Bratislava before spilling on toward Budapest. The principal town, Estergom is roughly an hour's car ride north of Budapest. Estergom was originally the eastern border fortress of Charlemagne's Empire and was called *Oster Rigun* or in Latin *Strigonium*. The name was later changed to the Hungarian Estergom. It was the seat of the first Hungarian dynasty, that of the Arpads. The principal hill was used as a fortress town for many years, later to become in the 10th century the site of King Bela's palace. The hill is now crowned by the Cathedral, whose foundation stone was laid in 1822. It is the largest church in Hungary. A visit to this cathedral is certainly worthwhile not simply for its architecture but to see the fine collections of gold and church articles in the Treasury. The view behind the cathedral overlooking the Danube far below is not to be forgotten. Across the river lies Czechoslovakia.

VISEGRAD This town is located just south on the Danube from Estergom and is the site of the former palace of King Matthias, though it was first constructed by Charles Robert of Anjou who came to Hungary in 1308. Additions were built by King Sigismund (1387-1437) and finally King Matthias (1458-1490). Matthias was married to Beatrice, daughter of the King of Naples. When Beatrice came to Hungary she brought with her many Italian artisans whose efforts and designs did much to create the beauty that was originally Visegrad Palace. It was only in 1943 that evidence of the ruins came to light, the Palace having been all but destroyed by the Turks in 1542. It must have been quite a place for they talk of two fountains, one of red marble (still to be seen) and the other white. These fountains would flow with wine on state occasions. The entire area is forested and certainly not to be missed.

SZENTENDRE This town is an artists' colony. Originally it was a Roman fort and remains of the Old Roman colony have recently been discovered. It is an interesting location for an afternoon's stroll.

There are no hotel facilities near any of these towns, though there are camp grounds. Should you be in Estergom try the restaurant directly across the road from the local Municipal Tourist Office. It is named *Kis Pipa,* and the food is simple but very good.

Hotels

GELLERT The Gellert is considered by many *the* address in Budapest and is located in Buda just off the west bank of the Danube River directly at the foot of Gellert Hill. From the rooms you will have a thrilling view of the Danube, the passing boats and apartments of Pest on the east bank of the River. The Gellert is situated directly on the Vienna-Győr highway, so should you enter the city from Hegyshalom (Vienna's Main Door to Hungary), stay on the west side of the Danube following Highway #1 through Buda directly to the hotel.

The north end of the mezzanine is occupied by the Winter Dining Room (very pleasant) and a large terraced dining area covered by colorful awnings known as the French Restaurant. Small enclosed dining here, too. Music in the evenings. Service is fair; the food mediocre at best. To the right of the main lobby is an excellent bar and cocktail lounge with some of the best music I heard east of Vienna. This lounge is very popular with the Budapest younger set and foreign guests alike. Drink prices are reasonable.

The mineral baths located to the rear of the hotel may be reached from an outside entrance or by elevator from your floor of the Gellert. Look for directional signs. There is a sulphur carbonic bath that gives the impression of bathing in a pool full of soda water. Outside the building, in an attractively landscaped garden surrounded by terraces, trees, is a large pool with a mechanism for creating artificial waves. This pool could be fun when not packed with other swimmers. A cafe is located nearby.

The Gellert has 224 rooms; 150 without bath. All rooms facing the Danube have been updated in furnishings while rooms to the side of the building retain their mahogany and walnut furnishings but are minus bathrooms. Corridors are wide, well-lighted. Floor service, particularly room service, is very good. Double rooms usually consist of narrow beds pushed into a foot-to-foot position, or beds may occupy the corners of the room. Should you reserve a double, special care should be taken that you do not receive what is actually a single with the couch (resembling a bed) made up as a bed. They look somewhat alike. For those of you who value your rest, I would either limit your stay in Budapest because of streetcar noise or request rooms on some hotel court, for almost all hotels in this capital front on busy streets. The Gellert sits on something of an angle to the Danube, therefore, the south end of the building is some distance from the entrance to the bridge, thus more removed from the screeching of the streetcars.

ROYAL Visiting Budapest for business reasons, for an active tour of the town, for conferences with the Hungarian Government? I recommend the Hotel Royal. Located on Lenin Avenue in the heart of the Pest district, the Royal is within five to eight minutes by car from almost all the important commercial and governmental establishments. What's more, the food here is just plain good!

There is a bar on the mezzanine and a nightclub under the lobby. A garden cafe is located in one of the courts around which the hotel is built. The restaurant is quite large, rather bleak decor-wise, but most pleasant and as I said, serves excellent food in a prompt, efficient manner. I was told that during some seasons there is tea dancing in the garden. An orchestra plays during dinner each evening.

There are 14 apartments in the Royal, all nicely furnished with French double beds (twins connected by a single head and foot board), three wardrobes and TV in the small sitting room. TV broadcasting seems to be only on Tuesdays and Fridays and only after five or six in the evening. Most apartments face the front (street side) of the hotel. Rooms other than the apartments are inclined to be rather drab in styling—comfortable, but nothing outstanding. Singles and doubles are available with bath; the former priced at about $13, the latter $24 (with board). The quieter rooms are located in the courts or on the higher floors. Apartments are good in every sense. Noting that the Gellert is really rather isolated in location, I would say the Royal was the more preferable shopping, business and probably tourist-wise.

GRAND For those of you who are anxious to just browse, walk and generally relax in an atmosphere totally devoid of traffic noise and the usual hustle and bustle associated with city streets, the Hotel Grand is highly recommended. The Grand is located on Margaret Island in the center of the Danube. The hotel is situated at the northern end of the island, surrounded by green lawns and within walking distance of mineral baths, swimming pools, outdoor theaters, restaurants and all the paraphernalia associated with summertime entertainment and relaxation. It is an old hotel (of ninety years vintage, I understand!).

A large sunny restaurant is located at the rear of the lobby overlooking the park that surrounds the hotel. Immediately outside the inside dining area is a summer garden where diners are served in the evening; there is dancing to a good orchestra. Food at the Hotel Grand is mediocre, meals served outside tended to be cool on delivery. The inside dining room is usually jammed for dinner; long waits for tables not being exceptional.

Rooms on the front or east side are inclined to be drab, dark and somewhat noisy; they are located over the kitchen and main entrance. The rear at the Grand is actually the better side as it overlooks the gardens and summer garden. I would certainly specify "West—Summer Garden Side" in requesting rooms. Rooms on the west side are much better furnished, certainly much quieter. Single persons should try to reserve the very pleasant southwest corner rooms with neat little balconies complete with deck chairs. Cost? Just the same as other singles. One or two suites (apartments) are available at 500 forints (roughly $22) per night. A parlor can be connected with the single room on the opposite side. In the season, doubles with bath run about $23; singles with bath $13. Book well before you arrive in Hungary.

Bathrooms at the Grand require a bit of special explanation. They are large, rather old in style but fairly clean. But the Grand is situated over a mineral spring. When you turn on the bath it is quite probable that water as black as coal will pour into your tub. You are on the way to a refreshing, curative mineral bath which will, contrary to suspicion, not leave you dirtier than before the soaking. They tell me "the blacker the better" as far as the water is concerned.

Entrance to Margaret Island can be either from the Arpad Bridge to the north or the Margaret Bridge to the south. The island is bisected by a single road running between the exits to the two bridges.

SZABADSAG A hotel of startling contrasts! Rakoczi Boulevard is one of the principal avenues of Pest, each side of this thoroughfare lined with shops, stores, pastry houses, etc. At the far end of the Boulevard is located Budapest's East Station where you will arrive from or leave for Vienna. In front of the East Station is a large traffic circle; directly opposite the station, across this circle, is the Hotel Szabadsag. The hotel is a convenient stopping place for those in Budapest for only a few nights.

Actually the Szabadsag is a combination of three older hotels, one of which was torn down. The new section has been grafted on to the older section, thus providing one large hotel of 403 rooms, of which 300 are brand new.

At one side of the restaurant a too narrow flight of stairs leads up to a large, smartly decorated nightclub, the only such lounge in Budapest serving hot food along with the usual cold snacks and cocktails. Music for dancing. This room is open from ten in the evening until four.

The new section of the hotel faces the traffic circle, therefore, I would recommend rooms on the upper floors. New rooms run from medium to spacious. Apartments occupy corner locations and consist of two good-sized rooms, radios, couches and tables all done in smart colors. The bathrooms are in green or white and are in good condition. Double rooms can be small with beds tucked into corners, or large and roomy, the beds being of the French double variety. Since the price is the same, I would suggest that you book French double and get the most for your money.

PALACE The Palace is not a first category hotel but don't let that dismay you. Prices run about at the same level as those hotels outside of Budapest. Located in downtown Pest, the Palace has a rather dark, small lobby and an elevator that could stand a bit of mechanical tinkering. Rooms number 180, only 100 having baths. Rooms on the front are preferable. Most all rooms are decorated in a turn of the century style, overpowering but clean. So are the bathrooms.

The double rooms are well furnished, particularly those located on corners of the building. Radios are available in all rooms. Double doors tend to eliminate corridor noise. Single rooms run small, but are also well furnished.

Single rooms here run, with bath approximately $8; without bath $5. Doubles with bath $15, without $8. These are seasonal rates and do not include meals. Remember: Full board is required during the season so figure $9 more on the double.

The restaurant at the Palace has a reputation of being among the best in Budapest. Gypsy music in the evening. The restaurant is styled in the potted palm and fern manner of the early 1900's. The room looks comfortable, cozy and intimate.

CITADELLA This structure was constructed in 1851 as a fort designed to permit the Hapsburgs in Vienna to keep an eye on their rebellious subjects in the environs of Budapest. Seldom used and eventually vacated, the building was renovated and in 1961, employing the same outside walls, the Citadel became the Citadella Hotel. Used primarily for large groups of tourists or families with several children, the Citadella Hotel is particularly well adapted for younger people for it is somewhat out of the city. Arrangements are perfect for entertaining groups of young people. The central lounge overlooks Budapest.

Hotel rooms with four beds cost 16 forints per night (per bed) and with three beds, 22 forints. Naturally, you can rent a room with four beds only for two persons by paying the charge for the extra sleeping accommodations. There are wardrobes for each person, tables and chairs, the latter rather rustic in style. All rooms have washbowls, but guests are obliged to use common showers and toilets. The dorm rooms, sleeping up to thirty people, are usually on the court or inside of the building, the beds constructed in double or triple bunk fashion. The entire building is scrupulously clean and really very well constructed.

SPORT This hotel boasts a lake nearby. Every room a double with bathroom. The Park Restaurant (*Etterem*) is nearby. Photos show a rather elaborate layout; I judge it compares interior-wise with the style of the hotels at Balaton. From appearance, I would inquire about this facility only in an emergency.

Restaurants

FORTUNA Easily the most elegant spot for dining in the city. The Fortuna is located in Buda, not far from the Matthias Church on Castle Hill; approximately a ten-minute taxi ride from the Gellert. Be sure to reserve, and dine late. Several rooms make up this restaurant. Wooden furnishings, green draperies, red candles, white tablecloths. Excellent food and fine service. The Fortuna provides a good orchestra playing typical Hungarian melodies as well as the gypsy rhythms we know so well. The worst tables are those near the orchestra for the kitchen lies in this direction.

ALABARDAS On Castle Hill, almost directly under the spires of Matthias Church you will find the very small, intimate Alabardas. Reservations are a must! Again, as at the Fortuna, dress well. White walls, modern furniture, a two-piece orchestra. You'll have a good to excellent meal at Alabardas. Reserve your table, and set aside an evening for this fine little restaurant.

KIS ROYAL In Buda, on the west side of the hills lining the Danube, is the Kis (Kish) Royal. This restaurant is but a ten-minute drive through the tunnel under Castle Hill from the Gellert Hotel. You will find a medium-sized restaurant built around a small but attractive summer garden where guests are served in warmer weather. The food here is fair to good; the staff most certainly attentive and anxious to please. Menus are in English. You can have fun here! Gypsy music paints a background atmosphere for what will probably be a most enjoyable evening. Dress fairly casually.

THE THREE BORDERS This restaurant is fifteen minutes by car, bus or taxi up into the hills somewhat north of Budapest on the Buda side of the Danube. A wide terrace affords a magnificent view of the city below, the Danube, even distant towns. The food is average to good. Woodsy decor with flags on your table indicating nationalities. Gypsy music, the orchestra weaving in and out of the various rooms onto the terrace. This restaurant is simply not for intimate, quiet dining for one couple. It is recommended for tours. Average to high prices.

HUNGARIA Heartily recommended! Located in downtown Pest. Excellent food (with no pseudo-International menu!) prepared in delectable fashion and served in informal fashion befitting one of the capital's oldest restaurants.

The decor? Picture twisted and fluted columns, gold leaf, balconies, mirrors by the hundreds, balustrades, stairs up and steps down. In the past as at present, the meeting place for Budapest's literary crowd. Frequented by numberless foreigners but saved from that touristy atmosphere associated with some other local dining spots. The restaurant is open all day; a cafe occupies the front of the main dining area. Prices are average.

BERLIN The Berlin is in downtown Pest. Good food and prompt service. Again, like the Hungaria, the Berlin is not for the eat-and-run tourist or businessman. Prepare to relax and enjoy the meal. A cafe occupies the very front of this restaurant.

MATYAS PINCE This restaurant is located at the east end of the Elizabeth Bridge, to the right when entering Pest from Buda. Several rooms for dining. I particularly liked the rear room to the right. Low beams, wooden booths, completely rustic in design. Very good food served in fairly prompt fashion. Open for lunch and dinner. I would suggest this restaurant as a good stop between business appointments or on a shopping tour. Medium prices.

KARPATIA This restaurant is rather near the main IBUSZ office. Somewhat like Hungaria but not as extreme in decor. Two or three large rooms. The food is average.

SZEZEVES Don't expect anything elaborate in this small restaurant located in Pest just one block from the Danube. The rooms are almost monastic in appearance, wooden booths in one room, large tables in the second. A gypsy duo provides music during the evening dining hours. Szezeves is quite popular with student groups. Note the mark on the wall indicating the level reached by the waters of the Danube when that river flooded in the late 19th century. Dress informally. Food average.

BUDAGYONGYES Set in a charming surrounding, this restaurant can be dropped from your list of spots to visit.

CITADELLA RESTAURANT This medium restaurant is very intimate, with a pleasant atmosphere and a terrific view of the city below. The food here is served at your table directly from iron kettles. The informal Citadella restaurant is perfect for that evening of relaxed dreamy dining.

APOSTOLIK This is a very original little restaurant located just behind the IBUSZ main office in Pest. Prepare to share a booth for the booths are large, the rooms small and the guests numerous. Very informal! Food is simple but excellent. Try the goulash served from small miniature iron kettles. Be sure to eat the retes here. A dessert speciality, resembling a strudel; so light and so good!

ROZSADOMB This quite colorful eating establishment cannot be recommended for its services and food are somewhat below average and prices considerably out of line.

PILVAX Don't miss this spot! Located in central Pest, Pilvax has all the atmosphere of a true mid-19th century restaurant. Capably managed, serving very good food to the lively tunes of a good gypsy orchestra, this restaurant is one of the few in Budapest which have managed to walk the narrow path between the over-bleak surroundings of post-war Middle Europe and the gushy folderol usually connected with those places set aside strictly for tourists. Dress reasonably well.

VOROSMARTY A pastry house, tea house, bit of the Old World located on Vorosmarty Square in downtown Pest, Vorosmarty has been popular since the last century. Large rooms, though a bit on the cheerless side; small tables; usually very crowded. One of those places where a glass of water will hold you a table—for hours. Small sidewalk sipping and sitting area for those who prefer their lemonade out in the sun and breeze. More pleasant out-of-doors in summer. Select your pastry (you'll be handed a number) and then locate a table. Once seated, hand a waitress your slip, order your tea, coffee, ice or lemon squash and relax! Quite a place to view the burghers of Budapest.

CAFE EMKE Located on the corner of Lenin and Rackoszi ut, not far from the Hotel Royal, this modern version of a pastry house is very popular and is recommended. Ignore the rather black surrounding and too modern furnishings. The cafe is clean and pleasant. More important: the pastries are good!

RUSZWURM My idea of a fine old pastry house exhibiting all the trademarks of old Hungary though none of that atmosphere of brooding regret. Ruszwurm is located high on Castle Hill, quite near Matthias Church. Very small but well maintained. You'll like the Old School waitresses, similar to those working at Demels in Vienna. Fine pastries, etc. Take note please of the displays along the walls, an exhibition of pastry arts of bygone years. Keep in mind that a bakery shop occupied these very premises as long ago as 1500. This is the oldest pastry shop in Hungary.

Note: This very small but charming two-room pastry house serves only coffee; no tea.

LAKE BALATON

Trans-Danubia is that region of Hungary lying between the Danube River (which bisects Hungary) and the western borders of the country. Rich in minerals, agricultural lands, fruit farms and mineral baths, this area's most fertile regions lie close to Lake Balaton, located in Central Trans-Danubia. The lake flows in a northeast to southwesterly direction, its shallow waters lapping against beaches, vineyards, bordering small towns, fishing villages and resort areas.

Lake Balaton is some 48 miles long, its width varying from 8 miles to 1 mile. At one point the Lake reaches a depth of 36 feet; the remainder is however quite shallow varying from 10 to 12 feet. The shores of the lake are sandy, the slope toward the water being unusually gentle. The temperature of the water in summertime can reach as high as 80 degrees. The northern side of Balaton is bordered largely by vineyards, orchards and occasional villages. Two or three prominent resort areas are to be found along this shore. The southern side of the lake seems to be more popular from a tourist standpoint, despite the presence of International Highway #7 running from Budapest to Zagreb, Yugoslavia. The drive along Balaton's northern shore is delightfully scenic. The road runs some distance from the lake, winding through vineyards, past colorful little villages and along the edge of numerous camping areas. Traffic is much less of a headache here.

The towns which have the best facilities for tourists are as follows: Siofok, Balatonfured, Keszthely and the Tihany Peninsula, though sprinkled along either side of the lake are innumerable camping areas.

Balaton is great for all the family if you are searching for a resort providing marginal facilities which include clean beds and good food, water in which to swim and a sun from which you may derive a tan. Lake Balaton is perfect for the low-cost holiday! Take the bus or train (your car if you wish!), pack your suitcase, bring the kids and figure on day after day of sun, swimming, average food, clean rooms (or tents) in the company of thousands of other tourists just like yourself collected along the shores of this attractive lake.

BALATONFURED

This small town is located on the northern shore of the lake. Quite evidently an old summer resort, Balatonfured spills over the small hills that line the lake shore. There are two sections to the town, not unlike resort communities the world over.

Within the tourist area are several hotels, restaurants, the IBUSZ offices, one or two nightclubs plus other rather run-down appurtenances usually associated with a summer resort. The principal hotel is located just off the highway, some ten minutes' walk above the beach.

Hotels

ARANY CSILLAG This is a four-storied structure, including a restaurant set in a small grove of trees directly off the highway. It is rambling, with rooms at ground level, stairs running every which way, no elevator, an outside garden for dining (used mostly by the help). There are 117 rooms in all, only one with bath and this room is not acceptable because of its poor location. Eight rooms have phones; 8 have radios. Public baths are in fair condition; toilets are clean. Double rooms cost about 90 forints, singles 50; there is an extra 18 forint charge for an extra bed. Single rooms are frequently used as doubles but only an 18 forint charge is made for the extra bed. There are no extra deductions for group bookings. No room service except in an emergency. Rooms are clean and comfortable though rather sparsely furnished. The Arany Csillag is booked to capacity during the season (June through September).

It is the best available in Balatonfured. Rooms can be airy and are generally clean. The distance from the lake is one negative factor. One spends a large part of each day "en route." There are no views as the hotel is situated between two narrow streets and the highway.

The restaurant at the Arany Csillag serves average to good food and is inundated with diners for three meals a day. Indoor dining rooms plus the small terrace facing the street are much too small to accommodate the number of guests, much less other summer residents who come in off the highway.

ASTORIA Assuming the Arany Csillag is booked to capacity and you just must see Balatonfured, the Astoria would probably provide you with protection from the elements, but this inadequate structure is a sorry excuse for a tourist facility.

Restaurants

HOTEL ARANY CSILLAG Indoor and outdoor dining facilities. Not particularly clean; slow service by rather unpleasant waiters. An average menu. Open for three meals a day.

BARICSKA CSARDA This restaurant is situated on the off-lake side of the main highway leading from Balatonfured to Tihany. It is situated in a vineyard atop a small rise affording a fine view of the distant lake. Dining rooms are clean; the kitchen in good order. This restaurant offers a very wide terrace with long tables to be occupied by several parties each. There are also two or three small inside dining rooms but you must reserve well in advance. Hungarian country decor in this sixty-year-old inn.

TOLYFACSARDA North of the highway and somewhat above Balatonfured, the Tolyfacsarda is not easily located. You will want to ask directions. The name means "Oak Tree Inn." Age of the inn? Only 100 years. There is a very pleasant dining room and a wide selection of food. The wine cellar has been made into a form of private dining room.

KESZTHELY

This is the site of the Georgikon, one of the first agricultural colleges in Europe founded in 1797. Nearby is the beautiful castle of Gyorgy Festetics housing the 40,000 volume library of the former owner who, in the late 1800's, played host to a group of progressive thinkers here at Keszthely.

Located some fifty yards or so from the shores of Lake Balaton is the Keszthely Motel. Keszthely is situated at the far northwest end of the lake, so the motel affords a fine view of the entire lake region.

The motel buildings are temporary structures purchased from the Belgian World's Fair (1958) and placed at various points around Lake Balaton. The double rooms all have two beds, nightstand, washbowl and bidet. The walls are thin. Public showers and toilets are fairly well maintained. There is also a form of hotel structure here at Keszthely

Beach which I understand has baths but the building gives the appearance of providing absolutely no creative comforts.

There is a restaurant on the grounds some four minutes' walk from the motel. It is an old building lacking the most fundamental features of decoration or comfort.

Should you wish to visit Keszthely (and it is an interesting little town), I would suggest that you find sleeping quarters elsewhere. Keszthely is only a little over an hour's ride from Siofok, roughly an hour from Tihany. At both these resort areas you will find much better accommodations.

HEVIZ *(Bath town near Keszthely)*

Three and one half miles from Keszthely is the thermal spring, warm water lake resort of Heviz. The season at Heviz lasts from the late summer months of August and September through October. You might enjoy the unique experience of bathing in this lake whose surface is covered with the rose-colored Egyptian lotus and whose temperature varies between 82 and 100 degrees Fahrenheit. Hotel facilities are available.

TAPOLCA

You might stop by the Gabriele Hotel here at Tapolca, a delightful town some forty minutes drive north of Keszthely. The hotel, a "tourist" accommodation, is named after the Viennese Poetess Gabriele Baumberg who was married to the Hungarian Poet Janos Batsanyi. The surrounding area is delightful.

TIHANY

The old town and resort area, Tihany, is located on a small peninsula jutting out from the Lake Balaton's northern shore. You must not pass by too quickly for the main highway between Keszthely and Budapest passes somewhat north of the peninsula. Just west of Balatonfured a small road will swing off the main highway, carrying you around the full perimeter of the peninsula. From the tip of Tihany Peninsula to the south shore of the lake is but a mile's distance. Regular boat service is maintained between Tihany and the opposite shore, thus saving tourists the long drive around the lake.

Tihany is a national park; geysers shoot forth their hot mineral waters and unusual forms of fossils can be found on the peninsula. In summer large fields of lavender cover the slopes of the high hills which form the center of the narrow finger of land protruding into the lake. Cradled within the hills is the Inner Lake and nearby, the old town of Tihany. The Romanesque crypt of the Abbey of Benedictine Church is one of the oldest pieces of architecture in Hungary. The remains of King Andrew I, an 11th-century ruler of Hungary, are buried here. The Old Town provides interesting bits of architecture. Incidentally, there is a little cafe located just to the right of the church. Enjoy a fine view of the surrounding lake while you have an aperitif or tea.

Down at the lakeside you will find camping and swimming permitted along the entire periphery of the peninsula. No sandy beaches on the peninsula, just grass. Swimming along this northern shoreline of Balaton can be a bit tricky for you will find yourself entering the lake over either rocks or mud. Benches and walks are available for those who wish to stroll. About five minutes from the main highway you will reach the ferry docks from which boats depart regularly for the south shore. Just beyond these docks is the hotel-motel-camping complex at Tihany.

Just to the west of the camping area (though quite separate) are 13 small individual units built of stone and angled toward a wide grass and sand area bordering the lake. One small room offers four beds, bath and toilet and rents for 120 forints for four persons; an additional 98 forints can be figured for meals per person per day.

TIHANY The Motel is set somewhat back from the beach in a shady area surrounded by parking areas and gardens. There is a large lobby with fountain, TV and many windows. Dining facilities are in a building nearby. The 250 rooms are exactly like those in the other motels scattered about at Keszthely, Balatonfoldvar and Siofok. Two beds, desk, bidet and washbowl. Central showers and toilets. The entire atmosphere, though cramped, is somehow bright and pleasant.

The Hotel Tihany is a six-story modern structure located directly on the lake. There are 135 rooms in all with beds in foot-to-foot position. Wood-paneled ceilings add a touch of atmosphere. The furniture in the rooms is in good condition.

Rates here are approximately 150 forints for a double. There are no eating facilities within the hotel building. Guests are obliged to use the restaurant near the motel, a five minute walk. The Tihany is one of the best hotels available in the Balaton area, if not the best. Here you can live in comparative comfort by the lake, enjoying a number of entertainment facilities nearby.

ANNEX (TO HOTEL TIHANY) This Annex building is located on the beach just east of the Hotel. Acceptable though the hotel is considerably better.

THE TIHANY RESTAURANT Serves the campers, motels and hotel. Two large rooms, one serving 450 persons; the second (adjoining walls) 350. The larger has a folk orchestra; the second loud dance music. Service here is acceptable; the food average.

TIHANY BAR Located on the beach directly across from the motel. Cocktail lounge; music for dancing. A small admission fee of 50 forints will be deducted from your bill. No bathing suits or shorts permitted. There is a fine view of the lake. Dancing is on an open terrace. The pleasant bar is open only in the evening.

SIOFOK

The Balaton is a beautiful lake with its Lombardy poplars, cannas, geraniums, roses, lake reeds, orchards and vineyards. The lake offers fishermen carp, fogas, pike, garda, perch and bass (hatcheries are continuously. restocking the lake). Trains will carry you from Budapest; buses, too. Or you might hire a car. Hotels in Siofok are grouped in an area of two to three blocks; most of them are directly on the lake shore. Surrounded by wide lawns, trees, gardens and restaurants, the modern hotels erected by IBUSZ really appear most attractive. Many parks with walks and benches separate the town from the nearby lake. The entire residential area of Siofok is one of quiet beauty and a certain charm.

Your life at Siofok will revolve largely around the immediate lake area. There, by the hotels and restaurants, you will find those tourist attractions designed to increase the pleasure of your stay. The town proper is busy, with noisy streets, dust, an occasional restaurant, only one of which could be of any interest.

Hotels

Most hotels at Siofok do not have restaurants on the premises. All the hotels are quite new and modern.

EUROPA Located at Siofok and with a design similar to the other three hotels located along the Lake Shore, the Hotel Europa has an integral extra feature, that being a restaurant located within the building proper. The restaurant serves comparatively good food; the service is generally good. An attractive intimate bar on the top floor boasts an impressive view of the surrounding lake area. Coffee and pastries are sold in addition to liqueurs, champagne, etc. Rooms at the Europa are functional, clean and not unattractive. Beds are in a foot-to-foot arrangement. A small balcony off the bedroom, complete with deck chairs affords the guest a striking view of the lake and Siofok. Beds are comfortable, bathrooms clean with showers.

LIDO Four modern, smart-looking hotels line the waterfront at Siofok. Built between 1963 and 1966 the Lido, Hungaria and Balaton and the Europa appear much alike to the new arrival. The furnishings are much the same; the atmosphere quite different.

At the Lido there is a large lobby, two elevators, souvenir stand and porter service. The hotel is colorfully decorated, in good taste. Located immediately beside the lake, the Lido has an east-west exposure. None of the rooms overlook the lake as lakeside frontage is occupied on each floor by large lounges. Rooms in the Lido are much like those in the three other hotels. Medium-sized with small balconies, rather stark but comfortably furnished; bathrooms (shower) and telephone outlets. There is no food facility in this hotel. No radio or TV in bedrooms; both are usually located in public rooms in the hotel.

HUNGARIA My, it is quiet here! There are the same services as at the other hotels. As is usually the case here at Siofok, rooms are clean and neat. The Hungaria is roughly two minutes' walk from the restaurant. There are no telephones in the rooms and TV only in public locations. Again lounges at the end of each floor facing the lake.

BALATON The hotel fronts the lake, and you can walk from the lobby directly out onto the lakefront terrace. Private beach. Rooms are the same as described above for the Lido. All the hotels are informal in environment; the Balaton is by far the most popular, if crowds prove a measure of popularity.

VENUS I rather like this place. It is a modern three-story hotel boasting 60 rooms, located a little over one block from the lake. No elevator. Baggage assistance. The eating facilities are located directly across the street. Rooms are clean, airy and generally appealing, and include baths plus hand shower. Foot-to-foot beds, two comfortable chairs, floor lamp and a small dresser. Fairly large balconies with each room; table and lounge chairs. Reserve on the upper floors here, "northern exposure."

VENUS MOTEL This motel is located on the same small park just to the left of the Venus Hotel. Avoid this place unless you are budgeting your trip to include only this type of facility. All doubles, with only public toilets and showers. Rooms contain bidets, washbowls and a small closet. The Venue Hotel and Motel are heavily booked during the season.

Restaurants

VENUS A large structure with inside and terrace dining. Breakfast served until ten; lunch "from noon"; dinner seven to ten. Music in the dining hall from seven until approximately eleven-thirty. The dining hall is kept remarkably clean. Service is fairly quick, the food is average.

THE LAKESIDE Serving the Balaton, Lido and Hungaria Hotels, this modern restaurant is nicely decorated and enjoys a good view of the Lake. The restaurant is serviced from a clean, up-to-date kitchen. It's just so big! Interesting wall designs, paintings, etc. For warm weather dining, there is a terrace overlooking the Lake. Meal hours here are the same as at the Venus Restaurant. One difference, the music "carries on" until 2:30 A.M.!

I enjoyed a delicious meal in this restaurant. Though this restaurant is big and crowded, throughout the season, I'm sure you'll enjoy your meals.

MATROZ CSARDA ("FISHERMAN'S INN") Located near the entrance to the harbor in western Siofok, the "Fisherman's Inn" offers enclosed dining in several small rooms or dining on a large open terrace fronting on the street. The rear of the restaurant is directly off the docks where boats from Balantonfured, Keszthely, etc., tie up. The harbor side of the restaurant includes an espresso, also more informal dining. Of course, the whole operation is casual, nothing fancy, just plain *fresh fish*. Prices are on the expensive side. Other foods are offered should fish not be on your diet.

BORHARAPO Feel like a little singing, swinging, wining in the comradely atmosphere of a smoky wine cellar with a few of your fellow tourists? Starting at four-thirty in the afternoon you'll have your chance at the Borharapo. Wear your old clothes, hold your breath and descend into the depths of this establishment.

The Borharapo is located directly on the Fö Utca, at the west end of Siofok.

REV CSARDA ("FERRY INN") You shouldn't miss this spot. Best orchestra and food combined with good service to be found outside of Budapest. Be certain to make reservations. Ask for the room with the orchestra. The food is good. Many specialities. Red and white wines (no selection) are served in carafes. Menus in German and Hungarian. Tables arranged for two to twenty. You may have to share. Arrange to be there by seven-thirty. The Ferry Inn is actually a very old establishment, recently renovated but left "as was" except the kitchen. In one building, if you are so inclined you can cook your own meal on an open range. In another part of this group of buildings you can, by candlelight, test various Hungarian wines.

FOGAS Located directly on the Fő Utca, the Fogas is not outstanding. Average food in a more than average surrounding.

TÜNDE BAR The Tünde Bar is located in what was obviously an old home. It is very popular with the younger set. The place is small and fills fast. Dress informally.

EDEN BAR A new daytime cafe doubling as a night spot after eight, the Eden Bar recently opened next to the Hotel Hungaria.

CURRACZARDA Why not try this rather attractive restaurant located on the main street in the center of Siofok? The attractive terraces, flowers and over-all appearance of the place make a good impression.

EGER

The history of this very charming little town dates from the year 1009 when the first Hungarian king, Saint Stephen, founded an episcopy at the foot of the Bukk Mountains. In 1241, Mongols ravaged the area and somewhat later rebel tribes (the Cumanians) set fire to the town. From 1280 to 1526, Eger developed into a prosperous community, the wine industry being founded at this time (for which the area is so famous). After the Battle of Mahacs and with the succeeding Turkish occupation, Eger passed through several sieges. In the year 1552, a Turkish army of 120,000 under the dual leadership of the Turks, known locally as Ahmet and Ali, laid siege to Eger. A Hungarian garrison of 2,000 men held off the Turks, who were forced to withdraw after severe losses. This ignominious defeat at the hands of soldiers stationed in what the Turks called a "Sheepfold that has the impudence to call itself a Fort" was not soon to be forgotten by the defeated. Forty-four years later, in 1596, the Turks advanced again, this time to fight troops supplied by the Austrian Emperor. These soldiers evidently appreciated the "sheepfold" characteristics of their surroundings and being far from home, capitulated. Eger thus experienced 91 years more of occupation. In 1687, the town was at last freed from Turkish domination, only to fall under the domination of Imperial Austria. Within the years immediately following the War of Independence (against the Austrian Hapsburghs in the early 18th century), the present outline of Eger began to take shape, namely the charming, thoroughly delightful Baroque style of architecture.

Every street, every corner of the town will amaze those of you who, like I, have never lived in a town which is such a jewel of Baroque-style architecture. And it is not at all like some weary museum-town frequently seen in various sections of Europe. The parks, the narrow streets, the statue of Istvan Dobo, the Minaret, the Fortress, the beautiful Lyceum (with its works of art displayed for the tourist), all the small houses, iron grillwork, patios and churches that make up this delightful town, are a delight to see, to inspect, to photograph. Do not forget the street of beautiful women, a line of caves from which one may purchase bottles of wine straight from kegs. Have a couple of drinks on the spot. In any location try some of the Bulls Blood, a well known wine from Eger.

Hotels

PARK One of the most delightful hotels I have visited in many years. Not a new hotel, the Park has been maintained in such good fashion that its facilities belie the years. Near the lobby is the restaurant, a very attractive breakfast room and a small bar serving coffee and liqueurs. There are 60 rooms. Singles with bath are limited, and in every instance singles are without toilets. Fourteen doubles have baths; only ten with toilets. Your reservations must be quite specific. Rooms at this hotel are very well maintained—clean, neat, sunny! Four of the double rooms on the second floor have private balconies overlooking the large garden to the side of the hotel. These rooms have baths and toilets but are on the dark side. The balconies are quite large and are covered with a glass roof; breakfast here could be a pleasure. Furnishings of these particular rooms are unexceptional, but acceptable and complete.

The restaurant at the Park serves average to good food as quickly as the overworked waiters can move from table to kitchen and back. The restaurant (indoors) is closed at noon; luncheon is on a pleasant, sheltered terrace overlooking the hotel's private garden. A cool and charming locale on a hot summer afternoon! In the evening, a good gypsy orchestra plays in such a manner as to make your long trip to Hungary completely worthwhile. Tea, ices and liqueurs are served from a small birch hut located at the side of the dance floor.

EGER The Hotel Eger located to the rear of the Hotel Park is under the same management. No food here; guests must eat at the Park a two-minute walk away. The Eger was built in 1962; it is a modern structure totally out of context with its surroundings. There are 62 rooms in all with a total of 200 beds. Singles number 50, none of which have bathrooms. Only four doubles with bath to a floor. Those rooms with bath also have toilets. An extra guest in a room costs 18 forints. A double with bath costs roughly 90 forints. Baths are kept in good condition. The best double rooms are located at the end of the hotel west and have medium-sized balconies. The Eger is well-maintained and comparatively comfortable.

DEBRECEN

The history of this city (Hungary's third largest) can be traced back to prehistoric periods when the Great Plain on which Debrecen is located was occupied, in turn, by the Celts, Scythians, Dacians, Huns until the area was eventually overrun by the Magyars in the 9th century. The name of the city apparently stems from "Debrezun" one of the three small 13th century villages from which Debrencen originated. Through the period of the early Arpads, of the Mongol invasion and well into the reign of King Robert Karoly of Anjou (supported in his claim to the throne by the "Squire of Debrecen"), the city has prospered as a trading center. Even during the years of Turkish occupation, Debrecen was able to maintain a modicum of freedom in that taxes are paid directly to the Sublime Ports in Istanbul; the town was considered an "estate" of the Sultan, thus remaining free of local mercenary activities.

As the gateway to Transylvania, Debrecen played an active part in the economic and political affairs of Catholic Austria, Transylvania (predominantly Protestant) and Moslem Turkey. The town grew rich on the trade which passed through its gates as the European Powers vied for positions of political advantage. The Thirty Years' War resulted in efforts to gain national independence in Hungary, the town of Debrecen standing firmly at the side of the Protestant (and independent) Kingdom of Transylvania. Debrecen was known locally as the "Hungarian Geneva." Printing presses were in operation here in approximately 1561, and in 1588 advanced courses were instituted at the Latin School which later developed into the College of Debrecen. During the Counter-Reformation, many students from this college studied in Calvinist Basle and Wittenburg, bringing back thought trends which bypassed the black-out imposed by authoritarian Vienna. When trade with the Ottomans was monopolized by Vienna, there was a loss of revenue to the city of Debrecen and commercial life suffered accordingly. During the 1848-49 War of Independence, Debrecen became temporary capital of Hungary. The First Republic of Hungary was decreed at this time, though it was later quashed by Vienna. After this last spark of advanced thinking Debrecen slowly stultified under Hapsburg rule, becoming little more than a country town.

At the end of World War II Debrecen was one of the first towns to be entered by Russian troops. A ball-bearing factory, pharmaceutical plant, meat processing plants, a fine museum and two universities (Lajos Kossuth and the University for Medical Science) are located in and around the city. I would suggest that you visit the various churches, the university grounds and the Deri Museum. The wooden carving on Saint Anna Church is particularly worth seeing. The Great Church, built in 1803, is notable for on April 14, 1849, it was from the pulpit of this church that Lajos Kossuth proclaimed Hungary free and independent of the Hapsburgs.

The *Nagytempiom* (Great Church) is the largest Reform Church in Hungary. The left tower supports the largest bell in Hungary (cast from cannon balls fired by Hapsburg troops). It is known as the Rakoczs Bell, named after a Transylvanian Prince. The church can hold 5,000 people.

Debrecen is an interesting town: simple, quiet, attractive and very hot in summer.

Hotels

ARANY BIKA This is a proud old structure that seems to have fallen on hard times. Located in the center of this medium-sized university town in Eastern Hungary, the Arany Bika offers great potential if only her facilities were updated, the decorations pepped up and service extended. There are 130 rooms of which 45 have baths. Telephones are in some of the rooms. Better rooms are located to the front of the hotel though there is something of a noise factor here. You might prefer a room off the court. Such rooms are pleasant, can have baths and are certainly much quieter. Doubles without bath are crowded and bleak. Washbowls. In many instances, rooms have couches instead of beds. These couches or beds have been decorated with large buttons placed with such diabolical cunning that sleep becomes impossible. Suggestion: place the comforter on top of the mattress and sleep under a sheet. If the weather turns cool, raid the other bed for coverings. Certain rooms are very pleasant—on the old-fashioned side, but airy, clean and generally quite good.

The cafe is the most updated of the hotel's public rooms. It is very pleasant and quite popular with local people. You can have a full breakfast here. Next door, the grill offers gypsy music during dinner and is more informal than the large restaurant. It is a bit too brightly lighted, however. Service is good; food fair to good.

HORTOBAGY CSARDA (HORTOBAGY PUESZTA) So in telling you of the Hortobagy Csarda, let us preface our comments with a capsule outline of the geographical and physical surroundings of the Inn, namely the Puszta (or Steppes). The Puszta is a vast lowland, 75,000 acres of it, covering the greater part of east central Hungary. Few bushes, no trees, an occasional windmill and large humps of soil showing the location of a village deserted by its occupants long ago. Drive south from Eger toward Tiszafured and on toward Debrecen. As you leave the Matra Mountain area close to Eger, the road will descend until quite suddenly you will find yourself driving across a land as different from your point of origin as day from night. First there will be the hills and trees, flowers, gardens and curving roads. Then by the time you have reached Tiszafured the road will have as many angles as a yardstick.

A sturdy strain of fine cattle is raised out here. Some of the principal breeding farms for the full-blooded Hungarian horses are located on the Puszta.

Combine the elemental features of the Puszta mentioned above, the cowboys, the various animals, add a few creature comforts such as the beef and veal dishes for which Puszta is famous, some wine and the ever present gypsy music and you have a combination not easily forgotten.

Located in the heart of this great prairie, the Hotrobagy Csarda (or Hortobagy Inn) built in 1699, sits along a tributary of the Tisza River, a stone's throw from the famous and picturesque Nine Hole Bridge, built in 1827. Hortobagy Inn stands exactly as built, the furniture styled as in the typical Hungarian country home. Such luxury as there is stems from the total naturalness of the surroundings. The Inn offers no great comforts; it is rustic and in fact primitive in many aspects. Guests should expect to rough it.

The restaurant consists of two long rooms in the form of a "T." Tables near the door (and kitchen) are reserved for residents of the Inn. You will share your table with other guests. Flags on the table identify the nationality of the guests. The food is good. You will have a choice of two or three main dishes plus soup and dessert. Service is similar to that in a hunting lodge in our country. Lunch and breakfast are served (weather permitting) in the small garden that separates the Inn from the highway.

Be sure you don't miss a ride out to the Puszta in one of the open carts for hire locally. It is an unusual treat that will possibly include riding exhibitions, visits to the local stud farm, a general tour of the cattle and sheep grazing areas and the Puszta stretching out as far as the eye can see.

KECSKEMET

Hotels

ARANY HOMOK Kecskemet is a delightful town, green with trees, colorful flowers, the glistening tile roofs of municipal buildings reflecting the summer's sun. During your stay in Kecskemet I would certainly set aside some time for sightseeing; the architecture of the buildings is most striking. Few are truly old, the most elaborate having been constructed in the early 1900's. But wait until you see those ceramic roofs, the towers and turrets. Splendid is the view presented to Hungarians and tourists alike.

ARANY HOMOK ("GOLDEN SANDS") Built in 1962; it is a modern structure. This hotel fronts on small parks, a fountain and is situated in a relatively quiet area of the town. Rooms here are quite comfortable, bathrooms frequently large and usually well maintained. Small balconies on front rooms overlook a small park and fountain. There is no appreciable noise problem here though church bells can, on occasion, bring out the agnostic in those guests trying to complete a night's sleep.

The restaurant serves very good food and should not be confused with an open air beer garden (complete with a very lively jazz orchestra) located nearby. The restaurant maintains a large (and good) gypsy orchestra. In the rear of the hotel there is an intimate cocktail lounge of good size; well-lighted. Entrance from either the street or through the hotel bar.

PECS

They call Pecs the "Two Thousand Year Old Town," for human habitation of the area was known to exist that long ago. The climate is dominated by the Mecsek Hills which lie to the north of the city, these hills blocking the northern breezes giving Pecs a rather Mediterranean climate. Hungary's springtime weather comes first to Pecs. The hillsides are covered with lilies-of-the-valley which are sold in decorative corsages throughout the town. Apricots, almonds and grapevines grow in the Mecsek Hills. A bishopric was founded here by Saint Stephen in 1009 and the cathedral construction was begun the same year. One of the oldest universities in Europe was established in Pecs in 1367. When the Turks occupied the town they built several mosques. Turkish baths and minarets can be seen throughout the city.

The Cathedral of Pecs (known as Saint Peter's) has been standing for ten centuries, but the stones of an ancient Christian basilica incorporated into the structure go back to the 4th century. The Cathedral was started under King Stephen I but was completed only after the Mongol Invasion, in 1241. It was a mosque during the Turkish period and was later converted to its proper role. Inside the Cathedral one can see a Renaissance Tabernacle dating from 1506. The walls of the building are decorated with murals by Szekely and Karoly Lotz, these murals completed in the late 1900's.

When in Pecs be sure to visit the Wilhelm Zsolnay ceramic factory. It will be interesting for you to note how an outstanding designer of ceramics (1870-90) conformed to the blatantly crude styles of the early 1900's. The display tells much of the story of design changes encouraged by the wealth stemming from the Industrial Revolution that swept Europe in the 1890's.

Pecs is truly a pleasant town. Its hillside location, the temperate weather, the pace of the community; the not inconsiderable antiquities, the Mecsek Hills with their walks, pines and streams, coupled with the good service provided by the Hotel Nador, make Pecs a worthwhile stop for the tourist.

Hotels

NADOR AND PANNONIA The Hotels Nador and Pannonia will for the sake of clarity be treated as one unit. Actually they are two old hotels built in 1812, connected by service halls and sharing certain public rooms. The reception is in the Nador, hotel offices in the Pannonia. The Nador faces the central square of Pecs with its old Turkish Mosque and is actually the principal of the two units. The Pannonia is on a narrow side street, quieter by night, more stuffy (and possibly hot) by day. The Nador offers the foreign visitor its best rooms fronting on the central square directly over a street that is a main traffic artery. Throughout the night therefore, the silence of your comfortable room is ripped by the hissing of air-brakes, the shouts of drivers and the roar of engines.

The Pannonia has 110 rooms including 3 singles with bath plus 12 to 14 doubles with bath. All with period furnishings. On the roof of the Pannonia are sunbathing facilities complete with shower. The

Nador boasts 85 rooms including 3 singles and 9 doubles all with bath. Two apartments; the latter cost 220 forints. There is also a single for 50 forints without bath, but as I recall it was a room whose window overlooked an inside corridor. There are broad corridors throughout the hotels; no elevators but easy stairs. Corridors are well lighted.

Restaurant facilities are very good at the Nador. Plan to dress for dinner. A new bar is planned for the Pannonia. A ballroom is available in this section of the hotel. In the Nador, the Hunt Room has been set aside for private parties and on the balcony above, the Peasant Room, a small area decorated in an Hungarian country motif. Next door to the Nador is the "Golden Room," a pastry house by day, a "Boite" by night. Meals are a la carte in all party rooms. To the left of the entrance is a "brauhaus" or "beer bar," paneled and appropriately "lusty in motif." The Nador also boasts a fine cafe for breakfast, mid-morning coffee or snacks. It is fashioned, not too sunny with just that touch of comfortable informality. The breakfast rolls are very good.

FENYVES High in the Mecsek Hills with a spectacular view of Pecs, the Fenyves Hotel is nothing for us. If you like to hike and care little for the commercial or touristic attractions of Pecs, you might want to stay up here. A new hotel, the Fenyves or "Pine Tree" Hotel has no parking space and no bathing facilities. I would come up here for lunch. The restaurant looks attractive.

Camping

Located not far from the Fenyves Hotel up in the Mecsek Hills is a new and attractively designed camping area under seemingly able management. Opened in July 1965; 10 forints for car space; 18 forints for the use of camp site; 7 forints per person. Use your own tent or rent one locally. Rubber mattresses are also available. The public toilets and showers are modern, well designed. Facilities are available for outdoor cooking in up-to-date facilities. The location, high on the hills beneath the pine trees, is truly delightful.

Restaurant

OLYMPIA The Nador Hotel has the best restaurant in Pecs, no doubt about it. However, should you be in town for several days and desire a change of scenery, why not drive out to the Olympia some evening? Located on one of the broad streets of the so-called Uranium Town, the restaurant will prove quite pleasant. There are two large rooms, a restaurant and cocktail lounge. Quite colorful! Should you be searching for a pleasant eating place completely free from touristic influences I recommend the Olympia.

SZEGED

When I think of Szeged several delightful memories come to mind. First are my favorable impressions of this lovely Hungarian town situated in the southern section of the country along the banks of the Tisza River. Parks; broad avenues; interesting statuary in the town's central parkway. Swimming pavillions along Tisza River; motor boat races; the music festivals. Historically Szeged shares a past not unlike that of Debrecen, Eger and many other Hungarian towns. See the paprika fields, where are grown the red and green vegetable exported to worldwide markets; taste the excellent salami, the fish soup (a local speciality) flavored with the Mako onions, also exported.

The Szeged Open Air Music Festivals are held in front of the enormous Votive Church throughout late July and early August. Ten thousand persons can occupy seats for each performance of the festival. When in Hungary try to visit Szeged for the Festival.

Hotels

TISZA A fine hotel in a beautiful town. The Hotel Tisza, named after one of Hungary's largest rivers which flows through Szeged, is situated on an attractive park in the center of town roughly two blocks from the river. Szeged is approximately a four-hour drive northeast of

Pecs, 12 miles from the Yugoslavia border and 26 miles from the Romanian border. I'm sure you will like this tourist facility from the minute you enter the front door. There is a relaxed feeling as if the staff wanted to see you entertained in the most satisfactory yet efficient manner possible. Actually the Tisza has been restored to its inn-keeping function for only three years. Built some 60 years ago, the hotel building was for some time used for municipal purposes, then completely renovated to offer the comfortable surroundings you see today.

Upon entering you will find a large, airy, attractive lobby off of which is located a cafe, very popular with the Szeged younger set, as well as a restaurant serving fine food in pleasant surroundings.

There are two floors of well-decorated, well furnished rooms—7 singles (4 with bath); 76 doubles (10 with bath). Singles cost 87 forints with bath, 52 forints without. Doubles 147 forints with bath, 92 forints without. There are three apartments, the bedrooms simply alcoves off a large sitting room. All rooms have telephones. All rooms here are neatly furnished, with attractive pictures on the wall. Bathrooms are particularly good. I would suggest that you book rooms on the "front" or "off park" side.

The restaurant at the Tisza consists of two large rooms. The first encountered when entering from the lobby has high ceilings, nice decor but is not the main room. The restaurant fronts on the park side of the hotel and has an entrance directly from the street. It is much smaller than the former room and much more in demand, particularly in the evenings. A gypsy orchestra plays from approximately seven-thirty on. You must reserve a table, or you will be shown a table in the other room. Service is fair, food good.

Restaurants

FISHERMAN'S RESTAURANT A local fish house IBUSZ raves about. Don't forget the *Halaszle,* or fish soup. It's a speciality here.

VIRAG CAFE The Virag Cafe is located on Kossuth Square just across from the Municipal Tourist Office. Very pleasant, especially on a hot day. Good ices. Especially fine orange juice. Try a speciality named *Somlay Galuska.* Very popular and very crowded come four o'clock on a summer's afternoon.

Poland

The traveler to Poland will find much to enjoy: the lakes and forests of Mazuria, the flower gardens and little inlets of the Hel Peninsula, the Baltic beaches, the towering Tatra Mountains. Chopin's birthplace at Zelazowa Wola and the gardens there would inspire etudes in the ear of the tone-deaf; situated among hollyhocks, asters and zinnias, Chopin's charming home overlooks a small lake spanned by a Japanese-style bridge. And Warsaw: a view of that turreted, metropolitan Phoenix seen from across the River Vistula during a summer's shower evoked the desire to paint on canvas the imposing yet charming scene. From the Oder River across the Vistula to the Bug; south from the Baltic Sea through the plains of central Poland and the pine forests of Mazuria to the peaks of the High Tatras, Poles walk in a wealth of natural beauty. Yet the Pole seems less a product of his environment than a temperamental diva; to meet a Pole is to shake hands with an explosion.

One would think that surrounded by such beauty the Pole would be at peace with the world—a little more concerned with roots, less tempted by the stars. Yet, strangely enough, the tumbling, foaming, roaring Dunajec River typifies the Polish spirit to me. The Pole is a drifter, colorful, a little aimless. Rather than a "summer's breeze," the Pole is a winter wind, a September storm over a gray sea; turbulent, violent, unaccountable for the damage that accompanies his natural temperament.

The Poles seem to be experiencing a period of self-sustained—and entirely incorrect—doubt as to the worthiness of their tourist establishment. When an enthusiastic, would-be traveler to Poland presents himself to some Polish authorities, they all but ask: "But why do you want to visit our country? We are only a small nation bordering on the road to nowhere." While proud of their country, Poles seem unable to grasp that within the confines of the Polish State there exist natural and historical attractions that would be of interest to the foreigner. I believe the Pole is wary lest his hospitable gestures toward the tourist be laughed off as inadequate and his small, painful efforts toward the construction of up-to-date tourist accommodations held up to ridicule. The Polish Government has both positive and negative attitudes toward tourism that stem from a variety of origins, most of which can be remedied by the encouragement of tourist exchanges between Poland and the United States.

Polish hospitality is inadequate commercially—in hotels, restaurants, guest services, etc. The true warmth of the Polish welcome manifests itself in small, personal deeds. Item: my car's battery desperately needed distilled water but none was available. A conversation ensued between the mechanic at the service station and the owner of a car parked nearby. The Pole entered my car and rode with me across town to a store where the water was available. I never would have found the place alone.

Item: one rainy evening in the town of Dancut I was obliged to leave my hotel in search of a dining spot since the dining room was closed to all but the initiated in anticipation of a Party banquet. With no idea where to go, I stopped a man on the street to inquire the location of a restaurant. Unable to make me understand the direction—I knew no Polish—the gentleman took me to a restaurant and introduced me to some friends who located a table for me in the overcrowded room, ordered my meal, called for beer, joined me during dinner and then paid the tab before I realized what was going on! The man then invited me to a bar nearby where we joined another group who insisted that I join them in a bottle of wine. As a result, I returned to the hotel accompanied by my new friends who bade me goodnight and a good vacation in Poland.

In Poland you must appreciate that while hotels are average and restaurants largely drab, your real hosts are not the innkeepers and restaurant managers. You must rely on the basic cordiality, the domestic welcome, of the Polish people. Traditional Polish hospitality has remained unchanged throughout the years. I sense the Pole's only regret is that he is not able to do more for you. Within the versatile Polish character, with its enthusiasm for life, entertaining personality and traditional warmheartedness, you will surely find a friend.

HISTORY

The 10th century saw the Polish tribes of the Vistula and Oder regions united under the leadership of the Piast dynasty. Mieszko I, a member of this dynasty, was baptized in the year 966 and at that point Poland became a Catholic nation. Three decades later Boleslaw the Brave, son and heir of Mieszko I, was assured by Otto, the Holy Roman Emperor, of the total sovereignty of the Polish land, and in 1025 Boleslaw was crowned king of Poland. Today's reader can easily understand that peace was difficult to secure, particularly at a time when the marauding German tribes to the west and the Slavs and Mongols not a great distance to the east continually sought new villages and new fields for their restless clansmen. While Poland was establishing contacts of a cultural nature with the nations of "Atlantic Europe," she was constantly under attack by her immediate neighbors. Foreign intervention succeeded to that point where members of the Piast dynasty began to quarrel among themselves; the nation was at the mercy of its own rulers.

During the 14th century Poland's great king, Casimir the Great, achieved something of a "millenium" by unifying the nation and subsequently codifying the laws. A central government administration and a university were established at Krakow. In 1386, the Jagellonian dynasty was created through a marriage between the Piasts and members of the Lithuanian royal house. The forces of this union defeated the Teutonic Knights in 1410 at the battle of Grunewald. King Sigismund (1548-1572) had no heir; therefore, to prevent possible dissension between the royal houses of Poland and Lithuania, it was decreed that one king and one parliament would rule the combined countries.

Members of the Polish Parliament (the Seym) gradually gained influence at the expense of the king and it was at this period that members of the Seym established the practice of defeating any resolution by the means of simply denying passage to any act against which even one parliamentarian should vote. With the eventual disappearance of the Jagellonian dynasty (through normal attrition), the throne was made elective but was so limited in its functions by the Seym that actual control of the kingdom was held by that legislative body. Despite the dramatic, history-making success of King John Sobieski, who in 1683 thoroughly trounced the Turks outside Vienna, the power of the Polish State was rapidly declining. Minor wars, internal problems and foreign intervention had greatly weakened the country.

Prior to 1772, Poland's borders stretched approximately from the present western border with Germany south toward Slovakia and east into what is presently Soviet Russia's Lithuanian province. A great university was founded in Krakow as early as the 14th century. Prior to and through the 16th century, Poland enjoyed great cultural and economic gains.

In 1772, as a result of military and political gains provided at the expense of Polish sovereignty, emissaries from Prussia, Russia and Austria convened, scalpels in hand, to finalize what countless earlier attempts at intervention had failed to realize—the final dismemberment of Poland. In 1795, after three successive agreements between the governments of the aforementioned countries, Poland ceased to exist as a national entity. The remains were equitably divided between the power-hungry monarchs of the three great European powers.

The agreements mentioned above between Austria, Prussia and Tsarist Russia in the years 1772, 1793 and 1795 resulted in a series of partitions of Poland, the last of which eliminated it as a country from the map of Europe. To this day, Poland has never completely recovered. There were serious revolts against the foreign rulers in the years 1830 and 1863, the results of which were so devastating for the Poles that prominent Polish women wore not only black gowns but black jewelry as well. Some gains were achieved in the first 50 years of the 1800's when the rulers of Russia, Austria and Prussia emancipated the serfs. In the late 1800's, the region known as Galicia (the area around Krakow), was granted partial autonomy by the Austrians, thus becoming the cultural, the progressive, center for the captive Poles.

Following World War I and the defeat of Germany and Austria, as well as the virtual withdrawal of Russia from the international scene, Poland partially regained its national identity. The creation of Czechoslovakia and the demands of Hitler's extending Third Reich resulted in a Polish State of rather truncated dimensions. The Poles held central Poland and were provided a slender corridor to the Baltic. The Baltic Sea coastline was occupied by Germany, as were large sections of Poland's western provinces.

Despite nonaggression pacts with both Germany and Soviet Russia, Poland was invaded by Germany on September 1, 1939, and by

Russia on September 17 of the same year. The Poles continued their fight for freedom only to be completely occupied first by the Germans and then toward the end of the war, by the Russians. A Government-in-Exile was established first in France, later in London. Polish men and women fought on the Allied side during World War II.

In July of 1944, the Polish Committee of National Liberation was set up by the Home National Council; it was to be the first government in Free Poland. In January, 1945, Warsaw was finally liberated by the Polish and Russian armies. The city was, however, by that time virtually destroyed. Hitler had personally ordered that Poland's capital be systematically razed.

Further statistics on Poland's plight at the end of World War II: of a population of 30 million prior to the war, six million were killed; two and one-half million were deported for compulsory labor in Germany; 500,000 were permanently crippled. Property losses were evaluated at $50 billion.

At the Yalta Conference, 46 per cent of Polish territory was given to Russia. As compensation for this loss, the Potsdam Conference in 1945 placed German territory east of the Oder-Neisse Rivers under Polish administration, pending a final settlement at a German peace conference that still seems scheduled in the indefinite future. (Meanwhile, the area in question has been thoroughly "Polified;" this I state from first-hand investigation.) At Yalta, the presiding heads of government, without Polish participation, also decided that the future government would be based on the Polish Committee of National Liberation plus elements of the Government-in-Exile group in London. The United States and United Kingdom eventually recognized this government. In 1945, a Polish-Soviet treaty of friendship and cooperation was signed on the border between the two countries; local elections in 1947 saw the defeat of the Polish Peasant Party, and the Party's leader Stanislaw Mikolajczka, then fled the country. The Workers' Parties and Socialist groups dominated the elections.

A new constitution was enacted in 1952 and a year later Poland and the government of Germany's east zone agreed on the Oder-Neisse line as the border between their countries. In May, 1955, Poland signed the Warsaw Pact providing for friendship, mutual assistance and economic ties between Poland, the Soviet Union and the countries of Eastern Europe. The Polish United Workers' Party made policy changes in its structure, and brought back as Secretary, Wladyslaw Gomulka, who had been isolated from the political scene since 1948. He still maintains his position in Poland.

GEOGRAPHY AND CLIMATE

Poland has a land area (121,666 square miles) roughly approximating that of New Mexico, and a population of 29½ million, somewhat more than the number of persons residing in the States of New York and Ohio combined. Except in the southern regions of the country where the Carpathian, Tatra and Sudeten mountain chains form a natural border with Czechoslovakia, Poland is largely lowland; less than half the land area is over 500 feet above sea level.

The central sections of the country are covered by open rolling plains; to the northeast, in the Mazurian Lake region, which was once part of Prussia, the country resembles certain regions of Wisconsin with wide, deep lakes and streams, conifer forests, rock formations; this is a largely uninhabited area, dependent in the main on summer tourism for its income. Poland's northern Baltic coast runs from the Bay of Danzig in the east (shared by Poland and the Soviet Union) to the Gulf of Pomerania, which forms part of the border between Poland and East Germany. The Gulf is largely under Polish control.

The mighty Oder (or Odra) River flowing into the Pomeranian Gulf is fed by the Neisse and Warta Rivers; the former combines with the Oder to form the presently disputed boundary between Germany and Poland. The Warta is located wholly within Poland. The Vistula (or Wista) River fed by the Bug and Narew, flows north into the Bay of Danzig.

The Baltic coastline is comprised of a series of bays and peninsulas; the Hel Peninsula north of Danzig is prominent. The wide beaches bordering the Baltic make excellent bathing sites. At Deba, west of the port of Gdynia, one may see the former German V-2 missile launching sites of World War II.

The highest point in Poland is Mount Rysy (approximately 8,000 feet), located within the Tatra Mountain range. Rich mineral deposits are known to exist in this region.

Seventy per cent of the forests are coniferous (mostly pine); birch, beech and elm trees are also plentiful. Fish and birds inhabit the lakes and forests throughout the country. Animals such as the bison, moose and tarpan (wild horse) are infrequently to be seen.

Weather in Poland is roughly the same as in Western Europe. The north is warm and has greater than average rainfall in the summer; it is quite cold during winter. Only in the southern regions is there much humidity. Daytime summer temperatures average around 70° Fahrenheit.

The largest cities of Poland are Warsaw (Warszawa), the capital, with a population of 1.1 million; Lodz, in central Poland (626,000); Krakow (461,000); Wroclaw, formerly Breslau (410,000); Poznan, formerly Posen (392,000); Gdansk, formerly Danzig (266,100); Szczecin, once Stettin (254,000); Pydgoszcz, also Bromberg (224,000); and Katowice (209,000). These figures are based on a 1959 census.

LANGUAGE

Luckily for us, Polish is written in the Latin alphabet, but most Poles would agree, I'm certain, that for the uninstructed ear the Polish language provides a dilly of a challenge. It's those blasted consonants! There are several regional dialects including something in the area around Gdansk, called Kashubian, thought to be an entirely different language. Poles, particularly in the western areas, are conversant in German; many Poles also speak Russian. Should you be "up" on some other Slavic tongue, you'll probably manage in Polish as well. As for me, I was a miserable failure—I just didn't understand anything, however I tried, but I did pick up a few clues for you.

Take the combination "sc"; this results in the sound "che." "Sz", I understand is sounded "sr." "Rz" is soft, while "cs" seems to be hard. There are about eleven of these "fateful combinations." Some are spiced with an "l" that is not an "l" because it has that little line through the stem thus making the "l" a "W" (Lods, a town, is pronounced "Wooch"). When speaking Polish vigorous jaw-action helps a lot. Want to send your kindest regards? Try *"Moc serdecznych pozdrowiern."* It seems that my trouble is that I get into the middle of one of these phrases and become so involved in the pronunciation that I forget what I'm trying to say!

But don't panic! In the large cities menus are generally printed in several languages and waiters as a rule know a bit of "restaurant English." Many of the younger Poles speak English quite well. In the countryside you are pretty much on your own unless you speak some Polish, Russian or German. If you should choose some intermediary language for communication purposes, establish your nationality in the first sentences; the citizens of some countries are not as popular in Poland as they would have us believe. Anyway why not let them know you're an American?

In Poland more than in any other Central European country the natives seem anxious to speak with English-speaking tourists, but not all conversations are harmless. In your eagerness to make verbal contact with those about you, don't fail to "size up" the person with whom you are conversing; you may find yourself face to face with a black marketeer or with someone who is out to determine your political connections.

I would not venture out into the countryside without a guide if I did not speak Polish. I'd also take an interpreter when I went shopping. If you are more adventurous than I, try the "gesticulation method" or simply point; you may end up with salami instead of ice cream but you can have fun in the process. You can depend on the gentility of the average Pole. They will be happy to help you out whenever possible.

CURRENCY

The Polish monetary unit is the zloty which is made up of 100 groszy. The official exchange rate is four zloty to the dollar, thus one zloty is roughly the equivalent of 25c. However, the special exchange rate for tourists is 24 zl. to the dollar—quite an improvement! Nonetheless a wide-open black market exists which offers as much as 100 zl. to the dollar.

Now hear this: tourists should also be advised that when they exchange $20 or more they will receive in addition to the equivalent amount of Polish currency computed at the special tourist rate ORBIS coupons amounting to approximately 16 zl. to the dollar. For example, if you exchange $30 you will receive in return 720 zl. in cash plus coupons to the value of about 480 zl. (I say "about" 480 zl. because there is some disparity between the stated bonus rate of 16 zl. to the dollar and the amount actually received; the exchange clerk consults a table of figures and pays you the indicated number of coupons. These coupons may be used to pay for hotel rooms, gifts, meals, gasoline, etc. Signs displayed on windows and in offices throughout the country indicate where these coupons may be used.

This business of the tourist exchange rate plus bonus coupons should be considered in the light of prepaid trips to Poland. I cannot emphasize one point enough: a fully prepaid trip, with all meals and hotel rooms paid for in advance results in greater expenditure of funds on your part than would be the case if paid for the same accommodations and board within Poland. You can understand that by traveling prepaid you will have less opportunity to take advantage of the "dividend" granted those who cash dollars or travelers checks within the country. It's foolish to prepay in the belief that it helps the American economy because Poland gets the cash in any case — so why not take advantage of an offer that will save you money?

The following banknotes are in circulation: 20, 50, 100 and 500 zlotys. Coins come in the following denominations: 1, 2, 5, 10, 20 and 50 groszy; 1, 2, 5 and 10 zlotys. Spend a few minutes getting familiar with the banknotes, and note that size is not a reliable indication of value.

The importation or exportation of Polish currency is forbidden. Any amount of foreign currency can be brought into Poland, but at customs you will be required to make out a written declaration regarding all currency in your possession, and you can't take out more than you brought in. I would encourage you to be forthright in filling out these forms. Moreover, I would not try any monkey business such as attempting to smuggle Polish currency into the country.

You will be required to retain your currency declaration during your stay in Poland. Whenever you cash dollars or travelers checks, notations will be made on this form. The form must be surrendered when you depart the country. Loss of the form could abrogate your rights to export those personal articles and currencies with which you entered the country. In short, if you lose the currency declaration you stand a good chance of leaving Poland with literally only the shirt on your back!

Money may be exchanged at offices of the Polish National Bank, at the border stations and at ORBIS desks in hotels and ORBIS offices within each town. In many small towns ORBIS desks in the hotels are not authorized to exchange travelers checks; you will therefore be obliged to visit the local ORBIS offices. When leaving the country, excess Polish currency can be left with border control personnel who will fill out and give you a form of depository note. This is redeemable in Poland any time within a year by you, or any one else you name providing he has a written document from you authorizing him to accept the funds.

A word to the wise: as you walk briskly down the Krakowskie Przedmiescie some summer evening, you may suddenly find yourself accompanied by a gentleman who has seemingly appeared from nowhere. He will most likely mutter something in Polish and when you quite naturally mumble "I don't speak Polish," you will hear the fateful words—"Change money?" Shades of the Place de l'Opera, Paris, circa 1949!

Now if you are the wise person you will shake your head "no" and move on. The very fact that the man spoke to you in Polish (to determine whether you actually were a foreigner) is evidence of the risks involved in dealing with these people. Furthermore, my guess is that some of these gentlemen may be less interested in exchanging your money than in determining your reaction to their approach. If this is too subtle, let me put it another way: some of these men are quite probably salaried by an agency of the government. Make note: "Any exchange of currency by the intermediary of unauthorized individuals is incompatible with the provisions of the Polish Exchange Regulations, and will, therefore, have legal consequences." They said it, I didn't, so be careful! If you feel the need to exchange some dollars at a rate higher than the tourist rate, speak with your Polish friends, persons you can really trust.

There is an amusing little anecdote related to the "change money business." I had been approached several times, usually in the evenings, by men wanting to make financial deals or by youngsters wanting gum, cigarettes, a light, etc. I became fed up with these interruptions and so one evening, while returning from a restaurant to my hotel, I blurted out, "I don't want to exchange money and I have no gum!" to two young men coming toward me. With that one boy said in fluent English (he was probably a university student!) "But sir, we only wanted to ask you the time!" So much for American-Polish relations.

VISAS AND CUSTOMS

A visa is necessary and may be obtained through your travel agent or directly, by yourself, from the Consular Section, Embassy of the Peoples Republic of Poland, 2224 Wyoming Avenue, N.W., Washington, D.C. Allow a *minimum* of two weeks to have the visa returned; I recommend that you apply for your visa at least one month ahead of your departure date. The cost of a regular (tourist) visa is about $9. Visas *cannot* be obtained at the Polish border.

In addition to your passport you must forward to the Embassy two visa application forms, two recent passport-size photo portraits (signed on the front), the visa fee and either a voucher showing that hotel reservations have been prepaid or, if camping or visiting relatives, a receipt for ORBIS coupons to cover a minimum per diem charge for the length of your stay.

When filling out the application forms you will have to indicate the places in which you plan to enter and exit from Poland. You will be obliged to enter and leave the country from the points on the dates indicated on your visa application.

However, once you are in Poland you can arrange through ORBIS to leave the country by an exit other than that indicated on your application. Visas may be extended once you are in Poland, but payment must be made in foreign currency for room and board for the extra number of days for which your visa is extended.

Visitors must register with the provincial or country militia within 72 hours after arrival in Poland. If you are staying at an ORBIS hotel the formalities are taken care of by the Reception Desk staff.

Besides the regular tourist visa two types of transit visas are issued, one valid for 48 hours and one for 72 hours. The former permits the visitor an overnight non-stop crossing through Poland; the latter allows the visitor to spend a night in Poland within the period of validity of the visa. Transit visas may not be extended.

Should you be visiting relatives it is required that you purchase "exchange orders" (redeemable in Poland) costing about $10 first class or $7.50 second class per day. The number of these "exchange orders" you must buy depends on the length of your stay. Minimums established (second class) are as follows: for one-month visa: 10 per diem ORBIS coupons at a minimum cost of $75; a two-month visa: 17

ORBIS coupons at a minimum cost of $127; for three-month visa: 22 ORBIS coupons at a cost of $165.

Persons entering Poland on a regular tourist visa (and not visiting relatives) must give evidence to the Polish Embassy that room and board charges have been prepaid for each member of their party. A voucher from your travel agency will do the trick. Hotel and board reservations cost approximately $12.50 deluxe, $10 first class and $7.50 second class. I have found that some American travel agents charge a flat rate of $15 per day per person for each day of one's stay in Poland, in spite of the fact that the maximum charge for a deluxe hotel room is about $12.50. The $2.50 per day difference is not the agency's service charge, and so I am at a loss to explain why they feel it necessary that we invest such an unnecessarily high amount, particularly when pre-payment in the United States has already limited (if not eliminated) the bonus we would receive by exchanging money in Poland. So it pays to shop around a bit for your travel agent. Not all agents are authorized to deal with the national travel offices of the Middle European countries but try to find one that is well informed on travel to this area, and that is prepared to give you the best trip at the best price.

With reference to visa applications, you may be told by the Polish visa section that applications for visas can be filed with the Polish offices in Washington and the visa itself entered into your passport in some European capital city. Visitors to Poland should be alerted to the fact that such a procedure sometimes results in the tourist having to pay the visa application fee (about $9) twice.

I personally filed my visa application papers in Washington, complete with $9 fee. Some few weeks later in Vienna, when picking up the visa applied for in Washington, I was required to pay another visa fee even though Polish Embassy officials were apprised of the previous payment. A request made to Polish officials in Washington that the original visa payment be returned brought no reply. So you see why I suggest that visitors to Poland allow themselves time to apply for and receive their Polish visa from the same Polish Embassy.

Scandinavian readers should note that they can enter Poland on an "excursion visa" provided, of course, they have a valid passport. Persons holding "excursion visas" must enter and leave the country through the Polish port of Swinoujscie and they may travel only in the three Polish provinces that border the Baltic Sea, unless they are on an ORBIS tour. However, a regular visa may be applied for in Poland and a person who obtains such visa may leave the country through any of the normal exit points. The "excursion visa" is only for the use of Scandinavian visitors to Poland; all other foreign visitors to Poland must enter the country in possession of a 48-hour or 72 hour transit visa or regular tourist visa.

You may bring into Poland items of personal wearing apparel, toilet articles, a radio, books and jewelry for personal use. Portable radios are permitted (though possession of same may be noted on your passport), as well as cameras, films (a few rolls, not a few dozen rolls). Also guns and ammunition provided you have a permit from one of Poland's consular officials abroad. One hundred rounds of ammunition for sporting guns can be imported as well as 25 rounds for revolvers (*if* guns accompany the ammunition). Medicine for personal use is acceptable. Thirteen pounds of foodstuffs is permitted, though chocolate, mushrooms (they export the things!) and "stimulants" are limited by specific order. A couple of quarts of liquor, 200 cigarettes, 50 cigars or nine ounces of tobacco is permitted per person providing the visitor is *over* 17 years of age.

Sporting equipment (in logical amounts) is okay and your baby may be trundled across the border in his carriage (baby carriages *are* permitted specifically), but don't try leaving little Oscar at home and filling the carriage with booze. Showing off? The Poles will permit you to stagger across the border carrying your "prizes and souvenirs received at international events." You can even "import" a diploma. Now let's see, there's my Bachelor of Arts degree, my certificate of graduation from the Wee Wisdom School.

Seventeen-year-olds who travel on their own passport can bring in goodies whose worth shall not exceed the value of 1500 zl. providing such items are shown to be for personal use. They sure have this thing down to a fine point.

Should some of your luggage be traveling through freight channels be certain that you declare same when passing through customs or you may lose such exemptions as exist when the boxes or luggage are finally opened for customs inspection. Be sure to retain all declaration forms used when entering the country for presentation when exiting from Poland.

TRAVELING TO POLAND

By Air

Poland's LOT airline (LOT standing for Polskie Linie Lotnicze) has a good reputation and excellent connections to cities throughout Europe. Planes flown are usually Soviet-built Ilyushins, though you may occasionally have a ride on a Viscount. Flights are frequent; service is acceptable, though without frills. The offices of local carriers throughout Western Europe (Austrian Airlines, Sabena, SAS, etc., can advise you of the schedule particulars as LOT usually runs in conjunction with these other lines. For example, Austrian Air Lines has flights to and from Warsaw three times a week while LOT operates flights on the alternate days.

I advise that you have in hand round-trip or continuing-flight tickets when flying to Warsaw. This may save you considerable trouble once you are in Poland. However, should you be purchasing a ticket in Poland for a return flight from Warsaw, keep in mind that all ticket sales within the country are handled by ORBIS or LOT, *not* by the representatives of foreign airlines. Some foreign airlines maintain offices in Poland but these function mainly as maintenance-centers and information outlets and do not handle ticket sales. The central booking office for LOT in Warsaw is located at Warsaw ul. Warynskiego 9, but I suggest you deal mainly with ORBIS, whose main office is located in the Hotel Europejski directly across from the Hotel Bristol.

One may travel to Poland by ship on the Polish Ocean Lines. The liner Batory sails between Halifax, Canada, and the Polish port of Gydnic; the twice-a-month sailing will take you to Poland via Montreal, Southampton and Copenhagen. ORBIS is in charge of ticket sales. I understand that Polish Ocean Line ships make infrequent cruise calls at east coast ports of the United States. Contact your travel agent for the particulars.

Ferry service is maintained between the Polish port of Swinoujscie (Swinemunde) and the Danish port of Bonne and the Swedish port of Ystad. Should you wish to enter Poland via this route be certain you have a regular tourist or transit visa; the "excursion visa" mentioned above is only for Scandinavians.

By Rail

Important international railway routes link Warsaw with most of the European capitals. The more important of these routes are: London-Paris-Berlin-Warsaw-Moscow; Rome-Vienna-Warsaw-Moscow; numerous trains to Prague; Warsaw-Budapest-Belgrade-Sofia (the "Polonia Express"); Warsaw-Lvov (the Soviet Union); Bucharest (the Karpaty Express); and Krakow-Katowice-Berlin (East). Sleeping cars and dining cars are available on international runs. The arrival and departure point for trains in Warsaw is the Dworzec Glowny (main station).

Keep in mind that tourists who purchase return rail (or air) tickets for international travel must pay for same with foreign currency, not with zlotys. This is one reason I recommend that you come to Poland equipped with round-trip tickets.

By Auto

A quick glance at the map will show you that Poland has no common borders with countries to which American tourists normally travel. It is necessary for the visitor to pass through Russia, Czechoslovakia or East Germany when traveling by land. Most Americans who go to Poland by auto enter at one of the Polish-Czechoslovakian border points.

I would urge that you acquire an International Drivers License plus some form of liability insurance prior to your arrival in Poland; White Cross Insurance (with its green card) is acceptable. Should you not have proper insurance you will be required to purchase some at the border. Cost? About $6 for 15 days.

TRAVEL WITHIN POLAND

Motoring

Traffic regulations are pretty much what you find throughout Europe. In open areas there is no speed limit; within populated areas keep below 30 miles per hour. Use of your horn is *not* permitted in larger towns. The Polish authorities ask that you pay particular attention to horsedrawn vehicles that do not always obey the traffic laws. Traffic moves on the right. Be sure to use your turn signal indicators at appropriate times. International road signs are displayed. Highways are fairly well maintained though there is a considerable difference between the Class I, Class II and other highways running throughout the country. Keep to the principal highways as much as possible. The routes running between large cities are usually constructed of concrete and kept in good condition. Motor traffic is usually light; it's the people, cattle, mules, geese and carts that keep your hair standing on end. In recent years the Polish Government has made considerable efforts to improve the condition of all primary roads. One is now able to maintain an average speed of at least 50 miles per hour on most principal highways. A planned program of small restaurant-inns is under way and motoring in Poland is becoming a most pleasant experience. The countryside is truly delightful—most scenic!

Gasoline stations are scattered throughout the country and when I say "scattered" I mean just that. Do not leave any metropolitan center with a half-filled tank; you might find yourself returning by foot! Not every station carries the grade I (87 octane) gasoline your car will most likely require. This higher octane gas costs about 6½ zl. per liter. Grade II (80 octane) costs 6 zl., and I wouldn't recommend going further down the octane scale unless you enjoy hearing your motor knock itself to death. "Extra" quality motor oil costs about 25 zl. per liter.

ORBIS petrol vouchers which provide tourists with a 30 per cent discount on the price of gas are to be had at the ORBIS offices located throughout the country. These vouchers are purchased with foreign currency or bonus coupons received when cashing travelers checks or dollars.

If you plan to drive in Poland I recommend that you take along some extra oil, brake fluid, transmission fluid and an additive which when poured into the gas tank tends to thicken the fuel before it enters the engine. In any case, know your car before leaving Western Europe. Further, I would add new oil to old rather than to drain all the oil from the engine. Since gas stations are rather few and far between, I also suggest you carry a little extra fuel as well.

State stations for the servicing and repair of cars are located in the principal cities. Beyond going to one of these few rather well-operated garages there is little you can do in Poland should there occur some primary malfunction in your engine. Remember: service stations in Central Europe are only for fuel and oil; few are prepared or equipped to actually "service" your car. My recommendation: keep the scotch tape handy and your fingers crossed!

When you rent a car in Poland you'll get a Volga and a quite uncomfortable ride it will be, too. The springless darling will rent, without driver, for about $6.50 per day plus 6c a kilometer. Lower daily rates are in effect on longer rentals. With driver, the same five seated car costs $1. an hour, plus 10c per kilometer or $12 for the entire day (plus 10c a kilometer). You will probably be required to leave a deposit of something around $100 when accepting the car without a driver. The deposit is of course refunded on your return to the renting agency. Gasoline will be "on you" and you will be required to possess or to take out liability insurance before operating the vehicle.

Be sure that your car is parked in official parking areas on overnight stops. The cost is minimal and varies somewhat from town to town. These locations, usually close to the principal hotels, are called "parking Strzezonym." Watchmen are on duty at all times.

By Bus, Streetcar, and Taxi

Poland is covered by a dense network of bus routes which provide the chief mode of transportation for most of the population. Bus stations are usually located near the railway terminals and buses operate in conjunction with railroad schedules. Look for PKS, the sign of the Polish Bus Lines. Tickets are available at ORBIS a week in advance of departure; on the day of departure, tickets can be purchased at the bus terminal or on the bus itself.

Regular bus schedules are maintained between Warsaw and all principal Polish cities. During the summer months service is expanded to include such resort areas as Augustow and Ruciane. Fares are inexpensive.

For local travel, buses and taxis are available. The latter charge about 2½ zl, per milometer, but the rate doubles after 11 at night. On buses and streetcars the honor system is employed throughout the country. Be sure and have the correct change when boarding streetcars for there is frequently no ticket collector. Collection boxes are usually found in the rear of cars.

By Train

Trains within Poland run on regular schedules but service is rather infrequent, so if you have a flight schedule fly wherever possible. On the main routes, trains are usually electrified or diesel. In case you have a layover some place keep in mind that most railway stations in Poland maintain all night service in their restaurants.

Sleeping car tickets may be obtained at ORBIS offices. Coach tickets for short trips can be picked up at railroad stations, but you had better know some Polish or take along an interpreter. Be sure that you book sleeping car space in advance through ORBIS; trains, particularly overnight runs, are usually jammed. During July and August and during the winter holiday season (end of December) advance reservations are particularly necessary.

By Boat

Coastal and inland steamer service is maintained throughout the summer months. A trip between Sopot and the Hel Peninsula proved most enjoyable for me. I only wish that boat schedules might be posted in one other language in addition to Polish. It took three trips to the pier at Sopot before I understood that boat service had been interrupted for two days! Trips along the Vistula and Elblag Canal can prove most delightful.

By Air

LOT, The Polish national airline, operates daily flights between all the principal cities of the country. Planes flown are generally Soviet-build Ilyushins; service is good and the staff are well-trained and courteous.

ORBIS

Responsible for every facet of the tourist's stay in Poland. Founded in 1923, ORBIS presently controls outright hotels, boarding houses, restaurants and bars. Theater tickets, tours, tickets for trains, buses and boats are available through ORBIS offices to be found in hotels, train stations and airports. ORBIS also maintains money exchange facilities throughout the country. ORBIS headquarters in Warsaw at ul. Bracka 16 are largely devoted to administrative functions and the offices on the main floor seem largely concerned with the travel activities of Polish citizens. Your inquiries should be directed to the Visitors' reception center located in the Europejski Hotel (Krakowskie Przedmiescie 13) directly across the street from the Hotel Bristol.

ORBIS receptionists in Warsaw are pleasant, hard-working and eager to be of service, but I was not impressed by ORBIS personnel located in bureaus outside the capital. Unfortunately, I left Poland with the impression that ORBIS does not really take the tourist's well-being to heart. ORBIS personnel function adequately but are aloof and do not go out of their way to be of service.

ORBIS could increase its effectiveness by having more multi-lingual personnel in its bureaus, particularly outside of Warsaw. I was forever running into receptionists and clerks who not only could not speak English but also seemed unable to speak any other foreign language in acceptable fashion. The activities of ORBIS personnel situated outside of Warsaw seem frequently to usurp the prerogatives of the regular hotel employees, resulting in more than the normal amount of confusion at hotel reception desks. ORBIS should clarify for the benefit of hotel employees, the ORBIS staff and guests alike which functions are to be performed by the representatives of ORBIS and which are the prerogatives of the hotel administration.

ORBIS, which controls the path to a closer relationship between United States tourists and the average Polish citizen, seems to be lacking any depth of understanding of its own business, which is primarily that of encouraging tourism. At the present time ORBIS certainly makes little effort to encourage the foreign visitor's interest in revisiting Poland.

As indicated above in the section entitled "Visas and Customs," tourists are not granted visas unless they purchase ORBIS coupons to cover room and board expenses for the length of their proposed visit.

Before you leave the United States your travel agent will provide you with a voucher or vouchers indicating that you have paid so many dollars for each night's accommodation in Poland. The names of your hotels will be noted and the class of accommodations paid for. The single voucher must be surrendered to the ORBIS representative in the first hotel or town in which you have hotel reservations; or in the case of individual vouchers, to that hotel for which the specific voucher is intended. In the event that you enter Poland with only one hotel voucher (which would of course cover meals as well) you will receive zlotys or coupons in the total amount to cover all your rooms and meals during your entire trip. This sum in zlotys will be the equivalent of the amount you paid your travel agent prior to your departure (the agent's fee naturally deducted). However you should enter Poland with separate vouchers for the individual hotels, fewer zlotys will change hands as each hotel will automatically deduct from your voucher the price of the room while providing you with meal coupons or zlotys to cover meals in the hotel for the length of your visit in that town. If you enter the country with a single voucher covering all rooms and meals you had better provide yourself with an extra copy of the voucher from your travel agent because the original will remain with the first ORBIS representative you meet after crossing the border. In the event of individual vouchers applicable to specific hotels you will of course be covered by always having the needed voucher in hand. This latter plan seems preferable to me and I recommend that you ask your travel agent to provide a separate voucher for each hotel on your itinerary.

Funds paid to your travel agent are allocated by ORBIS to the hotels in which you have reserved space. It is not advisable to stay at a hotel other than that one where rooms have been reserved or in any way to alter your itinerary. Keep to your original travel program. Re-scheduling can be worked out once you are in the country, but believe me it involves considerable book work on the part of all concerned.

HOTEL RATES AND ACCOMMODATIONS

The best hotels in Poland have been set aside by ORBIS for the almost exclusive use of foreign visitors. Naturally, such hotels have restaurants, bars, car hire services, theater ticket desks, money exchange booths, etc. ORBIS has also designated certain hotels in every city (sometimes the only good hotel in the town) as a kind of reception center for incoming foreigners. Here you can reserve room in an ORBIS hotel should you not already be in possession of a reservation. If you should be in Warsaw and in need of a hotel reservation, contact the ORBIS personnel at the Grand Hotel ul Krucza 28.

In ORBIS hotels, clothes may be laundered (see maid), clothes pressed but not dry cleaned, shoes cleaned, rail and air tickets reserved and theater seats engaged. In Warsaw, at least, there are usually doormen to assist you with baggage; room service is available. The Warsaw hotels also boast quite a variety of restaurants, bars, kawiarnias (coffee houses) and other pleasant public rooms. Look for the word Club in the lobby or on the mezzanine of hotels in the capital; in this semi-private room you can find American and British newspapers (albeit slightly dated!) and you may entertain in a quiet fashion guests whom you would rather not invite upstairs.

I have toured or slept in the majority of deluxe or first class hotels in Poland; I know what these establishments are prepared to offer you. I urge that you not expect the "ne plus ultra" in accommodations and that you stick to the establishments recommended herein. Hotels in Poland are generally either new (and therefore quite stark) or old and in need of refurnishing. You will find few "homey" type surroundings. The hotel in Poland is less a center of civic interest than simply an establishment for the housing of the visitor.

Hotels in Poland are classed as "S" (for Superior), class I and class II. There are also class III hotels but I recommend them only to the younger crowd on a shoestring who can put up with dormitory rooms without running water. There are only three "S" category hotels: the Europejski and Grand Hotels in Warsaw and the Grand Hotel in Sopot. Price per person in these three hotels, with board, is about $12.50 per day. As previously stated, though you are obliged to book reservations in Poland on the basis of lodging plus three meals a day, you will not be required to eat these meals in the hotel in which you are lodged unless you elect to use the food coupons offered by the hotel. All "S" category accommodations have private bathrooms.

Class I accommodations also include private baths and cost about $10 with full board. A class II room without bath costs $7.50. Apartments can run as high as 160 zl. (figure 24 zl. to the dollar) for one person; for two persons up to 240 zl. A single room with private bath, up to 80 zl.; with shower, 90 zl. Double with private bath runs, around 160 zl. ("S" category). Beds in dormitories cost 30 zl. and when you trip down around the hall for a bath you are charged 10 zl. "per plunge." During the summer season at Gdansk and Sopot and during the International Fair at Poznan, hotel rates rise as much as 50 per cent. Come time for winter sports in Zanopane, hotel prices there increase 25 per cent. This higher rate also prevails in the summer hiking season in Zanopane. A 50 zl. "city tax" is usually added to your bill.

On the following pages we will discuss the specifics of the more prominent hotels in Poland, those in which you will most likely stay during your journey. Hotels controlled by ORBIS will be indicated by an asterisk. Three hotels managed by ORBIS, not outlined here in detailed fashion, are located in the towns of Bydgoszcz, Lodz and Plock. I did not tour these hotels personally.

When exchanging your food and lodging vouchers purchased in America you will receive, as well as food coupons, a hotel coupon covering your night's stay in the hotel in which you have reserved. The hotel reception desk will take this coupon immediately after you have exchanged your Stateside voucher with the ORBIS representative. With that your room is paid. The next morning (or whenever you plan to leave) you need only turn in your key and leave the hotel. This assumes, of course that you have had no charges beyond meals and lodging. Such items as phone calls, drinks in your room, etc., must naturally, be paid for separately. One coupon covers one night's lodging. The value of your voucher and the value of the coupons are related. Your travel agent should not issue vouchers for more than the actual total cost of each night's lodging plus your daily food allowance. Should you not have hotel or food coupons, your hotel bill is to be paid at the time of your departure.

Should you plan to spend a considerable time in Poland, say two weeks or more, give some thought to making deluxe or first class reservations for only the first days of your stay, and arranging for tourist class accommodations for the remainder of your visit in hotels that also provide deluxe or first class space. Once you are in Poland you can upgrade your reservations and take advantage of the bonus rate in the process. Of course, this approach carries with it the risk that deluxe or first class hotel space may not be available when requested.

I suggest that you do not book deluxe accommodations except in

Warsaw and possibly Krakow. Throughout Poland first class space is very adequate. Should you be going to Warsaw or Krakow (and who would wish to miss these interesting cities?), a request for deluxe accommodations will insure you larger rooms, more elaborate bathing facilities, fancier quarters. But here again first class is acceptable. Under no circumstances book deluxe for your entire trip through Poland. Except in the large towns and one or two resorts, deluxe accommodations simply do not exist, so you will either be excluded from many towns due to your request for such space or will overpay the American travel agent and find yourself in Poland with the extra *zlotys* which ORBIS representatives will be required to return to you in the absence of deluxe accommodations at certain towns along your route. By such action not only will you lose out on the bonus coupons, but will also end up with unwanted Polish currency.

When hotel reservations are confirmed, full payment must be made for the entire duration of your stay. In the event that your reservations are to be cancelled, the travel agency will send a Telex to the Eastern European country concerned requesting cancellation of space. For this service you will be required to pay a fee and will, in all likelihood, lose a quarter to one half of the monies paid depending on the speed with which your cancellation is received. You should, therefore, make every effort to avoid any change in your Eastern European travel program.

Room service in Polish hotels? In Warsaw, okay. If you can make a connection with the kitchen enabling you to place your order. And, assuming the connection is made, let's hope that you are not faced with a language problem. If the telephone number for room service is not posted in your room, contact the receptionist or "nail" the maid who will be most likely lurking somewhere along the corridor outside of your room. Once in contact with the waiter, shriek: "*Herbata* (tea) — *chleb*(bread) — *dzem*(jam)!" Now, if you insist on a more American meal and have the courage to "press on" in Polish, you might try "*smynka-jujko*," at which point the waiter will probably ask you "How?" you wish your eggs; and then my friend, you are on your own! In provincial hotels—in fact, even in many larger towns, you must be prepared to "go down" for breakfast.

The electric current generally used in the larger hotels throughout the country is 220 volts at 50 cycles. However, I noticed in my hotel room in Warsaw that the current used was 110. Therefore, I would suggest that if you use an electric razor you provide yourself with one which can be regulated for either 110 or 220 volts. In an effort to find an outlet in which to plug my razor cord, I have moved beds, desks, couches, wardrobes and have often gone unshaven. Suffice to say that arrangements for electric shaving are nebulous at best. If you do not find an outlet which permits you to use your normal razor plug, I would suggest that you contact the maid who will provide you with an adapter. Quite frequently the hotel management will permit you to keep the adapter in your room until your departure from the hotel.

When checking into a hotel, state your name and on request present your passport and hotel coupons; the former will be returned the next day. Prior to my most recent trip to Poland I had heard rumors that on occasion confirmed space is not available when the would-be guest arrives. The rumors are true! Space is frequently not reserved even though previously confirmed. On such occasions I can only advise that you raise the dickens and take another acceptable room while demanding that on the following day the proper space as confirmed be made available to you. A bit of controlled temperament can on such occasions prove quite rewarding.

Residence cards are now employed by the principal hotels in Warsaw. When checking in you will be handed a wallet-sized blue and white paper folder which will list your name, hotel, rate, date of arrival and room number. This card must be presented when requesting your key. Don't lose it. This residence card will also list important hotel telephone numbers, such as housekeeper, room service, how to place long distance phone calls, etc. The reception desk in the large hotels will be willing to arrange theater tickets, movie tickets, make reservations in local restaurants, etc., at your request.

Polish regulations require citizens of that proud country to bid their hosts adieu following any late night divertissement. They are not permitted to pass the night in any hotel or lodging place within the district in which they are domiciled. So better plan your evening's fun with the thought in mind that taxis are scarce, buses run infrequently late at night, the late night air is cool and Poles who live in the immediate area of your hotel cannot remain on the premises even if you offer to pay for a room or for an extra bed. The Polish tourist authorities are in the process of establishing or refurbishing small inns all over the country for the convenience of travelers by bus and private car. These units will be much the same design with small restaurants downstairs and dormitory-type bedrooms upstairs. Each will specialize in food of the region and most likely offer same in cafeteria style. The atmosphere here will be informal; a blessing for the travel-weary. All the inns will carry the blue sign "Turysta" or "Zajazo Turystyceny." Polish authorities soon intend to issue a map on which will be noted the location of all such eating establishments which will number 250 before the construction program ends.

At present there are no motels in Poland. Without a doubt, prodded by the impetus of similar type accommodations in other Middle European countries, Poland will soon provide motel units for tourists. The nearest thing I found were some bungalows outside of Leba, near the seashore. I have not seen the interior of these accommodations but understand they are small, brightly painted wooden structures, sleeping two persons. Full pension rates per person in a "bungalow" for two about $3.50. In a unit sleeping four, the rate per person is about $3. Rates have been established on the basis of 8 *AL.* occupancy.

CAMPING

There are approximately 47 camping sites in Poland at the present time. These are located in the main throughout the Mazurion region of northeastern Poland, an area of lakes, pines and rolling hills; many are also to be found throughout the central and western parts of the country. There are two camp sites in the Carpathian Mountain area of southeast Poland.

Camp sites are scenic sections of ground where tents may be erected under the most informal circumstances. It is safe to assume that the tourist is expected to provide for all his needs at these camp sites. Electricity is provided at some such sites; caretakers are usually housed nearby and the location of the camping sites is marked by the usual international road sign showing the outline of a tent and trailer in black against a white background. The areas are fenced off. These camp sites are usually located along the main highways which run through the resort areas. The campsites at Rusiane, Mikolajki and Gteycko (in the Mazurion Lakes region) are particularly well situated for persons who enjoy swimming, fishing and water sports. To enter the camp sites you will be expected to show your passport.

In some of the tourist areas controlled by the PTTK (the Polish Tourist Association), vacation equipment may be rented. The "lending stations" are generally located near the tourist cabins and tourist hostels scattered about resort areas. However, should you undertake a camping trip, I urge that you come prepared for all emergencies rather than expect to rent camping equipment, for there is the possibility that no lending station may exist at the camp site of your choosing.

Persons who stay at a camp site *with their own equipment* a minimum of seven days can avail themselves of the "tourist" rate of about $2.50 per person per day, provided they are able to pay in zloyts.

SPAS

Health spas in Poland feature cures lasting four weeks and costing approximately $6.50 per day may be enjoyed at the following locations: Inwroclaw, Arknica, Kudowm, Polanica, Busko and Skncajscie. (There may be one or two other spas in Poland.) Rates cover room and board, medical care, treatments, necessary medicines, entertainment and excursions. The cures begin on the first and third day of each month and are never shorter than three weeks in length; they may be extended beyond four weeks on the advice of the physician. Adults taking a cure may *not* be accompanied by children.

DINING

Polish food is inclined toward the heavy side; lots of sauces, stewed vegetables and meat, thick soups. A dietitian would abdicate all responsibility and most likely join the pack. Dumplings stuffed with cabbage; sausages; smoked salmon (for a price); "bigos" (sauerkraut stuffed with meat); borsch; mushrooms in every possible culinary custume; goose stomachs (mushroom sauce!); calf's foot jelly (it is quite probable that I passed this up!); smoked goose breasts; rolled steaks; cooked tongue (do you get the impression the Poles make use of every part of the beast?) and game of every dimension: hare; roast wild boar; deer! For dessert: gingerbread; jelly-filled doughnuts; fruit; cheese. The pastries can be exceptionally good.

Smoked meats are usually quite good, as we know in this country from experience with Polish hams. Food is certainly varied. It is in the preparation that matters often go astray. So-called international cuisine is an abomination in every country; the very phrase should warn the customer that the cook was tempting fate by straying from his own special field of culinary art. And it is this international monkey business that one most frequently finds in large hotels all over Eastern Europe not just in Poland.

Food is not inexpensive in Poland; meat, fish and poultry are particularly expensive. Naturally, you will be eating in the "better" restaurants, so be prepared to pay a fairly good sum for your meals. If you stick to soups, salads, cheese and the like, you can hold down the budget a bit. When you want to live it up, order roast goose; it is delicious and a specialty.

Wine is quite expensive so you may find yourself drinking vodka with your meals: it's a good chaser for the rather heavy food. Polish wines are not exceptional. I recall the honeyed vodka called *Soplica* that was excellent as an after-dinner drink. Fact is, we went through two bottles! Polish vodka is outstanding! The dry vodka, known as *Vodka Dyborowa*, is good before and during meals. Perhaps you would enjoy the sweet, honeyed *Krupnik* as a cordial. Bulgarian *Pliska* brandy is also available and not nearly so expensive as its French counterparts.

Restaurants open for breakfast, close late in the evening. Some hotels have several restaurants and use one for breakfast, another for lunch and still another for dinner. But few hotels in Poland have such elaborate dining facilities and generally all three meals are served in the same room. Breakfasts are, by and large, well served and very tasty. Try the delicious Polish ham with eggs, boiled, fried or scrambled; rolls, jam and tea. Some hotels have orange juice. Price for a full breakfast comes to roughly $1.25. Don't plan to eat lunch before one. Figure on not less than an hour for the meal, even if you are having a light lunch. As for dinner, plan on eating about seven at the earliest. The hours of 7:30 to 9:00 P.M. find restaurant tables fully occupied. In small hotels it is better to be a bit early; in big city hotels I would not plan to go down much before 7:30. Many restaurants in Poland are so large, drafty and lonesome-looking that you will feel like a waif (possibly with a lost appetite) before the crowd arrives.

When you want breakfast, tea or a cognac before retiring, head for a kawiarnia (coffee shop). These pleasant, bustling places are always crowded, especially from noon onward, might be said to be the center of Polish social life. If you prefer to avoid a heavy noon meal, see what your local kawiarnia is offering. You might get by with a "soup 'n' sandwich."

Meals at ORBIS "S" (Superior) first class hotels cost as follows: Breakfast about 40 zl., lunch 75 zl. and dinner 25 zl. In other words, dinners in the better establishments cost about $2.00.

When you exchange your American travel vouchers (which state that you have paid a certain amount for room and board), you will most likely be given food coupons which are used as follows: the value (in zlotys) of each coupon is printed on the back. When the check is presented at the end of the meal you must give the waiter vouchers equally in the amount of the bill. He will give you zlotys if change is due you. I recall one meal when I used a dinner, breakfast and lunch voucher in one swoop! Some hotels along your route will automatically hand you the food coupons; others will inquire whether you wish coupons or cash. Keep in mind that you do have a choice and can request cash. Coupons are valid only at the hotel by which they are issued. If you are using cash instead of coupons circulate a bit. Chances are good that your hotel will have one of the better kitchens, but the atmosphere may well be "poisonous." This is to say that Polish hotel restaurants run toward the cavernous. Then too, ORBIS seems to have a penchant for large tables seating six to eight persons. During my stay in Poland I was very frequently obliged to occupy a "below the salt" position at some table at the opposite end of which sat a Polish family or some other "lost tribe" of uncomfortable foreign tourists.

In Poland I found the waiters to be rather casual in both dress and serving habits; moreover, they are incredibly slow. Even in the best restaurants I sensed that the employees had not had sufficient training. Meals sort of come at you in a rather distracting fashion; quite often soup and meat arrive at the same time. And things disappear disconcertingly, also. Once when I ordered a bottle of wine (it is expensive!) and failed to finish the bottle that evening, I asked the waiter to reserve it for me until the next day. Well, ORBIS has evidently failed to explain to restaurant personnel that the wine that waiters consume in the kitchen after hours has been paid for by the guests. So my policy is now either to drink up the wine, or, with chin up and shoulders erect, to walk out of the restaurant with the partially consumed bottle under my arm. Some may take me for a crook, but at least I have saved the wine.

You should not expect to be "seated" by a headwaiter when entering a restaurant in Poland. The usual approach is to leave your coat in the check room, then stride directly into the restaurant. See an empty table in a location acceptable to you? So okay—sit down! No table? Then eventually a table is emptied, dive, don't walk to take possession. Never mind whether it is cleared or not. This is a question of "possession being nine points of the law"; the table can be cleared while you look over the menu. Are there headwaiters? Yes, quite a few of them, in fact; but their job is evidently to hand out menus and to watch the waiters "wait." And don't rely on that sly maneuver called "I'll wait in the bar." You'll wait most of the night, for the headwaiter to whom you addressed the remark will most likely forget, or will not understand the fine point of your remark to begin with. A more aggressive person will end up at the empty table. And what if there are no tables for two? So take a table for four or six. Need a table for four? Not available? There's a table seating ten—sit down! In short, you are in a restaurant to eat. Accommodate yourself as best you can. It's every man for himself!

In Polish restaurants be prepared to share your table with another person for this custom is more the rule than the exception outside of Warsaw. Enjoy your aperitif, order your dinner, enjoy the meal (take along a magazine or a book to encourage your composure!), pay the bill and leave, with a parting nod to your table companions. Don't feel you have to engage a stranger (particularly a couple) in conversation. (Chances are there will be a language problem anyway.) In short, mind your own business! For the average Pole, a "night on the town" is a special occasion reserved for the entertainment of his guests, not a talkative stranger. Let the Pole (or the couple) engage you in conversation, if he wishes. And as a postscript to this paragraph, please keep in mind that your manners, clothes, jewelry, speech habits—in fact just about everything about you—will be of intense interest to your tablemates as well as to other Poles seated about you. So understand that whether they speak to you or not you are probably being studied in an informal, friendly fashion by someone in your immediate surroundings. The fact that a surprising number of Poles speak at least a little English should alert you (if "alerted" you must be!) to the fact that it is unwise to comment on Polish habits, food, dress, etc., in a public room. Your opinions about the host country are best kept to yourself until you are in private, or, better yet, out of the country.

It must truthfully be stated, with regret, that I did not leave Poland with any outstanding good impressions of Polish cooking. Now there will be Americans of Polish descent who will cry out in insulted fashion, pointing in reproach to the sumptious meals prepared by Grandmother. Well, it happens there's a Polish-born gentleman attached by marriage to my family at the present time and I know how he speaks of the almost Providential Polish kitchens of some years back. But let's face it! I visited Poland twice, ate in restaurants large and small all over the country and continue to state that I did not find the Polish cooking presently available to the foreigner particularly appetizing or in the least memorable. I sense that home-cooked meals in Poland may be less elaborate in style but much more tantalizing taste-wise — nutrition-wise. But I had no occasion to eat at home, so I must speak for those of you who, like I, will remain in the commercialized atmosphere of a hotel dining room.

I can recall having had very good meals at the following restaurants: Hotel Grand (Warsaw); the Krokodyi Restaurant (Warsaw); Hotel Francuski (Krakow); Hotel Bazar (Poznan); Hotel Grand (Sopot); Hotel Monopol (Katowice); and the Poraj Restaurant (Zakopane). These seven restaurants represent less than a quarter of the total number of Polish eating spots that I have frequented. I must add that I ate well in other restaurants, however, the meals in other locales were nothing to write home about. There is, in fact, one restaurant in Warsaw named the Balaton that is a disaster. Why one prominent author includes this joint (and it is a joint) in his guide covering Poland I cannot understand.

All in all, eating in Poland is something of a hit or miss affair. Later on in this section I will indicate just what to expect when you enter various restaurants in towns throughout Poland. It is oft times something of an experience. Reference tippings, make it 10 per cent; and when the service is slow skip the tip. It is unnecessary to tip the headwaiter unless he has performed some special service.

When driving from one town to another, do not plan to stop somewhere on the way, for Poland at present just isn't prepared to feed the touring foreign motorist. Instead ask your waitress at breakfast to boil a few extra eggs, they buy some pastry, maybe a bit of cheese, some bread and fill a thermos with hot tea. There are many delightful spots along the road where one may enjoy lunch. However, you might inquire whether there is by chance one of the delightful new regional inns (discussed in the Hotel Section) on the way to your destination; if so, your meal problem is solved.

SHOPPING

Gift purchases may be made in a number of shops honoring the ORBIS coupons, for example, the Jubiler shops (silver and jewelry); DESA shops (antique); but first determine which articles may be exported from the country. "The export of works of art from Poland requires among other things, an opinion of the Conservator of Historic Art objects." Books and publications before 1945 may *not* be removed from Poland. If you are an antique dealer ask for the *List of Prohibited Exports*. Copelia or many of the small ORBIS gift shops are actually your best bet for folk art objects. I would also urge that you visit some of Warsaw's large department stores; interesting items may frequently be purchased there or in the small shops located nearby along the main shopping streets. Warsaw's principal shopping center (and the department stores) is located on or near Jerozolimskie Avenue, some fifteen minutes from the Hotel Bristol and Europejski. A walk from these hotels to the shopping center will take you past many interesting stores. Should you be at the Grand Hotel, when leaving the entrance turn right and walk two blocks and you'll be in the principal shopping district.

KOMIS STORES are maintained largely for Polish citizens who have something they wish to sell, usually a new article and one most likely sent by relatives in the States. When sold, Komis takes a 15% commission and returns the remainder of the previously established sale price to the owner. Tourists can also make purchases here, although the Polish Government makes no effort to promote these shops.

PKO (or *Polska Kasa Opieki* shops) are located in every large city, in most of the large tourist hotels, at entrance points into Poland, etc. Here one may buy items of Polish and foreign fabrication. Prices are reasonable; payment must be made in a foreign currency (preferably dollars).

In the PKO one finds all sorts of goods of foreign manufacture, ranging from whisky to motor oil. I suggest you arrive in Poland adequately equipped with these items, but if you run out, don't hesitate to visit the nearest PKO store.

I avoid these "dollar-earner" stores except for purchasing products of Polish origin. Very high quality Vodka is available at very reasonable prices, well below what such items cost in Western Europe.

A number of shops display goods from other of the Middle European countries, e.g. Bulgaria, Romania, etc. Should you not plan to visit these countries here is a very good chance to buy some interesting little souvenirs. All in all, the broad avenues of Warsaw, the narrow shopping streets of Gdansk, Poznan and Krakow make interesting, delightful "walking tours." This is the only way really to see these fascinating old cities.

TOURS

Group travel is naturally less expensive than touring individually. Rates vary according to the length of the tour, class of accommodations, number of participants and so forth. All foreign tours fall under the direction of ORBIS the Polish Travel Office. Such tours would travel through Poland by train or bus, often arriving by plane or train.

There are at least three main tours available to guests of ORBIS. Prices run from $100 to $165 (double); $127 to $188 (single). These rates include first class board, room and travel facilities. Towns included are Warsaw, Krakow, Zakopane, Szestochowa and on the more expensive trip, Poznan.

The tours referred to above can be made by individuals "any day throughout the year."

Tours beginning on specific dates for larger groups of people cover the same towns, last from six to eleven days (the independent tours last a week to nine days) and cost from $75 to $165 (per person). The most expensive of these tours (called "Grandeur of Poland") provides a fairly good look at towns in east-central and south-central Poland. To the above prices must of course be added your fare to Poland (about $680 by air from New York in high season), and miscellaneous expenses such as laundry, insurance, wines, etc.

To participate in any such tours you must comply with the requirements outlined in the section entitled "Visas and Customs." Guides are furnished by ORBIS. Perhaps for your first visit to Poland you would prefer to participate in a group tour, but bear in mind that your itinerary will be limited if for no other reason than that many areas are simply not equipped to handle large groups of people.

All tourists to Warsaw please note the excellent tour originating at the ORBIS central reception office in the Europejski Hotel each morning at ten. The three hour tour covers the entire city and its immediate environs and costs about $3.

GUIDES

I do not feel that the service of a guide is necessary in Poland. However, I recommend that tourists employ a guide in the larger cities, particularly if they do not speak any language but English. Tourist groups touring cities and towns other than Warsaw are directed by guides who usually speak either French or German as a second language. I took a delightful if somewhat uninformative tour of Krakow's Wawel palace under the leadership of a guide who spoke Polish to some guests, Italian to others.

My advice is to cross the country on your own and to pick up a guide in the larger towns. Local guides in any case are more interesting than those you might "import" from another area. Of course, if you are a member of a tourist group traveling through Poland this problem is automatically solved. Once in a large town take the local tour if you wish (after first determining whether the guide speaks English) and then employ a private guide to re-visit those points you found most interesting.

Rates for guides "with a knowledge of a foreign language" run about $1.50 per hour. Naturally, if you take a guide cross-country you are obligated to cover his board and lodging costs, as well as the cost of his transportation home.

One should not forget that guides employed throughout an entire journey can describe much of the local scenery, monuments, castles, etc. They can also tend to isolate you from the people. If you speak some German, Russian or Polish I would certainly keep guides to a minimum. Half the fun of any trip is really getting out and meeting people. This becomes difficult with a guide continuously under foot.

AUTO MAPS

AGPOL, the foreign Trade Advertising and publishing Company division of the Polish Government, has published an excellent series of books giving specific routings, maps, descriptions of towns and historical data on all Poland. The series is called Poland-Travel Guide and is available in seven volumes. The paper-covered books of approximately 90 pages each are nicely illustrated and provide a good indication of routings (particularly through cities). Each book covers one specific topic or section of the country. For example, one provides the reader with a very thorough review of general information about Poland, including such items as geographical features, the theater, art and literature. It contains many beautiful colored illustrations of Polish manners of dress from past centuries as well as some instruction in the Polish language. This book gives an excellent insight into the tourist's Poland. Another volume is concerned only with central and eastern Poland; a third covers northern Poland, and so on. The sixth book in the series provides the tourist with a review of regulations which apply to him during his stay in that country. I have found these books very helpful and recommend them to all prospective tourists of Poland. Inquire of the Polish Embassy in Washington about how to obtain them.

The Poles have also issued a very good road map with a blue cover on which has been printed the words "Polska" and "auto map" in five languages. The map is easily read and nicely printed. It covers the present boundaries of Poland, disputed or not. On the rear side of the folding map are specific routings through the principal cities of Poland. The map is available at ORBIS offices.

When purchasing maps of Middle Europe in Western Europe bear in mind that many cartographers have hesitated to situate present-day borders as the latter were determined by the postwar conferences

(Yalta, Potsdam, *et. al.*) As a result you will find maps that indicate that the Baltic coast of Poland is controlled by the Germans. Using one of such maps I planned to cross from Czechoslovakia into Poland but found Germany where I had understood Poland to be presently located! Wroclaw was still called Breslau on the map I purchased in Zurich. So be cautious! Such maps, while quite logical in the absence of a German "peace conference," can be dangerous as well as confusing. Using them a non-European could quite easily think himself in West Germany and innocently blunder over the border into the east zone. A visa to the east zone of Germany plus such a map could land the traveler in Poland. Some day borders on such maps may be marked "Temporary-rending settlement of National boundaries," but in the meantime I urge you to use maps distributed by the countries in which you plan to tour. Peace conference or no, the fact remains that the borders are recognized in their present locations by the governments of Central and Eastern Europe.

TAKING PHOTOGRAPHS

Each visitor is permitted to bring into Poland one still camera, a movie camera and a limited amount of film. You won't have trouble importing such equipment as long as it doesn't have commercial connotations. A notation may be made in your passport specifying that you possess a camera or two, the purpose being to discourage the sale of the article in Poland. Film may be exported (undeveloped) and I advise you to have your films developed at home or in Western Europe.

You may not take photographs of military bases, army or police barracks, naval installations (including harbors). No photographs are permitted from aircraft flying over Polish territory. All this, with the possible exception of the last, seems rather logical.

HUNTING, FISHING, AND HORSEBACK RIDING

There exists quite a variety of animals to be hunted in Poland. The hunting seasons are very carefully controlled due to the decreased number of animals following World War II. Therefore I urge you to check with ORBIS representatives as to the seasons when the various animals may be hunted.

Roebuck is common in the areas around Poznan and Bydgoszoz. Roedeer are to be found in the eastern areas of the country, though some of the best shoots have been held in central Poland. Wild boar are found throughout the country and must be shot exclusively with bullets. It is, incidentally, forbidden to hunt during the night. Fallow deer are poorly represented in Poland, though there is a limited hunting season in the regions around Katowice and Cpole. Lynx can be hunted in a limited season (November till March) in the Carpathian regions and in the east. The wolf is found to be in the out-of-the-way areas of the eastern region; there is no closed season on this animal. Foxes are found throughout the country; the season is October to February 20.

Among the birds, the partridge is the most common. Pheasants may be hunted during an extended winter season. The capercailzie (males only) may be shot during the mating season which lasts from approximately April to mid-May. Other birds include the woodcock, wild duck, wild geese and black cock.

Cost to the hunter for board, lodging and interpreter runs from $6 to $10 per day depending on the size of the group. For groups of 6 to 14 persons, the cost per day is $5 for each person, plus $100.00 extra for the entire group. Prices for the individual game killed are listed in ORBIS brochures.

Rather strict rules govern fishing in the lakes and rivers of Poland, and so I would contact the Polish Anglers Association before attempting this sport. Moreover, rules covering angling change from county to county, so be certain you are well-informed by local officials. Salmon, trout, perch and pike are to be found throughout the country. No sturgeon may be fished. Hostels and boating stations are available for the convenience of fishermen.

Foreigners wishing to fish in Poland's inland waters must apply for a permit at the district Anglers Association. Permission must also be obtained for deep-sea fishing in the Baltic; contact officials at Gdynia, Skczecin or Koszalin. Angling in private or state-owned waters also requires permission.

Care for a relaxed, refreshing canter along the beach in the soft light of a summer's dusk? Near the Baltic Sea resort town of Sopot you can enjoy this fine sport at a local riding school, under the guidance of well-trained instructors. Riding holidays can also be arranged at the various stud farms in the area and throughout Poland.

To obtain information concerning the riding classes or cross-country tours, inquire at the reception desk of the Grand Hotel in Sopot or at the local ORBIS agency. Arrangements for cross-country rides can also most likely be made through the main ORBIS reception center in Warsaw. Prices for these rides are reasonable.

CABLES, WIRES, PHONE CALLS, AND MAIL

An ordinary letter will travel to Western Europe by regular post at a cost of 2.50 zl; a postcard, 1.50 zl. Airmail (inside Europe) costs .90 groszy for every 20 grams. Airmail to the United States and Canada costs 1.50 zl. for every five grams.

The minimum rate for telegrams within Poland is 6 zlotys. Urgent wires travel at double this rate. Local telephone calls from booths costs 50 groszy. Telephone calls to Western Europe can be made from almost all points within Poland in a space of 15 minutes to half an hour. The cost is reasonable.

Mail service in Poland is terrible. Figure on a big delay in all your mail coming to Poland. In the first place, all international mail goes through Warsaw. Mail is very frequently opened and occasionally a censor's stamp appears on the outside of the envelope. Quite frequently mail is not delivered, simply returned to the sender. I suggest that a person traveling in Poland either establish one or two hotels as mailing addresses or have mail held *outside* of Poland until his arrival. The latter course is preferable in my opinion.

WARSAW

The visitor must keep in mind that much that seems old in Poland is actually new. The port city of Gdansk (Danzig) was seventy per cent destroyed during the war; Warsaw 86 per cent destroyed, Wroclaw (Breslau) a ruin. The Poles set about with infinite patience to rebuild their cities at the same location and in the same style of architecture. Therefore, large sections of the cities that you will see seem untouched by war, just as they stood in the 16th century, while in fact the actual construction of the buildings was completed during the past decade.

In Warsaw, there are narrow, dimly lighted streets; cobblestones; archways framed by leafy vines; a late night's mist settling over an old market place where during the 14th century the Dukes of Masovia lived.

It should be added here that many bombed buildings will remain until a determination is made as to whether the building is to be reconstructed as a national monument or torn down, its bricks to be used for new units.

A statistic for those interested: of the 957 buildings of historical interest in Warsaw prior to World War II, 782 were totally destroyed; 141 were left in a state of semi-ruin. A total of 750,000 inhabitants of the city died between 1940 and 1945. All this is to say that today's Poland stands as a monument to that nation's past.

Sightseeing

There are many sights to see in Warsaw, not the least important those encountered on a casual walk through the main shopping area off Jerozolimski Avenue. The taxis are a bit shabby, the streetcars overly crowded, but throughout the city there is a certain verve, a dynamic sense of movement that must be felt to be understood.

While in Warsaw, I particularly enjoyed long walks through the city parks, along the crowded boulevards, and "tours." You will see many small coffee houses, soft drink stands or spots for a bit of revelry such as the vista of the Vistula from the Plac Zamkowy. Actually I found the openness of the city, combined with the animation of the people, stimulating. Be sure to hear the National Philharmonic. The Opera is sumptuous; see if you can locate a pair of tickets. Not easy!

Be sure to inquire at the ORBIS central reception about other interesting side trips which you may make individually or in groups in the Warsaw area.

A tour arranged by ORBIS through this proud city will cover many of the following sights:

UNKNOWN SOLDIER'S TOMB Set in a beautiful park near the Hotel Europejski.

THE OLD TOWN Not completely rebuilt. Contains many museums, the Basilica of Saint John, and Warsaw's cathedral.

BARBICON Originally built in the 15th century.

HOME OF MADAM CURIE The famous scientist once lived here.

PLAC ZAMKONY Brass statue of King Sigismund II built in 1644. Blown up by the Nazis, and restored in 1949. Nearby is the contemplated restoration site of the former Royal Palace.

CHURCH OF SAINT ANNE Frequently destroyed by fire, this church was restored in Baroque style in 1788. Note the altar and rococo organ.

WARSAW UNIVERSITY Here, too, are the Staszic Palace built in 1823, and the Kazimifrizowski Palace used as a royal summer residence.

NOWY SNIAT AVENUE Long, narrow, and so busy. Look for the *Belweder*, the former summer residence of Grand Duke Constantine of Russia (now headquarters of the Council of State).

LAZIENKI PARK A fine place for a summer's day's walk. Here is the Lazienkowski Palace, floating (it seems!) above a small lake, known also as The Palace on the Water. Also the Orangerie and the Island Theater dating from 1790, summer houses, statues and the Mysiewicki Palace, the site of numerous talks between the ambassadors of Red China and the United States. You might want to visit the Tenth Anniversary Stadium completed in 1955, seating 100,000 spectators. The stadium is unique as it has been quite literally constructed atop piles of rubble brought across the Vistula from the 1945 ruins of pre-war Warsaw.

MONUMENT TO THE HEROES OF THE GHETTO The ghetto itself has been totally replaced by modern apartments.

PALACE OF CULTURE AND SCIENCE A gift from the Soviet Union. This addition to the skyline of Warsaw can be seen from every section of the city.

MONUMENT TO THE HEROES OF THE CITY Across from the Opera.

KAMPINOS FOREST A national park area roughly an hour's drive from Warsaw. Here you will find sand dunes, oak and birch trees, and a thick undergrowth of juniper and hazel shrubs. Here, too, are defensive ramparts built on dunes, these fortifications having survived the uprisings of 1863 and the more recent German occupation of Poland from 1939 to 1944.

ZELAZOWA WOLA Home of Frederic Chopin. Here among charming gardens, woods and lakes you will see the house in which Chopin was born on February 22, 1810. Concerts of Chopin's music are given here on summer Sundays and holidays.

WILANOW PALACE Roughly a fifteen-minute bus ride outside of Warsaw. The 17th-century residence of King Jan Sobieski is truly a must for the foreign visitor. Though Warsaw was 86 per cent destroyed during the war, Wilanow remained intact and is the only state building surviving from past centuries. Dating from the early 17th century, Wilanow was constructed in the fashion of Versailles though it is a much more intimate, warm, livable structure. The palace was used as a residence through the 1930's. Numerous sections are given over to galleries where excellent portraits of Polish nobility are displayed. The remainder of Wilanow has been decorated in tasteful, traditional styles, giving a charming insight into Polish decorations, furnishings and the like from past centuries.

    A round-trip ride by taxi to Wilanow should not cost much more than three to four dollars. English-speaking guides are available at the Palace. Tours operate from the side entrance at the Palace every ten minutes from 10 A.M. until 3 P.M. The cost: 3 zl. Wilanow can be reached by train as well as by bus. Tours can be arranged through ORBIS though I personally preferred touring the Palace with small groups of individual tourists. You will be required to wear felt slippers over your shoes.

Taxicabs

Some drivers speak German or French; the majority can be depended upon to converse only in Polish. Therefore, ask the reception clerk to write down the proper address of your destination. This can be handed to the cab driver, thus saving you valuable minutes. Between 6:30 and 7:30 P.M. Warsaw's taxis seem to disappear from the streets. Keep this in mind should you have a six-thirty engagement. Along the way ask the hotel doorman to locate a cab for you.

The same applies for the trip home from a restaurant late in the evening. By late evening most cabs are off the streets. Don't leave any locale late in the evening expecting to "walk half way."

Since rates for taxis are so low, almost every citizen of Warsaw can take a cab for the slightest errands, for the shortest distance. Frequently it is necessary to line up at a designated place to wait for a cab. Taxi stands are located near most of the large hotels and throughout central sections of the city. Should you arrive at a taxi stand and find none available, simply take a position at the end of the queue. Usually your wait will not be too long for the distances are not great in Warsaw.

Hotels

EUROPEJSKI* Your visit to Warsaw will, in my opinion, be enhanced by a stay at Warsaw's leading hotel, the Europejski. The old world charm, the elegant lobby, the well-trained reception staff, attractive restaurant and efficient floor personnel staff make this hotel the best in Poland. Prices are high, a single running more than $10.00. The hotel is within easy reach of most of the main business and government offices of the Polish capital. Damaged during the war, the Europejski was rebuilt and modernized prior to its opening in 1962.

Off the lobby of the Europejski are a large restaurant, a cafe and, on the mezzanine, the hotel club where one may entertain visitors and read foreign magazines and newspapers. A hairdresser and coffee bar are off the main floor. The central reception desk of ORBIS, the Polish tourist agency, is on the ground floor. There are 278 rooms in the Europejski, 255 of which have private bathrooms. There are also two and three-room deluxe apartments. All rooms have hot and cold running water, central heating, telephone and radio. Bedrooms are decorated in modern fashion; apartments are period style. Rooms overlooking the large interior court are relatively quiet and pleasant, though dance music from the restaurant can prove a bother until midnight. Room service is prompt, breakfast particularly well served. Television is provided in some of the apartments. Laundry and pressing can be handled by the maid. Corridors are well lighted. There are small lounges located on each floor of the four-story building.

The restaurant, while serving tasty food moderately priced, is too barnlike and its modern furnishings are not in keeping with the overall appearance of the hotel. Service is good, however; the personnel acceptable. The restaurant is obviously geared to the evening; for there is a large dance floor, the orchestra playing during evening meals as weil as for after-dinner dancing. Should you be having lunch, table reservations are unnecessary. In the evening, reserve a table, for the room is popular and frequently very crowded. Men should wear business suits, and women should take along a sweater for the large room is drafty.

GRAND* The Grand, opened in 1958, is within a block of the main commercial center of Warsaw. A rather bleak structure, the Grand's 11 floors are reminiscent of a dormitory. There are 427 rooms, all with private bathroom. Businessmen take note: more than half of the rooms are singles. This hotel also provides 21 apartments for two persons, 28 apartments for one person. A no-nonsense lobby, functional to the extreme, is presided over by a well-managed reception desk.

The Grand is also the main ORBIS hotel reservation center where the visitor may reserve rooms in other cities of Poland.

To the right and left of the reception desk are the elevators, souvenir shops and money exchange desks. The hairdresser is nearby. At each end of the lobby are the entrances to the various restaurants and the cafe bar. Baggage assistance is available.

The price range at the Grand runs between 150 zl. and 300 zl., depending on the type of accommodation you select. All rooms are decorated in "mid-Thirties Modern." Rooms are not too appealing, but they are functional and convenient. Rooms and bathrooms are clean. Halls are wide and well lighted. For laundry and pressing service, contact your maid. Radios are available. There are telephones and room service.

Street noise is no particular factor here. Equidistant from all points of the city, the Grand is roughly a ten-minute walk from the U.S. Embassy. There is an indoor swimming pool.

Luncheon or dinner is served in either the large restaurant to the rear (where guests may enjoy variety acts in the evening) or in a small, more intimate restaurant to one side of the lobby. I recommend the latter. To the rear of the smaller restaurant is a nightclub where in the late, late evening music is furnished for dancing by a local jazz group. Menus in all the restaurants are in several languages. A number of the waiters understand English. Service, particularly in the smaller restaurant, is quite good. Meals at the Grand are tasty and well served, costing approximately $2.50 for one person. For the evening meal I would certainly reserve a table and be on time for reservations. I understand there is a cafe on the eleventh floor; meals are not served there. For breakfast, guests should visit the cafe off the lobby known as a "Kawiarnia." The breakfasts are hearty, promptly served and inexpensive. Planning a trip outside of Warsaw? Ask your waitress at breakfast to pack you a small lunch. Simply point to items on the menu you want to have included. Remember to provide a thermos for tea or coffee.

BRISTOL* Built between 1898 and 1901 by the Italian architect Marconi, one of the original owners of the Bristol was Ignacy Jan Paderewski. The Bristol is in central Warsaw, an extra dividend being its location directly opposite the main ORBIS reception center in the Hotel Europejski. The lobby is large and bleak, not at all inviting. Off the lobby are the restaurant, hairdresser and small bar. There is also a small banquet room, wine shop and kawiarnia. A gift shop and money exchange desk are situated near the main entrance to the hotel. Very limited parking facilities are available in front of the hotel.

Of the 248 rooms, 123 reportedly include bathrooms. Another estimate of the number of baths was 75. Tubs and toilets are so old they defy repair. For rooms without private facilities, public toilets are located on the main hall. Many rooms are located on an inside court and are frequently filled with kitchen-odors plus the pulsing late hour rhythms originating from the orchestra below. Furnishings are grim, in fact downright shabby. When reserving at the Bristol, make sure your request stipulates an outside room.

Room service is available, though usually for breakfast only. Breakfast costs between 50 and 75 cents including service.

I enjoyed a delicious lunch at the Bristol, but I must report the service, though pleasant, was very slow, the atmosphere mediocre. Menus are of the typical international variety including Hungarian, French and other Continental dishes.

WARZAWA Located on a large plaza in central Warsaw, the Warzawa is a monolithic, neoclassical structure which gives one the feeling of being lodged in the local jail. A small dark lobby. All rooms in the Warzawa are quite small and furnished in very simple fashion. I do not recommend this hotel though I would not hesitate to encourage you to try its restaurant.

The restaurant is again too large a room, with bright lights, dark corners, the patrons usually in varying degrees of dress. The entire decor reminded me of an operetta class 1880. The food is good and very tasty. The meals here cost approximately $1.75 which may include soup, an omelet, salad, cheese, beer and coffee. Waiters speak no English but some French.

Restaurants

BALATON This restaurant is listed in ORBIS travel folders as well as in other guides, but I state here unequivocally that it is a neighborhood restaurant of the meanest variety, serving food which I found inedible. Menus here are in Polish only. There is dancing. The restaurant is smoky, dark, crowded.

KROKODYI The Warsaw "Jockey Club," "Pump Room," etc. Located in the "Old Town" marketplace approximately 15 minutes' walk from the Hotel Europejski, 5 minutes by cab. It is somewhat difficult to find but once located, a delightful spot. Down a flight of stairs are four dining rooms, the best directly at the bottom of the stairs, near the orchestra; the next choice is the room to the left of the orchestra. Be sure you reserve ahead as the Krokodyi is one of the most fashionable dining and dancing spots in Warsaw. The food, service, and entire atmosphere of this place all are thoroughly delightful. Good dance orchestra. Dress well, though not in extreme clothing. The Krokodyi is not overly expensive compared with restaurants in the main hotels.

AMICA Also known rather familiarly as the "Jewish Restaurant," Amica is short on atmosphere and very long on food which is Kosher. Located in what seems to have been an abandoned air-raid shelter, this restaurant is approximately 10-minutes' walk from the Hotel Europejski. The entrance is not directly off the street but is tucked inside a small courtyard. A popular place; any person can point it out to you. Dress informally. The service, though rather slow due to a limited staff, is excellent. A four-piece orchestra plays for dancing.

SHANGHAI I did not visit this restaurant but all of Warsaw seems to approve. Both Chinese and Polish menus. It rates alongside Amica. Lunch and dinner. Not dressy!

RYCERSKA Quite near the Krokodyi, the Rycerska is located on Szeraki Dunaj Square in the Old Town. The food and service are good. The supper club atmosphere is pleasant. Dress well. Music for dancing. Reserve through your hotel reception desk.

HAMIENNE Enjoy breakfast or lunch in a quiet, noncommercial atmosphere, almost like a pleasant, private home. No dinners served. Don't try to reserve a table; the rule is "first come, first served."

CRYSTAL Hungarian cooking. I did not have an opportunity to visit this spot, but the Crystal is considered among Warsaw's best.

FUKIER No food served here. Fukier is a wine cellar located just a few doors from the Krokodyi. It closes at 10 P.M. Nice atmosphere, and the wines are good. Early evening and late afternoon are the best times to visit this spot.

There are a number of other restaurants and coffee houses in Warsaw which I could not visit. Some of them are mentioned in pamphlets issued by ORBIS. Undoubtedly you will find that the most intimate and charming are located within the environs of the Old Town. Those in the more central sections of the city are usually large and somewhat lacking in atmosphere, though the food may be quite good. Check with ORBIS for specific recommendations.

Note: Most bars, wine cellars and the like serving beer, coffee, wine, etc. close at 10 P.M. Your best bet for a drink late in the evening is in the restaurants of the large hotels.

BYDGOSZCZ

This good-sized town located in Central Poland was badly damaged by retreating Nazi armies in 1945. You might like a visit to the Church of Saints Martin and Nicholas (15th century) near the Bydgoszcz Canal linking the Vistula and Oder Rivers and at Koronowo, 25 kilometers to the north, the Gothic Cistercian Church of the 14th century. There has been considerable industrial development in Bydgoszcz since the war.

Hotel

POD ORLEM All of the conveniences supplied without frills, modesty being the byword of this small hotel. There are 67 rooms with a total of 118 beds; 13 rooms with private baths. Telephones, central heating, hot and cold water plus room service are supplied to all rooms. Two elevators. A money exchange desk is located in the lobby. A large restaurant seating 400 persons serves three meals a day and is a place for dancing in the evening. This is the social center of town.

GDANSK

Gdansk (Danzig) was first mentioned in a record of the year 997 A.D. Since that time the town has been developed as a port, then razed; raided, tossed back and forth between the Germans and Poles not unlike a territorially errant ping-pong ball. When peace between Poland and the Teutonic Order was finally established in 1466, Gdansk began to show rapid growth. Its free port status prior to World War II is well known, though most of us scarcely appreciate the damage incurred by the city and its environs during that war. The reconstruction of Gdansk is truly a marvel. A large number of the buildings I passed on a walking tour of the city had been rebuilt only in the past ten years.

Sightseeing

The Height Gate, Artus Court, Dlugu Targ Square, the Zielona Brama ("Green Gate") fortifications, bastions, Saint Mary's Church, the Old Town Hall and Neptune Fountain, all are to be seen on a regular tour of Gdansk. It is also interesting to make a boat tour of Gdansk Harbor, especially the basin of the Motlawa River. Reservations for these two-hour tours can be made in advance at the landing stage at Zielowa Brama or through your hotel reception desk. Don't forget to take in the Westerplatte Peninsula where on September 1, 1939, a small garrison of 200 Poles took the full brunt of Hitler's opening attack on Poland, which led ultimately to World War II.

While you are in Gdansk, I advise you to stay at nearby Sopot rather than in the city. In any case you should take a drive to Sopot and Gdynia, Poland's principal harbor for transoceanic shipping. It is at Gdynia that the Polish liner Batory docks on arrival from Halifax. You can get a fine view of the harbor from a number of sites along the hills.

On your itinerary Oliva, a suburb of Gdansk, should be inscribed in Capital Letters for the Church of the Holy Trinity here is a delight. Don't let the exterior of this 14th and 15th century church throw you, for it is bleak, almost forbidding. Renaissance tombs and pews; rococo ornamentation; a magnificent pulpit and the Abbot's Throne, all these magnificent pieces plus the enormous 17th century altar call forth the greatest enthusiasm. And the organ is an incredible late 18th century triumph, the work of a monk named Michal Wulff. Near the church is a rock garden, a conservatory and a large alpine garden. Inquire at your hotel about the scheduled organ concerts at this Church.

MALBORK CASTLE, roughly an hour and a half's drive from Gdansk is a pleasure to the eye of young and old alike. Here, during a two-hour tour, you can imagine yourself back in the 14th century. Malbork until 1457 was the seat of the Grand Master of the Teutonic Knights. Moats, crenellated walls and other ornamentation, kitchens, the Grand Master's private apartments, an old flour mill all are in a remarkable state of preservation. This dramatic sight cannot fail to impress any visitor.

You will without doubt enjoy a day's outing on the Hel Peninsula, just north of Gdynia. The Peninsula juts out into the Bay of Gdansk separating the latter from the Baltic Sea. Visit the village of Puck, a small fishing community dating from the 15th century. Nearby is Jastarnia, an old Kasubian village dating from the 14th century. Typical vacation facilities are here, such as restaurants, apartments and boarding houses. On the Peninsula you will find many places to swim, walk and relax. There are good roads, wide beaches, usually better weather than on the mainland. Good food at Jastarnia's private restaurant, Oaziz. Boats run on frequent schedules (during the summer months) from Sopot.

Hotel

MONOPOL* This rather uninspired, though modern and efficient, hotel is located directly across from the main railway station, a 10-minute walk from the main shopping areas. Prominent landmarks of Gdansk are also within easy walking distance. The hotel enjoys a location which excludes a great deal of the disturbances usually associated with busy commercial streets. Noise is negligible.

The Monopol has 121 rooms, 70 with private bath. All rooms have hot and cold water, telephones and radio. The hotel is centrally heated. There is elevator service. *Important note*: Be certain in your reservation to specify "private room with bath *and toilet.*" Inexplicably, there are a number of rooms with private bath but no toilet. Rooms are functional, quite clean, pleasant, and well maintained. Prices run as follows: for double with bath approximately 160 zl. plus tax; a double with no bath, 140 zl; single with bath, 100 zl. Single without bath, 80 zl. The apartment, which includes a bedroom and sitting room, TV and piano, 240 zl; two-bedroom unit including bath and toilet, 240 zl. Prices will be higher in season, July 15 to September 15.

A cafe opens off the main lobby where one may have breakfast and/or tea and coffee throughout the day and evening. A pleasant second-floor restaurant serves lunch and dinner. The food is good, the service pleasing and efficient. Dancing in the evening.

The Monopol is the only hotel in Gdansk of any significance. Should you be traveling to Poland by ship, the chances are your first night in the country will be spent at the Monopol. The port city of Gdynia offers no hotel accommodations for foreign tourists. I recommend the Monopol to travelers who find it necessary to stay over in

Gdansk. Otherwise, I suggest you seek reservations at the Grand Hotel in Sopot, visiting Gdansk as a side trip. The Monopol is really not designed as a tourist facility.

Restaurants

The Hotel Monopol serves the best food in an attractive atmosphere. However, you might plan a meal at Jantar or Gedania.

GDYNIA

Restaurants

THE POLONIA Recommended. It is informal, very "local" and on the small side.

In Gdynia, on the south edge of town, there is a very pleasant and comfortable kawiarnia. You will find it on the right of the principal highway just after you enter the city from Sopot. Coffee, tea, fine pastry, alcoholic beverages. I would recommend this cafe for breakfast, a before-lunch aperitif or an after-dinner drink.

KATOWICE

Hotels

MONOPOL This medium-sized hotel is located in the heart of a bustling commercial and industrial city centrally situated in upper Silesia. It is directly opposite the main Katowice railroad station. The hotel has 118 rooms, 180 beds and 4 common bathrooms; furniture is modest but comfortable. Rooms are good size. All accommodations are provided with hot and cold running water, central heating, telephone and radio. Room service is available for breakfast. There is elevator service. A hairdresser is located off the lobby. An old building with limited parking facilities, the Monopol is in desperate need of renovations.

I heartily recommend the restaurant at the Monopol for the food is excellent, the atmosphere most congenial. The restaurant seats 254 guests, and nearby is a cafe seating 144. There is dancing every night in the restaurant.

KATOWICE Hotel Katowice is available to visitors of this industrial town in the heart of Silesia. It is popular with European tourists; reservations should certainly be made in advance. The restaurant at the Katowice is reputed to be quite good.

Restaurant

BIEKITNA This is one of the outstanding local restaurants serving good food in a pleasant atmosphere, with good service. The name means "Blue Restaurant." It is located on Mickiewicza Street.

KAZIMIERZ

Kazimerz, a delightful old renaissance town located on the Vistula River in south central Poland, boasts several good restaurants. Here is a fine combination of historical tourist attractions plus good food in typical Polish surroundings.

Restaurants

U CYGANA One of the few privately owned restaurants in Poland. Small, with menus in Polish only. The atmosphere in these eating places is usually homey, the food delicious.

ARCHITECT'S RESTAURANT Located in the Press House on the Old Market Square, this informal restaurant is heartily recommended by Polish gastronomical authorities.

KRAKOW

Krakow is a thoroughly interesting town. A visit to this Polish city of old is certainly not to be missed by anyone interested in ancient culture, architecture of the Renaissance and Gothic periods, the famous Jagellonian University, the bastions and Barbicans of Medieval Europe. Take a drive along the Planty Parkway encircling the old city where the ancient fortifications once stood; note the Saint Florian Gateway and the remaining walls named after the Guilds. The former arsenal now houses a branch of the State Museum containing such paintings as "The Girl with the Ferret" by Da Vinci and a landscape by Rembrandt. Move on to the Barbican; visit Fiorianska Street with its small shops and famous coffee houses such as "Jama Michalikowa" and "Zielony Bjonih," each a delightful place for an aperitif or coffee.

Here is the magnificent and unusual architecture of the Cloth Hall which dominates the Market Place in the center of the Old Town. You will want to explore the Church of the Virgin Mary (Mariacki) built in Gothic style in the 14th or 15th centuries. Note the uneven spires. From the taller tower, on the hour, one can hear the lonesome, almost eerie bugle call of a watchful sentry of bygone centuries.

Notice the magnificent 15th century altar in Saint Mary's, a wood carving depicting the life of Christ and the Virgin Mary. The stained-glass windows are particularly lovely. Nearby is the little Church of Saint Adalbert, a section of which was built in the 11th century and is reputed to have been the location where the Saint preached before being killed by the Prussians. There is the Gothic Town Hall Tower, and not far from this spot the step where Tadeuse Kosciuszko called the nation to arms against Russian intruders in the year 1794.

No visit to Krakow would be complete without a visit to Wawel Hill, the ancient royal seat of Polish Kings. Built prior to the year 1000, Wawel was originally a fortification towering over the Vistula. From the 14th to the 17th centuries this site was the heart of the former Polish capital city. Kings were crowned, they fought, and were buried in Wawel Cathedral. Unused during the 17th and 18th centuries when the capitol was moved to Warsaw, Wawel suffered during the 19th century occupation by Austrian troops. It has since been restored. The buildings represent a marvelous combination of early Renaissance, Gothic, Romanesque and Baroque styles of architecture.

A more formidable architectural potpourri you could not find outside of Prague. I am certain you will find a trip through this famous old castle (and the Cathedral) a very interesting and certainly worthwhile occasion. Be certain that your guide speaks English!

I recommend a guided tour of this city, after which you can re-visit the more outstanding sights at a leisurely pace. A quiet walk up the Wawel certainly is a moment to be treasured. Krakow is a town in which it is a pleasure just to amble.

Hotels

KRAKOWY* Opened in July, 1965, the Hotel Krakowy is located at an important junction of the Warsaw-Zakopane-Katowice Highway on the north edge of Krakow. Fifteen minutes' walk from the heart of the Old City and ten minutes from the Jagellonian University, the Krakowy is truly representative of modern structures being built in Poland today. Broad walks, boulevards and parklike areas surround the hotel.

Upstairs the five-story Krakowy offers five apartments for two persons and five apartments for one person. Seventy-five per cent of the hotel has been given over to single rooms, fifty of which have bath and shower. The remaining seventy-five per cent of the rooms are doubles, all rooms with bath. TV sets are provided for apartments; all rooms have telephones and radios. The hotel accommodates 700 persons. The rooms, though small, are nicely and comfortably furnished. Rates are similar to those at the Europejski and other superior class hotels. There is a decided noise factor should you have a room toward the front. The convergence of several highways to the front and side of the hotel will bring the sound of screeching brakes and roaring engines into your room from 6 A.M. on.

In the building you will find nearly every convenience a Polish hotel can offer the foreign visitor! Hairdresser; ORBIS office; RKO shop; jeweler; etc. A large parking area is available for the cars of guests. Help with baggage is available. Personnel at the Reception Desk are most pleasant, helpful and more important still, are well trained.

You will find a delightful cafe located to the right of the main entrance. Here also is a pleasant terrace for that evening coffee or brandy. Behind the cafe, a very smart supper club with good decor, dim lighting and music for dancing. The restaurant at the Krakowy is located to the extreme rear of the hotel. Food is good; the service quite slow. Music for dancing after 10 P.M.

FRANCUSKI* An excellent hotel restaurant-wise, an average-to-good facility hotel-wise. The Francuski is located on one of the noisiest streets in Krakow. All front rooms are subject to a great deal of disturbance from cars, taxis and pedestrians.

Rooms in the Francuski have been renovated to some extent and are furnished in a practical manner. There are 59 rooms in all, 30 with private bathrooms. All rooms are provided with hot and cold running water, telephones and room service. An elevator is available although it is of little use because of its size and age. Rooms are comparatively clean. Floor service seems to be limited, therefore maids are hard pressed to cover all the rooms of this popular hotel. Bathrooms are large; beds are wider than in most hotels in Poland, also longer. Rooms are less stark than in many hotels in Poland. There are eight apartments in the hotel. Rates here run from approximately 160 zl. with bath (double) to 240 zl. for an apartment.

There is an excellent restaurant at the Francuski, neat in decor, with quick service and fine food, seating roughly 80 people. It is open for lunch and dinner. At lunch-time plan to arrive around twelve forty-five for tables are quickly occupied. Menus are distributed around one. For dinner be on hand by seven. After dinner coffee is served in the foyer. Breakfast in a cafe near the restaurant. Don't miss the very small, very intimate cocktail lounge offering good dance orchestra for late evening fun. Good bar. Late snacks are served here.

GRAND The Grand is located in the older section of Krakow two blocks from the Francuski. Lacking the class of the Francuski, the Grand certainly has quieter surroundings. The Grand's best rooms are on a side street and benefit from a southeastern exposure. There are three floors of rooms. The rates are somewhat lower as the hotel is not first class. Many rooms are cavernous in size, with high ceilings and big doorways. Apartments, renting for about 180 zl, consist of two rooms with bath and hall, two wardrobes and large bath, the latter complete with couch for post-ablution relaxation. Double rooms with twin beds and bath are quite large and cost approximately 120 zl. A double without bath can be quite pleasant, for about 80 zl. Limited

English is spoken at this hotel. The personnel are quite pleasant and helpful.

Restaurants

WIERZYNEK Wierzynek restaurant located on Old Market Square has an outstanding reputation which could stand an extensive re-evaluation. The Wierzynek is very pleasant in decor, particularly the upstairs rooms. The first dining room is quite elegant boasting a small string orchestra (no dancing). Connecting rooms down a short flight of stairs are pleasant, informal and comfortable. The service at the Wierzynek is acceptable, the food average. The meals here do not compare to the Francuski. Prices for lunch and dinner are equivalent to those in superior hotels.

JAMA MICHALIKOWA Located at Florianske Street, this cafe whose name in English means "Michael's Den," was founded 60 years ago and is connected with the names of many prominent Polish artists belonging to the "Mloda Polska" (young Poland) group. A very interesting coffee house where one may have light snacks, aperitifs, etc. A rather modern entrance leads to back rooms decorated in the manner of the early 1900's. You'll see chairs which are truly period pieces, pencil drawings, Polish folk-lore. Smoking in the front room only. Open until ten. Prices are reasonable.

LANCUT

A visit to the town of Lancut should not be missed. Lancut is roughly four hours' drive due east of Krakow over a comparatively well-maintained road. A delightful side trip. The palace was built as a fortress during the 17th century by Prince Lubormirski. In the 18th century, the palace became the property of a Count Potocki. Remarkably little damage, if any, was done to the property during and after World War II. You will find a trip through this delightful museum a rare treat. Polish women, under the guidance of the very able director of the Lancut National Museum, have maintained the entire property in an intimate, delightful fashion. Many family photos are on display revealing interesting insights into royal life in Poland during past decades. Kaiser Franz Josef of the Austro-Hungarian Monarchy was a visitor of Lancut twice during the early years of this century. Here also is a marvelous collection of 53 carriages dating from the early 1800's. These coaches are maintained in fine condition along with the magnificent saddles and bridles, some embossed in silver and gold. And you will see at Lancut one of the first hot houses of Europe used for the cultivation of orchid plants.

Hotel

ZAMEK The Hotel Zamek at Lancut is located on the grounds of and directly connected with Lancut Palace: "Zamek" is the Polish word for palace. About 1908 the owners of the palace added a servants' wing to the structure. It is within this four-story wing that you will be lodged. The hotel has approximately 30 rooms, some with shower and toilet, others with no running water. Lodgings are furnished with very comfortable beds, chairs, tables and a large radio. Pamphlets found near the radio contain complete schedules of the Polish Airlines. Bathrooms, both private and public, are in exceptionally good taste. Larger and more comfortable rooms face onto a large courtyard; they are remarkably quiet. Try to reserve a double on one of the lower floors. There is no elevator service. The stairs are formidably steep and no help is available for carrying your luggage.

The restaurant consists of two rather dreary but clean rooms to the rear of the hotel and is called the Zankowa. The food is quite good and well served at moderate prices. The management of this restaurant is exceptionally good. Open 8 A.M. until 10 P.M.

Cars are not permitted to remain within the palace grounds. Leave your locked car at the gate and contact one of the women at the small house to the right of the main entrance gate who will make arrangements for transporting your luggage to the hotel or arrange to have the gate opened to permit your car to enter the palace grounds. After removing your luggage from your car, the car must be immediately removed from the palace grounds. You will find a large public parking area two blocks away in the center of the small town of Lancut.

Located quite near the Hotel Zamek on the grounds of the palace are tennis courts, an indoor volleyball court, a basketball court and other gymnasium facilities. The surrounding countryside is particularly well suited for cross-country horseback rides.

The language problem is formidable; I would not encourage travelers speaking neither Polish, French or German to visit here as overnight guests unless accompanied by a guide or Polish friends. Menus are in Polish, the staff speaks very limited German or French.

The Palace of Lancut is frequently used by the Polish Government as a "guest house" for visiting foreign dignitaries. If your visit unhappily coincides with one of these political visitations, you will most likely find that your reserved room with bath has been exchanged for a bathless, toiletless, waterless but nicely furnished rookery on an upper floor.

LODZ

Lodz is the second largest city in Poland, based on population figures, and the center of the textile industry. Few monuments remain, more than sixty per cent of the city was destroyed by the retreating German armies. However small towns in the environs of Lodz, especially Leczyca and Tum offer a few interesting monuments from the 14th and 15th centuries.

Hotel

GRAND A very pleasant hotel located in this good-sized industrial town some 120 miles southeast of Warsaw. The Grand is located on the main street of the town, a short walk from the railroad station. There are 248 rooms, 333 beds. The Grand has 11 apartments; 54 rooms with private baths. All rooms have hot and cold running water, telephone, radio and room service. A hairdresser is located off the lobby. There is an elevator. The restaurant, seating 330 persons, is reputed to be the best in Lodz. The kawiarnia seats 170. Dance music is provided in the evening in the "Malinowa" Dining Room.

OSWIECIM (Auschwitz)

Some of you may wish to make a trip to the former Nazi concentration camp at Oswiecim. Approximately two hours' drive from Krakow, three quarters of an hour from Katowice, the camp is located on the edge of a small town of the same name. It may be reached by rail or bus. All the former grim characteristics of this prison have been carefully restored by the Polish Government. The inscription over the main entrance to Auschwitz reads "Arbeit Macht Frei"; all other street and building signs from the 1940's remain intact.

OLSETYN (Allstein)

The Mazurian Lake section is primarily a summer resort and is famous for its hunting and fishing; its outdoor life can be a delightful experience for Poles and foreigners alike during the months of July and August. There are large game preserves located in the area around Bialystek. A drive through the Mazurian area can be roughly compared to a tour of the Wisconsin and Minnesota lake regions. Olsztyn is the county east of the Mazurian area. A delightful old town (much of which has been reconstructed since World War II) Olsztyn offers the visitor a happy blending of the old and the new; of hills, parks, historic old churches and modern movie houses.

Hotel

WARNINSKI (OLSZTYN) The Warniski is probably the only hotel in this area which provides facilities acceptable for foreign guests. Located in the new quarter of Olsztyn, the Warniski seems to have been built roughly in 1950 but includes an addition constructed quite recently. The rooms at the Warniski are comfortably furnished. Though not outstanding, the bedrooms are clean. Bathrooms are just large enough for a washbowl, toilet, bathtub and one person; moreover, they are not clean.

A restaurant and cafe are located on the main floor of the old section immediately off the street. The cafe (or kawiarnia) is nondescript and should be used for breakfast only. Expect to pay a cover charge before entering the restaurant which will be deducted from your check. You must sit at the table assigned to you at the door although this may entail sitting with another couple. The food is average to good, the service acceptable. You will find this restaurant extremely popular and therefore crowded on Saturday and Sunday nights. It is a good place to meet local people, to enjoy an evening of night life in the provinces. The orchestra is loud.

PLOCK

The city of Plock dates approximately from the 9th century. Plock contains a number of fine historical sites, many dating from the 16th century. Visit Gora Tumska (Cathedral Hill) where in the great 12th century cathedral (rebuilt in the 16th century), lie the remains of Polish kings. A large petro-chemical plant is located near Plock, hence the name of the Hotel Petropole described below.

Hotel

PETROPOLE* The modern Petropole opened its doors to guests as recently as 1964. This eight-story structure contains 68 single rooms, 40 doubles and 4 two-room apartments. The latter have baths, all other rooms simply showers. Every room is equipped with a toilet and washbowl. There are radios and telephones in every room, TV in the apartments. The hotel has a restaurant seating 100, plus a kawiarnia; off the lobby is a hairdresser, a newstand offering foreign publications and a money exchange desk. Garages are located near the hotel; an attendant for parking is available.

POZNAN (Posen)

The city of Poznan, situated on Poland's western border, is bisected by the Warta River. During the 15th and 16th centuries Poznan

(Posen, in German) enjoyed its greatest period of growth though buildings of that period were largely destroyed during the fires following the year 1936. Architectural styles in later periods changed from Medieval to Renaissance, an Italian style of architecture eventually predominating. The Reformation found deep roots in Poznan resulting in the founding in 1519 of Lubranski College. Wars with the Swedes during the 17th century again left the city in ruins, however. Heavy taxation by both the Swedes and the Brandenburgers caused the city to decrease in commercial wealth and subsequently general prosperity declined. In 1793 Poznan was made a section of the German province of Prussia. The Napoleonic Wars saw the city included in the Grand Duchy of Warsaw, while the 1815 Treaty of Vienna once again awarded the city to Prussia and the Poznan area became known as the Grand Duchy of Posen. The year 1848 witnessed a rash of anti-German activities in the Polish area, resulting in the dilution of Prussian authority; nonetheless the "Germanization process" predominated through the early years of the 20th century markedly changing the entire architectural pattern of the city. During World War II the German armies destroyed 55 per cent of the city, 90 per cent of the Old Town was razed by bombing and subsequent fire.

Sightseeing

In Poznan the Museum of Musical Instruments is particularly interesting, as is the Town Hall with its 16th-century Renaissance Chamber. In the Old Poznan Parish Church don't miss the Man of Sorrows, a carved figure completed in 1435. The Spanish and Italian schools of art are represented in the National Museum. Poznan is also the home of the well-known Industrial Fair which has its permanent site on the west side of town not far from the Hotel Merkury. All in all, Poznan is a town better explored by foot than toured by bus. There has not been the "verified rebuilding" in Poznan that one sees in Warsaw and Gdansk. The countryside hereabouts is really delightful.

Hotels

MERKURY* This ultra-modern, seven-story hotel was opened just prior to the 32nd International Poznan Fair in 1964. It is situated on the western edge of town near the fair grounds, about a 10-minute walk from the railroad station. The lobby is bleak, poorly furnished. Off the lobby are located a souvenir shop, flower shop, a money exchange desk, hairdresser, restaurant and cafe. You will find bellhops to help you with your luggage. The grounds are well landscaped and include a large parking area. Immediately to the rear of the hotel is the main ORBIS office for Poznan.

The Merkury can accommodate 648 persons in 53 single rooms, 60 double rooms, 196 semi-apartments (the latter comprising one or two rooms), 38 small, two-room apartments, and four large three-room apartments. Seventy rooms have baths with showers, the remainder only baths. There are telephones and radios in all rooms; the apartments have TV sets. On each floor there is a pleasant central lounge. Corridors and public rooms are colorfully decorated. The price for a single with bath overlooking the main street is approximately 170 zl; large apartments rent for about 240 zl. plus tax. The smaller apartments rent for 225 zl. A double bedroom with bath is 140 to 160 zl. The four single apartments with bedroom, bath and living room cost about 160 zl; a single with shower, 70 zl.

The hotel restaurant seats 172 persons and includes, besides the main restaurant, three large banquet halls, a cocktail bar and a coffee bar. On the mezzanine there is a hotel club where one may entertain guests, read magazines or newspapers. Also on the mezzanine are a kawiarnia and small bar. The food in the main restaurant is substantial but flavorless and limited. In the brightly lit restaurant there are many large tables seating six to eight and not enough seating for couples or singles. Waiters are pleasant and the service is prompt. The Merkury restaurant is quite popular with the local people, perhaps because loud jazz music is played throughout the evening meal.

BAZAR* This small-sized hotel is located in the center of Poznan. There is a traditional, warm atmosphere quite different from the modernistic surroundings at the Merkury. At the well-maintained Bazar you will find 98 rooms, 12 with private baths, 25 with shower. There are 2 apartments. All rooms are provided with hot and cold running water, modernistic if stark furniture, telephones and radio. The hotel is centrally heated, television is available in the apartments. The two apartments overlook a main square of Poznan, one of them boasting a piano played by Paderewski during his visit to Poznan while he was prime minister. These apartments are comfortably furnished. Room service is available on a 24-hour basis, exceptional in Poland. Rates here for double rooms with bath are approximately 150 zl.; a double room without bath costs about 120 zl. Single rooms with shower range around 85 zl. and with bath 100 zl. Rooms without either bath or shower run in the neighborhood of 75 zl. per day. The large apartments cost 240 zl. plus tax.

The restaurant is open from 7 A.M. until 12 midnight, offering guests an excellent cuisine. There are two medium-sized restaurants and a cafe. All meals are served in the main restaurant where the service is prompt, the food truly delicious. The restaurant is a bit bleak, perhaps a trifle shabby, but don't be deterred. The food is good. After-dinner coffee, the pre-dinner aperitif, afternoon tea, all are available in the cafe (or kawiarnia).

POZNANSKI The Poznanski enjoys a central location, directly across the street from the Hotel Bazar. Guests have easy access to the Bazar Restaurant. The chief drawback of the Poznanski is a lack of eating facilities; only breakfast is served. The rooms and apartments are comparatively clean and comfortable. The lobby is one of the most attractive in Poland. Prices are low as the Poznanski is not controlled by ORBIS. This hotel rates high second class.

Restaurants

ADRIA This restaurant is near the main entrance to the Poznan Fair, about four blocks from the Hotel Merkury. The Adria is in a fair building of same vintage, but the interior is completely modern. The restaurant overlooks both the street and the fair grounds. Large and bleak, the Adria was evidently constructed for swirling crowds of late evening dancers. This restaurant is well liked in Poznan and considered first class. The food is good but not exciting. Waiters are efficient and pleasant, speaking several languages. Prices are in the first class category.

SMAKOSZ This restaurant is about two blocks from the Hotel Bazar in the middle of the shopping-theater-commercial district. The Smakosz ia a delight if only because of its relative, intimate setting.

Three small- to medium-sized rooms with modified lighting, no music and blessedly devoid of that Grand Central Station look. The food is good. Menus in English are available; service is prompt. Try some of the typical Polish dishes that seem not to translate into English. They are really good! Open late. Informal.

ARKADIA Down the street from the Smakosz and closer to the Hotel Bazar is the Arkadia, a combination restaurant-dance hall in what appears to be the former lobby or ballroom of an old private club. You will be required to pay an entrance fee which you will eat or drink up during the course of the evening. I do not recommend the food. Go around nine or nine-thirty for a beer, vodka or coffee and listen to the music or join the dancing. The music is quite good, the crowd is largely young and fun to watch.

MAGNOLIA The Magnolia serves quite good food, the service is acceptable, but the atmosphere is "medieval mausoleum." An entrance hall leads to a flight of stairs where you find a veritable "hall of columns." High ceilings, stone walls, high windows, with numerous small tables scattered about the enormous room. Those diners present are clustered in one section of the room seemingly for warmth and protection. A back room near the kitchen is far more pleasant. Prices are the same as in other first class dining spots. Music in the evening. There is a pleasant bar on the third level.

POD KOZIOLKAMI On "Old Market Square," some few blocks behind the Hotel Bazar, the Pod Koziolkami is known as one of Poznan's older and better restaurants. Not dressy. The food is not on a level with the Hotel Bazar.

SOPOT

This small town, some ten minutes north of Gdansk and just south of Gdynia on the principal north-south coastal highway, is a typical beach resort directly on the western shore of the Gulf of Gdansk. The town is attractive in a rather run-down fashion, high life here being restricted to the beach areas during the July 15 through September 15 season. Local activities are largely centered at a point on the beach from which Sopot Pier extends some three hundred yards or so out into the bay. On the pier and along the shore are coffee houses, restaurants, jazz festivals (during late July and August). A main shopping street offers the seasonal visitor shops, restaurants, movie houses and cafes.

Hotel

GRAND* The Grand is one of the last surviving hotels which Authoress Vicki Baum must have had in mind when she wrote her famous book. Built by the Germans in 1920, the Grand is a proud five-story structure located just a few yards back from the Baltic beaches and situated in a lovely park paralleling the sea. It is approached by means of a circular ramp extending from the street up to the first floor. One enters a large, pleasant lobby which opens on a circular cafe quite popular with the local jet set.

The cafe parallels the large restaurant, a very warm, attractive room facing directly toward the sea. No large tables here, rather more emphasis on tables for two, four and six. The restaurant is open for breakfast, lunch and dinner. Food served here is above average, rather hearty but very good. Service is acceptable, if on the slow side. There is an English menu available. Luncheon crowds come in late as a rule, between one-thirty and two o'clock. Dinner finds the room the most crowded between eigth-thirty and ten. Prices for food at this restaurant are higher than average comparable to those of the Hotel Europejski in Warsaw.

Dancing from 10 P.M. in the cocktail lounge, a large room near the entrance of the hotel. The cocktail lounge adjoins a small supper club where food is served; dances are held here. During the summer months, dancing also takes place in front of the hotel near an outdoor pavilion.

Cars may be parked across the street at a city garage opposite the hotel. The charge is rather stiff, approximately $1 a day at the official rate of exchange.

A small garden extends beyond the restaurant were you will find benches for reading or just resting. The Sopot Pier is but a short distance away where you can walk out over the Baltic, sit in the sun, watch the boats and generally relax. Boats leave this pier for the Hel

Peninsula every morning; the round trip taking roughly two hours and forty-five minutes. Boats leave for Gdansk in the afternoon.

The Grand contains 128 rooms, a total of 253 beds, and 4 apartments. Double rooms at the Grand are quite comfortable as are the singles. Be sure to request a seaside location, preferably on the lower floors. Upper floor bedrooms, while attractive, suffer from exposure to food odors and soot from chimneys located nearby. Rooms are pleasantly decorated with few frills. Maid service is good; room service available. For laundry service, see your maid.

The Grand's central location between Gdansk and Gdynia, with access to the Hel Peninsula, the beaches at Leba and the castle at Malbork make it an ideal location for a summer's visit. The Grand with its cocktail lounges, good food and fine service will, I'm sure, measure up to your standards for a pleasant mid-summer's "Baltic Holiday." Remember, don't go before mid-July as it is just too damp and cold.

Restaurants

HERMITAGE The best place for food is the Grand Hotel. The Hermitage is rather small with an intimate and not unpleasant atmosphere. Good for a diversion.

ALBA Cafeteria downstairs; bar upstairs. There is dancing in the evenings. The Alba is very simple but the food is fair. Don't forget that in the cafeteria the cash register comes *before* the food is served. You must make your selection of food from a menu on the wall, pay, and then you will receive the soup, meat, vegetables, etc.

SZCZECIN (Settin)

Szczecin has been in a state of flux since the 14th century. A northwestern province of the Polish State, it later joined the Hanseatic League. Still later, ascribing to Protestantism, ties were broken with Krakow (then the Polish capital). Eventual rule by the Swedes was realized through the incursions of the Swedish King Gustav Adolph. For 200 years, the province of Pomerania (which surrounds Szczecin) was divided between the Swedes and Germans, Szczecin being awarded by the 1648 Treaty of Westphalia to the Swedes. Some decades later, Sweden's Pomeranian provinces were sold to the Germans, this in the early 1700's. Polish influence at this time was for all purposes nil. Szczecin became, because of its position at the mouth of the Oder River, one of Germany's leading ports. The harbor was deepened; boulevards were widened and extended in a radiating design. The city became a "Free Port," its trade with cities overseas extended, and Stettin, as it was then known, became the leading German port city on the Baltic Sea. At the time of World War II Greater Stettin had a population of 400,000. Because of the fierce fighting during the war, the entire city and port area were almost totally demolished. Following the war Szczecin was returned to Poland.

Sightseeing

Once in Szczecin, visit the Terrace of Mly Gkrobrego overlooking the Oder River far below; on a fair day a visitor can see some distance beyond the city toward the forests of Gory Bukove and Golenion. The Church of Peter and Paul, built in the 15th century, is an interesting tourist attraction, as is the Castle built in Renaissance style during the 14th and 17th centuries. Take a car or bus tour through Szczecin as it extends over an extremely wide area, embracing the former German port city of Swincujscie (Swinelumde). Much of the Old City is still being reconstructed.

Want to cruise the Oder River? "White Boat" tours can be arranged through the Reception Desk at the Continental. The boats are located at the bottom of the bluff overlooking the Oder River. The boats leave on a regular schedule; the trip takes approximately two hours.

Hotel

CONTINENTAL* The central location of this very well run hotel provides ready access to the sights of Szczecin. Very clean rooms, fine service. A new lobby and central reception center were recently opened.

The restaurant at the Continental serves excellent food and is run in a very efficient manner. A good orchestra plays nightly for dancing. A cafe is located at the corner of the hotel where, until noon, one may have the usual delicious Polish breakfast of tea, eggs, ham, bread and jam. You will undoubtedly have to share a table here. Inquire of those seated if you may sit down (gesture will do!).

Restaurant

KASKADE Two floors of dining facilities. A cover charge must be paid before entering. The second floor is out, for on that level it is something of a "sailor bar." When buying the entrance ticket ask for a table on the main floor. Good orchestra, floor show and dancing. The atmosphere is quite pleasant. Waiters serve in acceptable fashion; the food is adequate. Nice as a diversion from the Continental.

WROCLAW (Breslau)

Wroclaw (Vrosuave) is a city of historical significance that a visit here should certainly be included in your itinerary even though over fifty per cent of the city was destroyed by German armies in the latter part of World War II and many of the original structures are no longer to be seen. In origin, Wroclaw was a Polish settlement dating from the 10th century. The two experienced a substantial development during the 12th century based largely on the prosperity of the city's cloth and weaving industries. Wroclaw enjoyed trade relationships with such countries as France, Germany and Belgium; a large number of Walloons from the flatter country having settled there in the late 12th century. Following a Mongol invasion at the height of its development, Wroclaw developed during the 14th and 15th centuries to such an extent as to compete with the more industrialized cities of Frankfort and Oder and Ypres. There was something of a Germanization of the town in the 16th century though the Poles managed to maintain their own social and cultural characteristics. Although incorporated in the then largely Germanized area of Silesia in the 1700's, the Poles maintained their national entity; street signs, school books and the like were largely in German or in the two languages. Polish influences were weakened during the period when Bismark assumed the Chancellorship of the German provinces. The area around and including the city became totally Polish after World War II.

Sightseeing

Sights here include the Town Hall (15th century Gothic); the Historical Museum with its collection of rare Gilesian coins; the houses of the burghers (many are restorations undertaken with great care); the Gothic Church of Saint Elizabeth (14th century); the Gothic Cathedral (18th century). Also see the many other interesting churches, university buildings, and what is known as the Popular Hall seating 10,000 people and boasting one of the largest cupolas in Europe. Any visitor would certainly be interested in visiting the Youth Center located in the basement of Wroclaw's 15th century Town Hall. Here, in four or five large rooms with vaulted ceilings, are displayed paintings and sculptured pieces by modern Polish artists. Also there are a small theater, a cafe, and a room for dancing. The decor of these centuries'-old rooms (now restored) is in good taste. The entire project is certainly most commendatory and seeming much appreciated by the young people of Wroclaw.

Hotel

MONOPOL* There is no other hotel of the Monopol's category in the city. This old-timer is located in the center of town. Of medium size, the Monopol has 92 rooms including 3 apartments and approximately 38 rooms with bathrooms, 8 with showers. Every room has hot and cold running water, telephone and radio. The hotel is centrally heated. Apartments are equipped with television. There is an elevator. The rooms, corridors and public bathrooms are clean and well-maintained. Insist on an outside room: do not accept a room on the court to the rear of the hotel (because of fumes from the kitchen). Maid service is prompt and pleasant. Prices are similar to those of other first class establishments.

The restaurant of the Monopol serves good food. An orchestra plays nightly for dancing in one of the three large rooms comprising the dining area. You will find that demand far exceeds tables so simply sit at any table on which no reserved sign has been placed. Menus are in Polish. Breakfast at the Monopol is taken in the cafe (or kawiarnia) located at the far end of the first floor corridor. There is afternoon dancing in the cafe.

ZAKOPANE

Don't miss making a side trip to this pleasant little resort town which is a two-hour drive south of Krakow. Zakopane is situated at the foot of the Tatra Mountains, on the Czech-Polish border. Here are ski jumps, a slalom track and sports stadiums; mountain railways and many hiking paths. You might drive up to Morskie Oko Lake in the Higher Tatras. A rather primitive restaurant located at the side of the lake serves excellent potato soup and sausages; for these tasty dishes as well as the marvelous view, I certainly intend to drive up again some time.

Hotels

GIEWONT* Located ten minutes from the railway station, the Giewont is situated at the crossroad of the main streets of the town. What once was an outstanding hotel has been reduced by fire and war to just another establishment in the ORBIS string of hotels. The design will seem quite familiar to those of you who have visited the Bavarian section of Germany or the Saltzgammergut in Austria. A sizeable lobby and lounge are located near the front entrance, providing a pleasant introduction to the hotel. There are 47 rooms at the Giewont; three apartments; 25 bathrooms in all. There is hot and cold running water in all rooms plus central heating, telephone and radio—TV in the apartments. I found the double rooms spartan, totally uninteresting in decor and in need of general refurbishing.

A separate entrance permits visitors to enter directly the large and rather ornate restaurant. It is open for lunch and dinner. An orchestra plays for dancing in the evening. The restaurant serves mediocre food, the service is average, the surroundings pleasant. Prices are on the high side. A cheerful cafe located across the front of the restaurant is also available for breakfast. Good service, good food!

ZAKOPANE (SPORT HOTEL) Built for the 1962 Winter Olympics held in Zakopane, this hotel is the principal structure in what the Poles eventually hope to develop into an Olympic Village. The modern hotel is run as a Pension. Two hundred guests may be accommodated in the very pleasant rooms. All accommodations are modern, quiet and antiseptically clean, with three-way radios and showers. In season doubles rent for about 120 zl.; singles 60 zl.

Also located in this very modern hotel are flower shops, a travel bureau, a private theater showing sport films, a cafe, a smart little bar and nightclub, plus a pleasant dining room for guests only. To the left of the main entrance you will find rooms containing complete medical facilities, with trained nurses. These facilities are made available to sportsmen engaged in track and field events, winter sports, etc., for which this hotel provides the main base.

A gymnasium is joined to the hotel building, complete with basketball and volleyball facilities; also locker rooms. A handicraft room adjoins the gym. There is seating in the gymnasium for approximately 300 people. Training in various sports is available for youngsters and grownups alike.

The site of the Hotel Zakopane is surrounded by quiet woods, a pleasant residential district and the sports facilities mentioned above.

DOM TURISTY A large north-woods-like structure one block from the main street in a quieter location than the Giewont. Rooms are pleasant and well attended. This hotel is associated with local tourist groups who enjoy favorable rates at their "club" hotel.

The Dom Turisty is more a hostel than a hotel.

Restaurants

PORAJ This restaurant is quite small, with only eight tables. Service is prompt and efficient, the food excellent. This is a privately owned restaurant where one may enjoy home cooking. The food is typically Polish. You must have someone along to help language-wise, but by all means go! Here you will find some of the best if not the best food in Poland.

KMICI CAFE A very pleasant cafe located in an old home approximately five blocks from the Giewont Hotel. There are several small rooms and a large lounge with piano. A very informal but extremely pleasant atmosphere, a good place to relax and talk from morning to night. Nice for late morning coffee, or an after-dinner drink. Food is not served. The interior of this cafe is very pleasant, very warm.

EUROPFJSKI CAFE The Europfjski Cafe is open from 10 A.M. to 10 P.M. and is extremely popular with local people, especially the younger set. The Europfjski is not unlike the Kmici though it is more crowded during the late afternoon. No food served, but one may have tea, soft drinks, wine, aperitifs, etc. These cafes are good spots in which to mix with local residents.

RESTAURANT AT LAKE MORSKIE OKO Don't forget to enjoy the dramatic drive past waterfalls, through small gorges to this spectacular lake situated near the base of the High Tatra Mountains. There is nothing fancy about the restaurant; usually it is jammed with sightseers and table sharing is a must. Try the potato soup, sausages, some bread and fruit; the food tastes good up there in the mountains. Rustic but entertaining with a spectacular view.

Side Trips from Zakopane

DEBNO CHURCH Located some thirty minutes from Zakopane and about ten minutes from the town of Nowy Sarg, this interesting church built in the 1500's is a sight not to be missed. Debno Church has been the subject of international attention for the past few years because of its interesting interior design and religious relics. Many relics dated from 1375. The building is in its original state: it is not a restoration. The small village of Debno, rural rusticity at its best, is located nearby. The town and church were located some 400 years ago direction on the "Amber Road," the caravan route leading from Constantinople to St. Petersburg via Vienna and Budapest. The church was constructed with the aid of robbers who used the steeple section of the wooden structure as their lookout point. This alliance between church and thieves actually resulted in the active support of the church by the thieves. Relics stolen from the caravans are in many instances contributed to the church's decoration. Planking in the ceiling and walls of the church contain motifs featuring the designs used by 77 different countries or areas of the 16th century world. Scandinavia, Ottoman, Turkey, Arabia and France are among those areas represented. Some of the planks must have been painted by artists from the caravans, others by the thieves themselves. The outstanding feature of these varied and strange motifs is that the color has never faded or been retouched. The blues, reds, oranges, etc. retain the same color they were some 400 years ago. A tract has been prepared by scientists recording efforts to determine what substances had been used in this paint. Actually the wood seems to have been impregnated with some form of dye. It could be that a stencil was used. One strange item in this unique church is a small hand xylophone discovered (and quite evidently stolen) by the thieves "somewhere in the East." The xylophone is presently used during the Mass. The unusual instrument has a very clear, fine tone.

NIDZICA CASTLE Some fifteen minutes down the road from Debno, one can see two castles located on high promontories overlooking the fierce, beautiful Dunajec River. One of the castles, Nidzica, is now a retreat for Polish artists but can be viewed from inside during certain hours. Both castles were built in approximately the 15th century. Visit the beautiful spot before its savage primitiveness is tamed. As you climb up to Nidzica Castle note the fine quality of the air. Its freshness and clarity are remarked throughout Poland.

Poland has a very great deal to offer the tourist. You will experience a worthwhile and memorable trip. The Poles are fine hosts who will make every possible effort to make you feel at home. Their country offers an extensive variety of scenery, a wealth of history, accommodations that are reasonably comfortable, food that can be very tasty. But most important, you will meet some of the most interesting, individualistic, and kindly people in the world.

Romania

Romania is a vacationer's paradise! Few countries offer such a tremendous variety of scenery, such an array of antiquity, and such diversity of entertainment and sports activities within resort areas. One is hard pressed to find a section of Romania which does not offer some attractions designed to lure vacationers, historians, bibliophiles, sportsmen or those of us who delight in art exhibitions of outstanding merit.

My confession will without a doubt startle my Romanian friends, but I must admit that prior to a first visit to their country my knowledge of Romania was built, for the most part, around mental footnotes conjured up by news clippings of the Thirties. Names such as Magda Lupescu, Queen Marie and Prince Michael ranked second only to phrases such as "Bucharest, The Paris of the East," a place where men rouged their cheeks, and in dimly lighted cafes danced the tango with ashen-faced ladies sporting sequins and bobbed hair. How wrong I was!

Even that previously remote-sounding, geographically sinister area called Transylvania, replete with the echoes of Count Dracula's carriage wheels and the screams of vampires, proved to be about as sinister as Yosemite National Park, and equally as beautiful. As for the Carpathian Mountains, the very name shrieked of historical intrigues, while words such as Bessarabia, Moldavia and Valachia spoke to me of romantic interludes stemming from song and verse. My imaginings came closest to reality when they concerned the city of Ploesti, which reminded me of oil and Allied bombings during World War II; nowadays the rebuilt city of Ploesti is little more than a place for lunch on the road from beautiful Brasov to "rougeless" Bucharest, a junction as you drive from Bucharest to the Danube Delta area around Galatzi.

So out of fairness to facts let's recognize romanticized recollections for what they are. From the wide sandy beaches of the Black Sea resorts, to the climbing trails of Breaza in the Transylvania Mountains, Romania offers an almost endless number of delightful tourist attractions any one of which make that country a repeat feature for your future trips to Europe.

GEOGRAPHY

Romania is shaped something like New York State and has a land area somewhat smaller than that of Oregon. The population of Romania (well over 18 million in 1960) is roughly a quarter more than that of our Empire State. Romania's northeastern border adjoins the Soviet Union for some 825 miles, while on the west Romania borders Yugoslavia for 339 miles and Hungary (to the northwest) for 264 miles. To the south Romania is bounded by Bulgaria, while from the Russian to the Bulgarian border Romania has 152 miles of shore line along the Black Sea.

The Carpathian Mountain chain swings south into Romania from the Soviet Union, turning west toward Yugoslavia in the central section of Romania, thus forming a giant reverse "L." This southern section of the Carpathians is known as the Transylvanian Alps; one peak (Mt. Negoiul) reaches a height of 8,346 feet. The Eastern Carpathians reach to a height of approximately 6,000 feet in some areas.

These mountain chains running in north-south and east-west directions divide the country into the various regional provinces. To the east and south of the Carpathian ranges lie the provinces of Moldavia (east) and Walachia (south). The central region, tucked inside the beautiful mountain ranges, is the "Transylvanian Basin," bisected by the Mures and Somes Rivers. The area called Banat lies west of Transylvania on the Hungarian-Yugoslavian border, while Dobrudja forms the rugged coastline east of the Danube, paralleling the Black Sea. Romania's capital, Bucharest, is situated in Walachia.

The Prut River forms Romania's border with the Soviet Union.

After providing a natural border with Bulgaria, the mighty Danube swings north into Romania and eventually flows east into the Black Sea in the region known as the Danube Delta near the Russian border.

The Carpathians are not unlike many mountain areas in the United States; remarkably scenic, they are covered with pine forests and inhabited in the more sparsely populated regions by the brown bear, wolf, lynx, boar and fox. Walachia and Moldavia are comparatively flat and covered with grasslands as well as wheat, sugar beets, corn and potatoes. And hear this: all of these regions, with perhaps the exception of Benat, contain fine vacation areas and/or regions of considerable historical interest. Hunting, fishing, climbing, scenic drives; swimming, boating, Danube River cruises and camping! The range of tourist activities in Romania is provided by the beautiful topography.

HISTORY

Geography provides an emphatic clue to Romania's historical background and certainly plays a very large part in contemporary Romanian affairs—social, cultural and economic, as well as political and religious. It is, in fact, extremely interesting to drive from Brasov in Transylvania through the Prahova District and the Predeal Pass toward Ploesti. This well-surfaced road takes you from the forested mountains occupied for centuries by people of German and Hungarian descent down to the Walachian Plains which were in turn greatly influenced by the Turks and to some degree, the French.

Dacia was one of the eastern provinces of the Roman Empire between the 2nd and 3rd centuries A.D. Following Rome's withdrawal, the Dacian-Romanic peoples were subjected to continuous invasions from the east and eventually withdrew to the mountains or to the areas bordering the Danube River, in what is now southern Romania (or Walachia). Here they came under the influence of the Slavs, and in the 7th century were known to the world as the Vlachs (or Walachions). These people were dominated by the Mongols in the 13th century.

The early 15th century saw the Vlachs people form two provinces: Walachia and Moldavia (to the east, bordering Russia). With the advance of the Ottoman Turkish forces through Bulgaria, the two provinces once again found themselves, from the late 15th century to the early 18th century, occupied by the Turks. With the advance of Russian influence, the Romanians found themselves eventually partitioned between the Turks and the Russians; the latter peoples annexed a section of Moldavia known as Bessarabia, thus bringing Russia's borders to the Prut River. By this time Turkish influences were on the wane.

Partial autonomy was provided for the two Romanian provinces following the Crimean War (1856); at that time the southern section of Bessarabia was returned to Moldavia and the Russian border was reestablished to the north, at the Dniester River. A union between the two principalities was formed in 1859 under Alexander Cuza and in 1866 the German house of Hohenzollern-Sigmaringen established a monarchy under Carol I. At the Congress of Berlin in 1878, Romania obtained full independence at the price of returning southern Bessarabia to Russia. It was at this time that Romania became a full economic and political national unit.

During the Balkan Wars of 1912-13, Romania gained Southern Dobrudja from Bulgaria. Carol I died and was succeeded by Ferdinand I. In World War I, Romania joined the Allies and obtained Bukovina (the German name for a section of northern Moldavia) from Austria, Transylvania from Hungary and Bessarabia from Russia. Postwar treaties (such as the Treaty of Neuilly) formally established the political reality of the greatly expanded Romania. Immediately after the war, Ion Bratianu, premier under Ferdinand, succeeded in obtaining considerable agrarian and electoral reforms. Bratianu and Ferdinand both died in 1927. After a short regency under Peasant Party leader Iuliu Maniu, Romania witnessed the return of exiled King Carol II and the establishment of a royal dictatorship. In 1940 the Nazi regime forced Romania to cede northern Bukovina and Bessarabia to Russia, Transylvania to Hungary and southern Dobrudja to Bulgaria. Carol II abdicated in favor of his son Michael (Mihai) and Germany occupied the country. The wartime regime of Antonescu was overthrown when Soviet forces occupied the country in 1944 and Romania joined the Allies against Germany. In 1945 Premier Peter Groza established a coalition government dominated largely by forces favorable to the Soviet Union. King Michael abdicated on December 30, 1947, and the Romanian People's Republic was proclaimed.

The Paris Peace Treaty signed in 1947 fixed Romania's borders as they existed in January, 1941, with the exception of the Transylvania area where the border issue was related to the year 1948—which meant that Romania regained Transylvania but lost southern Dobrudja to Bulgaria. That section of Moldavia known as Bessarabia remained a region of the Soviet Union. During the summer of 1965, internal policies decreed that henceforth the Romanian People's Republic would be called the Romanian Socialist Republic.

This capsule history of Romania does not begin to emphasize the important effects the Austro-Hungarian monarchy had on the country. Transylvania was a division of Hungarian territory for centuries prior to World War I, and the area still shows the tremendous influences of the Hungarian people as well as those of the Austrians and Germans who settled there in the 18th century. The historical towns known to the Austro-Hungarian subjects as the "Sieben Burgen" (seven castles) remain today much as they did during the times of the Crusaders. Many distinctions—architecture, manners of dress, customs—set the Transylvanian people apart from their brother Romanians living in the southern or eastern sections of the country. Actually I found Transylvania to be a completely different "world," and a nice one at that! In any case, each area has its own interesting, exciting past, which dictates everything from mood to food.

We have previously spoken of Dobrudja, that section of Romania bounded by the Danube on the west and the Black Sea to the east, the Bulgarian border to the south and the Danube Delta region to the north, along the Russian border. Along the 152-mile stretch of land by the Black Sea coast lie some of the most important antique ruins on the European continent. Four archaeological sites founded by the Greeks during the 7th century B.C. should certainly not be missed by the tourist. Later in the book we will give the locations of museums, open-air gardens, maps, etc., around Constanta that deal with the early Greek period in Romania as well as the Roman period which followed. Suffice to note here that Romania fell heir to some treasures which will delight even those to whom ancient civilizations are something less than exciting. The present city of Constanta was founded by the Greeks 2,500 years ago and was named Tomis. Through this port city passed the Persian Emperor Darius before engaging to battle with the Scythians; Alexander the Great camped here in the 4th and 3rd centuries B.C. Tomis was eventually incorporated into the Roman Empire in the year 8 A.D. by the Roman Emperor Octavian Augustus. The present name Constanta sprang from the naming of a nearby village after the Byzantine Emperor Constantine.

North of Constanta was located the ancient city of Histria. During the 7th century A.D. Histria, now the oldest city on Romanian territory, was an important trading center and port until the port silted up and the city was abandoned.

South of Constanta is the beach resort town of Mangalia, originally named Callatis; this city which boasts a fine museum, was founded by Dorians. The fourth fantastic old city is called Adamclisi and is noted particularly for its "Tropaeum Trajani" monument commemorating Roman victories in the 2nd century against the Dacian tribes. The base of the monument still exists, covered by bas-reliefs depicting scenes of the battle.

Legend has it that the Argonauts, returning from their search in Colchis for the Golden Fleece, stopped in ancient Tomis on their way home. Further, it is a fact that the Roman poet and writer Ovid lived the last years of his exile in Tomis, and wrote some of his greatest works at this restful, beautiful site overlooking the sea.

LANGUAGE

Ninety per cent of the Romanian language is based on elements of Latin. It is substantially a Romance language and bears striking resemblance to Italian; a knowledge of Italian will certainly aid you in Romania. The non-Latin words scattered through the Romanian language come largely from the Slav; a few come from Greek, some from Hungarian and a few from Turkish.

The cedilla under the letter "c" provides the sound "ch," as in "Charley"; under the letter "s" the cedilla gives a "sh" sound. A cedilla under the "t" provides a "z" sound, as in Miorita (Mioritsa).

Because of its high Latin content, many Romanian words are recognized by people who know a Romance language. The spoken language is not too easily understood, for the Slavic tones tend to disrupt the Latin harmony. The Romanian however appears less volatile, less energetic in his speaking mannerisms when compared with other nations having a Latin-based language. Romanian sounds more "eastern" than Serbo-Croation, an effect due partly to the use of the hands and certain Romanian speech inflections.

CURRENCY

The Romanian units of currency are the leu (plural lei) and the ban (plural bani). One hundred bani equal one leu. As of this writing the "premium" exchange rate is 18 lei to the dollar. Metal coins in circulation are in the denominations of 10, 15, and 25 bani, and 1 leu and 3 lei. Notes are issued to the value of 1 leu and 3, 4, 10, 25 and 100 lei.

The importation and exportation of Romanian currency is strictly forbidden. In 1967 currency controls in Romania were modified and undeclared foreign currencies could be introduced into the country. Romanian officials indicate that these relaxed currency controls will continue, but it's best to check on this point at the last moment before your trip.

Exchange stations have been set up at the borders. Money may also be exchanged at branches of the national bank. As in every country of Eastern or Central Europe, save the slips given to you when you exchange money; you may be asked to show them at the border when you exit. Moreover, they are very important should you wish to purchase souvenirs and the like in special discount stores (see below).

The official exchange rate is 6 lei to the dollar. This "premium" exchange rate of 18 lei to the dollar is only for tourists visiting Romania. Tourists in transit through Romania exchange money at the rate of 12 lei to the dollar. There is even a distinction between various forms of foreign currency. The American tourists in a category with the citizens of the hard-currency countries of Western Europe—the Dutch, French, Swedes, West Germans, British, Canadians, Belgians and Austrians—can avail themselves of the 200 per cent "premium" exchange rate. Indians, Australians, Finns, Egyptians and a few other "less fortunate" peoples receive only a 150 per cent tourist rate.

VISAS AND CUSTOMS

In the United States you can make application for a visa to Romania through your local travel agent or the Romanian Embassy at 1601 23rd Street, N.W. Washington, D.C. No charge! Visas are also obtainable at the Romanian frontier. No visa charge here either. Your travel agency will provide you with a duplicate copy of your reservation slip, which is occasionally requested by the Romanian agency issuing the visa. It is not necessary to indicate in your visa application at which frontier point you intend to enter Romania. You may enter wherever you wish, whenever you wish, though naturally within the limits prescribed by the validity of your visa. Visas are usually issued for six months.

Hotel reservations are not required to enable you to obtain a visa to Romania. This fact seems not generally understood by many travel firms in this country.

Here again and in brief are the principal features of Romania's regulations regarding visas. The visa is available on request at no charge. It may be obtained at embassies, legations, travel agents, at the Romanian Frontier and at airports. Members of diplomatic missions, businessmen and persons participating in conferences in Romania may apply for tourist visas at Carpati, the National Travel Office in Bucharest.

Should you wish to visit relatives in Romania, note on your visa application the address at which you will reside. There is no charge for this type of visa either. Groups of tourists who wish to visit Romania for a short period (not longer than 48 hours), and who are coming to Romania under the auspices of Carpati tours, may enter the country with an access permit (a form of landing card).

Frontier points are as follows:

From Yugoslavia: Stamora (by train) and Moravita (by road).

From Hungary: Bors (by road); several entrance points are available by train.

From Bulgaria: Giurgia (by train, car and boat); the Danube separates the two countries at this point; Negru Voda (by car and train); good connections to and from Constanta.

From the Soviet Union: Sculeni and Siret (by car); other points available by train and ship.

Bucharest's international airport is at Baneasa.

Customs and other frontier formalities are handled in varying fashion depending on the particular frontier point involved. I once crossed the Romanian border at Bors where the Hungarian and Romanian border officials work together (the Hungarians in brown uniforms, the Romanians in grey-blue). When the Hungarians completed their formalities, my Romanian hosts took over, asking to see my passport and providing me with a blank form concerned with importation of currencies. I was asked whether I had in my possession a rifle or ammunition, a portable radio, typewriter or camera, and appropriate notes were made in my passport. I was asked to raise the lid on the trunk of my car as well as the engine hood. I found the Romanian customs officers direct, polite and quite efficient. The entire customs proceedings generally take only eight to ten minutes (longer if you must obtain a visa too).

When entering or leaving the country you may be asked to sign a declaration stating that you have neither imported or exported any Romanian lei. Prior to leaving Romania, be cautious in exchanging lei so as not to be caught with additional Romanian currency.

When coming from Bulgaria and entering Romania at Giurgia I found that customs formalities take place at opposite ends of "Friendship Bridge," a road and rail span high above the Danube. Just beyond the gate on the Romanian side there is a small house which comprises the Romanian official "presence" on its southern border. At the northern border there were mainly the grey-uniformed frontier officials, whereas at Giurgiu it seemed as though a platoon of troops stood "at ease" about the customs platform. I was impressed by the unusual height and bearing of these men. But don't get me wrong; these soldiers aren't standing around as a "defense" against the tourist, so relax. Once when I was exiting from Romania I had a good laugh after the customs formalities were completed when a corporal asked if I would raise the hood of my car. Customs inspectors, soldiers and all crowded about. As I raised the hood I smiled and asked one of the inspectors: "For customs?" "Nu, nu!" he said, indicating that the men were just plain interested in the engine.

Delays in entering Romania are usually related to the going over given Romanian citizens returning from a trip abroad, that is if they are not traveling in an official capacity. One point cannot be emphasized enough: a similarity between governmental systems does not necessarily confirm the existence of a mutual spirit of brotherly love. Visitors from the eastern sections of Europe generally receive a remarkably thorough going-over when entering Romania. Those who prattle of the constancy of any economic or political factor, irrespective of outward appearances, are practicing that sorry art of self-delusion.

Passport inspectors and customs officials will come to your car during the passport formalities. However, I did not find that these men had the authority to permit entry without first checking with some "Mr. X" who usually inhabited the customs house. I was under the impression that the oracle was consulted before acting on the entry or exit of any tourist arriving by car. Some of this routine seems unnecessary but it doesn't take too long a time. I recommend patience as bureaucracy is bureaucracy in every entry of the globe. Leave your car and turn in your passport. Then "take a break!" Admire the scenery, lean on a tree, smoke a cigarette, observe the frontier formalities, watch that little stream running under the wooden bridge. Don't approach the soldiers or officials unless they speak to you, and then be pleasant and, most important, be friendly! I have found that these people will (1) want to complete their task as soon as possible and (2) be interested in looking over your car largely out of curiosity.

On trains and planes hand over your passport to customs officials and relax. These men are as anxious to do their job and get on with other work as you are to get through the inspection. Trains in Romania are crowded, airports frenetic, so accept the passport and customs check as an opportunity to take your first long look at these very proud but friendly people.

TRAVELING TO ROMANIA

By Car

We have indicated in the preceding section the main entry points into Romania. Roads are well maintained; the highway system being extended and improved upon each year. Special limits are 50 m.p.h. in the country, 15 m.p.h. in towns (strictly controlled). The same car papers required in Western Europe are valid for travel to Romania: White Cross insurance (with that ever-requested green identification paper) and an International Driver's License. When entering the country your engine number will probably be noted on your visa and you may receive a special slip for car owners, to be turned in to the authorities when you leave the country.

By Plane

International airlines serving Bucharest's Baneasa airport are Austrian Airlines, Sabena, Lufthansa Aeroflot, Malev plus Czechoslovakian, Polish Airlines. Charter flights by international lines may land directly at the Constanta air field for passenger connections by bus to Mamaia. There are quite a number of such flights between West Germany and Constanta. Tarom, the Romanian Airline, has regular connections to Copenhagen, Brussels, Vienna and Paris, as well as Athens and other Eastern European capitals. Flight time Paris to Bucharest is about four hours.

I have had the opportunity to fly with Tarom, the Romanian National Airline, and can report very satisfactory arrangements. The aircraft are generally the Ilyushen 18 prop-jets, and seatings in two and three. Cabin decor is a bit drab, and the food is simple (usually a cold buffet-type affair) but good.

I found customs at Baneasa airport to go smoothly, but the money-exchange business there is slow moving and badly organized.

Taxis are available at the airport and the 10-minute ride into Bucharest costs about 20 lei.

By Train

The international train service to Bucharest is frequent. I can't personally vouch for the condition of the wagons, but views of similar trains passing through Budapest indicated jammed second class sections and reserved accommodations in first class. Dining cars and sleeping accommodations are available on the Arlberg-Orient from Paris east through Basel, Zurich, Vienna, Budapest to Bucharest north; the Orient-Express from Paris with connections from Munich and Strasburg via Salzburg, Vienna west and Budapest; the Baltorient Express from Stockholm and Oslo via Berlin east with connections from Warsaw and Prague to Bratislava, Budapest and Bucharest. The Carpati-Express and Danubius travel between Romania and the Soviet Union.

Rail and train tickets may be purchased at Carpati offices; air tickets can also be purchased at Tarom offices.

Persons wishing to secure first class accommodations or wagon lit sleepers between Bucharest and neighboring countries be advised that such reservations can be secured at a central ticketing office located in the New Post Office Building on the Calle Victoria in central Bucharest. Do not attempt to visit the train station (the Gare Nord) for there are few there who speak foreign languages. Moreover long queues are usually found before the "International Trains" window. Space on international trains coming through from the Soviet Union or Western Europe may not be secured at the station until two hours before the departure of the train from Bucharest. Since a number of these trains arrive rather early in the morning, the purchase of tickets at the station involves being at the ticket window anywhere between 6 and 7 A.M. in order to be provided with a seat for a 9 o'clock departure. Go to the New Post Office Building; save time and gain sleep. Anyone will point the way.

By Ship

Frequent boat service is maintained between Constanta and such ports as Varna (Bulgaria), Odessa (Soviet Russia) and Istanbul. Navrom (the Romanian Steamship Lines) operates the S.S. Transylvania with a 400-passenger capacity; this ship offers a 3-day cruise to Istanbul from June through September. A suite costs approximately $65; a first class double about $50.

CARPATI

The Oficiul National de Turism (O.N.T., also called Carpati) is charged with the housing, transportation and feeding of all foreign tourists in Romania. As is the case in most of Europe, Carpati is an agency of the state but unlike Western Europe or National travel bureaus it has the sole responsibility for every facet of the tourist business.

Want a hotel reservation? Go to Carpati! Train ticket? Car rental? Carpati! Plane and train reservations. Guides. Tours. Money exchange. The works! The main office of this organization is at 7, General Magheru Blvd., in Bucharest. The name Carpati is Romanian for "Carpathian," Romania's principal mountain chain.

Carpati (I will use the name known best abroad; Romanians

usually refer to the outfit as "O.N.T.") maintains offices at airports in towns of interest to tourists, major cities, ports and frontier stations. The main office, a modern structure on one of Bucharest's busiest thoroughfares, is located near the best hotels. Carpati maintains exchange desks and information service in all hotels. This first class travel firm is a member of the International Union of Official Touring Organizations with headquarters in Geneva, Switzerland. Carpati is represented abroad by many well-known travel firms and it is through Carpati that your travel agent will book your reservations in Romania.

Carpati does not necessarily own the hotels in which tourists are lodged. The hotel may be state-owned, but Carpati is charged with the responsibility of reserving the best sections of the hotel for foreign guests, the size of the areas "blocked" or booked depending on seasoned demands. There is evidence that should the demand suddenly exceed the number of rooms reserved by Carpati in any one town or resort, Romanian guests may find themselves hustled out into the night, the bedroom hastily cleaned and the incoming guest never the wiser.

One would not be wrong to suggest that Carpati suffers from disorganization. I am still trying to figure out the reason (excuse?) for the Carpati approach to hotel reservations. No matter how far ahead your agent may have booked a room, chances are even though confirmed to your agent and yourself months before, the room will not actually be set aside until five to fourteen days before your actual arrival. The disaster potential here seems obvious. Example: your agent books in April for a room in Brasov come July 12; the reservation is confirmed to your agent say four or five weeks later. Roughly seven days before your arrival, say on July 5, Carpati in Bucharest sends a Telex to Brasov to reserve your space. Can Carpati be so certain that tourists will be so few in number that there will always be space in the hotel? More incredible still, is it possible that rooms are blocked off for Carpati in such numbers that the traveler without reservations stands no chance of finding a room. Do Carpati rooms stand idle awaiting an influx of tourists booking through Carpati from abroad?

As the reader may have guessed, there are evident tendencies toward a duplication of activities within the Carpati organization. This is regrettable, for confusion at the organizational level reflects throughout the Carpati offices in the entire country. In Oradea my hotel voucher copies were forgotten; in Sighisoara there was no hotel reservation; in Constanta I was advised by a Carpati employee that Bucharest had ordered the cancellation of my hotel space at Mamaia, this contrary to any plan of mine and despite the fact that I was following to the letter an itinerary programmed in the early part of March.

Carpati offers a great potential but not unlike many large organizations, the personnel structure needs a bit of clarification, the lines of communication need to be simplified. And should there be some form of intra-agency problem here (and I am certain "problem" is putting it mildly) the sparring should be exposed to the public.

Carpati must become less "group oriented." Without realizing it, this agency has arranged most of its facilities—bus trips, night time tours, airport facilities, restaurant accommodations, etc.—largely for groups of persons numbering 15 to 30 and up. As a result, individual visitors, responsible for their own passport formalities, table reservations and tour programs, are to a large extent left to fend for themselves, and sad to say, are at the mercy of a completely disinterested bureaucracy. This situation should not be allowed to continue. Competent hostesses at airports, more bi-lingual receptionists in hotels, areas of dining rooms set aside for individuals, these things will all help make Romania a tourist's delight.

At present Carpati's pride and joy are the three new hotels opened at Mamaia in 1966, which add 1,000 beds to that resort's sleeping capacity. Named the Bicaz, Sirat and Dorna all are in the tourist category. By 1970 Romania expects to have an additional 32,000 beds for foreign tourists, 20,000 of them in new hotels with many at Eforie Nord, Eforie Sud, Mangalia and Media. Camping facilities and motels will also be enlarged and new facilities will be built throughout the country.

In the 1965 tourist season there were 288,000 tourists sent to Romania by travel agents (this total does not include tourists who entered Romania without prior reservations). Up to September 1 of 1966, a total of 300,000 tourists had entered the country. It is expected that 1,200,000 foreign visitors will travel to Romania yearly in 1970. Income from tourism is split in Romania between state and local authorities. Romanian officials have expressed hope that the American tourist will be more interested in the cultural side of their country and are therefore expecting that fewer tourists from the United States will visit the Black Sea resorts. The O.N.T. people invite inquiries about their new program for one-family villas with kitchens and gardens to be constructed in resort areas about the country. The rental price for these villas has not yet been established.

HOTEL RATES

When it comes to hotels, I most earnestly urge you to follow my recommendations. Obviously, I have not visited every hotel in the country, but I have seen many and I know how good and how unacceptable they can be. Romania has a right to be pleased with a number of her tourist accommodations, even though others can well stand improvement. The hotels recommended in the following pages are all clean, comfortable and pleasant. The food they serve is good; the furnishings are adequate; the service is pleasant and efficient. Stay with these hotels and you won't go far wrong.

Rates for hotel accommodations are pretty much the same throughout the country. The following will give you a general idea of what you can expect to pay for various accommodations. Daily rates below are per person with full pension and private bath or shower.

Apartment deluxe, $13; *Room deluxe*, $11.
Apartment first class, $9; *Room first class*, $7.50.

Most rooms are doubles and if they are occupied by one person the rate is somewhat higher than that indicated above. On the other hand tourists traveling on a guided tour basis usually receive a somewhat lower rate.

Deluxe accommodations usually have a telephone and TV (on request). First class rooms usually lack phones and TV, but radios are generally available. Both types of rooms have private bath or shower.

Let me emphasize that you cannot hope to travel across Romania deluxe and still expect to really see the country. Deluxe accommodations simply do not exist in many of the places you will want to visit. I suggest you request deluxe space where available, and first class rooms elsewhere.

As mentioned earlier, evidence of confirmed and prepaid hotel reservations is not necessary when you apply for a visa. However, there are still reasons why it is a good idea not to pop off to Romania on the spur of the moment without reservations of any kind. I have already said that Carpati blocks off or reserves space in the principal hotels; we have no reason to believe that the space is unlimited, once it is entirely possible that you could not get suitable accommodations at the last moment. This leaves you in a desperate condition, because in many areas there is little choice of hotels. Also, Carpati books the best, and when the best is booked to capacity, life immediately becomes rough to tourists without shelter. Since the number of good hotels is severely limited, I would urge that you have in hand confirmed reservations before leaving on your trip. Fair warning: from May through September the best is booked solid in advance.

When you arrange reservations your travel agent will give you a voucher listing your hotels. This voucher should be presented at the first Carpati office you encounter on arrival. You will be given (1) cash to pay for your meals while in Romania and (2) vouchers to be handed to each hotel reception desk along the way as evidence of confirmed reservations. The amount paid in the United States for hotel space is simply channeled directly to the state hotel organization.

Be certain that this first Carpati office provides you with copies of your original voucher; these should be handed to the reservation clerk at each hotel you visit and should list hotels and dates as well as the length of your stay in each town.

In Oradea the Carpati agent, a rather pompous young man (since transferred) forgot to give me any vouchers for the hotels. As a result, there was a cry of rage and frustration from every hotel manager between Transylvania and Constanta. Had it not been for my guide, I fear there might have been some serious difficulty in explaining the absence of identification in order to obtain the reserved room. As it was, there was a veritable snowfall of Telex forms trying to right this mistake.

Registering in a hotel is a simplified procedure in Romania, in fact throughout Eastern Europe. The simplification is however the oversimplification found only in a paternalistic cultural pattern. When you enter a hotel in which you hold reservations and approach the reservation clerk, he takes the voucher (copy) and you receive the key. Period! You are "in" for the length of time stated on your voucher. One mistake and wheels grind to a stop.

Should you be traveling without confirmed reservations, head for the first class hotels listed in this book. There is always a chance that one room or a suite might become available for a night or two. That failing, check with Carpati with reference to a room in a private home. I prefer a private home to lodgings in a second or third class hotel.

Here in Romania particularly, there is little difference between deluxe and first class but second class can be rather like stepping into an elevator shaft. Private homes demonstrate "pride of home."

Keep in mind that hotels "block" rooms for Carpati. Separate rooms are kept available for individual, unexpected guests. Check with *both* the hotel and Carpati before ruling out any particular inn. One organization might know what the other does not.

Travel agencies do not as yet seem abreast of hotel developments in Eastern Europe. Be certain that the hotel offered by your agent as being deluxe or first class actually does have such accommodations. Quite frequently I found myself prepaid for a deluxe hotel in towns where such facilities did not exist.

Remember don't attempt any deluxe or first class travel program on the basis of a prepaid per diem which specifies only deluxe or first class accommodations throughout Romania. As I have noted above, you will encounter towns on your itinerary where deluxe or first class accommodations cannot be found. Your travel agent naturally will collect a commission on the full amount you pay him. Carpati—or any other national travel office—will be obliged to determine for which town you have overpaid and to return to you the difference in lei. As a result you will end up with extra foreign currency for which you may not have a need. Accept the recommendations of this book; select a hotel from those listed and pay the deluxe, first class or tourist rate accordingly. Do not plan to visit any town or city in Romania without first determining the class accommodation in which you will be lodged.

Tourists visiting Romania prepaid should bear well in mind that payments made to an American travel agent will seldom if ever be refunded by Carpati despite assurances by the officials of the Romanian National Travel Office. When my wife and I found our guide was less efficient than we had hoped we terminated his services one week earlier than originally planned. Though we were repeatedly assured by Carpati that the money paid for this guide would be refunded to us in dollars, such funds were never received. So, if cancel you must some portion of your trip while in Romania, I suggest that you accept the refund in Romanian currency and give no consideration to the possibility of any form of dollar refund. Carpati should either not make refunds and so state or follow through with their promises by making refunds available to their guests at the earliest date possible.

DINING

Food in Romania is substantial, tasty, thoroughly appetizing. One notices the definite influence of the Slavish and Turkish cuisine and quite naturally in Transylvania the Hungarian and Viennese kitchens. Dishes are hearty and inclined to be quite filling. I waded through a couple of lunches in provincial towns that left me scarcely fit for an afternoon of sightseeing.

Menus in the larger hotels boast a great variety of dishes, running the gamut from canapes, through soup and eggs, grilled meats, the works! Try those wonderful "mititei," small grilled sausages that are eaten as a first course or with a salad as a complete luncheon. Spicy and delicious! Perhaps for a heartier dish, the "varza da cluj," beef prepared in the manner of a town in Transylvania. Delicious! Or "dovlece," a form of stuffed squash available in the late summer. Omelets are popular and are served in a variety of ways.

Other interesting foods include "corbas," creamy soups; "sarmales," meat wrapped in cabbage leaves usually served with sauerkraut; and "mamaliga," a form of maize mixed with milk or water, something like our hot breakfast cereals only thicker in consistency. Cashcaval, a yellow cheese, can be excellent. Fish, fresh salads, fresh fruit and chicken dishes are in plentiful supply during the summer tourist season. Prices range from 6 lei (the highest) for soups to 10 lei for beef, an average of 8 lei for fish course and 2 lei for fruit. These are the prices in a first class hotel restaurant.

For the most part menus in hotels are printed in English, French and German as well as Romanian. Though hotel menus may list a seemingly providential number of dishes from which to make your selection, your choices should be based on the prices listed on the right-hand side of the page. This is not quite as mercenary a suggestion as it may sound since prices in this case indicate availability. No price! No have!

The "coffee break" in Romania is quite an occasion. Special shops sell the product for home consumption or provide facilities for drinking it on the spot. Buy your ground coffee for a few lei from the counter girl and line up at the expresso machine. Tell the girl how many sugars—*et voila*! freshly made coffee, Italian style. Rum and brandy are also available. A pleasant Romanian custom. Coffee (Turkish filtered and impresso) is also available at your hotel. Coffee served in the small shops does not contain the grounds at the bottom of the cup usually associated with Turkish coffee. Should you order Turkish coffee at your hotel, remember to sip. If you gulp it your mouth will become so full of grounds you'll feel like "Gravel Gertie!"

I recommend that tourists drink only bottled water throughout Eastern Europe.

Keep in mind that 18 lei equal one dollar. Some representative prices for food at deluxe Romanian hotels are: filet of beef, nine lei 39 bani; pork chops, 9.40; beefsteak with eggs, 12.15; omelet with fines herbes, 4.45; potatoes with onions, 80 bani; rice, 85 bani. Should you think to request Worcestershire Sauce, *don't*! One tablespoon runs about $2—and ketchup! forget it! Worse yet, black caviar (if you can get it) runs about $5 a portion whereas carp caviar costs 14 cents!

DRINKS AND DRINKING

Now in the hard drinking department, a few pointers choice-wise and price-wise: Just about every divertissement is available if you are willing to pay the price. Three Star Hennessey, 50 lei; Gordon's Gin, 14 lei; Dubonnet, eight lei. See what I mean? A zero added to these prices gives an idea of the cost of a bottle; But why not try some of the local products? *Teuica,* a powerful fruit brandy is good! There are also various local brandies and the good Bulgarian *Pliska.* Czechoslovakian beer, the famous Pilsner variety, runs roughly six lei per bottle. Local beers, which are acceptable, cost one or two lei less.

I won't bother to quote wine prices because they are uniformly inexpensive. All rieslings are good. A favorite of mine, *Feteasca Regala,* is an excellent light, white wine. *Cabernet* is very dry. *Otonel* from Arad is dry and white. *Dealul Mare* is also white and medium dry! Wine sales are inclined to be regional. If you fail to find a particular wine in one place, ask in another town. The first wines mentioned here were all available in Transylvania; the last one in Mamaia. *Tirnava,* a riesling, is quite good as is *Odobesti. Algeote* is dry but bitter.

Other wines which are my favorites in Romania are *Tirnave* and *Cotnari.* Both are white, fairly light and dry. Red wines in Romania are inclined to be the full-bodied Burgundy type.

Syphon bottles of soda water are available (brought to your room) in all leading hotels in Romania. In those hotels that don't have soda you will most likely be provided with an acceptable form of mineral water. Ice and a large bottle of soda water in Bucharest's leading hotel via room service costs two lei. Not bad for "set-ups."

The old adage "a fool and his money are soon parted" is particularly well applied here in Romania. Food prices are comparatively low but keep in mind that the per diem is also rather low ($11 deluxe). This is to say that dinner brandies, tend to approach a rather formidable total. If you plan to lean heavily on your travelers checks, so okay—eat, drink, be merry! On the other hand, if you are determined to live within your prepaid travel budget without recourse to extra funds, take it easy.

MOTORING

Drive to the right, observe the speed limits and watch out for any object too large to be covered with a thimble. A truck driver in Giuriu who had stopped at the curb without warning, suddenly raced his vehicle backwards. He learned of the presence of a motorcyclist when he first heard the scream.

Gas stations are found somewhere along the edge of every good-sized town. You may have to do a bit of looking around before finding one and some waiting in line once you've arrived. Use the 97 octane variety which costs almost 2 lei per liter. This gas comes from tanks painted with a blue stripe.

Car owners whether you drive your own or rent abroad, know your car; that is, before entering Eastern Europe try to learn something of the car's innards so that you can explain the vehicle to folks not acquainted with the latest European and American cars. No need to seem boastful; of course not! Open the doors, raise the hood, open the trunk, explain the functions of the various parts and the buttons on the dashboard. Men (and some gals, too!) ages five to eighty will crowd about asking all sorts of questions. Someone in the group usually speaks English, German or French. The questions will be pointed and many in number. This can lead to lively contacts with the local people.

Garages have gas, water, oil, pails—and a lot of enthusiasm. The modern service garage at Mamaia makes up in effort what it lacks in supplies. Take along brake fluid, extra oil, transmission fluid and a set of tools. Soap for car washing is also suggested. Should you manage a dent somewhere along the road, you'll be surprised how the garage mechanics can straighten it out.

Police

Throughout Romania, on the outskirts of each sizeable town you will notice what seem to be small guardhouses manned by police officers (usually sporting red patches on their collars). Originally built and staffed to control the flow of traffic from town to town, from one area of the country to another, these huts are presently little more than traffic control centers. The police stationed here are not concerned with foreign tourists as long as they abide by local traffic regulations. They will, however, frequently direct traffic or nod, perhaps salute as you drive past. It would be thoughtful if you acknowledged them by a wave or smile for their job is a lonely one and then, they are the law. Romanian drivers and motorcyclists are frequently stopped by these officers and required to show drivers license, to check the weight of their trucks, etc.

Forbidden Areas

Do not bring your car to a stop in front of any military base, barracks, military airport or the like. Should you have—as did I—a flat directly in front of one such establishment, go about the business of changing the tire and get the heck out as soon as possible. As I wrestled with the tire, a corporal on guard at the gate came over to explain that his sergeant had instructed him to tell us to M-O-V-E (this passed to me through my guide). It was hot, sultry and the tire as flat as could be. We asked the corporal if he expected us to drive on the rim of the wheel. Later the suggestion was made that perhaps rather than stand there he might be of some service so that we could leave more quickly. He left us. That was that! So don't become overly concerned about trouble with authorities.

If you should have a breakdown on a stretch of road along which are posted several international road signs indicating "No Stopping" (a blue circular sign trimmed in red with a red diagonal slash running from upper left to lower right, across the face of which may be written the words "Opires Interzisa"), I urge that you raise the hood of your engine as a form of distress signal and attempt to stop the next car that comes along. If the trouble seems momentarily insolvable, ask for a tow or push to a spot well beyond the area of these signs usually posted only a short distance along a main road near highly restricted areas. Chances are the first car to stop will be a military car as such areas are well patrolled.

Maps

Highway maps distributed by the Romanian government show all kinds of roads in tip-top shape (principal highways at that); yet I know of a number of instances where the pavement has not even been adequately surfaced. Travel on such roads is mighty wearing on car and rider, if not downright hazardous. Better check with your hotel before leaving on the next lap of your journey. The main stretch of highway from the Bore border (from Hungary) through Orades-Cluj-Alba Iulia-Sibiu-Brasov to Bucharest is particularly well maintained and a beautiful trip to boot.

Romania puts out a particularly good map for motorists which can be purchased locally. The front section outlines the "rules of the road" (largely the same as elsewhere) in five languages, including English. The principal section of the folded paper booklet provides numbered sectional maps, the numbers tieing in with an outline toward the front of the booklet. A single sheet up-to-date road map of Romania is also available.

As stated previously, check with your hotel or Carpati desk before starting out on any drive. Maps do not always show the incomplete state of some roads.

Car Rentals

Self-drive and chauffered card (and complete information thereon) are available through the National Travel Office (Carpati). When you rent a car in Romania you are required to make a cash deposit of about $70. The type of car available to you will most likely be a Hillman "Minx." The minimum amount of time for which you may hire a car is one day (24 hours). If you hire a car for several days, you will not be charged for any delay in returning the car that is less than six hours; delays exceeding six hours will be charged as one day. Costs for care hire are as follows: for one to six days, about $5 a day; seven days to one month, $4.50 per day; for over one month (or 30 days) $4 per day; plus, in each instance, 5c per kilometer. These prices include insurance against damage and third-party risks, lubrication and washing, radio maintenance and a motoring map. Tariffs do not include gasoline, garage and parking fees or damage not covered by insurance.

Chauffeur driven cars (without guide) are available. The Zim, a Russian four-seater, rents for 15c per kilometer; the Chevrolet and three-seater Volga for 12c. These are out-of-town rates; in town, the aforementioned cost is $3 an hour. The maintenance of the chauffeur added to the above-mentioned tariffs runs $5 for the day out of town, or for six hours in town. In the case of motor coaches and Mini-Buses, the chauffeur maintenance runs $10 a day. The rent for motor coaches out of town runs 30c per kilometer (with a minimum charge for 200 kilometers per day). Mini-Buses rent for 20c a kilometer outside of town (with a minimum charge for 200 kilometers per day).

SHOPPING

Tax free shops are located throughout the country at all ports of entry, in the principal cities and at resorts such as Mamaia. These stores display Romanian goods such as carpets, national costumes, ceramics, leatherwork, woven materials, wood objects, liqueurs, and so on. When you purchase goods in one of these stores (the addresses can be obtained at any Carpati office), show the slip given to you at the bank or tourist office in which you exchanged your dollars for lei. This will immediately entitle you to a 20 per cent discount on any purchase that costs at least 100 lei. You may also buy special travelers checks at the national bank which allow for the 20 per cent discount. However, I feel your regular exchange slip mentioned above is adequate.

Naturally you can also buy goods here without the discount being applied. Actually, I cannot see why you could not exchange say $40 and then traipse about the country applying this one money exchange transaction to each one of your discount store purchases. Anyway, save the bank slip! The items in these shops are colorful, of good workmanship, interesting in design and even in some instances practical, such as towels or beach sandals at Mamaia. I found many items to be over-priced. Goods may be shipped directly to your home address. My recommendation: take them with you! No duty is charged on goods purchased at discount houses.

Purchases can be made in Romania of woodcarving, ceramics, table covers and wooden slivowitz bottles, also colorfully costumed dolls. Prices are generally medium to high, with those fine pieces of linen completely overpriced.

While in Moldavia you may find the black on black ceramics (vases, plates, etc.) interesting and may wish to make a purchase. Don't delay! Though a number of items displayed in these discount stores are to be found throughout the country, these particular ceramics seem limited to Moldavia. I would call your attention to the fact that black sometimes becomes gray when the item is exposed to water.

SIGHTSEEING

Guides

I would emphatically urge any American motorist visiting the hinterlands of Romania for the first time to employ a guide from the moment he crosses the border until his arrival in Bucharest. Unlike Budapest or perhaps Prague, the Romanian capital is centrally located and some distance away from the borders with neighboring countries; therefore, with the exception of travel between Bulgaria and Bucharest, visitors arriving by car from other lands must pass at least their first night in Romania outside of the capital.

The hinterlands of Romania are full of historical sights, none of which should be missed. But seeing is not necessarily understanding; and a rudimentary knowledge of the language will not be enough. Unless you are well acquainted with Transylvania, Moldavia, Walachia and the other regions that make up this exciting country, without a guide, you can not possibly appreciate the museums, libraries, castles, spas and hillside towns that are to be explored. I feel a guide is also almost a necessity when one takes excursions outside Bucharest.

Just imagine being one of the first Americans to step through the door of a 16th-century palace turned into an art museum by its original owner, this museum now housing the works of such masters as Titian, Van Dyck and Rubens! Or climbing a hill topped by a fortress built during the Crusades in a town which never capitulated to the "terrible Turk"! Perhaps you would wish to visit a very small library which houses a collection of the original French Academy volumes of Napoleon's military expedition to Egypt. The library comprises a total of 110,000 books bought in the 1700's, in every instance a complete set of volumes as originally purchased. To learn the whereabouts of these towns, galleries, libraries and the many more sights to be found in Transylvania, *you must have a guide* — and a *good one*. Many of these historical treasures are in the most unlikely places, sections of a town to which you will not be directed by signs or pamphlets.

Carpati guides are paid $15 per day, all inclusive. They will meet you at the frontier and then accompany you to that pre-arranged point where you have indicated their service would be terminated. I feel that guides are absolutely necessary throughout Romania with the exception of Bucharest and Mamaia. You should, however insist that your guide be thoroughly trained for his work. One guide in my experience was extremely well versed in the historical background of all sections of Romania, while another man assigned to my party didn't know a restoration from a 13th-century original. If you find your guide to be unprepared for the tour which lies ahead, dismiss him at the first Carpati office available and demand that Bucharest send a replacement at no cost to you. Romania is rich in history; to wander through this sea of pre-Christian treasures, this art work of the Middle Ages, with an untrained guide is to lose the opportunity of a lifetime.

Sightseeing tours of towns with an interpreter-guide (entrance fees to museums included) using a Carpati car cost as follows: tour of Bucharest, half-day $10 for one person; $5.50 each for two persons; $3.75 each for three persons. An entire day's tour for one person $18, $9.50 each for two persons, $6.50 each for three persons. Night time tours of Bucharest including visits to two nightclubs cost $16 for one person, $10 each for two persons and $8 each for three persons. These rates are considerably reduced when the tourist uses his own car. Mini-Buses and motor coaches are available for charter at reasonable costs.

Tours of the Romanian coastline visiting such towns as Mamaia, Constana, Eforie Nord, etc., cost between $13 for one person by car and $1 per person by bus (minimum 15 persons).

The cost of a guide in town for one hour will be about $2; for a half day $6; whole day $10. A guide's services for a whole day outside of any town will cost you about $14. If the services of a guide are requested from and to the border point, transport expenses are added to the daily tariff in the place of sojourn.

Photography

Bring your camera along! Possession of a camera will be noted in your passport or on your visa by the customs official at the time you make a declaration of your currency. Take photos right and left for Romania is one of the most scenic countries of Europe. This is particularly true where architecture, national dress and resort areas are concerned. Photographs of Moldavian churches, the fortress hill of Sighisoara and the wide, wide beach at Mamaia will make delightful souvenirs of your trip. Take along enough film and have all the photographs developed when you return home, for the quality of processing the negatives is far better here than there. Don't forget some flashbulbs for those evening shots of national dancers performing at the open air theater at Mamaia or in some small clubs in Bucharest.

The writer assumes that you will be able to restrain the impulse to photograph a "No Stopping" sign; that you will beat back that impassioned suggestion to photograph the shipyards at Constana. Games are for children and such actions certainly smack of either infantilism or senility. When you aim your camera, select the correct light, the proper focus and a sensible background.

Tours

The Romanian government offers a wide selection of activities which may be enjoyed by those persons visiting their country. Such programs are under the immediate direction of Carpati. Itineraries for Romanian holiday group tours are available at all Carpati offices. In the U.S. see your travel agent for information regarding such packaged tours through Romania.

Sightseeing trips out of Bucharest revolve around five basic itineraries lasting from 1 to 12 days. Costs of these tours run from $8 to $140 per person and provide fairly extensive coverage of Romania. Accommodations are in the first class category.

A number of excursions originate from the Black Sea resorts of Mamaia, Eforie Nord and Eforie Sud. Included are excursions to North Moldavia, Bucharest, Histria and the wine region Murfatlar. Transportations for such tours is by bus and plane. Excursions from Constanta to Istanbul, as well as to Odessa are available to visitors either by plane or by ship. Prices for both local and foreign excursions originating at the Black Sea resorts are reasonable, in fact quite advantageous to the foreign visitor. Payment for all excursions must be made in foreign currency.

CAMPING

Camping areas are located near the following towns and resorts: Mamia; Sibiu (Dumbrava Park), Orades (1 Mai Health Resort); Bicaz; Timisoara; Cluj at (Foget); and Bucharest (Snagov Forest). At these locations the camper will be provided with electric light, running water, toilet facilities and parking area. Food stores and restaurants are located nearby. Tents and camping equipment are usually available for rental. Foreign tourists can use their own tents or park their trailers in these camping areas. No permits are required for camping. Camping equipment can be brought into Romania by tourists duty free.

There are additional camping grounds providing less elaborate facilities for campers in the Out Valley at Ilisesti (Suceava); at Lake Saint Ana (Tusnad); at Lake Bucura (in the Retezal Mountains); and at Teliuc in the Cerna Valley (Hunedoara). The charge for camping, including one tent or trailer, is 50c a day. The camping season runs from June 1 to September 30.

Most bungalows comprise four rooms with two beds in each. Toilets, showers and laundry areas are located nearby. Hot and cold running water is supplied. The Carpati tariff listing fails to advise us of the bungalow rates; however, I know that at Mamaia the cost per person runs about $4 per day, $1 of which is for the accommodations, the remainder for meals. Children between the ages of four and ten are entitled to a 50% reduction; this includes an extra bed in the parents' room and half an adult portion at meals. There is also a 15% reduction granted in off-season.

Rooms at student hostels include two beds, hot and cold running water and toilets. Meals are served at restaurants nearby. Prices (between June and September, including room and full pension) are about $6 per person per day. Note should be made that in all hotels, bungalows and student hostels there is a supplementary charge for a single room). Student hostels are located in Bucharest, Brasov, Cluj, Timisoara and Jassy.

SPAS

The health spas of Romania are under the direct supervision of the Romanian Institute of Balneology and Physiotherapy. The best known spas are at Eforie Nord, on the Black Sea coast 16 kilometers south of the port city of Constanta; Herculane, in the Cerna Valley not far from the Danube River; Sovata, in the northern part of the Transylvania Plateau; and Govora, located near Rimnicu-Vilcea at a fairly high altitude in wooded hills.

Contact Carpati for specifics regarding the treatments offered at the above health spas. Daily tariffs for individual tourists in high season run from $1.50 at Herculane to $2 at the other named spas. First class accommodations including meals are available at Eforie Nord and Herculane; second class accommodations at Herculane, Sovata and Govora. Tourists arriving in the off-season (apply to Carpati for specific dates regarding the "seasons") will benefit from a 20% reduction.

HUNTING AND FISHING

The range of birds, game and fish offered to the sportsman in Romania is almost endless. The principal regions for hunting and fishing are the

Danube Delta, the Romanial steppe (Walachia), the Carpathian forests (Transylvania), the "Alpine Zone," and the streams and lakes of the High Carpathians. Egret, heron, cormorant and species of duck and geese live in the Delta region, as do otter, ermine, red fox, wildcat, muskrat, wolf and deer. The steppe areas offer such birds as the bustard (large and small), partridge, quail, pheasant, doves and pigeons. The forest areas harbor such game as roebuck and boar, foxes, martens, wildcats, polecats, weasels and other smaller game. In September the three-month season for tracking the magnificent Carpathian stag commences. Bears, capercailzie and grouse live in the deeper forests. In the "Alpine Zone" one may encounter the chamois. The lakes and streams of the mountain areas furnish such fish as trout, grayling and huck.

Carpati can furnish you with a very complete pamphlet giving the exact dates of the hunting seasons for the various game and fish. Specific prices for game killed (or missed) are also included. Some examples: Carpathian stag with antlers weighing up to 6 kg., $300; on those from 9 kg. to 9.5 inclusive, $1,000 and so on. There is a $100 charge for a miss and $200 for a wound. Roebucks run about $200 maximum, fallow deer average $400, chamois average $150 to $200 and bear $1,000; hare, pheasant, pelican, swan $30 with other small birds about $10 each. There are $10 charges for a miss with these smaller birds and animals. A $10 charge is also applied if the hunter hunts but does not shoot the animal though the game was available to him.

Cost of the stay at the hunting ground is $18 daily for the hunter, except in the Danube Delta where the cost is $20 daily. Members of the hunter's family are charged $10 each daily. These charges cover room and full pension, an interpreter-guide, means of transportation in the hunting grounds and, in the Delta, a boat. (Boat charges are about $7 per hour when running, half that when idle.) Payments are best made either in advance or in Bucharest before leaving for the hunting areas.

Thirty rifle cartridges, 500 gun cartridges, one rifle-scope and a camera may be brought into Romania free of duty. Gun cartridges for shooting hare and pheasant are available in the country at 1.50 lei each. Veterinary certificates are necessary for hunting dogs brought into the country; such certificates must stipulate that not more than five months and not less than thirty days previously the animal had a rabies shot.

Hunting in Romania can be a mighty expensive pastime, but I can guarantee that the rewards for skill and marksmanship are great. The trout fishing is terrific, particularly in the area south (and high above) Fagaras.

CABLES, WIRES, PHONE CALLS, AND MAIL

The large hotels have mail desks where one may buy stamps, postcards, newspapers, magazines, etc. Letters are weighed on the spot. Register all mail! The cost (registered) to Western Europe is 3.20 lei; regular mail is 1.60; postcards, 1 lei. Tell your friends to register letters sent to you. These prices are all based on mail not exceeding 20 grams. Mail delivery is spotty. Figure not less than ten days for a letter to reach you from any point outside the country.

At hotels your mail will be handed to you when you request your key. Have your mail sent only to Bucharest unless you are remaining in the provinces for some length of time.

Telegrams and cables can be sent from the hotel mail desk, or you can visit the Telegraph Office (originally an American installation, by the way). However, I do not recommend sending wires from the telegraph offices for the formalities plus the language barrier are very discouraging.

Telephone calls can be placed through your hotel switchboard. Service to Western Europe takes several hours. For the fastest telephone service within Romania, ask for an extra-charge call; the charges are not excessive and the call will go through in a matter of minutes.

GUM AND CIGARETTES

No one spoke of chewing gum in Hungary; in Bulgaria the subject was not mentioned. But in Romania—phenomenon! Be sure to take along some extra sticks for the children. They love it! Rather refreshing to have a child ask for a stick of gum rather than cigarettes. Their parents like it too!

Some American brands of cigarettes and various European makes are available at stiff prices. Why not try the tasty, mild, well-packaged Bulgarian cigarettes? Ask for *Fila, BT,* or *Tresor.* Otherwise, bring along a couple of cartons from home.

BUCHAREST

I frankly do not credit Bucharest with more than a "C" rating as a tourist attraction, though the capital is a busy beautiful city of which Romanians can be justly proud. With the exception of one or two museums, the city's parks, restaurants and hotels, there really is not a great deal to see. I would suggest that three full days would be quite enough time in which to see the sights here.

Sightseeing

NATIONAL ART GALLERY Situated in the former royal palace just across the street from the Hotel Athens Palace. Important to check visiting hours, particularly during the summer. In any case, plan to get there not later than two o'clock in the afternoon.

CULTURE AND REST PARK The Romanian Government has erected a Village Museum along the banks of Lake Herastrau. You will find a very fine collection of 40 typical Romanian dwellings brought to Bucharest from all the varied regions of the country. Churches, shrines, stables, windmills and farm buildings are arranged in such fashion as to actually compose a small (though quite naturally polyglot) Romanian village of the 18th and 19th centuries. One house was actually built in the 1600's. The buildings are filled with household utensils, ceramics, carpets, costumes, wood carvings, all intended to give the visitor an authentic, well-researched look into Romanian village life over the past 200 years or more.

MUSEUM OF NATURAL HISTORY Located some ten minutes' ride on Bus #34 which passes directly in front of the Ambassador Hotel. Here you will see a very good collection of butterflies, animals, fish, etc. I was particularly interested in charts relating to the migratory habits of birds. Certainly interesting but not exceptional!

SCINTELIA HOUSE Near Banease Airport. A large printing establishment occupying a building whose design is strikingly familiar to buildings constructed in Warsaw and Prague. Maybe you'll like to tour!

COUNCIL OF MINISTERS BUILDING Located across from the Natural History Museum, the Athenaeum housing the Romanian Philharmonic (across from the Hotel Athenee Palace), the Opera and Ballet Theaters, the large new square containing the Palace of the Republic and so on. Most of these buildings are closed during the summer.

LAKE SNAGOV Northeast of the city as well as the Mogosoaia Palace, a museum of feudal art. Don't miss the many small art collections housed in the former homes of such artists as Aman; Zambaccian and Tatterescu.

PARKS Bucharest is surrounded by many lovely parks. As the city is quite hot during the summer months, these parks provide a wonderful relief on long August afternoons. Why not some boating on *Lake Herastrau* or a walk through the attractive park located not far from the New Opera House?

Hotels

ATHENEE PALACE Those of you who may have visited Bucharest prior to World War II will remember the Athenee Palace as the "Royal Athenee." This Hotel, directly across the street from the former Royal Palace, continues to be the capital's best hotel. Located on the wide and fashionable Calea Victoria, the Athenee Palace, a five-story structure, faces the National Art Gallery and the Concert Hall. The original structure boasts 179 rooms, 25 apartments, 80 doubles with bath and 17 singles with bath plus some singles with shower. There are also five garconieres or beds set in small recesses off medium-sized living rooms. All outside rooms have balconies. In 1965 the management opened a smart-appearing addition directly behind the main building and connected to it. There are 12 apartments and 125 doubles with bath and shower; a new restaurant seating 800, a summer garden, night bar and snack bar. Three automatic elevators lead to the seven very well furnished floors where almost every convenience has been provided for the guests. The lobby of the new structure has been joined to the older hotel area. Request a room in this new section—the accommodations are very pleasant. Maid service is good. Room service for breakfast. Telephones.

The restaurant looks into a pleasantly appointed garden where guests may enjoy after-dinner coffee or an aperitif. Service is fair. A section of the floor slides away to provide space for dancing. Near the main entrance is a very pleasant cafe (open for three meals a day). This informal cafe-restaurant is just the spot for lunch and is very popular for dinner, too. The food is tasty and nicely served.

The Athenee Palace is within walking distance of the main shopping streets, theaters, Carpati offices (three blocks from the main hotel entrance), art galleries and restaurants. Carpati maintains a service desk for foreign guests in the lobby staffed by English-speaking personnel. TAROM, the Romanian Air Line, also has an office in the Athenee Palace.

Note: Be certain your accommodations include a room with phone. A number of rooms do not have telephones. One could easily find himself completely cut off from all activities, functional as well as recreational, without that all important phone. Caution: Telephones, even when available, frequently do not operate correctly.

LIDO This hotel is comfortable, somewhat less aristocratic than the Athenee Palace, more casual. A very pleasant lobby, exchange desk and attractive cocktail lounge are off the main lobby. There is an inside (winter) dining room as well as an elaborate pool terrace and bar for summer dining. A popular "stand-up" buffet-type restaurant is located at the corner of the building which I do not recommend.

The Hotel Lido is located on the main business street, an area that can be somewhat noisy, so I would suggest that you reserve above the second floor. Book on the rear side of the hotel facing the gigantic swimming pool unless you are visiting during the summer when poolside rooms are just plain hot. There are six floors with approximately thirty rooms per floor. Lounges are on each floor with comfortable settees. There are only four single rooms and five apartments in this hotel. All rooms here have bath and telephones. Radios on request. The five apartments are acceptably furnished in a comfortable fashion. In the apartments you will find two rooms plus entry hall and bath.

The main restaurant opens in September. During the summer months, guests and visitors are invited to use the attractive, large terraces around the enormous swimming pool available for breakfast, lunch and dinner. The food is very good and served with surprising speed. This restaurant remains open quite late in the evening. Dress well. The umbrellas, awnings, planting make this a gay spot. Entertainment in the evening. The hotel restaurant provides music for its intimate evening dining seven days a week during fall and winter months. The Hotel Lido also boasts a very intimate, nicely lighted, attractively decorated cocktail lounge a few steps down from the main lobby. Good drinks, well served, at reasonably high prices. I would be extremely cautious about making friends in this particular locale.

NORD Now here is a smartly designed and decorated modern hotel boasting the latest conveniences, backed up by up-to-date hotel management. Located two short blocks from the North Railway Station, the hotel is surrounded by a large parking area and sits well back from the very busy roadway.

A spacious lobby opens into a smart little "day bar" where breakfast is also served. The bar is quite near the restaurant which can seat approximately 450 persons. There is music for dancing in the restaurant every evening.

Off to the side of the restaurant and lobby is a large patio furnished with tables and chairs.

All rooms in the Nord are double so you will be charged a double rate for single occupancy. Baths throughout the building. Hand showers may be affixed to wall brackets. Rooms are very clean; bathrooms well designed. Apartments at the Nord do not exist; instead there are two double rooms joined by connecting doors, one such unit to each floor of the building. I recommend that you take rooms to the rear side of this hotel to avoid street noises.

The one drawback is the distance from the main shopping centers and government offices. By car, the Hotel Nord is roughly six minutes from central Bucharest. The roads between the Hotel and the broad avenues of the capital are not in the best condition. There is a cab stand nearby, and frequent bus and streetcar service.

AMBASSADOR Directly across the street from the Lido and somewhat to the right and across from the main Carpati offices. It is cluttered, noisy and ill-lighted. Off the lobby are (1) a small cafe-bar and (2) the second class restaurant for short orders and low spenders. The main restaurant is quite pleasant, seating over 300 people. The food is good; service willing! An orchestra furnishes music during the evening hours.

Rooms until the seventh floor are much the same, floor by floor. Practically every other floor of this approximately 14-story building has a different room arrangement. There are 256 rooms in all, most with baths, others with shower (usually singles). All rooms have telephones; apartments are wired for TV, and radios are available to guests.

When making reservations, be specific as to your desires. To describe all the rooms here in the Ambassador would be impossible. Large apartments, small apartments, garconieres (beds in an alcove adjoining a small sitting room); apartments have terraces, with chairs, without chairs. Large rooms run about 230 Lei and up; singles at 56 Lei. Oh yes, and specify your sex. Rooms are available in portly walnut or pretty pink. If you don't like the room you have, ask to see another style. Remember: a glass-doored *empty* bookcase can up your price.

Restaurants

PARCUL TRANDAFIRILOR Located not far from the Ambassador, Lido and Athenee hotels. This restaurant has slipped to such an extent in food, service and surroundings that it can no longer be recommended. Those of you who enjoy the "Big Beat" music popular in mid-sixties Bucharest might like to stop by here for a drink after dinner.

CINA Located directly across the large plaza to the front of the Athenee Palace Hotel, the Restaurant Cina provides inside dining in winter and a garden location under striped awnings for summer dining. Music in the evening. Good food. Service makes every effort to keep up with demands—and the demand is heavy. Tours eat here en masse between eleven thirty and one. Plan your lunch time accordingly. A nice informal spot in which to recover from a morning's tramp around the National Art Gallery. Prices are right!

A Bodega (or inexpensive beer, wine and snack restaurant) occupies the side of the Cina nearest the Athenee Palace. Not fancy, but if it's a cold beer in lazy surroundings you're looking for, this is the place.

PESCARUS Lake Herastrau is the cooling-off locale for Bucharest during the hot, hot summer months. The Village Museum, the Park for Culture and Rest, swimming pavilions, boat rental stalls, plus various restaurants are located near this attractive little lake. The Pescarus is one such summer eatery. Rustic in architecture, the Pescarus, has an enclosed section, an open terrace overlooking the lake as well as an open-sided covered area. You have your choice of locations here depending on the weather. Reserve in advance and dress well. No sport shirts, open collars and shorts here in the evenings. Go late, not before eight-thirty. Figure a 10 minute car ride from your hotel. The Pescarus is well within the city but in a secluded, quiet area. Food is good. Service fair. Prices are up a bit here. The orchestra is imported from the Athenee Palace Hotel.

MIORITA Again on Lake Herastrau, the Miorita is located next to the Village Museum. If you wish, take Bus #34 from downtown Bucharest (in front of the Hotel Ambassador); ask the ticket seller to tell you where to get off. This restaurant is particularly pleasant on a hot summer's day. Lunch or dinner! Covered terraces overlooking the lake. A very clean kitchen and public toilets. Service is pleasant. The food is average to good. Music in the evening. Dress informally. Menus are in French as well as Romanian, though the waiters, however pleasant, seemingly speak only Romanian.

BUCURESTI A very intimate, nicely furnished restaurant serving excellent food. About a four-minute ride from the Athenee Palace. One section of this restaurant is a cafe while other rooms around the corner are more elegant, more intimate. Eat in this second area. Though formal, there is decidedly more atmosphere. Fine food; fair service. No music, at least in the summer. Dress well.

BERLIN This restaurant is off the Calea Victoria on a side street quite near the House of the Army. This average-sized informal restaurant is open for lunch and dinner, serving in a prompt affable fashion.

The Berlin comprises two large rooms plus an outdoor dining facility and maintains an orchestra for dancing during the dinner hour. Arrive not later than seven-thirty as this place is popular and all seats are occupied by eight o'clock. The situation is further complicated by the Berlin restaurant's willingness to cater to group tours. Dress informally but not too casually.

THE MELODY BAR Located directly beneath the Patria Cinema across from the Carpati office on Boulevard General Magheru. A 50 Lei person entrance fee is charged, to be deducted from your bill. Proceeding down a flight of narrow stairs you will find yourself in an elaborately decorated room; tables surround the dance floor on four sides.

You should not plan to visit this particular location much before ten o'clock nor would I suggest eating here. It would be best to go to the Melody Bar to enjoy an after-dinner drink and see the floor show. The Melody Bar is a clean, pleasant, high standard locale.

CONTINENTAL The Melody Bar's competition for the favors of foreign visitors and Romanians alike is the Continental located near the Romanian National Airlines office, TAROM. An entry fee must be paid and again one must go to the basement level. (A balcony seats approximately 200 guests. It is virtually impossible to see the floor show from the balcony.) I found the atmosphere not glamorous, crowded but nonetheless intimate and congenial. Again I would not consider a meal here though food is served; rather, a bottle of wine, a brandy, tzuica, champagne, whatever you will. Perhaps you might have fruit or nuts brought to your table. Entertainment is extremely good.

CARUL CU BERE Located in a central section of the capital, the "Beer Wagon" Restaurant was highly recommended by Romanian friends. Restaurant is also open for lunch.

PADUREA BANEASA This rather informal but extremely pleasant restaurant is located in a small, cottage-like structure deep inside Baneasa Park just north of Bucharest's principal airport. Surrounded by gardens and deep forests, the restaurant has both inside and outside dining facilities and on a warm summer's day the terraces are usually overflowing with diners. Parking facilities are located nearby. The food is fair to good, prices for meals are about average for a first class Romanian restaurant. The Padurea Baneasa Restaurant is frequented by local people, giving some measure of its popularity. Below is a wine cellar where the service is more informal and one may experiment with local vintages.

PARCUL PRIVIGHETORILOR This restaurant is certainly recommended. Ten minutes walk down the road from the Padurea Baneasa Restaurant and again just to the east of the northbound road to Ploesti, the Parcul Privighetorilor Restaurant is a folk-style restaurant built in the style of a Romanian country inn. Here one will find a broad open terrace on which are cages for birds and animals. An orchestra plays during the dinner hour. The interior is designed in a rather homey and colorful style; waiters and waitresses are dressed in local costumes. In short, if you wish a rather folksy atmosphere, colorful and very pleasant, with the prices up a bit from the Padurea Baneasa Restaurant, then I would choose the Parcul Privighetorilor.

ALBA IULIA

Enroute to Sighisoara from Bucharest you might enjoy lunch in the small town of Alba Iulia. Here is a rickety-clickety restaurant directly on the highway in the center of town. The building is desperately in need of repairs but rise above it. Though the service is slow, the food is good; the kitchen in acceptable shape. Don't let appearances throw you. It is a popular place with cross-country travelers.

ARAD

Hotel

MURESUL Located on Arad's main shopping street, the Muresul is a quiet, old-fashioned hotel, comfortably (if a bit sparsely) furnished, with no elevator and a formidable staircase. There is no restaurant, although breakfast ordered the night before will be brought in at the hour requested. I suggest you request Apartment 163 which boasts a bathroom. There are also two doubles with baths, a three-bedded room with bath, another with shower. All other rooms have only washbowls. There are 64 rooms in all. Prices run generally lower than average. I find the Victorian atmosphere relaxing if it's clean (as it is here).

Restaurant

MURESUL This is a very pleasant place for dinner—enclosed restaurant and large garden area for summer dining. Dance music. The service is quite good and the food excellent. It is priced a bit high compared to other local restaurants. There is a second Muresul Restaurant located just up the block to the left of the Hotel Muresul with inside dining, good food, acceptable service, music.

BACAU

Restaurant

BISTRITSA Driving from Iasi to Brasov you might enjoy lunch at the Hotel Bistritsa Restaurant located in this good-sized, fast-growing industrial town and next door to Communist Party Headquarters. Good food, pleasant surroundings, average to good service. Keep in mind that the Bistritsa offers no fast meals for the "traveler on the go."

BAILE HERCULANE

Founded in 1864 by the Austro-Hungarian Emperor Franz Josef, Herculane has continued to thrive mainly as a Spa. I am told that the resort was visited as early as 107 A.D. The spa is in south-central Transylvania set in a deep valley surrounded by beautiful tree-covered slopes. Herculane is actually only one narrow street lined with clinics and bath houses.

Hotel

CERNA Sits on a small rise not far from the entrance to the Spa. Built in the pseudo-Arabesque motif fashionable in the early 1900's, the Cerna is just off the main promenade. It is quiet and well managed. There are no phones in the rooms. Beds are comfortable. There are small balconies off many rooms. The resort is open year round, rooms are heated. Fourteen singles with bath, 36 doubles with bath and hand shower; 4 apartments. No radio or TV.

The restaurant here is an experience. Crowded? People seem to be eating at all hours! The kitchen is clean, the food average and the waitresses remarkably sane, crowds, hours and demands considered. You'll really get a chance to meet the people. I would recommend the Cerna to those people who wish to know Romania just a bit better; to see Romanians on their vacations. Plan to stay not longer than two or three nights. The resort is simply not designed for foreign guests; the environment doesn't offer enough diversion from the primary business of "taking the baths."

BRASOV (Kronstadt)

Five-hundred year old Brasov is one of the most attractive cities of Europe. From her broad boulevards, to the narrow streets of the town's older sections, whether you look up to the mountains or through the windows of the many interesting small shops lining the street, you will really love Brasov. There are the small restaurants, the Old Town Square with its centuries-old guild and municipal houses and the tour of Bran Castle at Risnow—about 30 kilometers southwest of the city. There is so much to see in and around this city, particularly if you enjoy hiking, climbing, fishing, exploring (trails or shops), that a stay at Brasov should not be limited to less than three nights.

The Black Church here in Brasov is interesting to some; here you will see old carpets donated by merchants returning from the east. The Museum of History and Art might interest you, also the organ concerts at five every afternoon in season. The name of this church was derived as a result of a fire. The Black Church, originally Catholic, was one of the first Transylvania churches to be "Lutheranized" during the years of the Reformation.

There is a fine little souvenir shop located just up the street behind the older section of the Carpati Hotel. You will find the shop nicely furnished with embroidered blouses, handbags, ceramic articles, etc. And keep your eyes open for antique stores. There is one located not far from the Old Town Square in the direction of the Hotel Postavarul.

Hotels

CARPATI Both sections of this hotel (modern, 1936 version and ultra-modern) now go under the name of Hotel Carpati and are beautiful. The older section is neatly joined to the new wing by a series of roof bars, terraces and patios. There are nine floors with two apartments per floor. A very nice lobby; breakfast room; two elevators. There is a swimming pool on the roof of the 1936 section where light snacks and cocktails are served. In both older sections the view from the roof bars is magnificent. In one direction the Old Town and the Carpathians; in the other direction a view across broad boulevards toward the northeast and the distant plains stretching toward Moldavia.

Bedrooms in the older section are very comfortably furnished, and would be a credit to any hotel. Two singles and two doubles on each floor are without baths; all others have bath and hand shower. Rooms on the back overlook the patio and the old town. The view is quite dramatic. Front rooms are equally nice. The new section of the Hotel Carpati is a sight to behold. On the main floor of the new section is an enormous lobby, with black leather chairs, a moss green carpet, the walls decorated with futuristic sculpturing of the talented Romanian architect-artist-sculptor Ioan Vlahos. Here are the reception desk; a day bar and a small tree-filled patio which connects with the older building. It is a truly spacious, beautifully appointed lobby.

As you enter the new section of the Carpati you will see the space occupied by the National Travel Office "Carpati." These offices are only for foreign guests (as distinguished from other Carpati offices for Romanian tourists). A desk for cashing foreign currencies stands opposite the reception. Note the magnificent stained-glass window at one end of the cafe which adjoins the hotel. Completed in Sighisoara, this window is truly a fine exhibit of local craftsmanship.

There is a night bar in the new section as well as a roof terrace complete with Japanese gardens. Food is served on this terrace, and what a view!

Apartments in the new section consist of a long living room, two bedrooms, dressing room, several halls, luggage space and baths. Apartments face the mountains. French double beds or twin beds are available. Furnishings are modern and inclined to be somewhat stark. Baths are very large; there are elaborate dressing tables in dressing rooms with full-length mirrors. Food carts are located in each apartment.

There are seven floors in this new section. Heating and air conditioning are controlled on each floor. Ducts are located in the ceiling which is seemingly soundproofed and insulated. There are balconies off each room.

The restaurant attached to the older section of the hotel is very modern, quite large, serving good food from an elaborate menu. Service is good! Dinner music; later jazz or dance music. Dress smartly here. The atmosphere calls for it. Don't forget that little bar off the cafe in the older section.

POSTAVARUL Centrally located on the main shopping street of Brasov, the Postavarul has a pleasant lobby, a summer garden for dining and dancing as well as an indoor restaurant (closed in summer). You will also see an attractive day bar. The Postavarul has singles and doubles with and without bath. There are also rooms for three with bath. Bathrooms are rather old but kept well cleaned. Rooms without baths have washbowls. Furnishings throughout the hotel are on the "rooming-house" side; generally frumpy, frilly, dowdy.

Restaurants

CERBUL CARPATIN This is an outstanding restaurant you must visit several times in a three or four-hundred-year-old house. It is the leading restaurant in this beautiful city and, I should add, could well be one of the more delightful eating spots of Romania. Folklore and local color play a large part in the delights of this place. By the way, be sure to make reservations.

The restaurant is comprised of four main sections; upstairs you will find a first class dining area which is cold, unnecessarily formal and uninteresting. To the left is the second class restaurant, decidedly warmer, livelier and recommended for lunch. On the ground floor and open only in the evening is the small, but certainly lively wine testing room where you will enjoy appetizers while "testing" (that is to say "guzzling"!) local wines. Because of its limited size this room is usually reserved only for groups. Also on the ground floor, once again open only in the evenings, is the large, long room where you may eat, drink, dance and be entertained by professional singers and waitresses and waiters demonstrating local folk dances. Reserve well ahead, for this main room is usually fully booked with large groups of West European tourists. Go about eight and dress casually but well.

CRANA POSTAVARUL This restaurant is rather close to the old Carpati offices. Garden dining in summer. Try it for lunch. Informal — nothing fancy, but good!

GRADINA POIANA Garden and "keller" dining. Try this for lunch or if you're feeling particularly adventuresome, for an evening meal. Informal. Located on the main thoroughfare near the Hotel Carpati. Clean and certainly far from staid. There is a typical wine cellar with meals eaten off wooden tables; barrels with leather cushions for seats. Bring your own food, if you wish. The main event is the wine. Food is served but it is nothing outstanding. Colorfully decorated.

POIANA BRASOV

The Kitzbuhl of Romania is the district above Brasov called Poiana Brasov, a delightful spot situated at an altitude of 1,020 meters, roughly three and a half to four miles from Brasov proper. A summer resort as well as a well-known sports paradise, Poiana maintains excellent ski facilities including jumps, slalom courses, skating rinks, bobsled runs, etc.; ski lifts are available.

Hotel

SPORT Situated among a cluster of other smaller hotels, chalets, rest homes and private villas around which is spread the typical fir forest of the region. This delightful Sport Hotel is certainly my idea of a retreat. The best time for a visit is during the mid-summer months or between January and late March. The Sport Hotel provides the visitor with two fine restaurants (dancing while dining in the upstairs restaurant) and an intimate, well-furnished cocktail lounge (open only at night) with a small terrace boasting a delightful view of the mountains. Rooms are well furnished in the main structure as well as in the annex.

If you don't have the time to visit Poiana Brasov for several days, at least go up for lunch. It's worth the extra effort, and the food at the time of our visit was delicious.

CLUJ (Klausenberg)

Cluj is a wonderful old town founded 2,000 years ago as Napoca. Between the magnificent churches and the delightful architecture, you'd swear you were within a block of Vienna's Sacher Hotel. Cluj once was one of the principal centers of Hungary's commercial life and was "home" to many members of the Hungarian nobility. Visit the beautifully maintained Saint Michaels Church built between 1435 and 1500; the bell tower is a restoration from 1702. Gothic in style, Saint Michaels dominates the principal town square directly opposite the Hotel Continental. Pay particular attention to the original altar, the Baroque pulpit from 1870 and the original frescoes painted in 1450. To the side of Saint Michaels, note the magnificent statuary by the sculptor Fudras. Visit the Banfe House built by Italian artisans in approximately 1755 for the Margrave of Klausenberg—truly a touch of Old Florence here in Romania. There is the smaller Franciscan Church dating from 1396 with its marble carving completed during the early 19th century, and the home which was the birthplace of King Matthias originally built in 1400 and ordered restored by the Emperor Franz Josef of Austro-Hungary in the late 1800's. Visit the botanical gardens containing 10,000 species of flowers from all parts of the world. The Cathedral of the Romanian Orthodox Church certainly should not be missed. Note particularly the gold and jewel-covered ikons over the former king's chair. These are the only such ikons on display in Romania. The Cathedral is comparatively new; the interior is interesting and beautiful.

Hotels

CONTINENTAL Ignore the unimpressive lobby of this hotel. Instead take the elevator to one of the three or four floors of what is truly a delightful, comfortable hotel. Your impressions will immediately change. Spacious lounges are on each floor, well furnished and decorated with plants, mirrors and paintings. The building must have been constructed in the early 1900's and was, I understand, originally built as a hotel. After World War II the building became the headquarters for one of the local political parties and only recently was returned to its former function, that of housing foreign visitors to Cluj.

Double rooms have twin beds; single rooms have the Romanian-bed-table complex mentioned elsewhere and which I rather like. Doubles cost about 100 Lei with bath. Singles about 60 Lei with bath; apartments cost 168 Lei for two persons and 195 Lei for three persons. Apartments are quite elaborate, consisting of a bedroom, sitting room and work room or study. Apartments occupy the corner of the building and have a fine view of the magnificent Saint Michael's Church in the park just across the street. All rooms facing outside are with bath. Those on the courtyard are without bath. Most rooms have phones. Radios are available on request.

A large, ornate cafe on the corner of the hotel serves breakfast as well as light snacks and beverages throughout the day. A very richly decorated restaurant serves lunch and dinner. Music in the evening is played by a good orchestra that features light classics until eleven or so, switching them to dance music and jazz. The food and service are both quite good.

SIESTA This is an informal, rather small hotel located on a side street not far from the local Carpati offices. Not the hotel for a lengthy stay, still it is clean, relatively comfortable and boasting a quiet location. No restaurant. Single and double rooms. No baths except in rooms for two or three persons. Telephones and radio. The Siesta is a clean, well-managed little tourist accommodation.

PARTIZANUL One of those "well perhaps," propositions. Located at the side of a happy, little river in the dead center of town, the view may excite the temperament of some contemporary artist. There is a Bohemian quality to this hotel with its pleasant lobby, the positively infernal-appearing elevator mechanism and the dark corridors emptying into small, rather drab little rooms. No radio or phones. No restaurant. There are singles with and without baths; four doubles; numerous rooms for parties of three or four persons.

Restaurant

BUCHAREST Should you be in Cluj for several days and yearn for a change from the continental food, you might try the Restaurant Bucharest, located quite close to the Hotel Partizanul. The restaurant opens its rear section for lunch and the entire room for dinner; dancing and floor show. The rear section is modern in design and very bleak. The front is rather ornate with emphasis on gold and blue walls, drapes, etc. The food is acceptable.

CONSTANTA

Hotel

CONTINENTAL Be sure to reserve in the older section! Rooms there are larger, airier, more pleasant in every respect. The newer units overlook a vegetable market on one side, the busy main street (or highway) on the other. The accommodations are so small that the beds scarcely fit.

The lobby is pleasant. Upstairs halls are pleasant but too dark. Lounges are located in the newer section. There are 150 rooms in all. The older section has 10 apartments, some boasting a refrigerator and

TV. Comfortable furnishings. The older section has 50 doubles with bath; cost 98 Lei with bath (72 Lei without). A single with bath is 52 Lei.

The restaurant here is pleasantly furnished though offering very poor food. There is a keller with lively music (dance and typical Romanian songs) offering food, liquor and beer. Usually very crowded but fun. Nothing fancy but you can unwind. Prepare to share a table.

Restaurants

ZORILE On a bluff overlooking the Black Sea is a modern restaurant serving simple food. The cheese, wine, fruit, sausages all taste wonderful. I was here for lunch and dinner. At lunch the place is less crowded though the view is equally delightful. In the evening there is music for dancing. Informal. Take a sweater for protection against those damp late evening breezes coming in off the sea.

MODERN This restaurant is located about three blocks from the Hotel Continental. In the summer, the front of the restaurant is closed. Go around to the side entrance. Very good food, very nicely served! Reasonable prices. Dance music played with a roar. Pleasant atmosphere; trees and flowers.

CASINO A large white building located directly on the sea. The Casino is quite near the Archaeological Museum. Should you be touring antiquities some morning, drop over to the Casino for lunch. The Casino is a pleasant place for lunch, and not much else.

DEVIN

Hotels

DACIA A true robber baron's castle! High on a hill overlooking the prim, proper, clean little town of Devin, located in the northwest section of Transylvania. During the 1640's the castle was used as a gunpowder storehouse for revolutionary purposes. The Dacia combines an old with a new section. You should specify new! There are 60 rooms. Baths are available with apartments, doubles and singles. I would not encourage reserving an apartment as they are decorated cum dining room. No full length mirror. TV and good radios are available on request. A neat hotel, despite the unpleasant lobby. Incidentally, noise is no problem here despite the central location.

BOULEVARD I believe this will be the hotel in Devin. Day and night bars, a restaurant seating 200 persons; music and garden dining. There will be accommodations for 400 guests in this hotel which boasts better location than the Dacia. I would request deluxe or first class space here.

Restaurant

PERLA Located at the rear of a park at the top of a short, unpaved road. Several summer terraces are covered by a trellis and canvas. There is an open dance floor, also an enclosed dining area (closed in summer). A very popular spot. Food is inclined toward the greasy so I should stick to meatless dishes. A very pleasant atmosphere.

TRANSYLVANIA A combination short order house and cafe located in the Hotel Dacia. Not recommended.

ORADEA

Hotels

TRANSYLVANIA Will most likely be your first stop or possibly your exit point from Romania. Only apartments (suites) have bathrooms. All other rooms, single and double provide only washbowls for the guests. There are 72 rooms in all. The apartments cost about 165 Lei with bath; doubles about 60; singles 40 Lei. All accommodations are clean and functionally furnished; short on decor but quite comfortable. You will find that Romanians are enthusiastic about the "bed unit"; that is, a so-called Hollywood bed arrangement, considerably more elaborate than anything I have found in the United States. The head of the bed forms a night stand, a back which serves as a storage for pillows and blanket, etc. The rooms are well maintained.

Near the entrance is a modernistic cafe where a good breakfast is available on the upper level of this medium-sized room. There is language problem here if you speak anything but Romanian. A large and rather opulent restaurant occupies the front side of the hotel. Usually very crowded! Music in the evening. In this restaurant the combination of vibrant Romanian melodies, the smoke, the animated conversations of well-dressed couples, the wine coolers covered with dots of moisture and filled with champagne, beer or perhaps the cooling "Otonel," white wine of Arad, will provide an exciting, high-point of your Romanian Romp.

RASARITUL If you cannot locate a room in the Transylvania then accept the Rasaritul. No food in this hotel. A large, gloomy lobby recalls a walk-up rooming house in an Eric Ambler thriller. Roughly a block from the Carpati office. No help with luggage. No elevator. Not much parking area near the hotel. There are 72 rooms, 7 with baths. Baths are old but kept in fair condition.

PARTIZANUL Carpati won't put you here unless they are desperate for space. The front overlooks the very crowded, narrow, noisy main street; the rear windows provide an onlooker with the more intricate workings of a box factory.

Restaurants

ORADEA Almost directly opposite the Hotel Transylvania. Decor? Humble Turn-of-the Century. Dress simply. Menus are in Romanian. The food is hearty and good, the restaurant clean. The entire atmosphere is what you would expect to find in some small American town. Average prices.

GRISUL REPEDE An airy, pleasant "short order" restaurant. A sidewalk dining area under colorful awnings. Recommended mainly for light lunches and breakfast.

LACTO BAR A nice little restaurant! Not fancy. Sport clothes okay. The food is good; service small-town style. Inquire about specialities which are numerous in the main course and dessert lines. Recommended. This restaurant is located on the main shopping street just beyond a movie theater. These lacto bars originated as purely milk bars but when they proved so successful, the Romanian Government gave them permission to enlarge on their selection of food.

SOUVATA A newly refurbished "beer parlor." Garish in decor and lighting. However, it is good for a cool brew and snack some afternoon.

PLOESTI

Driving from Basov to Bucharest? There's a good lunch stop in Ploesti. This oil city lies about three hours by car from Brasov south of the exit from Prahova Valley. The restaurant is directly on the highway in the center of town. Don't take the by-pass if you plan on eating here. The restaurant will be to your right driving south. The atmosphere is similar to small-town-restaurants the world over. Menus in Romanian only. As always in Romania, portions of food are plentiful. Good service and clean.

SIBIU

In Sibiu you will be greeted and delighted by architecture from the 14th, 15th and 17th centuries, in some instances lined up in a row so that you have a living model of architectural development in Middle Europe. Tour the city, but by all means take a guide. See the old churches, the guild houses, the old market; the barracks from Maria Theresa's time. Here is the Bruckenthal Museum, its rooms containing old coin collections, an ethnographical section, as well as the display of such great artists as Rubens, Van Dyck and Titian. See the Iron Bridge built in 1859; the old walls, moats, the incredibly old buildings. A fascinating town with a fascinating history. Incidentally, the first printed book in Romania was produced by the Sibiu Printing

Works in 1544. Metallurgical, mining, food and chemical machine industries dominate the city's economic pattern today. I would particularly recommend the Cooperative Arta Manuals Tricotage at 20 Str. (street) Balescu. This shop has a more limited stock than the one across the street but the materials are a better quality. (Incidentally this is quite a shopping street. At five in the afternoon you will really see Mr. and Mrs. Romania on the move. It is fun, interesting and very educational.)

Side Trips

When in Sibiu you might like to take a drive through the lovely Olt Valley occupied during the 2nd and 3rd centuries by the Romans in their wars of conquest against the Dacians. You will see the 14th-century Cozia Monastery reconstructed in 1707, containing the tombs of the ancient Princes of Walachia. The town of Rimicu Vilces is the principal population center of the region, part of the town constructed in a style common to the area many years before. The vineyards of Dragasani are nearby.

Hotels

ROMISCHER KAISER The "Roman Emperor" is truly a delightful hotel which I highly recommend. Located in the center of Sibiu (just behind the Bruckenthal Museum), the hotel offers a very pleasant lobby, two modern elevators, two ornate restaurants and very smartly decorated private rooms. Rooms are modern in good taste. Doubles have a "head to head" arrangement of beds with a table between. Singles are singles with no other bed in the room. Singles do not have a bath or shower; baths are off the main corridors and are very clean. Large apartments on the front side of this four-story structure face the main street where noise becomes something of a factor. Two large rooms (sitting and bedroom) are separated by a curtain. TV and radio are provided in apartments as well as bookcases and other more elaborate furniture. Again, colorfully and wisely decorated. Singles for the most part are located on a court overlooking the restaurant, and are noisy. The orchestra quits around midnight.

One of the restaurants is used largely for tours, breakfast, and light (and faster served) meals. The large ornate restaurant is Bohemian in atmosphere. The service was slow, the food mediocre.

The Romischer Kaiser is a fine hotel needing only a good dusting off, service-wise, to make it one of Europe's best. A fine hotel and certainly recommended! The combination of an exciting historical city and a deluxe hotel should mean much to the travel-weary tourist.

BOULEVARD Located directly on Highway #15, the Boulevard is a clean hotel with a central location. However, it should be avoided except in emergencies. Not recommended.

SIGHISOARA

Just walk and walk and walk and walk! Plan to spend at the least two nights here if you are at all interested in walking back into the 14th century. One of the cities first settled by the Crusaders, Sighisoara finally became a region of the Austro-Hungarian Empire, later Hungarian and now Romania. From its newest suburbs to the 14th and 15th century ramparts, the enormous walls, the somehow "eastern" flavor of its streets and shops, Sighisoara is a delight! You will see people living in houses restored in the original 15th or 16th century style of architecture. I could have wandered for days.

Hotel

SIGHISOARA A surprisingly fine little hotel located at the crossroads of history. The crowded, noisy streets, the towering citadel, the wealth of historical interest all about you here in Sighisoara make the hotel seem quite out of place (but, I may say, a very welcome sight!). The accommodations here are very comfortable and include wall-to-wall carpeting. The rooms are small but furnished in such a way as to give every appearance of careful planning. The bathrooms here are particularly good-looking. Colorful and clean! There are 72 rooms in all. Well-lighted halls and lounges on each floor.

SINAIA

Located at the southern end of the Predeal Pass, the main route leading from Bucharest through Ploesti to Brasov. Sinaia is a resort famous for its mineral waters providing treatment of gallstones and other gastro-intestinal disorders.

Here also are the reputedly excellent ski runs as well as the location of Peles Castle, the summer residence of the former Romanian royal family. This palace should be a "must" on your agenda. The castle was located at Sinaia to provide the Romanian royal family and their guests with a summer's escape from the hot dry climate of Bucharest. Surrounded by waterfalls, pine trees, mountains and total tranquility Peles truly is a wonder to behold! The magnificent crystal, the statuary, all the furnishings and carpeting are exquisite examples of 18th and 19th century royal living. You will see the "Turkish Salon," the collections of armor, the magnificent dining room, the gold and crystal private theater, even a glass ceiling that opens electrically. The woodwork is magnificent.

Tours cover the downstairs of this beautiful home several times during the day. A small entry fee must be paid at the gatehouse. There is a parking area for cars, roughly a ten-minute walk from the Gate House.

Hotel

PALAS The Hotel Palas is located among theaters, casinos, restaurants and the like in this typical summer and winter resort community. Rooms are very comfortable. Public lounges and writing rooms, terraces and corridors are spacious and airy. The restaurant serves very fine food. Limited parking space available.

SOVATA

In Sovata, a spa located in east-central Transylvania, the large hotels are presently used as sanitoriums for various trade unions. Therefore, don't bother making inquiry about rooms in the large buildings that line the central street and promenade. Should you be enjoying a couple of days here at this country bath resort, famous for its cures in the field of gynecological and rheumatic afflictions, stay at Villa #41 or Villa #7 set aside for "guests from Western countries." These are fairly new, comfortable, medium-sized houses with 9 double rooms on two floors, 4 baths and toilets off the hall. Facilities are clean and in good shape. The entire area around Sovata reminded me of the Denver region, pines, hills and lakes. By the way, while here you might want to visit Praid, an enormous salt mine from the Roman period, located approximately five miles from Sovata. There is also hunting in the area—wolves, foxes, boars are present as well as various types of fowl.

Restaurant

CIUPERCA This is the only acceptable restaurant here outside of the clinics and rest homes. Acceptable. Nothing outstanding.

TIRGU MURES

A fascinating town! Don't miss it! A center of minority cultures. See if the local Carpati office can't arrange a tour of the town's incredibly beautiful theater which was built in the twenties at tremendous expense.

Do not miss the Teleke Library located at the top of a small hill directly behind the Hotel Transylvania. Development of this library by a Count Teleke and his son was begun in 1759. The roughly 110,000 books were bought in the 18th century for 800,000 Forints. At the time of these book purchases 1,000 Forints was considered to be a very high income for one year. The Library also contains 60 or more valuable Incunabula, two of such books dating from the years 1437 to 1493. These books, fully cataloged in the 1700's and relating to the development of our present age in every field of endeavor are, incredibly enough, available for reference work of a scholarly nature and are housed in the old Teleke family home.

Hotel

TRANSYLVANIA A very pleasant up-to-date hotel of which this town may be quite proud. There are 118 rooms with a sizeable lobby, exchange office and souvenir shop; also a cafe and barber shop. Singles here have no bath or shower. Doubles have a shower. Surprisingly, the larger the room the smaller the bathroom. Large doubles have hand showers. Ask for beds "side by side" or you may be booked into a smaller "foot to foot" arrangement. Apartments are available. Traffic noise is no problem here for the best rooms face a well-surfaced parkway.

Restaurant

MURESEL Local best! Non-existent decor. Acceptable but far from outstanding.

TIMISOARA

Timisoara is recommended largely as evidence of the present Romanian Government's efforts to modernize and develop truly attractive cities unhampered by the design or architecture of past generations. A pleasant town of broad streets, parkways, fountains and up-to-date shops. A business and political center.

Here is a dynamic, progressive, clean, modern town of which the Romanians are justly proud. Many folks would like to move here but owing to certain restrictions, the town is closed to newcomers unless such a move is with a purpose (e.g., a job) and is approved. Wide avenues and many new buildings.

Hotels

BANATUL Timisoara is located in the region of Banat, hence the name Banatul.

There are two hotels here and I rate the Banatul first. A large lobby opens into a pleasant reception area. Rooms are decorated in a not-displeasing early 1900-type furnishing. A restaurant on the premises is closed in the summer. A garden restaurant to the rear of the hotel serves guests in warm weather. There are only seven rooms in this hotel with bath; seven with shower, so reserve well ahead. Baths and toilets are also located off the main corridors and are kept clean.

PARTIZANUL Built in 1934, the Partizanul is a surprisingly modern building, rather tall, on the bleak side with a small lobby. Limited parking on adjoining streets. Centrally located. As this hotel is built on a curve, corridors and rooms must conform to the bowed architecture. The rooms are cramped and vaguely reminiscent of a mid-thirties Y.M.C.A. dorm. There are 42 rooms, no apartments. The restaurant serves average to good food. A pleasant garden restaurant is open in the summer.

Ask for first category at the Partizanul. At best, doubles without baths are cramped and showers in all cases are small. Furniture is acceptable. Single rooms with shower are quite pleasant. Despite the cheerless "climate" the Partizanul is quite acceptable.

Restaurant

CINA This is a very pleasant garden restaurant with good food, fair service. This restaurant is particularly pleasant at noon.

Northern Moldavia

Though Carpati considers a trip into the northernmost reaches of Moldavia a "side trip" from Mamaia, the region deserves more specific mention, especially for those who are even mildly interested in the history of religious art, church architecture and particularly the al fresco painting employed by 15th and 16th century artisans under the patronage of King Stephen the Great. The churches of Vcronet (1488), Humor (1530), Sucevita (1580), Arbore (1503) and Moldovita (1532-37) are absolutely magnificent examples of early church art. The walls, painted in wonderfully luminous colors depict not only biblical but historical scenes as well.

IASI (Jassy)

Jassy is the capital city of Moldavia, throne city of Stephen the Great, the most famous Prince in Romanian History. An intriguing, truly interesting city. Jassy seems of another century. Its charm, architecture, the somehow romantic quality of the air, the narrow side streets, the flowers, will say to you "stay longer"!

Hotel

CONTINENTAL This is a comfortable old structure located in the center of this imaginative, rather charming and certainly interesting old Moldavian capital city. There is no restaurant, though breakfast can be served in your room or in the cafe off the lobby. The lobby itself is comfortable, airy. Rooms can be large and are acceptably furnished. *Note*: Steer clear of rooms on the corner. Streetcar tracks running directly under the windows of these rooms create a considerable noise. The Continental is certainly an acceptable hotel, but is not recommended for a lengthy stay.

Restaurants

BOLTA RECE Jassy has a number of good restaurants though only two are in this immediate vicinity of the Hotel Continental. The Bolta Rece is primarily a folk restaurant re-designed during the past few years for the benefit of tourists. However, the Bolta Rece maintains a strictly Romanian flavor. Food here is good; the authentic Romanian orchestra is excellent. You will need a Romanian-speaking person with you here for menus are in the local language. Prices are average. Heartily recommended!

MOLDAVIA A first class restaurant located a short distance from the Continental Hotel. The Moldavia is considered one of the best eating establishments in town.

COTNARI A deluxe restaurant located in the "new town" or industrial section eight to ten minutes from the Continental Hotel. Here you may find music for dinner and dancing. The restaurant is a recommendation, but is not exceptional.

SUCEAVA

Hotel

SUCEAVA A relatively new structure located in the center of Suceava's modern, recently completed downtown area. This hotel is a businessman's locale as well as one for those tourists who visit the beautiful monasteries located within an hour of the city. No rooms with toilet, some without shower. All the rooms are small, cluttered, the washing facilities quite primitive. This hotel is a convenience for the traveler, little more.

The restaurant of the Hotel Suceava is quite another matter. It is a large and airy dining room. The food is quite good. Reserve your table some hours before dining as the restaurant is popular with local people, too.

Restaurant

BUKOVINA Carpati has attempted to create a folk atmosphere for the benefit of visitors flown to Moldavia from the Black Sea beach resorts. Unfortunately, the travel agency has fallen somewhat short of its goal. Waitresses wear national costumes while serving guests, the one large room is furnished in the manner of a country inn; table settings are colorful, the service is adequate. There is a limited selection of foods, all mostly Romanian national dishes. This restaurant is acceptable for a single visit.

MAMAIA

You are in for quite a surprise! Following my arrival in Romania, I heard considerable comment from local travel people concerning the

Mamaia (Ma-my-a) Beach development. Mamaia was developed in 1910 in much the same manner and style of construction as the East Coast Florida developments of the twenties. The original wooden structures of the Mamaia resort burned and are nowhere in evidence today. During the thirties, King Carol built a summer palace here (now used as a government guest house) and in 1934 the Albatros, an apartment-hotel was constructed. The present Hotel International was built in '35. I have been advised that this was largely the extent of the construction here prior to World War II. Between 1957 and 1961, the Romanian Government in cooperation with Carpati built some 30 hotels with a sleeping capacity of 15,000 people along the five-mile stretch of beach which comprises the Mamaia resort. Restaurants, open-air theaters, camping sites, nightclubs, garages, clinics and a post office were built to accommodate guests from abroad. Since 1961, several more hotels have been opened and present plans call for hotel facilities to be developed along Romania's Black Sea littoral which includes such towns as Mangalia, Eforie Nord, Eforie Sud and Trkirghiol, a lake famous for its curative mud baths.

Mamaia is delightfully situated between sea and lake, the hotels surrounded by landscaped gardens, parks and fountains. There is not the over-cemented, loud rather brassy atmosphere common to many resorts we know. Mamaia certainly has its negative aspects but Mamaia is designed in such fashion as to permit maximum relaxation in healthful, tranquil, attractive surroundings with a variety of sports activities. The great Black Sea resort of Mamaia is, of course, a must for every tourist to Romania. However, I suggest that you tour the central regions of the country first—Transylvania, Banat, Walachia, Bucharest, and Moldavia—and make Mamaia your final stop. There are several good reasons for this recommendation.

First, you cannot possibly get a feeling for Romania, her charming people, delightful customs and open-hearted hospitality without venturing outside of Mamaia, for Mamaia is not representative of the country as a whole. It is international in atmosphere and crowded with foreign tourists. Folk evenings at Mamaia are largely directed at those tourists (and there are many of them!) who fly directly from Western Europe to Mamaia via Constanta. The "sampling" of local color at Mamaia's theaters and restaurants provides only a tantalizing tidbit of the wealth, beauty and culture that lies west of Lake Siutghiol.

Secondly, Mamaia itself can better be judged after touring the country. The Romanian government has made great strides in the development of the country's resort facilities, so to appreciate the full measure of this effort you should first come to know the "local" or if you will "domestic" Romania before involving yourself in the totally international resort climate.

Lastly, any auto trip can be tiring, whether from New York to Savannah, Cherbourg to Zurich or Orades to Bucharest. This is especially so when you spend much of your time popping in and out of the car to marvel at the sights on all sides. So I suggest that Mamaia be used for exactly that purpose intended by Carpati, namely to provide you with a chance to relax, sun, read and generally rest after your trip through the interior. Why fly first to Mamaia, relax in the sun and then plow through the Carpathian foothills? If you can arrange your trip accordingly, fly or drive to Bucharest, arrange your sidetrips either as you approach the capital or use Bucharest as a basis and take daily journeys outside of the city. Then drive or fly to Mamaia.

Keep in mind that Mamaia is to Romania what Miami Beach is to America. Do not base your decision to visit Romania on your opinion of facilities at Mamaia. Mamaia is five miles long and one mile deep whereas Romania covers an area of over 91,000 square miles. Transylvania, Moldavia, the capital at Bucharest, all offer wondrous and truly Romanian sights to thrill the foreign visitor. But when you do eventually reach Mamaia you'll thrill at the fine buildings, the gardens, the wide beach, the nightclubs. Don't miss this resort, but *"See Romania First"!*

Resort life seldom changes, whether ye be in Cannes, Palm Beach, the Mondsee or Lake Geneva in Wisconsin. Mamaia is no different. Sunburns, tarred beach sandals, orange peelings, perfume liquor and ssssex. Mamaia is a form of "compound" where anything goes, especially if that "anything" happens to be a liquor-fueled Scandinavian blonde making with the glances in the direction of a sad-eyed gentleman from Milan. Anything goes, that is as long as what "goes" is foreign! And brothers and sisters, hear me good! The "compound" known as Mamaia is a world unto itself. Tenderly nourished by Carpati since 1957, this mighty pretty beach resort is about ready to come of age to compete with Nice, Viareggio and Sardinia.

In the chapter on Bulgaria, I commented on the apparent laxity of life guards, particularly at Golden Sands. At Mamaia it is quite another matter. Lifeguards are stationed in high wooden structures not unlike those seen in the United States. When the guards are absent a small flag is flown indicating that the beach is unguarded.

The beach at Mamaia has a gentle slope and where there is something of a drop (a long distance from the water's edge) there are protective nets with floats to warn the swimmers. Guards are also stationed in small boats that continuously patrol the swimming area. These boats are beached in the late afternoon. Keep the kiddies out of them. The beaches are patrolled in the evening and the guards are understandably strict about children and young lovers using the boats as hideouts. Beaches are cleaned and rolled nightly.

Performances at Mamaia's outdoor theater can be exceptionally interesting, entertaining, colorful and just plain thrilling. During the summer season, folk song and dance companies provide the guests at Mamaia with a wondrous insight into the intricacies of Romanian folk dancing plus the thrill of Romania's sizzling national rhythms. Theater groups also provide the audiences at Mamaia with dramatic skits, contemporary music written by some of Romania's young composers, comedy sketches and the like. The Bucharest Summer Theater season is held at Mamaia. Film festivals take place at the modern, elaborate summer resort theater. Prices are low but seating is limited. Better try to obtain your tickets somewhat in advance. Check with the Carpati bureaus or at the theater some days before. The Indoor Theater is located at the south side of the resort near the Hotel Perle. The Outdoor Theater is centrally located not far from the Casino nightclub.

Prices for tickets to sports events, concerts and theaters run between $2 and $4 per person. Museum entrance fees run about 15c per person.

I am certain there must be several locations in Romania where riding horses are available, but the only such place that really caught my attention was at Mamaia. Morning and evening I saw people trotting by my hotel room, right along the beach. I had to find out more about it. Ride I would!

The stables in Mamaia are centrally located at the resort. Riding times 9-11 A.M.; 4-6 P.M. (but better recheck these hours). They seem to prefer groups and will probably leave you flat should you come a little late. Price about 25 Lei an hour. You will be accompanied by an attendant who, I might add, is usually more concerned over the horses than the guests! In our group, one gentleman from Munich took a tumble. His horse left for the stable; the attendant followed the horse and Herr Fritz was left to check for broken clavicles and to walk back to the stables unassisted.

Horses fall into the usual public stable category. Short-necked and soft-mouthed seems to categorize them. But boy, that ride down the beach at five o'clock with the sun dipping low and a soft breeze off a calm sea and the soft splash of the waves—beautiful.

Facilities for camping at Mamaia are located at the extreme north end of the resort and cost $2.50 if you use your own tent, $3 if you rent the local equipment. This charge includes meals. Restaurants for campers are located at the beach immediately adjacent to the camping area. Showers, toilets and parking areas are also available. There is a small charge (about 1.50 Lei) for use of the camping site, that is, for the space. Repeat: the camp location is directly on the beach and is really beautiful. Not a bad idea for those who decide at the last minute to make the trip and are caught without hotel space.

The institution known throughout most of the western world as the cocktail hour has not, however, pervaded the otherwise international setting of Romania's Mamaia. To avoid that let-down feeling when freshly showered and shined you march into the bar at seven only to find the room locked, filled with swimsuited tourists or, worse yet, empty, let me suggest the following: get out the scotch, bourbon, vodka, wine vermouth or Mastika (Kummel), order some soda from the desk, dig out the cheese or pretzels and have yourself a nice little party right there in your room. Dinner at night, with wine if you like, and the evening is made. Believe me, this is the most satisfactory solution to an as yet unsettled "hour" in your Romanian (or Bulgarian or Hungarian) resort life.

Hotels

Deluxe hotels will cost you (per person) on a per diem basis approximately $11; first class, $8; tourist, $5.

Romanian resort philosophy seems to be this: the European continent is small. European resort prices are high. The proportion of folks with ample cash who seek a summer vacation away from home is small in comparison to those people seeking a real economy vacation. Therefore, the resorts must be geared to accommodate the economy class tourist. Mamaia, for all the glitter and glamour of the modern highrise, beautifully landscaped structures, is substantially a "tourist class" vacation spot. Is Carpati wrong in their philosophy, their planning? Not at all! Seeking a happy-go-lucky, clean, warm inexpensive vacation, the Scandinavians, the English, the Hollanders and the West Germans are chartering buses, planes, anything on wheels to pack the Mamaia resort from June through September. Rooms are small, elevators crowded, the restaurants are jammed; yet the water is warm, the beach exceptionally wide and clean, there are sports facilities nearby, the beer and liquor only a bar's length away and the sun, bless it, shines hot and true throughout the summer months.

The tourist class hotels and restaurants comprise the greater number of guest units here at Mamaia but I cannot recommend these facilities to Americans with the exception of two categories of visitors: the 16 to 25 age bracket and those American tourists well accustomed to second class West European accommodations.

The failure to recommend these tourist class hotels is actually not a criticism. I found most of the hotels at Mamaia to be clean, well-staffed, airy, generally pleasant and attractive dwellings. But, these 10 to 14-storied buildings, these 5 or 6-storied units, those with views and those without, all are packed! For youngsters and those of you who have traveled in Europe enough to know what to expect from a youth hostel, Mamaia's tourist class facilities will seem just what the doctor ordered. Noisy, fun-filled, as clean as the crowds allow and very functional — with toilets, showers, clean and comfortable beds. Restaurants nearby serve average food at reasonable prices. But stay clear of those tourist hotels if you are not addicted to communal living with a vengeance.

What about the eight first class hotels? They are slightly less crowded, have somewhat larger restaurants offering a more diversified menu, better furnished rooms and more extensive public accommodations. Moreover, frankly speaking, except for the decreases in the size of the surging hordes, I saw little substantive difference between first and tourist class.

PARK AND PERLE These tall, modern structures are located at the south end of the resort, separated from the beach by a narrow roadway. Both are new and boast sun decks and roof bars. Both provide a fine view of the seacoast from their roofs and upper floor rooms. The lobbies of both the hotels are rather small; the elevators are not adequate for the size of the buildings. The Perle is a bit better in this respect. Each hotel is set in an attractive park-like surrounding with rose gardens, fountains and well-groomed lawns. Rooms in both hotels are quite similar; generally average to small in size, with beds in either a "foot to foot" or "L" position and one or two chairs, vinyl floors, a table or desk plus a small shower room. Light-weight curtains block out the hot bright rays of the five o'clock morning sun. Both hotels have hand showers, meaning the hand spray must be clutched in one hand while the other hand applies the soap. The rooms in both hotels are clean. Corridors are well lighted. No air-conditioning. Apartments are available. Corner rooms enjoy quite an expanse of windows. Rooms to the north have the better view. No telephones.

Restaurants are located near both hotels. The Perle has a particularly nice dining area, quite large but built in such fashion to eliminate the armory effect. There are terraces, gardens, open sections in the roof and at night, music. But you still can't escape the fact that these dining areas with their original architecture, restful pastel colors, splashing fountains and music of Strauss and Lehar, are nonetheless designed to seat hundreds of people at each serving. Architecture, colors, fountains and music tend to be swallowed by the laughing, gabbing tourists. . . .

THE ALBATROSS Constructed back in '34, the Albatross was first an apartment. Renovations over the years have resulted in a quiet resort hotel set some three minutes walk away from the beach. Old-fashioned, a bit frowsy but generally comfortable and clean. Rooms are nondescript, somewhat on the stark side. Set around a small table are, surprisingly, stools in lieu of chairs. Baths are clean, though old-fashioned.

A new, very pleasant, terraced restaurant has been built just east of the Albatross and is connected to the hotel by a short enclosed corridor just off the lobby. Tastefully decorated, with good food, well served; dancing in the evening. You can dine and dance under open skies in one section of this restaurant. Guests from all hotels are welcomed at the Albatross. The hotel itself does not particularly impress me.

BUCHAREST Such architecture I have never seen at a resort. The Bucharest was constructed in 1957. Massive doors, cavernous corridors, a high ceilinged lobby. Two rooms are connected with one central bath which is convenient for a family of four who are prepared to rent two rooms. Otherwise, you are required to share the bathroom with strangers renting the other room off your individual small corridor. Toilets and showers are separated in these baths. There are only four single rooms per floor so the majority of the rooms in this hotel are doubles. Corridors are dark, long and rather lonely.

The Bucharest sits in a small park well back from the main resort road. Rooms on the front face the sea, those on the back another park-like area and Lake Siutghiol. Looking quite impressive from a distance the Bucharest does not stand up well under close inspection.

A very pleasant, if rather formal, restaurant occupies the first floor area overlooking the distant lake. Though I did not have an opportunity to sample the food, should it and the service echo the general atmosphere of the restaurant, it could be a pleasant place in which to dine.

DOINA, AURORA, PELICAN, MODERN These hotels vary in height (Aurora and Doina are nine-story buildings; the Pelican and Modern are four storied). The taller structures have three elevators, the other hotels two. Apartments are available at the Doina. All these hotels have showers and a so-called service unit on each floor including a refrigerator, electric iron and kitchenette. The view from the taller buildings is quite spectacular. Are you an early riser? If not, keep to the hotels with minimum height. Shades are an uncommon item in this part of the world and the more modern architecture of the tall structures finds no place for such clumsy items as shutters with which to close out the sun's glare at six A.M.

INTERNATIONAL A truly delightful deluxe hotel. Four stories and 90 rooms (doubles). Elevators, complete bathrooms (with tub), sunny lounges on each floor and balconies. You can say that this hotel is actually located on the beach. Rooms have an undisturbed, very beautiful view of the Black Sea and shutters to block out the crack of dawn blast of sunlight.

The rooms here are all doubles with bath and shower; 12 apartments are located on each corner of the four floors and are comprised of two rooms; large bath and showers. Eastern rooms overlook the sea while those to the west have a pleasant view of a small flower-filled park.

Showers and changing rooms are available to guests at the beach level of the hotel. Chair, umbrella and cabana rentals may be made on the ground floor as well. Shops on the street arcade sell beach towels, swim suits, sun lotion and other items for beach use.

The restaurant at the International is particularly pleasant. A large room overlooking a park to the west and on the seaside, a wide terrace extends out toward the beach. Open for three meals a day, the blue and white decorated restaurant is ably managed, serving good food in a manner that would do credit to the best European hotel. An orchestra plays nightly.

Here at the International you will find the best service, the most comfortable rooms, the most direct access to the sea, the most complete public facilities all wrapped up in very attractive surroundings. Be sure to reserve well ahead! Perhaps in May or September (late) you may be able to walk in and find a room. Otherwise, you'll be out of luck.

Restaurants

HOTEL INTERNATIONAL The food served at the International is tops at this resort. For dinner, dress as you would for a hotel restaurant in any of our large resorts. Be certain you reserve a table for meals.

MIORITSA Located directly on the shores of Lake Siutghiol within the shadow of the large, modern hotels which face toward the sea. A low, provincial-type structure, the Mioritsa copies its architecture from the Romanian country inns. A truly delightful atmosphere has been achieved here by the use of the country decor softened by candlelight, open air dining on a terrace overlooking the lake, employees in folk costume, typical Romanian folk music, and representative dishes from the typical Romanian kitchen. The first floor is composed of the dining terrace, a garden dining room (enclosed) and a small bar. A 25 Lei entrance fee will admit you to the second floor where Carpati has built an attractive, roomy cocktail lounge, a long bar (with comfortable bar chairs) a dance floor plus an international floor show. Reserve for dinner, say about eight. Then not later than eleven go on upstairs and join the fun.

Tuesday and Thursday nights at this charming folk restaurant guests enjoy a cook-out. Wear comfortable, informal clothes. The cook-out starts about nine-thirty, winding up at midnight. Bus transportation from your hotel. Folk music, singing and dancing. Food on the Ala Turkaside with lamb cooked Romanian (Turkish style on a spit)!

DELTA A fish restaurant. And fresh fried, finny fellows they are too! Directly off the beach with a rustic interior and a view toward the sea. Waiters are dressed as sailors, tables and chairs are shaped in circular fashion in the manner of booths (or extended nautical love seats). Tanks of live fish line sections of the wall, aquarium fashion. Strictly informal. Good place for that rainy day lunch or warm evening dinner.

MELODY BAR If the Romanians want to describe a two-story, glass-walled floating terrace structure surrounded by fountains and pool, the entire edifice bathed in colored lights as a bar, okay, but it's like no bar I've seen. Minimum entrance fee (a bit more if you indend to play roulette) paid as you enter the door opposite the beach. Gaming rooms to the left after entering. Show your passport and surrender your ticket. Roulette, baccarat and maybe poker if enough of a crowd turns up. The Melody Bar is extremely modern and decorated in excellent taste. Good orchestra; swell dance floor.

I suggest you visit here after ten or ten-thirty. If you wish, tables can be reserved in the supper club.

Side Trips from Mamaia

CONSTANTSA To visit the extremely interesting and well-organized Archaeological Museum which will provide you with an excellent review of the town's Greek and Roman past. The museum is located in the older part of town between the harbor and the Casino.

Follow the road coming in from Mamaia directly through town and down toward the sea. Also visit the small gallery of art and sculpture near the Archaeological Museum, the Ottoman Turkish mosque recently restored, offering Moslem services every Friday and during Ramazan. Finally, see the site of ancient Tomis where you will find a relief map showing the position of the former old Greek buildings. Constantsa is really an interesting, fascinating old town. On a hot day it's a delight to poke around the dusty streets, in the little shops or to sit under the trees down near the sea.

ISTAMBUL Earlier we discussed the tours available on the cruise ship Transylvania to Istanbul and return.

EFORIE NORD; EFORIE SUD; TRKIRGHIOL To visit the other seaside resorts; all are within an hour's drive of Mamaia.

MORFATIAR To visit the award-winning wine cellars. A bit of sampling goes on here.

HISTRIA To see the ruins of the oldest city on Romanian territory — Histria, the port founded in the 7th century B.C.

EFORIE NORD

Eforie Nord is located some ten to fifteen minutes' drive south of Constantsa, twenty minutes from Mamaia.

Hotels

THE EUROPA Was opened in July, 1966. A large section of this small resort community is occupied by summer homes of Romanian Government officials; the Hotel Europa lies at the southern edge of these homes. A very modern structure, the Europa is situated on a small rise overlooking a wide, golden Black Sea beach and commands a magnificent view of the entire coastline area. All bedrooms face the sea. Though not overly large, each room is of comfortable dimension;

all are doubles. Baths are good-sized and colorfully tiled. There are balconies. The bedrooms are bright, comfortable and well maintained.

The restaurant at the Europa overlooks a small park which rises above the sea. There is a terrace bordering the dining area. Music for dancing in the evening. The food is generally good. Be sure to reserve a table. Group tours take over large sections of the restaurant.

I heartily recommend the Europa if you are hunting for a modern hotel, well managed, in a quiet location with few other attractions in the immediate surrounding area. The beach is particularly wide here and the view of the beach and sea from all rooms truly outstanding.

The Danube Delta

This is a must! Take along your most comfortable clothes and plan to spend either a day or a week or month, depending on the extent of your interest in wildlife, particularly birds. There are 300 species of birds in the Delta including cormorants, cranes, egrets, swans, pelicans and woodcocks, to name only a few. Flowers such as roses, marsh marigolds, lilies and iris are here as well as the tamarisk groves and the forests of Letea and Caraorman. The wolf, ermine, hare and boar abound in the Delta regions. Here is a true paradise for those who either love nature or engage in two of man's most exciting sports: fishing and hunting. Sixty species of fish including carp, pike and sturgeon live in these waters.

Via the town of Tulcea you will be able to leave by car or boat (boat travel is certainly more fascinating) to such other centers as Sulina (a port on the Black Sea), Maliuc (the capital of the Delta) or Chilia Veche founded by the Greek colonists in the year 1000. The old windmills, ruins, fisheries and the new modern sections of some of the towns give evidence that the Danube Delta was and is one of Eastern Europe's primary sources of food, wildlife and the wellspring of many a civilization.

Turkey

What a cacophony of sights and sounds assault the senses of the visitor to the ancient land of Asia Minor. So it has been and so it will remain. No race or creed, no beggar's pack or silken robe can claim eternal right to a heaven which will be forever blue, a fragrant wind assuring inspiration, a tormented soil whose elements attest to the timelessness of this enchanted land. Even as no single oak can claim a forest or one lion authority over some tractless waste, neither can one man (or race of men) say to himself, "I have license over all surveyed. This is mine. I claim it all." Asia Minor will for all time remain a land of many men; heroes, cowards, kings and commoners will come and go as the centuries wax and wane. A timeless land, this Asia Minor, this Byzantium, this incredible land of minarets, bazaars, cold seas and arid hills, this Turkey—a land that I have often cursed, but truly love.

Coverage given to Turkey will be limited to Istanbul (and that city's environs), Izmir (and the nearby towns of Ephesus and Pergamum), Bursa, Ankara and Edirne. It is felt information relating to these cities and towns will be adequate for tourists visiting Turkey for a limited period of time. Turkey is included in this book largely for the convenience of persons visiting the country following a trip through Eastern Europe and the Balkans. Readers should be advised the southeastern and southern Mediterranean coasts of Turkey as well as those regions bordering the Black Sea offer outstanding tourist attractions to tourists with adequate time to engage in an extensive tour of the country. Towns such as Konya, Sivas and Isparta will prove interesting to those of you touring the interior. The larger share of eastern Turkey, including Erzerum and Erzincan, is restricted (for military purposes); travel to this region is dependent on the issuance of a pass by the Turkish Ministry of Defense.

GEOGRAPHY AND CLIMATE

The Republic of Turkey consists of two principal divisions: Asia Minor, or Anatolia, the larger section; and Thrace, a small portion of the east European land mass. Anatolia and Thrace are divided by three waterways which form a passage between the Black and Aegean Seas; the Bosphorus Straits (flowing from the Black Sea), the Sea of Marmora and the Dardanelles Straits (flowing into the Aegean Sea southeast of Salonica). Turkey controls a few minor islands located just off the Turkish coast, in the Aegeon. Turkey is bounded by the Black Sea on the north, the Aegean Sea on the west and the Mediterranean Sea to the south. Common political borders are shared with Bulgaria and Greece to the west, Syria and Iraq to the south and the Soviet Union and Iran to the east.

With the exception of the fertile coast lines bordering the Black Sea, Aegean coast, large sections of Thrace and the plains of Adand and Antalya (southern Anatolia), Turkey's topography consists largely of vast, semi-arid regions and in the eastern areas of the country, of vast mountain ranges. The highest mountain in Turkey is Mount Ararat (16,946 ft.), popularly associated with Noah's Ark; it is located near the intersection of the Turkish, Iranian and Russian borders. There are numerous high peaks in this region. The Tigris and Euphrates Rivers have their headwaters in eastern Turkey. There are few other rivers of importance in Turkey, though the Sakarya River in a west central region of the country has considerable historical importance related to the Turkish War of Independence. The largest lake in Turkey is Lake Van, in the far eastern section of the country; the Tuz Gölü (Salt Lake), in central Anatolia, has such a high density of salt that it is used for commercial purposes.

Turkey has, in all, 3,310 miles of coastline. The southern and eastern coastal regions enjoy a generally moderate climate. Istanbul can be quite damp and cold during winter months. The capital, Ankara, located in the more arid regions of the country, experiences hot dry summers and fairly cold winters. The capital's aspect has been altered in recent years by the extensive planting of trees on the formerly barren, dry plateau. There is a wide variation of climate within the several regions of Turkey.

HISTORY

Prior to 1922 what is now the Republic of Turkey was an empire governed by the Ottoman Turk. The Byzantine Empire was at its zenith following the Great Schism of 1054. While we need not deal in depth with the historical transition from the Byzantine period to that of the Ottomans, I feel it is important to construct our historical review of Turkey on a very brief summation of an era prior to the fall of Constantinople in 1453, which date provides formal acknowledgement of a fact actually accomplished some years before, e.g. the death of Byzantium or East Rome.

The Great Schism had its origins in a period of severe strife within the Catholic Church (1348-1417), at which time there were several claimants to the papacy. The Byzantine Empire was actually founded in 476 A.D. following the fall of the Roman Empire. The city of Constantinople, originally called "Byzas" after an ancient tribal chief, was located on a promontory overlooking the Sea of Marmora. The first settlers were known as Megarans and later as Aryans. Wars and tribal strife resulted in the gradual destruction of the small trading town and port. In 324 A.D. the Roman Emperor Constantine conquered the town, making it the seat of his empire. The port town was then called New Rome. In 330 A.D. the name was changed to Constantinople.

When Emperor Theodosius died in 395 the Roman Empire was divided between his sons: Byzantium was then split into two sections (west and east). The successor emperor to the son of Theodosius who had inherited east Rome was known as Theodosius II. It was he who established the complete dimensions of the Byzantine Empire. But years of war, scandal and uprising were to follow until Emperor Justinian ascended the throne. Justinian did much to bring Byzantium to a peak of wealth and great commercial prosperity. Construction of a number of famous buildings was undertaken at this time, including the Church of Saint Sophia.

The centuries following Justinian's rule were especially turbulent due to the friction between the two arms of the Catholic Church. Basil I, another Byzantine emperor, did much to assure the prosperity of his empire, though eventually antagonisms between the Latins and Greeks reached such a point that Constantinople was one victim of the

Fourth Crusade, falling to Latin troops in 1204. Baldwin eventually claimed the throne in the name of West Rome. Baldwin was crowned emperor in Saint Sophia. During 1261, due to poor military and economic control over her distant provincial capital city, Rome lost control of Constantinople, and a Paleologue, Michael of Nicea, assumed the throne. His heirs ruled Byzantium until the fall of Constantinople in 1453.

Prior to the capture of Constantinople the surrounding countryside, Anatolia, Thrace (including present-day Greece), Bulgaria and Serbia had fallen to the Turks. It should be remembered, however, that the Turkish armies which actually caused the collapse of ancient Byzantium were the second wave of a Turkish invasion which had been sweeping across Byzantium since the year 1071.

The original Turkish people moved westward from an area around Russia's Ural Mountains. One Turkish group reached Asia Minor approximately ten centuries ago. At the Battle of Malazgirt (1071) these Turks defeated the Byzantines. Settling in Anatolia, these people, known as Seljuk Turks, established their capital at Konya. Their domain, constructed within the Byzantine Empire, was exceptional for its great prosperity. The Seljuk Turkish Empire was eventually overthrown by a mongol invasion under Genghis Kahn in 1243.

In the west-central section of Anatolia, quite near the town of Bursa, there lived a tribe of Turks under the leadership of a man named Osman, a given name not uncommon in Turkey. With the withdrawal of the Mongols, this tribe of Turks expanded to embrace other tribes of nomadic Turks, until the Osman Turks spread across Anatolia. They encircled and finally overran all of Byzantium, except for the capital city of Constantinople. The Osman Turks are best known in the west as Ottoman Turks. In less than 200 years following the Mongol withdrawal, the Ottoman Turks occupied a large share of the eastern end of the Mediterranean.

By 1453, Constantinople was surrounded, cut off from the remainder of the anxiously waiting Western world. Byzantines and Venetian, Genoese and Greek tradesmen waited behind the walls of Constantinople for the attack. A previous assult had failed; they knew too well the city could not long withstand the second attack. A siege of some 20 days had seriously impaired the morale of the people. Galleys from Rome could not approach the city because of the presence of Turkish warships. Traffic from the Black Sea had been cut off one year previously by construction of an impregnable fortress at a narrows in the Bosphorus just north of the city. Huge rock-throwing devices had been employed to sink ships sailing south from Russia.

On the 21st of April, 1453, the Turkish Sultan Mehmet II ordered the overland transfer of a number of ships from his fleet. The boats were pulled along greased rails by sailors using cables, ropes and capstans. The boats were transferred from what is now Dolmabahce at the entrance to the Bosphorus to the present-day Kasimpasha in the "Golden Horn," an inlet separating two sections of Constantinople. Greeks arose after a sleepless night to find the Sultan's ships had been transferred, seemingly miraculously, from the Bosphorus to a point well behind a boom which had until that day closed the funnel-shaped "Golden Horn" to the enemy. At this time during a religious procession the ikon of the Mother of God slipped from the hands of its bearers to the ground; only with great difficulty was it lifted from the ground, and the curiously increased weight of the ikon was accepted as a grave omen. The next day a heavy fog shrouded the city; and as the Divine Presence was reputed to absent itself during such inclement weather, the city was thus understood to be abandoned by Heaven.

Great cannons had been cast by the Turks for use against the city walls, as well as the ships anchored in the Sea of Marmora. A fleet sent by the Roman Pope was attacked by the Turks and forced to stand away from the city. The Genoese and Venetian minorities began to desert the city. With the death of the great Italian General Giustiniani, great numbers from the ranks began to slip away to the countryside. This action was duly noted by the Turks. The Sultan ordered a pontoon bridge constructed across the "Golden Horn" to Pera, thus making the lengthy trip around the "Horn" unnecessary. Volunteers poured into the Sultan's camp while wine and bread became scarce in the city.

Near the Kharisios Gate the great wall surrounding the city collapsed, pounded by shot from Turkish cannons. The dome of Saint Sophia glowed blue-white in the turgid nighttime sky; the Emperor was killed while fighting with his men at the Gate of Saint Romanos. A Turkish flag flew over the Blachernae. It was May 29, 1453; the Sultan Mehmet II, the leader of the Ottoman Turks, had conquered the city of Constantinople. Byzantium had fallen.

The Sultan returned to Adrianople (Edirne). Constantinople became the capital of the Ottoman Empire in 1458. At that point and forever after, the city was known to the Turks as Istanbul; but it was not until 1926 that the Republican government of Kemal Ataturk formally advised foreign nations that from that year hence Constantinople was to be officially referred to as Istanbul by all those governments dealing with the Turkish Republic.

In 1516, the Turks conquered Syria; in 1517, Egypt. The year 1529 found powerful Turkish armies camped beyond that hill called Leopoldsberg at the edge of Vienna, Austria. This period is considered the high point of Ottoman power. During the reign of the truly great Sultan Suleyman (sometimes called the "Law Giver" or the "Magnificent"), Turkish authority stretched from Asia Minor across the Arabian Peninsula, along the northern coast of Africa, the Caucasus, Crimea (now part of the Soviet Union) through Eastern Europe to the Balkans. Turkish power waned during the 18th and 19th centuries due largely to the rise of nationalism principally throughout the Balkans. Twenty-eight Sultans succeeded Sultan Mehmet the Conqueror. The title of caliph was added to that of sultan when the Turks occupied Egypt; this title relates to the sultan's role as Protector of the Faith, the titular head of the Moslem religion in the empire.

The intervening years, stretching from 1529 to 1839, witnessed a parade of incredible rulers who were to govern the Ottoman Empire until 1922. Beginning with Sultan Selim (also known as the "sot") there came a series of men each seemingly more limited than the previous one in his capacity to demonstrate moral leadership. The harem and its screeching eunuchs assumed more than a measure of authority. Debauchery, corruption and eventually bankruptcy followed. One cannot completely blame these pathetic though dangerous historical figures, for they were members (and victims) of an autocratic governmental system without parallel in history. Threatened his entire life by incarceration, treachery and death, once he had assumed the throne the sultan was usually ill-prepared for the position to which he had been elevated. It was the sultan's undisputed right to dispose of any relative, any potential claimant to the throne he felt might endanger his rule. It was a custom to isolate regal pretenders within the royal circle to such a degree that the man (young or old) was quite literally cut off from all forms of civilized domestic (creative) activities. Sons and brothers of the Sultan were often murdered to assure that they would not attempt to sieze the throne. Even during the early years of the enlightened 1900's, reigning Sultans were known to have slept in different locations each night so that real and imagined assassins would be thwarted.

The year 1839 saw the sultan's imperial powers restricted by the issuance of the Tanzimat or Imperial Rescript. Further reforms were indicated by the Illustrious Rescript in 1856.

A constitution was promulgated in 1876 by Sultan Abdul Hamid only to be revoked the following year. Until the Young Turk revolution in 1908, an absolute monarchy again prevailed. At that time the constitution was reinstated. The Committee of Union and Progress assumed control of the government under Sultan Mehmet V in 1913 (the Committee was the action organization for the "Young Turks"). The leaders of this organization were named Tolat and Enver Pasha. Forced to commit their country to the side of the Central Powers during World War I, Enver and Tolat fled the country after Turkey's defeat. Turkey's willingness to side with Germany and Austria during the Great War stemmed from Kaiser Wilhelm's earlier defense of Turkish rights (with German political aims uppermost in mind) when the British and Russians convinced of Ottoman collapse, seized Egypt and Cyprus as well as the Caucasus and Crimea (Russia). France, meanwhile, occupied Tunis and Syria. Economic rights, called "capitulations," were claimed by a number of the Great Powers. Foreign governments owned outright such municipal facilities in Constantinople as the gas and electricity works, streetcar lines, etc. Nominal sums were paid directly to the sultan for these privileges which amounted to direct foreign interference in Turkey's internal affairs. Yet the sultan needed money and the officials of his government were so corrupt that the "sale" of such domestic activities seemed only a logical procedure. It should also be noted that the Ottoman Turks had for years left the tedious chore involved with domestic enterprise in the hands of ethnic minorities who resided in the capital. The Ottomans ruled; manual, even "mental" labor was considered quite beneath their rank.

Further emphasis should be given to the fact that between the Ottomans (the rulers) and the ordinary Turk (who farmed the fields of central Anatolia, living a mirthless life of ignorance) there existed an enorous gulf not easily understood by those of us brought up in 20th century America. Even the language written and spoken by the Ottomans was quite different from the native "Turkish" employed by the average citizen of Ottoman Turkey. The Ottomans spoke a language larded with Arabic and French words and phrases.

The Treaty of Sevres, issued on the basis of allied agreements determined prior to the end of World War I, decreed that Ottoman Turkey was to be stripped of all her non-Turkish areas and that the body of Asia Minor (central Turkey) was to be divided between Greece, Italy, England and France. Western portions of Asia Minor were actually occupied, particularly the region surrounding Smyrna (Izmir). The last sultan, Vaheddin, was actually a "prisoner" of the Allied powers, discredited in the eyes of the nationalist-minded Turk as a pawn of Allied policy.

Mustapha Kemal (later Ataturk, or "Father of the Turks") was a popular and well-known nationalist leader determined to fight the Allied imposition of the Sevres Treaty. Leaving Constantinople for Samsum (a town on Turkey's Black Sea coast), Ataturk rallied a large body of his followers and declared the Treaty of Sevres invalid. At the Sakarya River he attacked a Greek force moving eastward from Smyrna toward central Anatolia. The Greeks were driven back to the Aegean Sea. The city of Smyrna was burned as the Greeks withdrew. Successful in this military engagement, the nationalist group, with its governmental apparatus established at Ankara, gained international recognition. On November 1, 1922, the provisional government of Turkey declared the sultanate abolished.

In 1923, the Turkish Government at Ankara was able to negotiate with the Allied Powers the Treaty of Lausanne which recognized Turkish sovereignty over Asia Minor and a small section of Thrace. Abdul Mejid, a nephew of the last sultan, had been proclaimed Caliph of All the Faithful.

On October 29, 1923, the Republic of Turkey was proclaimed; Ankara (formerly Angora) was its capital city.

On March 23, 1924, the caliphate was abolished and all members of the imperial family were banished from Turkey.

The following years saw tremendous social and cultural changes in Turkey. Known as the Ataturk Reforms, they included the suppression of religious organizations and education, the legal advancement of women to a position equal with men, the replacement of the Arab script with Latin letters, the writing of a republican constitution based on popular sovereignty, the substitution of secular law for religious law and the abolition of the fez.

Turkey was neutral during World War II, though pro-Allied in her sentiments. In 1945, Turkey declared war on the Axis. A charter member of the United Nations, Turkey is also a member of the North Atlantic Treaty Organization and the now semi-defunct CENTO (Baghdad Pact). Ataturk remains a venerated figure throughout the country.

LANGUAGE

As we have noted above the Turkish language was deprived of its largely Arabic base by the language reform of 1928, when the Roman alphabet was substituted by means of enforced teaching programs instituted throughout the country. The President of Turkey, Kemal Ataturk, literally took to the blackboard in an effort to impose on his people the new system of writing. The American educator John Dewey played a large part in developing the modern-day Turkish language.

It was not until the years immediately following the founding of the republic that Turkish citizens adopted the custom of family names. Prior to the early 1920's (during the centuries of the Ottoman Empire) Turks were known by their family relationships: e.g. Tarik, son of Inal, Refet, son of Mehmet, etc. When the westernization program got under way, Ataturk required each citizen of Moslem origin to acquire a family name. Frequently men legalized their family nemes by referring to their profession: Balikoglu (son of a fisherman) or Kavunoglu (son of a melon grower), and so forth. Others simply took their father's first name and added the word son, thus Inaloglu; still others adopted the name of a village. For women, the practice was similar.

In addition to the standard Roman characters, the Turkish language uses the letters ğ (the accent makes the letter silent), i (with no dot over the letter, making a sound as in the word "it"), c (as in *Ch*arles); ö (giving a *"you"* sound); s (as in *sh*oe, and ű. There exists no "q" or "x" in the Turkish alphabet. The Turkish c is pronounced like our j; hence "John" is spelled "Con."

Despite many efforts to rid the language of numerous Persian and Arabic expressions, these continue to exist, though the spelling of most phrases is latinized. It has been said that if one is able to speak Turkish one can easily write it, and to some extent this is true. Turkish is an extremely phonetic language as the following words demonstrate: tennis, in Turkish—*tenis*; telephone, *telefon*; sandwich, *sandvic*; sport, *spor*; doctor, *doktor*; dance, *dans*; radio, *radyo*; reservation, *rezervasyon*; automobile, *otomobil*; etc. While there are thousands of other words not so easily understood by foreigners, it holds true that a Turkish word, once properly pronounced, can be spelled with ease. The following list of Turkish words and expressions will demonstrate the phonetic capacity of the language as well as provide you with a means of communication with the Turks, especially during those first hectic few hours in the country. Where the correct Turkish spelling is not strictly phonetic or involves an accented character, it is given in parentheses.

ENGLISH	*TURKISH*
Hello	Merhaba
Goodbye	Allaha Ismarlidik
Taxi	Taksi
Chauffeur	Shofor
Good Morning	Gun Aydin
Good Night	Allah Rahatlik Versin
Yes	Evet
No	Hayir
Good	Iyi
Bad	Fena
Very Bad	Cok Fena
Please	Lutfen
Breakfast	Kahve Alte
Lunch	Ogle Yemegi
Dinner	Aksam
Tea	Cay
Coffee	Kahve
Friend	Arkadas
Brother	Kardes
Sister	Kiz Kardes
Father	Baba

Mother	Ana
Mr.	Bay (Follows given name)
Mrs.	Bayan (Follows given name)
City	Shehir
Thank you	Teshexkur Ederim or Cok Merci
You're welcome!	Bir Shey Degil
Airport	Hava Alanya
Restaurant	Lokanta
Hospital	Hastane
Bridge	Kopru
Go	Gidiniz
Come	Gel
Sick	Hasta
How are you?	Nasilsiniz?
Not bad	Fena Degil
Wonderful	Fevkalade!
Beautiful	Guzel
Very beautiful	Cok Guzel!
Who?	Kim?
American Consulate	Amerikan Konsolugu
Information	Danisma
Beach	Plaj
Museums	Museler (A "ler" or "lar" at the end of a word makes it plural.)
Library	Kutuphane
Airline	Hava Yollari
Railroad	Demir Yollari
Steamship Line	Deniz Yollari. (The word "yol" means road or line.)
Hot	Sicak
Cold	Soguk
Open	Acik
Closed	Kapali
Islands	Adalar
New	Yeni
Old	Eski
Mosque	Cami
Bed	Yatak
Food	Yemek

Meat	Et
Vegetables	Sebzeler
Fruit	Meyvalar
Sweet Dessert	Tatli
One	Bir
Two	Iki
Three	Uc
Four	Dort
Five	Bes
Six	Alti
Seven	Yedi
Eight	Sekiz
Nine	Dokuz
Ten	On

There are a number of dialects spoken in Turkey and no one city or town has a monopoly on "best-spoken" or standard Turkish. There has been such an ebb and flow among the populace during the past 20 years that one can be fairly sure few Turks are now working in the town of their birth. Ankara is filled with former Istanbul residents, Istanbul overflows with villagers. The words listed above are, however, understood in all sections of the country. While local dialects may change the pronunciation to a degree, the difference is not so great as to create a language barrier among the Turks themselves.

The verb in Turkish falls at the end of a sentence. Example: I GO TO THE HILTON HOTEL EVERY DAY. *Ben Holton Oteli her gün giderim.* Note that the "i" or "e" at the end of a noun forms the article and makes it a specific hotel, bridge, restaurant, etc. The suffix of the verb, in this instance "im," denotes the person, in this sentence, the first person, I.

English is spoken throughout the major cities; and Turks, particularly the younger generation, take considerable pride in their ability to speak the English language. Thousands of Turks from all economic stratas have been trained in the United States, at factories and in our universities. Moreover, many Turks are married to American citizens. You will have some trouble in the countryside, but there also one comes across educated villagers who have picked up some English expressions from other tourists, while on a visit to the city, from the movies or from our military personnel. French, German and to a lesser degree Spanish and Italian are spoken by a number of people in the larger towns in the western coastal region.

If you run into language problems, the Turks will try to help you. Tourkish men and women sometimes project a rather obstreperous and off-handed attitude, but by and large they are an extremely hospitable people who will often inconvenience themselves to help foreigners. Turks admire Americans and despite the vagaries inherent in our diplomacy I believe we can count on them as being good friends for many years to come.

RELIGION

Ataturk and his followers separated the caliphate (religious leadership) from the sultanate (secular rule) and later abolished both institutions. The state has since assumed the role of official supervisor of the Moslem religion in Turkey. The maintenance of mosques and other religious properties, the licensing of religious instructors for the schools and the arrangements for such instruction are all functions of the republic. It should be noted, however, that in Turkey there exists no official state religion. Non-Moslems may worship according to their particular beliefs. At the last census it was determined that 98.9% of the Turkish population is Moslem. Greek Orthodox, Gregorians, Jews, Roman Catholics and Protestants are the largest minority religious groups. Secret religious sects are forbidden, but it is rumored that certain dervish orders continue to practice their unique form of worship.

The Turkish Constitution expressly forbids proselytizing by either the Moslem or non-Moslem population of Turkey. Theoretically religion is not permitted to play a role in politics, but this law has not been as scrupulously adhered to as some people would have us believe.

CURRENCY

You will meet no particular problem in learning to differentiate between the various denominations of bills and coins circulated in Turkey. Though frequently old and very dirty, the currency will cause no mind-wrenching calculations before paying that restaurant or hotel bill or while bargaining in the bazaar.

The Turkish lira (frequently referred to as the Turkish pound) is available to foreign tourists at the special rate of 12 TL to the dollar. The regular exchange rate is 9 TL to the dollar. A black market exists which offers 16 TL to the dollar, perhaps more; however, trading at this illegal rate is extremely dangerous. Dealing with the characters who peddle Turkish currency at unauthorized rates can lead to your arrest and imprisonment. Stay clear!

The lira or pound is divided into 100 Kurus ("kurush"). Coins in denominations of 5 and 10 kurus and 1 and 2½ lira are in circulation. Care should be taken not to confuse 1 and 2½ coins for they are similar in appearance. Notes come in the following denominations: 5, 10, 20, 50, 100, 500, and 1,000 lira.

Each tourist may bring into Turkey 100 Turkish lira, and the same amount of Turkish currency may be removed from the country. You may bring into Turkey any amount of foreign currency. It has not been a custom of recent years to ask tourists to complete money declarations; however, should such a declaration be requested of you I suggest that you declare all cash and travelers checks, for on your departure from Turkey you might be asked for the declaration slip to prove you did in fact import the currency into the country.

Turkish currency can be purchased at any bank and at airport exchange offices. Turkish hotels are also permitted to exchange travelers checks or cash (dollars) for lira. A hotel guest is considered a tourist and is therefore able to benefit from the tourist exchange rate. However, one must be a guest of the hotel where the transaction takes place or be prepared to show one's passport. Wagon-Lits Cook and the offices of various steamship and airline agencies also accept foreign currencies. My suggestion is to exchange your money at your hotel—there will be fewer formalities. Keep the exchange slips, for they will be needed should you wish to cash in any excess lira before leaving the country.

New bills are now being placed in circulation and they are frequently different in color from the old notes. Better check the denomination of the note carefully before passing it along. Most of the new notes are in the 5, 10 and 100 lira denominations. You will find that hotels usually dispense the new currency when cashing travelers checks.

VISAS AND CUSTOMS

A valid American passport will gain you immediate entrance into Turkey. No visa is required of American citizens nor is there any necessity for you to be in possession of hotel reservations before entering the country. However, this writer urges that you reserve hotel space in advance to assure yourself proper accommodations. A United States Health Certificate proving you have been vaccinated for smallpox is not necessary for entry into Turkey but is required by U.S. officials when you reenter this country. Should you plan extensive travel around the less inhabited regions of central and eastern Snatolia, I suggest you take the typhus and tetanus series of tests.

Passport formalities at all frontier points and at plane and rail depots are minimal. All foreign visitors, whether journeying to Turkey for business or pleasure, are required to fill out entry and exit forms. The entry card consists of a form on which is listed one's address in Turkey, passport number, date one's passport was issued and the reason for one's visit. This card will be handed to you by the stewardess on your plane, the porter on the train, or the frontier officials if you enter Turkey by car. Exit forms, completed when one departs from the country, are available at airports and at frontier posts. This form must be presented to officials before one passes through passport control at the frontier or at international airports in Ankara, Istanbul or Izair.

Visitors who wish to remain in Turkey for a period exceeding three months must visit local police headquarters (a special office exists for this purpose) to secure permission from local authorities for the extended stay. These offices are located in every major city or town in which foreign visitors might reside.

In Turkey it is *not* customary for hotel clerks to request that American visitors leave their passports at hotel reception desks when registering for a room; however, on occasion the hotel management may ask that your passport be left at the reception desk for a few hours or overnight.

Customs procedures at Istanbul's Yesil Koy airport or at Esenboga airport in Ankara are usually brief. A simple declaration of "personal effects" is generally adequate for the customs officials. Don't signal for the customs inspector until *all* your baggage has been brought to you by the porters.

One or two fifths of whisky and a reasonable number of cigarettes for personal consumption may be imported into Turkey. Gifts for Turkish friends should cause no difficulty and to the best of my knowledge (and experience) need not be declared. However, I urge that tobacco and gifts fabricated of cotton, ceramics, silver and gold not be imported. As these items involve raw materials exported by Turkey, customs authorities sometimes create problems.

Camera, film and sports equipment for personal use may be imported free of duty, as may be typewriters, automobiles, radios and stenographic equipment. Certain of these items may be noted on your passport to insure re-exportation.

Persons entering Turkey by car must have in their possession the green card issued by the American Automobile Association indicating that the owner of the car has third party accident coverage. The driver of the vehicle must be prepared to show his International Driver's License, also issued by the Automobile Club. An automobile may remain in Turkey only a limited time (usually up to three months) before it becomes necessary for one to register it with local authorities, obtain a local license, etc.

As a rule, passport officials in Turkey are coldly efficient. Be certain your passport and entry or exit papers are in good order before presenting them for clearance. These men are very methodical and moreover are not noted for their winsome personalities. Be patient and cooperative. Passport inspection is normally completed in a short length of time.

Customs officials check through your car at all frontier stations. Locate the engine and body numbers of your car (usually on the motor and inside the left front door frame) before calling the customs inspector. This saves time! At airports the customs clearance involves little more than a declaration as to the contents of your bags. The baggage itself will most likely remain unopened.

TRAVELING TO AND IN TURKEY

Turkey forms a natural land bridge between Europe and Asia. Because of its proximity to countries previously reviewed in this book, Romania and Bulgaria, it is included in this guide. Plane travel between Turkey and the aforementioned countries is severely restricted but rail traffic from such European capitals as Paris, London, Bern and Vienna enters Turkey through Bulgaria (or Greece) and terminates at Istanbul's Sirkeci Station.

This book deals with the countries of Balkan, Central and Eastern Europe. However, it is this writer's thought that many people would enjoy a trip which, instead of circling through Eastern Europe, moved directly southeast through Hungary and Romania (or Yugoslavia), to Bulgaria and finally to Turkey. In this fashion, whether one travels by air, car or train, one is in fact following the tidewaters of history from Western Europe to Asia Minor. Once in Turkey one can place one's car aboard a ship for Trieste, Venice or Genoa and then fly home. Persons with more time can sail with their car directly to the Italian ports.

Tourists visiting Romania's Black Sea resort of Mamaia near Constanta or Bulgaria's resorts at Golden Sands or Sunny Beach near Varna will have the opportunity to board a Romanian, Bulgarian or Russian ship for a cruise to Istanbul. Bulgaria's Thracian city of Haskovo (Haskoy to the Turks) is only a five-hour car ride from Istanbul (or 45 minutes from the Turkish border). Romania's Tarom airlines takes one from Bucharest to Istanbul in one hour and fifteen minutes. One travels from Nis in Yugoslavia across Bulgaria to the Turkish border within a normal day's drive, with lunch at Sofia to boot.

The geographical relationship between the countries of south and southeastern Europe and Turkey make the entire area covered by this book a natural travel unit, a new area to be explored—from Vienna to Istanbul. The 16th century saw the advance of the Turks through Bulgaria, Romania, Yugoslavia and into Hungary and the foothills near Vienna. Throughout the 19th century the Turks gradually withdrew as the Ottoman Empire came under strenuous attack by the peoples of southeastern Europe and Yugoslavia in their determined struggle for independence. It is only natural that one should witness this region of tumultuous historical event in its entirety.

By Plane

The Turkish capital of Ankara and Istanbul are connected to major European cities by daily, regularly-scheduled flights of many well-known air carriers. Both cities are stops on Pan American World Airways "Round the World" service. SAS, BEA, KLM, Air France, Lufthansa are among the best-known air companies flying passengers to Turkey. Swissair maintains excellent service from Zurich. Keep in mind that Turkey is one hour ahead of such Western European cities as Zurich, Vienna, Paris and Rome.

THY, or Turkish Hava Yollari (the Turkish national airline) maintains regular service to Athens, Rome, Frankfurt, Munich, Vienna, Amsterdam, Brussels, Zurich, Tel-Aviv, Beirut and Nicosia. This airline has recently purchased a DC-9 fan jet for use in its European service; other types of aircraft flown include Viscounts (pro-jets) and a number of the domestic routes are maintained with small propeller aircraft seating only 15 to 25 passengers.

Istanbul airport is known as Yesil Koy; Ankara maintains the Esenboga airport. It is approximately a 40 minute drive from the airport at Istanbul to the Hilton Hotel and the trip from Ankara to that city's airport takes approximately the same length of time. However, departing passengers are advised to allow a minimum of one and a half hours from hotel to airport in both cities. The taxi rate in both instances comes to approximately 40 TL. The airlines maintain bus service between the city and the airports.

THY maintains daily service between almost every important town in Turkey. The cost of a ticket on the one-class flight between Istanbul and Ankara runs 332 TL (approximately $30). Flights are conveniently scheduled and take roughly an hour.

Children between two and twelve receive a 50% reduction on domestic flights on THY; children under two years old only pay 10% of the full fare. There are reductions of 10% for group travel. Family groups also have a 20% reduction. (See your travel agent for further details on these tariffs.)

By Rail

During recent months even the most hackneyed television programs have commenced to reflect the total decline of the Eastern European railway lines as an attractive, comfortable, practical means of travel between Western Europe and Turkey. Throughout Eastern Europe these international trains provide an important means of travel and communication between the various regions and cities within one country or between two of the countries previously reviewed, such as Yugoslavia and Bulgaria. But as a means of tourist travel the trains have all but been eliminated by air travel. Still, as a comparatively inexpensive, leisurely and certainly instructive means of transportation trains such as the "Orient Express" continue to be of marginal interest.

Tickets for sleeping accommodations on the following international trains may be purchased at Wagon-Lits Cook offices all over the world, through your travel agent or at national railway terminals throughout Eastern Europe. Sleeping cars on trains running between Paris, London, Vienna, etc., and Istanbul go directly through from their point of origin to Istanbul. Passengers are reminded, however, that restaurant cars do *not* make the complete trip. See your travel agent for up-to-date fares on the international trains.

The Direct Orient Express connects Istanbul, Munich and Vienna (twice a week service). The Orient Express makes a similar connection between Istanbul and Paris. The Marmara Express provides service between London and Istanbul. Twice a week the Baghdad Express operates between Istanbul and the capital of Iraq.

Passengers traveling between Istanbul and Ankara are reminded that no bridge or tunnel connects the city of Istanbul with its suburbs on the east side of the Bosphorus. Therefore, persons arriving in Istanbul from Europe with connections for Ankara or points further east (e.g. Syria or Iraq) should keep in mind that trains coming from Europe terminate at Istanbul's Sirkeci Station on the *west* side of the Sea of Marmora. Passengers are thus obliged to travel either by car ferry or regular ferry (frequent schedules) to the opposite shore where at Haydarpasha Station they may entrain for the remainder of their journey.

The best train leaving Istanbul for Ankara (and vice versa) departs from each city at approximately 8:30 P.M. Tourists leaving Istanbul on the night-time Ankara Express (sometimes referred to as the Anadolu Express) should allow a minimum of two hours for travel between the hotel in Istanbul and Haydarpasha Station on the opposite shore. The trip by taxi costs approximately 50 TL ($4.25), ferry boat ticket included. There is usually a wait of 20 to 45 minutes for a place on the car ferry leaving from Kabatas on regular 10 minute schedules. These boats are always crowded during the 5 to 7:30 rush hour.

Should you find yourself five to ten minutes late for your train, ask the taxi driver to take you to Pendik (pay him 50 lira extra). It takes the train a half hour to reach this small seaside town after leaving the station at Haydarpasha.

A regular ferry boat direct to Haydarpasha Station leaves the Galata Bridge at Karakoy every 15 minutes or so. You will be obliged to handle your own luggage.

The Ankara Express departs Istanbul at approximately 8:40 P.M. for Ankara (this time is subject to change). Sleeping car service is available; a restaurant car serves acceptable food. The Express arrives in Ankara at 8:30 A.M. Besides this daily night-time service, the Turkish Demiryollari (state railway) maintains daily daytime service on the Bosphorus diesel trains leaving both cities between eight and nine in the morning and terminating about eight hours later. Meals are served at your seat. The trip is long and in summer very hot, but there's one good way to make the acquaintance of Turkey. I recommend you travel *from* Ankara *to* Istanbul. The scenery will prove more interesting, much more enjoyable as you go from the semi-arid Anatolian Plateau to the green shores of the Sea of Marmora. Only open (though comfortable) coaches on this train. Seats must be reserved. Sleeping tickets one-way to Ankara cost approximately $20.

By Boat

Somewhat slower, perhaps, than other means of transportation, but I kid you not when I say the most dramatic, exciting, colorful introduction to Turkey is aboard ship. From Naples, Genoa, Venice or Piraeus, regular sailings provide passenger service direct to Istanbul's docks at the mouth of the "Golden Horn." So fascinating was my introduction to Turkey that despite many comings and goings by car and plane over the past 15 years I have never forgotten that early summer evening 17 years ago when from the bow of my ship, the SS. *Tarsus,* I first glimpsed the minarets and domes of ageless Istanbul. As the ship drew closer I saw the Seraglio, the palace of the Sultans, outlined against the hazy August sky. Nearby were the incredible Saint Sophia and the ever-so-graceful minarets of the Sultan Ahmet Mosque. Across the bay, to the right of the tiny "Leander Tower," the windows of houses in old Scutari seemed as though fully aflame as they reflected the hot, unforgiving though splendid summer sun.

And then came the cries of the city: peddlers, stevedores, taxi drivers; it was as though the entire city had turned out to greet the incoming ship. And there were the odors known only to those who have traveled in the east: coffee, dust, horses, sweat, tar, fish drying (rotting) on the dock. The city is never still; Istanbul is not unlike some gigantic cornucopia, spilling out an endless torrent of sounds, sights and odors to impress the foreigner with the infinite, unimaginable facets of that flawed totality known as Man.

I will never forget that evening, nor will many tourists forget the night's passage from Piraeus, the early dawn as the ship enters the Dardanelles Straits. There on your right is the monument to the British soldier who died at Gallipoli; ahead are the 40-mile-long Straits, the Hellespont, separating Europe from Asia. What tales have been told of this one- to five-mile wide gulf representing historical legend, political greed and enduring dynamic drama. Lunch is served as the vessel enters the Sea of Marmora. Turkish fishing boats, Russian ships-of-war, Romanian oilers and American destroyers pass off the port bow. And then at dusk—Istanbul!

The voyage from Naples to Istanbul takes roughly three days. Italian and Turkish ships making this run offer acceptable accommodations and average to good food. Prices vary according to the class in which one travels. See your travel agent for specific information regarding individual sailings.

The Turkish Maritime Lines also offer service between Istanbul and Izmir, Istanbul and the Turkish Black Sea ports (along the country's northern coast) as well as international service to such ports as Haifa and Beirut.

By Car

Visitors may enter Turkey from the west (Greece) at Ipsala and Uzunkopru; the former is on the better route (Highway E5 (18)). Tourists traveling by car can cross the Turkish frontier at Kapikule along International Highway E97 (Turkish Highway #1). Southeast of Turkey lies Syria. Persons traveling north from Aleppo, Damascus, Beirut or Iraq (no access routes presently exist for tourists between Iraq and Turkey) may enter Turkey at the following points: Cilvegozu (between Aleppo and Antakya), Carablus, Akcakale, Resulayn, Derbesiye and (to the far east of Syria) Kamisli.

Keep in mind that Turkey's eastern provinces constitute a military zone to which entry is allowed only by official permission.

Visitors traveling from the Armenian regions of the Soviet Union use the Turkish border station located at Gűmrű ("Leninakan"). This trip is emphatically not recommended for the American tourist.

By Bus

Bus service provides the visitor and Turk alike with an easy mode of transport between the principal cities and towns of Turkey and the more remote areas to which rail lines have not been constructed. A number of private companies offer overnight bus service between Istanbul and Ankara to Izmir, the Black Sea coastal towns, etc.

I recommend bus transportation only when no other means of transportation is available. There was a time, not too many years ago when bus travel was recognized as the quickest, most convenient if not the least hazardous mode of travel to distant points within the country. With the advent of the Marshall Plan, the ever-increasing numbers of cars on the road and an improvement in the national highways, bus travel began to serve, largely, the farmers and shopkeepers, soldiers, etc., who lived or worked in remote areas. The night train and THY planes are presently the best mode of travel between the larger cities.

Of course, if you really want to "Meet the Turks" in their natural haunts on something less than a first-class basis, there's no better way of doing it than on a bus trip across Anatolia. But first brush-up on your Turkish, and be prepared to meet a few chickens, goats and cats along the way. As for me, I'll fly!

By Taxi and Dolmus

Turkish cab drivers are, on the whole, a mighty sorry group. Poorly educated, harried by their inability to speak with foreign tourists, bedeviled by crowded, frenetic driving conditions, they operate on a profit margin that promises economic extinction if they cannot meet competition or the car breaks down. And if all this were not enough, along comes a tourist who insists on bargaining for a ride between the Hilton and Taksim Square (actually a five-minute walk) that has cost five or six lira for the past five years.

Meters on taxis in Turkey are not operative. You cannot judge the fare by these devices installed years ago but to date unused by the majority of the drivers. Learn the correct fare between the hotel and your destination or between those points you expect to cover during the day prior to your departure from the hotel, then throw in an extra lira for good measure when you arrive at your destination. Be sure to have the correct change or close to it. Drivers frequently pull the "no money" routine, obliging one either to give them too much or to rush into some shop to break a bill. *If* you know the correct fare and give him a lira tip, you have done all that could be expected of you. However, the driver may well comment: Musu (a bastardization of monsieur), cok az (very little) his face assuming the look of one who has suffered from instant loss of faith in mankind. Walk away! He'd probably pull the "very little" bit if you paid him four times the correct fare. After all, particularly where tourists are concerned, "nothing ventured, nothing gained"!

Should you not have an opportunity to learn the correct fare, figure that in most instances a ten-minute ride from the Hilton will cost between 10 and 12 lira (that is if you stay within the city). Trips to out-of-town destinations should be arranged for in advance and the price settled before you put one foot into the taxi. Drivers frequently say you may pay whatever you wish but of course if you pay what you think the unpleasantly rough and careening ride should cost and your guess proves incorrect, you may well find the driver at your side as you enter the restaurant. The scene guaranteed to follow, although better forgotten, will be long remembered!

During the late evening and night-time hours Turkish cabs usually operate with the inside lights on. This is a hangover from the "Good

Old Days" (?) when authorities wanted to know who was going where with whom. You will feel like a goldfish in an illuminated bowl, but bear with it. Times are changing fast. Incidentally, "yavas" (yavash) means slow. I'm sure you'll have occasion to use it. Fast is "cabuk," but you'll get that anyway.

There is frequent but slow bus service between Yesil Koy airport and downtown Istanbul. I recommend a taxi as the best means of transportation. When leaving the airport you will be very literally besieged by a number of cab drivers all offering to drive you into town. Determine the price in advance! The drive to Istanbul should cost 45 to 50 TL (these prices include a five-lira allowance for rising costs). Do not pay more! If the driver declines to take you, look for somebody else. Forty in Turkish is pronounced "kirk"; 45 is "kirk besh." Start at 40 and hold to it. If in a jam, go to 45. But don't go above "elle" (fifty). I do not know why the Istanbul municipality cannot do something about this tiresome "bargaining" that has taken place for years at Yesil Koy airport. On my most recent trip to Istanbul the situation was exactly the same. One last point: make the porter hold on to your bag until you have settled for one driver. Possession is nine points, etc., and the driver who has your baggage in hand might prove nigh unto impossible to deal with once the suitcases have been stowed away. Keep in mind, too, that bargaining in Turkey is not considered offensive if you are quoting prices that are reasonably in line with fact.

There exists a critical shortage of conveyances for public transportation in all cities and towns of Turkey, and the buses and streetcars that exist are frequently laid up due to a shortage of spare parts, breakdowns, etc. As a result, shoppers, businessmen, office workers, high school students and the more intrepid of the foreign colony have learned to depend on the dolmus as the quickest, most convenient method of transportation between various points within the city. A dolmus is a privately-owned car or station wagon, perhaps even a mini-bus, operating over a specific route and carrying five to six passengers. Dolmus stations are usually located near municipal bus stops. For approximately 10 to 20 kurus more than the usual bus fare, one can escape the crowded city buses and join four or five other persons in a dolmus and ride to one's destination in comparative comfort. Better than a packed bus, at any rate. One may alight from a dolmus at any convenient point along the route; it is not necessary to leave the car at a pre-arranged "official" stop.

Dolmus drivers shout the destination of their particular trip and so you must know the general direction you wish to take or the name of the terminus you want before entering the car. The driver usually does not start until his car is full, though when business is slow he will attempt to pick up passengers along the way (much to the annoyance of bus drivers who are forever being forced to honk dolmus cars away from bus stops).

Once you have learned your way about town, I recommend the dolmus as the quickest, most convenient way of getting about in Turkey's cities. A dolmus is not as expensive as a taxi, either. Pay the driver when you leave the car. Be sure you have adequate change or small bills.

When looking for a taxi in Istanbul, be careful not to snag a dolmus instead. It is surprising how fast a dolmus can transform itself into a taxi when an innocent hoves into view. Taxis are usually better maintained, less likely to cruise.

HOTELS

I urge that you make hotel reservations well in advance of your planned trip to Turkey. The best hotels in Istanbul (reviewed on the following pages) are frequently fully booked months in advance. Hotels in Ankara (not as popular a tourist attraction) manage to stay well booked throughout the winter months. Izmir is always filled during the well-known Izmir Fair (a commercial exhibition, but very popular), and the best hotels there are also booked well in advance during the summer season.

You can travel to Turkey by ship, car, plane or train. No so-called international bus lines connect Turkey with bordering countries; most of the large buses you will see in Istanbul or Ankara are chartered by individual groups of tourists. Reservations for your trip to Turkey can be made through any authorized travel agency. I do not recommend that you undertake to program such a trip without the advice of a travel specialist. Distance, language difficulties and the need for prepaying a portion of your trip tend to complicate matters for those who seek to avoid the agent's fee.

Should you fly directly to Istanbul and plan no further stops in Turkey, reservations at the Istanbul-Hilton may be secured through the Hilton Reservation offices in New York City. Book well in advance; this hotel is extremely popular.

The best time to visit Turkey is during the late spring, summer and autumn months. Ankara is usually hot and dry during the summer. Istanbul has the advantage of the sea breezes but can still be quite hot and dusty. Ismir's climate is semi-tropical. Plan your wardrobe to include a large amount of warm weather gear. Winters in Turkey find Ankara quite cool but with very little if any snow; Istanbul is humid, rainy. Izmir also experiences considerable rain during the winter months.

Turkey has not shown herself to be among the more enterprising countries when it comes to the matter of tourist travel. It was not until the inauguration of the Istanbul-Hilton in 1955 that Turkish officialdom began to appreciate the importance of tourism as a means of obtaining foreign currencies. Those Turks interested in developing Turkey's tourist potential were frequently in no position to influence official action; some suffered from a malaise not necessarily peculiar to Turkey, but one which that country possesses to an abnormally high degree, namely bureaucratic laziness or the "God will take care of His own" syndrome. In short, little was done about new roads, care of old roads, construction of motels, hotels or restaurants (primarily for travelers), nor was there any great amount of propagandizing the virtues of Turkey as an interesting, let alone exciting, tourist environment. Tourists were left to rattle about the country as best they could with Istanbul engendering the greatest amount of enthusiasm, almost by default. International carriers could be depended upon to bring the tourist safely and dependably as far as Istanbul. From that magnificent city eastward it was up to the Turks and, with an official posture indicating almost total disinterest, few tourists demonstrated much enthusiasm for the uncertainties of travel into Anatolia. So through the early fifties, those of us who visited Turkey (with exceptions) whiled away our after tour hours on the balcony of the Park Hotel, watching the more intrepid of the pack embark aboard ferry boats physically if not spiritually geared for the journey by night express to Ankara.

Even in the late fifties, after the Hilton had proved such a tremendous success, Turkish officialdom displayed no great enthusiasm for developing the foreign tourist trade into a full-scale enterprise. Oh, there were rumors of a new beach here, a boat ride there, someone buying a property with the thought of building a motel, an improvement in the until then almost sleepless fiasco represented by the bucking, jerking Istanbul-Ankara night train. A few innocent little motels even opened up near Istanbul's international airport; a private beach resort or two along the Black Sea or in Antalya, one of the most beautiful locations on the Mediterranean Sea (and still largely untouched by commercial development). Still Turkish officials talked and talked and talked!

Due in part to a political upset a few years back, major changes were made in the Turkish Government and the approach to tourism was seen to change. How or what or when the change occurred cannot easily be ascertained, but since roughly 1962 increased official interest regarding tourist travel to Turkey has resulted in a fairly extensive amount of construction; hotels, restaurants and motels are now in greater supply. There exists an intensive effort on the part of Turkish officialdom to encourage foreigners to visit Turkey, where "Europe meets Asia," etc. Visitors will not be over awed by the size or variety of facilities offered by the Turkish tourist establishment, nor will travel agents swoon with amazement at the speed with which their bookings are confirmed, but "old timers" to Turkey will, I'm certain, take vicarious pride in the public and private steps taken to introduce such tourist facilities as the Grand Hotel Efes in Izmir and the Grand Hotel Ankara in the capital.

Here are my suggestions with regard to hotels in Turkey. Deluxe hotels are a rare breed—indeed to be found only in Ankara, Istanbul and Izmir. The majority of these hotels are located in Istanbul and that city's immediate suburbs. Unfortunately, not all hotels officially rated "L" (deluxe) are top notch; when visiting the towns reviewed in this book, keep to the hotels recommended.

Local hotel rating authorities in Turkey have a habit of permitting the aura of historical reference to gloss over physical disadvantages in a number of their tourist facilities. One example of this misplaced sentimentality is the Hotel Pera Palace in Istanbul which is rated (locally) as high class. The Pera Palace was once an excellent hotel and certainly it has played a major role in the bedding and feeding of many personages commonly associated with the transition from Ottoman Turkey to the present day republic (Kemal Ataturk lived at the Pera Palace during the early twenties). But presently the Pera seems just a little sad, as if aware that a fine view of the "Golden Horn" cannot make up for the grimy walls and dusty plush interior.

And, incidentally, the rating of high class strikes this author as less a matter of quaint mis-translation than an attempt to muddy the distinction between genuine first class and those tourist units the Turkish authorities wish were first class but are not!

In Turkey reserve either deluxe (L) or high class (1) facilities, and in the latter category only after assuring yourself that the high class rooms are really such. One exception to the above rule is the Celik Palas in Bursa, now rated a "good grade, well appointed" (2) hotel by the local authorities.

Book in advance and allow adequate time for each stop. Know in advance that hotels such as the Hilton will most likely be unable to extend your stay (much as they would like to do so!) Do not book into hotels rated (2) unless you have been advised the hotel is acceptable, and never into hotels rated (3) or (4).

The vast majority of foreign tourists in Turkey visit the region of Izmir and Istanbul and make their headquarters in those cities. Official and business contacts require frequent trips to Ankara on the part of public administrators and businessmen. Hence, these three cities provide the best hotel and restaurant facilities. There are several widely scattered resort areas providing comparatively good vacation facilities for foreign tourists. See your travel agent or check with Americans stationed in Turkey for information regarding these very attractive resort cities.

Deluxe and high class hotels in Turkey are generally clean and offer a wide range of guest services; they are adequately staffed, serve average to excellent food and from reception desk to waiter give the visitor an impression of being most anxious to please. Passports are usually not requested of American visitors upon registration. Deluxe prices can be quite steep; first (high) class rates are below those encountered in the United States.

Hotel reservations for your trip to Turkey should be secured through authorized travel agencies either in the United States or prior to your departure from Western Europe. The number of acceptable hotels in Turkey is severely limited even in the largest cities. It is mandatory that you arrange for suitable accommodations some weeks prior to your journey. Should you visit Turkey (particularly Istanbul) without advance reservations, there is a good chance you will find yourself passing a night either in totally unacceptable surroundings or at some second class motel far removed from the city you had planned to visit.

Reservations at the Istanbul Hilton, far and away the best tourist facility in Turkey, may be obtained at the Hilton Reservations Office in New York or through your travel agent. Once your reservation has been confirmed at the Hilton, you will be provided with a confirmation slip indicating your time of arrival and day of departure. As the Hilton is usually fully booked, it is suggested you be prepared to leave the hotel on the exact day specified on your confirmation slip. The Hilton reservations staff is continuously besieged by guests requesting an extension of their stay (the answer is usually, "Sorry, but no!"). So allow yourself ample time in Istanbul. It is always better to leave a day early than to be caught 24 hours short and forced to move or leave.

We have already noted that you need not have in your possession a hotel reservation prior to entering the country, that no visa is necessary for a tourist stay under three months. However, border police will ask for a local address when you pass the Turkish frontier. If you have not had an opportunity to make a hotel reservation, better give the American Legation (or Embassy) as your address and then move fast to obtain a lodging before nightfall. But I repeat, arrive in Turkey with your hotel reservations confirmed in advance, preferably in writing.

I do not recommend any form of boarding house or private lodging in Turkey. Facilities of this nature are of too uncertain a genre to permit their inclusion in this guide. Nor do I recommend camping facilities in Turkey, for reasons outlined in a later section pertaining to this particular activity.

We have noted that hotel rates in Turkey run the gamut between prices paid in our country's most luxurious tourist facilities down to 28 lira for a single bed with shower (but sure as shootin' you'll hike out of there "Quick Step"). To provide you an idea of prices I am quoting below the top price for a single and double room with bath or shower in Istanbul, Izmir and Ankara (breakfast not included unless specified). Also quoted are the top high class rates in each of these cities. A service charge of 10% is usually added to the bill.

	ISTANBUL	IZMIR	ANKARA
Deluxe (single)	170 TL	100 TL	100 TL (breakfast incl.)
(double)	210 TL	120 TL	160 TL
High Class (single)	120 TL	75 TL	65 TL
(double)	155 TL	85 TL	100 TL

Prices listed above cover rooms with bath or shower.

Breakfast at the Hilton will run you between 13 and 23 TL and believe me, the "13 TL special" won't do too much for you if a hearty Western-style breakfast is uppermost in mind. In Izmir breakfast costs a fraction less in deluxe hotels.

Provincial hotels charge between 65 and 80 TL for "high class" facilities for a single person. Smaller hotels charge even less. Better inquire ahead. If you are quoted a rate below 50 TL figure you are more or less literally "taking a dive" and stay clear. Ditto for the larger towns. Hotels in provincial cities are always lower priced, but you must be certain to obtain the facts on any small town hotel before your hour of arrival.

Naturally, food and other room services vary from town to town, hotel to hotel. Generally speaking, all forms of room service, whether related to food or beverage, laundry, pressing, are pleasantly and efficiently rendered by the staffs of the deluxe hotels. Delays are more frequently caused by the tremendous demands made on personnel than by inadequacies on the part of the staff. Breakfast service in your room at Istanbul's Hilton can sometimes be a time-consuming, frustrating affair; again demand is usually the reason. On the other hand, I have seldom experienced such fast room service as encountered at Ankara's Grand Hotel. On one occasion I seemed scarcely to have replaced the telephone receiver when breakfast was brought through the door.

DINING

Turkish food is outstanding. Vegetables and fruits are matched in quality and flavor in few other sections of the world. Seafood, from lobsters through swordfish to mussels, is excellent. Lamb is prepared in endless varieties and is outstanding. Pastry comes in all forms: whether prepared as a main dish, an appetizer or as dessert, Turkish sweets not only delight the palate while confounding visitors by the singularly unsubtle designations given some pastries (e.g. "Ladies Navel"). One needs no other clue as to the anatomical vantage point from which the sultan's chef evidently gazed upon the world.

Within recent years great strides have been made in the preservation and freezing of foods in Turkey. It is now possible to enjoy many of that country's exemplary foodstuffs throughout all seasons of the year. Not only does the food in Turkey make for an excellent meal, it is vitamin-full as well. Yogurt, melons, bread, meats—all are of such high caliber as to provide the Turk and visitor alike with unusual opportunities for a healthful daily diet designed to improve the body's inner resources and to please the most discriminating, homesick epicurean. In short, my friend, you'll eat well in Turkey. Even the bottled water tastes great!

I heartily suggest you forsake the standard fare—roast beef, hamburgers and omelets; there are just too many other fascinating dishes in Turkey. Most menus carry descriptions in English describing the various components of each dish. Example: the curious and amusing dish called "imam bayildi"—which means, literally, "priest fainted"—is concocted of eggplant cooked in olive oil and then served cold with tomatoes and onions. It proved so devastatingly delicious that the old friar keeled over in sheer delight. Such being the case, what must have happened when the old gent was confronted with a serving of *kadin budu* (ladies thighs) can only be imagined.

Let's detail some of those typical Turkish dishes before reviewing the wines and other beverages. The following list will set your mouth to watering, but keep in mind that it is a long, long way from being complete. There are just too many exciting dishes to include them all in this brief review of Turkish eating habits.

> *Biber Dolmasi.* Stuffed green peppers; meat mixed with rice is the usual filling.
>
> *Ic Pilav.* Rice mixed with spices, raisins and pine nuts. Ask for "Each Peelav."

Su Boreci. A pastry filled with cheese or meat; rather heavy but very tasty.

Zeytin Yagli Patlican Dolmasi. Literally, eggplant prepared in olive oil and stuffed with rice.

Fasuliye Piyazi. Dried bean salad; the beans are mixed with eggs and onions.

Kabak Kizartmasi. Thin slices of squash, fried and served with yogurt.

Sis Kofte. Small meat balls, served hot.

Kilic Sis. Swordfish grilled on a skewer separated by and flavored with bay leaves.

Midye Dolmasi. Mussels stuffed with spicy rice and cooked in olive oil.

Dungun Corbasi. Wedding soup (evidently to prepare one for or to help one recuperate from the nuptials) contains meat, egg sauce and lemon juice. Great!

Cacik. Cucumbers, olive oil, yogurt and garlic; a side dish.

Iskembe Corbasi. Tripe soup with egg sauce (well-known and *good!*

Kuzu Dolmasi. Roast lamb with spiced rice. (Rice, incidentally, is "pilav."

Yogurt Kebab. Grilled lamb served in medium-sized pieces, mixed with chunks of bread and covered with yogurt.

Sis Kebab. Lamb grilled on a skewer, but this dish you must know!

Kadin Budu. Meat balls, folks, fried at that!

Cerkes Tavugu. Circassian chicken. Excellent. A speciality usually seen only at parties. Chicken ground with walnuts, paprika, etc.

Kavun. Green melon.

Karpuz. Watermelon.

Kase. Cheese. (Try the goat cheese.)

Asure. Pudding made of corn, figs, hazelnuts, walnuts, etc.

Baklava. A very sweet pastry stuffed with almonds or walnuts.

Tel Kadif. Browned, wire-like semi-sweet pastry.

Kadin Gobegi. A round, indented, very sweet (what else?) dessert.

Breakfast in Turkey usually consists of orange juice (from Haifa oranges), sour bread (toasted with jam, usually from Bursa), goat cheese, butter and tea. You can also have eggs in every condition and bacon, etc., if you so desire. But that sour bread (or rolls) with the tart cheese, a bit of jam and strong tea really starts a guy's day off right. And for lunch, try a tomato salad with stuffed mackerel and a glass of white wine and follow it up with a piece of cheese and some Turkish coffee. That's how lunch should be every day of the week!

Turkish aperitifs are many and varied. A few of the more outstanding are: Raki, a grape brandy flavored with anise, similar to the Bulgarian Mastika; Salep, a root served in hot milk; Sira, a non-alcoholic grape cordial; Boza, made with fermented wheat; Ayran, a cold drink made with yogurt and water—great drink on a hot day. The local brandy, Konyek, is okay with soda or straight with coffee.

Turkish coffee deserves special mention for it is served in three flavors. Like it sweet? Then ask for "Sekerli." The semi-sweet version, the kind most frequently served, is called "Orta." With little or no sugar it's "Sade." A drop of water, incidentally, will settle those grounds if you are in a hurry. In any event, do *not* gulp or you'll get a mouthful of sediment. Served in very small cups, Turkish coffee is excellent. It would be a thoughtful act if you tipped the girls in Turkish national dress who serve the Turkish coffee in large hotels. Coffee is frequently served when visitors meet with Turkish officials or local business people. You can order "American coffee" at large restaurants and hotels.

Tea in Turkey is frequently served in small glasses devoid of what is to me that so necessary handle. Don't burn yourself. I have yet to learn the fine art of balancing the little saucer on top of which is precariously balanced the steaming hot glass of tea, all the while conversing with acquaintances. The trick is to talk, balance and occasionally sip without burning either your fingers or gullet. A table on which to place the fiery concoction? Well, that's usually on the far side of the room.

Drink bottled water at all times, particularly in Istanbul.

Turkish wines can be quite good. My favorites are Kavaklidere (white and red) from Ankara; Klup (red); Yakup Damglasi ("Drop of Ruby"); and Doluca, "Doluja" (white).

Whiskies (Scotch), French wines, cordials, champagne as well as other assorted imports are available in the leading hotels and restaurants for a stiff price. Better bring a bottle or two with you (pick them up at those duty-free shops located at all international airports). If you don't drink them up, they'll make excellent gifts for local friends. Customs will say nothing about that "export" box carried with your hand luggage.

Meals can be extremely expensive at Istanbul's leading hotels and restaurants. You'll pay stateside (New York) prices for even the most simple dishes—figure 30 to 50 TL per person for dinner. In Ankara and Izmir, prices are somewhat lower; the food there is good but less elaborate. Service is included in the bill, but you might add 10% to 15% if the waiter's work has been particularly good. In the countryside you can eat well at minimal cost. Keep to grilled meats, fresh vegetables, bread and fruit. Smaller restaurants will run 15 to 20 TL per person for a three-course meal. Wine is not expensive.

Food service in Turkey is so-so. Waiters at leading hotels have been trained on a crash basis. It has been 14 years since the Hilton set the pace in Istanbul and today, after years of stumbling, fumbling service guided by French, Swiss and Italian maître d's, the Turks seem at long last launched in the right direction. Elsewhere, even in Istanbul, service is only average. The Grand Hotels in Ankara and Izmir provide their guests with acceptable service. I'll tell you one thing: the Turks are eager to learn, for their livelihood is at stake. Sounds refreshing, doesn't it?

People have asked me, "Do Turks drink alcohol?" Well, Moslems are not supposed to drink alcoholic beverages but nonetheless many of them do. There are many Turks who do not touch alcoholic drinks, but in the cities and among those Turks who maintain active contact with the European and American colonies you will find few abstainers.

SONGS AND DANCES

Well, now, here is a subject I would just as soon ignore. Effusiveness is, quite frankly, not in over supply where this writer is concerned and when it comes to Turkish music that particular trait is totally lacking. For my first six years in Turkey I tried, how very hard I tried, to develop an appreciation for the impassioned bleatings issuing from my radio at various times during the evening hours. On weekends, while eyeing my pile of too frequently played LP records, I would tune in a musical from Radio Ankara and try to find the rhythm, harmony, even purpose in the distressing sounds. Failing to achieve the slightest blush of satisfaction from the sounds, thoroughly distracted by lyrics telling of a lady's misery that her "Ahmet" had been confined to a local jail, I once again found solace in my warped, slightly cracked recording of "Wien, Wien, nur Du allein" played by the Wiener Volksőper orchestra.

But let's be fair; Turkish music, with its seeming aversion to pure tones and chords is an art form in itself. The instruments — many of Asian, Spanish, Egyptian, even Scottish origins — tell a story of musical development in composition and style which has yet to be fully appreciated by those of us weaned on harmonic orchestration. The music will be better understood when used as an accompaniment for dances than when played in support of the vocal stylings of a contemporary Turkish folk singer.

Turkish songs are written in the everyday language and sometimes employ dialects to emphasize some phase of the story told in a form of melodic rhythm. The average foreigner failing to grasp the import of the words issuing forth in half or quarter notes, is usually thunderstruck that his Turkish host seems on the verge of tears. The story told in an average Turkish song is usually one of impassioned but unlucky love. The songs speak of sadness, intense jealousy, grief or sublime joy.

Turkish dances fall into distinct groups: folk dances performed by men (the Zeybek, Horon, Sword and Shield); those performed by men and women (Spoon Dance, Bar Dance), those danced by women alone (the sensuous, forever popular *Ciftetelli*, known to the trade as the "Belly Dance"). As the above dances suggest, the dancers strive to depict scenes of battle, or courting, playfulness, etc. Costumes are usually simple in cut but elaborate in their trimming. It should be emphasized the *Cliftetelli* is many times more graceful than similar dances performed in Arab countries. In Turkey this dance relies less on gymnastic quiverings and quaverings than on the artful use of hands, arms, head and other more "southwardly" sections of the anatomy. The *Zeybeck* is an equally classic dance performed throughout the country, though usually associated with the Aegean area. Black Sea dances are extremely lively; the dancers not only make warlike gestures but also permit their bodies to shake as if from nervous excitement.

It is not difficult to gain access to a performance of these colorful folk dances. Should you not be in Turkey for one of their national holidays when folk dances are arranged by local civic organizations, then visit one of the several nightclubs in the Istanbul area featuring these attractions. Don't fail to attend one of these performances for they are exceptionally entertaining. The Hilton Hotel in Istanbul does a meritorious job of arranging nightly programs by dancers featured at the hotel on a year-in, year-out basis.

Speaking of national holidays, take in the Janissary Marching Band which frequently parades in costume to their own strange, warlike marching songs. One look at those men, their drums, swords and slow march cadence, and you will better understand the incredible fear Turkish armies inspired as they marched with terrifying determination through the Balkans, Transylvania and Hungary to besiege the incredulous Viennese.

Will you hear modern dance music, enjoy contemporary jazz programs in Turkey? Darn right you will! The Turks are true aficionados of beat-style tunes and dance them with a vengeance. An evening at the Hilton Roof Bar should convince you that no nation can claim a monopoly on the twist, frug or whatever form of calisthenics is on the upswing at the time you read these words.

KARAGÖZ AND HACIVAT

The Turkish Shadow Theater is world-famous. The two principal characters of this unique theatrical production are Karagöz and his rival Hacivat. The Shadow Theater refers to the construction of the characters, two puppets fabricated of a very thin vellum-like substance of which permits the light to shine through and around them as they dance, prance and fight, animated by hidden strings and wires. The figures are painted in elaborate colors. Keep in mind the little figures are actually only profiles.

THE TURKISH BATH

Unlike the overly vigorous but so healthy (I'm told) saunas found in Finland, the Turkish hamam has not gained its fame from a unique approach to bathing but rather from the obvious objective of building a facility in which the populace was provided with a means of keeping clean. It amounts to a passion for cleanliness resulting in a determined search for springs, wells and fast-flowing rivers and the construction of elaborate bath houses. All in all it is the religious motivation that has made the Turkish hamam so famous throughout recorded Turkish history.

A hamam (or bath house) usually consists of an entry hall, a central room protected by a domed ceiling and containing a large pool of hot mineral water plus assorted small rooms for private baths and rubdowns (in the more up-to-date facilities). Smaller anterooms where women and children may bathe may also be available. Some of these hamams are quite elaborately decorated (colored tiles, cupolas, etc.). It is the historical importance of these baths that has made them significant. In Hungary, Yugoslavia, Bulgaria and Romania we have found evidence of the Turks' unending search for sites at which they could construct hamams for their armies, officials, guests and kings. Frequently these sites had been famous as Roman baths centuries before the Turk marched through Eastern Europe.

The Moslem religion calls for frequent intervals of prayer throughout a 24-hour period. Before entering a mosque or engaging in prayer, the Turk is required to wash certain areas of his body, usually those parts which touch the ground when the kneeling posture is assumed for prayer. This requirement led to the construction of a fountain (or "cesme") in the courtyard of the mosque. But even more important, the Koran set down strict rules regarding cleanliness. It was therefore mandatory that the Turk locate his settlements, bivouacs, etc., near a source of clean water. And if a mineral spring could be found—perhaps one producing hot water and thus providing the bather with curative benefits—so much the better.

A great deal of significance was attached to bathing facilities constructed by the Ottomans. Many of these edifices remain with us today so great was the care with which they were constructed. These buildings give impressive witness to an empire that marched against its neighbors behind a green flag testifying to an irrefutable belief in the invincibility of Allah, who through his prophet had decreed that men should obey the Commandment of Cleanliness.

In later years of the Empire the Hamam achieved a certain social distinction by providing mothers with an opportunity to arrange matches between their sons and the daughters of fellow bathers of acceptable social status. Mothers and their young sons frequently visited the hamams with the sole aim of arranging a suitable "alliance." The feelings and thoughts of the offspring were of secondary importance.

In today's Turkey, the hamam perhaps has less religious importance and, except in the villages, is of only limited importance socially. Still, for young and old, rich and poor, a visit to the mineral baths continues to be a pleasurable occasion. A number of hotels, such as the Celik Palas at Bursa, maintain baths on the premises. There guests may visit the hamam or simply enjoy the mineral waters in the privacy of their own bathroom.

RELIGION

The Turk is a deeply religious person, more so perhaps than even he realizes. It has been my impression that Turks try to abide by their faith even though there is little outward demonstrativeness. However, orthodox religious practices do not play a great part in the life of the better educated, economically advanced Turkish citizen. It is, to a large extent, the farmers, resident of smaller towns and the elderly (and probably less educated) persons who make an effort to conform today to religious requirements, many of which are at odds with modern domestic and business practices.

The Turkish language is riddled with references to "Allah," but much of this phraseology is automatic; mere verbal reflex reactions to situations or, perhaps simply conversational gentility. Nonetheless, under this guise of sophistication there exists in each Turk an abiding faith in the sublimity of his religion and its ordinances. Americans could learn a great deal by analyzing the depth of a Turk's religious commitments as well as his sense of national pride.

The Turk is quite broadminded when it comes to understanding the religious beliefs of non-Moslems. Moreover, the Turk is not at all reluctant to show the visitor his mosques and religious artifacts or to permit the Christian or Jewish visitor to witness a Moslem religious service—providing the visitor evidences respect for the occasion.

When visiting a mosque remember to remove your shoes before entering the interior. At some of the more historic shrines slippers are available which may be worn over one's shoes. (Be most careful not to "walk out" of the slipper, something easily managed without the wearer noticing his *faux pas*.) You will note Turkish women may not move to the front of the mosque but are obliged to remain seated in special sections at the rear of the building. Women among tour groups who wish to walk about the mosque may do so without fear of reprimand, though I would urge that *all* visitors remain at the rear should there be a service underway at the time. Turkish men must cover their heads when entering a mosque for a religious function. (Note how handy is the rimless feature of the fez when participating in a Moslem service. As the head must, at times, touch the ground the fez and baggy trousers of old were a worthwhile part of a Turk's garments. For this reason the "golfing" cap so popular among the farmers was adopted following the ban on wearing of the fez. By turning the hat in reverse the wearer could participate in the religious worship without interfering with custom.)

ATTITUDE TOWARDS WOMEN

Visitors will be invited to visit the Harem in the Sultan's Palace (the Seraglio) at Saray Burnu, a point of land separating Halic (the "Golden Horn") from the Sea of Marmora. It was in this building that many of the more infamous occasions in Turkish history took place, though these incidents have acquired a romantic patina down through the centuries. Today lechery, torture and intrigue now seem idle concepts when one views the aging panels and faded silks of this historic monument to an empire's proud though frequently shabby past.

The harem as an institution ceased to play an important part in the Ottoman monarchical institution in the late nineteenth century and was largely relegated to the past prior to World War I. With the dissolution of the monarchy the harem ceased to exist. With the conception of the republic, multiple marriages were forbidden; in fact, such practice was never pre-ordained by any Moslem religious teaching.

The women of Turkey have been legally advanced to a position equal to that of men though in some circumstances (particularly in the more remote areas) they continue to occupy a secondary role in both public and domestic affairs. Gone is the harem with its latticed windows, gone the veil, gone the homes so constructed that "separate but equal" facilities for men (the "Selamlik") and women (the "Haremlik") were provided, with the men occupying the more elaborate quarters. Women in Turkey play a role not dissimilar to that of their counterparts in Europe and the United States. The Turkish woman is active in civic affairs and has attained a prominent role in the fields of education, law, literature, politics and medicine as well as in many other areas of public and private endeavor.

Turkish women are extremely style-conscious and follow the latest trends in designs from Rome, Paris and the United States. They love to dance, thus providing charming company to the travel-weary bachelor, and are excellent homemakers for their devoted (and very frequently jealous) husbands. Yet there exists something of a social problem in Turkey. For instance, it continues to be difficult for a Turkish woman to meet in *public* with some man (a family friend, uncle, etc.) without arousing a tirade of gossip, most of it malicious, in all social circles. Moreover, it is difficult for any young woman of any nationality to walk the streets of Turkey without being subjected to the most odious comments, the most flagrantly rude actions on the part of many less-educated Turkish men. I know of one instance when the young Swedish wife (and mother) of a Turkish friend of mine was literally stoned by youths for failing to acknowledge their "amorous" remarks. It would behoove all women to take care that their teenage daughters do not go out on the streets of Istanbul or Izmir without benefit of proper escort. A mini-skirted youngster on a crowded city street in Turkey is emphatically asking for trouble.

Turkish women are extremely feminine. One seldom sees women who so artfully—in fact, soulfully—represent the many attributes thought to embody the "mystique" of the female sex. (We are, of course, for the most part dealing here with the educated, or semi-educated, Turkish woman.) Turkish women love clothes, perfumes and good food. They dress artfully and with great care. The Turkish girl is extremely conscious of male appraisal, yet seems to project her femininity in such a disarming manner as to deny a posture of super-sophistication. Istanbul girls in particular are extremely sophisticated. Women in Turkey, certainly teenage girls, are usually chaperoned. We have stated before that even in their middle years it is difficult for Turkish women (housewife, salaried employee, professional) to meet with men in public without causing comment. You seldom see younger Turkish girls lounging about in public facilities open to foreigners; rather they are usually found with close friends at sports clubs and on the beach, with members of their families frequently nearby. Most of the young (and old) women seen unescorted in public places are not Turkish.

I would be unfair if I did not also state that I find many women in Turkey to be incredibly vain as well as astonishingly gossipy. But here again we have introduced two of the less attractive but certainly well known facets of femininity. After all, that "harem heritage" certainly must have rubbed off some place.

THE TURKS

Turkish men are as masculine in their outlook on life as the women are feminine. They love sports, particularly "futbol" (or soccer), boating, tennis and swimming. On a perhaps less educated level Turkish men are great extroverts but remarkably enough at the same time extremely shy. There are few bachelors in Turkey, though marriages do not necessarily occur at an early age. On some social levels the Turks appear quite aggressive; language and gesticulations tend to give this impression though actually the Turkish male is not much different than men in any other country.

There is no real guide to understanding the Turkish mentality. Better men than I have studied this question for longer periods than my twenty-some-year association with that country. Truly, I don't believe the Turks understand themselves. They will say yes rather than decline an offer, lest they hurt a friend. As a result the "friend" may become an enemy. They may say no when a friend offers to do some kindness (albeit ill-timed). As a result pride stands between friends. Yet to have a Turk as a friend is a "possession to be valued beyond price."

There is no prototype of a Turkish man or woman. So many races and ethnic groups of both European and Asian origin have crossed Asia Minor since the earliest periods of recorded history that it is ludicrous to say Turkish women are "fair-haired" or Turkish men are "swarthy." Turkish men are generally shorter than their American counterparts, but what they have lost in height is usually made up for in physical strength. Turkish women are not much different in size from women of other countries bordering the Mediterranean Sea. Though slender in youth, many tend to gain weight about the hips after reaching thirty.

Both sexes adore children and make fine parents. Young married couples remain quite close to their parents though frequently living apart. A great deal of respect continues to be shown elderly people, even those outside a direct family relationship. Foreigners are generally welcomed to Turkish homes; Americans continue to be quite popular in Turkey. I believe the most important word to be applied in your contacts with the Turks is "naturalness." Be yourself. Don't be patronizing, over-eager or a "show-off." The Turks are an extremely natural, rather easy-going yet very sensitive folk and can appear quite friendly toward you in public. Quite another matter, though, this business of meeting a Turk's wife, mother, sister, etc., in their domestic environment. Still, if you continue to demonstrate an honest interest in his country, from an historical point of view as well as on a day-to-day domestic basis, chances are you will find yourself drawn closer to the family.

SHOPPING

To my knowledge there are no official discount stores in Turkey. Stores and shops along Istanbul's Istikial Caddesi or on Ataturk Boulevard in Ankara maintain fixed prices. Goods are usually marked and prices are indicated both inside the shops and in store windows.

Attention should be directed here to the question of bargaining. Many tourists (and I can assure you Americans are far from the worst in this practice) visit Turkey with the idea that bargaining or haggling for the lowest price is a common practice in all bazaars, stores, shops and markets throughout the country. This is emphatically not so! Whether you find yourself in the flossiest dress shop in Istanbul or the vegetable market in Ankara, accept the price quoted to you by the sales person or the price marked on the ticket attached to the merchandise. Even in Istanbul's Grand Bazaar the prices of many goods are fixed by local trade unions or, in the case of jewelry, by the prevailing price of gold and silver.

Istanbul, Izmir and to some degree Ankara abound in shops specializing in items of interest to the tourist. There are hundreds of items on display; a few are outstanding, many are interesting or amusing, and the rest, actually the greater part, is just junk. Be guided by two rules; (1) remember for whom you are purchasing the gift and where the item will be displayed and (2) note that many small souvenir shops are to be found in large cities, so shop around a bit for the best price. Souvenir shops stock such things as ceramic vases and small water pipes, clay pipes with the bowls carved to form turbanned heads, dolls, copperware of every ilk, brass ashtrays in many forms, rugs of good and poor quality, figurines, pins and necklaces (again of good and poor quality), mediocre filigreed silver, glassware and plaques of brooches sporting the Imperial Seal of Emperor Abdul Hamid. My Turkish friends readily agree that the Istanbul souvenir shopkeeper is particularly adept at fashioning little Turkish delights to charm the already harrassed and confused foreign visitor. Your shopping motto should be: Relax – shop around – buy cautiously! Don't be either soft-soaped or antagonized by the usually glib-tongued, loquacious sales personnel; these people are past masters at the art of selling. Truly a breed apart, they are often amusing as well as effective.

Articles of outstanding worth and superior workmanship are available in a number of the stores located near the "Tunel" in Istanbul (Istiklal Caddesi), that is at the showroom two to three blocks down the street from the French Consulate near Taksim Square. At this place prices are high but the silks and satins displaying centuries' old motifs and designs are magnificent. The girls who prepare this material are keeping alive traditional fashions in handwork that were almost lost during Turkey's turbulent centuries.

Shopping hours are rather lengthy, lasting from eight in the morning until seven in the evening, but many shops close during the early afternoon. Offices are closed on weekends.

Bitex

If you arrive in Turkey without your favorite shampoo, go to "Bitex." If you want a jar of Planter's peanuts, a cheese spread, a jar of olives to go with cocktails, get them at "Bitex"! Band-aids, cereal, a can of peaches, in fact, just about any American product available in U.S. Military Stores abroad can be found in the "Bitex" shops. All purchases in local currency only, please.

"Bitex" shops are something of a phenomenon – the "legalization" of a dubious practice for the benefit of a have-not market starved for luxuries. Ankara seems to be the center for this side-door handout; there the "Bitex" shops are located on the ground floor of apartment houses two blocks west of Ataturk Boulevard, in the Yenisehir section of the capital. I attempted to learn the meaning of the word "Bitex," and the answer I got was that since civilian stores associated with the American military establishments are called a Post Exchange (or "PX"), the analogous Turkish phenomenon is called BITEX.

My sole purchase at these curious little stores was one bottle of a well-known American shampoo for which I paid just short of double the State-side price. And my, oh my, what a range of other goodies lined the walls of that 8 by 10-foot shop opening onto a passageway occupied by 10 to 12 other stores selling almost identical products. It is interesting to note how canned hams are featured next to jars of vaseline which in turn give way to stacks of a chewing gum company's contribution to the defense effort. How these shops secure their weekly allotments and on what basis the "swag" is divided would provide a gold mine of information relative to the foibles of the human animal. Of course the rather obvious loss of public funds through the medium of this semi-official black market also figures in here. But if I say more I'll be cordially disliked by both parties to this commercial "bridge-building" operation. Quite obviously if there existed no demand there would be no market for the tons of corn flakes, whiskies, detergents and bath oils found in these shops. So let's conclude by stating that the "Bitex" shops provide many a Turkish housewife with wondrous opportunities to provide her household with the ultimate product once she scrapes together enough lira to pay the fine. Meanwhile, some person or persons within the American military establishment must be living rather well in Turkey from the not inconsiderable percentage gained from sales of the most expensive oatmeal and shaving soap east of Trieste.

How to Bargain

It has already been noted that most shops maintain set prices which they will quote to you or mark on small slips attached to the sale article. In such stores, do not bargain. If you do you'll be given the deep-freeze treatment and will most likely lose your sales clerk in the process. Neither should you attempt to jimmy down the price in restaurants, hotels, bars, etc. Unless you are certain you are being overcharged, pay the price asked (after checking the bill, naturally!) and go quietly.

Really, the only two areas where bargaining is acceptable in Turkey are: (1) with cab drivers in reference to "long haul" rates and (2) in Istanbul's Bazaar, and there only at certain small shops. Oh sure, in small provincial towns or with repair men called to do some work around your home, a "compromise" can be worked out with reference to the price of goods or service. But this is a delicate negotiation requiring fluent Turkish.

Individuals who run the hundreds of jewelry shops, souvenir

stands, antique and rug stores in the Bazaar expect the customer to bargain, and he who fails to bargain is usually overcharged. Keep in mind that articles of fair to good workmanship fabricated of gold or silver offered by the jewelry shops have a base price relating to the value and quantity of the precious metal used in the article. But with this exception, all sales are made at a mutually agreeable price. It is expected, however, that the customer knows what he's talking about; in other words, you must have an appreciation of the true worth of the article you wish to purchase. To suggest a price far below the real worth of the goods is to invite scorn, derision and a cold shoulder from the shop keeper.

As you have probably been advised before, don't show your eagerness for an article which you in fact can't wait to buy. Purchase some other small item, look about the shop, let your face portray just a hint of disdain. Give the impression that you usually don't come into such ill-lighted, cold (hot), loud (empty) shops, and that you just might walk out if they don't treat you well. Keep your offer a good many liras below his offer so there will be plenty of room in which to bargain. Figure the shopkeeper will be asking several times the worth of the goods. Once the figure has been settled, or he is only 200 or 300 liras above you, show him the cash to cover your offer and say you are satisfied, to wrap it up — in short make an effort to terminate the discussion. Appear anxious to leave, sober, wearied by all this "bos ver" (cheap talk). If he won't meet your price at this point, leave the shop. This usually brings interesting, and very quick results. And if the shop owner or salesman should fail to follow you down the covered street, you can always go back, right?

In Turkey, a sharply upraised tilt of the head means no. This motion is frequently accompanied by a lisping or clucking noise made by pressing one's tongue against the back of one's teeth. A sideways, rather slow motion of the head indicates agreement. These motions are almost the complete reverse of the signals used by English-speaking persons; don't get mixed up.

In bargaining, three points to remember if you are seriously after some unique article or one of exceptional worth: (1) To the shopkeeper, bargaining is a way of life. It is not demeaning to him or to you. (2) Don't get angry or take the shopkeeper's reactions as a personal affront. You wanted to bargain, so give as good as you get. (3)

If you are offered coffee or tea, even in the middle of the bargaining session, even if you are in a hurry, accept the drink. This is a wise (and pleasant) custom designed to take the edge off the discussion, to give you both time to think over the offers made.

MOTORING

Auto garages are located throughout major cities and along principal highways across the country. Usually associated with gas stations, these repair facilities are frequently under the supervision of well-trained mechanics. Many Turks attended factory schools then worked in Germany prior to World War II and again during the late 1950s. For this reason, Turkey can offer average to excellent car-servicing facilities.

Should you require some particularly special service for your car, keep in mind that large installations are maintained in Turkey by prominent West European and American car manufacturers. See the hotel reception desk clerk for details regarding the location of these wholesalers and purveyors of specialized auto repair units.

High octane gasoline is just not available in Turkey, so you'd better have your engine adjusted accordingly if you plan to spend some time in Turkey. The lower octane gas costs approximately 55c per imperial gallon (equals 1-1/5 U.S. gallons).

Rental cars are available with or without chauffeurs through travel agencies located in the principal cities. In Istanbul check with Doktoroglu Seyahat Agentesi, Istanbul Turizm or Covo Turist Agentesi. The American Hertz Car Rental firm maintains offices in Ankara and may be contacted at the number listed in the local telephone book.

Although I realize that to really see the country auto travel is a must, I cannot recommend extensive car trips through Turkey unless one is fully prepared for what is almost always an extremely wearing experience. Roads are far from the best, traffic is heavy (along the few main routes) and Turkish drivers take incredibly dangerous risks, particularly the truck and bus drivers who careen from one end of Turkey to the other in their overloaded vehicles. Rent a car if your requirements dictate but try to keep within the environs of one town. Be extremely cautious, drive with great care and avoid driving after dark. I have known truck drivers to leave their vehicles parked without lights in the middle of the main Ankara-Istanbul highway! Other hazards on the roads are animals, farmers, children and carts. Turkish drivers turn off their headlights when approaching another vehicle from the opposite direction. What follows is a nerve-shattering game of "lights on, lights off" until two vehicles pass each other.

Turkey is not a large country but travel distances are increased by the limited number of acceptable roads. The highway system comprises approximately 38,000 miles. A lack of bridges and tunnels under the Marmora Sea, across the Bosphorus and Gulf of Izmit has greatly complicated matters for those traveling.

Tourists wishing to rent a car must be in possession of a valid international driver's license and must be able to present proper identification (e.g., passport). The minimum age for those renting cars is 21. Free pick-up and delivery service is available for those arriving by plane, train or boat.

The Turkish Ministry of Tourism and Information, 500 Fifth Avenue, New York City, has a number of road and city maps which I am certain you will find valuable, truly of considerable assistance in finding your way about the country or through specific cities, such as Ankara and Istanbul. New road maps are issued annually.

GUIDES

Guides may be secured through local travel agencies or the Information Bureau of the Ministry of Tourism. The National Union of Turkish Students also provides guides but these must be contacted through the Ministry's Information Bureau. I urge that you either employ a guide of unquestioned capabilities or join tours of Ankara, Istanbul or Izmir offered by local travel firms. Try to find a tour group that is restricted in size, for too many people limit the worth of the touring experience. But by all means take a competent guide with you when touring the multitude of historical sights in such cities as Izmir and Istanbul. Fees are nominal.

TRAVEL AGENTS

This writer is singularly unimpressed by the great number of so-called travel agencies in Turkey. With the exception of such large international organizations as Wagon-Lits Cook, most are little more than pastimes for the offspring of wealthy Turks or else are operated on a shoestring by unprofessional and inexperienced persons. Many of Turkey's travel agencies are not even prepared to perform such functions for the tourist as cashing or selling travelers checks, issuing rail or air tickets, and the like.

I suggest that you contact your hotel reception desk, the local airline office of your carrier, Wagon-Lits Cook, the United States Information Service (in Istanbul or Ankara) or another responsible organization before making car rental or touring (including guide service) arrangements with local travel firms. Obtain first-hand information from these sources before approaching the local agents.

PHOTOGRAPHY

Turkey is a beautiful country and provides the amateur and professional alike with outstanding photographic raw material. Be certain not to forget your camera when visiting Turkey. All types of cameras, still and movie, plus film, may be imported into the country for personal use.

There are no unusual requirements with reference to photography in Turkey. I would refrain from photographing warships, military installations or troop movements. Do not take photographs from airplanes while flying over Turkey. On the other hand, picturesque shots of shipping in the Bosphorus, along the "Golden Horn" and in the Dardanelles Straits are acceptable to local authorities. I think you know as well as I what is permitted and what is not; try to stay within "the rules."

MOTELS AND CAMPING

Motels are located at the towns and cities listed below. I have not had an opportunity to investigate each one; however, quite a number, particularly those located in resort areas and at the seaside, are unique in location and architecture (a blending of Turkish design with up-to-date functionalism). In many instances there are several motels located within the environs of one community.

This list will only advise you that a motel is located in these communities. You would do well to inquire in advance as to the caliber of specific facilities on your route. In many of the sea resort towns (e.g., Aydin) the motels are far superior to the local hotel accommodations.

Antalya (well-known and particularly beautiful resort area on Turkey's southern Mediterranean coast)
Aydin
Balikesir
Bolu
Burdur
Bursa
Canakkale
Denizli
Edirne (at the Bulgarian Turkish border)
Edremit
Icel
Istanbul (all Mamora Sea resort areas): Kiliyos, Kartal, Pendik, Kumburgaz, Yemikoy, Floriya.
Izmir: Cesme, Bergama, Gumulduh, Selcuk
Kayseri
Kocaeli
Kutahya
Sakarya
Tekirdag

Visitors to Turkey should keep in mind that new motels are built each year. The above list runs through the 1968 tourist season only. Make inquiry in Turkey if there seems no motel along your planned route.

Wtih reference to camping, I would urge that you restrict your camping activities to those specific locations allocated by the Turkish Government for that precise purpose. In short, lay off the "self-elected site." Turkey is a rugged country, and it is possible that certain minor instructions could upset your outing. Camp sites are clearly designated by the blue and white International Camping signs on which are outlined either the symbol of a tent (camp site) or of a trailer ("caravan" or trailer camp) or both.

The following "Mocamps" include such facilities as telephone, water, shower, beach or pool, first-aid, a staff member who speaks a foreign language, electric lights, car repair outlet, gas station, souvenir shop and post office. Some camps maintain additional facilities. All the sites have restaurants except those marked with an asterisk (*).

>   *Edirne** (The Ipsala Keravansaray maintains restaurant facilities nearby.)
>   *Istanbul* (Bakiroy*)
>   *Ankara**
>   *Bursa* (Mudanya)
>   *Canakkale** (Intepe Camligi)
>   *Izmir*
>   *Antalya*
>   *Mersin*

TELEPHONES, CABLES AND LETTERS

Local pay telephones in Turkey are operated by means of tokens (jetons) purchased at post office counters for 50 kurus each. Telephone calls between Turkish cities can be mighty slow in going through unless you place them on an "express" or "urgent" basis. The latter type of call costs two or three times the normal rate.

Telephone conversations within Turkey (as well as those placed to some individual overseas) can be not so much expensive as wearing. Calls are frequently delayed for many hours and then when completed are subject to noisy, often interrupted connections. Rates are approximately 14 TL per minute from Turkey to Europe, 47 TL per minute between Turkey and the United States.

The tension concomitant in the inter-city telephone calls in Turkey is a wonder to behold. After contacting the operator one is required to remain close at hand, as the length of time required to complete the call is usually indefinite. Once one's party has been reached, one is summoned to the phone in almost unseemly haste. I would suggest you arrange for the utmost privacy before picking up the receiver because connections are frequently so poor that you will be required literally to bellow throughout the entire call. It has been said by a few uncharitable souls that a connection with Ankara from Istanbul might better be undertaken by simply shouting toward Ankara from an east balcony of the Hilton Hotel.

Regular mail within Turkey costs 50 kurus; 60 kurus for air mail. Air mail to Europe runs 1.30 TL; to the United States, 2.20 TL.

Telegrams within Turkey cost 2.50 TL for 10 words, plus 20 kurus for each additional word. Rates differ between Turkey and other countries; better consult the post and telegram desk in your hotel or else visit the local post office. A word to the wise: only limited English (if any) is spoken by clerks in the main offices. Better deal with the mail clerk in your hotel or contact the reception desk. Incidentally the Hilton in Istanbul maintains a very efficiently run mail desk.

HUNTING AND FISHING

The hunting season in Turkey lasts from September 15 through April 15. Licenses may be obtained at recognized hunt clubs; contact the Turkish Tourist Information Office for details regarding rates, bag limits, etc.

Animals which may be hunted year around (with a license) are the lynx, wild boar, panther and tiger. Those animals that may be hunted without restriction (license required) during the hunting season are the wild cat, badger, rabbit, squirrel, fox, bear, boar, partridge, duck and goose. The following animals are restricted and may not be hunted deer, ram, wild goat, porcupine, pigeon, dove, pheasant (the Ministry of Tourism uses the word "peasant" but I assume no form of genocide is actually contemplated by that sedate government bureau! stork and owl.

No license is required for the following fresh water fish: trout, catfish, carp, pike and bass. I suggest you contact the Ministry of Tourism for information relating to salt-water fishing before casting a line into Turkish waters.

SERVICES

Laundry is usually returned in time, acceptably cleaned, clothes neatly pressed. Costs are reasonable. I do not recommend the dry cleaning in Turkey unless, perhaps, it is handled at the Hilton. Pressing is acceptable in any of the recommended hotels. You'll find floor personnel eager to please though there exists a fairly substantial language problem. For all floor services in the large hotels, see the Directory located near the telephone.

ANKARA

Visitors approaching Ankara by train or car will spot the capital's Citadel some minutes before reaching Ankara's city limits. Twin peaks form the heart around which this very old city has developed with increasing speed since its selection as capital of the Republic of Turkey in 1923. There is evidence that Ankara was inhabited as long ago as 5000 B.C. (the Stone Age). Artifacts have been discovered acknowledging the presence of Hittite Tribes in this area 1200 B.C. The Phrygian King Midas made the town his capital and called it "Ankyre." It was the town's misfortune to lie on an informally acknowledged border between civilizations to the west (Roman) and those of the east (principally the Persians). Following the Phrygians came the armies of Alexander the Great and then, in the 3rd century B.C. a race of Celts known as Galatians.

The Romans granted the Galatians who had settled in the region of Ankara a form of local autonomy. A temple was built at Ankara in honor of the Roman Emperor Augustus. In 74 B.C. the Roman Emperor Pompeius incorporated Ankara into his "Asia Province." The Ankara "Citadel" is believed to have been constructed by the Galatians during the Roman Period. The round shape of the towers was something of a hallmark of the Galatian people. It is thought that upwards of 200,000 people lived in the immediate area of Ankara during the time of the Early Romans.

During the Byzantine era, Ankara was the seat of the Orthodox Metropolitan. Between 695 and 806 the town was exposed to almost continuous plundering by Arabs under the leadership of the well known Harum-al-Raschid. What had been one of the main centers of Christianity in Asia Minor was totally under Arab control. With the eventual extension of Byzantium's borders toward the East, Ankara was again secure against Arab raids. Considerable assistance was provided the Byzantines by the intercessions of the Crusaders who in 1101 returned Ankara to the authority of Constantinople replacing the Seljuk Turks who had captured the town in 1073.

In 1127 Ankara again became part of the domain ruled by the Seljuk Turks, Byzantine power being continuously restricted to regions bordering the Aegean coast and the Bosphorus. In 1354 the Ottoman Turks under the command of Suleyman captured the town following an invasion by the Mongols under Genghis Khan. And on the wide plain near Cubuk, not far from Ankara (then "Angora") the forces of Ottoman Sultan Beyazit fought (and lost) against the invading hordes of the infamous Mongol Timurlane.

In 1920 Kemal Ataturk chose Ankara as his capital in an effort to break with foreign as well as Ottoman influences prevalent in the former capital city of Constantinople (or "Istanbul" to the Turks). Ataturk chose Ankara over two other towns considered fitting as capital cities, Konya and Kayseri. Ankara was by this time little but a village on the semi-arid, hot and windy Anatolian plateau. When vast populations had moved, where empires had fallen little remained. On that April day the Turkish National Assembly was convened in Ankara. Ataturk proclaimed the establishment of a Turkish Republic, October 29, 1923. On that date roughly 40,000 people lived in Ankara. This was a capital for the Turks, a *Turkish* town, centrally located in a northwest section of the central Anatolian Plateau. Though the capital had moved east geographically, the policies of Turkish governments including those of Ataturk have always been oriented toward the West.

Ankara is a comfortable city, in which you can move about with great facility. Trolley buses connect the important points within the city, taxis and the ever-eager "Dolmuses" are always available. Ankara runs in approximately a north-south direction with small suburbs located east and west of town. Ulus is the main business and financial area of the city; Yenisehir, the main shopping section. Broad Ataturk Boulevard connects Ulus and Yenisehir with that area of the town comprised of government buildings (Bakanliklar). South of this government section, composed of the Parliament, the Ministries of Defense, Education, the Foreign Ministry, etc. is an attractive tree-shaded avenue (actually an extension of Ataturk Boulevard) leading upwards toward the residential subdivisions of Cankaya and Kavalikdere. Here reside important Turkish officials and here are the official residence of the President, the Government Guest House, Ataturk's former home (now a museum), embassies, apartments, etc. Nearby are other select residential areas, the many homes commanding a magnificent view of distant Ulus some miles to the north. The Grand Hotel Ankara is situated at the northern end of Cankaya Boulevard as the latter swings up toward the official residence subdivision.

The majority of historical sites are in Ulus. Restaurants and the better hotels are located in Yenisehir and Cankaya. It is approximately ten minutes by cab from Cankaya to Ulus. Cab fares are quite low. Ankara's airport (Esenboga) is situated roughly an hour north of town as you exit from Ulus. Figure a cab fare of approximately 50 TL and plan to leave your hotel at least one hour and 45 minutes before the departure time of your plane. In winter better figure a minimum of two hours, if not more. The railroad station is located midway between Yenisehir and Ulus not far from the Opera. Plan on leaving your hotel a half hour to 45 minutes before train departure time. Porters are available at both the airport and rail station.

At any time of the year Ankara is a pleasant city in which to visit. In winter there can be a fair amount of snow. The weather is usually cold but fairly dry. In summer Ankara is quite hot and dry. Turks tend to leave Ankara on the slightest pretext during summer months. Men, women and children all love the sea and there is a wholesale migration to the shores of the Aegean, the Black and the Mediterranean seas. Restrict your business trips to the fall and winter months.

Ankara *is* Turkey. The Turks are proud of Ankara and justifiably so. Buildings are comparatively new, there are no large bodies of water nearby for bathing and historical sights are limited. But you do want to meet the Turks? Then don't miss Ankara!

Sightseeing

THE CITADEL First constructed in the year 278 B.C. by Alexander the Great; there are also Byzantine and Turkish battlements. Final construction work was completed by Ibrahim Pasha (Egypt) in 1833. The Alaettin Mosque was constructed in 1178 by a Seljuk Sultan. Notice the mimber (pulpit) made of walnut. The Augustus Temple is a Corinthian Temple built to the god Kybele and the Moon God Men by the Galatians. In the 4th century the temple became a church. Note the wall in the entry hall giving praise to Emperor Augustus in Latin and Greek. The Haci Bayram Mosque was built in the early 15th century. It is near the tomb of Haci Bayram Veli. The Aslanhane Mosque is the largest in Ankara; built in 1290. Note the pulpit and altar, the latter in the blue and black tiles of the Seljuk style. The pulpit is made of walnut. An outstanding well-preserved mosque.

THE HITTITE ARCHEOLOGICAL MUSEUM Near the Citadel. It was originally a bazaar and has a famous collection of 35,000 cuneiform tablets; Hittite relics. The Anit-Kabis was constructed between 1944 and 1953 as the tomb of Kemal Ataturk; this mausoleum dominates the western skyline of Ankara. The Roman Baths were constructed by the Emperor Caracalla between 212 and 217 A.D. discovered in 1926. You will see here the various rooms for cold, warm and hot water bathing. The Ethnographical Museum contains ceramics, carpets, handwork, etc. The Ataturk Farm is west of town and was the semi-official residence of Ataturk; a good place to walk or lunch. The farm is roughly ten to fifteen minutes by car from the center of Ankara. Ataturk's Home where Kemal Ataturk resided during the War of Independence. Entry is limited to special times on certain holidays, Sundays, etc. Inquire at your hotel.

There are a number of excursions to locations some distance from Ankara such as to Gordium, capital city of the Phrygians founded in the 7th century B.C., also to "Karagol" or Black Lake, a crater lake near the town of Cubuk. Inquire about all such tours at your hotel.

Hotels

THE GRAND HOTEL ANKARA Constructed approximately seven years ago the Ankara (it is not referred to as the Grand) enjoys an excellent location in Ankara situated as it is on the main avenue leading into the best residential quarter of the city. This hotel was financed by the Government Employees Pension Fund.

All rooms at the Ankara provide an excellent view of the city. I would suggest that you either "face north" or "face west." Higher floors provide the more spectacular panorama. However, stay clear of floors 12 through 14 as they are directly beneath a restaurant where guests dance until the wee hours.

Bedrooms are very comfortably furnished in what could be called "American Executive" styling. Corridors are well lighted, colorful and well arranged. Room facilities include comfortable beds, three-way radios, a desk, large closets, wall-to-wall carpeting, comfortable chairs and indirect lighting. Bathrooms are modern, tiled, well arranged. Telephones in bedroom and bath. I do not recommend the apartments. Though comfortably furnished they conform to the design of the building and are therefore angled. Moreover these rooms are rather cut up. Double rooms are furnished with small twin beds located in the corners of the room (though some "French Doubles" are available). Singles are particularly commodious and therefore recommended. All rooms bath/toilet/bidet.

There is day and night food service (in rooms) at the Ankara. Every Thursday and Sunday the Management offers guests a Smorgasbord by the pool (summer). The restaurant serves average to good food, the service fair. Room service is very good.

The Baskent is the main restaurant; there is a bar at the entrance to this room. On the roof, dining after eight until all hours. There is a great view of the city from this roof restaurant. It is one of the best night spots in Ankara.

KENT My choice of hotels in the capital should you not wish to reserve at the modern, super-deluxe Ankara. Though located a great distance from the Government buildings, the Kent is situated near the Ministry of Health, a section of the Ministry for Tourism, near all major airline offices and in the center of the principal Yenisehir shopping area. There is some street noise but this is no great problem.

You will find the lobby one floor up. A large restaurant and dining terrace are located near the reception. The food is reputed to be very good. There is a cocktail lounge upstairs. On the roof is a small grill room open only in winter. There are two wings to this hotel, one built in '63, the new section in '67; not a great deal of difference between the two. Rooms are comfortably though not elaborately furnished. Accommodations on the rear might be quieter. All rooms have full bath and shower. Prices at the Kent are well below those at the Hotel Ankara. The Kent has a particularly attractive, warm atmosphere the Ankara fails to capture. While fewer facilities, gadgets, public rooms, etc., are available to guests, those guest conveniences at hand are more than satisfactory. You won't go wrong reserving at either the Kent or Ankara. The latter is more splendid, more "grand" as its name implies. The Kent is more homey, and less expensive.

DEDEMAN A comfortable though not extravagantly furnished hotel located roughly two or three blocks off Cankaya Boulevard and quite near Bakanliklar and the Government offices. The Dedeman falls somewhere between a family hotel and a strictly commercial enterprise. Large lobby and bars; souvenir shops and hairdresser. The second floor restaurant appears quite pleasant. I judge the food would be average to good. On the roof is a nightclub with music for dancing. Piano music in the restaurant during evening meal hours. Bedrooms at the Dedeman are fair-sized, furnished in a comfortable fashion though actually the rooms are somewhat nondescript. Apartments are actually large rooms for three persons. All rooms have bath/shower. Rear rooms overlook a small park owned by the hotel. The Dedeman is situated in an area of Ankara which has seen a tremendous surge of building during the past five years. Surrounding the Hotel are many apartments of a notably unattractive design. I feel the Hotel suffers from its location in this rather featureless section of town. The Dedeman is far from exceptional, rather simply "an accommodation away from home." Comfortable, comparatively clean, convenient. Guests should not be troubled by noise as the hotel is situated on a primarily residential area. Rates are somewhat below the Kent Hotel.

BULVAR PALAS Situated directly opposite the majority of Turkish Government offices at Bakanliklar at a point just north of Cankaya Boulevard as that street climbs toward the embassy section. The hotel sits somewhat back from the street though there will be a noise factor here. The Bulvar was for years one of Ankara's best hotels. Food at the Bulvar continues to receive the plaudits of local gastronomes. Bedrooms are all on the small side; rather cut up in appearance. Nothing outstanding. Only a few singles without bath or shower. Rates are approximately the same as at the Kent and Dedeman. All Room Services.

The Bulfar Palas is certainly recommended. Though rooms are smaller, the facilities limited to some extent, this hotel provides its guests with clean, well-managed accommodations.

BARIKAN Recommended in the event the aforementioned hotels are fully booked. Location is poor as are certain of its facilities.

Restaurants

KAZAN Presently one of the best restaurants in Ankara. The Kazan is situated high on the hills of Cankaya. Front window table diners have a splendid view of the city stretching out toward the Black Sea away to the north. Excellent service, good to excellent food. Rustic decor (stone walls, iron ornaments, etc.) though The Kazan is a fairly dressy restaurant. Reserve your table the day before if possible. The Kazan serves dinner until eleven or so. It is also open at noon.

The Kazan is small, tables being located at various levels across the colorfully decorated room. Try to arrange a table near the windows. The restaurant is expensive by local standards.

BEKIR Situated just around the corner from Ataturk Boulevard, centrally located in Ankara's Yenisehir shopping district.

Bekir consists of two or three small rooms (always packed during meal hours, particularly at noon) and a small outdoor patio. Service is good; the food excellent. It is a popular spot with Turkish businessmen, tourists, foreigners. Prices are reasonably low.

WASHINGTON A very informal restaurant recommended for noontime dining only. It is quite near the Bekir restaurant, roughly three blocks to the east of Ataturk Boulevard in Yenisehir. There is no decor here to speak of; service is rather casual. The food is very good. I feel the Washington comes closer to being a real Anatolian-type restaurant than any other acceptable dining place I found in Ankara.

HATTUSHA Want to try out a few Turkish specialties? What about lunch at Hattusa located on Carnation Street (Karafil Sokak) in Yenisehir. This restaurant serving lunch only will be found on a street running behind the Bulvar Palas Hotel and immediately paralleling Ataturk Boulevard to the east.

MERKEZ LOKANTA (CENTRAL RESTAURANT) The Central Restaurant can be found at the Ataturk Free Farm (Orman Ciftligi) approximately three miles, perhaps less, from Ankara. At the "Farm" you will see a house once occupied by Kemal Ataturk, visit a small zoo, perhaps see where yogurt is made and then have an opportunity to enjoy a tasty lunch in the garden of this informal, inexpensive restaurant. The food and service are far from exceptional, but with the sun, dry air, cool breeze and rustling poplars you will, I'm sure, be in the right mood for a cool glass of Ayran, cucumber and tomato salad, a plate of Doner Kebab and for dessert, some grapes or fresh pears. Recommended for lunch only.

Night Clubs

The Grand Hotel Ankara, Hotel Dedeman and Hotel Kent offer night-time dining and dancing during both the summer and winter months. There is also the Kazan restaurant for delightful noon and night dining (no dancing).

BOLU

For those of you interested in historical facts, Bolu was the ancient residence of the Bythniem Kings, later named "Claudiopolis" by the Romans. Here was born Antinoos, known as the Favorite of the Roman Emperor Hadrian. Today, Bolu's greatest claim to fame is the super-excellence of the cooks trained by the masters of this region.

Hotel

HOTEL ABAND When motoring between Istanbul and Ankara, you might like to spend one night at the Aband Hotel just outside the

Anatolian town of Bolu. It is delightfully situated in a splendid stand of pines; the fragrance and "whispering" of the trees is seldom forgotten by guests of this informal little establishment. Rates are low.

BURSA (Brussa)

Situated at the foot of a mountain called the "Mystic Olympus" (or "Ulu Dag") Bursa has for some years been something of a Shangri-La for this writer. The green slopes and rocky crags, the winding roads and fruitladen apricot trees, the baths, minarets and silk bazaars have forever occupied a favored niche within hailing distance of fading recollection. Bursa was constructed six years before Christ on the site of an early settlement. Originally the town was founded by King Prusias II of Bythnia (186 B.C.). It was here the fleeing Hannibal sought refuge. The town later came under Roman authority and was physically transformed when a Roman Governor, Pliny the Younger, was appointed to the region. Plinius built roads, public baths, a library and a bazaar. In the year 950 A.D. it was destroyed by the Arabs. Prior to the 11th and 12th centuries Bursa formed a section of the strategic defenses of the Byzantine Empire. A palace and bath were built at nearby Cikirge by the Emperor Justinian. Bursa became a part of the Seljuk Turk Empire during the 11th century, later being returned to the Byzantines.

Following a nine-year siege, Bursa fell to the Ottoman Turks in the 14th century. We have already spoken of the Battle of Ankara between the Turkish Sultan Beyazit and Timurlane. Following this victory Timurlane had his nephew Nirsa march to Bursa, then the capital of the Ottoman Empire, burning it to the ground (1402). The city was largely rebuilt by the Celebi family (Sultan Mehmet I). Following the fall of Byzantium, the Turks moved their headquarters to Constantinople making it their capital city a few years later. Thus Bursa declined in political importance. Nevertheless the town continued to be the center of architectural art for the Ottoman Empire. Bridges, baths, mosques and mausoleums were constructed during the centuries to follow. The town was badly damaged by an earthquake in 1855. Nonetheless, an innate charm of past centuries has not been lost. The pinks, blues, greens and whites—the colors of Bursa—are not easily erased from the earth, much less the mind.

Sightseeing

ULU-CAMI Built between 1379 and 1421, that is, before the fall of Constantinople in 1453. This mosque was built by Sultans Murad I, Beyazit I and Mehmet I. Note the engraved pulpit made of ebony (no nails were used) and of great value; nearby a golden Koran dating from approximately 770 A.D. Note the roof supports and the unique water fountain. Outstanding examples of the Arabic calligraphy are to be found on the walls. Twenty small cupolas cover the roof.

YESI CAMI (The "Green Mosque") Built between 1413 and 1421 by Mehmet I. This particularly beautiful, four-sided mosque contains a marble fountain in the entry hall. Note the altar and pulpit formed by interlocking pieces of black, gold, white and dark blue tiles. The main door is decorated with a section of the Koran. The facade of the mosque is covered by white and pink tiles.

YESIL TURSE Mehmet I's mausoleum and that of a large part of the famous Celebi family (who by the way continue to live in Turkey today). The Turbe is near the "Green Mosque." The ceramic on the outer walls is a reconstruction from the 19th century.

ORHAN CAMI One of the earliest Ottoman mosques. It was built in 1453. Once destroyed by Karamanoglu, the Mosque was ordered restored by Mehmet I.

YILDIRIM BAYEZIT CAMI A 14th century mosque restored in 1855.

MURADIYE CAMI The mosque of Sultan Murad I from the 14th century; it is the oldest mosque in the town.

There are many other turbes and mosques in Bursa. You should also pay a visit to Kara-Mustafa-Pasa Hamam where the water contains a strong radioactive quality. Perhaps you might wish to visit Ulu-Dag Mountain. The drive passes through some wild country.

Spring and early summer is a particularly lovely time in Bursa before the heat of summer sets in with its accompanying dust, hot nights, etc. Be sure to tour the bazaar, for Bursa silk was once famous throughout the world, in great demand in Western Europe. Between the hotel, the bazaar and turbes and mosques you'll find your time well occupied in Bursa.

Hotels

CELIK PALAS This is the only hotel of any significance within the city limits of Bursa. Situated atop a slight rise at the foot of Mount Ulu-Dag, Bursa's "Steel Palace" hotel commands a delightful view of the surrounding countryside including fruit orchards that have made Bursa famous. The Celik Palas is somewhat outside the main commercial section of the town which is all to the good. A four minute car ride will find you at the gates of the magnificent Yesil Cami or the Ulu Mosque. The Celik Palas is of modern design though not of recent construction. The newer building was something of an innovation during the late thirties hence the rather pompous appellation.

The Celik offers its guests every convenience. Cleanliness is stressed, for the Celik is also a spa for guests wishing to enjoy the nearby mineral baths. (*Note*: Mineral water is piped directly into the hotel. It is not necessary to visit the Hamam located across the small garden to the rear of the hotel. Still, here's a chance for you to investigate a genuine Turkish Bath.)

There are only three singles with bath at the Celik; 109 doubles with bath or shower. Reserve ahead, for the Celik is almost always crowded. Be sure to specify "new building/front" to assure acceptable accommodations as well as a pleasant view. Rates run approximately 70 TL top for a single with bath, 100 TL double (or $14.00). Apartments are available as are telephones, elevator, room service.

The restaurant serves average to good food though nothing outstanding. I suggest ordering grilled meats, vegetables, salads and fruit. Prices are reasonable, the service fair.

BUYUK OBERJ Located high atop Bursa's Mount Ulu-Dag the Büyük Oberj Hotel is a very popular resort facility providing a base for summer hiking, a delightful lodge for winter sports enthusiasts. The hotel can be reached by "le teleferik," or cable car from a central station in Bursa.

The hotel offers no singles and only six doubles with bath so reserve well ahead of time. Three apartments are available as well as twelve rooms with three beds. You will find 58 rooms (doubles and three bedded) without bath or shower. Rates for the doubles (bath) run between 195 TL and 220 TL with full board. The hotel is centrally heated. Facilities at the "Auberge" are not outstanding but comfortable and convenient.

Side Trips from Bursa

Iznik was for a time under the authority of Rome during the 4th century B.C. Later the town was known as a provincial capital under the Byzantine Palaŏlogen Dynasty between 1204-1261, eventually being destroyed in the 3rd century (sacked and burned by Goths and Huns). When rebuilt, Iznik housed the First Ecumenical Council in 325, the Seventh Ecumenical Council in 787. Captured by the Seljuk Turks, then returned to the Byzantines, the town became part of the Ottoman Empire in 1326. This is a fascinating little town with remarkable relics from the Byzantine Period (walls), Roman Period (aqueducts; amphitheater), the Seljuks (small "Bey Bath" only) and Ottomans (mosques and tombs). The town suffered an earthquake in 1065, a fire in 1922 (War for Independence) therefore many of the relics are in ruins. Yet the site of this historically important little town on the Sea of Iznik is truly lovely.

EDIRNE (Adrianople)

Situated in the barren, semi-desolate hill country of Western Thrace, ten minutes' drive from the Bulgarian border (a somewhat lesser distance from Turkey's border with Greece) Adrianaople continues to enjoy the strategic prominence attained during the 2nd century. It should be emphasized that Edirne's history is of such importance, the city's mosques so outstanding, that many tourists make the long, rather tiresome drive out from Istanbul just to absorb the unique environment.

There are no tourist facilities of note in Edirne though a motel may be found close to the customs house on the Turkish side of the Turkish-Bulgarian border.

On the horizon to your left (entering from Bulgaria) you will see the outline of the magnificent Selimiye Mosque, its tall, so very graceful gray minarets seeming to pierce the sky. To your right will intersect Saraclar Caddesi, a narrow street lined with countless small shops and restaurants. Considering the number of invasions, plus the continuous movements of armies and "carpetbaggers" throughout this region, it is a wonder any complete buildings were left standing. Yet a great deal remains to be seen.

Sights

SELIMIYE CAMI (Sultan Selim Mosque) Considered the finest mosque in Turkey. It was constructed between 1569 and 1575, the architect being the famous Sinan who was responsible for many important structures throughout the country. The "Selim Mosque" is considered his masterpiece. It was Sinan himself who said the Sehzade Mosque in Istanbul was his apprentice work, the Suleymaniye Mosque (Istanbul) his occupation and the Selim Mosque his masterpiece. The cupola is 45 meters high with a diameter of 31.2 meters. The four minarets are 81 meters high with three encircling walkways or galleries each. Note the small marble pillars as well as the 16 pillars from the Dionysos Theater in Athens. Note also the altar (the faience work) and the eight porphyry pillars holding up the cupola. The entire building is an architectural wonder.

UC-SEREFELI CAMI (The Three Galleries Mosque) Another architectural marvel constructed by the architect Alaeddin between 1438 and 1448. Note the marble and 18 cupolas over the pillard entryway; also the colored bricks on the highest minaret. Also see the Yildirm Mosque (Lightning Mosque) from the 14th century, the oldest in Edirne; originally a Byzantine Church.

BEDESTEN The Antique Bazaar includes 19 cupolas, 4 entrances and 50 sales-rooms. Many other mosques, baths and bazaars are to be seen here including several bridges constructed during the 15th and

16th centuries. There is also the Rustem Pasa Karavansary (16th century) noted for its two-floor construction. The mosques, bazaars and karavansary (or "hans") mentioned above are all within a two or three block radius of the highway.

Because of the lack of proper room and board accommodations I think you'll want to continue your trip before nightfall. In any event, don't get caught on the Edirne-Istanbul highway after nightfall. There are far too few filling stations, lights and away too many trucks, people, animals and the like along the road.

ISTANBUL

Istanbul, more than just an ancient city, a busy port or gateway to the Middle East seems particularly during the months of April through June a tonic designed to remove all the cares of the world. Near the *Eyüp Mosque* mimosas bloom, the fragrance seeming to fill the city; the pink, red and purple tulips wake in gardens near the old Seraglio. On a clear spring day the seas seem full of dancing light, the boats so white, the wind so clean and fresh. Laundered sheets flap from rooftops across Para, seeming not unlike the sails of Sultan Mehmet's ships as they were pulled by ropes toward Kasimpasa. Sirens shriek and wail, a boat departs the Galata Bridge for Yeniköy or Sariyer filled with sightseers bound for lunch along the Bosphorus. And all the odors of the universe seem to assail your nostrils as you pass through crowds of fish vendors, "kahvecis," shoeshine boys and small children selling violets and lilacs. People not the monuments should be the special object of your involvement with this ancient, incredibly fascinating city. Through them you will better understand the Byzantine-Ottoman heritage which provided the poorest Turkish peasant with a source of strength.

Istanbul was founded some 657 years before Christ as a Megarian colony under the leadership of a man named Byzar of Megara. Situated on the small point now called "Saray Burnu" a small trading colony grew within a few short years. The town was named "Byzanz" after its leader. Due to the town's prominence both as a port and a mid-point on the high road between Europe and Asia, "Byzanz" suffered continuous attacks, sieges and massacres until it was reduced to little more than a trading village. The Roman Emporer Septimius Severus was responsible for the redevelopment of the colony. In 324 A.D. Emperor Constantine transferred "Byzanz" to his Empire calling it New Rome. In May of the year 330 A.D. the name was changed to Constantinople. The city enjoyed extensive development during these early years. Then, after a short period of decline, Constantinople again experienced active civic progress under the reign of Theodosius II under whose reign the name "East Rome" or "New Rome" was changed to Byzantine Empire.

Sightseeing

Because of the extensive suburban area, it is important for a tourist to realize that rather elaborate tour programs must be undertaken if he is to become acquainted with the important historical and geographical features of the entire city.

Istanbul proper lines on the west bank of the Bosphorus, a body of water flowing in a north-south direction from the Black Sea into the Sea of Marmora. The city is situated at the confluence of those two bodies of water; divided by the so-called Golden Horn or Halic, a four-mile long, narrow inlet separating the Old Town (Stamboul) on the south bank of the Golden Horn from the newer sections of town (Pera or Galata) on the north bank. The Horn is bisected by two bridges connecting Pera or Galata with the Old City made up of districts with such exotic names as Suleymaniye, Sultan Ahmet, Bayezit, Sirkeci, Eminonu and Sarayburnu. The latter is the small point of land crowned by the Seraglio, or Palace of the Sultans. Across the Horn in Pera you will find the districts of Beyoglu, Taksim, Harbiye (the Hilton is located here), Macka, Sisli (good residential areas), etc.

Across the Bosphorus, in Asia to speak rather pedantically, you will find the suburbs of Uskadar (or "Scutari"), Kadikoy, Suadiye and Erenkoy, largely summer residential areas, though a great many Turks live there year around. Stretching along both sides of the Bosphorus are numerous small towns which form an integral part of Istanbul. These small residential centers are too numerous to mention here but they include, particularly on the European (or west side) of the Bosphorus some of the most delightful summer resort areas to be seen in this region of the world. These suburban centers are connected with the city by road or water. A great many people working in Istanbul commute by boat between their homes along the Bosphorus and the city. No bridge or tunnel connects the Asian shore of the Bosphorus with communities, including Istanbul, on the west bank.

In the Sea of Marmora directly off the coast of Anatolia are located the four Prince's Islands or Adalari. Fast boats departing from Karaköy near the Galata Bridge connect these islands with Istanbul and the Anatolian shore at Kadikoy. The Prince's Islands are primarily summer resorts. The smallest island as you leave Istanbul is known as Kinalli, the second Burgas, the third (and second largest) being Heybeli-Ada, and the last and largest, Büyükada.

The majority of historic sites in Old Istanbul are located in that region of town south of the Golden Horn. Here are the great mosques, old palaces, the University, Covered Bazaar and the ruins of Byzantium. In Pera (or Galata) north of the Golden Horn lies the commercial center spreading along the hills between the Golden Horn and the Bosphorus. Consulates of foreign delegations, hotels, large residential centers as well as the main shopping districts of the city are situated in this district.

Sightseeing

SAINT SOPHIA Aya Sofia or Hagia Sophia was built on the site of an earlier church; the church was built between 532 and 537 A.D. during the reign of Emperor Justinian. Many outstanding pieces of classical architecture from the pre-Christian Era were incorporated into the structure. The Church became a mosque during the Ottoman Period; many great frescos and pieces of art work were defaced or plastered over by the Ottomans. Minarets and supporting buttresses were added to better capture the "mood" of a mosque. With the formation of the Republic the church became a museum. Restoration work was then undertaken.

SULTAN AHMET MOSQUE The Blue Mosque was built between 1609 and 1617; the six minarets on this mosque proved excessively expensive for the Sultan. His order to the architect to include the six required his paying for the construction of two additional minarets on the Great Mosque at Mecca. It was inconceivable that the most sacred mosque in the Holy Land (with five minarets) should be bettered by the "Blue Mosque" in Istanbul.

SAINT IRENE MUSEUM Near Saint Sophia; built in the same period.

GALATA TOWER The Ancient Tower of Christ was built by the Genoese who lived in Constantinople. It is now a Fire Watch Station.

TOWER OF BEYAZIT Constructed in 1808. It commands a fine view of the city. Located on the grounds of the University of Istanbul.

SULEYMANIYE MOSQUE Built by Sinan during the years 1550-1587; the proportions and structural design are unique; its silhouette dominates the city. It is located in Old Stanbul above and right of the Galata Bridge.

TOPKAPI PALACE Built between 1465 and 1478; additional buildings were added to the Palace through the 19th century when the Sultan constructed a new palace on the Bosphorus. It is considered one of the wealthiest museums in the world; outstanding displays of jewels (the film *Topkapi* was based on a theft from this building) and ceramics. Five to six thousand people lived here. All the intrigues and fascinating stories of the Imperial Ottomans originated on these grounds.

DOLMABACHE PALACE Built in 1854 and designed to awe the civilized world. Sultan Abdul Mecit was the first Turkish Ruler to move from Topkapi.

SULTAN SELIM MOSQUE Built during the reign of Sultan Suleyman. The dome is outstanding, the architecture of the best in Turkey.

FATIH MOSQUE This mosque was constructed between 1453 and 1471 at the order of Sultan Mehmet the Conqueror. Historically the mosque is outstanding.

YENI MOSQUE Outstanding because of the "independent" construction of the various portions of the building. Yeni means "new." It was built in 1663.

FOUNTAIN OF AHMET III Near Saint Sophia; famous for its cupolas and marble reliefs.

BINBIRDIREK "One Thousand One Pillars." It is a cistern constructed as a water supply for old Constantinople.

HIPPODROME Constructed in 203 by Emperor Septimius Severus and completed in 330 by Emperor Constantine. Little remains of this outstanding monument to Byzantium.

WALLS AT YEDIKULE The Seven Towers are a commemorative gate, "Golden Door," and a defensive structure built during the Roman Era; used (in sections) as a treasury and later a prison. Sultans and foreign emissaries were imprisoned and executed here.

BLACHERNAE PALACE This ruin is the former residence of the Emperors of Byzantium (1150-1453); destroyed in 1453 (the attack on Constantinople began in this area of the city).

OBELISK OF THUTMOSIS III Built between 1501 and 1448 B.C. it was brought from Karnak, Egypt, by Emperor Theodosius in 390 and modified to include reliefs of the Emperor and his family.

EYUP MOSQUE Located at the narrow tip end of the Golden Horn; it is the most sacred mosque in Istanbul, built honoring the Standard Bearer (Abu Eyűp Ansari) of the Prophet Mohammed who died here.

COVERED BAZAAR The "Kapali Carsi" is a fascinating collection of shops, fountains, restaurants and what all covered by a roof so that shopping in all sorts of weather is possible. Enter through the Egyptian Bazaar immediately opposite the Yeni Mosque at the south end of the Galata Bridge continuing up hill toward the Bazaar.

MUSEUM OF ARCHEOLOGY Greek, Roman, Phoenician and Byzantine works of art are displayed here.

MUSEUM OF MOSAICS Near the Sultan Ahmet Mosque and has exhibitions of mosaics found in 1935.

TOWER OF LEANDER Located in the center of the Bosphorus at that point where the Straits enter the Sea of Marmora; the name is a misnomer as Leander swam the Dardanelles.

North of Istanbul along the Bosphorus you might visit the famous Rumeli Hisar, a fort constructed by Mehmet the Conqueror at the time Turkish troops first crossed the Straits in an effort to isolate Constantinople. By occupying Rumeli Hisar ("Roman Fort") as well as the installation at Anadolu Hisar ("Anatolian Fort" directly across the Bosphorus), Mehmet could control shipping north of Constantinople for this is the narrowest stretch of the Bosphorus. Inside the Fort is a Janissary Mosque.

Beaches

Now would you, after all these museums, palaces, mosques, bazaars and fortresses, maybe, like to go for a swim? West of Istanbul near Yesil Kőy airport are Bakirkőy, Floriya and Yesil Kőy Village. Hotels, restaurants, changing rooms, all sorts of facilities are available. Beaches are excellent. On the Bosphorus: Altim Kum, or "Gold Beach" (end of the line — the last boat station at the north end of the Bosphorus) and Tarabya, the hotel. On the Anatolian side east of Uskadar, there are numerous resorts, one of the best being Moda, another Suadiye. Naturally the Prince's Islands offer fine facilities for swimming. There is also a fine beach at Kilyos on the Black Sea north of Istanbul.

Hotels

ISTANBUL-HILTON One of the most beautiful hotels in the world, it is set in a small park well isolated from the noise of the busy streets nearby. The Istanbul-Hilton commands a magnificent view of the Bosphorus. The hotel is situated a ten-minute walk from Taksim Square in the heart of one of the best shopping and residential districts of Istanbul. The hotel building itself appears not unlike a huge white ship outlined against the azure Turkish sky. You will find the main lobby of the Hilton a wonder to behold. Those individuals responsible for the design and decoration of this area have done a magnificent job. You will find paneled walls, lime green carpeting, shopping arcades set around a small patio shaded by shrubs and flowers and tiled walls expressing a uniquely Turkish design through the use of wondrous blue and green ceramics from Kutahya. This vivid interior setting provides a magnificent counter-balance to the dramatic panorama of the Bosphorus and distant Anatolia as witnessed from the deep lounge chairs informally grouped along the Hilton terrace. There is bar service on this terrace as well as in the adjacent lobby. Tea concerts are held in the lobby every afternoon at four.

Beyond the three elevators, a wide flight of stairs sweeps down to the ground floor where guests will find the Karagöz Bar and the Sadirvan Night Club. The Sadirvan serves a late dinner, offering a nightly floor show. Again beyond the elevators, are located the hotel post office, barber shop, a carpet store and several fashionable shops in which women's apparel of unique design and good quality may be purchased. At the end of this picturesque corridor, its large windows and sliding doors facing the Bosphorus, you will find a cafe (or Coffee Shop) serving light meals and snacks from early morning to late evening. Drinks are served here as well. Counter service, also tables. On the roof of the Hilton you will find the Marmara Roof Bar and the Roof Rotisserie recommended for dinner. Small bar. Piano music during dinner hours. Reserve ahead as this restaurant is very popular; truly one of the world's most elegant restaurants. The Marmara Roof Bar opens at ten though you can go in somewhat earlier for an after-dinner coffee or brandy. Dancing to good small orchestra. Intimate atmosphere.

Only rooms in the new wing (north wing) are air-conditioned so be specific when reserving, particularly if you are arriving in Istanbul during the mid-summer months. Rooms are all much the same in design, furnishings and decor with the exception of the apartments which include a sitting room. All bathrooms are alike including bath/shower and bidet. All room services. Beds are usually of the convertible type, one located in a corner, the second in the center of the room. Radios; balcony.

Attention those of you who like to sleep late: The Istanbul-Hilton offers guests with Bosphorus-side rooms a magnificent view. However, heat from the early rising eastern sun can turn these front bedrooms into saunas at 5 A.M. during mid-summer months.

Prices at the Hilton range from about 130 to 170 TL for a single room; 170-210 TL double. Apartments cost between 450 TL and 1400 TL. *NOTE:* U.S. credit card holders (American Express; Carte Blanche) may charge the bill to their stateside accounts. The amount paid at home will be the dollar equivalent of the room rate listed in Turkish Liras. Purchases made in shops within the hotel may be placed on the guest's hotel bill.

HOTEL DIVAN Located within a five minute walk of the Hilton, the Divan has striven mightily (and with some success) to maintain the quality of management, food, service, et al. adhered to by its opulent neighbor. This hotel is situated on a particularly noisy, busy corner of Cumhuriyet (Republic) Avenue quite near the office of many major airlines and five minutes' walk from Taksim Square, Istanbul's not unattractive commercial center dominated by a statuary group commemorating an event in the life of Kemal Ataturk. Nearby the hotel is Taksim Park and the Municipal Casino (restaurant-night club).

The Divan offers guests a cafe terrace (very popular with local people) and a restaurant serving tasty, substantial food. Service is fair to good. A souvenir shop is located near the front entrance. There are no apartments. Doubles run about 140 TL a night; singles (with bath/shower) 90 TL. Rooms are on the small side here though respectably furnished and clean.

HOTEL PARK An old standby, an old friend, the Park was the hotel in Istanbul prior to the opening of the Hilton. Quite near Taksim Square, the Park occupies a reasonably impressive location near the enormous German Consulate, front rooms commanding an excellent, very dramatic view of Istanbul's busy harbor and Sea of Marmora. The hotel fronts on a small garden providing guests with limited parking space. Off the rather bleak lobby is a large restaurant offering diners a view of the Sea. Food here is quite good though service is perfunctory. A small, very pleasant, intimate cocktail lounge is located behind the reception desk. Tables on the small balcony again provide a fine view of the harbor, a natural setting for forgetting the blues.

Bedrooms at the Park can be cavernous or monastic in size. But you must book to the front and should reserve well ahead. There are singles as well as doubles here (mostly at the rear of the building) without bathing facilities. Book "Front-Bath" and you'll be satisfied. Don't expect much in the way of furnishings. Singles at the Park will run you between 70 and 120 TL; doubles go from 100 TL to 155 TL. Twenty apartments run between 150 TL and 275 TL. These apartments are usually large bedrooms with extended balconies. All front rooms include private balconies.

HOTEL CINAR The Cinar is located very near Yesil Köy Airport, in fact, nor more than an eight-minute drive from that international "fugplatz." The Cinar is actually a resort hotel, situated as it is directly on the Sea of Marmora. Still, most of you will be in Istanbul during summer months so this could provide better than a perfect answer to your problems for here is a deluxe hotel facility located on the Sea within a 45-minute car ride from central Istanbul. (NOTE: train connections are available from Yesil Kőy to Istanbul's Sirkeci Station.)

All rooms at the Cinar with bath or shower; telephone, parking, all room services. Balconies. Prices range from about 90 TL for a single to 160 TL for doubles. Apartments cost upwards of 300 TL. The restaurant here serves good food; terraces overlooking the Sea.

The Cinar is a comparatively new hotel, centrally heated, open all year round. So should you find yourself scheduled to visit Istanbul, the family primed for a well-earned vacation and the "Sold Out" signal is heard from downtown Istanbul, inquire about the Cinar. You'll be satisfied. Services are not top standard but rooms are comparatively clean, employees doing their best to satisfy. And you can swim, sun, boat and fish to boot.

THE GRAND Once upon a time, in the charming Bosphorus resort town of Therapia there was a delightful old hotel constructed of wood, staffed by eager hometowners and surrounded by bougainvillae, mimosa and roses. In approximately 1954 time ran out for this old hotel when a devastating fire swept through the entire structure. And so, on that unique promontory overlooking Therapia (or Tarabya) Bay guests no longer had an opportunity to look from their rooms directly out on passing freighters, Black Sea passenger ships and warships of the ever-haggling Great Powers. Recently some capable authority has taken it upon itself to rebuild the Grand Tarabya Hotel and once again from a modern, concrete and glass structure foreign guests in Turkey have a great opportunity to enjoy unique surroundings in a particularly comfortable hotel.

The Grand is situated directly at the edge of a small promontory jutting out from the ever-irregular coastline on the west bank of the Bosphorus. Only the highway (and a narrow one at that!) separates the hotel from the black, swift waters of that historic waterway. Tarabya is a very small town, a little port located some 30 minutes from Taksim Square in central Istanbul. Cabfares to Tarabya are moderate; boat and bus transportation is also available.

Rooms at the Grand are clean and comfortable. All room services are offered. There is a restaurant on the premises serving good to excellent food (the view from this restaurant is quite dramatic!) as well as a nightclub offering facilities for dancing and dining. Bar. Capably managed.

Rates at the Grand Tarabya approximately 100 TL for a single, 110 to 140 TL for a double and between 225 and 800 TL for an apartment. Book "southeast" or "east" for a startling view of the Bosphorus plus a bit of Europe and Asia. Try not to reserve on the upper floors for you lose something of the drama of the waterway if you are high in the clouds. Settle for the fourth or fifth floors; this will eliminate some of the not-inconsiderable traffic noise while still permitting you a view of the Bosphorus without too much neck-craning.

NOTE: Though this hotel is centrally heated, the Grand is exposed to the strong and bitterly cold winds blowing down the Bosphorus from Russia's frosty steppes. In winter the Bosphorus is not the best location so I would try to book in the city proper. Secondly swim only at "controlled" locations here at Tarabya for the current is extremely swift.

Restaurants

ABDULLAH'S FARM RESTAURANT It would not be overly fanciful to suggest there are those among us who would fly to Istanbul for an evening meal if assured a table at Abdullah Efendi's. Once the owner of two locations, a restaurant in Beyoglu (near Taksim Square) and at Emirgan on the Bosphorus, Abdullah has now closed the Beyoglu location largely because of the severe traffic problem existing in Istanbul. I would urge that you make a date for lunch or dinner at Abdullah's Farm Restaurant at Emirgan when that opportunity first presents itself. Emirgan is approximately half an hour north of Istanbul, directly on the Bosphorus. This restaurant is situated on the hills somewhat west of the town. Be sure to make reservations. Lunch or dinner. Dress according to the time of day but dress well. Vegetables, grilled meats, fish, salads, in fact all Turkish specialties as well as the international dishes are prepared in superb fashion. Expensive but not out of line.

PANDELLI Located in the former Egyptian Bazaar Restaurant, Pandelli is one of Istanbul's best restaurants. Local specialities are tops.

Go up the flight of stairs to your left as you enter the Egyptian Bazaar. This Bazaar is located across the wide circular street opposite the Yeni Mosque at the south end of the Galata Bridge in Eminönü. Recommended for lunch only. A good place from which to start or pause during those tours of the Old City. Several small rooms. Try to find a table near the windows. Reserve if you wish.

KONYALI This place is well recommended. It is located directly across from Istanbul's Sirkeci Railroad Station. No liquor served. Informal surroundings. Turkish specialities are recommended. Again, a good location for those of you doing the Old Town.

LIMAN LOKANTA The "Docks Restaurant" is part and parcel of the terminal building at which passengers debark from ships; located at the north end of Galata Bridge. The district is called Karaköy. Unkempt surroundings, but the food is good. Moderately priced. From your table you'll be able to watch the loading of ships passengers, the passage of small boats, fishermen and I don't know what all.

CANLI BALIK The "Live Fish" restaurant is located at Sariyer some 45 to 50 minutes north of Istanbul on the Bosphorus. In a rather old-fashioned surrounding, the Canli Balik offers a diverse menu; food and service are not exceptional, rather "fair to good." Recommended for lunch only. Canli Balik is situated on the boat dock at Sariyer; tables overlook the Bosphorus. Fish specialities are naturally suggested. You will find the combination of a hot summer's day, a broiled fish, a cold bottle of wine and some fruit or cheese can really make life one big smile. Reasonable prices. Dress casually.

SUREYYA Sureyya has opened a new establishment at Bebek, fifteen minutes or so up the Bosphorus from Istanbul. The actual situation of the nightclub is rather unfortunate but the interior is lush, the wine dry, the food excellent and the company — well, this is the place to bring along the one with whom you plan to spend many pleasurable hours.

KERAVANSARAY The Keravansaray is situated just beyond the main gate of the Hilton Hotel in an apartment house facing Cumhuriyet Caddesi. Open evenings only. Restaurant and nightclub. The restaurant is not recommended because of the distinctly "touristic" approach fostered by the management. The room is usually packed to the rafters, waiters hard-pressed to fill the sudden demand for drinks as tour groups pour into the club. Turkish folk singers invite audience participation, encouraging men in the audience to join them in the "bump and grind" of dances for the benefit of audience and photographers alike. The crowd usually thins out a bit after the show; then you'll be able to relax somewhat.

LES PARISIYYEN Leave the wife at home! Les Parisiyyen can be found roughly two to three buildings to the left of the Main Gate of the Hilton, again in the Lower Regions of an apartment building off Cumhuriyet Cadessi. Go after dinner, say around ten or ten-thirty. Continuous entertainment.

IZMIR (Smyrna)

The region surrounding Izmir is truly delightful. Make a special effort to allow some days for a visit to fabled Smyrna (now Izmir) situated on the eastern perimeter of the Aegean Sea. In Izmir you will find a remarkable blend of ancient and modern architecture, of Turkish social customs and "international living." Izmir offers you luxuriously comfortable headquarters while you enjoy excursions to such famous towns as Pergamum and Ephesus. The climate of Izmir is predominantly Mediterranean with mild, rainy winters and hot, dry summers.

Izmir is believed to have been founded some 3000 years B.C. at Tepe Kule on the north coast of the gulf of Izmir near the present day town of Bayrakli. Together with Troy, Izmir was considered one of the centers of social and cultural development during the pre-Christian Era. The region was under the domination of the Hittites during the 20th to 12th centuries B.C. During the 9th century a second town was founded by the Aeolians which by 900 B.C. came under the authority of the Greek Ionians. It is understood that Homer lived in Izmir during this period. In 575 B.C. the city was destroyed by Alyattes, King of the Lydians. It was the task of the Romans to restore the city. Alexander the Great commissioned his Commanders Lysimachos and Antigonos to build a new city further to the south at the Pagon Mountain near the present town of Kadifekale. In the 3rd and 2nd centuries B.C. the new town experienced great economic progress, being considered one of the main cities of Ionia. During the 4th century A.D. Izmir became part of the Byzantine Empire. The city and nearby Ephesus suffered something of a decline during this period.

Between the 11th and 13th centuries following continuous attacks by the Arabs Izmir came under the domination of the Seljuk Turks. The city of Izmir was returned to the Byzantines following the First Crusade. Again Izmir was ceded to a new dynasty when captured by the Sultan of Aydin in 1320. This was a small Anatolian Kingdom later to be absorbed by the Ottomans. The Crusaders swept through the region in 1344 giving the city to the command of the Italian military order, the Johanniter (later known as the Knights of Malta). Following the invasion by Timurlane, the city of Izmir accepted Ottoman rule in 1415 some 48 years prior to the fall of Constantinople. The city remained in Ottoman hands until the end of World War I. The early twenties saw a particularly bitter period for the citizens of Izmir as the Greek regime of Premier Venizelos undertook the occupation of their city as part of an over-all effort to occupy other regions of Turkey under provisions of the ill-starred Treaty of Sevres. However, forces of the newly formed Turkish Republic moved west from regions east of the Sakarya River to engage Greek troops. During this engagement (1922) the Old Town of Izmir was burned.

The modern city of Izmir is now the second largest port of Turkey lying at the end of the 18-mile Gulf of Izmir. Izmir has a population of 427,410 people and is the third largest city of the Turkish Republic. The region's best known products are figs, cotton, grapes and tobacco. There are many very attractive and valuable carpets woven throughout this area of Turkey. The town besides offering the tourist a variety of sights (some originating with the Pre-Christian Era) is a resort town of not inconsiderable importance. There are not many cities in the world that can offer you antiquity, a uniquely Turkish environment and the Aegean Sea all within ten minutes' drive from your hotel.

Sightseeing

FORTRESS   Dates from the era of Alexander the Great. An excellent view of Izmir from this prominence.

AGORA   The first Agora built by the Hellenes was destroyed; this second Agora was constructed during the reign of Marcus Aurelius. Note the imposing basilica supported by great pillars; statues of Poseidon (God of the Sea) and Goddess Demeter.

AQUEDUCT AT KIZILCULLU   Particularly outstanding (over the River Kemer); also the one on the road to Selcuk.

KIZLARAGASI AND CAKALOGLU CARAVANSARAYS   Built during the 18th century; they are interesting examples of Ottoman architecture.

GRAVE OF TANTALUS   Ruler of Izmir in the 7th century B.C. near Acropolis.

KONAK SQUARE   Note the beauty of the entire area. Colorful tile buildings; marble work.

ACROPOLIS   Built in the first half of the 1st century B.C.

ARCHEOLOGICAL MUSEUM Most interesting with findings from Old Smyrna, Ephesus, Sardes, Pergamum plus other ancient Greek communities.

CULTURE PARK The site of the yearly Business Fair for the Near East.

HISAR CAMI AND SADIRVAN CAMI Most interesting mosques built in 1597 and 1636.

Side Trips

EPHESUS 77 kilometers south of Izmir near Selcuk is one of the foremost cities of the Greek (Ionian) Empire. Founded some 1400 years before Christ; located at the delta of the Kucuk Menderes River (the ancient "Kaystros") as the River enters the Aegean. It was ruled by King Androcles in the 2nd century B.C.; later occupied by Romans who drained swampy areas to make the town more habitable. Saint John was reputed to have preached in Ephesus between 55 to 58 A.D.; in 97 A.D. the Saint was said to have lived here writing his Gospels. Many interesting sites including Greek, Roman and Seljuk ruins remarkably well preserved.

PERGAMUM One of the three great cities of the East Roman Empire; independent Kingdom of Pergamum founded from part of the Roman Empire in 283 B.C.; later the capital of East Roman province. It was burned by Arabs in the 7th century A.D. and reconstructed by Seljuk and Ottoman Turks after the 15th century. See Aesculapium built in honor of God of Medicine (an ancient medical center) famous throughout written history; Ethnographical Museum; Acropolis; Roman Theater; Amphitheater (built 3rd century A.D.); Agora; Palaces; Gates, Temples.

NOTE: It is essential that you either employ a guide for your trips to Ephesus and Pergamum or study material relating to the towns prior to your visit. The region is beautiful, the historical detail incredible.

Hotels

BUYUK EFES The Grand Hotel Efes is truly a splendid structure designed and furnished to provide you with the near ultimate in accommodations while visiting the beautiful and historic town of Izmir. Situated within a minute's walk from the sea, the Efes is a modern structure whose facilities include nine and five-storied units housing hotel guests. The larger building overlooks the Aegean Sea (front), the swimming pool (rear rooms). The small building overlooks the pool (front rooms). Nearby are cafe and bars, one bar constructed so as to provide an underwater view of bathers in the pool. The Efes is located directly off the "Kordon" (Boulevard along the Sea) in the center of Izmir. A golf course is associated with the Hotel properties. Telephone; elevators; central heating.

Bedrooms at the Efes are well furnished in a simple, functional pattern befitting the semi-tropical climate in this region. All Room Services; very complete guest accommodations. Prices at the Efes run between $7 and $10 a day without meals.

NOTE: Izmir at fair time is crowded with tourists, businessmen, government personnel, etc. Unless you enjoy a carnival atmosphere I would keep away from Izmir during the thirty day period August 20-September 20. To be sure, the town is spruced up to greet visitors at this time but desk clerks are harried, waiters rushed, food not as well cooked, etc. For those of you who take pleasure in relaxed, tropical surroundings, an unhurried walk through the town or among those magnificent historical treasures, why not visit Izmir between mid-April and July?

The Drive from Istanbul to Izmir

So you want to see some of the countryside, tour a few antiquities, get to know the Turks? There is no better way than to drive from Istanbul to Ankara or Istanbul to Izmir. The first trip is less interesting than instructive — you may see little of historical note but you are sure to become better acquainted with the Turks. Driving from Istanbul to Izmir will take you through some extremely interesting countryside, past sites of great historic importance.

Do not drive via Bursa and Balikesir, however. The road has not been completed. Leaving Istanbul, drive instead toward Tekirdag (west of Istanbul), then on to Kesan and Gelibolu. Car ferry service is provided across the Dardanelles Straits. You can then proceed south toward Izmir via Canakkale and Bergama. This drive is not easy by any means. Roads are not the best but you certainly will get an eyeful both of history and contemporary Turkish village life. Figure a minimum of two days for this trip. Be certain you have a competent driver.

IN CONCLUSION

If you want really to enjoy your stay in Turkey while experiencing a total involvement with this nation of extroverted, unpredictable, sly, amusing, frustrating and so very proud people, you had best bring along your walking shoes, casual clothes, practical slacks and wade into the tide of humanity that is Turkey. Sure, you'll be driven wild by the shoe-shine boys ("Shine, musu, shine?"), the street urchins ("Money, musu, little para?"), the temperamental cabbies, the over-eager salesmen and Lord knows what. But one wonders why the journey, if you want to avoid those less attractive features which are, in fact, part of a whole that comprises today's Turkey!

On every visit to Turkey I attempt to leave behind in my air-conditioned, comfortable hotel room, that person in me who dislikes crowds, dust, noise, and other less formal environmental circumstances which characterize my daily existence at home. I walk from my hotel onto the street not unlike an Olympic swimmer taking a first dive, concerned with achievement yet living life to the limit while realizing total enjoyment from the environment with which I have elected to surround myself. Try it! Run to catch a bus; jump for the ferry as she leaves the dock; buy flowers at a streetside stand; dodge that dolmus; bargain in the bazaar; drink coffee sold by the "kahveci" (coffee-seller) aboard a boat to the Prince's Islands; eat roasted chestnuts at Kucŭk Su some September afternoon; drink too many beers on the beach at Suadiye; laugh, talk, yell, argue, live—live—live! You know, it's wonderful if you can lose a few of those inhibitions, and Turkey is just the country to make that trial run. Try to leave just a portion of that formality behind, won't you? Life will, I know, seem a lot sweeter.

Yugoslavia

Yugoslavia can be one of the most delightfully interesting vacation spots you have ever experienced.

The American visitor to Yugoslavia should realize that he is about to embark on a trip to the reliquary of Europe's greatest historical treasures, to the melting pot of Illyrian, Roman and Slavic cultures. Yugoslavia was the unpolished jewel over which the Roman Catholic and Orthodox faiths fought for centuries, the terrain for which great empires expended centuries of blood and treasure. Here the Greeks built their trading colonies; the early Romans their forts and military roads to the East. For 500 years, as the Ottomans sought to achieve military and political supremacy over Europe, they chose the Balkans as their source of manpower and raw materials.

Today's Yugoslavia is witness to the centuries-old dream of all South Slavs — that of being united under a government founded by and composed of people of Slavic origin.

Yugoslavia combines history and scenic beauty; sports, rhythmic dance and melodic song.

The weather in Yugoslavia is warm throughout the summer months, even into mid-October. The Adriatic Sea is cool blue, and the streams and lakes stocked with fish.

Prices are consistently reasonable; the highways in fair to good condition; hotels, private rooms, camps and motels well-maintained and competently managed.

Here are some highlights of the country:

Sarajevo, the town where, in 1914, a boy named Princip shot the Austrian Archduke Franz Ferdinand, is of particular interest because almost 90% of its population is Moslem and its shops and restaurants provide a unique insight into a section of Europe almost more Eastern in flavor than Instanbul itself.

Skopje, the capital of the Roman province of Dardanien three centuries before Christ, a town in Macedonia, was leveled by an earthquake in 1963.

Dubrovnik, located on Yugoslavia's south Adriatic Coast, was founded in the 7th century and is a monument to the architecture, social and religious customs of the Middle Ages.

Petrovaradin has a 16th-century fortress built high on bluffs overlooking the Danube.

Opatiya at Croatia's delightful year round resort, you'll find the most elegant hotel in Europe—the Ambassador, located directly on the Adriatic Sea.

Yugoslavian wines are excellent. Fishing is the order of the day, and comes in several varieties—lake, river and deep-sea angling. Folk dances and singing are exciting occasions, especially when you can participate in the fun.

Yugoslavia's highways are for the most part in good condition.

Geographically Yugoslavia can best be compared to California. It has mountains, seacoasts, forests and arid plains.

All types of sports are available. Restaurants and hotels cover all price categories. One can eat in elegant surroundings or cook over an open fire; sleep in a deluxe category hotel, or camp beside a river or the sea. Trains, planes and highways serve almost every important tourist location. The weather during summer is almost always ideal. And prices are low!

HISTORICAL BACKGROUND

The existence of Slovaks, Slovenes, Serbs and Czechs in separate regions beyond political demarcation lines may occasionally be confusing to the traveler. The Yugoslava, or "South Slavs," originally journeyed to the South Balkan Peninsula from regions surrounding the lower Danube Basin, Poland and Russia. All Slavs have essentially the same ethnic background. Religious, regional and political differences serve as guideposts to the essential divisions within the Slavic races.

In the mid-14th century all of Macedonia, Albania, Thessaly and Epirus were under Serbian control. There followed the "Time of the Turks" who captured Constantinople (İstanbul) in 1453. Macedonia, with a heterogenous population due to its location between Greece, Serbia and Bulgaria, met the same fate as Serbia, and was occupied by the Turks until 1912.

Montenegro, (Black Mountain) is essentially a mountainous, non-agricultural, woodcraft, semi-industrial republic. At the time of Serbia's defeat by the Turks, the Montenegrins retired to the central sections of their rugged kingdom and were never actually subdued by the Moslems. Bosnia-Hercegovina was placed under Turkish authority and the Bosnians converted to the Moslem religion in great numbers. The mark of those four centuries of Turkish rule can easily be witnessed when visiting in Banja Luka or Sarajevo.

South Slav tribes were converted to Christianity as early as the 8th and 9th centuries. Due to the schism in the Catholic Church occurring in 1054, the northern South Slavs remained within the Roman Catholic Church whereas the Slavs in the southern regions, Serbia and Macedonia, followed the Orthodox Church. Today approximately 35% of the Yugoslavian population remains Orthodox while upwards of 13% is Roman Catholic. The remainder consists of Moslems, Protestants, followers of a few other faiths, and non-believers.

Following the Russo-Turkish War of 1877, Serbia became a kingdom. During the 18th and 19th centuries, South Slav political activities were suppressed not only by the Turks, but also by the Austro-Hungarian Empire. Slovenia was a specific section of Austria proper and Austrian influence continues to be seen and felt throughout this republic. Croatia, the largest of the Yugoslavian republics, was also a sector of the Austrian Empire. Following World War I, the kingdom of the Serbs, Croats and Slovenes was formed; in 1929 the area took the name of Yugoslavia. Originally a member of the Little Entente (England, France), Yugoslavia in 1939 showed favor to the Axis powers. In March, 1941, the pro-German regency of Prince Paul was overthrown and the reign of King Peter II was declared. Germany, Italy, Hungary and Bulgaria immediately overran the country and partitioned Yugoslavia. Croatia declared itself independent and collaborated with Germany. Between 1941 and 1945 1,700,000 Yugoslavs lost their lives, many in guerrilla wars against the occupation troops. Fighting also continued against the homegrown Croatian Uptasi (a local fascist movement) as well as between Serbian Tito. Allied support went to the latter faction in the late years of the war. Following the war, Yugoslavia received the semi-peninsular land area of Istria from Italy. The question of Trieste was settled by plebiscite.

The monarchy was dismantled after World War II, and a Federal People's Republic established. In 1948 Yugoslavia was expelled from the Cominform, a regional economic union dominated by the Soviet Union. Since this time economic and social contacts with Western Europe and the United States have been developed.

LANGUAGE

The official language of Yugoslavia, Serbo-Croatian, is spoken in Bosnia-Hercegovina, Montenegro, Croatia and Serbia. In Slovenia one speaks Slovenian; in Macedonia, Macedonian; all three languages are closely related. To the south, primarily where the Orthodox religion is predominant, Cyrillic characters are used; to the north, Latin letters are employed. The Slovenian language is written with Latin characters; the Macedonian with Cyrillic. The essential difference in the spoken language lies in the manner of pronunciation. A long *e* may be heard in one region and a short, flat *e* in another area.

In regions where the Cyrillic characters are chiefly used road signs and street names are usually spelled out in both Latin and Cyrillic characters. The following list of expressions are employed throughout Yugoslavia unless a specific region is indicated.

Please	Molim *(to the south)*
Please	Prosim *(in Slovenia, largely)*
Excuse me	Oprostite
Thank you	Hvala (sounds like the French voila)
Thank you very much	Hvala lepa!
Good morning	Dobro-justro
Good day	Dobar dan
Good evening	Dobro vece ("veche")
Good night	Laku noc
Goodbye	Dovidjenja *(the second j sounds like a y)*

Hello	Zdravo
Waiter	Konobar
What is your name?	Kayo se zovete?
Menu	Menu
Bill	Racun (the c stands for a ch sound)
Gas station	Benzinska stanica
How much?	Koliko?
My name is David	Moje ime je ili zovem se David (or more simply Zovem se David)

Yugoslavs in the northern republics speak German quite frequently when addressing foreigners; in the Belgrade region French is frequently heard. In the principal hotels, airports and large restaurants English is also spoken. In the provinces you'll need to rely on sign language. The Yugoslavs are very hospitable folk and will be ready to help you with your language problems.

GEOGRAPHY AND CLIMATE

Yugoslavia is a land of varied topography and so a journey by car through the various regions will prove delightful. Yugoslavia is about as large as Oregon (98,766 square miles) and has a 1,238 mile coastline. The Julian Alps in Western Slovenia are the country's highest mountains; some peaks reach 9,000 feet at Triglav. The region east of the Albanian border is comparatively rugged and extremely scenic.

Yugoslavia borders on Austria, Hungary, Romania, Bulgaria, Greece and Albania.

The Yugoslavian State is comprised of six federal republics: Slovenia, Croatia (the largest), Bosnia-Hercegovina, Serbia, Montenegro (the smallest) and Macedonia. Belgrade is the capital of Serbia as well as the seat of the national government; Ljubljana is the capital of Slovenia, Zagreb the capital of Croatia, Sarajevo of Bosnia-Hercegovina, Titograd of Montenegro and Skopje of Macedonia. The region directly paralleling the coast is somewhat arid though between Split and Dubrovnik there are many forests of pine and cypress. Farther northeast are birch forests, while in the southwest-central sections are deep forests where may be found great numbers of wild animals. Fish abound in rivers and lakes as well as in the Adriatic Sea. Pheasant, partridge and wild duck are also plentiful.

The chief agricultural area of Yugoslavia lies in the east-north-east, from eastern Slovenia to the Pannonian Plain on the Romanian border. The principal rivers in Yugoslavia are the Danube, Sava, Tisa, Drink and Drava; the first three are navigable. Summers are usually warm and dry; winters are damp and rainy along the Adriatic coast, while inland it is cold with snow.

CURRENCY

The chief Yugoslav monetary unit is the dinar, which consists of 100 para. At this writing $1 equals 12 dinars and 40 para. There exists no special tourist rate. Whenever you change money in Yugoslavia, whether at banks, your hotel or some travel agency, you will receive the same amount for your dollar. Coins come in the following denominations: 5, 10, 20, 50 para and 1 dinar. Bills are not quite so simple a matter. There are at present two sets of currency in circulation since devaluation some five years ago. The old currency runs in higher denominations: 500, 1000 and 10,000 dinar notes. Knock two zeros off in order to determine the present-day value. A 500 old dinar note is equal to a five new dinar note (45c); a 1000 old dinar note equals 10 new dinars (approximately 85c). Both old and new 5, 10 and 100 dinar notes are in circulation. I suggest that you separate the new bills from the old, thereby lessening the risk of handing out 100 new dinars to cover a 100 old dinar account. As a rule Yugoslav trades people add up charges in the old currency. A taxi driver will tell you the trip to Belegrade's airport will run you six to seven thousand (old) dinars. Restaurants often list prices in both the old and new currencies; the new dinar prices are usually in the right-hand column. Waiters in Yugoslavia are quite proper in adding up checks, and I didn't come across anyone trying to take advantage of the somewhat confusing situation.

Any amount of foreign monies may be imported into Yugoslavia, but only 100 new Yugoslav dinars may be imported (in 10 new dinar notes); only 50 new dinars (per person) may be exported. Retain your exchange slips, they'll be required of you, to reconvert Yugoslav currency into dollars.

VISAS AND CUSTOMS

Since the International Tourist Year (1967) the Yugoslav Government has not required visas of most foreigners entering the country. However, this provision is extended on a year to year basis, so check with your travel agent or the Yugoslav State Tourist Office, 509 Madison Avenue, New York, N.Y. 10022 for up-to-the-minute rulings on this question.

Visitors arriving by car may enter Yugoslavia without payment of any road tax. They are required to have an International Driver's License (available through AAA) and the "Green Card" insurance (including third-person coverage) issued through local automobile clubs.

Customs formalities at Yugoslav borders have been reduced to a brief formality. As regards imports, the primary rule to follow is—take along only what you believe reasonable for your personal comfort. Two still cameras, several rolls of film plus two movie cameras and film are acceptable; also a typewriter, radio, TV, camping outfit, a boat without motor, one shotgun with 50 shots, and a fishing pole. Declare these items orally to the inspector. Larger quantities of these objects will necessitate a written declaration; and naturally, on your departure you will be expected to give an adequate explanation if any of the listed items are no longer with you. Dogs, cats, etc., may not be imported without a certificate showing that the animal has been vaccinated within the previous six months.

Items may not be exported from the country in quantities that would suggest commercial transactions. Items of archeological, ethnological, historical or cultural value may be exported only with a special permit, but contemporary paintings by local artists may be exported without permits. One must be able to prove, if challenged, that goods were paid for by exchanging dollars for dinars or be able to show a slip from the discount store where the items were purchased.

PLANNING YOUR TRIP

A trip to Yugoslavia requires little advance preparation other than a valid passport and a steamship or air ticket. (Be certain you have a valid smallpox vaccination card for your re-entry into the United States.) Prepaid hotel reservations are not required, and the Yugoslav authorities require no minimum per diem. However, unless you are willing to hazard a few nights without hotel space, develop something of an itinerary with your travel agent and then reserve rooms at each place you plan to visit. Some form of travel schedule and advance reservations are particularly necessary for the resorts in the summer months when Yugoslavia overflows with foreign tourists. Tourists are permitted to travel freely in Yugoslavia.

NATIONAL TOURIST ORGANIZATIONS

In all the other countries discussed in this book the travel firms are all controlled directly by the national government. Romania has its CARPATI, Hungary as IBUSZ, in Czechoslovakia it is CEDOC. Yugoslavia has a different approach to foreign tourist travel—semi-independent travel associations responsible for tourism within the various specific regions. These associations receive only a minimal amount of direction from Belgrade. The Yugoslav State Travel Organization, PUTNIK, collaborates directly with these individual regional firms.

When you visit a specific locality a travel firm organized for that particular region will be responsible for your stay; guides, tours outside the city, cruises, car-rentals, theater tickets, etc., can all be arranged through this one organization. Hotel reservations are arranged between Belgrade and the hotel association of the town in which you plan to visit. The following list gives the most prominent travel agencies in the various important cities:

Tourist Agency	City
Atlas	Dubrovnik
Dalmacijaturist	Split
Generalturist	Zagreb

Kompas Ljubljana
Kvarner-Express Opatiya
Montenegroturist Titograd
Putnik Belgrade

Each agency maintains an office in other principal cities to handle customer referrals.

Plane reservations may be arranged by contacting directly the JAT offices located in every major town and resort area.

Hotels in Yugoslavia have an arrangement similar to the travel offices and also fall between private enterprise and the stricter forms of socialist reform. (In fact, these associations appear to me to be closer to a pure form of communism than what may be seen in other sections of the world.) Hotels within one specific town or resort are usually members of an association owned, in the main, by the workers themselves. All the personnel have a say in the development and operation of the hotels in their association. It is seldom that every hotel in one town will belong to one association; on the contrary, in large resort towns there may be one, two or three associations, each maintaining hotels in all price categories. It is for the associations themselves to make decisions regarding enlargement, modification, installation of air conditioning or the financing of a loan. Hotel associations are grouped together under the wing of Belgrade's Jugohoteli, an organization which reviews local planning and passes along opinions. Restaurants are also organized into similar associations; in fact, such employee groups presently dominate all sections of the Yugoslav economy.

TRAVELING TO AND IN YUGOSLAVIA

By Plane

Yugoslavia is easily accessible by air from all the capitals of Europe as well as from New York via Pan American World Airways. Modern airports in Yugoslavia to which you fly directly from Europe are located in Zagreb, Ljubljana, Dubrovnik, Titograd, Belgrade and Split.

In addition to JAT (Yugoslav Air Transport), the majority of Europe's prominent airlines maintain services to Yugoslavia on regular scheduled flights.

JAT is the sole representative of foreign airlines in Yugoslavia. Do not attempt to book out of Yugoslavia through the ticket offices of a foreign airline. The offices of other international airlines are maintained in Yugoslavia simply for informational purposes and aircraft maintenance. Reservations can be made for you aboard flights of foreign carriers, but all bookings and payments are handled through JAT.

Purchase continuing or return-trip tickets prior to embarking on the journey. This advance planning eliminates a number of potential problems once you have arrived at your intermediate destination; funds need not be exchanged to purchase tickets, your ticket is in hand and you need only secure reservations. The more programming that can be completed in advance, the easier matters become once one is enroute.

The capitals of each Yugoslav republic are connected with each other by air via Belgrade and also maintain flights to such well-known seaside resorts as Dubrovnik and Pula and such mountain resorts as Ivangrad. A flight from Ivangrad to Belgrade costs 100 ND or approximately $8.

Excursion flights on such well-known international carriers as Swissair, Lufthansa, SAS, AUA can be arranged from almost any point in Western Europe to Yugoslavia's resort areas.

By Rail

Yugoslavia is connected by rail with the major European cities. The following is a partial list of international trains carrying sleeping cars which serve Belgrade; Simplon Express (from Paris); Orient Express (Paris); Yugoslavia Express (Munich); Tauern Express (Ostend to Zagreb); Balkan Express (Vienna to Rijeka or Zagreb); Polonia Express (Warsaw via Bratislava and Budapest); Pannonia (East Berlin via Prague and Budapest); Acropolis Express (Munich via Belgrade to Athens). From mid-summer to mid-September, international trains such as the Dalmatian Express, Adria Express, Jadran and Opatiya Express connect Ostend, Munich, Vienna and Stuttgart directly with Yugoslavia's Adriatic coast resort areas. All the above-mentioned trains carry, in addition to sleeping cars, reclining chair cars and dining cars. Children under the age of four not occupying a seat travel free of charge. Children from four to ten, occupying a seat, travel for half fare. Tickets are available at Cook Wagon-Lits or through any travel agency.

By Boat

The entire coastline of Yugoslavia, from Rijeka to Dubrovnik, is connected by steamers making daily voyages between coastal towns and resorts. The trip from Rijeka to Dubrovnik takes 24 hours; accommodations are rather cramped and the food only average.

Greece, Turkey, Lebanon and Italy maintain shipping routes connecting Yugoslavian ports. The liner "Dalmacija" leaves Venice every other Monday for a two-week cruise through the Adriatic, Aegean and Mediterranean. During summer the liner "Jadran" makes seven-day trips from Venice, traveling as far east as Pireaus. The ship "Jedinstvo" makes a similar run with fewer stops in Yugoslavia but more port calls among the other Greek islands. A Yugoslav cargo ship carrying 50 passengers makes a New York to Rijeka trip regularly.

Italian and Yugoslav ferry boats operate between the Yugoslav port of Bar (in Montenegro) and the Italian city of Bari, and Zadar (in Croatia) and Ancona.

During the summer months several of the large islands off the Yugoslav coast are connected to the mainland by car ferry and passenger ships. I understand there are also trips aboard hydrofoils out of Split to islands in the vicinity of that Adriatic port. Another nice trip by hydrofoil is from Belgrade to Kladovo; this is a form of cruise down the Danube to that point where the river leaves Yugoslavia through the Iron Gate Gorge to enter Romania, and thence on to Bulgaria some 30 miles farther south. It is an all-day trip; one departs Belgrade around 7:30 A.M. and returns roughly 12 hours later. Well worth it if you have the time.

One point I should like to emphasize while on the subject of cruises. Unless you have a surfeit of time—are in Yugoslavia for many weeks and have five or six days or more set aside for one seaside resort alone, don't let some local Yugoslav travel official book you aboard a "Sunny Day's Cruise to Korucula," or some such island hideaway. These cruises cut deeply into the visitor's time and often the object of the trip is not worth the extensive voyage.

By Bus

Yugoslav bus lines maintain regular schedules to points throughout the country. Bus travel is on the increase, most likely because the buses are well operated and fairly comfortable. I cannot recommend bus travel between provincial towns, but the capitals of the six republics are connected by good and reasonable bus service. Passengers entering Yugoslavia from Villach, Klagenfurt, Vienna and Graz (Austria), Venice or Trieste will find regular seasonal service.

MOTORING

Diesel oil and two grades of gasoline are available in Yugoslavia. Premium quality (86 octane) retails for about 1.60 ND (new dinars) per liter. Superior grade (98 octane) costs 1.80 ND per liter. I recommend superior made for all American cars as well as for newer makes of European cars. Diesel oil runs about 1.10 ND per liter.

Gasoline coupons available in Western Europe at banks and tourist associations will save you the bother of exchanging money for fuel within Yugoslavia. When leaving the gas station be sure to tip the attendant; one dinar will do the trick. If paying with coupons, ask for gas to an amount one dinar less than what you intend to pay; the extra dinar can be applied as a tip. Good quality foreign motor oils are available in larger towns; they cost between 10 and 13 ND per liter.

Repair services are available throughout the country, but do not rely on the efficacy of these outfits when driving a new car or some make infrequently seen in Yugoslavia. For a trip through the country I suggest you rent a Volkswagen, Fiat, Ford "Tanunus," Opel, or a British make, such as Morris, Austin or Hillman. These cars are more easily repaired. The number of repair service units in each town is listed on the reverse side of the Yugoslav "Tourist Auto Map."

Highway service cars, usually yellow Volkswagens, will be seen throughout the country. The drivers of these cars are there to assist in elementary roadside repairs, to give information on road conditions, and to lend a hand in removing obstacles in the road. These men can also give first-aid treatments. Don't hesitate to call on them.

Firms specializing in car rentals and tourist agencies authorized to provide rental cars for their guests may be found in every major city and tourist area in Yugoslavia. Two major firms are authorized representatives of American firms—Autotehna (Hertz) and Kombas (Avis). Cars may be rented from Hertz or Avis in any major European city and later left with the representative of the firm within Yugoslavia. Similarly cars may also be driven from Yugoslavia to a West European city.

Two other local companies handling car rentals are Putnik and Inex. These firms maintain depots in many Yugoslav cities and resort areas. Rates are reasonable. Chauffeur-driven cars are also available, as are guides.

The Adriatic Coast

Yugoslavia is composed of six republics and two autonomous provinces associated with the Republic of Serbia. Only two republics have provinces bordering on the Adriatic Sea—Croatia and Montenegro. Thus it is with these two republics we must concern ourselves when seeking out a low-priced summer's vacation by those blue Adriatic waters in regions of magnificent geographical contrasts and incomparable natural beauty.

Although the bulk of Croatia lies many miles from the coast, two of its provinces, Istria and Dalmatia, lie directly on the sea. On the sunlit sandy beaches, within the rocky coves and in the azure or turquoise waters of the Istrian and Dalmatian coastline you will enjoy one of the finest vacations of your life. To the south and immediately joining the Dalmatian region lies the coastline of Montenegro. Though less extensive than the maritime region of Croatia, Montenegro possesses some 200 miles of coastline stretching from Kotor south to Ulcinj. This region of stark though magnificent physical contrasts boasts a number of excellent vacation areas, many already adapted to resort life.

The charms of the Adriatic coastline are great indeed: deep-sea fishing, swimming, camping, climbing, good restaurants and fine hotels. But if time permits, you must visit the interior of Yugoslavia, that extremely interesting, fascinating world of canyons and mountain peaks, grilled meats and heavy wines, gypsy melodies and dancing bears and tranquil monasteries. You should not miss a visit by car to Mostar half an hour from the coast, to the Plitvice Lakes and national forest, two hours from the coast, or the magnificent drive through the mountains from Titograd to Ivangrad.

Dalmatia extends from the Gulf of Kvarna to the Gulf of Koto, 233 miles along the Adriatic Sea, and 45 miles inland from the sea through the Dinaric Alps. The capital of the province is Split or Spalato. Some 725 islands are included in the Dalmatian region; among the more noted are Krk, Rab, Korcula, Mljet and Pag. The Dalmatian coast is bisected by two principal rivers, the Krka, entering the Adriatic between Split and Zadar in the north, and the Neretva, flowing toward the sea through mountain passes from Bosnia-Hercegovina. Dalmatia's primary agricultural output consists of olives, vegetables and wines; one-third of Yugoslavia's better wines originate in this region. There are great limestone deposits as well as bauxite in the area of Sibinek. The strip of land bordering the coast is quite barren; cliffs rise directly from the sea. Away from the immediate coastal area are many fertile valleys. An excellent road parallels the entire coastline.

The Illyrians were a tribe of people judged to have settled in Dalmatia in the pre-Christian era. Essentially Indo-European, their presence was encouraged by the Greeks during the 4th century B.C. as a protection against warring bands from northern Europe. They were eventually subdued and then absorbed by the early Romans. In 155 B.C. Dalmatia became a Roman province with its capital at Delminium. The Roman Emperor Diocletian was a native of Dalmatia and when in 3 A.D. he retired to his homeland, a great palace was built for him at Split (Salona). Large sections of this palace and the Emperor's tomb form an integral part of modern-day Split.

Following the Emperor's death, Roman generals warred over the region for decades, and there followed invasions by Goths, Huns, Avars and Slavs. As Byzantine influences waxed and waned there developed in the period of approximately 1000 A.D. a notable trend toward Slav leadership. As Venetian influences began to increase, the Slavs and Venetians were continuously at war. Rome sent Franciscan and Dominican monks into the region and these religious orders eventually extended a significantly beneficial influence over the entire region by means of their teachings, beliefs and social and economic modes of living.

Between 1420 and 1797 Dalmatia was under the influence of Venice. It was the period of the "uskoki," a guerrilla band formed by the Slav knight Peter Krusic to fight the foreign armies. In the Treaty of Campio Formio (1797) Dalmatia was ceded by the Venetians to Austria. In 1805 the Treaty of Pressburg saw Dalmatia come under Napoleonic authority and Dalmatia's change of government this time did much to encourage the idea of Slav unity. Yet once again, in 1815, following Napoleon's defeat, Dalmatia was placed under Austrian authority as a Crown Land of the Hapsburgs.

Following World War I all of Dalmatia was joined with Croatia, with the exception of four coastal islands and the area surrounding the town of Zadar. During World War II the entire region of Dalmatia was joined to Yugoslavia, and a plebescite later directed that Trieste and that city's environs be returned to Italy.

While Dalmatia is presently little more than a remarkably picturesque province of Croatia, its importance from the historical point of view is tremendous. When you visit Dalmatia, see its coastline, hear the tales of historical intrigue, view primitive mountain fortifications; you will comprehend why for centuries this land has been coveted by the greatest powers of the world.

Istria, a component part of Croatia, is a small but rather wide peninsula from the Croatian Coast north of Rijeka (Fiume) and south of Trieste into the Adriatic Sea. Principal crops are rye, wheat and oats; beechwood, oak and oils are other main products. Figs and melons are also grown in large quantities.

The name Istria evidently stems from the old belief that an area of the Danube reached out from Hungary to empty into the Adriatic. (The Greek name for the Danube River is Istra.) Istria was also known as the port from which the "Illyrian" pirates preyed on North Adriatic shipping.

Montenegro possesses a coastline of approximately 200 miles, stretching from Ulcinj in the south to a point some 20 miles south of Dubrovnik in the north. One should not overlook Montenegro as a fine vacation area. The proximity of this coastal region to the splendid mountain regions, little over an hour's drive to the northeast, should be given consideration. For those who enjoy climbing, spectacular drives through forests and splendid canyons, and sunny beach areas, Montenegro's coastline is an ideal location. Another point of significance: most of the tourists visiting Yugoslavia's Adriatic coast each summer seem to settle for camping and vacation resort towns farther up the line, particularly in the region between Dubrovnik and Split. You will certainly be far from alone on the Montenegrin coast, but it can be stated that the mass of vacationers confronted on the Dalmatian coast thins out somewhat in the south.

The coastal regions of the two republics, Croatia and Montenegro are grand seaside vacation areas. I urge you to extend your trip, time permitting, to as many towns and resorts in the interior as possible. Second, see if you cannot plan your trip, preferably by car, so you may first visit the interior of the country, returning to the coast for relaxation and some genuine vacationing. Travel is tiring, so save the most effortless part of your trip for the last. Moreover, Yugoslavia's geography is so arranged that travel toward the sea provides more thrilling panoramas of the country.

I have been advised by Yugoslavian authorities that within the next few years the coastal region between Split and Ulcinj will be the object of an extensive development program designed to create a form of "tourist zone" providing 700,000 to 800,000 beds for Yugoslavia's anticipated foreign guests. The Yugoslav coast, Istria, Dalmatia and Montenegro, will become the world's first truly international seaside resort boasting a 1,238-mile beach.

The Bohemian Isles region of Slovenia will see further developments with an eye to the tourist trade. At the same time Macedonia will witness the construction of winter sports facilities in the region of the Sava Mountains.

Those contemplating the purchase, rental or lease of a home in Yugoslavia for vacation purposes should be advised that the law concerned with such transactions has not as yet been acted upon by the Yugoslav Parliament. Until the government of Yugoslavia has issued specific regulations with regard to such sales, leases and rentals, Yugoslav authorities urge that you avoid entering into any financial or property transfer arrangements with Yugoslav citizens.

DINING

Yugoslavia can be neatly divided into four food categories. The first category should be called the "Mixed Grill Circuit." This area extends from the eastern border of Slovenia south through Serbia, Macedonia and Montenegro. Throughout this area pork and lamb are prevalent except in small enclaves in Zagreb and Belgrade where one finds a more international type cuisine and therefore more variety. Beef dishes are available but not featured as are lamb cutlets and pork chops. Fish is seldom found except in the international enclaves. Throughout this first food region you will eat very well: omelets, tomato and paprika salads, soups, fresh fruit and the ever-present palacinke (crepes suzette filled with jelly, nuts, cream). Prices are reasonable. Aside from the usual broths, eggs with mayonnaise, omelets and spaghetti, you might select Dalmatian ham as a first course. Thin slices of this world-renowned prosciutto-type, air-dried ham combined with a green salad can make a delightful lunch in itself. Dalmatian ham is called Dalamatinski prsut—don't miss it. Also available is breaded, semi-broiled cheese (pohani sir); rich, very filling and quite tasty.

Main courses run the gamut from the ever-present "Mixed Grill" or cebacece (kebap on some menus) to plates of various types of grilled meats. Try the goulash, stuffed cabbage, mutton with cabbage, and pork cutlets with paprika. Dyuvec is another favorite of mine, as is choolbastia, a form of Balkan beefsteak.

Food Category Two covers the restaurants located in the interior of the "Mixed Grill" area which serve a more international cuisine. This category of restaurant features a more varied menu and is usually more expensive. Such restaurants are usually in deluxe hotels or are the stars of one or another restaurant association; the Dusaney Grad in Belgrade is one outstanding example.

Category Three covers the coastal areas from Ulcinj north to Porterz. Here you will be treated to numerous Yugoslav specialties and a delightful dash of seafood lost to you while traveling in the interior. Throughout the Adriatic resort areas you will be able to enjoy in addition to the usual cevap and baked cheese diet—shrimp, mussels and oysters plus several fine fish specialities. In Dubrovnik a fish called osman is excellent. There is also mullet, dentex and, in Ohrid, excellent trout. Trout is also found in the mountains at Ivangrad and in the Plitvice Lake region.

In Category Four are the numerous privately owned restaurants found in every large town or city. In some cities hotel receptionists hand out introductory pamphlets indicating the whereabouts of these restaurants. The private restaurants have a bit more style, more original decor and often a picturesque location. By and large they are somewhat away from the central sections of the city, in suburbs, along the docks or in the woods. Don't miss them. Service is usually excellent, the foods diverse and delicious, prices only slightly higher than those charged by the restaurants owned by the workers' associations.

Along the coast, in association restaurants, fish, shrimp and oysters run between 9 and 12 ND a serving. Meat dishes cost 14 or 15 ND; salads and vegetables, 2½ ND. Usually the most expensive item in association restaurants is something like Chateaubriand, which can cost 25 ND. In private restaurants "specialities" shoot up to 48 ND ($4) on occasion. Except in hotels and some eating places in small towns, menus are a la carte.

Breakfast usually consists of tea or coffee, rolls, jam, butter; all of this is usually included in the price of your room. In the deluxe hotels, juice and a boiled egg ("Vienna breakfast") may also be included. Yugoslav tea is not particularly titillating, so you might bring along your own if you really like tea. American and Turkish coffee are generally available in Belgrade, at resorts and in the larger cities; in the countryside coffee is always Turkish style, meaning small cups and thick liquid. By the way, coffee is kava and tea is caj, pronounced "chi."

All manner of drinks are available: cordials, aperitifs, whisky, beer, wine, soft drinks—all at reasonable prices. Let me give you an idea of what is available along with the prices for some of the drinks. Don't forget: $1 is about 12 ND.

Scotch whisky (shot)	10 ND
French cognac (shot)	13 ND
Cinzano vermouth (shot)	5 ND
Local champagnes (bottle)	40-70 ND
Local beer (bottle)	2-4 ND

With respect to local aperitifs, I recommend the following: *Slivovitz* (stara), a fiery drink; *Vlahov,* a liqueur somewhat like but better tasting than the Italian Fernet Branca; *Pelinkovac,* rather sweet but tasty locally produced vermouth; and *Maraskino,* cherry brandy. Also *Mastika* if you like the taste of anise. Naturally, *vodka* is available; should you like it with tonic water, the mixer can be found in most leading hotels—ask for "Indian tonic water." If you want bottled water, ask for *Radenska Voda*, famous throughout Europe; it is inexpensive (roughly 3 ND per bottle) locally bottled and good. Soda water is also available—3 ND delivered to your room.

As for the beer, in Slovenia you will find *Schwerter Brau*, an import from Graz, Austria. The famous *Pilsner Urquel* is available in all leading restaurants and hotels. *Svetlo Pivo* (pivo meaning beer) is produced in Serbia; it is fair but must be served very cold. *Slatibor Pivo*, from Serbia, is light, quite good.

Soft drinks are available, including *Pepsi-Cola*. Blackberry juice is quite tasty; when served cold with soda it is even more refreshing.

Wines

Now to the wines. The following is a partial list of good and, in many cases, excellent Yugoslav wines. They are reasonably priced—say 10 to 16 ND per bottle. In some instances the wines are available only within the immediate district in which they are produced. Try all; you'll enjoy them immensely.

>*Merlot*: a semi-dry red wine (Croatia)
>*Riezling Karlovacki*: a semi-dry white (Serbia)
>*Zilavka*: white, rather fruity and very popular throughout Yugoslavia (Bosnia)
>*Ilocka Grasevina*: excellent dry white, reputedly served at the wedding of Britain's Queen Elizabeth II (Serbia)
>*Zupski Rieszling*: a white, dry wine; rather light (Serbia)
>*Kratosija*: dry red wine (Montenegro)
>*Blatina*: dry red wine (Herce-govina)
>*Vranac*: dry red wine (Montenegro)
>*Ritozoccan*: (my spelling may be off here); white and dry (Slovenia)
>*Plavac*: dry red wine
>*Rebula*: white, light, rather fruity (Slovenia)
>*Malvazija*: dry white wine, very good (Istria-Croatia)

Tips are included in the bill (10%) but I suggest adding another 8 to 10% for the waiter if the service is good. For room service there is usually at 15 to 20% service charge added to the bill. Breakfast may be taken in bedrooms or in a special room set aside for that purpose.

The food in Yugoslavia is generally good, inexpensive, rather on the hearty side. If traveling in the interior for an extensive period, you would be wise to vary your diet as much as possible; include omelets, vegetables and, when available, fruits and stay clear of kebabed meats as much as possible. Inquire regarding the availability of types of kebabs other than mixed grills; some are especially delicious—ground mutton, seasoned and rolled into long finger shapes, then grilled, for example. When on the seacoast eat as much fish as possible; it is delicious. When visiting private restaurants be certain to inquire regarding their specialities; by and large, those will be memorable.

HOTELS

Tourist accommodations in Yugoslavia are grouped into five categories: *L* (for deluxe), *A, B, C,* and *S.* Boarding houses and resort area tourist accommodations are similarly rated.

Whether in a city or at a resort you will find a complete range of tourist facilities that will certainly include some type of room, camping area, private house, apartment or complete bungalow to meet your needs. The regional Yugoslav hotel associations, grouped together under the larger country-wide Jugohotels, maintain high standards for their 208 hotels and restaurants located throughout Yugoslavia's six republics.

To adequately satisfy the interests and vacation customs of the thousands of foreign guests that pour into Yugoslavia each summer, the hotel associations have not relied simply on the construction of individual hotels within cities, towns and villages. They have introduced a unique approach to foreign tourist lodging, specifically the construction of "resort villages" at intervals along the 3,798 miles of coastline stretching from the Albanian border in the south to the Italian border near Trieste. Located within each of these resort villages you will find deluxe hotels, both large and small, economy priced hotels, bungalows for several families or individual houses for a single family group. Also lounges, bars, a restaurant or two, dance pavilions, souvenir shops, barber shops and hairdresser shops, medical facilities. These are, thus, resort units totally independent of whatever town may lie nearby. In such historical resort towns as Dubrovnik maximum utilization is made of the large hotels centered within or near the Old Town. However, outside the city limits of Dubrovnik you will find excellent resort areas designed for camping, dining or simply a day's outing while boating and swimming.

Yugoslavia is bent on becoming one of the foremost tourist havens, if not the foremost tourist locale, in all Europe. Private U.S. Foundations and the United Nations have developed real interest in seeing the Yugoslav tourist development blossom into a foreign moneymaker of which any country can be proud. I can state that without exception I have never seen such a display of efficiently managed, clean, well-situated hotels, bungalows and tourist apartments — whether in towns, the mountains or at the sea.

Yugoslav travel authorities occasionally encourage foreign guests to cable specific hotels within the country directly when requesting hotel space. I do not concur with this idea. I feel it is best to deal with a travel firm, whether at home or abroad. This is a far less risky approach to securing hotel space. Foreign languages, geographical distances, failure to advance return cable funds, failure to confirm — all these hazards are risked when one attempts to make reservations for oneself. Select your hotel and then book through an authorized travel agent. I suggest that a full itinerary be mapped out before requesting any reservations. Keep in mind that Yugoslav hotels are heavily booked during the summer season.

Unlike other countries in Eastern Europe, you will *not* be issued food coupons. Either your meals will be included in your prepaid reservations or you will cash travelers checks in Yugoslavia to cover the cost of your meals. Breakfast, I repeat, is included in the price of the room. I do not recommend that you book hotel space on a full-board basis unless you are going to spend a long period of time in a resort area where there are not many interesting restaurants. Full board means that you eat all meals in your hotel.

Unless you are traveling with a group, be certain you have separate hotel vouchers for each hotel on your itinerary. These vouchers will state the type of accommodation reserved, whether full board or simply breakfast is included with the room, your dates of arrival and departure. Upon arrival at each hotel or motel, this voucher should be handed to the reception clerk, who will give you a key to your room. Other than the presentation of your passport there is no other registration formality. Persons traveling without hotel reservations will, of course, have no hotel voucher and will, therefore, register on arrival and pay their hotel bill on departure. At the time of your departure be certain you have your passport in your possession!

Hotel vouchers are usually not issued for the Esplanade Intercontinental Hotel in Zagreb; guests with confirmed reservations there are provided with a confirmation slip indicating that a room has been reserved for such and such a night. In this instance the guest is responsible for payment of hotel charges. This exceptional practice seems to stem from the fact that this hotel maintains a reservation office in New York (its parent organization is a subsidiary of Pan American World Airways). Diner's Club credit cards are accepted by hotels in all major Yugoslavian cities and resorts.

Here is an indication of hotel rates in Yugoslavia. Keep in mind that an individual person, living alone in a room, pays more than half the cost of a double room. Note also that full board gives you a substantial reduction in your overall rate. Tourists who stay in any one hotel less than three days pay 10 to 20% extra. Here then is a general look at deluxe hotel prices for single and double rooms with bath. The second range of prices is for full board. Prices are indicated in dollars.

	Single	*Double*
CITY	$7 to $9	$10 to $14
	$14 to $16	$12 to $14
LAKE	$5 to $6	$8 to $10
	$8 to $9	$7 to $9
SEASIDE	$7 to $12	$10 to $24
	$10 to $11	$8 to $16

Most deluxe and first-class hotels in Yugoslavia offer the full range of services usually found in tourist facilities of such categories. Room service, laundry and pressing, baggage assistance, morning maid service, elevators and in most instances, car parking space or garage. Also the usual number of public rooms—bars, nightclubs and restaurants. A number of hotels have private swimming pools, barber shops and masseurs. Laundry and pressing should be handed directly to the maid; the charge will appear on your bill. Prices for laundry and pressing are not exhorbitant and the work is well done.

In Yugoslavian bathrooms, "H" on the faucets stands for *Hlanda*, meaning cold; this knob is usually located to the left. "T" is for *Toplo,* meaning hot. Occasionally the English "H" and "C" are used, but watch out; sometimes knobs read this way, but the hot water gushes from the right-hand ("C") knob anyway!

The men's room is generally indicated by a picture of a man's shoe; the ladies' room by — you guessed it! — a high-heeled pump.

Spring on the Adriatic can bring some mighty cool days. And summer days can be mighty hot. Inquire of your travel agent about the availability of heat and air-conditioning. Central heating is generally available in city hotels; air-conditioning is exceptional everywhere.

It is not necessary to tip hotel personnel inasmuch as their services are included in the price of the room. Employees of these hotels, almost without exception, perform room services pleasantly. Don't feel you have to tip, but everyone is so pleasant you'll wish to demonstrate your appreciation.

SHOPPING

Discount stores offering 10% off on all purchases made with foreign currencies are located on the principal thoroughfares of all large cities and resorts. The merchandise available is of excellent workmanship and representative of all sections of the country. Prices are right. There are other souvenir shops and galleries not offering discounts for dollar purchases. I recommend you set aside several dollars for purchases in discount shops.

CURRENCY

If you find yourself having to cash travelers checks for dollars or must re-exchange dinars so as to buy dollars you will be required to visit the National Bank. Hotel exchange desks are not allowed to exchange travelers checks for foreign currencies (e.g., dollars).

A wide variety of merchandise is available to tourists. Wooden plates, dolls, finely woven tablecloths and towels, ceramic pitchers, vases and wall hangings and bottles of local liquors and Slivovitz. Even fur coats are available!

In addition to the shops offering no reduction for foreign currencies and the discount shops there exists a third category in Yugoslavia. These are the galleries which display the works of local artists. As a rule these are private operations representing the artist for a percentage of the income. The articles available are usually reasonably priced. One such shop is located near the north gate of the "Old Town" in Dubrovnik; another is in the summer palace of the Emperor Diocletian in Split. Local artists in Novi Sad, Belgrade and Dubrovnik will be pleased to open their studios so you can view their paintings and sculpture.

Be sure to retain money exchange slips as proof that goods were purchased with dinars secured by exchanging dollars. Also retain slips on all discount shop transactions to show that purchases were made in foreign currency.

GUIDES

It is essential that you hire a guide in such towns as Dubrovnik, Split, Ljubljana, Zagreb, Sarajevo, Skopje, Chrid and Belgrade. You stand to gain a great deal from a guide who can explain the historical or political importance of your surroundings. Guides for these cities should be hired locally. Rates are very reasonable. If you feel you want a guide in a smaller town simply visit the nearest local tourist office. I do not recommend that you employ a guide to travel with you about the country. Points of interest in Yugoslavia are rather isolated from one another and there will be moments when you will long for solitude.

TAKING PHOTOGRAPHS

Yugoslavian authorities have given little emphasis to the question of restrictions on photography. It is wise to impose a little self-discipline with regard to one's photography program: avoid taking photographs near military bases, near harbors, at airports, or large industrial plants. Stick to the esthetic and historical points of interest and the inevitable family shots.

CAMPING, BUNGALOWS AND SPAS

Yugoslavia offers the camper literally hundreds of camp sites located the length and breadth of the country, with special emphasis on the coastal regions, lake districts and mountainous regions. You need no "camping permit," and camping gear may be imported into Yugoslavia free of duty. All camp sites are indicated by the international "Camping" road sign, a trailer superimposed on the outline of a tent, or individual signs directing one to camp sites privately owned or of special importance, such as those associated with large resort hotels. Bungalows associated with large hotels are classified as "paviljoni." These buildings are usually located at the center of camp sites and consist of a small room containing two beds, chair and table. Management of the two types of units is usually lodged in a building near the entrance to the resort. The bungalow locations are referred to as "Turisticko Naselje"; the name of the campsite usually follows: e.g., "Turisticko Naselje Verudica." Toilet and bathing facilities are located nearby.

Camping is not premitted at sites other than those authorized by local authorities or, frequently, by the owner of the private property. This regulation has been established in an effort to provide maximum sanitary arrangements for foreign guests as well as sports grounds, running water and kitchens at the more elaborate sites.

Charges are based on the number of persons, with children paying half the adult price, and with an extra charge for cars. In a few places one pays according to the space one occupies. Camp site charges per person per night run between three and seven new dinars. More elaborate camping areas are higher. A visitor's tax may add one or two ND per person to your bill. The camp management will ask to see your entry card and passport when you register.

Tourist accommodations in private homes are readily available in Yugoslavia and are usually less expensive than rooms in large hotels. The decision to live in a private dwelling naturally depends largely on the extent to which one wishes to involve oneself with the local citizenry. The increase in private rooms stems largely from the limited number of hotel facilities available near the popular resorts and from the demand for less expensive accommodations.

Rates for rooms in private homes depend on the facilities available to the guest. A seaside location, large garden and increased guest privileges with use of kitchen will of course cost more than a bare room without a view. Category Five rooms, the cheapest, cost between 5 and 10 new dinars; Category One accommodations run about 8 and 23 new dinars.

Lists of private rooms for let may be obtained at local tourist offices. Select the room you desire and upon completion of your visit, settle your bill with the tourist agency. Hotel reception desks are also usually able to provide you with information of private rooms and if you obtain the name of a private home from a hotel, pay the owner of the home, not the tourist office, when you depart. If you have some specific location in mind rooms may be reserved in advance by writing to Turisticko Drustvo at the town or resort you wish to visit.

I found the Yugoslavian camp sites, bungalows and private rooms to be generally well maintained, ideally located and popular with every type of European nationality. If the impersonal, more formal approach is for you, keep to the hotels. But for really meeting the Yugoslavs, there's nothing better, or less expensive, than a vacation spent in a private home.

SPAS

Yugoslavia has quite a number of outstanding health resorts noted for the treatment of various diseases. Some of these resorts are open the year around. Contact your local travel office or the Yugoslav National Tourist Office for lists of the frequently very attractive cure locations. The thermal springs are located in Slovenia, Bosnia, Montenegro and Croatia.

HUNTING AND FISHING

Yugoslavia offers some of the finest hunting preserves in Europe.

Special licenses are required for the various species of game hunted. There are the usual rules regulating the catch, season, weapons, handicaps and sport photography. I suggest you contact local authorities for particulars regarding these activities. Field sport organizations the world over will be able to provide you with such details.

In Yugoslavia there are over 2,000 hunting preserves controlled by game associations; additional preserves are controlled by the game and forestry commissions. The more important hunting preserves are laid out with roads, trails, and bridle paths incorporated into the general layout of the hunting areas. Guide and game keeper services are available. Deer can be hunted in the old preserves located around the Sava, Drava and Danube Rivers. The brown bear can be found in the mountains of Montenegro, Macedonia, Bosnia and southern Slovenia; chamois, ibex, wild boar and roe are found in various areas of the country. The lynx inhabits certain less settled regions of Macedonia. Hare, fox, partridge, pheasant, grouse, woodcock and quail may be hunted in sections of Hercegovina and Dalmatia. Geese and duck are found in certain preserves near the smaller rivers.

Fishing in Yugoslavia falls into several categories: pastime fishing, fishing for game, underwater fishing and freshwater fishing. No rules govern the first of these categories. Visitors may fish from shore or a boat with a line, nets or pots. Game fishing is another matter. Should you want to try for larger varieties of the 300-odd species of fish inhabiting the waters of the Adriatic coastline, contact local tourist officers, who will give you up-to-the minute details on where and how to obtain your license. This will also give you an opportunity to learn the whereabouts of the best fishing waters.

Underwater fishing is strictly controlled by local organizations but it is a very popular sport in Yugoslavia, due largely to the uniquely clear water found along the coast. You should have no difficulty arranging your program with local authorities. There exists a local underwater fishing organization which you may join at a cost of 30 ND per year. From this association the latest news and information may be gained regarding this particular sport. Licenses are usually valid for one specific area. However, as a member of the afore-mentioned association you will be able to obtain licenses at half-price and be able to pursue the sport at any location along the coast. Equipment can be purchased locally, but Yugoslav authorities advise that you bring your own since you might not be able to rent the exact type of equipment to which you are accustomed.

Freshwater fishing in Yugoslavia is particularly good. There are more than 200 types of freshwater fish to be caught in the hundreds of miles of streams and 70 freshwater lakes. Fishing licenses are valid for one to 30 days, depending on local regulations. Fees vary from place to place. The licenses will specify the number of fish that may be caught, and two licenses may be taken out in one day. Small fish must be returned to the stream or lake. Certain areas are periodically closed to fishing because of spawning periods.

Underwater photography is a common pastime in Yugoslavia, especially along certain stretches of the Dalmatian coast. Antique hunters may decide to forsake the shops in favor of diving gear when they learn of Yugoslavia's azure blue waters and the wealth of the old coastal cities. Check with local authorities before high-tailing it over to Austria with your latest find, as regulations regarding the exportation of antiques can be messy.

If you are interested in mountaineering, you'll find some excellent locations in certain regions of Montenegro and Slovenia. Comfortable hotels and hostels are nearby for those who, once up, need liniment, a hot bath and Scotch to ease the pangs brought on by our over-enthusiasm.

Alphabetical Listing of Resorts and Tourist Attractions on the Adriatic Coast

BAR

An attractive small town located directly on the coastal highway some 15 minutes south of the Titograd road, this is the terminus of the Bar-Bari (Italy) ferry. There is a large harbor with interesting archeological diggings nearby. Fine fruit orchards and olive groves. Excellent beaches about one kilometer in length. Some 25 miles to the northeast is Lake Scutari forming a portion of the border between Yugoslavia and Albania. Ruins of the Venetian Fort Topolica are also nearby. No hotels are recommended here. I would suggest Bar as a pleasant camping site somewhat removed from the more frenetic locales farther north.

BRELA

Brela is a thoroughly delightful resort development roughly a 45-minute car ride along the coastal highway south of Split. Pay attention to signs along the road; the town of Brela is rather too casually designated. The upper town is situated in the hills, the smaller resort area lying directly on the sea 1.5 kilometers below the highway. Lovely pine forests provide a refreshing, scented atmosphere; the beach is quite stoney—some form of cork or rubber sandals would be advisable to ease your way into the sea. Beach equipment is available. A small port is located in the village adjacent to the hotel area. Tours may be arranged to nearby islands.

Hotel

MAESTRAL This is an excellent hotel plus two annexes. The hotel units were constructed in 1965. The restaurant has pleasant decor and serves good food; service is pleasant. Dinner from seven to ten; lunch around one; breakfast until nine or nine-thirty.

Rooms are comfortable and well arranged, with all facilities. Clean baths, balconies and telephones. I would book "seaside south," that is, toward the south end of the hotel.

Should rooms be unavailable in the Maestral, don't hesitate to ask for the annex, Marina. The rooms here are very pleasant; somewhat smaller in dimension, but clean and comfortable. The annex Marina seems a bit dark, less interesting in atmosphere. Breakfast and cocktails are served at the annexes; all other meals must be taken at the main building. I would take full board here. Prices are quite reasonable, little difference—maybe $1.00 or $1.50—between rooms in the main building and the annexes.

BUDVA

This town, primarily thought of as a resort center, was founded in the 4th century B.C. and was surrounded by a fortress well in the 15th century. Little remains of the old structures. Instead, one finds a rather sleepy, sunny seaside town located just off the main coastal highway. Southwest of the town you'll see a fortress wall from the Middle Ages. Nearby is the 8th century Church of the Holy Ivan in which one can view paintings of the Venetian School; nearby is the Church of the Holy Trinity representing both the Catholic and Orthodox faiths. The Cloister Church is now an archeological museum exhibiting articles from the Greek and Roman "Nekropol" or "Dead City." Aside from the structures of historical interest, Budva maintains a fine sandy beach excellent for bathing or underwater sports.

Hotel

AVALA Recommended. Located on the sea, with private beach.

Restaurant

VIDIKOVAC Highly recommended by tourist agencies. The restaurant is located off the main highway north of Budva.

DUBROVNIK

When planning a trip to Dubrovnik, keep in mind that this is first a town of great historical importance and second, a pleasant resort town where a person could spend weeks lying beside a swimming pool or the sea, enjoying the best food and drink that life could offer.

The town of Epidarus was destroyed in the 7th century, its citizenry fleeing to the present site of Dubrovnik; however, the present format of the old town was laid out between the 12th and 17th centuries. A severe earthquake in 1667 did extensive damage to the buildings, but all was rebuilt much as before, though the principal thoroughfare of the town, the Placa, originally a canal, was rebuilt as a street. The original name of Dubrovnik, at least as it was known outside of Croatia, was Ragusa.

A few sights not to be missed: The two city gates, the Gate of Ploce and Gate of Pile; the architectural shape of the walls and fortifications; the Onofrio Fountain; the Franciscan and Dominican Monasteries; the Priljeko with its old merchants' homes; the 15th century synagogue; the Old Fort; the Rector's Palace where summer operas are performed; the Cathedral on Marin Drzic Swuare, whose origins are associated with a vow of Richard the Lionhearted; the Church of Saint Blaise and the Sponza Palace. There is also a Maritime Museum and Historical Museum. The pharmaceutical display in the Monastery of the Franciscans is most unusual.

Dubrovnik developed from a fishing village and a hideaway for slaves to an aristocratic oligarchic commune in the 13th century. It was the crossroads of Europe and from this position, the people of Dubrovnik managed to forge alliances through trade pacts and treaties of mutual security. The Dubrovchani minted their own money; set up a public health service; founded a home for the aged; banned the slave trade. Surrounded by Venetian armies they made pacts; endangered by the Turks, they proclaimed neutrality. In 1808 Napoleon added their town to his Illyrian Provinces. After Napoleon's fall, Dubrovnik became part of the Austro-Hungarian Empire under whose domination it remained until World War I.

The Gothic-Renaissance architectural beauty of Dubrovnik can never be forgotten. One remains aware of 20th-century "annoyances," yet the complete absence of cars, buses and the like—barred from the Old City—plus the old street maps and the music from a Mozart opera played in a nearby square, create a mood of indescribable peace.

Tours by Boat and Bus

Trips to the islands some distance from the Dubrovnik shoreline can be arranged through local travel offices. Korcula, for example, is the birthplace of Marco Polo. This is a day long trip which should be undertaken only if you have sufficient time to see Dubrovnik first. On Korcula you can visit the Cathedral of Saint Marco; the 15th-century Dominican Cloister, as well as the jewelry displayed in the Bishop's Palace. Night-time boat cruises are also available.

Boat trips may also be arranged to the Island of Miljet and the Island of Elaphita where there is a 14th century Roman town and botannical gardens. One trip booked as the East Riviera Cruise includes a visit to the villa of Maximillian, Emperor of Mexico and brother of

Vienna's Emperor Franz Josef. Perhaps you'll also find time for a visit to the sandy beaches at Lapad and Kuparis.

City tours of Dubrovnik may be arranged daily except Sunday.

Tours are also available by car and bus to Mostar, Trebinje, the ancient capital of Montenegro, Sveti Stefan and a number of other interesting locations.

Hotels

ARGENTINA This is my choice of the Dubrovnik hotels. The atmosphere is relaxed. Located approximately two minutes up the street from the Old Town, the Argentina commands a delightful view of the sea as well as the Old Town from front room balconies. The Argentina comprises four buildings. First a modern structure, completed approximately three years ago and built on several levels.

Next door you will find a second building, the original hotel with large, homey, early 1900-style rooms. All have bath, shower and phone. The new hotel is more commercial, the older more intimate, somewhat overstuffed in its decor. There is also an annex across the street which is not recommended. Rooms at the Argentina are air-conditioned, modern and furnished in acceptable fashion. Bathrooms are up-to-date.

The Argentina restaurant serves excellent food; service is tops. Dress well though not formally. Terrace dining in summer; the inside dining room is open only in late fall. The bar located under the older building is quite pleasant. Room service is available for all meals.

EXCELSIOR There are those who believe the Excelsior the best hotel in Dubrovnik. The Excelsior maintains two sections, old and new, side by side somewhat down the street from the Argentina and a little closer to the Old Town. Entrance to the new section is through a small street-level lobby where boys will assist you with your baggage. As the Excelsior is constructed below the roadway, one is obliged to descend to the lobby and later ascend by other elevators to the bedrooms. There is a large ornate lobby; capable reception staff. Off the lobby are a television room, small bar and a large sitting room overlooking the sea. Public rooms are superior at the Excelsior.

Front bedrooms are air-conditioned. The seaward view is stunning as the hotel is located directly on the beach. Apartments are available and have TV and radio; telephones throughout. From the balconies off the front rooms a splendid view of the harbor and Old Town. The rooms are very comfortable. Back rooms are not air conditioned. The old section of the Excelsior is again in the folksy, early 1900-style but quite comfortable.

The Excelsior Restaurant serves excellent food, lunch is a particularly pleasant occasion when enjoyed from the terrace overlooking the swimming area, Adriatic and Old Town. Service is the best. The Kafana, or cafe, at the north entrance of the hotel grounds is a very popular night spot. Italian orchestra, as a rule; garden surroundings by the sea; entrance charge. One of the best night locales in Dubrovnik.

VILLA DUBROVNIK This attractive small hotel is situated in a garden setting directly over the sea, and is located south of the main road some 15 minutes' walking time from the Old Town. It is more of a family hotel; clean, less commercial and quiet. There are 100 rooms in all, including an annex. All rooms have phone and bath; many have a fine view of the sea. Rooms are rather dowdy but pleasant. Back accommodations are equally pleasant though they lack the sea view.

The restaurant is informal and attractive. If relaxation, a less hectic pace and a need for less elaborate facilities agree with you, the Villa Dubrovnik is ideal. Pleasant, capable management; English spoken. Prices are much the same as those at the Excelsior and Argentina; the Villa Dubrovnik is a member of the same hotel association.

IMPERIAL Located in an old residential section north of the Old Town, smack in the commercial area of the New Town. Other hotels mentioned are on the sea south of town. The Imperial has no outlet to the Adriatic. It overlooks a small park owned by the hotel, which has a coffee terrace featuring an orchestra nightly. The Imperial is approximately 100 yards or so from the north gate of Old Town.

There are 17 rooms with bath and shower and balconies overlooking the park; 64 doubles with shower, 11 singles with shower. Rooms are somewhat Spartan decor-wise but otherwise clean and relatively comfortable. The atmosphere is certainly more "Dubrovnik-like" than other more modern establishments on the sea. I would book "south side" thereby missing cafe noises as well as the clanging of street cars on a nearby thoroughfare. East-side rooms are the best, but face the

Cafe. Book on the second or third floor which may help matters noise-wise.

The restaurant is a typical long, mirrored salon of the early 1900's; rather cold in appearance. During the summer months meals are served in the garden. Public rooms are average; the management is most pleasant and helpful.

I cannot recommend the Imperial. The structure is of a bygone age; its location is unfortunate, furnishings are in desperate need of updating. The summer garden and cafe are a hangout for the local population; full of children and singing youngsters.

Restaurants and Nightclubs

LABERINT This rather unique, but not exceptional night spot is a two minutes' walk inside the south gate of the Old Town, with the entrance directly in the town wall. It is Dubrovnik's largest night-time, non-cultural attraction and is interesting. An entry fee of 1000 old dinars must be paid at the door; then you continue through a modern lobby and down a flight of stairs. A small patio provides an attractive place to sit, but is usually filled up early. Surrounding the patio is a terrace and nearby another large room and bar. The place appears quite new, modern and attractive, though somewhat rustic. Fair orchestra; floor show. No food; drinks are reasonably priced; atmosphere is casual.

JADRAN An attractive place located just inside the north Old Town Gate right behind the Onofrio Fountain. A piazza-type arrangement, with terraces on three sides, an enclosed restaurant to the east. The entire facility is surrounded by a large building housing art galleries, theaters and the like. I would recommend the Jadran for lunch. In the noon sunlight, the shadowed court is delightful, quiet and somehow remote. At night the Jadran seems to be "Mila" Dubrovnik's favorite hangout.

GALERIE Located directly across from the north entrance to the Excelsior Hotel, this restaurant seems more a cafe than a restaurant. A very large terrace overlooks the Excelsior gardens. Quite pleasant for coffee or a drink. Not surprisingly, the Galerie is in an art gallery.

GRADSKA KAFANA On Marin Drzic Square immediately by the Cathedral. Located on the site of the 14th century Palace of the Grand Council, the cafe occupies a building built in 1862. It is a good location for afternoon or morning coffee or for a quick drink. The cafe is quite near the Rector's Palace where operas are staged. Front rooms at Gradska Kafana are more formal and service somewhat quicker. Time permitting, however, go to the back of the cafe toward the section overlooking the Old Port. There is lots more atmosphere here; music for dancing. The rear terrace of this cafe is extremely lively in summer.

Side Trip to Mostar

Should you be in Dubrovnik for four or five days and not be planning a car trip through central Yugoslavia, it would be well worth your time to make the 301-mile round trip to Mostar. Easily a day's drive you will find yourself in another world. A sharp turn to the northeast at the Neretva River delta, a few miles of hilly plains and suddenly you'll think yourself beyond the Yugoslav borders. There are sharp cliffs, a sunny river valley, mosques, primitive fortifications and quite another type of people. Mostar offers attractions that will really not occupy you for longer than one or one and a half hours following your lunch but what there is to see is extremely interesting. It is a trip into an environment quite close to the sea, yet so different from the Adriatic area in character.

HVAR

Hvar, an island in the Adriatic Sea, is located southwest of the Dalmatian coastal town of Split. It can be reached by boat from Split or by ferry from the town of Drevnik. At Hvar you will see some outstanding examples of the Dalmatian Renaissance style of architecture: a clocktower, 16th century cathedral, a municipal building from 1515, and a 1612 theater. In the Franciscan Monastery, now a museum, you can see Ungoli's *Last Supper* and also works by Tiepolo and Titian. The outstanding feature of Hvar is the tropical environment. The island is covered with ferns and oleanders. Hvar is, in fact, referred to as the "Madeira of the Adriatic." I'd suggest you investigate the Hotel Dalmacija. Located on the sea; private beach.

KOTOR

When driving from Titograd to Dubrovnik or perhaps from Sveti Stefan to Dubrovnik you would enjoy a lunch stop at Kotor. Kotor lies at the far end of a wide gulf. Kotor was founded by the Byzantines prior to the 12th century, and until the 14th century the town was part of the Kingdom of Serbia; since 1918, it has been associated with Yugoslavia. It is worth visiting to judge the impact of Byzantine, Serbian, Venetian and Austrian rule on the culture of the people. There are many buildings and artifacts from the 13th through the 18th centuries.

Hotel

FJORD Recommended as a luncheon stop when touring Kotor or en-route to Dubrovnik or Sv. Stefan. Recently remodeled, the restaurant overlooks the gulf and has a small terrace. The food is good; service fair. Clean and pleasant.

MAKARSKA

Founded at the time of the First Roman Emperor Augustus, Makarska is well known because of resort developments within the community. Historically there are few outstanding sights—two museums, a Franciscan Cloister and a library containing an original copy of the first world map. The beach at Makarska is roughly one mile long; nearby is a modern sport center. The area is popular both with Yugoslavs and foreigners. I do not recommend this resort; there are more outstanding town vacation areas nearby.

OPATIYA

An outstanding, if not the outstanding, summer and winter resort on the Adriatic Sea. Originally known as Abbazia, Opatiya was founded in the late 1800's by a family named Scarpia who counted among their guests members of the Austrian Imperial family. Opatiya is blessed with amazingly fine weather, the Kwarna Mountains blocking winter winds to such an extent that Opatiya enjoys mild temperatures the year round. A further dividend is the approximately 12 kilometer walk along the immediate shoreline, the path uninterrupted by buildings or other commercial distractions. There are no historical monuments of note in Opatiya. It is strictly a resort town dedicated to the convenience, entertainment and comfort of guests. There is a fine botannical garden in the center of the town, nearby an outdoor theater presenting plays, opera and specialty acts during summer months, as well as a casino, the Villa Rosalia. Bordering both sides of the main street there are souvenir shops, restaurants, cafes, a post office—all the usual appurtenances of resort life. Day and night-time activities at Opatiya are largely centered around the hotels for there are few restaurants of note; the summer theater is the only entertainment other than that offered by the hotels.

Hotels

AMBASSADOR   A very fine hotel. Opened during the past two years, it provides every possible facility for complete enjoyment. A modern structure set slightly back and above the sea, the rich interior decorations blend splendidly with the surrounding semi-tropical environment. The Golden Room cocktail lounge and restaurant are air-conditioned, and both rooms are attractive. On the top floor are a nightclub and an a la carte restaurant (open at eight); music for dancing. Nearby is an attractive bar room. There is good service in all these rooms.

Rooms are extremely pleasant and commodious. All rooms have bath and hand shower. Apartments occupy corner locations, with singles next door. Specify whether you wish double bed; twins are available. All rooms have balconies and are recommended, though you should reserve on the sea side of the building. The Ambassador is surely one of Europe's better hotels. The resort town is roughly a day's drive from the Austrian border.

BELVEDERE Second best. Has a location on the sea, excellent restaurants, tennis courts, casino nearby. Public rooms and bedrooms are informal, clean, quite pleasant. Double rooms have baths; singles a shower. A pleasantly decorated restaurant overlooks the sea; a small, well-stocked bar is located nearby. Balconies off the front rooms are delightful, rather resembling small sun rooms. Don't let the lack of phones or the sleepy atmosphere of the hotel scare you away. This is a hotel in which you can relax.

BRIONI A small hotel also located near the sea, though somewhat back from the shore than the Ambassador and Belvedere. A large, "Gemütlich" restaurant with a small aperitif bar nearby. No nightclub here. Double and single rooms have showers. Rooms are clean and comfortably furnished.

Note: The three hotels mentioned above are particularly recommended for your stay in Opatiya because of their proximity to the sea. With the exception of the old Hotel Kwarna, all other hotels are on the main road, facing the traffic. Guests of the Ambassador, Belvedere and Brioni will find their rooms facing towards the sea, quiet gardens or relatively peaceful side streets. The following hotels are fine facilities but simply don't have the advantageous location of the first three.

PALMA Approximately one block from the sea. Front rooms face the Botannical Garden; rooms to the rear overlook a parkline area. All bedrooms are clean, bathrooms are frequently large. Accommodations can be arranged for family groups, the Palma being somewhat of a family-type facility. The restaurant here appears very pleasant. There is also a night club.

PARIS Quite near the Palma along the main thoroughfare. Rooms at the Paris are clean if starkly furnished. West rooms can be quite hot in summer. Keep in mind the Paris is a "garni" hotel, that is, breakfast is the only meal served on the premises. The breakfast room is pleasantly decorated. Prices are somewhat lower here because of the meal situation.

KWARNA The Kwarna and its annex, the Villa, were the first two hotels constructed in the town. Both buildings are set in a small park quite near the sea and the summer outdoor theater. Rambling architecture and Victorian in appearance inside and out. I found the bedrooms sparsely furnished, the location too close to the municipal swimming area. Upper floors are decidedly gloomy. However, I do urge that you visit the hotel for meals. The main restaurant is a delightful throwback to the good old days; crystal chandeliers, light colored furniture, the wide salon with the orchestra balcony. There is also a terrace for outside dining and nearby a very pleasant bar. In the basement, be sure to visit the Grill Room, open evenings only.

Restaurants

PLAVI PODRUM This is a small private restaurant located near a very picturesque fishing port in a section of Opatiya called Voksko. This district is sometimes called the "Yugoslavian Portofini." It is a delightful locale that should not be missed. This is essentially a fish restaurant. I would recommend the fish soup and lobster, the tray displaying the fish being offered. Not recommended for large groups; the atmosphere is intimate, perfect for tables of two or four. Prices here are reasonable; the food excellent.

VILLA ROSALIA Open only in the evenings, the Villa Rosalia is Opatiya's gambling casino. The Rosalia was the home of violinist Jan Kubalik. The gracious salons with high ceilings and crystal chandeliers provide an interesting setting. English is spoken. The Casino is operated as a joint enterprise with Austrian financial interests; the Yugoslav Government is the second partner. No orchestra but there is a bar.

POREC

One of the most delightful towns I have ever visited, the oldest town on the Istrian Peninsula. Founded in the 2nd century B.C. as a Roman settlement, Porec was under Venetian authority from the 13th until the 18th centuries. Now Porec is one of the most popular resort locales in northern Yugoslavia. To reach Porec one need only drive south from Trieste along the road paralleling the coast. The town sits directly on the sea some 15 minutes drive west from the main highway.

At Porec you will find a number of unique historical attractions: the Roman war camp, constructed two centuries before the Christian era; the Mars and Neptune Temples; numerous palaces; the Lion of Saint Mark statue, and picture galleries. In nearby areas are several camps boasting fine grounds for tenting or bungalow living. The Plava Laguna is one, the Bellevue Villas another.

Hotel

NEPTUN This small but attractive hotel was opened in 1869. Located opposite the port area away from the noise of the cobblestone streets, the Neptun has a pleasant terrace and functional lobby. The restaurant is decorated in a semi-rustic style, the service is prompt and the food good. Nearby is a small well-furnished bar. Rooms are attractive. Two apartments are beautifully furnished in an informal fashion. The apartments boast every convenience including television and a refrigerator. All rooms have bath or bath and shower. This is a perfect place to get away from it all for five days or a week. The casual, attractive surroundings, historical displays, the proximity to Yugoslavia's Italian border, these and other points make Porec one of the better tourist finds in Europe.

PIRAN

Here is a delightfully picturesque little fishing port located some five minutes by car northwest of Portorouz. Piran was founded by the early Romans, and later was under Venetian rule. Between the years 1797 and 1919 the town was included in the Austro-Hungarian Monarchy. In 1945 it was returned to the Italians. You will be impressed by Piran's Italian style of architecture as well as the general layout of the town, situated as it is around a small port rising to considerable heights in the town's eastern sectors. The narrow streets, small shops, and multitude of colors all combine to make Piran a photographer's heaven. Visit the Tartini monument, the 19th-century City Hall and the 13th-century cathedral.

There is no hotel of note in Piran. I would recommend that you enjoy the tourist facilities in Portorouz making side trips to the neighboring towns.

PORTOROUZ

Portorouz is approximately a 45-minute drive from Trieste on the northern coast of Istria. The town was formerly controlled by the Italians. With its remarkably interesting sister town of Piran, Portorouz should be visited if only for lunch on the way to Opatiya or Ljubljana. It is dedicated to total relaxation with no emphasis on the historical. Piran, on the other hand, is designed to lure those interested in Old World architecture. The two towns provide a perfect balance of the old and the new; resort life and historical attraction.

The beach at Portorouz is particularly good—sandy and comparatively wide. The principal hotels have access to beaches and resort life revolves largely about the hotels. The three largest and best hotels, the Palace, Lucija and Riviera, maintain complete facilities; all are located across the principal thoroughfare, a three-minutes' walk from the beach. The climate in Portorouz is sub-tropical, comparable to north-central Florida during the summer months. You can enjoy vacation houses and camp sites as well as the curative effects of thermal baths. However, resort life at Portorouz means "hotel life" with a capital "H."

Hotels

LUCIJA Located on the coast road entering Portorouz from the south. The large, rambling chocolate and white structure is situated some distance from the road, surrounded by lawns and flower gardens. To the right, and separated from the main building, is the restaurant; to the rear and somewhat above the hotel is the annex. The annex is where I suggest you make your reservation; it is named Vesna. On the opposite side of the road lying directly on the beach are the Grill Room and nightclub.

All bedrooms are the same dimensions, with bath or shower. Rooms in the Vesna are more elaborate; furnishings richer, less commercial.

The restaurant is a two-storied structure quite modern in design. You will have a choice of terrace or inside dining. Dancing at the restaurant three times weekly. The entire layout is appealing, functional, very pleasant. Meals are average to good; service acceptable.

PALACE Built in 1912 the Palace has a large lobby, long corridors and a restaurant boasting Venetian mirrors and crystal chandeliers. Of typical Italian design, it is situated at a central section of the resort, somewhat northeast along the coast road leading away from the Hotel Lucija.

The Palace offers private beach bathing as well as thermal or mud bath treatments. Front rooms have bath and shower; all rooms are equipped with telephone. There are 200 rooms in all; double and twin double rooms available. Some rooms have extra large balconies.

The restaurant at the Palace serves very good meals, waitresses are most obliging. Be certain you are assigned to a table. Terrace dining during summer months.

The Palace is a fine old hotel, though somewhat gloomy. It is well managed, offering average to good floor and restaurant service. Baths have been built into many of the rooms making them less spacious; moreover, the bathrooms are rather cramped and dingy. The Palace is recommended if you are interested in the thermal baths and love an Old World flavor.

RIVIERA This is a clean, well-managed hotel located at the northern end of town with beach facilities, restaurant and nightclub. The Riviera lies directly on the road so the better rooms do experience some traffic noise. Bedrooms are light and airy though somewhat sparsely furnished. Baths and telephones are to be found only in apartments; all other rooms offer showers. The restaurant, built in a circular design overlooking the street and nearby beach, appears quite pleasant.

PULA

Pula is the cultural and business center for the Istrian Peninsula, as well as an important port for commercial and military purposes. Founded by the Early Romans in the 2nd century B.C., there is evidence the region was inhabited during the Early Stone Age. Between 1896 and 1918 the town was occupied by Austrians, being the site of the Imperial Monarchy's most important naval base. The area around the town is craggy, the beaches partially covered with gravel and rocks. There are a number of important historical monuments in Pula, including a Roman Amphitheater which is now the site of operas and film expositions. In the principal square (Forum) are the ruins of municipal buildings and temples. You might also visit the 14th-century Gothic Church of Saint Franco, the archeological museum and the Lapidarium.

Hotels

The hotel facilities at Pula are under the management of an association named Veruda. These hotels are not located within the immediate confines of the town but rather some two miles beyond the more populated area. It is a resort complex or resort village. Within this area is the Zlatne Stijene (Golden Rock), a combination of hotel and bungalows, the Verudela Park Hotel, the Verudela Hotel Complex and the Ribarska Koliba cottages. All are located either within a pine forest or immediately along the coast.

VERUDELA PARK HOTEL I found this to be clean—period. I cannot recommend it to you. Furnishings are grim; service, perfunctory at best.

ZLATNE STIJENE Top prices run about $12 per person, double room, with meals; $40 for two persons in an apartment. Rooms are equipped with showers. However, until the management feels compelled to fulfill obligations to their guests by honoring their previously paid reservations, I cannot encourage you to visit this resort. Another negative feature is its distance from the town.

RAB

Rab is a small town located on an island of the same name in the Adriatic Sea south of Rijeka. Frequently billed as the "Island of Love," because of a nudist colony near one of the beach areas, Rab was originally the site of an Early Roman camp. Buildings on the island show the influence of the Middle Ages. I would recommend Rab only for a day's sea excursion. The beaches are sandy and boat trips from the resort town of Opatiya can easily be arranged.

RIJEKA

Rijeka is the second largest city in Croatia and the principal port of Yugoslavia. It is perhaps better known to Europe and America by the name Fiume. Naptha and ship engines factories are side by side with enormous shipyards and the harbor. A large percentage of goods destined for Austria passes through Rijeka. During the late 19th-century and throughout the early 20th-century Rijeka was first a possession of Hungary and later Italy and great competition continues to exist between Rijeka and the Italian port of Trieste.

Rijeka has a number of historic sites: the 17th-century Church of Saint Veit, the old Cathedral, the National Museum, a small Zoological Garden, the Naturalogical Museum and a number of other churches and palaces—but it is first and foremost an industrial and commercial city.

There are few restaurants of outstanding note, though many small cafes and beer houses line the dock area. If you must stay in Rijeka the best hotel is the Bonavia. Otherwise I would book rooms in Opatiya, an outstanding beach resort town 10 minutes away and $5 away by taxi.

ROVINJ

Rovinj is an interesting old town located on the west coast of the Istrian Peninsula. The central section seems to be straight from the Middle Ages, with narrow streets and overhanging buildings. Originally a hideout for sea pirates it was connected to the mainland in 1763. It was the one principal commercial city of the Venetian Kingdom. Beaches in the area are largely rocky with large boulders strewn about, and very crowded during the summer months.

Hotel

PARK The only hotel to be recommended in Rovinj is the Park, and even then I can scarcely be enthusiastic. It is a modern structure standing on a slight rise overlooking the sea. There are limited bathing facilities; bleak lobby. Rooms are modern, starkly furnished though clean.

SENJ

Senj, founded four centuries before Christ, was known as the town of the "Uskoki," where warriors banded together and fought against the Turks and later the Venetians. Though the town was forever engaged in wars it nonetheless became a cultural center for the Croatians. Though seemingly only a small resort town on the Adriatic, Senj is one of the most interesting, attractive towns along the entire coast. Nearby is the Seniska Draga Gorge and during winter months one may frequently encounter winds of tremendous velocity. Not far from the town you can see the fortress of Nehaj; palaces from the 15th to 17th centuries and a Franciscan Church. Senj is an extremely popular summer resort for tourists from all over Europe. The beach is not wide but bathing can be excellent. One is able to walk some distance from shore without coming to water of great depth. Be certain to take a sightseeing trip to the Plitvice Lake area. The only hotel to be mentioned here is the Nejag, a B-category facility.

SIBENIK

Sibenik is located on the Adriatic Coast approximately 75 miles north of Split on the coastal highway at the south of the Krka River. Since the completion of a by-pass, the main road passes somewhat east and north of the town. There are three outstanding tourist attractions in Sibenik: a beautiful waterfall formed by the Krka River; the Cathedral of Saint Jacob, and the Municipal Building. Founded in the 10th century by King Peter Kresimir IV, between 1918 and 1921 as well as between 1941 and 1945, Sibenik was under the control of Italy. Today it is an industrial center for aluminum processing, woodworking and fish processing.

Note: The waterfalls on the Krka are located at Skradin some 18 kilometers from Sibenik. You can reach the falls by boat in a shorter time than by car. A 16th-century Franciscan Cloister is located on an island in the river.

Hotels

JADRAN This thoroughly modern, small hotel is located opposite the fishing port, on the seaward side of Sibenik. You must travel to the parking area in the center of town, then descend the road to your left. There are 15 single rooms and 21 doubles. Some rooms include telephones, all rooms are sparsely furnished though clean. Only a few rooms have baths.

I do not recommend the Hotel Jadran for more than a one-or-two night stay. It might be wiser to include Sibenik on a trip from Split to Zada.

MOVESAK-ZAGREB This motel is located directly on the main highway between Sibenik and Zadar. The motel sits on the west side of the highway at the northern end of a modern bridge spanning the Krka River. A small tourist facility, this motel offers the visitor a choice of double rooms, with showers, pleasantly decorated and comfortably though sparsely furnished. No singles or apartments. The rooms facing the river gorge have the advantage of a spectacular view with Sibenik in the distance. There is a good restaurant with terrace overlooking the gorge. Food is acceptable.

SPLIT

Here is a fascinating tourist stop. Split combines the dramatic qualities of a busy port city with the romantic, exciting attractions of a historic past. Centrally located on the Dalmatian coastline Split is equidistant from both Dubrovnik and Rijeka. Within the immediate surroundings are many outstanding resort and historic attractions. While Split itself does not warrant an extensive stay, a two-to-three night stop should be considered so you may enjoy the local sights as well as a number of excursions originating from the city. Split also offers a first-rate hotel.

Split is the largest town in Dalmatia. Founded originally in the 7th-century as the Roman town of Salonae, it was the summer capital of the retired Roman Emperor Diocletian. Split was for some time governed by Venice, followed by the Hungarians and once again was under the Venetians until 1797 when, with the exception of some years of French authority, she remained a division of Austro-Hungarian Monarchy.

The town of Split now is divided into several distinct sections: the Old City plus the main shopping area and port, is centered across broad boulevards from the port itself. Along the harbor to the north stretches a promenade area including hotels and parks while to the south, away from the port, we find a modern subdivision of apartment houses and shopping centers.

Among the sights to be seen in Split are the Diocletian Mausoleum. Diocletian's original aim in constructing his palace at this site was related to the existence of a thermal spring. An Ethnographic Museum is located in a central square near the Palace. Also you might like to visit the Franciscan Monastery, and hear a concert in the charming cloisters.

Hotel

MARJAN Here we find a modern structure quite out of place among the monasteries, temples and mausoleums which comprise downtown Split. The restaurant serves good food, and offers fine service. The cafe on the main floor is used for breakfast as well as afternoon tea. English is spoken throughout the hotel. The casino is one room containing roulette tables and slot machines and is far from the lively setting one would expect to find in such an establishment.

Rooms at the Marjan are completely furnished in a rather dormitory-like style. There is a fine view of the harbor from the upper stories. Small bathrooms with half-baths and shower. Large apartments on the upper floors are not exceptional. The Hotel Marjan is recommended as a fine hotel for a stay of several days when sightseeing or simply driving through town.

Restaurants

CAFE CENTRAL This cafe is directly across from the Ethnographical Museum, and is a good place for coffee, tea or a drink.

MARJAN A small restaurant, just up the street behind the Dalmatian Tourist office and located on the central quay, the Marjan is nothing outstanding though the food is good. Dress casually. Recommended for lunch only. Average price.

ZAGREB By far the best restaurant in town. Located near the main post office, it is 10 minutes' walk from the Hotel Marjan. Always crowded between one and two-thirty. The food is very good. Casual dress.

SARAJEVO Reputedly the best restaurant in Split although this writer did not find it so. A narrow, ill-lighted dining room beside which is located a small and seemingly not too clean patio. I cannot recommend this restaurant.

Shopping

LOZICA ALTALIER Located in a section of the Diocletian Palace, actually a covered passageway leading from the Mausoleum to the Titova Obala, or the main boulevard along the quay. It is approximately a 10-minute walk from the Marjan Hotel, midway between Marmontova Ul and Jrvojeva Ul.

Within this well-lighted, spacious corridor a private organization has established a gallery in which interesting, original and in many cases outstanding works of art by contemporary Yugoslav artists are displayed. These items are for sale; the gallery collects a commission from both artist and purchaser. On display are such items as glazed ceramic ashtrays, pottery, amphora jugs, icons, paintings and graphic sketches. Prices are not out of line.

Excursions from Split

Boat trips to Hvar, as well as to the islands of Brac, Solta, Vis and Bisevo, may be arranged through local travel agencies. Dalmacijaturist with offices on Titova Obala is the leading travel agency in Split. Rates for the boat trips are reasonably low, the tours leaving Split in the morning, returning in late afternoon. Hydrofoils are employed on some of these trips to nearby islands.

TROGIR An outstanding historical attraction, Trogir was founded four centuries before Christ as a Greek colony. The town is located on a small island midway between the main coast and the island of Ciovo and is connected to the mainland and Ciovo by bridges. It was once one of the principal Greek trading and commercial colonies along the Dalmatian coast. The entire town is an architectural monument to Venetian Gothic design and maintains many of the characteristics of the Renaissance Period. Trogir is approximately 45 minutes by car along the northbound coastal road from Split towards Zadar and Bijeka. I would urge that you treat Trogir as an individual side trip from Split and not as a stop.

The entire town is a museum, two of the more outstanding sights being the Cathedral of Saint Lorenzo and the nearby Italian Campanile or bell tower. Other buildings of historical interest: the Municipal Building; several palaces and a loggia built for a marshal of Napoleon's armies, and the Fort of Saint Marco. An outstanding historical trip and one you should not fail to include. No hotels or restaurants are recommended.

SVETI STEFAN

Saint Stefan is a unique resort experience. The village seems to have its origins in the 15th century, when all along the coast the fishermen and their families banded together as protection against sea pirates who preyed on all forms of commerce along the rugged, indented coastline. Thus was born the small island village of Sveti (or Saint) Stefan. Originally Sveti Stefan was connected to the coast by a sandbar, but later a short stone causeway was constructed. The island lies only 100 yards or so from the beach and is located on the Montenegrin coastline some 136 kilometers south of Dubrovnik and 57 kilometers from the Montenegrin capital, Titograd. The resort can be reached from airports located at Titograd and Dubrovnik or by boat from Bar, Kotor and Budva.

There is little of historic note here. In 1960 Sv. Stefan was opened to the public as a hotel accommodation. The entire island is composed of bungalows, apartments, hotel rooms, bars, casino, restaurants and all the other appurtenances of modern hotel life. There are two Orthodox churches on the island. From a small plaza in front of the upper church one can see for miles across the Adriatic and along the rugged coastline.

The Sv. Stefan hotel consists of 36 buildings, some new, some old but all recently renovated and providing accommodations for 209 guests. Minimum prices here run about $10 plus tax in single villas, large apartments run as high as $14 plus additional charges per person. A single person can pay $7 for room and breakfast or $11 with full pension which is, of course, desirable if a person is staying for some length of time. A double room will run $10 per person, $9 with full pension per person. Half pension plans are also available at somewhat less cost. Special rates are available for children.

Sleeping facilities at Sv. Stefan come in all shapes and sizes. There are the usual hotel rooms, apartments and two complete bungalows for family use. The apartments and bungalows are complete units with bedrooms, baths plus a large sitting room and one walk-in closet. Bathrooms are large. Single or double rooms also may be in duplex-type buildings, two units to one building.

The restaurant at Sv. Stefan is comprised of two large inter-connecting rooms plus a small cafe and dining terrace. There is also a second roof terrace for after-dark entertainment and dancing; orchestra nightly except for those evenings when folklore programs are arranged which is once a week during summer. Food is average to very good; service fair. Breakfast is served on a terrace off the restaurant.

Water skiing facilities are available as well as boats for excursions. Beaches at Sv. Stefan are wide and sandy, though not long. Guests of the hotel should use the beach to the left of the causeway as you leave the hotel. The other beach is for public use.

I would urge that you plan, at a minimum, a three day stay at Sv. Stefan for it is a most unusual experience. Be sure to take along your camera—the colorful and exotic flowers, shrubs and trees make for exciting color snaps.

ULCINJ

The town of Ulcinj is the last stop for any tourist traveling south along Yugoslavia's 1,000-mile coastline. A couple of miles farther to the south or east will place you in Albania. Ulcinj is, in fact, only a small spit of land extending along the coast enroute nowhere. Founded by the Byzantines in the 6th century, Ulcinj was the home port of a particularly dangerous group of pirates during the 16th and 17th centuries. The road between Bar and Ulcinj is extremely narrow and in many places permits the passage of only one vehicle at a time. There is little habitation along the road, no filling stations or restaurants. The drive south from Bar, in daylight, will take you approximately 45 minutes. By night it is well over an hour of miserable driving.

Within the town is an interesting old marketplace, a votive church and a number of mosques. The entire town has a distinctly Oriental flavor. As you approach Ulcinj, drive straight through the older areas to the resort complex, which is located somewhat above the town. Watch for a street leading up to your left with signs pointing toward the hotels. The main road continues toward the harbor. Beaches at Ulcinj are wide, of fine sand with particularly excellent areas for bathing by inexperienced swimmers and children. Hotels are some distance above the bathing area.

Hotel

GRAND HOTEL GALEB After reaching the top of the small hill overlooking the town, be prepared for a second turn to your left and a sharp incline to the area of the Hotel Galeb. This is a modern hotel in the "B" category but one offering pleasant facilities for its guests.

There are two sections to this hotel; the older section, with a fine view of the sea, is not recommended until alterations have been completed. Then and only then, ask for the corner rooms with shower and sea view. The new section was completed in 1963. Book a "double-room-seaside"; singles and doubles to the rear of the newer section are without bathing facilities; singles to the front as well. Double rooms are pleasant though with only rudimentary decor and functional furnishings. Seaside rooms do not overlook the sea, but rather an attractive pine grove beyond which is the Adriatic and the swimming area.

The hotel restaurant is on a lower level of the building, below the lobby. Outdoor dining with music every night but Monday. Below the hotel, nearer the beach, is a cafe with dancing nightly except Monday open also during the day for the benefit of swimmers. You might enjoy dining on the terrace beyond the restaurant. It is particularly pleasant for breakfast.

Restaurants

PALMA A private restaurant reputed to have fine food, some distance downhill from the Galeb.

HOTEL JADRAN Directly across the bluff from the Galeb is the Hotel Jadran. It is not recommended as a hotel but the view from their nightclub terrace is exceptionally lovely. Dancing nightly. There is an intimate little bar very popular with the younger crowd.

ZADAR

Zadar is an interesting, unique port town located along the north central coast of Dalmatia. It is a town over which I cannot be enthusiastic. There are however, attractions of historic value as well as resort facilities. Zadar, founded as an Illyrian fortress town four centuries before Christ, suffered extensive damage from allied air attacks during World War II. Buildings of historic worth were located between the harbor and Zadar Canal so civilian casualties and damage to buildings were great. Originally an island, Zadar was connected with the mainland some centuries later. The principal tourist attractions are located on this island. Historic buildings, the Forum and churches, are located just off Obala Marsala Tita, an avenue paralleling the Zadar Canal — this is, on the island. This section is some distance from your entry into the town from the highway. Among the sights of interest in Zadar: the Basilica of Saint Stosije and the Church of Saint Illipa. There are other churches in the area as well as the Porta Marina.

Hotels

FORUM Should history be your interest make reservations at the Hotel Forum, which is located immediately within the range of the historic buildings and ruins.

The Hotel Forum is a four-story structure built within a new complex of buildings including book stores, groceries and a theater. Bedrooms are functional and clean; there are two apartments. All rooms have telephone; laundry service; showers.

BORIK HOTEL ASSOCIATION: (HOTELS PARK, SLAVIA AND ZADAR) The Borik group represents Zadar's leading hotel association. There is no connection between these hotels and the Hotel Forum. This is strictly a resort operation, 10 minutes by car away from the historic sections of the town. The Borik Hotels are well beyond the north edge of Zadar and occupy a large tract of land directly on the Adriatic. Though the hotels are of similar construction, I can recommend only the Hotel Zadar for from this building you have a view directly onto the sea and a restaurant is on the premises. At the Zadar we find clean, purely functional rooms with showers only. The corridors are bleak; no elevators; toilets in each room; English spoken. Bedrooms here are what you might expect of a third-rate hotel in the United States—they are, however, clean. The saving grace of the Hotel Zadar is that it faces the sea; also the bar and restaurant face wide lawns surrounding all hotels. Food is very good; service is acceptable and pleasantly rendered. You might enjoy breakfast and lunch on the broad, umbrella-shaded terrace that runs the length of the building.

Slovenia

Slovenia is the most northwesterly of the six republics comprising the Socialist Federal Republic of Yugoslavia. The Julian Alps form Slovenia's geographic border with Austria. The principal rivers flowing through Slovenia are the Mur, Drava and the Sava. The topography is comprised largely of rolling hills, green pastures, dense forests and many lakes. Principal crops and farming industries include the growing flax, sugar beets, sunflowers, hemp, soy beans and chicory. Animal husbandry is practiced on farms throughout the region. There is heavy industry located throughout the republic. Some of the most famous grottos of Europe are located southwest of Ljubljana, the capital and largest city of the republic. The people of Slovenia are generally industrious, courteous, very candid in their observations, deserve praise for the efficiency and individuality of their tourist programs.

BLED

Bled, approximately one hour's car ride from the Austrian town of Klagenfurt, is located in a beautifully forested, semi-mountainous region of northern Slovenia. Situated at the end of a lake it has been for years an outstanding summer and winter sport center for central Europe. In the center of Lake Bled is a small island on which are the church of Saint Mary of The Lake and the Castle Blejaki Gradue, a restaurant and museum. A promenade stretches along the lakeshore; nearby are cafes, restaurants, hotels and souvenir shops. Boats are available for rental.

Hotel

GRAND HOTEL TOPLICE This is the best hotel at Bled, without exception. Located directly on the lakeshore, it was constructed in 1935 and renovated in 1968. There are three annexes to the Grand but if the main building is unavailable I would urge you to consider only the Annex Jadran. It is the older building and here one can find pleasanter double rooms overlooking the lake. Nose is a factor to be considered if you are in an off-lake room. Book "lake view" or in the Jadran. Concerts or dance music in the main salon every evening in season. The restaurant, overlooking a terrace and the lake, is located on a level below the salon. All meals are served here and the food is very good. All rooms lakeside have fair sized balconies. Double rooms are rather small; book twin-bedded room located at the *south* end of the building. All rooms are pleasant and comfortable.

LJUBLJANA

The capital of Slovenia is Ljubljana, a city of approximately 178,000 inhabitants. Beautifully laid out along the Ljubljanica River, the city is composed of the famous Old Town (Baroque style), a university, fair grounds and central business sectors. While in Ljubljana you should certainly visit the Baroque Town and Castle Hill; art galleries; a cathedral, and souvenir shops. This is a vital city in which to spend, at a minimum, two to three days. Or use Ljubljana as your headquarters while making tours about the countryside.

Hotels

LEV A modern, well-equipped, efficiently managed hotel on the northern edge of the central shopping area of Ljubljana, overlooking the river. Single rooms face the park and river; doubles face on a quiet, narrow street. All rooms have shower, bath and phone. Singles run approximately $8 and doubles $15 (twin-bedded). Should you wish a snack for lunch, eat in the cafe off of the lobby; for a quicker lunch or dinner try the first dining room to the right of the elevators. A more leisurely meal, with music in the evenings, is available in the second dining room. A pleasant little cafe-terrace is located just beyond the second dining room. Food and service are very good; no dancing; orchestra until ten.

SLAN Built in the mid-thirties, the Slan has recently undergone renovation and is reputed to have a fine restaurant. However, the hotel itself is located on a rather noisy street in midtown Ljubljana and is devoid of a view.

Restaurants

Ljubljana offers the tourist a number of private restaurants where you will enjoy an excellent meal at reasonable prices, surrounded by the typical decor of a Slovenian household. These eating places are usually small, family-owned and not easily accessible for those without means of transportation. Yet all are within a five to ten-minute drive from the Lev or Slan. Your hotel receptionist can arrange reservations for yourselves or even for a large party, as these restaurants encourage party groups. In Ljubljana you might try the Restaurant Machek, the Jasper, the Urshka or the Katrca. Open for lunch and dinner, most of these locations have outside and inside dining facilities. Food is usually quite good.

MARIBOR

The town of Maribor, or Marburg, lies astride the principal highway running between Graz and Zagreb. This midway location makes it a good place to spend the first night when driving to Yugoslavia from Vienna. It is also within a day's drive from Ljubljana, Rijeka and Zagreb. In Maribor it would be of interest to visit the Old Town where are such sights as the cathedral and the 16th-century Municipal Building.

Hotels

SLAVIJA An extremely modern building located directly on the main highway between the Austrian border and Zagreb and Ljubljana.
   Be certain to book on the west side during summer months. The

east side rooms are intensely hot in early mornings. All bedrooms are the same size here with the exception of the three apartments. Comfortable though there is considerable street noise. The restaurant, complete with orchestra, seems to be something of a place for local beatniks, emphatically provincial. Food is mediocre.

POHORJE

Hotel

BELLEVUE Pohorje is a summer-winter resort frequented by many tourists from Italy and Yugoslavia. The Bellevue offers clean, simply furnished rooms in rustic surroundings. A double with shower and telephone will cost about $4 to $5; a single without shower $2. This is a typical ski hotel with an out-of-door atmosphere — souvenir shops, restaurant, bar and terrace cafe. Many group tours here. I would recommend the Bellevue to young people and those who enjoy a hike in the woods. The food is fair. Try it for lunch, the cable car ride should prove amusing and an afternoon in the woods could only be a pleasure diversion.

OTOCEC

Otocec, pronounced Otochecz, is located an hour or less on the main highway north of Zagreb.

To the right of the highway is the Motel Otocec; to the left the Grad Hotel. On a small island in the center of the Krka River is one of the most charming settings imaginable.

GRAD HOTEL OTOCEC A 14th-century Romanesque castle destroyed during the Turkish Wars, was rebuilt in the 17th-century. It is a beautiful setting with wooden bridge, willow trees and swans gliding and small boats. Park your car outside the main gate of the castle to enter by foot. Across the courtyard is a central hall, off of which are located a dining terrace and a long wood-paneled restaurant. Food is quite good here and well served.

There are two apartments, 10 doubles with bath, water heated electrically. Rooms furnished in Period style. Apartments are enormous including sitting room and study and large bathrooms. All rooms with hand showers. Rates for apartments approximately $15; the doubles approximately $10. Singles without bath cost $4. These are prices with board, for the "with meals" arrangement is necessary as the hotel is quite apart from any town. Excellent fishing and hunting in the region surrounding this hotel. The Grad Hotel Otocec should not be missed, if only for a lunch stop. Plan to spend some hours here for a leisurely lunch, exploring, and browsing.

OTOCEC This motel consists of two sets of motel buildings, the first units built in 1968, the older units a few years before. Newer rooms are constructed in the form of a duplex, two double rooms sharing one building. They are quite modern and set into the landscape in appealing fashion. The hotel is east of the highway away from the Grad Hotel and Krka River. All doubles with shower; restaurant and cafe in an adjoining building; nice terrace for afternoon coffee. If you wish, your meals could be taken at the Grad Hotel a five-minute walk away.

POSTOJENSKA JAMA

The year 1968 celebrated the 150th year since the discovery of the Postojenska Grottos, and some six million visitors have streamed through these fantastic grottos formed by underground rivers. Covering an area some 20 miles in length, the Postojenska Jama might be better known to you as the Adelsberger Grottos, the German name carried for many years. Small electric trains run some distance through the caves. Wear a heavy sweater, for the temperature can become extremely cool. Your head should also be covered as protection against water dropping from the roof. You might also enjoy a visit to Predjamski Grad, a Baroque castle of the 15th-century. This region of caves, castles and grottos is only 52 kilometers from Ljubljana and 64 kilometers from Opatiya; Zagreb is 186 kilometers away.

ROGASKA SLATINA

This spa is famous for its spring water as well as for the hot alkaline saline mineral water used in the cure of liver and gallbladder diseases. Rogaska Slatina is located in an attractive region of southern Slovenia some 70 kilometers south of Maribor. The spa is midway between the two towns and can be used as a relaxing location for lunch. A majority of hotels in Rogaska Slatina have been occupied by trade unions as rest and cure locations for their members.

Hotel

SLOVENSKI DOM Located directly on the highway, remains open to the public. The hotel is clean but somber. The restaurant is quite cheerful. There is a medium-sized terrace to the rear of the hotel where one can overlook the woods. The food is good; service fair. As a lunch stop between Maribor and Zagreb or as an outing from Zagreb, the environs of Rogaska Slatina are pleasant.

Croatia

Croatia has a great cultural heritage, one that almost spans the period of the Christian Epoch. Much of its social, religious and political development stemmed from the time of the struggles between those forces favoring the religious teachings of Rome and those leaning toward the Orthodox teachings which stemmed from Byzantium and Pope Gregory VII. Eastern Croatia is composed of farms and a number of fair sized towns, the chief occupation being agriculture. Here and there are large industrial combines. Excluding Istria and Dalmatia there are only two attractions of tourist importance to be seen in east central Croatia, namely Zagreb and the Plitvice Lakes.

PLITVICKA JEZERA (The Plitvice Lakes)

The Plitvice Lakes are an outstanding tourist attraction located in a national park 140 miles southwest of Zagreb or two hours from the Dalmatian coast. Within a splendid pine forest are 16 lakes. Throughout the park are many walkways and beaches. Fishing is permitted in some areas and with a license. Leave your car in order to enjoy your surroundings. Excursions to the Plitvice area may be arranged through your hotel reception desk in Zagreb, Senj, Rijeka or Split. From Zagreb or Senj, by car or bus the trip will occupy your entire day. Should you be driving through, have lunch at the Hotel Plitvice near the eastern end of the park.

Hotels

PLITVICE Located deep within the Plitvice Lakes National Park, the Hotel Plitvice provides good food served either on a wide terrace overlooking the forests or in a rustic indoor dining room. The hotel is built on several levels with access from the south side. Ample parking; pleasant lobby. Bedrooms are twin-bedded with baths, telephones and room service. There is a total of 70 rooms and 4 apartments. The food is very good—the trout in particular. For those interested in a relaxing, undisturbed few days in a particularly beautiful forest surrounding, I would recommend the Hotel Plitvice. The atmosphere is informal, the food creditable, the service average to good.

VILLA IZFOR An annex of the Hotel Plitvice. A 10-minute drive up a road to the right of the restaurant terrace of the Hotel Plitvice. The road leads nowhere but to this villa plus a number of small camping and fishing areas along the way. The Izvor consists of 14 double rooms and 4 apartments; all rooms are on two levels. A double room has a short staircase to the very spacious bedroom, beautifully furnished in semi-rustic style. Every comfort is available—large bathrooms; all room services. The double rooms occupy one wing of the villa. Apartments occupy the other wing and consist of a dining room and sitting room on the first level, a large twin-bedded room, dressing room and large bath up a short flight of stairs on the second level. Should you be traveling with a group of friends or on one of the more expensive European tours, book your group into the Villa Izvor for at least two or three nights. Fishing, hiking plus beautiful seclusion. The Villa Izvor is a Government Guest House occupied on occasion by President Tito.

ZAGREB

Zagreb is a busy, crowded, rather unattractive city not unlike many in the United States—but 700 years older. When it's hot in Zagreb the populace wilts; should there be a heavy rain, taxis disappear; in winter the streets are a pedestrian's obstacle course. Streetcars, broad boulevards, narrow side streets and crowds. It will seem like home to those acquainted with Baltimore and Chicago. Zagreb is Yugoslavia's second largest city and the center of commercial traffic for the entire country. Here you will find a university, technical school, an Academy of Arts and Sciences. Located on the Save and Medveaica Rivers, it is called a "City of Three Cities," composed of a Lower Town, Donji Grad, largely a modern commercial center; the Upper Town, Goraji Grad, location of the district and Croatian Government offices and, lastly, the Capital City, Kapitol, a slightly higher area surrounding the Cathedral. Zagreb during the Napoleonic times was a frontier town of considerable political influence. Today Zagreb is internationally known as the site of the yearly Spring and Autumn Industrial Fairs. There are a number of outstanding historic sights, most of them located in the Upper Town. The more outstanding are: the view of the city from Upper Town; the frescoes in the Catharine Church and Saint Mark's Cathedral. Museums and art galleries are of special interest in Zagreb. The Ethnographic Museum is particularly interesting, also the Modern Gallery. For those who enjoy opera, concerts or the theater, inquire of your hotel reception regarding the programs.

Hotels

ESPLANADE-INTERCONTINENTAL One of the best hotels in Yugoslavia and has been leased by the Intercontinental Hotels Corporation, a subsidiary of Pan American World Airways. It is an old hotel. Since its new ownership it has experienced a wholesale face lifting that has provided a luxurious, yet local atmosphere for the foreign, as well as local guest. Off the lobby is the Rubin Restaurant and Bar, a delightful room for evening dining or lunch. The restaurant has a broad terrace for outside dining during summer months. The Golden Lions Bar is one floor beneath the reception area, a well decorated, smart nightclub. Low lights, drinks and service the best. Directly across from the Golden Lions is the Taverna Rustica, a national food-type restaurant closed during summer months. This could be interesting for those who have little time to explore other regions of the country to see the national dress and test local foods.

To reserve a room at the Esplanade you can have your travel agent contact Intercontinental's New York office. You will be provided with a slip noting the date of your reservation and the amount of the room. This is not a prepaid voucher. Rooms at the Esplanade come in all shapes and sizes; what's more, to the front are streetcar tracks and immediately to the rear of the hotel is the main railroad station. One other side of the hotel can be intensely hot during summer months. Book on the upper floors overlooking the terrace.

Apartments and doubles occupy corner rooms. All sleeping accommodations are well furnished and very comfortable. Room services for food and beverages are beyond fault.

Rates at the Esplanade are a bit up from other hotels in Yugoslavia; the hotel is not a member of the usual trade associations. Figure about $16 a day per person for a double room and about $12 for a single. There are rooms running somewhat less in each category. These rates do not include meals. Larger rooms are equipped with radio and TV.

PALACE Across from a large park, about two blocks from the railroad station. It is somewhat more centrally located than the Esplanade only three blocks from the commercial area. The United States Information Service Reading Room, the Archeological Museum and Modern Gallery are nearby. Bedrooms on the side of the hotel are smaller, but quieter. Front rooms are larger but noisier due to streetcars and traffic on a main boulevard. Better rooms are designed in a turn-of-the-century style.

BRISTOL This small hotel is located on a comparatively quiet side street in a central section of town. Should you be looking for something less formal and a bit smaller make inquiry regarding the Bristol. It has possibilities and appears far less institutional than the other large hotels.

DUBROVNIK On a central square in the center of the commercial district and is more of a commercial or transient hotel. Good management; elevator; all room services. Rooms are clean though somewhat starkly furnished. Singles are quite good; baths appeared clean. The lobby of the Dubrovnik is most unimposing; the restaurant located one floor beneath the lobby is almost grim in appearance. Reserve on Republike Square upper floors.

INTERNATIONAL Located at a junction of the Belgrade-Ljubljana highways in a quiet, newer area of the city near the university. You will have a choice here of twin or double beds. Only half the rooms in the older section have bath or shower. Location is the chief factor here as the International is just off the two main highways and within walking distance of the university and fair grounds. There will be ample parking when the new section of the hotel is finished. The International is some distance from the central commercial area of Zagreb and at the opposite end of town from the historic Upper Town.

Restaurants

VESELI KUTIC A delightful private owned restaurant located in a residential area five minutes by car from central Zagreb. It is easily accessible by car, a taxi ride costing you approximately 1700 OD. Located on a side street the Veseli Kutic sits in a small tree-shaded yard surrounded by homes and apartments. At night a gypsy orchestra can be enjoyed until eleven. Indoor dining in a large room seating 100 persons, but the garden is preferable during the summer months. Service is somewhat slow but the food more than compensates for the delay. Prices are not unreasonable, though perhaps somewhat higher than the average restaurant. Not too many tourists at the Veseli Kutic — so enjoy an evening of good food to the accompaniment of melodic music in one of Zagreb's best restaurants.

KORNATI Approximately a 10-minute walk from the Hotel Esplanade; go left on the first street to your right after exiting from the hotel. The Kornati will be on your right about five blocks from the Esplanade. Those staying at the Palace and Bristol will find the Kornati nearby. Formal restaurant downstairs, a small cafe to the front. I would suggest you eat in the garden patio to the rear of the building. The food is good, service fair. Dress well, though informally. Prices are somewhat up but not exceptionally so.

TAVERNA Located two minutes' walk from the Upper Town. The restaurant is reputed to be among the best in Zagreb and is popular with local people. Dress conservatively and well. Buffet to the left of the entry hall, the main restaurant to the right. A long paneled room seats about 50 people at 30 tables. Wooden benches and low lights; the entire atmosphere is on the pseudo-rustic side. Service is fair, the food average.

Bosnia-Hercegovina

The Republic of Bosnia-Hercegovina is located in the south central region of Yugoslavia and is bounded by the Una and Drina Rivers. It occupies upwards of 51,000 square miles in central Yugoslavia. The Republic's northern region is the most fertile with the production of tobacco a principal occupation. The southern regions are more arid with considerable limestone deposits. Pine, beech and oak forests are found in the south. Serbs and Croats made up two thirds of the population; the Croats associated with the Roman Catholic faith, the Serbs being Orthodox. Followers of the Moslem religion comprise the remaining third of the population. These people are centered mainly about the towns of Sarajevo, Mostar and Banja Luka.

BANJA LUKA

The second largest town in Bosnia is Banja Luka. The surrounding areas are generally rural, and the town is best known as the gateway to Vebas River Valley. One senses a decidedly eastern character in the town—suddenly one sees sheep, wooden carts, local costumes all just 40 miles southwest of the highway. In Banja Luka one should visit the 16th-century Perhad Pasha Mosque, located in the Old Town; the Arnaudi Mosque; a Bazaar, plus the remains of assorted castles and forts of the Middle Ages.

AUTHOR'S NOTE: Since this manuscript was originally written, this town was almost totally destroyed by earthquake.

Hotel

BOSNIA I cannot recommend the Hotel Bosnia for other than lunch. The hotel is quite antiquated, reminding one of a mid-1900's lakeside resort. The food is good, service equally so, prices average. A good lunch stop enroute to Sarajevo from Zagreb.

JAJCE

If you are interested in a picnic here is the perfect opportunity for such an outing. Jajce lies approximately 72 kilometers southwest of Banja Luka on the Vrbas River road. It is not a fast 60 miles by any means for the road winds between arid cliffs and small green meadows. You'll want to make this a leisurely trip. Jajce, pronounced as Ya-tsay, was founded in the 15th-century and rests among the cliffs lining the Vrbas and Pliva Rivers. The area is stark, almost violent in its primitiveness. During the last years of World War II, Jajce was the site of a conference designed to lay the groundwork for the present Yugoslav State. Now it is the location of large chemical and hydroelectric plants, plus related industries.

When entering Jajce from the direction of Banja Luka, do not follow the main highway directly to the Jajce exit. As you approach the town you will see a sign indicating that Jajce may be reached either by following the asphalt or concrete highway to your left—the main road—or by taking a secondary gravel road to your right. Follow the secondary road! This will provide you with a much more picturesque view while bringing you directly into the central section of the town. When leaving the town, follow the bridge from the walled section of the town and return to the main highway.

The outstanding attraction in Jajce is a waterfall where Pliva Lake drops to the Vrbas River—the rustic old water wheels are even more interesting. Here, among the many small rivulets and streams, rocks and trees is an ideal spot for your picnic. There are a number of grassy meadows suitable for this purpose. Other local sights are the many small mosques, the Roman Walls, Franciscan Monastery and the 1404 castle catacombs.

No hotel is recommended in Jajce, though you might check out the Tourist Hotel should you find yourself running late. It's a long drive between Zagreb and Sarajevo (418 kilometers) with many sights to see enroute. A picnic actually is in order here for it will save you a tedious wait in some restaurant. If the time permits only a drive through the town, see the falls and the old mills. The drive between Jajce and Sarajevo is particularly lovely; the fruit orchards, tobacco fields, small town, the farmers in colorful costumes all make for an unforgettable day's drive.

MOSTAR

Mostar, the capital of Hercegovina, is a town of 55,000 situated on the banks of the Neretva River. The name stems from the fantastic bridge built across the Neretva River in 1566, during the Turkish occupation. Mostar refers to the "Bridge Watchman" or "Guardian of The Bridge." The Old Bridge is located in the central part of town. Park your car near the small park opposite the Hotel Neretva and walk westward along the second street paralleling the Neretva. This will take you through the old Turkish quarters and bazaar area to the bridge. It is not possible to drive your car into the area immediately surrounding the Bridge. The bazaar area, at the south end of the Bridge, is mainly a tourist attraction, with postcards, crafts and souvenirs. Also to be seen is the Karadjoz-Beg Mosque, the Kajtaz House; plus other assorted mosques and artifacts from the Turkish occupation. The Partisan War Cemetery contains an outstanding example of memorial architecture.

Hotels

BRISTOL I cannot be enthusiastic about the Hotel Bristol, the entire atmosphere is dismal. It is located on the north bank of a modern bridge spanning the Neretva. During summer the hotel is largely in the shade with a breeze sweeping down from the mountains. The Bristol is actually not a tourist hotel; it is far too commercial.

HOTEL NERETVA Located at the opposite end of the new bridge, the Neretva is a gaudily designed building representatve of the good old days. I do not recommend the Neretva as a sleeping accommodation, though I found the restaurant particularly pleasant for a noon meal.

Restaurant

LABYRINTH Located several yards from the Old Bridge within the so-called bazaar sector. With brass pots swinging, the stew bubbling and dust rising from the sidewalk, you may eat on a very narrow wooden porch from small wooden tables. You will also feel yourself to be very much on display. Try the terrace at the rear of the Labyrinth. There, for the price of a beer, you will enjoy a splendid view of the Old Bridge and the Neretva River. In the evening the "labyrinth" (cellar) itself could be pleasant, decorated as it is in national colors, rugs and rustic furniture.

SARAJEVO

Sarajevo is a famous old city whose origins can be traced into prehistoric epochs. Located in the center of Bosnia-Hercegovina it is 189 kilometers east northeast of the Adriatic Sea. Sarajevo the capital city of Bosnia-Hercegovina, is situated on the Miljacka River, which bisects the city and has a population of 218,000. Located in Sarajevo is the seat of a Roman Catholic Arch-Bishopric, the offices of the Metropolitan of the Orthodox Church as well as the Reis-ul-Ulema, the highest authority of the Moslem religion. It was here that the heir apparent to the Austrian throne was shot in 1914, resulting in political reverberations which led to World War I.

Sarajevo consists of three principal sectors. As you enter the town you will see the modern apartments, streetcar lines, express roads of the new city. Farther in, toward the central sections of the city, you will see the hodgepodge of old and new-style architecture, the crooked streets, churches and mosques. Finally, to the east lie the hills covered with the homes of Moslems who make up 80 per cent of Sarajevo's population. The Miljacka River flowing directly through the center of the town, in some areas, forms a border of sorts between the European sectors and the area which is largely Moslem. However, the line is not so definitive, for Moslem religious, commercial and social activities are located throughout the entire eastern half of the city.

Here you will see the Chusrev-Beg Mosque (1531), the best known mosque in Yugoslavia. Farther on are the Moslem religious school and the Clock Tower. There is the bazaar where one can find many woodworking shops and jewelry of gold and silver filigree. To walk about the bazaar district you would swear you were in the Middle East, so Oriental is the entire atmosphere. Near the bazaar is the Careva Dzamija (Sultan's Mosque) the location of the Reis-ul-Ulema and the Parliament of the Republic. Farther on, the Princip Bridge, where Franz Ferdinand was shot.

Sarajevo is not particularly impressive when first viewed by the tourist. It is a sprawling, not outstandingly attractive town. It can also be quite hot. This is a romantic city nonetheless, especially when a moon rises over the Moslem quarters and the aroma of roasting Turkish coffee and oleanders wafts through the hot night air. I would suggest that a stay of two nights is necessary to fully appreciate the sights in Sarajevo. Longer visits are not recommended unless you are a student of some particular facet of historical note.

Hotel

EUROPA I can recommend only one hotel in Sarajevo and even this recommendation is proffered with marginal misgivings. The first section of the Europa Hotel must have been constructed in the late 1800's; an addition was completed in 1961. It is located in the central downtown area two blocks from the Voivode Stepe Obala.

There are 233 rooms in the nondescript hotel including five apartments and an annex of 52 rooms, the latter all without baths. I would urge that you book "double bath" at the Europa, for singles with bath are scarce and usually in terrible locations. Doubles are larger, airier and generally lighter. Doubles in the older section are larger but have no particular view. The smaller 1961 section doubles have a breathtaking view of the Old Town though there is some disturbance from the open-air cafe located on a terrace outside.

Apartments with two rooms and connecting bath cost about $15. They are furnished in the comfortable style of the 1900's. Doubles cost approximately $6, and singles with bath, $5. Rooms without toilet or bath facilities cost about $3. Reserve a "double with bath" whether traveling alone or with another party. The difference in price is well worth it.

Restaurant service includes an inside room for lunch or dinner, the first room as you enter being used for breakfast. The terrace dining section is frequently reserved for tours. There is a bar on the lower level; open late.

Restaurants

DAIRE RESTAURANT Here is a fascinating surrounding in which to enjoy a meal cooked in local fashion. Recommended for dinner only. The Daire is located approximately a six-minute walk east of the Hotel Europa, in the bazaar sector. The building was originally a Moslem structure and a number of small rooms open onto a central courtyard. Eat outside, weather permitting. Service is fair; the food acceptable although heavily spiced. Prices are reasonable. Casual dress.

JAJI BAYRISCH In the Old Bazaar area, this is purportedly an excellent private restaurant, small and very informal.

CENGIC AND BASCARAIJA RESTAURANTS These two restaurants are also recommended by the Yugoslav Tourist Office.

HAMAM BAR A former Turkish bath converted into a very elegant cocktail lounge. Leather seats, brass tables, music for dancing. I believe dinner may also be served here. The Hamam Bar is located on the main thoroughfare two blocks from the Europa. There is local-type music here — one of the few chances one has to hear Yugoslav music as public entertainment. Reasonable prices. Go at a late hour.

TUZLA

Beside the fact that Tuzla has an outstanding thermal spring, lies astride a main road between Belgrade and Sarajevo and is a large industrial and railroading center, the city also offers the traveler a pleasant location for enroute dining. There is nothing historical here.

Hotel

BRISTOL A large modern structure in the residential area of Tuzla. An excellent spot to lunch when enroute to Belgrade, although it is rather dank, dark and sepulchral inside. After wending your way through the assorted halls and public rooms, you will reach a delightful dining terrace off the kitchen to the rear of the hotel. Rather Grecian in design, the restaurant offers excellent food at reasonable prices; service is tops. I recommend this restaurant for a peaceful, enjoyable break during a cross-country drive.

Montenegro

Montenegro may be the smallest of the Yugoslavian Republics (just under 14,000 kilometers) but what the region lacks in size it makes up for in determination. The principal towns of Montenegro are Titograd, the capital, Cetinje and Niksic. Outstanding resort areas are located near the towns of Ivangrad, Herceg-Novi, Bar and Ulcinj. The distance between Montenegro's seaside resorts and towns and her mountain resort areas can be covered in less than a day's drive. The republic's principal airport is located at Titograd, though daily flights are also available between Ivangrad and Belgrade.

The landscape of Montenegro is extremely rugged except for those regions paralleling the coast. The highest point in the country is Mt. Lovcen, "Black Mountain," from whose district the Republic takes its name. The principal religion of the Montenegrins is that of the Orthodox Church.

During World War II Podgorica was almost completely destroyed by air attacks. The city has since been rebuilt and renamed after the President of Yugoslavia.

You will find the Montenegrin people delightfully droll, outspoken and most hospitable. Anxious to attract tourism to their republic, they will welcome your opinions about their tourist establishment while evidencing every desire to make your visit a pleasant one. Should your itinerary carry you toward Belgrade or along the coast to Bar, be certain you drive into the interior of this republic. Your stay will be a memorably pleasant one if for no other reason than the interesting, dynamic people you will meet.

IVANGRAD

Ivangrad is a developing industrial town located at the northern exit from Serbia's Cakor Pass, about two hours by car east of the capital city of Titograd. The drive is pleasant; the road follows canyons carved by the Moraca River. The cliffs, pines and swift stream provide a wonderful setting whether by car or foot. The more prominent industries in Ivangrad are a paper pulp and manufacturing plant, leather factory and coal mining settlement. The town is located on the Lim River, which divides the old and new sections of the town. The surrounding area is covered by forests and fruit orchards. Of historic note: archeological diggings, which prove the evidence of former Roman and Illyrian colonies in the region, the Monastery of Djurdjevi-Stubovi and a Folk Museum containing ethnological displays. Historically, Ivangrad has less to offer than many towns throughout southeastern Yugoslavia. There are excellent opportunities for fishing, and streams in the area abound in trout plus other river fish. You can walk through the older section of town and view the houses with their slate roofs; you might wish to picnic at Lake Pesic, a beautiful location or you might walk through the woods or climb nearby mountain peaks. Ivangrad maintains a small airport with restaurant and bar facilities five minutes from the Hotel Berane; daily flights are maintained between Belgrade and Ivangrad aboard Yugoslavia Air Transport's Douglas plane.

Hotel

BERANE Overlooking the Moraca River, the Hotel Berane is at the northern end of a new bridge connecting the hotel area with the town of Ivangrad. Entering the town, drive directly down the main street until reaching the bridge—you will spot the Berane across the river to your right. A modern structure, the Berane offers 3 apartments, 96 beds in all. Rooms are small, clean and comfortably furnished. Nothing luxurious, but convenient and comfortable, it provides an excellent stop when driving through. Should you be looking for some fishing or plan a climbing trip, use the Berane as your headquarters. All rooms with shower, apartments with bath. Book toward the front for a better view of the surrounding countryside and mountains. Off the lobby is a very large cafe and bar and the restaurant. Off the restaurant is a large terrace for dancing or dining during summer. Service at the Berane, in both the rooms and the restaurant, is very good; the food, though not exceptional is tasty and nicely served.

KOLASIN

Hotel

BJELASICA A recommended lunch stop when driving between Titograd and Ivangrad. The small town of Kolasin is approximately one hour east of Ivangrad toward the Adriatic coast. You will see the hotel to your right as you ascend toward Ivangrad. The Kolasin region is noted for its beautiful National Park, which is a starting point for climbing trips, hunting, fishing expeditions and for boat trips along the Tara and Drina rivers.

TITOGRAD

Historically Titograd, as Podgorica, disappeared in a rain of rubble during World War II. Since 1946 a completely modern industrial town has been built over the ruins of the past. There remain some Turkish mosques, a clock tower and above the town, forts and aqueducts from the Roman Period. North from Titograd you will see the centuries' old city of Diocles, built during the time of the Emperor Diocletian.

Hotel

CRNA GORA An exceptionally fine hotel located on Nemanjna Obala in the center of Titograd. Wide terraces and a large garden surround the hotel. Bedrooms at the Crna Gora, are very commodious, furnished in a comfortable fashion. Nothing elegant, but functional and in good taste. Large baths; twin-bedded rooms are available. Apartments are particularly pleasant. The Crna Gora is recommended should you wish a few days relaxation, in a non-resort area of limited historic interest.

Serbia

The Serbs are of Slavic origins and are ethnically related to the Croats. Their written language is expressed in Cyrillic lettering with certain other "sounds" added to correlate with the Serbian tongue. The Orthodox Church is predominant within Serbia. The Serbs crossed the pages of history 900 years after Christ following the migration of a primarily pastoral people from the Dniester area of Russia in the Balkan Peninsula during the 6th century. Serbia's political past is laden with centuries of warring and occupation by the Turks; the First and Second Balkan Wars, and the subsequent economic development of the republic within the context of the present Yugoslav State.

BELGRADE

The capital of the Serbian Republic and the Federated Socialist Republic of Yugoslavia is in central Serbia and picturesquely situated on a promontory overlooking the confluence of the Danube and Sava rivers. The bluff immediately above the two rivers is occupied by the ruins of the Belgrade fortress, Kalemegdan. Belgrade was the capital of the Serbian Kingdom at the end of the 19th century, becoming the capital of Yugoslavia in 1944. Sites of interest in Belgrade are not numerous, due to the severe destruction suffered during World War II. It is nonetheless an interesting and hospitable city. Tourist accommodations are excellent, restaurants are some of the best in Yugoslavia, the shops well worth inspection.

Sightseeing

Sights to see include the National Gallery; Ethnographical Museum, with exhibits of clothes and household effects of all the Yugoslavian provinces, and the Kalemegdan Fortress, in the center of the old Roman Sector. Near the Fortress is the City Zoo.

AVALA You might enjoy a ride out to Avala, a cool, very pleasant park of pines and firs, about 45 minutes by car. At the top of the one-way road is a gigantic green-marble block memorial to Yugoslavia's Unknown Soldier; the artistry of Sculptor Mestrovic. Nearby, the Yugoslav State Television antenna; at the top of the structure a restaurant providing guests with a thrilling view of the countryside.

HYDROFOIL TRIP TO THE "IRON GATES" Recommended for those spending upwards of three days in Belgrade, this is an all-day trip to a point on the Danube, through a series of cliffs in a particularly picturesque area of Serbia. Reasonably priced; daily trips throughout the summer.

DRIVE THROUGH DEDINJE TO TOPCIDER AND KOSUTNJAK This hour-long trip can be arranged with any taxi chauffeur. Dedinje is the suburban residential area of many embassies as well as the official residence of President Tito. Near the President's home is the palace of the former royal family.

Topcider and Kosutnjak form a large summer playground for residents of Belgrade. I recommend this very pleasant drive through the thickly wooded area, a 10-minute drive from downtown Belgrade. Within the park are the Yugoslav film studios, national sports training center, camping areas and a number of good restaurants.

TITO MUSEUM This is a comparatively new exposition housed in a modern building lying between Dedinje and Topcider. Displayed are the gifts presented to Marshal Tito by various Chiefs of State on the occasion of their visit to Yugoslavia.

FRESCO MUSEUM Here you will find copies of the most outstanding frescoes to be found in churches and old public buildings located throughout Yugoslavia.

NATIONAL DANCES Four nights weekly, during the summer, the National Kola Dancers of Yugoslavia perform at the Concert House located on the University Park in central Belgrade. A lively program in which regional dances are performed by groups representing the various republics and provinces of the country.

SHOPPING

Belgrade boasts a number of large department stores within walking distance of the main hotels. You'll enjoy touring these interesting stores and shops displaying merchandise of every type for the Yugoslavians as well as for tourists. Here are a number of shops selling various types of handwork; most items are reasonably priced.

Hotels

METROPOL Considered to be Belgrade's best hotel though I have second thoughts on this matter. A rather overwhelming modern structure, it is situated so that rooms on upper floors have an excellent view of the Danube. The hotel is two blocks from the National Bank, the central JAT office as well as the main post office. The Parliament is three blocks away.

Off the large lobby is a breakfast room which also is used as a lounge. To the right is a rather bleak bar area through which one continues to the restaurant. Dining facilities at the Metropol are austere and ornate. Piano in the evening; terrace at the rear of the hotel for outside dining. Food is excellent; service good. Prices are definitely higher here than elsewhere in the capital.

All rooms at the Metropol include bath and telephone. Upper rooms are inclined to be quite warm during summer months. The six apartments run about $24 per night, the price including breakfast. Streetside rooms catch the late afternoon sun making them warmer than rooms facing the park and Danube. There is also considerable noise. Book "off street side." Rooms are comfortably furnished though inclined to be more functional than attractive. Doubles and singles have the same size baths; apartment bathrooms are larger. The Metropol is much too big in every respect; too institutional. The very size of the structure defies any hope of intimacy. But it is clean, well serviced, adequately staffed, serving excellent food.

EXCELSIOR Located in the Kneza Milosa, a wide avenue along which are located a number of embassies, the Ministry of Defense, as well as the American Club. It is within two minutes walking time from JAT, the Parliament and 10 minutes by foot from the central shopping area. Facing a large park and former royal palaces, it is exposed to minimal traffic noises and provides a pleasant, intimate atmosphere. Small lobby, nicely decorated; restaurant with fine food and prompt service; bar.

Telephones and bath in all rooms; five apartments, doubles and singles. Toilets are separated from bathrooms. Rooms are clean, not large but comfortable. The Excelsior serves as a "home away from home" for a number of foreign businessmen obliged to remain some time in Yugoslavia. If an informal, more intimate surrounding is for you, I would certainly urge that you consider the Excelsior.

SLAVIJA An ultra-modernistic structure located at the end of Marshal Tito Avenue, a 15-minute walk from the central shopping area of Belgrade. Owned by the same association as the Metropol, the Slavija is a functional, clean hotel. The lobby seems ever full of loud milling tourists, most of them in groups. Reception personnel are polite though understandably harried. Off the lobby are a cafe terrace, bar and restaurant, which serves very fine food. Restaurant is very crowded at lunch time and tour groups do not improve matters. In the evening you might seek a reprieve by dining in the grill room on the mezzanine. Corridors are too narrow, the rooms positively Spartan. Rooms are comfortable, well lighted and clean. The Slavija is acceptable if you are not particularly conscious of your surroundings, and simply want something efficient, clean and available. The food is excellent; menus are varied and prices reasonable. Rooms with an eastern exposure are preferable during summer.

MAJESTIC Situated on a quiet street one block from the main shopping area. Telephones and baths are planned for all rooms; restaurant, bar and Belgrade's contribution to the casino trade are located on the premises.

PALACE A quiet, rather Left Bank atmosphere pervades this pleasant old hotel, located approximately three blocks off Belgrade's main thoroughfare. You may expect to find 40 doubles, 20 singles; approximately 135 beds with bath available. Rooms are furnished in a comfortable, old-fashioned style. Apartments include two rooms with double beds. Clean; all services. Rates are somewhat lower here at the Palace. There are two restaurants, one off the lobby and a Grill Room on the top floor. Dinner music; closed during summer.

MOSCOW Recommended only on an emergency basis. This hotel is, quite simply, from a time long past. Rooms are commodious and fairly clean; old-fashioned decor. Bathrooms, when available, are large. A severe noise factor here, as the Moscow is located on a main thoroughfare in the center of the principal business section. The restaurant here appears very clean, with a glass-walled kitchen to the rear. The room is, however, very stark in appearance. A cafe-terrace is located directly off the street and is crowded all day.

Restaurants

BEZISTAN Located in a busy shopping plaza in downtown Belgrade, the Bezistan would seem an excellent place for a quick snack. It is immediately inside the plaza in a section called "Terazije." Informal, quick service and average food. Fountains nearby cut the hustle-bustle of pedestrian traffic. Borba newspaper offices are nearby.

MARS NA DRIMU This is a nicely decorated, average sized restaurant located five minutes by taxi from the leading hotels. Clean. It is evidently popular with local people.

STADION Located within the confines of Belgrade's stadium, occupying a section of the ground floor and including a wide, tree-shaded terrace as well as indoor facilities. Music in the evening. Food is quite tasty here particularly if you order local specialities. Try the "Cebacece," or Shish-Kebab, salads, kaymak (cheese).

ZONA ZAMFIRKONA This restaurant is located a five-minute walk from the Hotel Slavija. Upstairs, strictly an informal restaurant decorated in the manner of a pub. Don't make the mistake of having your meal upstairs. Go to the basement level which is also very informal. It is one of the few places where you can eat while listening to Balkan music. Food is average to good – not outstanding – average prices.

DUSANOV GRAD One of the most outstanding restaurants in Belgrade. This restaurant occupies two floors of a building in the main shopping and business area of the capital, approximately half a block below the Hotel Moscow. The snack bar on the first floor is not recommended. Open for lunch and dinner, the Dusanov Grad's main dining facility is at the top of a short flight of stairs, directly above the snack bar. Dress casually but well. The pleasantly illuminated room is decorated with typical Serb motifs, weaponry and the like are employed in the design. Seats away from the windows are somewhat quieter. Excellent service. The food at Dusanov Grad is varied, tasty, and outstanding. Prices are somewhat higher here. The atmosphere is good, as you would expect to find in a first class restaurant in Vienna or Los Angeles. You will want to make more than one visit to the Dusanov Grad.

DVA JELENA This restaurant is outstanding for its game, dishes being prepared according to local recipes when such specialities are available. The Dva Jelena comes highly recommended by local food authorities.

DOM LOVACA Here Serbian specialities are reputed to be outstanding. Local authorities continue to favor this restaurant.

VINOGRAD Located somewhat outside of Belgrade. Judging from the name the wine should be particularly good and it comes highly recommended by many friends and associates in Belgrade. Fish and other local specialities are served and the location is particularly pleasant. Informal; luncheon is served.

ACA DEVETKA A particularly fine private restaurant, the Aca Devetka is located in the Kosutnjak section of Belgrade. Indoor and outdoor dining facilities are available in this delightful, intimate restaurant located deep in the forest of a suburban park. The Aca Devetka is located on the main road, approximately a 10-minute taxi ride from central Belgrade. National food served in attractive rural surroundings; informal; open for lunch and dinner during summer.

Night Life

Belgrade must be placed in that category of capital city in which "after hours" preoccupations center mainly about private or diplomatic functions. Restaurants in Belgrade are open until eleven or so and bars a bit later. You may enjoy good food, wines and dance music in most of the hotels, also in a few restaurants. Beyond that, there is little to offer the visitor.

KRYSTAL BAR Located in the sub-basement of an old building in downtown Belgrade. Guests are obliged to pay an entry fee. It is a large room dimly lighted, dank, cluttered, totally without appealing atmosphere.

Note: Eat late in Yugoslavia. Figure lunch hours between 1:30 and 3:00, dinner from 7:30. Naturally, there are many locations in which you can eat prior to these hours, but then you'll find yourself out of step with local tour programs, the office hours of higher officials and businessmen.

DECANI

The small, small town of Decani is located within the province of Kosovo-Metohija, approximately 190 kilometers northwest of Skopje and a few kilometers from the border of Albania. For the tourist Decani is but a turn in the road *except* for the magnificent Romanesque-Byzantine church which must be seen—the Monastery of Visoki Decani—the most outstanding church in Yugoslavia.

GRANCANICA

This particular monastery is located roughly a mile southwest of the town of Phistina on the main highway, and is approximately a 10-minute drive from the main road.

NIS

Nis is an industrial town in the southeastern section of Serbia, the second largest city in the republic and a junction point for visitors traveling between western Europe and Turkey. Situated on the River Nisava, it is approximately 75 kilometers from the Bulgarian border. Nis offers the tourist an archeological museum; a cathedral, and Turkish fort constructed during the Byzantine Period. As a token memento of the Turkish period, you may view the Tower of Skulls, constructed by the repressive Turkish occupation forces.

Hotel

AMBASSADOR A modern high-rise hotel constructed in the central downtown area of Nis. It is the only hotel in Nis recommended. The Ambassador was not open at the time of my visit. Appearances would indicate that the hotel would offer all the usual services including the usual quota of cafes, restaurants and bars. The Ambassador is rated as a first-class tourist unit and should be quite comfortable. An acceptable stop enroute to Bulgaria or driving through from the Adriatic.

Note: Enroute to Skopje from Nis, should you wish to avoid an extended lunch stop, you might tour the historic attractions in Nis, drive 50 kilometers southwest of the city to a roadside restaurant serving comparatively tasty food. Constructed as a combination fuel-food stop, this location is quite attractively situated. Food is served on the second level of the structure; the restaurant also offers a dining terrace.

NOVI SAD

Novi Sad presents an interesting opportunity to visit a portion of today's Yugoslavia, to witness the day-to-day activities of a particularly attractive group of Yugoslav citizenry living in one of Serbia's lovlier regions. Novi Sad is the capital of the province of Vojvodina. The town lies among the northeastern bank of the Danube River, linked by a bridge to the picturesque settlement of Petrovaradin situated on the opposite shore.

The year 1746 saw the declaration of the "Free Town of Novi Sad," and since that date the people have engaged in a remarkable effort to establish a manner of life independent of their surroundings, in the area of politics, commerce and cultural life. The first professional theater was opened here in 1861; three years later the well known Hungarian cultural institution, the "Matica srpska" left Budapest to be reopened in Novi Sad. There is a purposeful, yet semi-wistful, engaging quality in the inhabitants.

You should visit the Matica srpska library and its picture gallery. There is also the Bishop's Palace, in Byzantine style; the Uspenska Church, and the Zschorna Orthodox Church. The Gallery of Foreign Art displays paintings by Breughel, Veronese, Osterhuys and Rembrandt.

The Vojvodina National Park is located within a few miles of Novi Sad. Here you will find miles of hiking trails, one or two cafes and camping areas. Should you be interested in boating on the Danube, rowboats and small craft with outboard motors are available for rental through local tourist agencies. Take your boat up-river half a mile or so to a number of excellent locations for swimming, including a large municipally owned beach.

Hotel

PUTNIK This hotel is recommended as a lunch stop during your tour of Novi Sad. The Putnik is a congenial, clean, functional hotel located in downtown Novi Sad. Food, served on the terrace, is quite good; service adequate. Open for lunch and dinner. It is the availability of the magnificently appointed Hotel Tvrdjava in Petrovaradin that underlines my insistence you pass up the Putnik in favor of the Tvrdjava.

PARTIZANSKI VODA

The Zlatibor Plateau is in west-central Serbia, 250 kilometers due west of Belgrade in the direction of the Adriatic Sea. The summer and winter resort town of Partizanski Voda lies astride a secondary highway north of the Montenegrin border. Situated around a small but scenic lake, the resort is comprised of many small cottages, trade union rest lodges and the Hotel Palisad. There is not a great deal of social activity here; the emphasis is on rest, hiking or skiing and other sports. The resort is very popular with the Yugoslavs, many of them preferring Partizanski Voda to the seaside locations farther west.

Hotel

PALISAD Situated atop a small rise overlooking the Partizanski Voda Lake. Comprised of two separate buildings, it is encircled by green meadows and the rolling hills of the Zlatibor Plateau. A restaurant is located in the main building. The second building is an annex and it is in this unit that you should reserve your room.

Beneath the restaurant is a cafe, by day, and nightclub after dark. Oriented toward younger people, the place is jammed by nine o'clock. The restaurant cannot be recommended, a fatal comment when one realizes that no other public eating facilities are available for guests of this resort.

Nonetheless, the Palisad is an excellent place to meet the Yugoslavs, to draw a little closer to these people who, when not on a vacation, are usually too busy to relax.

Rooms in the main buildings are commodious, although lacking some of the more elemental amenities. I would book into the annex which is very pleasant, the public rooms furnished in a most delightful fashion with Serbian woodworking. A small, well stocked, bar is located on the ground floor as well as a pleasant cocktail lounge. Bedrooms in the annex are functional, comfortably furnished. Request a room with toilet; all rooms in the annex have showers except for the apartments. Cost of the rooms run around $6 with meals. The Palisad has its limitations, but you would enjoy one or two nights in this delightful location high in the mountains of west central Serbia.

PEC

Pronounced "Pech," this extremely interesting small town is located in the Kosovo-Metohija province of Serbia. It is the jumping-off place for your drive through the Cakor Pass to Montenegro. There is an extremely Oriental flavor to the town, part of this due to those Moslem settlements in the region as well as Albanian influences. For centuries Pec has been of importance to the Serbian Orthodox Church and, since the early Christian era, it has been known for the gold and silver filigree work done by local artisans. It is essential that you visit the Monastery of the Patriarch located at the western end of the town. Here you will find a Church School, a compound enclosing three or four separate churches uniquely joined together in a single building. The entire area surrounding the churches is a delight. A small stream runs through the compound from nearby mountains. Parking in the area is very limited.

Hotel

METOHIJA Named after the province in which the hotel is located. Truly a find. It is located near the western end of the town, approximately three blocks from the road running toward the monastery. Built of stone, the rather somber brown-colored building resembles an elaborate city hall. The interior is furnished in a comfortable mid-thirties style. All rooms with shower, apartments with bath; singles are available. Room rates are reasonable, doubles costing approximately $5 and apartments $8. Rooms to the rear include small balconies overlooking the dining terrace. Bedrooms are well furnished, comfortable and clean. The restaurant at the Metohija is exceptionally well managed and serves excellent food. I would suggest you eat on the partially covered terrace to the side of the restaurant as the Spanish surroundings are truly delightful.

PETROVARADIN

Mark this stop with four stars and plenty of exclamation marks. A visit to Petrovaradin is an occasion you will not soon forget. Among the sights of interest is the Petrovaradin Fortress, occupying the site of a former Roman settlement. It was rebuilt by Empress Maria Theresa of Austria to form an Austrian military frontier against the Turks.

Hotel

TVRDJAVA Following World War II, and up until 1966, the former barracks and storerooms of Petrovaradin were used as quarters for students attending the University in Novi Sad. Recently the Yugoslavian Government, working through local tourist offices, has remodeled the interior of the principal dormitory into one of the most sumptuous hotels I have visited. The hotel offers all possible services. Nearby, a second building houses a public restaurant, including a wide terrace for summer dining with a delightful view across the Danube to Novi Sad. The hotel restaurant, during summer, is open early for breakfast and lunch. Dinners may be enjoyed on the terrace of the nearby reataurant or in the enclosed dining room of the facility. Below the restaurant is a form of keller where in the evening a gypsy orchestra plays. Prices are moderate at both the restaurants and keller.

Decorations and furnishings of the entire hotel are magnificent. Three apartments are available, comprised of a sitting room, sleeping alcove and modern bathroom facilities. Bedrooms on the second floor are all doubles. All have baths; twin-bedded rooms to the rear. The third floor is somewhat more Spartan and informal compared to the heavier Empire styles used on the lower floors; all single rooms here. Rates for the apartments come to roughly $20 a day with breakfast; doubles $10; singles fall within the range of $6 to $8.

PRISTINA

The medium-sized town of Pristina is 87 kilometers northeast of Skopje among the gently rolling plateau country of west-central Serbia. It sits astride the main highway running from the capital of Macedonia to Belgrade; Pristina is a junction point for those driving from Belgrade or Skopje to Montenegro. For these reasons I review hotel facilities here. Pristina does not itself offer any outstanding historic attractions although the Monastery of Gracanica is located a mile southeast of town. Formerly noted for its mining and commercial interests, the central part is composed of relatively modern buildings, broad avenues and many small shops. See the Turkish Sultan's Mosque and an 18th-century clock tower. The infamous Battlefield of Kosovo is located not too far from here.

Hotel

KOSOVSKI BOZUR This is strictly a provincial operation. The Kosovski Bozur is in the central section of town, toward the southeast entrance to Pristina. The rear section is preferable, so book "Double and rear section"; only double rooms have bathrooms with toilets. The front section is somewhat older though subject to more street noise. The restaurant of the hotel serves comparatively good food. Nearby is a cafe or breakfast room, rather on the grim side but service is quick.

On the roof, a small enclosed snack bar serving drinks; terrace, music for dancing. Directly across the street from the hotel you'll find a local "pub" complete with Serbian music, a good opportunity to witness a true, provincial Yugoslav night spot. The Kosovski Bozur is strictly a stopover enroute one of the more outstanding tourist towns nearby. But don't hesitate to spend a night here. The hotel is clean and acceptably managed; the food average to good.

TITOVO UZICE

This medium-sized industrial town, situated in west central Serbia is historically noteworthy. One of the oldest towns in Serbia, it was the scene, in 1941, of an uprising resulting in the eventual return of Yugoslavian independence from the Germans. An imposing statue of Marshal Tito is in the main square, as well as a museum relating to the freedom movement. An old Roman fortress may be seen on the hills over the town.

Hotel

PALACE The town of Titovo Uzice is a good lunch stop on the way to Partizanski Voda. The Hotel Palace, situated just above a small park in a central section of town, has indoor and terrace dining facilities. The hotel is roughly a two hours' drive from Belgrade. Food is excellent; service above average.

Macedonia

Macedonia, which has been occupied by many nations, is today usually associated with either Greece or Yugoslavia for it is, in fact, these two countries who control the destiny of the Macedonian people. Following World War I the Treaty of Neuilly tended to fix the boundaries of Macedonia much as they are today, that is, as a distinct region within the boundaries of Yugoslavia and Greece. During World War II see the re-entry of Bulgaria into Macedonian affairs. By 1944, however, Bulgaria had withdrawn her troops and Macedonia finally came to rest within the provincial territorial limits prescribed by the 1919 Treaty of Neuilly. Approximately 900,000 people of the Macedonian region of Yugoslavia, living on upwards of 10,000 square miles of land, were finally incorporated into the Federal People's Republic of Yugoslavia in 1946. More than two million Macedonians now live in Greece.

BITOLA

Bitola is the second largest town in Macedonia, situated in a fertile valley of the Pelegonian Plain. It is a lovely area with numerous orchards and grazing areas, the rich soil standing out in sharp contrast to the barren cliffs and craggy peaks of nearby mountains. Those driving to Ohrid or farther on to Athens will pass through this town. You will want to visit the old mosques and churches grouped around the central Veliki Plostad Square bisected by the main highway. Here also are the Yeni Mosque and a clock tower and the Orthodox Cathedral of Saint Dimitrije. Nearby, a Turkish bath "Hamam" and covered bazaar. Driving toward Bitola note the picturesque river town of Tito

Veles, where buildings built over the river provide excellent material for photographs or paintings. The town of Tito Veles is one of the oldest communities in the Balkans, founded 216 B.C.

OHRID

Ohrid, a remarkably picturesque town of 19,000, lies on the eastern shore of Lake Ohrid in the southwestern tip of Yugoslavia. Site of Macedonia's annual Summer Festival, Ohrid plays host to artists from other Yugoslavian republics, the Macedonian National Theater, Belgrade Madrigal Choir, Chamber Music ensembles from Skopje while enjoying numerous recitals by leading performers of the Yugoslav concert world. Its historic background is exceptional and its geographical setting a delight. As a resort Ohrid is not important enough to merit the long, rather tedious drive from Skopje. You would be wiser to visit the Adriatic Coast. Resort facilities at Ohrid are far below the par established by seaside locales in Montenegro and Dalmatia, as well as the mountain and lake regions of Slovenia. Should you be interested in visiting historic old town of churches, forts, architectural and religious treasures, Ohrid fills the bill.

Lake Ohrid ranks with the Caspian Sea, Lake Baykal and the Nyassa Lakes as one of the rarest inner seas known to man. The water is quite transparent, giving impetus to the search for the many rare fossils to be found there. Various types of algae, two types of trout and several rare species of sponge are also to be found in this lake. Historic buildings and sites which should be visited include the Church of Saint Nikola Bolnicki; Church of Bogorodica Bolnicka; numerous other churches and the 5th-century Citadel, residence of King Samuilo. A thorough tour of the town, its churches, amphitheaters, castles and museum will occupy your time for two or three days.

Hotel

GRAND HOTEL PALACE Near Lake Ohrid, this is a modernistic structure with a total lack of appeal. A large lobby exits onto a partially enclosed terrace; a cafe terrace is nearby where there is dancing in the evening. The restaurant, with dining terrace, is mediocre. The best rooms at the Palace face the dining terrace and nearby lake, with a fair view of distant mountains and nearby Castle. These rooms are noisy until a late hour. Bedrooms are functional and that is all. Bathrooms were not clean.

SKOPJE

Skopje's importance was based on the city's strategic position midway between the Adriatic Sea and the Dardanelles Straits, between the Danube River and the Aegean Sea. It is only within the contest of this broad geographical panorama and the ever-shifting winds of political expediency that one can fully appreciate the turbulent tale of an incredibly brave people and their city. Skopje has recognized the authority of many masters: the Byzantines, Serbs, Bulgars and Turks, and natural disasters have on countless occasions attempted to stem the course of her physical development.

To the left of the River Vadar lies the Old Town, the center of Skopje's economic and cultural life for centuries. On the right bank of the river lies the modern city, to some degree recovered from the earthquake of 1963. The two sections of town are connected by the "Kameni most," 15th-century stone bridge. On the left bank is the National Theater; the Dimitrius Church, Library and the Daut Pasha Hamam (bath), built in 1466 and now an art museum. Up Marshal Tito Avenue is the Church of Saint Spas and on the top of the nearby hill is the Palace of Dusan. You certainly must take the time to tour the Bazaar.

You would do well to visit Skopje. There is, as yet, not a great deal to offer the tourist in the way of creature comforts. The hotel is far from tops; there are few theaters, restaurants and parks. But I feel it is important that we visit Skopje in an effort to witness the courage of a people who, in defiance of urban planning studies and the physical laws of nature, have shown a determination to reconstruct their city on the exact location it has occupied since the 5th century. Moreover, you'll find the Old Town interesting, the townspeople most hospitable.

Hotel

GRAND Skopje's largest and best hotel. On the right bank of the

Vardar River, the Grand offers the usual number of services on a most efficient, pleasant manner. The restaurant is located beyond the lobby and lounge, and has indoor and outdoor dining facilities. Dancing nightly on the nearby terrace. The restaurant of the Grand serves exceptionally tasty food; service is prompt and efficient. Bedrooms at the Grand are merely functional, but very well maintained. Bathrooms are clean. Most rooms offer only showers. Book your room on the dining terrace side, east wing of the hotel, where you will be less bothered by traffic noise. The Grand is situated at a busy intersection and rooms overlooking the front entrance can be quite noisy. The Grand escaped the 1963 holocaust as construction had only just begun, and what damage occurred was easily repaired.

Restaurants

MACEDONIA HOUSE Located in the Old Town directly beside the "Kale," the Macedonia House is a delightful restaurant made up of several small salons and porches, kellers and verandas. The entire interior has been restored to its original late 1890 design. Food and services are beyond reproach. Open for lunch and dinner; reasonable prices.

SARAJ The location of the Saraj is quite attractive, with willows, gardens, and parklike surroundings. Food and service-wise it is poor.

CARDAK

Ten minutes outside of Skopje lies the hillside monastery community of Mount Skopska Crna Gora. You may tour the monasteries; maps are available showing the location of each cloister. The general area of the monasteries is well beyond the Old Town section of Skopje, some distance from the Vardar River. Among this group of church buildings is the Saint Ijlen Monastery featuring the Cardak Restaurant. The Cardak, located in one of the first of the several monastery compounds, is open for lunch and dinner. Wine is served; prices are low. I recommend the Cardak only for a glass of wine or a cup of Turkish coffee while touring the monasteries. The food and service and generally disorderly appearance of the dining area are uninviting.

Index

INDEX

Aband Hotel, 406-407
Abbazia, *see* Opatiya
Abdul Hamid, Sultan, 353
Abdullah's Farm Restaurant, 421-422
Abdul Mecit, Sultan, 415
Aca Devetka Restaurant, 507
Academy of Arts and Science, Yugoslavian, 489
Acropolis, 425
Adamclisi, 282
Adand, Plains of, 348
Adelsberger Grottoes, 486
Adria Restaurant, 261
Adrianople, 136. *See* Edirne
Adriatic Coast resorts, 441-444; 445; 456-481
Adriatic Sea, 439
Aegean Sea, 348, 439
Aeroflot, 87, 145
Aesculapium, 426
Agora, 426
AGPOL, 238
Agrarian People's Union, 11
Ahmet III, Fountain of, 416
Ahmet, Sultan, Mosque, 367, 414-415, 417
Air France, 87, 364
airplane travel, 13, 86, 87, 88, 144, 145-147, 153, 218, 222, 287, 288, 363, 364, 371, 437-438
    Bulgarian, 13
    Czechoslovakian, 86, 87-88
    Hungarian, 145-147
    Polish, 222
    Romanian, 287
    Turkish, 364
    Yugoslavian, 437-438
Air India, 87
Akanara, 372
Akcakale, 368
Akheloy Restaurant, 68, 72
Alabardas Restaurant, 161, 181

Aladga Monastery, 64
Alak, Garden of, 65
Alba Iulia, 298, 314
Albania, 433
Alba Regis Days, 167
Alba Restaurant, 268
Albatros Hotel, 335, 340
    Restaurant, 340
Alcron Hotel, 102, 105, 108
    Restaurant, 95, 105, 108
Aleppo, 368
Alexander, II, Czar, 28, 48
Alexander the Great, 281, 401-402, 424, 425
Alexander Nevzky Memorial Church, 28, 29, 32
Allstein. *See* Olsetyn
Alpine zone, hunting area, 305
Ambassador Hotel (Bucharest) 307, 311, 312
    Restaurant, 311
Ambassador Hotel (Nis), 508
    Restaurant, 508
Ambassador Hotel (Opatiya), 430, 465-466
    Restaurant, 465
Ambassador Hotel (Prague), 107
    Restaurant, 107
American Automobile Club, 151
American coffee, 379
American Express, 92
Amica Restaurant, 249
ammunition, importing of, 84, 217, 305
amphora jugs, 74
Anadolu Express. *See* Ankara Express
Anatolia, 348, 350, 353, 366, 368, 372
Ancona, 439
Andrew, King, remains of, 189
Ankara, 347, 348, 364, 365, 366, 368, 371-376, 389, 393, 394,

399-406
 airport, 362
 campsites, 397
 Express, 365, 366
Antalya, 348, 368, 396
 campsite, 397
 motel, 396
antiques, 102, 103, 163, 164, 235, 456
Antonescu, 280
Apostolik, 183
Aydin, motel at, 396
aquaduct, 425
Arad, 314-315
Arany Bika Hotel, 198
 Restaurant, 198
Arany Csillag, 186
 Restaurant, 186, 187
Arany Homok Hotel, 199-200
 Restaurant, 200
Ararat, Mt. 348
Arbanasy District, 47, 48
Arbore, Church of, 332
Archaeological items, exporting of, 435
Archaeological Museums, 38, 50, 323, 343, 344, 417, 426, 471, 490
 Cluj, 323
 Istanbul, 417
 Izmir, 426
 Mamaia, 343, 344
 Plovdiv, 38
 Pula, 471
 Varna, 50
 Zagreb, 490
archaelogical site, 281
Archangel, Church of, 40
Architects Restaurant, 254
Arda Hotel, 68
Argentine Hotel, 460, 461
 Restaurant, 460, 461
Argonauts, 282

Arkadia Restaurant, 266
Arknica, spa at, 230
Arkutyno, 75
Arkutyno Restaurant, 75, 76
Arlberg-Orient Express, 287
Arnaudi Mosque, 493
Arpad Bridge, 174, 179
Artand, 142
art galleries, 29, 32, 307, 308, 311, 462, 476-477, 489
artists' colony, 176
Artus Court, 251
Ascension, Church of, 47
Assenograd, 40, 43
Assen Quarter, 48
Asia Minor, 348
Astoria Hotel (Baltonfured) 186
Astoria Hotel (Golden Sands) 56, 60
 Restaurant, 56
"asure", 379
Ataturk, Kemal, 352, 353, 354, 373, 400, 402, 406
 home of, 402, 406
 tomb, 402
Atlantic Hotel, 117-118
Atlas Tourist Agency, 436
Athenaeum, The, 308
Athenée Palace Hotel, 307, 308-309, 311, 312
 Restaurant, 309
Athens, 14, 76, 287, 438
AUA, *See* Austrian Airlines.
Ausgleich of 1867, 137
Augustine Monastery, 111
Augustow, 221
Austria, 433
Aurora Hotel, 341
Auschwitz, *See* Oswiecim.
Austerlitz, 80
Austria, 82, 86, 123, 134, 142, 147, 208, 209, 280
Austrian Airlines, 13, 87, 145, 218,

287, 438
Austrian cooking, 23
Austro-Hungarian monarchy, 137, 259, 281, 431
auto maps, 16, 98, 99, 152, 238-239
Autotehna, 441. *See also* Hertz
auto travel, 15, 16, 24, 25, 84, 85, 86, 87, 145, 150-151, 218, 219-221, 284, 286, 296-299, 362, 367, 368, 393-394, 440-441
    Bulgarian, 15, 16
    Czechoslovakian, 17
    Hungarian, 150-151
    Polish, 219-221
    Romanian, 286, 296-299
    Turkish, 367, 393-394
    Yugoslavian, 440-441
Avis Car Rental, 441. *See also* Kombas.
Avala Hotel, 458
Avala Park, 502
"ayran," 24, 74, 406

Bacau, 315
badger, 398
Baghdad Express, 365
Baile Herculane, 315-316
Baja, 170
    stud farm, 170
Bakirköy, Beach at, 417
"baklava," 379
Bakony, forest of, 171, 172
Bakony, Mountain riding trail, 171
Balassagyarmat, 86, 142
Balaton, Lake, 135, 156, 158, 159, 162, 167, 168, 171, 181, 184-195
    Riding tour, 169, 170
Balaton Hotel (Siofok) 192, 193
Balaton Hotel (Sunny Beach) 69
Balaton Restaurant, 234, 248
Balatonfured, 185-187, 189, 193
Balchik, 64
Baldwin, Emperor, 350
Baldwin Tower, 47
Balikesir, 396, 428
Balkan Hotel (Gabrovo) 51
Balkan Hotel (Sofia) 29, 30, 31, 33, 34, 40
    Restaurant, 34
Balkantourist, 16, 17, 18, 20, 21, 30, 31, 35, 53, 63, 66, 73, 76, 152
Balkantourist Hotels, 18, 22, 23, 37, 46, 47, 49, 50, 51, 74, 75
    in Haskovo, 37
    in Kavatsite, 74, 75
    in Rila, 46
    in Schipka Pass, 47
    in Stara Zagora, 51
    in Turnovo, 47, 49, 50
    in Vidin, 51
Balkantourist Motels, 52
Balkantourist training school, 57
ballet, 308
balls, 167
Balt-Orient Express, 14, 89, 147, 287
ban, 283
Banat Province, 278, 331, 335
Banatul Hotel, 331-332
    Restaurant, 332
Baneasa, 284, 285, 287, 308, 313
    airport, 287, 308
    park, 313
Banfe House, 320
Banitsa, 23, 24
Banja Luka, 431, 492, 493

Banreva, 142
Banska Bystrica, 122, 123, 127
Bar, 439, 456, 478, 479, 498, 499, 500
"baratfule", 162
barber shops, 31, 54, 448, 450
Barbicon, 243
bargaining, 389, 391-392
Baricska Csarda Restaurant, 187
Bari, 439
Barikan Hotel, 405
Barrel Restaurant, 70
Bartok, Bela, 174
Bascaraijä Restaurant, 497
Basel, 287
Basil, Emperor, 349
Baskent Restaurant, 403
bass, 398
Batchkovo Monastery, 39, 40, 43
Bath, Harkany, 170
baths, 188
 Turkish, 383-384, 514
Batory, The, 218, 251
Batsanyi, Janos, 188
Baumberg, Gabriele, 188
Baum, Vicki, 267
bazaars, 391, 392, 409, 411-412, 414, 493, 496, 497, 514
Bazaar Hotel, 234, 264-265, 266
 kawiarnia, 265
 restaurant, 265
BEA, 364
bear, hunting of, 305, 398, 455
Bedesten, 411-412
beef goulash, 96
"Beer Wagon" Restaurant, *see* Carul Cu Berr.
Beethoven, Ludwig van, 81, 116, 124, 167, 175
 concerts, 167
 piano of, 175
Beirut, 367, 368

Bekir Restaurant, 405
Bela, King, 174, 175
Belgrade, 32, 89, 147, 152, 219, 433, 437, 438, 444, 452, 498, 499, 500, 501-507
 Belgrade Madrigal Choir, 515
 Rakpart, 142
Bellevue Hotel (Pohorje), 485
 Restaurant, 485
Bellevue Restaurant (Stary Smokovec), 129
Bellevue Villa camping site, 468
belly dance, *see* Ciftetelli
Belogradchik, 77
Belogradchik Rocks, 77
Belvarso Templom, 174
Belvedere Hotel (Prague) 110
Belvedere Hotel (Opatiya) 466
 Restaurant, 466
Belweder, The, 243
Berane Hotel, 499-500
 Restaurant, 500
Bergama Motel, 396, 428
Berkovitsa Hotel, 77
Berlin, 89, 219, 287, 438
Berlin Restaurant (Bucharest) 312-313
Berlin Restaurant (Budapest) 182
Berlin Restaurant (Sofia) 35
Bessarabia, 277, 280, 281
Bethelehem Chapel, 103
Beyazit, Tower of, 415
Bezistan Restaurant, 505
Bialystek, 261
"biber dolmasi," 377
Bicaz, 303
Bicaz Hotel, 290
Biekitna Restaurant, 254
"bigos," 230
Biharkeresztes, 142
Bikel Hotel, 69
Binbirdirek, 416
Birth of Christ Church, 48

INDEX 525

Bisevo Islands, 477
bison, hunting, 211
Bistritsa Hotel, 315
Bitola, 514
Bitex Shops, 390-391
Bjelasica Hotel, 500
Blachernae Palace, 416
Black Bear Restaurant, *see* Cerny Medved.
Black Church, 317
black market, 212
Black Sea, 9, 348, 413
  excursion, 76
  resorts, 14, 18, 53-77, 278, 290, 334-344, 363
Blagoevgrad, 51
Blejaki Castle, 482
Bled, 482-483
  Lake, 482
Blue Mosque, *see* Ahmet, Sultan, Mosque
boar, hunting of, 101, 173, 305, 330, 345, 398, 455
boat travel, 167, 171, 172, 222, 366-367, 439, 477, 482, 500, 509
Bohemia, 79, 80, 81, 82, 88, 95, 96, 98, 116, 118, 120, 122
Bohemian cooking, 95, 96
Bojana, 29, 33, 34, 35
  Church of, 29
  Restaurant Folk Evening, 35
Boleslaw the Brave, 207
Bolu, 396, 406-407
Bonavia Hotel, 472
Bor Hotel, 36
Borevets Mountains, 36
Borharapo Restaurant, 193
Borik Hotel Association, 481
Boris III, 11
Bors, 284, 285
"borsch", 23, 230
Borsod Express, 147

Borszony, 172
Bosnia-Hercegovina, 431, 432, 433, 442, 454, 455, 492-498
Bosnia Hotel, 493
  Restaurant, 493
Bosphorus, 414
Bota Rece Restaurant, 333
Boulevard Hotel, 324, 328
  Restaurant, 324
Bourgas, 51
Brac Islands, 477
Braha Restaurant, 109
Bran Castle, 316
Brandenburger, 263
Brasov, 279, 288, 298, 304, 315, 316-319, 326, 329
Bratianu, Ion, 280
Bratislava, 79, 80, 81, 89, 91, 122, 123-125, 175, 287
  Castle, 79, 125
Breaza, 278
Brela, 457
Breslau, *see* Wroclaw
Breughel, paintings by, 123, 509
Brioni Hotel, 466
Bris Hotel, 59
Bristol Hotel (Mostar) 494-495
Bristol Hotel (Tuzla) 498
Bristol Hotel (Warsaw) 218, 223, 235, 247-248
  Restaurant, 247, 248
Bristol Hotel (Zagreb) 490-491, 492
Brno, 79, 80, 95, 100, 110-114
  Industrial Fair, 111
Bromberg, 211
Bruckenthal Museum, 326, 327
Brussa, *see* Bursa
Brussels, 287
Bucharest, 13, 55, 89, 277, 278, 286, 287, 288, 300, 301, 303, 304, 307-314, 326, 329, 335, 337, 363

Bucharest Restaurant (Cluj) 322
Bucharest Restaurant (Mamaia) 341
Bucharest Summer Theater, 337
Buchlov, Castle of, 81
Buchlovice Estate, 79, 81
Buchvata Restaurant, 70, 71
Bucovice, 111
Bucuresti Restaurant, 312
Buda Hills, 175
Budapest, 134, 135, 138, 139, 142, 145, 147, 153, 155, 156, 158, 167, 168, 170, 172, 173-184, 287
  International Fair, 167
Budagyongyes, 183
Budva, 457-458
Buk Forest, 172
Bukk Mountains, 170
Bukovina, *see* Moldavia.
Bukovina Restaurant, 334
Bulgaria, 9-77, 280, 281, 284, 288, 300, 348, 350, 363, 365, 433, 439, 508
  air travel, 13
  auto travel, 15, 16
  Balkantourist, 16-18, 20, 21, 30, 31, 35, 53, 63, 66, 73, 76, 152
  Black Sea resorts, 53-77
  Blagoevgrad, 51
  Bojana, 29
  Borovets, 39
  Bourgas, 51
  bungalows, 69-70
  camping, 52-53
  cars, 15, 16
  currency, 11, 12
  customs, 12
  Dimitrovgrad, 51
  drink, 23-24
  Drouzhba, 63-64
  food, 23, 24
  Friendship Beach, *see*
  Drouzhba.
  Gabrovo, 51
  Golden Sands, 55-62
  group tours, 25
  guides, 24-25
  Haskovo, 37
  history, 9-11
  hotels, 18-23, 29-34, 36, 37, 40-42, 43-44, 45-46, 47, 49-50, 51, 56-59, 63, 67-69, 70
  language, 11
  mail, 26
  money, 11-12
  motoring, 15, 16
  motels, 51-52
  Mramor, 51
  photography, 26
  picnics, 73-74
  Pleven, 37-38
  Plovdiv, 38-42
  Pomporovo, 43, 44
  Quiet Nest, 64-65
  restaurants, 23-24, 34-35, 42, 59-62, 63-64, 70-73
  Rila Mts. Area, 44-46
  Schipka Pass, 46-47
  sightseeing, 28-29, 38, 39-40, 44-45, 47-49
  Slunchev Bryag, 65-76
  Sofia, 28-35
  souvenirs, 26, 27
  Stara Zagora, 51
  Sunny Beach, 65-76
  table sharing, 27
  Tenha Yava, 64-65
  tourist industry, 16-18
  trains, 14, 15
  traveling in, 14-16
  traveling to, 13-14
  Turnovo, 47-50
  Vidin, 51
  visas, 13
  Zlantni Pyassatsi, 55-62

INDEX 527

Bulgaria Hotel (Plovdiv), 42
Bulgaria Hotel (Sofia), 29, 32, 33, 34
Bulgarian Orthodox Church, 45
Bulvar Palas Hotel, 404-405, 406
  Restaurant, 404
bungalows, 66, 69, 70, 75, 76, 229, 303-304, 448, 453, 454, 468, 471
Burdur, 396
Burgas, 9, 13, 14, 65, 74, 75,
Bursa, 347, 384, 396, 397, 407-410, 428
Business Fair for the Near East, 426, 427
Busko, spa at, 230
bustard, hunting, 173, 305
bus travel, 89, 91, 145, 149, 221, 368, 371, 440
Buyouk Mosque, 29
Buyuk Efes Hotel, 427
Buyuk Oberj, 409-410
Bydgoszcz, 226, 250
Byzantine Empire, 10, 28, 349, 350, 414, 416, 424, 442, 464

cab drivers, bargaining with, 391
cables, 102, 104, 173, 241, 306,
  Czechoslovakia, 102
  Hungry, 173,
  Poland, 241
  Romania, 306
  Turkey, 398
"cacik," 378
Café Central Restaurant, 476
Café Emke, 184

Café Lil, 119-120
Cakaloglu Caravansarays, 425
Callatis, *see* Mangalia.
cameras, 26, 99, 143-144, 165, 217, 239, 302, 362, 395, 435
camping, 52, 53, 76, 98, 100, 168-169, 176, 189, 202, 229, 230, 290, 303, 304, 338, 396, 397, 429, 441, 448, 453, 454, 456, 468, 488, 489, 502, 509
  Bulgaria, 52-53
  Czechoslovakia, 99-100
  Hungary, 168, 202
  Poland, 229-230
  Romania, 303-304
  Turkey, 396, 397
  Yugoslavia, 453-454
Campio Formio, Treaty of, 443
Canakkale, 397
Canli Balik Restaurant, 422-423
Capuchin Church, 174
Caraorman, forest of, 345
Cardak, 517
Cardak Restaurant, 517
car rental, 15, 90, 145, 150-152, 298-299, 395, 436, 440
car travel, 15, 16, 24, 25, 84, 85, 86, 87, 145, 150-151, 218, 219-221, 284, 286, 296-299, 362, 367, 368, 393, 394, 440, 441
Carol, King, 280, 335
carp, fishing for, 344, 398
Carpathian forest, 305
Carpathian Mountains, 82, 210, 229, 277, 278, 279
Carpathian stag, 305
Carpati, 284, 287, 288-291, 292, 293, 298, 299, 300, 304, 305, 309, 313, 318, 319, 321, 325, 330, 332, 334, 335, 336, 337, 339, 342, 436
  Express, 287

Hotel, 317-318, 319
  Tours, 284, 330
Carton Hotel, 125
Carul Cu Bere Restaurant, 313
cascade, 110
cashcaval, 294
Casimir The Great, 207
Casino Restaurant (Cluj) 323
Casino Restaurant (Golden Sands), 60, 71, 72
casino, gambling, 54, 62, 71, 343, 467, 475, 476
Caspian Sea, 515
castles, 79, 80, 81, 103, 104, 124, 125, 167, 170, 175, 316, 482
castle hill, 174, 181, 184
catacombs, 494
catfish, 398
cathedrals, 79, 175
cathedral hill, 262
caviar, 23, 295
caves, 122
"cebacece," 445, 506
CEDOK, 80, 83, 84, 89, 91, 92, 93, 95, 98, 99, 100, 101, 104, 108, 113, 114, 117, 130, 152, 436
  maps, 98, 100
  restaurant guide, 108
Celik Palas Hotel, 409
  Restaurant, 409
Cengil Restaurant, 497
cenotaph, 46, 47
Central Hotel (Brno), 110
Central Hotel (Karlov Vary) 117, 118
  Restaurant, 118
Central Restaurant, *see* Merkez Lokanta
Cerbul Carpatin Restaurant, 318-319
"cerkes Tavugu," 378
Cerna Restaurant, 316

Cerna Valley, campsite, 303
Cernin Palace, 104
Cerny Medved Restaurant, 113, 114
Cesky Krumlov, 79, 114-115
Cesky Krumlov Hotel, 115
Cesme, 396
Cetinnje, 498
"cevap," 445
Chaika, 68, 69
Chaika Hotel, 72
Chalupki, 86
chamois, 101, 305, 455
Charles IV, 104
Charles Bridge, 104
Charles Robert of Anjou, 176
chauffeurs, 15, 90, 298, 299, 393, 441
Cheb, 116
chepellare, 40
chewing gum, 306
children's fares, 14, 15
children's visas, 83
Chilia Veche, 345
Chinese food, 249
"choolbastia," 445
Chop, 86
Chopin, Frederick, 205, 244
churches, 29, 39, 40, 47, 48, 79, 111, 122, 255, 274-275, 317, 332, 458, 489, 515
Chusrev-Beg Mosque, 496
Cieszyn, 86
ciftetelli, 302
cigarettes, 84, 217, 307, 362
Cina Restaurant (Bucharest), 311-312
Cina Restaurant (Timisoara), 332
Cinar Hotel, 420
Ciovo, Island of, 477
circus, 120
citadel, 399, 401-402
Citadella Hotel, 180, 181

Citadella Restaurant, 183
Ciuperca Restaurant, 330
Clark, Adam, 174
Climate, 9, 135, 348, 372, 401, 429, 434, 451, 469
Cloister Church, 458
Cluj, 298, 303, 304, 320-322
coin collection, 326
Cominform, 432
Communism, 11, 137, 138
Compromise of 1867, 137
concentration camp, 261
concerts, 167, 308
Constanta, 13, 281, 282, 284, 285, 287, 288, 290, 302, 303, 335
Constantin and Elena, Church of, 39
Constantine, Emperor, 175, 349, 413, 416
Constantine, Grand Duke, 243
Constantinople, 136, 349, 350, 353, 400, 413, 431. *See also* Istanbul.
Constantsa, 343-344
Constanza, Romania, 55
Continental Hotel (Cluj) 320, 321
    Restaurant, 321
Continental Hotel (Iasi) 333, 334
Continental Hotel (Pilsen) 120, 121
    Restaurant, 95, 121
Continental Hotel (Prague) 113
    Restaurant, 113
Continental Hotel (Szczecin), 269-270
    Restaurant, 270
Continental Restaurant (Bucharest) 313
cook-out, 343
Cook Wagon-Lits, 92, 439
Co-operative Area Manuals, 327
Copenhagen, 287
"corbas," 294
cormorant, 305, 345

Corso Hotel, 119, 120
costume pageant, 167
Cotnari Restaurant, 333-334
Covo Turist Agentesi, 393
Cozia Monastery, 327
Croatia, 472, 487-492
Crana Postavarul Restaurant, 319
cranes, 345
Crater Lake, 402
Cristal Hotel, 119, 120
Crona Gora Hotel, 501
Crowns, Czech, 82
Crusades, 349, 350
crystal, 102
Crystal Restaurant, 249
CSA, 88, 89, 145
CSAD, 89
Cubek, 402
Culture and Rest Park (Bucharest) 307
Culture Park (Izmir) 426
Curie, Marie, home of, 243
Curraczarda Restaurant, 194
Currencies, 11-12, 82-83, 139-140, 212-214, 283, 359-360, 434-435, 451-452
    Bulgaria, 11-12
    Czechoslovakia, 82-83
    Hungarian, 139-140
    Polish, 212-214
    Romanian, 283
    Turkish, 359-360
    Yugoslavia, 434-435
Currency declarations, 140, 213
customs, 12-13, 83-86, 140-144, 145, 146, 147, 215-217, 284-286, 361-362, 435
    Bulgaria, 12-13
    Czechoslovakia, 83-86
    Hungary, 140-147
    Poland, 215-217
    Romania, 284-286

Turkey, 361-362
Yugoslavia, 435
customs free shop, 145
Cuza, Alexander, 280
Czechoslovakia, 20, 79-131, 134, 136, 137, 142, 147, 152, 208, 209
    airplane travel, 86, 87-88
    antiques, 102, 103
    auto maps, 98, 99
    auto travel, 17
    Banska Bystrica, 122-123
    bars, 109, 110
    Bohemia, 79, 80, 81, 82, 88
    Bratislava, 123-125
    Brno, 110-114
    bus travel, 89
    cables, 102
    camping, 99, 100
    cars, 17
    car rental, 90
    currency, 82, 83
    customs, 83-86
    CEDOK, 91
    Cesky Krumlov, 114-115
    excursions, 104, 105
    fishing, 101
    foods, 95-97
    geography, 81, 82
    Gottwaldov, 115
    group tours, 99
    guides, 97-98
    hotels, 91-94, 105-108, 111-113, 115, 116-117, 118-119, 120, 121, 122, 124-125, 126, 127, 128, 129-130
    hunting, 101
    Karlov Vary, 116-118
    Karlsbad, *see* Karlov Vary
    Kosice, 126-127
    Marianske Lazne, 118-120
    Marienbad, *see* Marianske Lazne
    money, 82, 83
    motels, 99, 100
    nightclubs, 109, 110
    Olomouc, 120
    Ostrava, 120
    photographs, 99
    Pilsen, *see* Plzn
    Plzn, 120
    Podbrezova, 127-128
    Prague, 103-110
    restaurants, 108-109, 113-114, 119-120, 125, 126-127
    shopping, 97
    sightseeing, 103, 104
    Slovakia, 121-131
    souvenirs, 102
    Spartakiade, 101, 102
    spas, 100, 101
    Stary Smokovec, 128-129
    Tale, *see* Podbrezova
    Tatranska Lomnica, 129-131
    telegraph, 102
    telephone calls, 102
    tours, 99
    train travel, 88
    traveling in and to, 86-90
    visas, 83-86
Czechoslovakian Air Lines, *see* CSA
Czechoslovakian Bus Lines, *see* CSAD
Czechoslovakian Embassy, 83
Czechoslovakian president, residence of, 103
Czechoslovakian Philharmonic, 104

Dacia, 279
Dacia Hotel, 323-324

INDEX 531

Daire Restaurant, 497
Dalibor Tower, 104
Dalmacija Hotel, 464
Dalmacija, The Liner, 439
Dalmacijaturist Agency, 436, 477
Dalmatia, 441, 442, 443, 444, 455, 475, 487
Dalmatian Tourist Office, 476
"Dalmatinski prsut," 445
dancing, 32, 62, 105, 107, 110, 112, 117, 119, 125, 126, 127, 130, 178, 179, 190, 246, 247, 248, 249, 257, 266, 267, 268, 270, 272, 311, 313, 318, 321, 323, 340, 343, 404, 405, 418, 463, 465, 478, 480, 497, 507, 513
Dancut, 206
Danube River, 9, 79, 80, 81, 123, 135, 138, 167, 278, 279, 305, 345, 434, 455
Danube Cup Motor Race, International, 167
Danubian, 14
Danzig, see Gdansk
Dardanelles Straits, 348
Darius, Persian Emperor, 281
Da Vinci, Leonardo, works by, 255
Deak, Ferenc, 137, 174
Deba, 210
Debno Church, 274-275
Debrecen, 134, 135, 145, 153, 196-199, 203
  College, 197
Decani, 507
Dedeman Hotel, 404, 405
  Restaurant, 404
Dedinje, 502
deer, 101, 172, 240, 305, 398, 455
Delta Restaurant, 343
Demanovska Grottos, 79, 122, 130
Derbeslye, 368
Dervent, 48

DESA shops, 235
Devin, 323-324
Devin Hotel, 124, 125
  Restaurant, 124
Dewey, John, 355
diet restaurant, 116
Dietrichestein Palace, 111
Dikilitash, 50
Dimitrov, Georgi, 11
  tomb of, 29, 32
Dimitrovgrad, 51
dinars, 434
Diners Club, 91, 450
Dining, 23, 24, 95-97, 161-163, 230-235, 294-295, 376-381, 444-447
  Bulgaria, 23, 24
  Czechoslovakia, 95-97
  Poland, 230-235
  Romania, 294-295
  Turkey, 376-381
  Yugoslavia, 444-447
Diocles, 500
Diocletian, Emperor, Palace of, 452, 476
Diocletian Museum, 475
Dionysos Theater in Athens, 411
Divan Hotel, 419
  Restaurant, 419
Djumaya Dyamiya Mosque, 39
Dlugu Targ Square, 251
Dobo, Istvan, 195
"dobostorte," 162
Dobrudja, 10, 280, 281
Dobsina, 80
Dock's Restaurant, 422
dogs, importing of, 435
Doina Hotel, 341
Doktoroglu Seyahat Agentesi, 393
Dolmabache Palace, 415
dolmus, travel by, 370-371, 400
Dolna Krupa Castle, 81, 124
Dominican Church, 111

Dominican Monastery, 459
Dom Lovaca Restaurant, 506
Dom Turisty Hotel, 273
"doner Kebab," 406
Donner, Rafael, 123, 124
Dorna Hotel, 290
Dospevski, Alex, 39, 45
Dounva Hotel, 51
doves, hunting of, 305, 398
"dovlece," 294
Dracula, Count, 227
Dragasani vineyards, 327
Dragon of Brno, 111
Drassenhofen, 86
Dresden, 147
Drevnik, 463
Drina River, 434, 492, 500
Drouzhba, 18, 53, 54, 63-64
Druzba Hotel, 120
Dubrovnik, 430, 433, 436, 437, 438, 439, 443, 448, 449, 452, 458-463, 464, 475, 478
Dubrovnik Hotel, 491
  Restaurant, 491
ducks, hunting for, 101, 305, 398, 455
Dunajec River, 205
Dumas, Elder, 116
Dumbrava Park, camping site, 303
"dumpling," 06
Dunaujvaros, 172
"Dungan Corbasi," 378
Duni Restaurant, 72
Dusaney Grad Restaurant, 445
Dusanov Grad Restaurant, 506
Dva Jelena Restaurant, 506
"Dyuvec," 445

Eastern Rumelia, 10
Edelweis Hotel, 59

Eden Bar, 194
Edirne, 347, 351, 411-4
Edirne Kapi, 136
Eger, 134, 153, 159, 162, 170, 194-196, 198, 203
Eger Hotel, 196
Eforie Nord, 290, 302, 303, 304, 335, 344
Eforie Sud, 290, 303, 335, 344
Elaphita, Island of, 459
Elblag Canal, 222
electric current, 227, 228
electrotherapy, 100
El Greco, works by, 175
English-speaking, 11, 105, 119, 121, 138, 139, 182, 212, 433, 461, 467, 475
English tourists, 55
Entry-points, 13, 86, 142, 284, 367, 368
    Bulgarian, 13
    Czechoslovakian, 86
    Hungarian, 142
    Romanian, 284, 286
    Turkish, 367, 368
Ephesus, 347, 426
Erlach, Fischer von, 111
Erzerum, 347
Erzincam, 347
escorts for ladies, 387
Esenboga Airport, 361-362, 364
Esplanade Hotel (Marianske Lazne), 95, 118-119
  Restaurant, 119
Esplanade Hotel (Prague), 89, 106, 107
  Restaurant, 106, 107
Esplanade Intercontinental Hotel, 450, 489-490, 492
  Restaurant, 490
Est Bar, 107
Este, Ferdinand d', 104

Estergom, 172, 175-176
Esterhazy Estate, 167
Ethnographical Museum, 29, 38, 39, 402, 475, 502
   Ankara, 402
   Belgrade, 502
   Plovdiv, 38, 39
   Sofia, 29
   Split, 475
Euphrates River, 348
Europa Hotel (Eforie Nord), 344-345
   Restaurant, 345
Europa Hotel (Sarajevo) 496-497
   Restaurant, 497
Europa Hotel (Siofok), 191
   Restaurant, 191
Europa Hotel (Sunny Beach), 69, 71, 72
Europejski Hotel, 218, 225, 235, 243, 245-246, 247, 249
   Restaurant, 245-246
Europfjski Cafe, 274
Excelsior Hotel (Belgrade), 504
   Restaurant, 504
Excelsior Hotel (Dubrovnik), 461
   Restaurant, 461
Excelsior Hotel (Marianske Lazne), 119
exchange rate, 23, 82, 97, 139, 140, 212, 283, 360
exporting of currency, 213, 283, 435
Eyüp Mosque, 412, 416

Fairs, 111, 167, 426, 427
   Brno Industrial, 111
   Budapest International, 167
   Business Fair for the Near East, 426, 427
"fasuliye piyazi," 378
"fatanyeros," 162
Fatih Mosque, 415
Federal People's Republic of Yugoslavia, 432, 514
Felibe, 38
Fenyves Hotel, 202
   Bar, 202
Ferdinand I, King, 280
Ferdinand of Saxe-Coburg-Gotha, 10
Ferihegy Airport, 141, 142, 145, 146, 147, 151
ferry boats, 218, 365, 366, 439
Fertöd, 167
Feudal Art Museum, 308
Fichev, Nikola, 48
fillers, 139
film, 26, 99, 143, 144, 165, 217, 239, 302, 362, 395, 435
Film Festival, 337
Finno-Ugaric Languages, 138
Fisherman's Bastion, 174
Fisherman's Hut Restaurant, 70
Fisherman's Inn, 193
Fisherman's Restaurant, 204
fishing, 79, 100, 101, 135, 172, 173, 240, 304-306, 316, 345, 398, 455, 456, 488, 489, 500
   in Czechoslovakia, 79, 100, 101
   in Hungary, 135, 172, 173
   in Poland, 240
   in Romania, 304-306, 316, 345
   in Turkey, 398
   in Yugoslavia, 455, 456, 489, 500
   underwater, 455
Fiume, *see* Rijeka
Fjord Hotel, 464

Restaurant, 464
Floriya, Beach at, 396, 417
"fogas," 162
Fogas Restaurant, 194
Foget, camp site at, 303
folk art, 235
folk dances, 381-382
folk singers, 423
food, 23, 24, 95, 97, 161-163, 230-235, 294-295, 296, 376-381, 444-447
  Bulgarian, 23, 24
  Czechoslovakian, 95, 97
  Hungarian, 161-163
  Polish, 230-235
  Romanian, 294-295, 296
  Turkish, 376-381
  Yugoslavian, 444-447
food shops, 163, 164
forbidden areas, 297-298
forests, 50, 172, 244, 345, 433, 434, 442, 488, 492
Forest's Corner Restaurant, *see* Gorski Kut
forints, 139
  vouchers, 141, 142
Fortress District, 174
Fortress, The, 425
Fortuna Restaurant, 161
Forty Martyrs, Church of the, 48
Forum Hotel, 481
Fountain Restaurant, 70
foxes, hunting, 240, 305, 330, 398, 455
Franciscan Church, 320
Franciscan Monastery, 459
Francuski Hotel, 257
  Restaurant, 257
Frantiskovy Lazne, 101
Franz Ferdinand, Archduke, 429, 495, 496
Franz-Josef, Emperor, 123, 259, 315, 321, 460

free port, 269
French tourists, 55
frescoes, 29, 40, 45, 48, 49, 65, 332, 414
  museum, 503
Friendship Beach, *see* Drouzhba.
Fukier Restaurant, 249
Furstenburg Palace, 104

Gabriele Hotel, 188
Gabrovo, 51
Galata Bridge, 366, 415, 416
Galata Tower, 415
galleries, art, 29, 32, 104, 307, 308, 311, 452, 462, 476-477
Gallipoli, 367
gambling, 54, 62, 71, 343, 467, 475, 476
game preserve, 170
gasoline stations, 16, 43, 90, 150, 151, 220, 221, 296, 297, 393, 440
  Bulgarian, 16, 43
  Czechoslovakian, 90
  Hungarian, 150, 151
  Polish, 220, 221
  Romanian, 296, 297
  Turkish, 393
  Yugoslavian, 440
gas vouchers, 90, 440
Gate of Pile, 459
Gate of Ploce, 459
Gdansk, 210, 211, 226, 236, 241, 250-253, 266, 268
Gdynia, 252, 253, 266, 268
geese, 96, 173, 305, 398, 455

INDEX 535

Gellert Hill, 174
Gellert Hotel, 176-177, 181
    Restaurant, 177
Gemenc, forest at, 172
Gemenc-Mecsek Horseback Riding Tour, 169, 170
Gemiyata Restaurant, 62
Genoa, 366
General Toshevo, 13
Generalturist, 436
Georgikon College, 187
geography, 81, 82, 134-135, 210-211, 278-279, 348, 433-434
    of Czechoslovakia, 81, 82
    of Hungary, 134-135
    of Poland, 210-211
    of Romania, 278-279
    of Turkey, 348
    of Yugoslavia, 433-434
German cooking, 95
German tourists, 55
Germany, 82, 86, 137, 138, 208, 209
Ghetto (Warsaw), Monument to, 243
Giant Mountains, 104
Giewont Hotel, 272, 274
Giorgione, works by, 175
Giurgia, 284, 285
Glarous Hotel, 58
Globus Hotel, 65, 67, 69, 71, 72
Gmund, 86
Gobelin Tapestries, 123
Goethe, 116
Gold Beach, 417
Golden Anchor Hotel, *see* Zlatni Kotva
Goldener Bearn, 109
Golden Horn, 366, 373, 380, 413, 414, 416
Golden Lions Bar, 490
Golden Sands, 18, 53, 54, 55-62, 63, 64, 65, 66, 74, 336

Gomulka, Wladyslaw, 209, 210
"Good Soldier Schweik," 109
Gora Tumska, 262
Gordium, 402
Gorski Kut Restaurant, 61, 62
Gottwaldov, 80, 115
goulash, 96, 161, 162, 183, 445
Govora, 304
Goya, works by, 175
Grad Hotel, 485, 486
    Restaurant, 485
Gradina Poiana Restaurant, 319
Gradska Kafana Restaurant, 463
Grafenburg, 101
Grancanica Monastery, 508
Grand Hotel (Ankara) 376, 380
Grand Hotel (Brno) 112, 113
Grand Hotel (Budapest), 178-179
    Restaurant, 178-179
Grand Hotel (Istanbul), 380
Grand Hotel (Izmir), 380
Grand Hotel (Krakow), 257, 258
Grand Hotel (Lodz), 260
    Restaurant, 260
Grand Hotel (Skopje) 516-517
    Restaurant, 517
Grand Hotel (Sopot), 225, 267-268
    Restaurant, 267
Grand Hotel (Stary Smokovec), 128, 129
Grand Hotel (Warsaw), 225, 235, 246-247
    Restaurant, 247
Grand Hotel Galeb, 479-480
    Restaurant, 480
Grand Hotel Moskva, 116-117
    Restaurant, 117
Grand Hotel Palace, 515-516
    Restaurant, 515
Grand Hotel Praha, 128, 129, 130
    Restaurant, 130
Grand Hotel Toplice, 482-483

Restaurant, 483
Grand Tarabya Hotel, 420-421
  Restaurant, 420-421
Grassalkovich Palace, 123
Graz, 440, 484
Great Church, The, 197
Greece, 9, 10, 12, 38, 74, 348, 439
Green Card Insurance, 87, 435
Green Mosque, *see* Yesi Cami
Grisul Repede Restaurant, 325
groszy, 213
grottoes, 79, 122, 130, 131, 486
Grotto Restaurant, 38
grouse, hunting of, 305, 455
Groza, Peter, 280
Gteycko, camping site at, 229
guides, 24, 25, 91, 97, 153, 166-167, 237-238, 300-302, 394, 426, 452
  Bulgaria, 24, 25
  Czechoslovakia, 91, 97
  Hungary, 153, 166-167
  Poland, 237-238
  Romania, 300-302
  Turkey, 394, 426
  Yugoslavia, 452
Gul Baba, Tomb of, 174
Gümrü, 368
Gumulduh, 396
Gundel Restaurant, 175
guns, importing of, 84, 217, 305, 435
Gustav Adolph, King, 268
Gydnic, 218
Gyekenyes, 142
gymnastic exhibition, 101, 102
gyongyos, 170
Gyorgy Festetics, Castle of, 187
Gypsy Ball, International, 167
gypsy music, 34, 125, 133, 134, 180, 181, 182, 196, 198, 199, 200, 204, 512
gypsy village, 122

Gyueshovo, 13
Gyula, Castle of, 167

Hadjiiska River, 71
Haifa, 367
Hajdo, 161
hairdressers, 31, 54, 111, 245, 246, 253, 256, 257, 262, 264, 448
Hairdressers Ball, 167
Halic, *see* Golden Horn
hamam, *see* Turkish Bath
Hamam Bar, 497
Hamienne Restaurant, 249
Hanseatic League, 268
Hapsburgs, 137, 174, 195, 197, 443
hare, hunting of, 101, 173, 345, 455
harem, 386
Harkany, 161
Haskovo, 37, 65
Hattusha Restaurant, 405-406
Haugadorf, 86
Haydarpasha Station, 365, 366
Hegyshalom, 142, 176
Height Gate, 251
hellers, 82
Hellespont, 367
Hel Peninsula, 205, 210, 222, 267, 268
Herastrau, Lake, 307, 308, 312
Herceg-Novi, 500
Herculane, 304
Hermitage Restaurant, 268
Heroes of the City Monument, 244
Hertz Car Rental, 393, 441, *see*

also Autotehna
Heviz, 170, 188
Hidasnemeti, 86
highways, 87, 89, 152, 220, 286
  service car, 440
Hilton Hotel, *see* Istanbul Hilton
hiking, 36, 45, 46, 79, 98, 100, 130, 316, 409, 487
Hippodrome, 416
Hisar Cami, 426
Historical Maritime Museum, 459
Historical Museum of Wroclaw, 271
historical village, 328
history, 9, 10, 11, 28, 135-138, 207-210, 279-282, 349-354, 399-400, 407, 410, 412, 413, 423, 424, 430-432, 442-443, 458, 514
  Bulgarian, 9, 10, 11, 28
  Hungarian, 135-138
  Polish, 207-210
  Romanian, 279-282
  Turkish, 349-354, 399-400, 407, 410, 412, 413, 423, 424
  Yugoslavian, 430-432, 442-443, 458, 514
Histria, 282, 303, 344
hitch hiking, 145, 149-150
Hittite Archeological Museum, 402
Hohenau, 86
Hohenzollern-Sigmaringen, house of, 280
Holy Ivan, Church of, 458
Holy Mother, Church of, 39
Holy Trinity, Church of, (Durbrovnik) 458
Holy Trinity, Church of (Gdansk), 251
Holy Virgin, Church of, 40, 50
Homer, 424
Horizante Hotel, 59
"horke parky," 96

Hornad River, 122
horseback riding, 100 134, 135, 153, 169-171, 240-241, 260, 337-338
  tours, 134, 169-171
  171
horse show, 167
Horthy, Admiral Nicholas, 137
Hortobagy Czarda Inn, 198-199
  Restaurant, 199
hostels, student, 304
hotels, 18-23, 29-34, 36, 37, 40-42, 43-44, 45-46, 47, 49-50, 51, 56-59, 63, 67-69, 70, 91-94, 105-108, 111-113, 115, 116-117, 118-119, 120, 121, 122, 124-125, 126, 127, 128, 129-130, 158-161, 176-180, 186, 189-190, 191-192, 195-196, 198-199, 200-204, 224-229, 245-248, 250, 252-254, 256-258, 259-265, 267-269, 271-273, 291-293, 308-311, 314-318, 320-325, 327-329, 331-334, 338-342, 344-345, 371-376, 402-405, 409-410, 417-421, 427, 448-451, 457, 458, 460-462, 464, 465-471, 473-476, 479-485, 487-491, 493-501, 503-505, 508-517
  Bulgarian, 18-23, 29-34, 36, 37, 40-42, 43-44, 45-47, 49-51, 56-59, 63, 67-69, 70
  Czechoslovakian, 91-94, 105-108, 111-113, 115, 116-122, 124-125, 126, 127-130
  Hungarian, 158-161, 176-180, 186, 189-192, 195-196, 198-204
  Polish, 224-229, 245-248, 250, 252-254, 256-265, 267-269, 271-273
  Romanian, 291-293, 308-311,

314-318, 320-325, 327-329, 331-334, 338-342, 344-345
  Turkish, 371-376, 402-405, 409-410, 417-421, 427
  Yugoslavian, 448-451, 457, 458, 460-462, 464, 465-467, 468, 469-470, 471, 473, 474, 475-476, 479-485, 487-489
hotel associations, 437, 448
hotel classes, 154-160, 225, 226
hotel reservations, 17, 20, 21, 22, 40, 41, 91, 92, 93, 94, 141, 142, 153, 154, 228, 283, 289, 290, 292, 293, 361, 370, 374, 375
hotel vouchers, 20, 94, 95, 449, 450
House of the Army, 312
Hradcany, 81, 103, 109
Humor, Church of, 332
Hunedoara, camp site at, 303
Hungaria Agency, 153
Hungaria Hotel, 192, 193, 194
Hungaria Restaurant, (Budapest), 182
Hungaria Restaurant, (Kosice), 127
Hungaria Restaurant, (Sofia), 34
Hungaria Riding Tours, 169
Hungarian Legation, 140, 141, 142, 154, 155
Hungarian National Travel Office, *see* IBUSZ
Hungarian Workers Party, 138
Hungary, 16, 82, 86, 133-204, 280, 433
  airplane travel, 145-147
  Balotonfured, 185-187
  Budapest, 173-184
  bus travel, 149
  cables, 173
  camping, 168, 202
  cars, 150-151

chauffeurs, 152
climate, 135
currency, 139-140
customs, 140-144
Debrecen, 196-199
dining, 161-163
Eger, 194-196
Estergom, 175-176
fishing, 172-173
food, 23, 95, 161-163
geography, 134-135
group tours, 165-166
guides, 166-167
Heviz, 188
history, 135-138
hitch-hiking, 149-150
horseback riding, 134, 135, 153, 169-172
hotels, 158-161, 176-180, 186, 189-190, 191-192, 195-196, 198-199, 199-200, 201-202, 203-204
hunting, 172, 173
IBUSZ, 152-154, 155-160, 166, 169, 173, 183
Kecskemet, 199-200
Keszthely, 187-188
Lake Balaton, 184
language, 138
money, 139-140
motoring, 151
Pecs, 200-203
photography, 165
river boat travel, 149
restaurants, 181-184, 187, 192-194, 203, 204
shopping, 163-165
Siofok, 190-196
Szeged, 203-204
Szentendre, 176
Taploca, 188
telephone calls, 173
Tihany, 188-190

INDEX 539

train travel, 147-149
traveling in and to, 145-151
visas, 140-144
Visegrad, 176
yearly events, 167
hunting, 79, 98, 101, 172, 173, 239-241, 304-306, 330, 345, 398, 454, 455
  in Czechoslovakia, 79, 98, 101
  in Hungary, 172, 173
  in Poland, 239-241
  in Romania, 304-306, 330, 345
  in Turkey, 398
  in Yugoslavia, 454-456
  lodges, 101, 305
  preserves, 454, 455
  seasons, 101, 239
Hus, Jan, 103
Hutnik Hotel, 126
  Restaurant, 126
Hvar, 436-464, 477
hydrofoil, 134, 149, 172, 439, 477, 502

Iasi, 304, 315, 333-334
ibex, hunting of, 455
IBUSZ, 145, 148, 149, 151, 152-154, 155, 156, 157, 159, 160, 166, 169, 173, 183, 436
  International Ball, 167
"Ic Pilav," 377
Icel, 396
icons, 40, 321
IDEGENFORGAIMI HIVATALA, 153,
154, 171, 172, 173-174
Illisesti, camp site at, 303
Iluyshin airplanes, 13, 14, 18, 76, 88, 145, 218, 287
Imperial Hotel (Dubrovnik), 461-462
Imperial Hotel (Kosice), 126
incunabula, 330
"indianfank," 162
Indian Village Restaurant, *see* Kolibite
Inex Agency, 441
Intercontinental Hotels Corporation, 489, 491
Interhotel, 91, 92, 93, 97, 111, 115, 119, 122, 130
International Air Travel Office, 87
International Boat Tour on the Danube, 167
International camping symbol, 100, 169
International Danube Cup Motor Race, 167
International Drivers License, 15, 87, 151, 219, 286, 362, 394, 435
International Fair (Hungary), 167
International Fair (Plovdiv), 41, 42
International Fair (Poznan), 226, 263, 264
International Hotel (Brno), 111, 112, 113, 114
  Restaurant, 112-113
International Hotel (Mamaia), 335, 341-342
  Restaurant, 342
International Hotel (Prague), 107, 108
  Restaurant, 108
International Hotel (Prague), 491
International Union of Official Touring Organizations, 289
Ipsala, 367

Iran, 348
Iraq, 348, 368
Iron Bridge, 326
Iron Gates, 502
Iron Gate Gorge, 439
"iskembe corbasi," 378
Isparta, 347
Istanbul, 14, 76, 89, 288, 302, 344, 347, 361, 363, 364, 365, 366, 367, 368, 370, 371, 372, 373, 374, 375, 376, 389, 393, 394, 396, 397, 406, 412-423
Istanbul-Ankara Express, 373
Istanbul-Hilton Hotel, 364, 371, 372, 374, 375, 376, 417-419
　Restaurant, 418
Istanbul, University of, 415
Istria, 432, 441, 443, 444, 469, 471, 472, 487
Italy, 439
Ivan Asan II, Tsar, 49
Ivan Aven II, 10
Ivanograd, 438, 442, 498, 499-500
Izmir, 347, 367, 368, 371, 372, 373, 374, 375, 376, 389, 394, 423-427
Iznik, 410

Jadran (boat), 439
Jadran Hotel, 474, 480
　Restaurant, 480
Jagellonian dynasty, 207
Jagellonian University, 255, 256
Jajce, 493-494
Jaji Bayrisch, 497

Jakuszice, 86
Jalta Hotel, 105, 106
　Restaurant, 105, 106
Jama Michalikowa Coffee Shop, 255, 258
Janissary Marching Band, 382
Janissary Mosque, 417
Janissaries, 136
Janske Lazne, 101
Jasper Restaurant, 484
Jassy, *see* Iasi
JAT, 438, 504
Javorina, 129
Jedinstuo Liner, 439
Jesenik, 101
Jewish Cemetery, 103
Jubiler shops, 235
Jugohoteli, 437, 448
Julian Alps, 482
Justinian, Emperor, 349

"kabak kizartmasi," 378
Kabatas, 366
"kadin budu," 377, 378
"kadin gobegi," 379
Kailuka Hotel, 37, 38
Kalemegdan Fortress, 501, 502
Kampinos Forest, 244
Kapali Carsi, 416
Kapikule, 368
Karlov Vary, 80, 101, 116-118
Karlsbad, *see* Karlov Vary
Karlstejn Castle, 81, 104
Kartal, 396
"kase," 379
Kashubian dialect, 211

INDEX 541

Kaskade Restaurant, 270
Karadjoz-Beg Mosque, 494
Karagöz Bar, 418
Karagöz and Hacivat, 383
Kara-Mustafa-Pasa Haman, 408
Karpatia, 183
"karpuz," 379
Katowice, 219, 253-254, 261
Katowice Hotel, 254
    Restaurant, 254
Katrca Restaurants, 484
Kavatsite, 74, 75
"kavun," 379
kawiarnias, 225, 232, 247, 253, 262, 264
Kayseri, 400
Kazanluk, 65, 77
Kazan Restaurant, 405
Kazimierz, 254
Kazimifrizowski Palace, 243
kecs, 82
Kecskemet, 134, 167, 199-200
Kelebia, 142
Kemal, Mustapha, *see* Ataturk
Kent Restaurant, 403, 404-405
Keravansaray Restaurant, 423
kessel goulash, 162
Keszthely, 185, 187-188
Keszthely Motel, 170, 187-188
    Restaurant, 187-188
"kilic sis," 378
Kiliyos, 396
Kinizsi, Pal, 170
Kinizsi Castle, 167, 171
Kis Pipa Restaurant, 176
Kis Royal Restaurant, 181-182
Kizlaragasi Caravansarays, 425
Kladovo, 437
Klagenfurt, 440, 482
Klastorisko, 122
Klein, 86
Klausenberg, *see* Cluj
KLM, 13, 87, 145, 364

Kloster Wine Stube, 110
Kmici Cafe, 273-274
Knights of Malta, 424
Kolasin, 500
Koliba, The, Restaurant, 128
Kolibite Restaurant, 62
"kolozvari rakottpakszta," 163
Komanom, 86, 142
Komarom Hotel, 171
Kombas, 441. *See also* Avis
Komis Stores, 235
Kompas Agency, 437
Konak Square, 425
Konopiste Castle, 104
Konopiste Motel, 100
Konsumtourist, 164, 165
Konya, 347, 400
Konyali, 422
Kopiter Hotel, 34
    Restaurant, 34
Koprivshtitsa, 77
Korcula, 442, 459
Kornati Restaurant, 492
Korucula, 439
Kosciuszko, Tadeuse, 255
kosher food, 249
Kosice, 122, 126-127, 131
Kosice Hungarian Restaurant, 95
Kosouvski Bozur Hotel, 513
    Restaurant, 513
Kosovo-Metohija, 507
Kossuth, Lajos, 137, 197
Kosutnjak Topcider, 502
Köszeg, Castle of, 167
Kotor, 441, 442, 464, 478
Koulata, 13
Kozeg, 142
Krakow, 207, 208, 219, 227, 236, 255-258, 261, 268, 272
    University at, 207, 208
Krakowskie Przedmiescie, 214
Krakowy Hotel, 256-257
    Restaurant, 256-257

Krk Islands, 442
Krka River, 442, 474, 485, 486
Krokodyi Restaurant, 248
Kromeriz Palace, 79
Kronstadt, see Brasov
Krumlov Hotel, 115
    Restaurant, 115
Krusic, Peter, 443
Krym, Cafe, 125
Krystal Bar, 507
Kuarna, Gulf of, 442
Kubalik, Jan, 467
Kudowa-Stone, 86
Kudowm, 230
Kukiri Restaurant, 62
Kumburgaz, 396
Kun, Bela, 137
Kuparis, 460
Kurus, 360
Kushlata Restaurant, 60, 61
Kutna Hora, 104
"kuzu dolmasi," 378
Kvarner Express Agency, 437
Kwara Hotel, 466-467
    Restaurant, 467
Kynzvart Palace, 116

Laberint Restaurant, 462
Labyrinth Restaurant, 495
Lacto Bar, 325-326
Lakeside Restaurant, 193
Lamartine, home of, 38
Lancut, 258-260
language, 11, 138, 211-212, 282, 355-359, 432-433
    Bulgarian, 11

    Hungarian, 138
    Polish, 211-212
    Yugoslavian, 432-433
Lapard, 460
lapidarium, 471
laundry service, 32, 33, 36, 41, 63, 67, 68, 111, 113, 225, 399, 450
Lazienki Park, 243
Lazienkowski Palace, 243
Lazour Restaurant, 72
Leander, Tower of, 417
Lebanon, 439
Leczyca, 260
Ledeburg Family, Palace of, 104
Ledenika Cave, 77
Lenin Square, 30
lei, 140
Letea, Forest of, 345
Letenye, 142
lev, 11, 12
Lev Hotel, 483, 484
    Cafe, 483
Levoca, 80, 122, 130
Liberator's Hill, 39
Liberation Memorial, 104
Liberation of Hungary, Anniversary of, 167
Lidice, 104
Lido Hotel (Bucharest) 309-310, 311
    Restaurant, 310
Lido Hotel (Siofok), 191, 192, 193
Liechtenstein family, 81
Lil, Cafe, 119-120
Lillia Hotel, 58
Liman Lokanta, 422
Linz, 114
Lippizan horses, 135, 170
Liptovsky cheese, 96
Liptovsky, Mikulas, 122, 131
liquor, importing of, 84, 96, 97, 143, 162, 163, 380, 446-447
lira (Turkish), 360

INDEX

Liszt, Franz, 174
Live Fish Restaurant, 422-423
Ljubljana, 437, 452, 469, 483-484, 486
Lodz, 226, 260
Loket, 116
Lokoshaza, 142
London, 14, 89, 146, 219, 365
Loretto Monastery, 108
LOT Airlines, 218, 222
Lotus Casino, 71
Lotus Restaurant, 71
Louis, King, 136, 175
Lounic Castle, 111
Lovcen, Mt., 498
Lozica Altalier, 476-477
Lubormirski, Prince, 258
Lubranski College, 263
Lucija Hotel, 469-470
    Restaurant, 470
Ludmilla wine, 97
Lufthansa Air Lines, 13, 87, 287, 438
Lvov, 219
lynx, hunting of, 240, 398, 458

Macedonia, 10, 11, 432, 455, 514-517
Macedonia House Restaurant, 517
Macedonia National Theater, 515
Macedonia Summer Festival, 515
Machek Restaurant, 484
Madrigal choir, 515
Maestral Hotel, 457
Magnolia Restaurant, 266
Magosoaia Palace Museum, 308

Magoura Cave, 77
Magyrs, 135, 136, 137, 196, *see also* Hungarians.
Mahacs, Battle of, 194
Mai Health Resort, camp site, 303
mail, 24, 26, 31, 102, 173, 241, 306, 398
Majestic Hotel, 505
Makarsk, 464
Mala Strana District, 95, 104, 108, 109
Malbork Castle, 251
Malev Airlines, 145, 147, 287
Maliuc, 345
Malokarpacke Zlato wine, 96, 97
Mamaia Beach Development, 287, 290, 299, 301, 302, 303, 304, 334-344
"mamaliga," 294
Mamora, Sea of, 367
Mangalia, 282, 290, 335
Maniu, Iuliu, 288
"Man of Sorrows," statue of, 263
maps, 98, 99, 238-239, 298, 394
Marburg, *see* Maribur
Marchegg, 86
Marco Polo, birthplace of, 459
Margaret, Princess, Islands, 174, 178, 179
Maria Theresa, 123, 512
Marianske Lazne, 101, 102, 116, 118-120
Maribor, 484, 485, 487
Marie, Queen, 65
Marienbad, *see* Marianske Lazne
Marina Hotel, 457
Maritsa Hotel, 68
Maritza Hotel, 42
Maritza river, 38, 39
Marjan Hotel, 475-476
    Restaurant, 475-476
Marmora Express, 365
Marmora Roof Bar, 418

Marmora, Sea of, 348, 351, 366, 386, 396, 413, 414
Mars Na Drimu Restaurant, 505
Martonvasar, 167
"mastika," 24, 73
Matra-Bukk Riding Tour, 169, 170
Matra Mountains, 198
Matroz Csarda Restaurant, 193
Matthias, King, 122, 136, 176
    church of, 174, 181, 184
Matyas, Prince, 182
Maximillian, villa of, 459
Mazurian Lake region, 205, 210, 229, 261
Mecsek Hills region, 168, 200, 201
Media, 290
medical facilities, 273
medicinal baths, *see* spas
medicines, 154
Mediterranean Sea, 348, 439
Mehmet I, 407
    mausoleum of, 408
Mehmet II, 351
Mehmet V, 353
Mehmet the Conqueror, 352, 415, 417
Melana Hotel, 58, 59
Melmet the Conqueror, 136
Melnik Castle, 104
Melnik wine, 96
Melody Bar (Bucharest), 313
Melody Bar (Mamaia), 343
Mendel, Gregor, 111
Merkez Lokanta Restaurant, 406
Merkury Hotel, 263-264
    Restaurant, 264
Mersin, camp site at, 397
Metohija Hotel, 511
    Restaurant, 511
Metropol Hotel, 503-504
    Restaurant, 503
Metropoli, Church of, 74
Metternich Summer Palace, 116

Michael, King, 280
Michael Karolyi, Prince, 137
Michael of Nicea, 350
"miche-mache," 23
Midasnemeti, 142
"midye dolmasi," 378
Mieszko I, 207
Mikolajczka, Stanislaw, 209
Mikolajki, camping site at, 229
Miljacka River, 495, 496
Miljet, Island of, 459
Milk Bar, 326
Mill Restaurant, 60, 64
mineral baths, 55, 79, 100, 177, 179. *See also* spas
mini-golf course, 58
Miorita Restaurant, 312
Mioritsa Restaurant, 342-343
Miskolc, H., 147
"mititei," 294
"mixed grill," 444, 445
Mljet Islands, 446
Mloda Polska Group, 258
Mly Gkrobrego, Terraces of, 269
Modern Hotels, 341
Modern Restaurant, 323
Modra, vineyards of, 81
Mohacs, 136
Mokova Hotel, 115
    Restaurant, 115
Moldavia, 277, 278, 279, 280, 281, 300, 317, 332-334, 335
Moldavia Restaurant, 333
Moldovita, Church of, 332
Monastery Tavern, 64
monasteries, 9, 39, 40, 43, 44-46, 48, 64, 108, 111, 327, 459, 479, 507, 508, 517
monetary declarations, 83, 140, 213
money, 11-12, 82-83, 139-140, 212-214, 283, 359-360, 434-435, 451-452

INDEX 545

Bulgarian, 11-12
Czechoslovakian, 82-83
Hungarian, 139-140
Polish, 212-214
Romanian, 283
Turkish, 359-360
Yugoslavian, 434-435, 451-452
Monopol Hotel, (Gdansk), 252-253
   Restaurant, 253
Monopol Hotel (Katowice), 253-254
   Restaurant, 254
Montenegro, 10, 456, 460, 478, 498-501, 511
Montenegroturist Agency, 437
moose, hunting of, 211
Moravia, 79, 80, 82, 88, 95, 96, 98, 110, 111, 116, 122, 135
Moravita, 284, 285
Morfatiar, 344
Morskie Oko Hotel, 57, 58
   Restaurant, 58
Morskie Oko, Lake, 274
mosaics, Museum of, 417
Moscow Hotel (Belgrade), 505, 506
   Restaurant, 505
Moscow Hotel (Golden Sands), 53, 58
Moser Glass Factory, 116
Moskva Hotel (Dimitrovgrad), 51
Moskva Hotel (Karlov Vary), 116-117
mosques, 29, 39, 367, 385, 402, 408, 410, 411, 412, 414, 415, 416, 417, 426, 493, 494, 496
Mostar, 442, 460, 463, 492, 494-495
motels, 51-52, 75, 76, 99, 100, 229, 373, 396, 411, 429, 474, 485, 486

motoring, 15, 16, 87, 145, 150-152, 219-221, 286, 296-299, 367, 393-394, 440-441
   in Bulgaria, 15, 16
   in Czechoslovakia, 87
   in Hungary, 145, 150-152
   in Poland, 219-221
   in Romania, 286, 296-299
   in Turkey, 367, 393-394
   in Yugoslavia, 440-441
motor trains, 89
moufflons, 172
Movesak-Zagreb Motel, 474
   Restaurant, 474
Mozart, 459
Mramor, 51
Munich, 14, 287, 438
Municipal Tourist Office, *see* IDEGENFORGAIMI HIVATALA.
Muradiye Cami, 405
Mures River, 278, 279
Muresel Restaurant, 331
Muresul Hotel, 314-315
   Restaurant, 315
Murillo, works of, 123
museums, 29, 32, 38, 39, 50, 103, 104, 111, 175, 255, 258-259, 263, 271, 301, 307, 308, 311, 317, 323, 326, 327, 343, 344, 402, 415, 417, 426, 459, 471, 472, 475, 476, 490, 502, 503
musical instruments, Museum of, 263
muskrat, hunting of, 305
Mysiewicki Palace, 243

Nador Hotel, 201-203
   Restaurant, 202, 203

Nagycazony, 170
Nagytempion, The Great, Church of, 197
Naples, 366, 367
Napoca, see Cluj
Napoleon, 123, 301, 443, 459
Narodny Dom Hotel, 122, 123
 Restaurant, 123
narrow gauge railroad, 129
National Art Gallery (Bucharest), 307, 308, 311
National Art Gallery, (Sofia), 29, 32
National Museum (Budapest) 175
National Museum (Prague), 103
National Museum (Rijeka), 472
national parks, 189, 488, 500, 509
National Theater (Prague), 103
National Theater (Skopje), 516
National Theater (Sofia), 49
NATO, 355
Natural History Museum, 307, 308
Naval Museum, 50
Navrom, 288
Navyvazony Castle Hotel, 171
Nehaj, Fortress of, 473
Nejag Hotel, 473
Neptune Fountain, 251
Neptun Hotel, 468
 Restaurant, 468
Neretva River, 442, 463, 494-495
Neretva Hotel, 494-495
 Restaurant, 495
Nessebur (ship), 76
Nessebur, 65, 67, 68, 73
Nessebur Hotel, 71
Nessebur Restauant, 74
Neuilly, Treaty of, 280, 514
Nevzky, Alexander, Memorial Church, 28, 29, 32
Nidzica Castle, 275
Niksic, 498
Niptoun Restaurant, 72

Nis, 363, 508
Nord Hotel, 310
 Restaurant, 310
Novi Sad, 452, 508-509
Nowy Sarg, 274
nudist colony, 472
Nuremburg, 89

Oak Tree Inn, 187
Obelisk of Thutmosis III, 416
Octavian Augustus, Emperor, 281
Oder-Neisse River, 209, 210, 269
Odessa, 76, 288, 303
Oficiul National de Turism, see Carpati
Ohrid, 515
OIH, 153
Olimp Hotel, 69
Olomouc, 79, 80, 111, 120
 Palace, 79, 111
Olsetyn, 261-262
Olt Valley, 327
Olympia Bar, 110
Olympia Restaurant, 203
Olympics, Winter, 273
O.N.T., see Carpati
Opera House (Bucharest) 308
Opera House (Dubrovnik), 459
Opera House (Kosice), 127
Opera House (Sofia), 34
Opera House (Varna), 62
Opatiya, 430, 437, 465-467, 469, 486
Oradea, 290, 298, 303, 324-326
Oradea Restaurant, 325
ORBIS, 212, 213, 214, 215, 216, 217, 218, 220, 221, 222, 223-

224, 225, 226, 232, 236, 237, 238, 240, 241, 242, 244, 245, 246, 247, 248, 249, 256, 264, 272
  coupons, 215, 216, 223, 235
  gift shops, 235
  hotels, 215, 216, 232
  tours, 242
Orient Express, 88, 89, 147, 287, 365, 438
Oroforio fountain, 462
Orpheus Hotel, 43
oscepek cheese, 96
Osman Turks, *see* Ottoman Turks
Ostend, 439
Osterhuys, works by, 509
Ostrava, 120
Ostrava Hotel, 120
Oswiecim, 261
Otocec, 485-486
Otocec Motel, 486
Ottoman Turks, 45, 349-354, 363
outdoor theaters, 74
Out Valley, camp site at, 303
Ovid, 282
owl, hunting of, 398

Paderewski, Ignacy Jan, 247, 264
Padurea Baneasa, 313-314
Pag Islands, 442
Palace Hotel (Belgrade), 505
  Restaurant, 505
Palace Hotel (Budapest), 180
  Restaurant, 180
Palace Hotel (Marianske Lazne), 119, 120
  Restaurant, 119, 120

Palace Hotel (Portorouz), 469, 470
  Restaurant, 470
Palace Hotel (Titovouzice), 514
  Restaurant, 514
Palace Hotel (Zagreb), 490, 492
Palace of Culture and Science, 244
Palace of the Republic, 308
Palace of Sultans, *see* Seraglio
Palace on the Water, *see* Lazienkowski
palaces, 97, 103, 104, 123, 167, 171, 174, 176, 243, 308
"palacinke," 445
Palas Hotel, 329
Paliffy, Count, 81
Palisad Hotel, 510
  Restaurant, 510
Palma Hotel, 466
  Restaurant, 466
Palma Restaurant, 480
Pan American World Airways, 437, 450, 489, 491, *see also* Intercontinental Hotels Corporation
Pandelli Restaurant, 422
Pannonia Express, 147
Pannonia Hotel, 201, 202
Pantakrator, Church of, 74
panther, hunting of, 398
paprika chicken, 162
Paradsasvar, 161
Parassapuszta, 142
Parcul Privighetorilor, 314
Parcul Trandafirilor Restaurant, 311
Paris, 14, 145, 146, 147, 148, 219, 287, 365, 438
  Peace Treaty, 280-281
Paris Hotel, 466
Parisiyyen, Les, Restaurant, 423
Park Hotel (Eger), 196
  Restaurant, 196

Park Hotel (Istanbul), 372, 419-420
  Restaurant, 419
Park Hotel (Karlov Vary), 117
  Restaurant, 117
Park Hotel (Mamaia), 339-340
Park Hotel (Zadar), 481
Park of Freedom, 35
Parks (Bucharest), 308
Park Restaurant, 181
Partizanska Polyana, 74
Partizanski Voda, 510
Partizanul Hotel (Timisoara), 332
  Restaurant, 332
Partizanul Restaurant (Cluj), 322
Partizanul Restaurant (Oradea), 325
partridge, hunting of, 101, 173, 305, 398, 434, 455
Pasaj Kavarna Restaurant, 107
Pasha Enver, 353
Paul, Prince, 431
Pearl Hotel, 59
Pecs, 135, 145, 153, 162, 168, 200-203, 511
Peles Castle, 329
pelicans, hunting of, 345
Pendik, 396
Pera Palace Hotel, 373
perch, fishing for, 240
per diem minimum, 142, 143, 146, 155, 156, 157, 215, 436
Pergamum, 347, 426
Perhad Pasha Mosque, 493
Perla Restaurant, 324
Perle Hotel, 337, 339-340
  Restaurant, 340
Pescarus Restaurant, 312
Peter II, King, 431
Peter Kresimir IV, King, 474
Petofi, Sandor, 174
petrified forest, 50
Petropole Hotel, 262
  Restaurant, 262
Petrovaradin, 430, 511-512
Pezinok, vineyards of, 124
pheasant, 101, 173, 305, 398, 455
Phillippopolis, 38
phoenix, 67
photography, 26, 99, 165, 239, 302, 395, 452-453, 455, 479
  underwater, 456
Piast dynasty, 207
picnics, 73, 74, 171, 234-235, 493, 494
Piestany, 79, 80, 101, 124
Pietet, works by, 123
pigeons, hunting of, 305, 398
pike, fishing for, 240, 344, 398
Pilsen, *see* Plzn
Pilska Hotel, 33
pilsner beer, 88, 97
Pilvax, 183-184
Piraeus, 366, 367, 439
Piran, 468-469, 470
Pirin Mountains, 68, 77
Pitka, 23
PKO Shops, 236, 256
PKS, 221
Plac Zamkony, 243
plane travel, 13, 86, 87, 88, 144, 145-147, 153, 218, 222, 287, 288, 363, 364, 371, 437-438
Plava Laguna, 468
Plavi Podrum Restaurant, 467
Pleven, 37-38
Pliny the Younger, 407
Pliska Hotel, 31, 32, 34
  Restaurant, 31, 32, 34
Plitvice Hotel, 488
  Restaurant, 488
Plitvice Lakes, 442, 487, 488-489
Plitvicka Jezera, *see* Plitvice Lakes
Plock, 226, 260, 262
Ploesti, 277, 278, 279, 326, 329
Plovdiv, 14, 36, 38-44, 52

Plzn, 116, 120-121
Podbrezova, 127-128
Podgorica, 498
Pod Koziolkami Restaurant, 266
"pohani sir," 445
Pohorje, 485
Poiana Brasov, 319-321
Poland, 82, 86, 205-275
    air travel, 222
    Auschwitz, 261
    auto travel, 219-221, 238-239
    boat travel, 222
    bus travel, 221
    Bydgoszcz, 250
    cables, 241
    camping, 229-230
    car travel, 219-221
    climate, 210-211
    currency, 212-214
    customs, 215-217
    dining, 230-235
    fishing, 240
    food, 230-235
    Gdansk, 250-253
    Gdynia, 253
    geography, 210-211
    guides, 237
    history, 207-210
    horseback riding, 239-241
    hotels, 224-229, 245-248, 250, 252, 253-254, 256-258, 259, 260, 261, 262, 263-265, 267-268, 269, 271-272, 273
    hunting, 239-241
    Katowice, 253-254
    Kazimierz, 254
    Krakow, 255-258
    Lancut, 258-260
    language, 211-212
    Lodz, 260
    mail, 241
    maps, 238, 239
    money, 212-214
    motoring, 219-221
    Olsetyn, 261-262
    ORBIS, 223-224
    Oswiecim, 261
    phone calls, 241
    photographs, 239
    Plock, 262
    Poznan, 262-266
    Restaurants, 248-249, 253, 254, 258, 265-266, 268, 270, 273-274
    rail travel, 219, 222
    shopping, 235-236
    sightseeing, 242-244, 251-252, 255-256, 263, 269, 271, 274-275
    Sopot, 266-268
    spas, 230
    streetcar travel, 221, 222
    Szczecin, 268-270
    taxis, 221, 245
    telephones, 241
    tours, 236-237
    train travel, 219, 222
    travel guide, 238
    traveling, 218-222
    visas, 215-217
    Warsaw, 241-249
    Zakopane, 272-275
Polanica, 230
polecats, hunting of, 305
Police, Romanian, 296
Polish Anglers Association, 240
Polish Bus Lines, *see* PKS
Polish ham, 231
Polish National Bank, 213, 214
Polish Ocean Lines, 218
Polish State Museum, 255
Polish Tourist Association, *see* P.T.T.K.
Polish Tourist Office, *see* ORBIS
Polish United Workers' Party, 209
Polonia Restaurant, 253

Polska Kasa Opieki Shops, *see* PKO
Polskie Linie Lotnicze, *see* LOT
Pomerania, Province of, 268, 269
Pomporovo, 43-44
Poprad, 89, 122, 129, 130
Poraj Restaurant, 273
porcupine, hunting of, 398
Porec, 467-468
pork chops, 96
"porkolt," 162
Portorouz, 468, 469-470
Posen, *see* Poznan
Postavarul Hotel, 317, 318
Potocki, Count, 258
Postojenska grottoes, 486
Postojenska Jama, 486
Potsdam Conference, 209, 239
pound, Turkish, 360
Poznanski Hotel, 265
Pracky Hill Peace Memorial, 111
Prague, 14, 79, 82, 87, 88, 89, 90, 91, 93, 102, 103-110, 114, 116, 122, 147, 219, 300, 438
    Castle, 103
praguerham, 96
Prahova District, 279, 326
Predeal Pass, 279, 329
Predel Hotel, 77
Predela Hotel, 51
Predjamski Grad Castle, 486
Preobrazhensky Monastery, 48
Presburg, *see* Bratislava
Presburg, Treaty of, 123, 443
Presov, 80, 122
Primate's Palace, 123
Primorets Hotel, 51
Prince's Islands, 414, 417
Pristina, 512-513
private homes, tourists in, 453, 454
Prussia, 208, 209
Prut River, 278
P. T. T. K., 230
Pula, 438, 471

Puszta, 134, 135, 159, 198, 199
Putnik Hotel, 509
    Restaurant, 509
Putnik Tourist Agency, 436, 437, 441

quail, hunting of, 305, 455
Quiet Nest, 64-65

Rab Islands, 442, 472
Rabafuzes, 142
rabbit, hunting, 398
"racpoity," 162
Radihaza stud farm, 170
radon baths, 100
Rafil, 45
rail travel, 14, 15, 88, 147-149, 219, 222, 287-288, 364-366, 438-439
    Bulgaria, 14, 15
    Czechoslovakia, 88
    Hungary, 147-149
    Poland, 219, 222
    Romania, 287-288
    Turkey, 364-366
    Yugoslavia, 438-439
Rajka, 86, 142
Ram, 398
Ramazan, 344
Rasaritul Hotel, 325
Rector's Palace, 459, 463
Regatta, International, 167
Reis-ul-Ulema, 495, 496
religion, Turkish, 359, 384-385
Rembrandt, works by, 255, 509

INDEX 551

Rental, car, 90, 221, 298-299, 393
reservations, hotel, 92, 227, 436, 449
restaurant associations, 445, 446
restaurant districts, 156
restaurants, 23-24, 34-35, 42, 59-62, 63-64, 70-73, 108-109, 113-114, 119-120, 125, 126-127, 181-184, 187, 192-194, 203, 204, 248-249, 253, 254, 258, 265-266, 268, 270, 273-274, 311-314, 315, 318-319, 322-323, 324, 325-326, 330, 331, 332, 333-334, 342-343, 405-406, 458, 462, 467, 476, 480, 484, 491-492, 495, 497, 505-507, 509, 517
    Bulgarian, 23-24, 34-35, 42, 59-62, 63-64, 70-73
    Czechoslovakia, 108-109, 113-114, 119-120, 125, 126-127
    Hungary, 181-184, 187, 192-194, 203, 204
    Poland, 248-249, 253, 254, 258, 265-266, 268, 270, 273-274
    Romania, 311-314, 315, 318-319, 322-323, 324, 325-326, 330, 331, 332, 333-334, 342-343
    Turkish, 405-406
    Yugoslavian, 458, 462, 467, 476, 480, 484, 491-492, 495, 497, 505-507, 509, 517
restricted travel, 347, 368
"retesh," 162
Retezal Mountains, 303
Rev Csarda Restaurant, 193-194
revolving theater, 115
Rhodin Hotel, 57
    Restaurant, 57
Rhodopes Mountains, 43
Ribarska Hizha Restaurant, 70
Ribarska Koliba cottages, 471
Rijeka, 438, 439, 443, 472, 475, 484, 485
Rila Hotel (Rila) 45, 46
Rila Hotel (Slunchev Bryag), 68
Rila Hotel (Sofia), 31, 32, 33, 34
    Restaurant, 34
Rila Monastery, 9, 44-46
Rila Mountain Area, 44-46
Rilsky, Ivan, 45
Rimicu Vilces, 327
Risnow, 316
river boats, 145, 149
Riviera Restaurant, 469, 470
road maps, 98, 99, 238-239, 298, 394
Rodina Tourist Agency, 15, 17
Rod Orlem Hotel, 250
Rogaska Slatina, 487
Romania, 9, 10, 20, 134, 137, 142, 147, 152, 277-345
    airplane travel, 287
    Alba Iulia, 314
    Arad, 314-315
    Bacu, 315
    Baile Herculane, 315-316
    Brasov, 316-317
    Bucharest, 307-314
    cables, 306
    camping, 303-304
    Carpati, 288-291
    car rental, 298-299
    car travel, 286, 296-299
    chewing gum, 306
    cigarettes, 306
    Cluj, 320-323
    currency, 283
    customs, 284-286
    Danube Delta, 345
    Devin, 323-324
    dining, 294-295
    drinking, 295
    Eforie Nord, 344-345

fishing, 304-306
food, 294-295
forbidden areas, 297-298
geography, 278-279
guides, 300-302
history, 279-289
hotels, 291-293, 308-311, 314-315, 316, 317-318, 320, 321-322, 323-324, 325, 327-328, 329, 331-332, 333, 334, 338-342, 344-345
hunting, 304-306
Iasi, 333-334
language, 282
mail, 306
Mamaia, 334-344
maps, 298
Moldavia, 332-334
money, 283
motoring, 286, 296-299
Oradea, 324-326
photography, 302
Ploesti, 326
Poiana Brasov, 319-320
police, 297
restaurants, 311-314, 315, 318-319, 322-323, 324, 325, 326, 330, 331, 332, 333-334, 342-343
ship travel, 288
shopping, 299-300
sightseeing, 300-303, 307-308, 327, 343-344
Sibiu, 326-328
Sighisoara, 328
Sinaia, 329
Sovata, 329-330
spas, 304
Suceava, 334
telephone, 306
Timisoara, 331-332
Tirgu Mures, 330-331
tours, 302
train travel, 287-288
travel to, 286-288
visas, 283-286
wires, 306
Romanian Embassy, 283
Romanian Institute of Balneology and Physiotherapy, 304
Romanian National Airline, *see* Tarom
Romanian Orthodox Church, Cathedral of, 321
Romanian People's Republic, 280, 281
Romanian Steamship Line, *see* Navrom
Romanian village, re-creation of, 307
Rome, 219
Roman, 38, 281, 327, 330, 410, 459, 471, 472, 494, 513
   amphitheater, 471
   fortress, 513
   occupation, 281
   relics, 410
   salt mines, 330
   town, 459
   walls, 494
   war camp, 472
Romischer Kaiser Hotel, 327-328
   Restaurant, 327-328
Ropotamo Restaurant, 35
Ropotamo River, 76
Roske, 142
roulette, 54, 62, 71, 343, 467, 475, 476
Roussalka Pastry Shop and Bar, 72
Rousse, 13, 14, 51
Rovinj, 472-473
Royal Athenée Hotel, *see* Athenée Palace Hotel
Royal Hotel, 177-178
   Restaurant, 178
Rozsadomb, 183

Rubens, works by, 301, 326
Rubin Hotel, 63
Rudolf II, Emperor, 114
ruins, 281, 344, 410
Rumeli Hisar, 417
Rusiane, camp site at, 229
Russia, 208, 209, 281, 288, *see also* Soviet Union
Russian Church, 29
Russian Club Restaurant, 34
Russian Memorial Church, 38
Russian Soldiers Monument, 39
Russian tourists, 55
Russo-Turkish War, 431
Rustem Pasa Karavansary, 412
Ruszwurm Restaurant, 184
Ruzyne Airport, 82, 84, 85, 87, 88
  free shop, 88
Rycerska Restaurant, 249
Rysy, Mt., 210

Sabena Air Lines, 13, 87, 88, 145, 218, 287
Sadirvan Cami, 426
Sadirvan Night Club, 418
St. Adalbert, Church of, 255
St. Andrew, Church of, 48
St. Ana, Lake, 303
St. Anna, Church, 174
St. Anne, Church of, 243
St. Constantine, Church of, 48
St. Elizabeth, Church of, 271
St. Franco, Church of, 471
St. George, Basilica of, 104
St. Helene, Church of, 48
St. Illipa, Church of, 481
St. Irene, Mosque, 415

St. Jacob, Cathedral of, 474
St. James, Church of, 111
St. John, Basilica of, 243
St. John Rilsky, Church of, 45
St. Marco Cathedral, 459
St. Marks Cathedral, 489
St. Martin's Cathedral (Bratislava), 123, 124
St. Martin, Church (Bydgoszcz), 250
St. Mary's Church, 251
St. Michaels Church, 320
St. Nicholas, Church of (Bydgoszcz), 250
St. Nicholas, Church of (Plovdiv), 40
St. Parasheva, Church of, 74
St. Peter's Cathedral, 201
St. Sophia, Church of (Istanbul), 349, 350, 351, 367, 414, 415, 416
St. Sophia, Church of (Sophia), 29
St. Stephen, 136, 194, 200, 201, *see also* Sveti: Stefan
  Cathedral of, 174
  crown of, 136
St. Stosije, Basilica of, 481
St. Vaclav, tomb of, 103
St. Veit, Church of, 472
St. Vitus, Cathedral of, 103
Sakarya River, 348
Salonae, *see* Split
Salonica, 13, 348
Salt Lake, 348
salt water fishing, 398
Salzberg, 14
San Stefano, Treaty of, 10
Saray Burnu, 386, 412
Saraj Restaurant, 517
Sarajevo, 429-430, 431, 492, 495-497, 498,
Sarajevo Restaurant, 476
"sarmales," 294
SAS Airlines, 218, 438

Satoraljaujhcly, 86, 142
Sava Mts., 444
Sava River, 434, 455, 482
Scandinavian tourists, 55
"schaschlik," 23
Schipka Church, 47
Schipka Pass, 9, 10, 46, 47
Schirnding, 86
Schwarzenberg family, 114, 115
Scilvasarad stud farm, 170
Scintelia House, 308
Seagull Hotel, 63
Sehzade Mosque, 411
Selimiye Cami, 411
Selim, Sultan, 352
    mosque of, 411, 415
Selcuk, motel at, 396
Seniska Draga Gorge, 473, 474
Senj, 477, 488
Septimus Severus, Emperor, 413, 416
seraglio, 366, 386
Serbia, 10, 350, 446, 501-514
Serbo-Croatian language, 432
Serdica, 28
service stations, *see* gasoline stations
Settin, *see* Szczecin
Sevastopol Restaurant, 117
Seym, The, 207
Sgraffito Palace, 104
shadow theater, 383
Shanghai Restaurant, 249
Sheepfold Restaurant, *see* Kushlata
ship travel, 218, 288
Ship Restaurant, *see* Gemiyata
"shish-kebab," 506
shooting, *see* hunting
shopping, 54, 97, 102, 163-165, 235-236, 299-300, 389-393, 451, 476-477, 503
    in Bulgaria, 57
    in Czechoslovakia, 97, 102
    in Hungary, 163-165
    in Poland, 235-236
    in Romania, 299-300
    in Turkey, 389-393
    in Yugoslavia, 451, 476-477, 503
"shopska salad," 73
Sibenik, 473-474
Sibiu, 303, 326-328
    Printing Works, 326-327
Siesta Hotel, 322
Sighisoara, 289, 314, 318, 328
Sighisoara Hotel, 328
sightseeing, 28-29, 38, 39-40, 44-45, 47-49, 79-81, 103-104, 242-244, 251, 255-256, 263, 269, 271, 300-303, 307-308, 320, 326, 328, 401-402, 408-409, 411-412, 413-417, 421-423, 425-426, 429-430, 458-459, 502-503
    Ankara, 401-402
    Belgrade, 502-503
    Bursa, 408
    Cluj, 320
    Edirne, 411-412
    Gdansk, 251
    Izmir, 425-426
    Krakow, 255-256
    Pleven, 38
    Plovdiv, 38, 39, 40
    Poznan, 263
    Prague, 103-104
    Sofia, 28, 29
    Sibiu, 326
    Sighisoara, 328
    Szczecin, 269
    Turnovo, 47-49
    Warsaw, 242-244
    Wroclaw, 271
Sigismund, King, 176
    statue of, 243
Siklos Castle, 170
Silesia, 79

"silivovic," 96
Simeon I, 10
Simplon-Orient Express, 14, 89, 438
Sinaia, 329
Siofok, 170, 185, 188, 190-194
Sirat Hotel, 290
Sirkeci Station, 365
"sis kebab," 378
"sis kofte," 378
Siutghiol, Lake, 335
Sivas, 347
skiing, 36, 44, 130, 272, 320, 329, 485
Skncajscie, 230
Skopje, 13, 430, 452, 507, 508, 516-517
Skopska Crna Gora, Mt., 517
Skradin, 474
Slan Hotel, 484
　Restaurant, 484
Slavia Hotel, 33, 34
　Restaurant, 34
Slavic languages, 11
Slavija Hotel (Belgrade), 504, 506
　Restaurant, 504
Slavija Hotel (Maribor), 484-485
　Restaurant, 485
Slavkov, 79, 80
Slav Sredeta, 28
sleeping cars, 89, 148, 365, 395, 439
"Slivowitz," 24, 127, 133-134
Slovak Hotel, 113
Slovakia, 79, 80, 88, 91, 93, 95, 96, 98, 101, 116, 121-131, 136, 137
　cooking, 95, 96
　language, 11
Slovan Hotel (Brno), 113
　Restaurant, 113
Slovan Hotel (Kosice), 126
Slovenia, 456, 482-487
　language, 432

Slovenski Dom Hotel, 487
　Restaurant, 487
Slunchev Bryag, 53, 54, 65-76
Snagov Forest, camp site, 303
Smakosz Restaurant, 265-266
smallpox vaccination, 361
Smetana Theater, 89, 101, 106
smorgasbord, 402
Smyra, 354
Smyrna, *see* Izmir
Snagov, Lake, 308
Snow White Hotel, 44
Sobieski, Jan, 137, 207, 244
Sofia, 11, 13, 14, 15, 18, 28-35, 36, 55, 63, 65, 219
Sofia Hotel (Golden Sands), 57
Solta, 477
Somes River, 278, 279
Somoskoujfalu, 86, 142
Sopot, 222, 226, 241, 251, 252, 266-268
Sopron, 142, 167
Souvata Restaurant, 326
souvenirs, 25, 26, 66, 97, 102, 236, 389, 451
Sovata, 304, 329-330
Soviet Union, 76, 82, 86, 135, 138, 142, 147, 152, 284, 348, *see also* Russia
Sozopol, 75
spa, 79, 80, 94, 98, 100, 101, 116, 124, 170, 230, 304, 315-316, 329-330, 409, 454, 487, 498
Spalato, 442
Spartakiade, 101, 102, 105
speed limits, 15, 152, 219, 220, 286
Spillberk Castle, 79, 111, 112, 114
　Restaurant, 114
Split, 433, 436, 437, 442, 444, 452, 457, 463, 474, 475-477, 488
Sport Hotel (Budapest), 181
Sport Hotel (Poiana Brasov), 320
　Restaurant, 320

Sport Hotel Partizan, 127, 128
  Restaurant, 127, 128
squirrel, hunting of, 398
Stadion Restaurant, 505-506
Stamboliski, Alexander Square, 39
Stara Zagora, 51
Staromestke Namesti, 102
Stary Smokovec, 79, 122, 128-129, 130
Staszic Palace, 243
steamers, 439
Stephen The Great, King, 332, 333
Stoletov, Mt., 46
Stolytov Monument, 9
Stotinki, 11, 12
Strahov Stadium, 102
"strapacka," 96
streetcars, 221, 222
Strsbke Pleaso, 122, 130
"Street of Beautiful Women," 134, 195
strudel, 162, 183
"Su Boreci," 378
Suceava, 334
Suceava Hotel, 334
  Restaurant, 334
Suceava Teliuc, 303
Sucevita, Church of, 332
Sudeten Mts. 210
Suleyman, Sultan, 352, 400, 415
Suleymaniye Mosque, 411, 415
Sulina, 345
Summerau, 86
Sunny Beach, see Slunchev Bryag
Sveti Stefan, 460, 464, 477-478
Sv. Stefan Hotel, 478
  Restaurant, 478
swans, hunting of, 345
Swinoujscie, 218
Swissair, 87, 438
synagogues, 103, 459
Syria, 348
Szabad Sag Hotel, 179-180
  Restaurant, 179
Szczecin 268-270
Szczeves Restaurant, 183
Szechenyi, Istvan, 174
Szeged, 135, 159, 162, 203-204
  Open-Air Festival, 167, 203
  Salami, 162
Szegediner goulash, 161
Szentendre, 176
Szestochowa, 236
Szilvasvarad stud farm, 135
Szob, 86, 142

table sharing, 27, 233, 234
TABSO, 13, 14
Tale, 121, 122, see also Podbrezova
Tantalus, grave of, 425
Tapolea, 188
Tara River, 500
Tarator soup, 23
"tarhonya," 161
TAROM, 145, 287, 309, 313, 363
tarpan, hunting of, 211
Tatras Mts., 79, 80, 81, 94, 97, 100, 101, 122, 130, 147 205, 210, 272
Tatranska Lomnica, 79, 122, 128, 129-131
Tauern Express, 14, 438
Taverna Restaurant, 492
tax-free shops, 299-300
taxicabs, 221, 245, 369-371
Tchaika Hotel, 63
tea, 380
teahouse, 72
telegrams, 31, 102, 173, 241, 306,

397-398
telephone, 31, 102, 173, 241, 306, 309, 397-398
Teleke Library, 330
Telex, 92, 160, 227, 289
Teliuc, 303
"tel kadif," 379
Tenha Yava, 64-65
Teplice Lazne, 101
tetanus shots, 361
Teutonic knights, 251
Theodosius I, Emperor, 349
Theodosius II, Emperor, 349, 413, 416
Three Borders Restaurant, 182
Three Galleries Mosque, *see* Uc-Serefeli Cami
Thutmosis III, Obelisk of, 416
THY Planes, 368
Tiepolo, works by, 463
tiger, hunting of, 398
Tigris River, 348
Tihany Bar, 190
Tihany Hotel, 190
Tihany·Motel, 189-190
Tihany Peninsula, 135, 170, 185, 188-190
Timisoara, 303, 304, 331-332
tipping, 92, 97, 163, 234, 440, 447, 451
Tirgu Mures, 330-331
Tisza Hotel, 203, 204
    Restaurant, 204
Tisza River, 135, 162, 203, 434
Tiszafured, 198
Titian, works by, 175, 301, 463
Tito, Marshall, 432, 489
    home of, 502
    museum, 502
    statue, 513
Titograd, 437, 442, 464, 478, 501
Titova Obala, 477
Tito Veles, 515

Titova Uzice, 513-514
Tolstoi, Alexander, 117
Tolyfacsarda Restaurant, 187
Tomis, 281, 282
Topkapi Palace, 415
Tornyosnemti, 142
tourist cabins, 37
tours, 25, 97, 99, 104, 165-166, 236-237, 301-302, 329, 459-460
trains, 14, 88, 89, 147, 287, 365, 366, 373, 438
    Ankara Express, 365, 366
    Arlberg-Orient Express, 287
    Baghdad Express, 365
    Balt-Orient Express, 14, 89, 147, 287
    Carpati Express, 287
    Danubian, 14
    Istanbul-Ankara Express, 373
    Marmora Express, 365
    Orient Express, 88, 89, 147, 287, 365, 438
    Pannonia Express, 147
    Simplon-Orient Express, 14, 89, 438
    Tauern Express, 14, 438
    Yugoslavian Express, 438
train travel, 14, 15, 86, 88-89, 145, 147-151, 219, 222, 284, 287-288, 364-366, 438-439
    Bulgaria, 14, 15
    Czechoslovakia, 86, 88-89
    Hungary, 145, 147-151
    Poland, 219, 222
    Romania, 284, 287-288
    Turkey, 364-366
    Yugoslavia, 438-439
Transylvania, 136, 137, 197, 277, 278, 279, 280, 281, 300, 301, 305, 315, 316, 323
Transylvania Hotel (Oradea), 324-325
    Restaurant, 325

Transylvania Hotel (Tirgu Mures), 330, 331
Transylvania Restaurant, 324
Transylvania (ship), 344
Trapezitsa, 47
travel agents, 20, 21, 22, 83, 84, 92, 94, 95, 141, 142, 143, 154, 155, 156, 157, 158, 165, 166, 216, 283, 290, 293, 371, 374, 395, 436, 449
Trebinje, 460
Trenchin, 79
Triaditsa, 28
Trieste, 432, 469
Triglav, 433
Trimontium, 38
Trimontium Hotel, 40, 41, 42
    Restaurant, 41
Trinity Monastery, 48
Trkirghiol, 344
Trogir, 477
trolley buses, 400
Tropaneum Trajani Monument, 282
trout, fishing for, 306, 445
Tsarevets Hill, 47
Tschuchura Restaurant, 70, 71
Tsuom Department Store, 29, 30
    Restaurant, 35
Tulcea, 345
Tum, 260
Tünde Bar, 194
Tupelov airplane, 88
turbes, 408
Turkey, 9, 12, 347-428, 439
    airplane travel, 364
    Ankara, 399-406
    bargaining, 391-393
    beaches, 417
    Bitex, 390-391
    boat travel, 366
    Bolu, 406
    Bursa, 407-410
    bus, 368

cables, 398
camping, 396-397
car travel, 367, 393-394
climate, 348
currency, 359-361
customs, 361-362
dining, 376-381
dolmus travel, 369-371
Edirne, 410-412
fishing, 398
food, 376-381
geography, 348
guides, 394
history, 349-354
hotels, 371-376, 402-405, 409-410, 417-421, 427
hunting, 398
Istanbul, 412-423
Izmir, 423-427
language, 355-359
mail, 398
maps, 394
money, 359-361
motels, 396-397
motoring, 367, 393-394
music, 381-382
photography, 395
plane travel, 364
rail travel, 364-366
religion, 359, 384-385
shadow theater, 383
shopping, 389-393
sightseeing, 401-402, 408-409, 411, 413-417, 421-423, 425-426
taxis, 369-371
telephone calls, 397-398
train travel, 364-366
travel agents, 395
traveling, 363-371
visas, 361-362
women, 386-387
Turkish bath, 383-384, 408, 497

INDEX 559

Turkish coffee, 294, 295, 379
Turkish dances, 381-382
Turkish Demiryollari, 366
Turkish Hava Yollari, *see* THY
Turkish invasions, 10, 28, 39, 46, 47, 48, 64, 136, 137, 194, 195, 201, 280, 431
Turkish Maritime Lines, 367
Turkish National Airline, *see* THY
Turkish State Railway, *see* Turkish Demiryollari
Turnovo, 47-50, 56
Turnovo Hotel, 47, 49, 50
Tuzex Shops, 90, 97, 105
Tuz Gölü Lake, 348
Tuzla, 498
Tvrdjava Hotel, 509, 512
    Restaurant, 512
typhus shots, 361

Uc-Serefeli Cami, 411
U Cygana Restaurant, 254
U Kalicha, 108, 109
Ulcinj, 441, 443, 444, 479-480
U Loretty, 108
U Loretty Restaurant, 95
Ulu-Cami, 408
Ulu-Dag Mountain, 408, 409
U Markyse, 108
U Medemase, 109
Una Rivers, 492
Urals, 135
U.S. Information Service, 395, 490
Uzhgorod, 86
Uzun Kopru, 367

vacation homes, 444
vaccination, smallpox, 154
Valachia, 277
Vald Stejnska Hopsoda, 109
Valley of the Roses, 77
Van Dyck, works by, 301
Van Lake, 348
Vardar River, 516, 517
Variety Bar, 72, 73
Varna, 9, 13, 14, 15, 19, 26, 50, 51, 53, 55, 56, 62, 63, 65, 66, 75, 76, 288
Varna Hotel, 50, 51
Varna Restaurant, 64
"varza da cluj," 294
Vassil Kolarov Hill, 39
Vassil Kolarov (ship), 76
Vcronet, Church of, 332
Venetian Nights, 70, 71
Venice, 439
Venus Hotel, 192
    Restaurant, 192-193
Venus Motel, 192
Verkovitsa Hotel, 51
Veruda Hotel Association, 471
Verudela Park Hotel, 471
Veseli Kutic Restaurant, 491
Vesna Hotel, 469-470
Vidikovac Restaurant, 458
Vidin, 77
Vienna, 89, 139, 145, 146, 147, 148, 152, 175, 219, 287, 365, 440
"Vienna breakfast," 446
Villa Dubrovnik Hotel, 461
    Restaurant, 461
Villa Hotel, 467
Villa Izfor Hotel, 488-489
    Restaurant, 488
Villa Rosalia, 465, 467
Villach, 440
Vindobona Motor Express, 89
vineyards, 81, 124, 327

Vinograd Restaurant, 506
Virag Cafe, 204
Virgin Mary, Church of, 255
Virzhdebna Airport, 13
Vis Islands, 477
visas, 13, 14, 18, 83-86, 91, 140-144, 146, 154, 215-217, 283-286, 361-362, 435

    Bulgaria, 13, 14, 18
    Czechoslovakia, 83-86, 91
    Hungary, 140-144, 146, 154
    Poland, 215-217
    Romania, 283-286
    Turkey, 361-362
    Yugoslavia, 435

Visegrad, 172, 176
Visoki Decani, Monastery of, 507
Vistula River, 205, 210, 222
Vitava, 81, 103, 110
Vitusha Mountains, 28, 33, 35
Vitusha Hotel, 68
Vlahos, Ioan, 37
Vltava River, 104, 109
Vodenitsata Restaurant, 60
Vojvodina National Park, 509
Volga Hotel, 51
Vorosmarty Restaurant, 184
Vranov, 81
Vratsa, *see* Ledenika Caves
Vrbas River, 494

Wagon-Lits Cook, 92, 148, 365, 395, 439
Waidhaus, 86
Walachia, 278, 279, 300
Wallenstein family palace, 104
War Museum, 104
Warninski Hotel, 261-262
    Restaurant, 261-262
Warsaw, 147, 152, 205, 209, 219, 227, 236, 260, 438
    University, 243
Warzawa Restaurant, 248
Washington Restaurant, 405
water skiing, 54, 479
Wawel Hill, 255, 256
weather, 9, 135, 348, 372, 401, 429, 434, 451, 469
Wenceslaus Square, 89, 103, 105, 106, 107, 109, 110
Westerplatte Peninsula, 251
Westphalia, Treaty of, 269
whirling dervishes, 64, 174
White Cross Insurance, 15, 151, 219, 286, 362, 435
Wierzynek Restaurant, 258
Wilanow Palace, 244
wild cats, hunting of, 305, 398
wine, 96, 97, 143, 162, 231, 233, 380, 446, 447
    cellar, 30, 42, 44, 64, 109, 127, 134, 249, 314, 319, 322, 344
    house, 114
    tasting, 71, 72, 153, 194, 319, 344
winter sports, 128, 226, 273, 319, 409, 444, 485
wires, 31, 102, 173, 241, 306, 397-398
wolf, hunting of, 240, 305, 330, 345
Wolfethal, 86
woodcocks, hunting of, 345, 455
Wroclaw, 241, 270-272

Yakasal Baba, tomb of, 64
Yalta, 76
    Conference, 209, 239
Yantra Hotel, 68
Yantra-Arda Hotel, 71
Yantra River, 47, 49, 50
Yedikule, walls of, 416
Yemikoy, 396
Yeni Cheri, 126
Yeni Mosque, 416
Yesi Cami, 408
Yesil Köy Airport, 361, 364, 370, 417, 420
Yesil Turse, 408
Yildirim Bayezit Cami, 408
Yildirm Mosque, 411
"yogurt kebab," 378
Yugoslavia, 9, 12, 14, 134, 137, 142, 147, 284, 365, 429-517

    Adriatic Coast, 441-444, 456-481

    airplane travel, 437-438
    Banja Luka, 492-493
    Bar, 456
    Belgrade, 514-515
    Bitola, 514-515
    Bled, 482-483
    boat travel, 439; 459-460
    Bosnia-Hercegovina, 492-498
    Brela, 457
    Budva, 457-458
    bungalows, 453-454
    bus travel, 440, 459-460
    camping, 453-454
    Cardak, 517
    car travel, 440-441
    climate, 434
    Croatia, 487-492
    currency, 434-435, 451-452
    customs, 435
    Decani, 507
    dining, 444-447
    Dubrovnik, 458-463
    fishing, 455-456
    food, 444-447
    geography, 433-434
    Grancanica, 508
    guides, 432
    history, 430-432
    hotels, 448-451, 457, 458, 460-462, 464, 465-467, 468, 469-470, 471, 473, 474, 475-476, 479-480, 481-482, 483, 484, 485, 487, 488-489, 490-491, 493, 494-495, 496-497, 498, 499-500, 501, 503-505, 508, 509, 510, 511, 512, 513, 514, 515-516, 517

    hunting, 454-456
    Hvar, 463-464
    Ivangrad, 499-500
    Jajce, 493-494
    Kolasin, 500
    Kotor, 404
    language, 432-433
    Ljubljana, 483-484
    Macedonia, 514-517
    Makarska, 464
    Maribor, 484-485
    money, 434-435, 451-452
    Montenegro, 498-501
    Mostar, 494-495
    motel, 486
    motoring, 440
    National Tourist Organization, 436-437
    Nis, 508
    Novi Sad, 508-509
    Ohrid, 515-516
    Opatiya, 465-467
    Otocec, 485-486
    Partizanski Voda, 510
    Pec, 511
    Petrovardin, 511-512

photographs, 452-453
Piran, 468-469
Plitvicka Jezera, 488-489
Pohorje, 485
Porec, 467-468
Portorouz, 469-470
Postojenska Jama, 486
Pristina, 512-513
Pula, 471
Rab, 472
Restaurants, 458, 462, 467, 476, 480, 484, 491-492, 495, 497, 505-507, 509, 517
Rijeka, 472
Rogaska Slatina, 487
Rovina, 472-473
Sarajevo, 495-497
Senj, 473
Serbia, 501-514
shopping, 451, 476-477, 502
Sibenik, 473-474
sightseeing, 429-430, 502-503
Skopje, 516-517
Slovenia, 482-487
spas, 453-454
Split, 475-477
Sveti Stefan, 477-479
Titograd, 500-501
Titovo Uzice, 513-514
tours, 459-460, 463
train travel, 438-439
traveling, 437-441
Tuzla, 498
Ulcinj, 479-480
visas, 435
wines, 447-448
Zadar, 480-482
Zagreb, 489-492

Yugoslavian Air Transport, *see* JAT
Yugoslavian Express, 438

Zadar, 439, 442, 474, 477, 480-482
Zadar Hotel, 481-482
    Restaurant, 481-482
Zagreb, 185, 436, 437, 438, 444, 450, 452, 484, 487, 488, 489-492, 493, 494
Zagreb Restaurant, 476
Zakopane, 236, 272-275
Zakopane, 236, 272-275
Zakopane Sport Hotel, 273
Zamek Hotel, 259, 260
Zankowa Restaurant, 259
Zanopane, 226
Zelazowa Wola, 205, 244
"zeytin yagli patlican dolmasi," 378
Zielona Brama Fortifications, 251
Zielony Bjonih, 255
Zlatibor Plateau, 510
Zlatne Stijene, 471
Zlatni Kotva Hotel, 56, 57
    Restaurant, 56, 57
Zlantni Pyassatsi, *see* Golden Sands
zloty, 212, 214
Zochova Chata Restaurant, 125
Zograf, Zahari, 45, 48
Zona Zamfirkona Restaurant, 506
Zoo (Budapest), 175
Zoo (Rijeka), 472
Zorille Restaurant, 323
Zsolnay, Wilhelm, ceramics by, 201
Zurich, 147